ENDOMETRIOSIS

Endometriosis

The Complete Reference for Taking Charge of Your Health

MARY LOU BALLWEG
& the Endometriosis Association

Contemporary Books

Chicago   New York   San Francisco   Lisbon   London   Madrid   Mexico City
Milan   New Delhi   San Juan   Seoul   Singapore   Sydney   Toronto

The McGraw·Hill Companies

Library of Congress Cataloging-in-Publication Data

Ballweg, Mary Lou.
    Endometriosis : the complete reference for taking charge of your health / Mary
Lou Ballweg and the Endometriosis Association.
        p.   cm.
    Includes bibliographical references and index.
    ISBN 0-07-141248-4
        1. Endometriosis—Popular works.   I. Endometriosis Association.
    II. Title.

    RG483.E53B348   2003
    618.1—dc21   2003011015

1 2 3 4 5 6 7 8 9 0   AGM/AGM   2 1 0 9 8 7 6 5 4 3

ISBN 0-07-141248-4

Interior design by Think Design Group
Illustrations in Chapter 7 by Gary O. Caviness

McGraw-Hill books are available at special quantity discounts to use as premiums and
sales promotions, or for use in corporate training programs. For more information, please
write to the Director of Special Sales, Professional Publishing, McGraw-Hill, Two Penn
Plaza, New York, NY 10121-2298. Or contact your local bookstore.

This book is printed with soy-based ink on recycled, acid-free, and partially chlorine-free paper.

To women and girls with

endometriosis, to their families, and to the hope

they will become active in the drive

to save our health and the health of our planet.

Together, we make a difference!

Contents

PART 3 RESEARCH LEADS THE ENDO MOVEMENT IN NEW DIRECTIONS

Foreword

Deborah A. Metzger, M.D., Ph.D.

Mary Lou Ballweg and the Endometriosis Association are to be congratulated for their innovative advocacy work for women with endometriosis, which includes the publication of this book. To women with endo, these philosophies, treatments, and lifestyle approaches seem logical and have benefited many. Unfortunately, the vast majority of physicians are unfamiliar with this big-picture view of the disease. Nevertheless, many women with endo have turned to alternative medicine for validation and treatment.

Conventional medicine thinks of endometriosis as a disease of black spots that must be eradicated with surgery and suppressed with side-effect-producing hormones. Alternative medicine approaches endometriosis as a systemic disequilibrium that must be corrected through diet, nutritional supplements, exercise, stress management, reestablishing normal bowel flora, identification and desensitization of allergies, and balancing hormones. Conventional medicine attempts to ameliorate symptoms with powerful drugs; alternative medicine strives to determine the cause of the disequilibrium and reestablish a normal balance.

For women who are frustrated by the diverse philosophies of the healing professions, hope comes in the form of "integrative medicine," a small, but growing form of medical practice that combines conventional and alternative approaches to medicine. The contents of this book demonstrate the extraordinary resources that can be made available to patients through an integrated approach.

As a physician trained in conventional medicine, I recall my frustration with not being able to offer women anything more than surgery or hormones for the treatment of endometriosis. I could ameliorate pain for a period of time, but patients still had to curtail activities because of fatigue, irritable bowel symptoms, fibromyalgia, or brain fog. It was only when I began to address diet, nutrition, allergies, intestinal dysbiosis [see Glossary], and integration of the mind and the body that I truly felt that I was a healer. I should add that in many cases, it was my patients who suggested trying these alternatives.

I now also appreciate that integrative medicine is more than just combining conventional and alternative medicine—it must draw on *all* fields of medicine to treat the entire person, not just her pelvis. Once a woman is diagnosed, all of her symptoms are assumed to be due to endo, when, in fact, they may be due to other disease processes.

Women with endo often have other sources of pain, are quite sensitive to medications, have multiple allergies, often have insulin resistance, and might be thought of as "exceptions to every medical rule." To address these diverse problems, a woman may have to work with multiple health care providers and become the coordinator of her own care. The ideal is to have a physician who specializes in treating all aspects of the disease and can primarily handle most of these health problems. The concept of specializing in managing all aspects of a disease is called "disease management" and is currently being applied to chronic diseases such as diabetes and cardiovascular disease, apparently with considerable success.

Although integrative medicine and disease management are intriguing concepts for women with endo, they are still not widely available. However, given what the Endometriosis Association has accomplished over the past twenty-three years, there is every reason to believe that a new age for the treatment of endometriosis is emerging so that many sufferers will be freed of years of pain and lost lives!

Foreword

Russell Jaffe, M.D., Ph.D., C.C.N.

Endometriosis may be described as enigmas wrapped in riddles. Apparently normal cells take up residence in atypical sites with a host of physical and psychospiritual consequences.

What a set of enigmas.

Typical laboratory tests reveal few, if any, abnormalities, yet too many with endo suffer greatly and function poorly. Molecular and functional lab tests are revealing an ever-broadening awareness of cell dysfunctions. Functional tests assess the operation of cell systems. This allows a more real-time assessment than the typical chemical or enzyme assessment tests usually performed.

What a set of riddles.

Perhaps endometriosis is . . .

- teaching us about the nature of health
- revealing the importance of subtle, significant control system functions
- illuminating a deeper level of human function than conventional lab tests allow

What is the evidence that this might be the case?

Comprehensive management of endo shows promise of improved outcomes. This involves assessment of three measures:

1. Functional immune responses
2. Hormone (and hormone mimics) actions
3. Neurochemical balance

Immune, hormonal, and neurochemical responses can be seen as aspects of a common human control system. In addition to the function of this control system, nutrition and personal attitude make up functional, comprehensive care.

The basis of this comprehensive care approach is as follows: Our immune defense and repair systems are designed to both respond to foreign invaders and repair us from normal wear and tear. Our hormonal and neurochemical systems depend upon a balance of activation and restorative rest signals. Technically, this means the balance of cortisol to DHEA hormones and adrenalines to serotonin neurochemicals. Nutritional biochemistry includes enough of the essential nutritives to keep our cellular machinery working efficiently. This also includes the ability to remove some environmental chemicals by detoxification. This, in turn, means chemically modifying the foreign chemical to a form that is less reactive and more easily excreted from the body. This process requires highly efficient cell catalysts and adequate essential nutrients, especially for hard-to-rid toxins like mercury and aluminum.

If multiple components are out of balance at the same time, single interventions are unlikely to be sufficient. This is particularly true if our care is symptom reactive rather than focused on repairing the underlying causes of the problem(s). An example is using medications to suppress the symptoms of allergies, rather than identifying and correcting their fundamental biological triggers.

In endometriosis, an increase in immune reactive substances is usually observed when functional tests for delayed reactions ("delayed allergies") are performed. Reactive substances commonly include dietary digestive remnants and xenobiotic chemicals that have accumulated in the body and become reactive burdens on the immune system. This can be documented by the ELISA/ACT LRA tests developed in our laboratory. These tests tell us, for each individual, what her immune system is tolerant to and what her immune system recognizes as a defense burden. A burdened immune system is less able to repair. People with burdened immune repair are more susceptible to endo and have more intense pain than people better able to repair.

Dietary substitution for the reactive substances reduces the burden on the immune system. This allows the immune system to attend to the repair of the body's infrastructure that may have been substantially deferred for an extended period of time. When needed repair is deferred over extended time, tissue permeability goes up and elective adhesion molecules necessary for directing cell placement and orientation may be underproduced. This means that cells may lose their orientation and be able to proliferate in unusual and nonnormal places. Paradoxically, misdirection of cell adhesion molecules at a microscopic level is clinically linked with overproduction of a type of collagen associated with internal tissue bonds (clinically called adhesions) that are often painful.

Our clinical experience supports the work on the importance of hormone mimics such as dioxins in endometriosis. Dioxins and other hormone competitors can reduce immune system defense against infection and interfere with needed body repair from daily wear and tear or distress. They can also serve as activators of hormone-sensitive sites in the nucleus. This is where cell division takes place. This is also where signals to produce new functional components in the cell originate. These chemicals can alter cell receptor sites where critical cell communication takes place. This increases the risk of symptomatic endo.

Endometriosis challenges us to think more deeply and comprehensively. Management of endo in an integrated fashion shows promise. In practice, integrated management of endometriosis involves several activities by patient and healthcare provider:

- Identifying the individual immune system burdens, and substituting for them to the extent possible
- Eating a diet that enhances repair—This is known as "the alkaline way." This means a diet having a healthy chemical balance to neutralize excess acids from distress or cell metabolism. Health restoration and maintenance depend upon reserves to neutralize these acids. Specific supplements are often needed to restore or enhance cellular repair functions and detoxification ability.
- Practicing restorative habits of daily living

Taken together, this approach shows promise to restore immune, hormonal, neurochemical, and essential nutritive resilience.

Endo's mysterious "enigmas and riddles" challenge us to think deeply about the causes of this life-disrupting condition. Identifying and resolving the causes are likely to bring constructive, comprehensive approaches out of the current frustration over care that merely reacts to and suppresses symptoms as they occur.

Preface

Mary Lou Ballweg

I am proud to present to you the Endometriosis Association's third book. If you are a woman with endo or part of an endo family, you will find yourself in this book.

For decades, women with endo suffered in silence. Endo and its related problems were dismissed as taboo, too stigmatized, and too unimportant to be openly discussed (or researched). Because of this long silence, the pent-up need to tell our stories overflows into the Association's hundreds of support groups around the world; the hundreds of thousands of letters, phone calls, and E-mail messages we have received; and our research and writing, including our books.

As you learn that many other women have felt exactly as you do, you, too, will feel validated (no, you're not crazy). We hope you are empowered to stand up for yourself, find and insist on respectful and knowledgeable care, and are inspired to join our mission to educate, research, cure, and prevent endo.

Because of the neglect of endo until recent times, the disease became, in our oft-repeated statement, a nightmare of misinformation, myths, taboos, lack of diagnosis, and problematic hit-and-miss treatments overlaid on a painful, chronic, stubborn disease. The hard work of many women with endo, as well as their families, researchers, and physicians working with the Association, has gradually, since our beginnings in 1980, made it possible to "create order, focus, and useful information out of overwhelming and complex sources of research and data," as Nancy, an Association member in Virginia, wrote in a letter to us.

It is not easy creating this "order, focus, and useful information." As immunologist Grace Migaki wrote after completion of her excellent article, "Understanding the Immune System's Role in Endometriosis" (Chapter 7), "When Mary Lou asked me if I would be interested in writing an article about the immunology of endo, I was only too happy to agree. I figured that my educational, research, and medical backgrounds would more than suffice for the task and that such an article would be a breeze to write. *Oy vey!* Much to my chagrin I found myself knee-deep in an undertaking that was far more work than I had anticipated. Simply introducing the language of immunology can be a challenge, and manipulating that language into a clear and understandable illustration of the intriguing subject was an even greater obstacle!"

Like most of the Association's comprehensive and groundbreaking features, Grace's article wound its way through a long process. First, we listen carefully to the experiences of women with endo—what insights, what new slants to the disease, what patterns are discernible? It is the coming together of women, the honest feedback on treatments as well as every other aspect of the disease, combined with the work of the staff and volunteers around the world, that gets us to solid information and insights on the disease.

Second, our staff and volunteers attend scientific and medical meetings worldwide, learning and sharing what *we've* learned. This is harder than it sounds. Most information presented at these conferences is piecemeal, unconnected to any larger whole or even, sometimes, to endo. The pace of research is rapid, and understanding the politics that sometimes wraps itself around the research also contributes to the challenge.

Third, because the Association conducts and funds research, we channel all we've learned into data gathering, experiments, and analysis. Often this is accomplished in conjunction with leading research groups such as the Endometriosis Association Research Program at Vanderbilt University School of Medicine and the team headed by Pamela Stratton, M.D., at the National Institutes of Health, with which the Association collaborates.

Next comes another hard step: distilling the information into an intelligible package for the lay or medical reader (we reach medical readers through a variety of scientific journals and medical textbooks to which we contribute). After struggling through this conceptualization stage and usually many drafts, we ask trusted Advisors to review the article. Then we sift through their comments and further refine the article. Finally, after publication, we await feedback from our readers, which further enhances our understanding of the topic. People are often amazed at the insights and synthesis of disparate information we achieve in our articles. It is because of this process and input from so many sources, and because the whole organization has contributed.

Our goal is always to make this vast body of information as accessible as possible. If you find that it's hard to grasp everything in *one* reading (some chapters are particularly packed with information), bear in mind that this book is meant as a resource that you go back to time and again as different aspects of the disease unfold in your life. Endo is a complex disease, so this book won't read like a fast-paced novel.

Remember that part of the confusion, too, is that many doctors—as Deborah Metzger, M.D., Ph.D., says in her Foreword—still see endo as just some misplaced black spots, rather than a whole range of health problems that have underlying them hormonal/immune dysregulation. As I wrote in *The Endometriosis Sourcebook*:

> *In the new picture of the disease which is emerging, one sees not only the traditional symptoms of endometriosis—chronic pelvic pain, pain with sex, gastrointestinal and bladder problems, infertility, and others—but also high rates of atopic (allergic) diseases in these individuals*

and their families including allergies, food intolerances, asthma, eczema, and sometimes debil-
itating sensitivities to environmental chemicals such as perfumes, cigarette smoke, cleaning
agents, and others; a tendency to infections and mononucleosis; problems with Candida albi-
cans; mitral valve prolapse, fibromyalgia, and chronic fatigue immune dysfunction syndrome;
and a greater risk for autoimmune diseases and certain cancers.

Unlike the feeling of déjà vu I had when working on our second book, *The Endo-*
metriosis Sourcebook, my feeling with this book was one of major progress. I felt as if
we are really moving to the "big picture" of the disease that our earlier work had fore-
shadowed. We've known from the early days of the Endometriosis Association that
something much bigger than "only" a pelvic, gynecological disease was going on with
endo and that efforts directed at just the endometrial implants were directed at just
the tip of the iceberg. Bringing the pieces of the puzzle together has taken many years
of talking with each other (after all, the disease starts in the patient, not in the research
lab), exploring, continuing to work with the world's largest research registry, and being
open-minded to new treatments.

Readers of this book will see a cohesive picture of endo as a whole-body hormone
and immune disease. The role of endocrine disruptors like dioxin has become quite
clear. These toxic chemicals act like hormones in our bodies, disrupting our own hormonal messages, as well as poisoning our immune systems so they can no longer protect us from certain cancers and even turn against us in the form of autoimmune
diseases. Worst of all, no one currently knows how to get these chemicals (which we
accumulate throughout our lives—starting even before birth) out of our bodies. But at
least now we have a focus and explanation for this unusual combination of hormonal
and immune symptoms which had baffled doctors for decades.

Endometriosis: The Complete Reference for Taking Charge of Your Health and *The Endo-*
metriosis Sourcebook are companion books. We have so much material to share; we have
tried hard to avoid duplication in this book (except the first chapter on the basics of
endo for new readers). So, if you have not yet read *The Endometriosis Sourcebook* (now
in its seventh printing), we recommend you do. It contains in-depth background on
drugs to treat endo, the whole range of surgical issues, pain management, hysterectomy, adhesions, endo of the bowel and urinary tract, traditional Chinese medicine,
relationships and coping with painful sex, basic background on dioxins and the early
research linking them to endo, and many other topics. The book is available from local
and online bookstores or the Endometriosis Association (see contact information at the
back of the book).

In addition, as you would expect, the Association will continue developing new
materials and topics as we learn more and as our research continues to unfold new
insights. For instance, we are currently working on in-depth, groundbreaking articles
to explain and explore the autoimmune diseases we now know occur in significant

numbers of women with endo. And we are exploring methods to detoxify dioxins and other chemicals deep in our fat cells, toxins not amenable to removal through any current detoxification method. Become a member of the Association, and receive our newsletter for this type of up-to-the-minute information.

We hope this book will inspire many women with endo and their families, as well as doctors and scientists, to become part of our worldwide movement to help change the pain and suffering of an estimated 89 million women and girls. With numbers that large, if we stand together, we *will* change everything about endo. Since so many are not yet diagnosed and some who are diagnosed are too sick to do the work of the movement (or, succumbing to the taboos and stigmas around the disease, are afraid to speak out and get active), those of us who are diagnosed and able to get well enough must act. The heartbreak of seeing the next generation, including sometimes our own children, caught up in the same nightmare moves many of us to action. Join us!

Joe with Endo

One of the most popular parts of our earlier books, *Overcoming Endometriosis* and *The Endometriosis Sourcebook*, is the cartoon series "Joe with Endo." Joe, a young man with endometriosis, seems to have helped thousands of people understand that endo should be taken seriously. He helps show, with humor, that if a disease like endo affected millions of young men rather than millions of young women, society would think of it differently. After all, if there were millions of Joes out there—young men whose dreams were in danger of being destroyed by a disease, whose ability to function sexually was at risk, whose fertility was at risk, whose ability to build a satisfying work life and carry out the normal activities of living was at risk, and who even would face the threat of castration—no one would dare say it was unimportant.

Joe also helps with his black humor. He helps me leave audiences laughing at the end of what can sometimes be discouraging meetings (because we don't yet have the answers we need for this disease). Joe is particularly funny when I share the podium with a doctor who is willing to take the part of Joe. (Camran Nezhat, M.D., had the audience rolling in the aisles when he did the part for a San Francisco Association chapter audience.)

Joe has also brought his important message to other parts of the world. This talented fellow speaks quite a number of languages and has helped women all over the world get the message out that society needs to take endo seriously. To see the earlier episodes of Joe from *The Endometriosis Sourcebook* and *Overcoming Endometriosis*, see the Appendix of this book. The new episodes start in Chapter 1.

We're thrilled that the very talented artist and teacher Meri Lau has again drawn Joe as only she can. Thank you, Meri!

We hope you enjoy Joe while recognizing the real tragedy behind him: that every-thing that happens to Joe is based on the actual experiences of millions of women with endo. Let's change that!

EDITOR'S NOTE Just as *multiple sclerosis* was shortened to MS decades ago, we made the decision to shorten *endometriosis* to *endo* for lay use. Educating about the disease and making it a little more manageable and a little less formidable starts with the public being able to pronounce its name.

We have retained the Canadian, British, Australian, and New Zealand spellings of certain words (gynaecology, humour) where the writer is from those countries.

We are thrilled that McGraw-Hill agreed to print this book with soy-based ink on recycled, partially chlorine-free paper.

Acknowledgments

This book would not exist without the Endometriosis Association—the thousands of members and supporters worldwide who are the Association's members, donors, chapter and group leaders, board members, Advisors, researchers, and volunteers. Without them, there would be no Association and without the Association, there would not be this book.

We would like to thank all of our Advisors who helped review various chapters in this book: G. David Adamson, M.D.; Marla Ahlgrimm, R.Ph.; Donald P. Braun, Ph.D.; John Dulemba, M.D.; Robert Franklin, M.D.; Mark Hornstein, M.D.; Wayne Konetzki, M.D.; Kay Lie, M.D.; Dan C. Martin, M.D.; Deborah Metzger, M.D., Ph.D.; Dian Mills, M.A.; Camran Nezhat, M.D.; David Olive, M.D.; Kevin G. Osteen, Ph.D.; David Redwine, M.D.; Togas Tulandi, M.D.; and Ian Tummon, M.D.

Also, we greatly appreciate our other reviewers: Alain Audebert, M.D.; Laura Becker; Louise A. Brinton, Ph.D.; Stella M. Ĉapek, Ph.D.; Cathy Corman; Jennifer Cox; James Dorr; Jackie Elliott; Aquene Freechild; Leo Galland, M.D.; D. Alan Johns, M.D.; Tony Luciano, M.D.; John Mathias, M.D.; Betty Mekdeci; Farr Nezhat, M.D.; Sharyle Patton; Donald Pittaway, M.D.; M. Steven Piver, M.D.; Shelley Raebel, Pharm.D.; Sherry Rier, Ph.D.; Judy Robinson; Monica Rohde; Ceil Sinnex; Eric Thomas, M.D.; Daniel Tsin, M.D.; Aristo Vojdani, Ph.D.; and Grant Yeaman, Ph.D.

We also appreciate our other Advisors: Leila Adamian, M.D.; Agneta Bergqvist, M.D., Ph.D.; Michel Canis, M.D.; Ming-Yang Chang, M.D.; Donald L. Chatman, M.D.; Michael P. Diamond, M.D.; W. Paul Dmowski, M.D., Ph.D.; Jacques Donnez, M.D.; Linda C. Giudice, M.D., Ph.D.; W. F. Howard, M.D.; Robert B. Hunt, M.D.; Stephen Kennedy, M.A., M.D.; Charles H. Koh, M.D.; Philippe R. Koninckx, M.D., Ph.D.; Marc Laufer, M.D.; André Lemay, M.D., Ph.D.; Subbi Mathur (Pillai), Ph.D.; Charles E. Miller, M.D.; Mette Haase Moen, M.D., Ph.D.; Mark Perloe, M.D.; Carlos Alberto Petta, M.D., Ph.D.; Robert S. Schenken, M.D.; Osamu Tsutsumi, M.D., Ph.D.; Johan Van der Wat, M.D.; Paolo Vercellini, M.D.; Michael W. Vernon, Ph.D.; and Robert A. Wild, M.D.

We deeply appreciate all our supporters who make our research possible. We especially want to thank Tracy H. Dickinson; the Fairleigh S. Dickinson, Jr. Foundation; and the Harry and Betty Quadracci family, including Elizabeth, Joel, Kathryn, and Richard.

A special thank-you to Ellen Agger, freelance writer, for her contributions to this book, including an enormous amount of work on the pioneering menopause chapter.

Also, a special thanks to Linda Duczman, who worked very hard with Mary Lou Ballweg on the groundbreaking chapters about cancer and surgical regulation.

A huge thank-you to our book production manager, Eileen Kopp, who put her heart and soul into this work. In normal times, Eileen is Mary Lou Ballweg's executive assistant. Thank you! We are also very grateful to Fay Campbell, our associate director, for her work on this book, and all the staff and volunteers of the Endometriosis Association who have contributed their knowledge over the last eight years (since the publication of *The Endometriosis Sourcebook*). A special thanks to Jerry Metz, who has been our operations manager for the last nine years. Thanks also to our wonderful copy-editor, Karen Schenkenfelder. Finally, we appreciate all of the professionals at McGraw-Hill, especially our editor, Judith McCarthy.

Disclaimer

The Endometriosis Association is an international self-help, nonprofit organization dedicated to providing support and information to women and girls with endometriosis, as well as to their families and friends; promoting awareness of the disease among the medical community, the public, and the media; and conducting and promoting research related to endometriosis. The Association is governed primarily by those with the disease, and independent of vested interests.

The contents of this book are not to be construed as medical advice, nor is the book a substitute for proper medical treatment. Unless clearly stated as such, treatment options are not recommended by the Endometriosis Association. The Association does not promote any drugs, treatments, or specific theories unless clear evidence of their efficacy emerges.

Letters published reflect the experience and/or opinions of the writers. Publication does not constitute endorsement of the letter writers' opinions or verification of their experiences. Likewise, articles published in the text reflect the research, experience, and opinions of the individual authors. The Endometriosis Association neither endorses nor disclaims specific theories or treatment recommendations in the articles unless such endorsement or disclaimer is specifically stated.

What Is Endometriosis?

Mary Lou Ballweg

E ndometriosis is a puzzling hormonal and immune disease affecting girls and women in their reproductive years. The name is derived from the word *endometrium*, which is the tissue that lines the inside of the uterus and builds up and sheds each month in the menstrual cycle. In "endo," as this disease is called for short, tissue like the endometrium is found outside the uterus, in other areas of the body. In these locations outside the uterus, the endometrial tissue develops into what are called "nodules," "tumors," "lesions," "implants," or "growths." These growths can cause pain, infertility, and other problems.

The most common locations of endometrial growths are in the abdomen—involving the ovaries, fallopian tubes, ligaments supporting the uterus, area between the vagina and the rectum, outer surface of the uterus, and lining of the pelvic cavity. Sometimes the growths are also found in abdominal surgery scars, on the intestines, in the rectum, or on the bladder, vagina, cervix, and vulva (external genitals). Endometrial growths have also been found outside the abdomen in the lung, arm, thigh, and other locations, but these are uncommon.

It is possible, though relatively rare, for endo lesions to become cancerous. In addition, recent research has indicated women and girls with endo are at greater risk for cancer, particularly ovarian and breast cancer, as well as melanoma. They are also at risk for certain autoimmune diseases, in which the immune system attacks the body's own tissues. Because of these risks and the life-disrupting nature of endo in many cases, women and girls are encouraged not to ignore symptoms.

Like the lining of the uterus, endometrial growths usually respond to the hormones of the menstrual cycle. They build up tissue each month, break down, and cause bleeding. However, unlike the lining of the uterus, endometrial tissue outside the uterus has no way of leaving the body. The result is internal bleeding, degeneration of the blood and tissue shed from the growths, inflammation of the surrounding areas, and formation of scar tissue (adhesions). Other complications can be rupture of cysts (which can spread endo to new areas), intestinal bleeding or obstruction (if the growths are in or near the intestines), interference with bladder function (if the growths are on or in the bladder), and other problems. Symptoms seem to worsen with time, though cycles of remission and recurrence are the pattern in some cases.

Symptoms

The most common symptoms of endo are pain before and during periods (usually worse than "normal" menstrual cramps), pain during or after sexual activity, infertility, and heavy bleeding. Other symptoms may include fatigue, painful bowel movements with periods, lower-back pain with periods, and diarrhea and/or constipation and other intestinal upset with periods. Many women with endo also experience a range of immune disorders, including allergies, asthma, eczema, and certain autoimmune diseases. Infertility affects about 30 to 40 percent of women with endo and is a common result with progression of the disease.

The amount of pain is not necessarily related to the extent or size of the growths. Tiny growths (called "petechial") have been found to be more active in producing prostaglandins, which may explain the significant symptoms that often seem to occur with small implants. Prostaglandins are substances produced throughout the body, involved in numerous functions, and thought to cause many of the symptoms of endometriosis.

Theories About the Cause of Endometriosis

The cause of endo is not known, but a number of theories have been advanced. One theory is the retrograde menstruation, or transtubal migration, theory. According to this theory, during menstruation some of the menstrual tissue backs up through the fallopian tubes, implants in the abdomen, and grows. Research shows most, if not all, women experience some menstrual tissue backup, so experts believe that an immune system problem and/or hormonal problem allows this tissue to take root and grow in women who develop endo. Another theory suggests that the endometrial tissue is distributed from the uterus to other parts of the body through the lymph or blood. A genetic theory suggests that certain families may have predisposing factors for the disease. Research spearheaded by the Association since 1992 has shown that environmental toxins such as dioxin and PCBs, which act like hormones in the body and damage the immune system, cause endometriosis in animals.

Another theory suggests that remnants of tissue from when the woman was an embryo may later develop into endo or that some adult tissues retain the ability they had in the embryo stage to transform into reproductive tissue under certain circumstances. Surgical transplantation has also been cited as a cause in cases where endo is found in abdominal surgery scars. However, endo has also been found in such scars when direct accidental implantation seems unlikely.

Diagnosis

Diagnosis of endometriosis is generally considered to be uncertain until proven by laparoscopy. Laparoscopy is a surgical procedure done under anesthesia in which the patient's abdomen is distended with carbon dioxide gas to make the organs easier to see and a laparoscope (a tube with a light in it) is inserted into a tiny incision in the abdomen. By moving the laparoscope around the abdomen, the surgeon can check the condition of the abdominal organs and see the endometrial implants, if the surgeon is careful and thorough.

A doctor can sometimes feel endometrial implants during a pelvic examination, and symptoms will often indicate endo, but it is not good practice to treat this disease without confirmation of the diagnosis. (Ovarian cancer, for instance, sometimes has the same symptoms.) A laparoscopy also indicates the locations, extent, and size of the growths and may help the doctor and patient make better-informed long-range decisions about treatment and pregnancy.

Treatment

Treatment for endo has varied over the years, but no sure cure has yet been found. Hysterectomy and removal of the ovaries has been considered a "definitive" cure, but research by the Association and others has found such a high rate of continuation or recurrence that women need to be aware of steps they can take to protect themselves. (Please see *The Endometriosis Sourcebook* and Chapter 11 in this book for more information.) Painkillers are usually prescribed for the pain of endo. Treatment with hormones aims to stop ovulation for as long as possible and can sometimes force the disease into remission during the time of treatment and sometimes for months or years afterward. Hormonal treatments include oral contraceptives, progesterone drugs, a testosterone derivative (danazol), and GnRH drugs (gonadotropin-releasing hormone drugs). New drugs are being tested. With all hormonal treatments, side effects are a problem for some women.

Because pregnancy often causes a temporary remission of symptoms and because it is believed that infertility is more likely the longer the disease is present, women with endo are often advised not to postpone pregnancy. However, there are numerous problems with the "prescription" of pregnancy to treat endo. The woman might not yet have made a decision about childbearing, certainly one of the most important decisions in life. She might not have critical elements in place to allow for childbearing and child rearing (partner, financial means, etc.). She may already be infertile.

Other factors may also make the pregnancy decision and experience harder. Women with endo may have higher rates of ectopic pregnancy and miscarriage, and one study has found they have more difficult pregnancies and labors. Research also shows there are family links in endo, increasing the risk of endometriosis and related health problems in the children of women with the disease.

Conservative surgery, either major or through the laparoscope, involving removal or destruction of the growths, is also done and can relieve symptoms and allow pregnancy to occur in some cases. As with other treatments, however, recurrences are common. Surgery through the laparoscope (called operative laparoscopy) has rapidly replaced major open abdominal surgery. In operative laparoscopy, surgery is carried out through the laparoscope using laser, electrosurgical equipment, or small surgical instruments. Radical surgery, involving hysterectomy (removal of the uterus) and removal of all growths and the ovaries (to prevent further hormonal stimulation), becomes necessary in cases of longstanding, troublesome disease.

Menopause also is believed to end the activity of mild or moderate endo, although little research has been done in postmenopausal women. Even after radical surgery or menopause, however, a severe case can be reactivated by estrogen replacement therapy or continued hormone production. Some authorities suggest no estrogen be given for a short time after hysterectomy and removal of the ovaries for endo.

Many alternative treatments, including nutritional approaches, immunotherapy, traditional Chinese medicine, allergy management techniques, and others, are being used by women with endo. A survey of 4,000 women with endo found some of these treatments to be the most successful of all the treatments they had tried.

Learning About Endometriosis

Endometriosis is without question one of the most puzzling diseases affecting women and girls. More is being learned about it as time goes on, and this knowledge is dispelling some of the assumptions of the past. One of these past assumptions was that nonwhite women did not generally get endo. This has now been shown to be untrue. Often nonwhite women were not getting the kind of medical care to have endo diagnosed.

Another myth about endo is that very young women do not get it—an idea that probably arose because formerly teenagers and younger women endured menstrual pain (often one of the early symptoms) in silence and did not get diagnosed until the disease progressed to unbearable proportions. It was also believed in the past that endo more often affected well-educated women. Now we know that this notion developed because well-educated women were those getting the best medical care and were more often persistent enough to obtain explanations for their symptoms.

Another assumption that has at times been made about endo is that it is not a serious disease because it is not a killer like cancer, for instance. However, anyone who has talked with many women with endo about their actual experiences with the disease soon learns otherwise. While some women's lives are relatively unaffected by it, too many others have suffered severe pain, emotional stress, have at times been unable to work or carry on normal activities, and have experienced financial and relationship problems because of the disease. Perhaps someday soon we will understand this perplexing disease and be able to end all the myths, pains, and frustration that go with it!

How the Endometriosis Association Can Help

The Endometriosis Association is a self-help organization of women and families with endo, doctors and scientists, and others interested in exchanging information about the disease, offering mutual support and help to those affected by endo, educating the public and medical community about the disease, and promoting research related to endo. Those affected by the disease help each other by ending the feeling of being alone, sharing with others who understand what one is going through, counteracting the lack of information and the misinformation about endo, and learning from each other.

The Association is an international organization with headquarters in Milwaukee, Wisconsin (USA), members in numerous countries, and chapters and activities worldwide. Elected officers guide the Association with help and suggestions from an advisory board of medical professionals and others. The Association was founded in Milwaukee in 1980 by Mary Lou Ballweg and Carolyn Keith and was the first group in the world dedicated to helping women with endometriosis.

The Support Program provides a wide range of services to help girls, women, and their families. These services include support groups, counseling/crisis call help, assistance finding knowledgeable doctors, a prescription drug savings plan, networking, and other help. At the local group level, meetings and activities are planned according to each group's wishes. Usually some meetings are planned to allow informal sharing of information and support. Other meetings offer speakers and presentations on various aspects of the disease. Group activities also may include fund-raising and outreach into the community to teach about endo.

The Education Program provides a wide range of literature, books, videotapes, audiotapes, CDs, and other educational items to help individuals, the public, and the medical community learn about the disease. Members of the Association receive a popular newsletter covering the latest treatment and research news, as well as activities of the Association. The Association also provides ongoing help to the media and medical community to aid in the dissemination of accurate information about endometriosis.

The Association's Research Program includes maintaining the world's largest database on the disease, a major research partnership with Vanderbilt University School of Medicine, and funding of promising research worldwide. The Association also serves as a clearinghouse for information on the disease. Researchers interested in working with the Association or seeking funding should contact headquarters. Donations to help continue the work of the Endometriosis Association are very much needed and appreciated.

This chapter is available as a brochure in quantity to gynecologists, hospitals, pharmacies, and women's clinics. Please specify the quantity and language(s) desired. Brochures are available in Arabic, Bulgarian, Croatian, Danish, Dutch, English, Farsi, Finnish, French, German, Greek, Hebrew, Hindi, Hungarian, Italian, Japanese, Korean, Lithuanian, Malay, Mandarin, Norwegian, Polish, Portuguese, Russian, Spanish, Swedish, Thai, and Turkish. Preteen and teen versions are also available.

Mary Lou Ballweg is president and executive director of the Endometriosis Association, an organization she cofounded in 1980. Besides founding and leading the Association, she has overseen the publication of the Association's three books and its educational videotapes, an extensive body of literature on the disease, and the development of two million-dollar-plus educational awareness campaigns, four public-service announcement campaigns, and many other outreach efforts. She is editor of the Association's bimonthly newsletter and has produced numerous articles and chapters for journals, magazines, newsletters, and medical textbooks.

Together with Karen Lamb, Ph.D., she established the world's first research registry for endo. She was responsible for a major breakthrough in research linking dioxin to endo, helped develop groundbreaking work on cancer and endo, and has collaborated with the National Institutes of Health on research on autoimmune diseases and endo. She was instrumental in establishing Association research programs at Dartmouth Medical School and Vanderbilt University School of Medicine.

Prior to founding the Endometriosis Association, Ballweg was a communications consultant with her own national business producing film and audiovisual materials and training programs on affirmative action and race/cultural/gender understanding in the corporate and social environments. Earlier she was a scriptwriter-director at a film and public relations company and managing editor of a monthly magazine. She was also one of the founders of a women's community health clinic and has been recognized in numerous Who's Who listings, including *Who's Who in the World*, *International Who's Who in Medicine*, and *The World Who's Who of Women*.

P A R T

TREATMENTS:
A BROADENING
SMORGASBORD
OF OPTIONS

1 Endo: What a Pain It Is!

NEW PERSPECTIVES ON ENDO PAIN

P. Fay Campbell, M.S.Ed.

The Problem with Endometriosis

Endometriosis is an enigma—a very complex disease affecting multiple systems in the body. It's associated with immune dysfunction, allergies, cancer, and many other diseases. The symptoms are various and assorted as well—diarrhea, nausea, fatigue, heavy bleeding, infertility. But for most women with endo, the biggest problem—the one that grabs our attention like a hammer on a thumb—is *pain*.[1]

There are several ways that endo causes pain, and we know that it's real regardless of what we have been told. It is real, it can be ferocious, it is shrouded in myth and misunderstanding, and like all pain, it is invisible. It sometimes seems that the more we learn about endo pain, the more complicated it becomes, and therein lies the problem. Endo isn't something that you can just take to your physician and say, "Fix it." There isn't an easy way to get rid of the pain of endo. That is not to say it is impossible. With patience, education, and perseverance, you can get some control over the pain of endo.

Relying on research and the knowledge and experience of thousands of women with endo, this chapter will explain the nature of endo pain, suggest treatments for relief, and show you how to become the director of your pain management team.

The Nature of Endo Pain

It is well established that pain, acute and chronic, is a major undertreated problem.[2] According to the American Pain Society, pain is the most common reason individuals seek medical attention. The society explains that physicians are used to dealing with problems they can measure objectively, such as temperature, broken bones, tumors, or skin rashes; but because pain is entirely subjective and people's reactions to pain are so individual, it's difficult for physicians to assess pain.

The symptom that brings women with endo to their physicians most often is unrelieved, uncontrolled pain.[1, 3] To understand the treatment of endo pain, we first must have a general understanding of pain. Pain is usually characterized as either acute (short-term) or chronic (ongoing for more than six months). Most women with endo pain have both. Treatment for chronic pain differs from treatment of acute pain because the mechanism of the pain may be different, and treatments that work in the short term may not work in the long term or be safe for long-term treatment.[2, 4, 5] What works well for the acute pain of a sprained ankle, for example, may not work for the chronic pain of endo.

> "After examining me and doing an ultrasound, my doctor said the only problem I had was in my head because I had not accepted the fact that I was a woman, and women were born to suffer!"
>
> —Rosemarie, Illinois

Acute pain or short-term pain that is a result of injury works like this: Tissue injury leads to inflammation, and pain signals are sent to the brain. The brain then signals the release of inflammatory mediators such as prostaglandins, substance P, and serotonin. As the tissues heal, inflammation resolves, and the central nervous system sends out fewer pain signals, which in turn results in decreased pain perception.

Acute pain can usually be controlled effectively by a variety of medications, including over-the-counter medications such as aspirin, acetaminophen, and nonsteroidal anti-inflammatory drugs (NSAIDs) like ibuprofen, or prescription medications such as short-acting opioids like Demerol or codeine. A physician may also prescribe anti-inflammatory medications or muscle relaxants or nondrug therapies such as heat and cold or behavior modification to ease acute pain. In the case of endo, as the disease continues, it causes new or ongoing trauma to tissue, resulting in ongoing acute pain. And that can result in chronic pain.

Pain is complicated enough, but endo pain is even *more* complicated. (We've always known we were special!) Because endo lesions are often microscopic, we can never be sure if surgery has removed all the endo. And even if it has, we still have to deal with the immune system aspects of endo. Endo can cause pain in a variety of ways, including the following:

- **Inflammation**—Inflammation can cause tissue damage that creates pain. (Tissue damage can also cause inflammation.)
- **Pressure/stretching**—Endo or adhesions may be pushing or pulling tissues. Pain may be triggered by exercise, bowel or bladder functions, or sex.
- **Adhesions**—Adhesions may damage nerves or strangle tissue, cutting off blood supply to areas of the body. Adhesions are caused by endo and may also be caused by surgery to remove endo.
- **Nerve involvement**—Nerves may be altered, entrapped, or damaged by the chronic irritation of endo.
- **Increased prostaglandin production**—Endo lesions create their own prostaglandins, which are hormone-like substances, some of which cause pain by causing strong muscle contractions and inflammation. Different types and locations of endo lesions may produce pain in different ways, and some types produce more prostaglandins than others.[6–10]

Often endo pain continues after surgery. Endo is, after all, a chronic disease. If the surgeon thinks he or she has removed all the lesions but the woman still reports pain, the surgeon may believe that the pain is imagined when, in reality, there may be microscopic disease left that the surgeon couldn't see or other factors causing pain. If so, there is ongoing trauma to tissue, causing pain. In fact, microscopic endo is very common. In one study, women undergoing laparoscopy for pelvic pain who did not have visible endo were biopsied in areas of the peritoneum (see Glossary) that looked normal. Of these, 50 percent were found to have microscopic endo.[10, 11]

W. F. (Dub) Howard, M.D., an endo specialist in Dallas, Texas, and an Advisor to the Endometriosis Association, has stated, "I have never laparoscoped a woman, of any age or parity, who had at least cyclic pain who did not also have signs of endometriosis. Sometimes you have to look very carefully, but the signs will be there!"

When long-term pain occurs, as is usual in endo, it can result in a lowered pain threshold and the spread of pain. The way pain is managed may have to change over the course of the disease, because the way endo causes pain may change.[7, 12]

Women's Pain

Even well-educated, open-minded, emotionally healthy women can be woefully unprepared when it comes to discussing endo pain because of preconceived ideas about women and pain, coupled with the extremely personal nature of endo pain. It is often difficult to discuss pain with sex or bowel movements or menstruation with a treatment provider. However, open communication is the cornerstone of effective long-term treatment.

Just as some women hold misconceptions about managing our pain, so do some medical professionals. A report in the *Journal of Law, Medicine and Ethics* states that medical professionals take women's reports of pain less seriously than men's and that women receive less aggressive treatment.[13] It is also likely that women experience pain differently than men. Research presented at a U.S. National Institutes of Health meeting suggests that hormones likely play a role in how pain is perceived. Women are more sensitized to some pain during the premenstrual period than in the postmenstrual period, and higher estrogen levels were associated with heightened sensitivity to temperature.[15]

> "Sometimes I would think that if I were just dead, the pain would be gone."
>
> —Brandi, Michigan

Women also experience certain diseases that produce chronic pain more frequently than men do. Women experience fibromyalgia nine times more frequently than men (in fact, many of these women may have endo) and experience migraine more than twice as often. Women are also more vulnerable to arthritis and temporomandibular disorders (that nasty TMJ, which can cause face, neck, and head pain and cause your jaws to snap, crackle, and pop!). In fact, of the leading causes of chronic pain, only back pain reportedly affects men as often as it does women.

A collaborative study between the National Institutes of Health and the Endometriosis Association shows a higher incidence of fibromyalgia, chronic fatigue immune dysfunction syndrome (CFIDS), rheumatoid arthritis, multiple sclerosis, and other autoimmune diseases in women with endo. That means women with endo are more likely to have multiple sources of chronic pain.[14] If a woman goes to her doctor and says, "My pelvic pain is terrible, my hands hurt, and my legs and shoulders are killing me," the doctor may be tempted to believe the woman is exaggerating because she has so many seemingly unrelated pains. In reality, these pains might be related for some women with endo. The woman who complains of these diverse pains may be suffering from rheumatoid arthritis, fibromyalgia, and endo all at the same time.

Attitudes that women can't handle "normal" pain, that we are hysterical, and that our pain is exaggerated abound. These misconceptions hinder appropriate diagnosis and treatment of our pain. Perhaps because physicians see more women than men with chronic pain, they may assume that many of them must be exaggerating.

To muddy the waters even more, there are gender differences in the efficacy of pain treatments. Research suggests that pain medications are metabolized differently by men and women and, of course, some medications work on some types of pain better than others. This issue becomes even more complex in the case of endo, since the pain is experienced in a wide variety of locations, at various times, and at different levels of intensity (see Figures 1.1 and 1.2).

Deborah Metzger, M.D., Ph.D., an Association Advisor and reproductive endocrinologist in Palo Alto, California, states, "I have had women break down and cry in my office when I told them I would treat their pain. They were just so relieved because no one else would deal with it."

When pain is caused by endo or adhesions, it may be even more undertreated and even more misunderstood than other pain women suffer. Major factors appear to be misinformation and stigma associated with the symptoms of endo as well as with chronic pelvic pain. It takes an average of nine to ten years between onset of symptoms and correct diagnosis of endo. Approximately half of that time elapses because women and girls have not reported the symptoms to their physicians. (See Chapter 13 for this data.) Friends and family, media, and society in general often tell women that "female pain," including painful menstruation and pain with sex, is normal. This is not true. The impression seems to be that if pain isn't a sign of superior femininity, at least it is a sign of normal femininity and must be accepted.

> "I vividly remember that I was staying overnight at my grandmother's house. All of a sudden, I felt extremely nauseated, I broke out in a cold sweat, and I had what I thought was the worst 'stomachache' of my life. . . . All throughout my high school years, I would spend the entire first day of my period lying down in the school clinic, writhing in pain, with a heating pad on my abdomen. I would only get up when I had to vomit. As quickly as I could, I would return to the couch to lie down and clutch the heating pad to my abdomen until the next wave of nausea hit me."
>
> —*Peggy, Texas*

This concept of justified pain leads to additional misunderstanding about the nature of endo. According to the Association's pain survey, 80 percent of women surveyed experience one to three days each month when they are unable to carry on their regular activities, including housework. However, many women reported anecdotally that no one took their endo pain seriously, even after endo was diagnosed, unless and until they had trouble conceiving. It's as if our pain doesn't matter because it's part of being a woman. But if we can't perform womanly duties (have children), then there is something wrong with us.

The Endometriosis Association has heard from physicians who consider giving birth to be proof that endo has been cured. We've also heard from women that their doctors have told them they can't have endo because they have gotten pregnant. The truth is, pain is the primary symptom of endo. Women with endo go to their gynecologist three times more often with a complaint of pain in a wide variety of locations, of differing intensities, and at various times than with a complaint of infertility.

Physicians' response to complaints of pain may be due in part to the fact that historically they were actually taught that pain with menstruation is psychological, and that idea has been slow to change. Additionally, Association data shows pain from endo is actually becoming more severe than it was in the past (see Chapter 13). Mark Per-

FIGURE 1.1 When Do You Feel Pain?

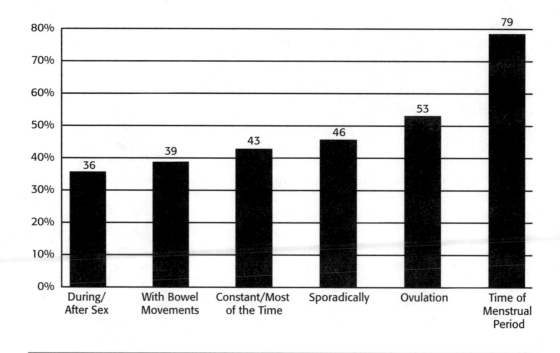

Note: Results based on responses from 819 women with surgically confirmed endo.

loe, M.D., is an Association Advisor and reproductive endocrinologist in Atlanta, Georgia, interested in treating the pain of endo. He believes many gynecologists are unprepared to treat chronic endo pain.

Some physicians fear treating pain aggressively because they perceive that pain medications have potential dangers (legal, social, and physical). They are afraid of being accused of being "pill pushers" or of having the medications they prescribe diverted for illegal purposes. People who are addicted to or abuse medications can be very persuasive in conning physicians into giving them prescriptions for pain medication, so physicians are understandably wary about prescribing the potentially addictive substances.

These barriers to appropriate treatment of pain can hurt your ability to obtain pain relief if your situation requires one of these effective but potentially addictive pain medications. The American Pain Foundation, in much of its literature, proposes that it is unwise to allow the behavior of deliberate drug abusers to dictate medical treatment of pain. They state that, among patients who regularly take opioids for pain and have no

FIGURE 1.2 Where Do You Feel Pain?

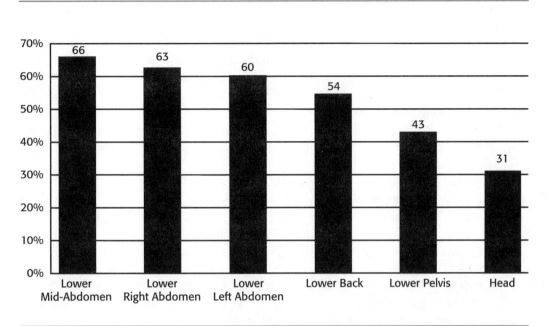

Note: Results based on responses from 864 women with surgically confirmed endo.

Most women with endo pain experience pain at the time of their periods; however endo pain occurs at various times and in various locations for different women. This information is compiled from the Endometriosis Association Pain Survey.

history of substance abuse, the incidence of addiction is 1 percent. That means 99 percent will not become addicted, but it's easy to understand why physicians are cautious.[16]

Many people, including physicians, confuse addiction and physical dependence. A person who is correctly using prescription medication for pain over a long period of time may develop some physical dependence—in other words, the body has gotten used to that substance. He or she may need to reduce the amount of medication used gradually, under the supervision of a physician, when the medication is no longer needed because some physical dependence has developed. This is not the same thing as being addicted to the drug. Addiction includes misusing or abusing the substance in order to get a "high"; not including proper use of the drug.

Women with endo are often told that their pain is exaggerated, imagined, or normal. Association research showed that 69 percent of women were told so by their ob-gyn! The opinions of family and friends add to that pressure, and women with endo are likely to begin to doubt their bodies and believe their pain is imaginary, somehow their own fault, or that they should just buck up and shut up—even though the pain is often disabling. Many women surveyed responded that they themselves had sometimes wondered if their pain was "all in their head."

When a woman doesn't fit the physician's idea of who gets endo or when the physician believes the endo is gone but the woman still reports pain, the physician may psychologically dismiss the woman. This can lead to additional isolation for the woman, and it certainly does nothing to relieve the pain. In essence, she is being punished for feeling pain and asking for help![15, 17]

So not only is there stigma involved with chronic pain, there is misunderstanding about the nature of pain in women and additional stigma attached to menstruation- or sex-related pain. This stigma and misunderstanding is fed by the belief that it is normal to feel some "womanly pain," even when that pain is disabling.

Our attitudes are often colored by a skewed sense of endurance or courage that causes us to believe that only weak people experience pain, or that tough people don't need relief but "tough it out." That is the conundrum of denial—a strong force at work in many women with endo. *Denial* is a psychological term implying knowing and not knowing at the same time. It is like refusing to acknowledge a given state such as having a chronic, incurable disease. Denial can apply to individuals and societies. In the short term, denial may allow us some time to get used to a situation, but in the long run, it can keep us from doing what we need to do to overcome the situation.

It takes a brave woman to accept that the pain means it's time to take decisive action. It is a strong woman who advocates for herself and does what it takes to truly be there for herself, her friends, her work, and her family. It takes courage to stand up to disbelief and face the treatments and lifestyle changes necessary to make sure endo doesn't rob us of our dreams.

Developing a Plan of Attack

In their training, physicians learn the importance of taking a detailed history, but in real life, they often do not have or take the time to listen to a patient discuss her symptoms in detail.[15, 18] Additionally, patients often feel inhibited about volunteering information. But with a complex disease like endo, we have to be proactive and maintain open communication with our physicians and other healthcare providers. We are the experts on our own pain. We must be prepared to give our physicians the information they need in order for them to help us treat our pain.

A woman with endo is very likely to have multiple symptoms and see multiple professionals such as a gynecologist, gastroenterologist, and chiropractor. If a patient needs to see multiple specialists and the treatment is going to be effective, someone needs to coordinate the care, and that's generally not a billable activity. Therefore, coordinating care is not likely something that medical staff is going to do. To make sure our treatment is as effective as possible, we need to become our own case coordinators and take the following steps.

Step 1: Get Medical Records

Get copies of your medical records, including test results from each provider you see. This way, costly tests are not redone, and each provider can build on the body of knowledge already collected. Review what has been written before you share it, and discuss with your new provider any area in which you disagree. Keep a copy so you have your complete medical history.

A woman with endo may have to see more than one physician in order to find one who works well with her, but if she has had the authenticity of her pain questioned in the past, she may not be eager to communicate openly with a new physician. She may think sharing information from the disbelieving physician would be counterproductive, but knowing what's been tried with what outcome, previous test results, even attitudes of previous physicians can be very helpful.

We often expect physicians to know everything there is to know about our pain. Of course, we need them to know as much as possible so they can help us. That means we have to be willing to share all the information we, as owners and operators of our bodies, have about our pain and other symptoms. If we give them inadequate or incomplete information, it isn't fair to go home and be silently angry because we got no help. Although you may be uncomfortable discussing very personal matters, it is important to report every symptom to your physician. (Diagnostic kits available from the Endometriosis Association help you track your symptoms and communicate frankly with your physician.) On the other hand, if our physicians refuse to listen to what we have to tell them, are too busy to look at a pain map or journal (samples in the discussion of Step 3, later in this chapter), or minimize the pain we describe—that is, if they aren't willing to be part of our pain treatment team—it's time to find a different doctor.

Step 2: Get a Videotape of Surgery

Ask that your surgeon videotape the surgery and give you a copy of the tape and the surgical report. Share the tape and the report with any other physician who treats you. Knowing where the lesions were/are, what type of lesions you had, and how they were removed can be very helpful. (Some surgeons may not want to videotape the surgery; see Chapter 3.)

Step 3: Keep a Pain Journal with a Pain Map

Your physician will probably want to examine you when you are in pain, and since it is very difficult for a person to verbally give an accurate and thorough history while in pain, journals are vitally important. Keep a pain journal that includes the name of the treatment, dosage if applicable, and frequency of use, along with the results. Include any activity that may have triggered pain or relief. Keep in mind that the smallest things may greatly increase your pain. For example:

Sample Pain Journal

July 1:

3:00 A.M.—level 2 pain. Took ibuprofen and used heating pad. Period started.

5:00 A.M.—level 7 pain. Took a hot bath; took Tylenol #3.

5:45 A.M.—level 4 pain. Went back to sleep.

9:00 A.M.—level 3 pain. Can't believe I slept so long! Still don't feel rested.

3:30 P.M.—level 3 pain. Appt. with Dr. Smith. Shared my journal and pain map with him. He suggested a topical and gave me a sample. I used it at his office, and pain was barely noticeable when I got home!

6:00 P.M.—level 2 pain. Pain is sneaking back. I used the topical again, and pain is gone.

July 2:

8:00 A.M.—level 2 pain. I slept really well last night. Period is very heavy.

2:00 P.M.—level 2 pain. Took ibuprofen and rested with heating pad.

2:30 P.M.—level 2 pain. Not too bad.

Be sure to include what you eat. Many times women with endo have food allergies that trigger pain. Having a record of what you eat and when you feel pain can be invaluable. One member told us that she had the best week in a long time but then ate wheat, to which she is highly allergic, because a restaurant person told her that the tortilla chips had no wheat in them. She had an extremely severe reaction and developed such severe pain that even Percocet didn't touch it. Consulting a good allergist and trying an elimination diet may be very helpful in determining if you have allergies to foods or other substances.

In conjunction with your journal, use a pain map. (For an example of a pain map, see *The Endometriosis Sourcebook*, pp. 84–85, or order a diagnostic kit from the Endometriosis Association.) Be as specific as possible in communicating where you feel pain and in describing the pain. Use a pain scale to report the intensity of pain. For example, rate your pain from 0 (no pain) to 10 (worst pain imaginable).

Step 4: Develop a Treatment Plan

Develop an individualized treatment plan that includes drug and nondrug treatments by all providers, as well as things you do yourself. Share this with each of your treatment providers.

Your plan should be comprehensive and include every aspect of your life. It will require some serious thought and introspection on your part, but it is the road map that will lead you to beating the pain. Here is an example of a treatment plan:

Date	1	2	3	4	5	6	7	8	9	10
Sleep goal: 8 hrs. per night	6 hrs.	7	7	8	5	8	8	8	8	8
Objective 1: no coffee after 5:00 P.M.	1 cup	X	X	X	1 cup	X	X	X	X	X
Objective 2: go to bed at 10:00	X	X	X	X	11:00	X	X	X	X	X
Objective 3: no TV in bed	X		X	X		X	X	X	X	X
Objective 4: prescribed sleep aid	X	X	X	X	X	X	X	X	X	X

The sample treatment plan shows a sleep goal. Poor sleep quality contributes to pain, which contributes to poor sleep quality, creating a vicious cycle. This person has set a realistic goal and objectives for her situation. She puts an x in each box when she reaches her objectives and records the hours of sleep she got each day. When she combines this information with her pain journal, she will easily be able to see patterns and be able to determine what helps manage her pain. Other goals for medication, exercise, and so on will be recorded the same way.

Communicate with Your Treatment Provider

Women are more expressive of their pain or express pain in ways that physicians may interpret as overly dramatic and find suspect. In American culture, it is more acceptable for women to talk about pain than men, but this might not be to our advantage when it comes to convincing a physician to treat it. The American Chronic Pain Association, Partners Against Pain, the Endometriosis Association, and many patient organizations encourage patients to openly discuss symptoms with physicians and to be active partners in health care. It only makes sense.

However, there seems to be a fine line between adequately describing pain and having it discounted as emotional, psychogenic, or not real. Exactly where that line is located differs from day to day, from physician to physician, from patient to patient, and from pain to pain. It is imperative that women in pain and their physicians learn how to communicate effectively and frankly about pain and its management. Working with your physicians on a treatment plan, taking in pain journals and medical records, and educating yourself about your disease will help show your physician that you are a proactive member of your own healthcare team and will increase good communication.

Include your primary physician in planning how to handle your pain when it comes up, as well as planning how to decrease or eliminate your pain. Have a frank discussion about what to do if the pain reaches a certain point. You and your physician should devise a plan that lets you know that something will be done if the pain gets too severe for you to handle. Imagine that it's the middle of the night and your pain soars to a 9.5 on the 10-point scale. Does your physician want you to call him or her? Should you go to a certain emergency room? Should you have a supply of opioid analgesic medications on hand that you save for such an event? These are questions that should be answered in your treatment plan.

Knowing that there is a plan in place and you won't have to face the worst pain alone is a great comfort. This is especially important for teens, who may feel especially isolated by their pain. Parents of teens with endo need to regularly reassure their daughters that they will help them in times of intense pain and will not give up on pain relief for them.

> "My ovaries feel like volcanoes. Yesterday was an eruption. They feel like they are pulsing out and going to blow up. They send waves of pain. I live in fear over this. The pain keeps building and growing. It begins to hurt when I walk from the reverberation of my feet touching the ground. It is extremely painful to sit, as I cannot even bear the pressure of the weight on my buttocks. Deep pains shoot out of the volcanoes. It becomes difficult to breathe, so I keep it shallow. I can't even touch my hand to my stomach because the pain is so intense now and I feel swollen all over. I'm completely doubled over. I'm on the floor in pain. I keep shifting on my hands and knees and side and back, like a dying animal."
>
> —Diana, California

Baseline

The first step in developing your treatment plan is to determine where you are in terms of pain. This is called determining your baseline. Your pain journal and map will give you a good idea of that. Chart your pain every day for a month on a calendar, recording your pain level on a scale of 0 to 10 (10 being the worst pain imaginable and 0 being no pain at all). Record your period on the same calendar, including how heavy the period is, as well as its duration. You will easily be able to see any patterns when you can look at three months at a time.

In your journal, chart behaviors such as sleep and diet. When you reread your journal, other patterns will emerge. For example, you may notice that the days after you sleep six or fewer hours, you experience more severe pain; or you may notice that whenever you eat ice cream, your pain rating climbs.

Goal Setting

Make sure your goals are realistic. It will be helpful to break down your goals into smaller chunks of time. You may have one-month goals, three-month goals, six-, nine-, and twelve-month goals. If you are currently unable to get out of bed due to pain three days a month and find it difficult to walk a block the rest of the time, it would be unrealistic to make your one-month goal running five miles every day. If you have four days at level 8 pain and the rest are lower numbers, your first goal may be to have fewer than four days at level 8. Other first goals may be to get at least seven hours of sleep every night and not eat any ice cream. Work with your health professionals to set realistic goals for yourself.

You will have goals in various areas of your life. Areas covered may include medical (what medications or treatments your physicians suggest), nutritional (dietary plans and supplements), exercise (may include physical therapist's or chiropractor's suggestions for exercises at home, yoga classes, etc.), spiritual, and attitudinal.

Don't overlook the importance of attitude goals. They will include getting rid of any harmful beliefs that you discover when you take a hard look at your belief system. Examples of harmful beliefs include the myths about women and pain or menstruation that might have taken up residence in your psyche such as the following:

MYTH	TRUTH
Strong people don't talk about pain.	Strong people seek help for pain.
It's normal for a woman to have severe menstrual pain.	Menstrual pain is not normal.
Women are weak, neurotic beings who exaggerate pain in order to get attention.	Women are wonderful, individual, strong, and valuable.

It's easy to distinguish the truths from the myths when it's all written down in black and white like that. Still, the messages are deeply ingrained in our culture, and we often behave as if they are true. In the quest for pain relief, it is important to go on a search-and-destroy mission to get rid of any hurtful ideas we are carrying around about pain and its treatment.

Objectives

Your objectives are things that you will do to reach your goals. You may have several objectives for each goal, or you may have just one. For example, your sleep objectives might be to go to bed every night at the same time; to eliminate caffeine intake after 5:00 P.M.; and to do some gentle stretching exercises, suggested by your chiropractor, before bed. Make sure you have a place to check off each objective as you complete it so that you have a record of what you've actually done rather than simply what you've intended to do.

Objectives for attitude goals might include attending a local support group, positive self-talk, writing and reading affirmations, or reading uplifting books.[19] This is a very individual matter. You may want to work with a counselor or go to a library or bookstore to find information on affirmations and self-talk. A positive attitude can't hurt, but it's essential to remember that just because positive thinking can help, it isn't true that your thoughts caused your disease. Feeling guilty because you aren't thinking positively enough is not productive. (There are many things about endo we don't know yet, but we can be fairly sure that it isn't caused by a negative attitude. Likewise, if you choose a different treatment than your friend with endo, it doesn't necessarily mean that one of you is wrong. Complex, multisystem diseases such as endo require individualized treatment. There is no place for guilt in this fight.)

Other objectives might be to take two aspirin at the first sign of pain, to use a heating pad, to take a hot bath, to exercise for twenty minutes every day, and to eliminate refined sugar from your diet. Your journal will record your pain level, and you can compare it with your treatment plan to see which objectives correlate with increased or decreased pain.

Treatments

There are probably as many diverse treatments for pain as there are types of pain that can be associated with endo. The Endometriosis Association Pain Survey reinforced what we hear from women with endo: What works for one pain or one person at one time may not work for a slightly different pain, a different person, or the same person at a different time.

Women with endo consult a wide variety of sources and try a variety of approaches to seek relief from our pain. Most women in search of adequate treatment of endo see more than one physician. Association data show that following the immunotherapy treatment approach, a change of diet, and exercise—all considered alternative—are often the most effective in relieving pain.

Learning About Medications

If your physician recommends a medication, learn about the drug before taking it. It's a good idea to look up information about every medication you take, even if you've been taking it for years. Ask your pharmacist for help. Every medication you use should be on your treatment plan and in your medical records and pain journal. Over-the-counter supplements and medications, as well as alcohol, tobacco, and recreational drugs, may interact with prescription medications or each other, so be sure to include them in discussions with your physician.

Remember, just because you can purchase a medication without a prescription doesn't mean the medication is completely safe. Never exceed the dosage suggested on the label of the medication. Also be aware that many prescription medications contain a narcotic and an over-the-counter medication because combinations seem to work better than either of the medications alone.[2, 9] Tylenol #3, for example, contains codeine and acetaminophen. If you are taking your limit of acetaminophen and then also take Tylenol #3, you may overdose on acetaminophen, which can be deadly.

When you are taking any medication for pain, whether it's by prescription or over the counter, and you do not get adequate pain relief, *do not* exceed the prescribed dosage. After a certain point, increasing the amount of medication taken does not increase its ability to relieve pain, but side effects and toxicity do increase. So if the bottle of acetaminophen says you can take two tablets every four to six hours, but two hours after taking it you do not have pain relief, do not take more. If you are a parent of a teen with endo, you should make sure she realizes that over-the-counter medications can be harmful, even deadly.

Aspirin relieves pain by working in the brain and throughout the body. In addition to being a pain reliever, at larger doses aspirin is effective as an inhibitor of the synthesis of prostaglandins and works as an anti-inflammatory. These large doses of aspirin should be taken only under medical supervision, because at this amount, there is greater chance of stomach ulceration and other adverse effects. Your physician can recommend brands of coated aspirin that are gentler on the stomach and can be taken at the dosage necessary to be anti-inflammatory. However, other side effects, such as increased bleeding time, are the same as for uncoated or buffered aspirin.[20]

> "For over ten years, I suffered with excruciating pain under my right rib cage. I was given several different diagnoses such as 'floating rib,' 'irritable bowel,' and one surgeon removed my gallbladder! I actually have diaphragmatic endo!"
>
> —*Pam, Illinois*

Other medications more commonly used in the treatment of endo, including NSAIDs (nonsteroidal anti-inflammatory drugs), narcotics, and some topical (used on the skin) medications, are discussed in *The Endometriosis Sourcebook*, and the discussion won't be repeated here. You can also look up any medication suggested by your physician in a drug reference book, such as the *Physicians' Desk Reference* (PDR), which is updated annually, or online at resources such as rxlist.com or nlm.nih.gov/medline plus/druginformation.html, or consult your pharmacist.

Relatively recent arrivals in the world of pain medications are the cyclooxygenase-2 inhibitors (COX-2 inhibitors) such as Celebrex, Vioxx, and Bextra. These (like aspirin at higher doses) work by reducing the production of prostaglandins released at sites of inflammation. They have less of the gastrointestinal side effects of aspirin and the other NSAIDs. Since endo causes pain in various ways, it's good that we have pain relievers that work in various ways as well.[20, 21]

Newer options on the market include topical analgesics specifically aimed at reducing cramping. Menastil and Menstrogesic are two of these over-the-counter options. Menastil is an oil that is rolled on the skin directly over the painful site. Menstrogesic is a cream that is rubbed into the site of pain. Neither agent has reported side effects, and both have been found to help some women. They seem like a good option to try.

Another option that has no known side effects and helps many women with pelvic pain is heat, including your trusty old heating pad. New products on the market, including one called ThermaCare, provide heat for several hours at a time (without having to be plugged into electricity) in a thin pad form that can be worn under your clothes.

Another treatment for chronic pain is the use of local nerve blocks (also called trigger point injections). A local anesthetic (like the Xylocaine your dentist uses) is injected near a nerve, anesthetizing the area. Repeated over time, these trigger point injections may "retrain" the nerves into not feeling pain.

Alternative Treatments

For our purposes, alternative treatment means treatments other than medication or surgery. These include acupuncture (see "An End to Painful Periods," following this article), massage, dietary changes, heat/cold, yoga, exercise, magnets, chiropractic—a seemingly endless list. Many treatments that we think of as "alternative," such as traditional Chinese medicine, have actually been commonly used in other parts of the world. (For a discussion of traditional Chinese medicine, see *The Endometriosis Sourcebook*.) As with any treatment, the responsibility to research the pros and cons rests with the person in pain or the parent, in the case of a minor.

Conclusions

Naturally, it is frustrating for physicians and patients when patients don't respond to treatments for pain. Finding the solution for the pain of endo is likely to be a time-consuming, often frustrating task for treatment providers and women with endo alike. It is a task that can only be begun in earnest once the pain is identified and believed. If a girl or woman with endo is ashamed to discuss her pain or her symptoms are dismissed or minimized by her physician, it is almost inevitable that her pain will continue untreated.

An eye-opener in researching this chapter was that most of the endo literature discusses pain as just one of the many symptoms of endo, which seemed to minimize the importance of pain. Pain is the *primary* symptom of endo. We challenge researchers and treatment providers to consider the concept that pain is "part and parcel" of the disease. Of course, we want to have the whole disease treated and cured, not only the pain. But let's not treat pain as if it's some minor annoyance. Endo pain shouldn't be relegated to two or three pages in the back of the medical texts. We deserve to have our pain taken seriously and treated aggressively.

Treating the pain of endo is difficult but not impossible. For some women, this will mean being totally free of pain; for others, it will mean a reduction of pain. Women with endo must be willing to take responsibility for seeing that their treatment is coordinated among all treatment providers and that they have all the information necessary to do their jobs. When women with endo and treatment providers work together,

After Joe's last surgery for endo and adhesions, he's having problems again.

we can find help for endo pain, and we will change the way society looks at endo pain, one attitude at a time.

AN END TO PAINFUL PERIODS: ONE WOMAN'S SUCCESS STORY

Jennifer Hochgesang

I was so excited the first time I got my period. At thirteen, I relished this sign of approaching adulthood. But the second time, it hurt so bad I could barely stand up. I was baby-sitting when the pain hit, and as soon as the child's mother came home, she gave me painkillers. She told me that monthly pain was normal, and for the next three years, I did the best I could with ibuprofen and heating pads. My gym coach instructed me to run it off, saying exercise would cure the pain, but my abdominal cramps made even walking difficult. By the time I was sixteen, I was missing at least three school days a month.

My mother, who'd been begging me to see a gynecologist, now insisted that I go. I was diagnosed with primary dysmenorrhea (painful menstruation), and the doctor prescribed birth control pills and muscle relaxants. But the next month was no better. My doctor then began to prescribe narcotics like Tylenol #3 [Tylenol with codeine, 30 milligrams] and Vicodin, and each month I had to choose between being bedridden with pain or knocked out on painkillers.

In researching my condition, my mother learned about endometriosis. Although I naively continued to believe that painful periods were just part of being a woman, my mother asked the gynecologist to test me for endo. My doctor recommended laparoscopic surgery.

I signed up for the surgery reluctantly. I was a seventeen-year-old junior in high school and worried about missing more than a week of school before final exams, especially since college entrance exams were approaching. I wished I could just ignore my aching body and the emotional pain it was causing.

When I woke up from the anesthesia, the agony was severe. The carbon dioxide gas that expands the abdominal cavity during surgery had not been adequately removed, leaving my abdomen bloated about four inches higher than normal. Frightened, my parents tried to get me more analgesics for the gas pain coursing through my body, but the doctors told them that the only solution was to wait for the gas to dissipate on its own. I overheard one nurse hint that I was exaggerating my complaints. What a blow that was. I began to think this was my fault, that I was weak and making a big deal out of nothing.

My doctor didn't find endo, but she decided to treat me as if she had. I began taking a high-estrogen birth control pill that stopped my periods but not my pain. (I later learned that estrogen encourages the growth of endometrial tissue.) After three months of agony, I was desperate and turned again to my doctor for guidance. She told me that if I were older, she would suggest that I have a child or a hysterectomy. I decided to see another doctor.

My new doctor had just been featured in a major newspaper because of his success in treating endo. Even though my previous doctor hadn't found endo during surgery, my mother still believed I had it, and after my first exam, the new doctor agreed with her. He suggested a new course of treatment: different birth control pills, hormones, narcotics, and muscle relaxers. None of them worked. I was sick of being sick. A year after my first surgery, I again reluctantly agreed to a second, more extensive one. At the very least, this procedure promised to alleviate my pain for a year. This time the doctor did find evidence of endo and destroyed the visible growths with a laser. The next month, though, I was suffering again. I tried to ignore it because I had less than two months of high school left.

The following fall I went to college in Ohio, eight hours away from my home in suburban Chicago. For the next year and a half, I tried almost every drug conventional medicine had to offer, but the side effects were almost as bad as the endometriosis: depression, migraines, soreness, nausea. I was still on birth control pills that prevented me from having a real period. I was trying to function like a normal college student, but I was tired all the time, and my grades were slipping.

To be close to my doctor and the support of my family, I transferred to a school in Chicago. My doctor suggested another surgery to manipulate or partially remove my presacral nerve, which transmits pain messages from the pelvic area to the brain. Again I was desperate and went along with the plan. But a week before surgery, I learned that my doctor had been accused of performing laparoscopies incorrectly. I immediately canceled my operation.

My next doctor was a reproductive endocrinologist who specialized in infertility. I liked him because he truly understood how much pain I was in. He also suggested a laparoscopy and a presacral neurectomy, which he said eliminates most of the pain in up to 90 percent of patients. The operation could result in a loss of sexual feeling, bladder problems, and constipation, but I didn't care about the risks. I wanted the promise of a pain-free life. In addition to the surgery, the doctor advised me to take Synarel, a GnRH agonist, for six months. He assured me this plan would work. I was twenty at the time.

When I woke up from the anesthesia of my third surgery, I was whimpering with pain. I stayed in the recovery room for six hours because my blood pressure kept dropping. Once at home, I vomited for two days and experienced dehydration, a bladder infection from the catheter, and a popped stitch. Three days after surgery, my period started again with the same torturous cramps. I refused to talk to my doctor.

> "We are taught from an early age to associate pain with our monthly cycle. The problem is that pain is a very subjective thing, and all of our pain thresholds differ. So when I would describe my pain associated with my monthly period, I feel that I was never taken seriously."
>
> —Sue, Wisconsin

Soon after I began taking Synarel, I was hit with menopausal symptoms like hot flashes, mood swings, and insomnia. I plunged into depression. The surgery had affected my bladder, causing me to go to the bathroom as many as five times a night. My relationships with friends and family grew tense, and I withdrew. It was not only the pain that was destroying my ability to function but the effects of so many hormones. I received some relief from Synarel, but when the six-month treatment ended, the pain returned. I thought I had lost all strength to fight.

My mom, though, had found a reason to regain her hope. She located other endo sufferers who had gained relief with acupuncture, and urged me to see a practitioner. It took me more than a year to make an appointment, because I didn't believe acupuncture would work, and I feared more treatments with more needles and—I assumed—more pain. After examining my tongue and the pulses on both of my wrists, the acupuncturist explained that the vital energy, or *qi*, that flows through my body was stagnant around my abdomen. He also said I had excess "heat" in my body, which was causing irritation and pain. Needles would be inserted into specific points on my body to clear the energy flow. I found his explanation simplistic and hard to believe but had nothing to lose.

I was twenty-one when I began the twice-weekly acupuncture treatments; I still saw my gynecologist and took birth control pills. The acupuncturist placed two long, thin needles around my navel, one on the outside of each knee, and one on each of my big toes. I felt a mild "electric shock" when two of the needles went in. With the others I felt a warm and almost itchy sensation. At times I experienced euphoria. In a private room with the lights turned low and calm music playing, the treatments soothed me. Initial sessions lasted only fifteen to twenty minutes, but they stretched to almost an hour as my abdomen became less sensitive. At the end of the sessions, I often was tired. My acupuncturist explained that my body was healing itself, which consumed energy. He also prescribed a horrible-tasting tea of several Chinese herbs, which I often couldn't bring myself to drink.

Unlike my Western doctors, my acupuncturist didn't consider my illness merely physical. Several times during each treatment, he would ask how I felt and, based on my answers, would either manipulate the needles, leave them alone, or remove them. I would often cry during a session for inexplicable reasons. He suggested I had been holding back emotions; he encouraged me to let them out in order to heal. I worked very hard on this emotional healing, which I consider instrumental in my recovery.

Slowly, it began to work. First, my premenstrual pain diminished, and I decided to stop taking birth control pills, even though my gynecologist didn't approve. At last I felt in control of my health. Half a year after my acupuncture sessions began, I could comfortably lie on my stomach and watch a movie—a feat that had been impossible for more than eight years.

I also started selecting foods that would naturally balance my hormone levels and lower inflammation. I avoid most dairy products as well as meat, high-fat foods, alcohol, caffeine, and sugar. I drink at least eight glasses of water a day and have begun swimming to improve my strength. I also had massages to reduce stress and ease the pain from surgical scar tissue.

Today, at age twenty-four, I've achieved almost total remission after two years of acupuncture treatment. I no longer have to plan my life around times of pain. Simply reducing stress, eating well, and exercising are keeping me healthy and pain free.

Looking back on all my medications and surgeries—which didn't help and sometimes worsened my condition—I feel like a fool. I now recognize how important it is to talk to other patients, get second and third opinions, and deal with the emotional drain of a chronic disease. Most importantly, I realize I know my body better than anyone. I know when I'm in pain and when my symptoms are real. I need to listen to myself.

EDITOR'S NOTE Readers need to realize each woman's experiences with endo and treatments are unique. Jennifer had a particularly difficult time with surgery; your experiences may be less difficult. See Chapter 7 of *The Endometriosis Sourcebook* for more information on traditional Chinese medicine, including acupuncture, and endo.

2 What You Need to Know About Treating Endometriosis Medically

MEDICAL TREATMENTS FOR ENDOMETRIOSIS: OLD STANDBYS AND NEW OPTIONS

David L. Olive, M.D.

The medical treatment of endo has been the dominant mode of therapy for over thirty years and today remains an integral part of the treatment approach to the disease. However, the design of medical therapeutics for endo is evolving scientifically, as new strategies are aiding in the attack upon this disease.

We now have a much greater depth of understanding of the growth and maintenance of endo, particularly at the molecular level. This has provided drug developers with new, precise molecular targets for treatment of the disease. Currently under development, these newer agents hold the potential of greater efficacy and flexibility with fewer total body effects.

This article will review those medications currently used as well as those under development for the medical treatment of endo. Doses, routes of administration, side effects, and efficacy will all be discussed.

"I would like to see the Association take a strong stand on the fact that no presently available medication can offer a 'cure.' Many women, myself included, have endured debilitating side effects, in addition to financial hardship, in order to pay for medication, in the belief that it was known to provide lasting benefit. In truth, the medication (partially) suppresses growth of endo tissue, but only as long as the medication is continued. When the medication stops, the endo continues. All I got from Lupron was six months of hell. Surgery eight months after Lupron revealed severe, deeply invasive disease—so what good was a medication that gave me mood swings and ate my bones? Choosing *not* to take Lupron or the other drugs is a valid choice."

—Susan, Texas

Types of Treatment Trials

Although many studies have been published regarding the medical treatment of endo, it is important to realize that not all are of equal importance. A hierarchy of clinical trial design exists that enables the discerning reader to determine which studies should be relied upon most heavily for validity and applicability.[1] These study designs and their place in the hierarchy are explained in the following list:

HIERARCHY OF EVIDENCE FROM CLINICAL STUDIES
1. **Meta-analysis**—Combining the results of many randomized trials of similar design to determine a single answer to a research question
2. **Randomized clinical trial**—Treating patients with either traditional or experimental therapy, with treatment type determined by random assignment (luck of the draw)
3. **Nonrandomized, concurrently controlled trial**—Treating patients with either standard therapy or an experimental treatment; the physician or patient determines which
4. **Historically controlled trial**—Treating a group with an experimental drug, then comparing the results with patients treated traditionally (or untreated) in the past
5. **Case control study or cohort study**—Evaluating a group of patients with a disease compared with the normal population or unaffected women of similar backgrounds
6. **Time series study or anecdotal case reports**—Evaluating a relatively small number of patients, not following them in a standardized way
7. **Expert opinion**—Drawing conclusions based upon clinical experience, not published data

Uncontrolled trials have limited value other than to suggest hypotheses to be tested by more rigorous designs. The same is true for historically controlled studies and concurrently controlled nonrandomized trials, each of which introduces significant biases into the results. The gold standard today is the randomized clinical trial, where subjects are randomly allocated to one of several treatment groups, often in a manner such that the assignment is unknown to the patient or physician until the conclusion of the trial. This type of design is referred to as a "double blind" or "double masked" study. This design is the least biased of all approaches and results in the most reliable conclusions.

Unfortunately, many randomized trials are too small to conclude there is no effect. This is because a large number of patients are often required to be reasonably sure that a small difference in outcome is not simply a chance event. The results of these studies may also differ from one another, due to slight differences in study design, different patient populations, or even as a result of random variation. For these reasons, when multiple randomized trials exist, they can often be combined into a single evaluation called a meta-analysis.[2] The meta-analysis allows us to gain a single, best answer to a question with a higher level of confidence than is usually possible with individual studies. However, it is important to keep in mind that a meta-analysis is only as good as the studies included in it. If poor-quality trials are placed into a meta-analysis, the resulting conclusions are as tenuous as those of the component studies.

> "After the surgery, I took monthly Lupron injections. They were wonderful! I felt so wonderful on the Lupron. I could only stay on that for six months. Six months after my Lupron therapy, my symptoms of endo returned. I thought the Lupron therapy should have kept me pain free for several years."
>
> —*Wendy, West Virginia*

Assessing Treatment Effectiveness

The value of a particular medical treatment upon endo will vary depending upon the goal of the treatment. With regard to endo, three outcomes can be used to determine drug efficacy: the anatomic endo, pain symptoms, and fertility status.

The anatomic manifestations of endo—implants and adhesions—can be assessed before and after therapy to determine whether the treatment is of value. However, such a simple comparison makes two assumptions. First, it is assumed that endo is an invariably progressive disease, never to regress on its own. This is not necessarily correct, however, as the disease has in fact been noted to regress in some instances in both baboons and humans.[3, 4] Second, it is assumed that once regression has occurred via medical therapy, it is stable. This, too, is not the case; endo is a dynamic disease that constantly changes over time. Thus, to adequately address the effect of a medical treatment upon endo lesions, a proper control group for comparison is needed, and patients need to be followed for a reasonable period of time and continually assessed to determine how they are responding.

A second outcome of interest is the effect of treatment upon pain symptoms. The first requirement of pain research is the need for a reliable method of assessing pain.[5] A second necessity in pain research is the need for assessing the patients over a period of time to see how they continue to respond to treatment. Finally, when assessing the value of a drug, it must be realized that the idea a patient is taking a drug may sometimes be enough to convince her or him that the pain is better after treatment, even if the treatment has done nothing. This is called a placebo effect. This phenomenon of relief by inactive drug (the placebo effect) occurred in as many as 55 percent of women with endo-associated pain in a 1979 study.[6] Thus, studies comparing experimental drugs to inactive drug (placebo-controlled trial) are needed to determine the absolute value of a medication. Comparative studies between drugs will allow determination of relative benefits of one drug versus the other.

The final outcome of interest is fertility enhancement. Women with endo-associated infertility rarely are absolutely incapable of conceiving, as is the case with women who have both fallopian tubes blocked or men who have no sperm. Instead, most women suffering from endo-associated infertility have a relative reduction in fertility.[7] Thus, they are able to conceive, albeit at a slower rate. To demonstrate improved fertility status after treatment, a comparison group of untreated women is clearly needed. Finally, the number of pregnancies depends upon how long a group of patients is followed; following them for two months results in a much different pregnancy rate than if they are followed for two years. To truly understand the effect of a drug on fertility, patients must be checked for pregnancy regularly over a reasonable period of time, generally at least six months and preferably one year.

From this discussion, it is clear that the best studies are properly controlled and randomized. In addition, it is important to have studies that have lengthy follow-up so that we can determine the long-term course after treatment. Studies such as these will be primarily relied upon in this article.

Medical Treatments

Danazol (Danocrine, Cyclomen)

Danazol is a derivative of the male hormone testosterone. It was originally thought to work by medically producing a hormonal state similar to menopause, but subsequent studies have revealed the drug to act primarily by diminishing the midcycle surge in luteinizing hormone (LH),[8, 9] causing a shutdown of ovulation. It may also work to interfere with the production of hormones[10] and increase the amount of male hormone in the blood, resulting in an antagonism of the effects of female hormones.[11]

The recommended dosage of danazol for the treatment of endo is 600 to 800 milligrams per day. However, these doses have substantial side effects, such as increased

FIGURE 2.1 Did the Treatment Help?

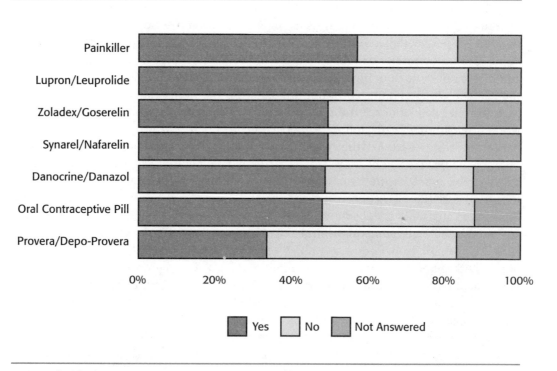

Note: Results based on survey responses from 3,751 women with endo.

This chart shows how 3,751 members of the Endometriosis Association fared with danazol, GnRH agonists, oral contraceptives, and Provera. For comparison, see the figures on surgical treatment in Chapter 3 and on alternative treatments in Chapter 4.

facial and body hair, mood changes, deepening of the voice (possibly irreversible), weight gain, and rarely, liver damage (possibly irreversible and life-threatening) and blood clots in the arteries.[12, 13] A change in serum cholesterol levels might also predispose long-term users to atherosclerosis (clogging and hardening of the arteries), although this has not been scientifically demonstrated. Studies of lower doses as primary treatment for endo-associated pain (50 to 400 milligrams per day) have been uncontrolled or with small numbers and thus contain information of limited value.[14]

Due to the many side effects of the drug, alternative routes of administration have been sought. Recently, the use of danazol vaginal suppositories[15] and a danazol-impregnated vaginal ring[16] have been described in small, uncontrolled trials. Preliminary results suggest side effects may be less severe when this drug is administered via the vagina.

An effect of danazol upon endo implants has been consistently observed. Uncontrolled trials have demonstrated implant resolution in the vast majority of treated patients.[17, 18] Questionable studies have shown a mean decrease of 61 to 89 percent of implant volume[19, 20] and a 43 percent decrease in classification score.[21] A single placebo-controlled randomized trial examined the effect upon implants six months following completion of drug therapy. The study found resolution of implants in 18 percent of the placebo group and 60 percent of the danazol treatment group.[22]

Pain relief has also been well demonstrated with danazol, with 84 to 92 percent of women responding.[23] A randomized placebo-controlled trial proved danazol reduced pain significantly better than no treatment for up to six months following discontinuation of the drug.[22] No good data exists for longer follow-up periods. Recent evidence suggests the average time to pain recurrence following discontinuation of the medication is 6.1 months.[24] Thus, the drug does seem to produce pain relief, but for a limited duration in many.

Two randomized, prospective trials have evaluated the effects of danazol upon fertility. In women with minimal endo, 37 percent of the danazol-treated women conceived within one year, whereas 57 percent of the untreated group became pregnant.[25] A second study included women with all stages of disease, finding a 33 percent thirty-month pregnancy rate in those taking danazol versus 46 percent in thirty months among those taking placebo.[26] Thus, neither study showed danazol to increase fertility; in fact, the opposite may be the case. Given this research, there is no evidence that danazol will enhance rates of conception in women with endo-associated infertility.

Progestogens: Medroxyprogesterone (Provera), Norethindrone (Aygestin)

Progestogens are a class of compounds that produce progesterone-like effects upon endometrial tissue. A large number of progestogens exist, ranging from those chemically derived from progesterone (progestins) such as medroxyprogesterone, to derivatives of male hormones such as norethindrone. The proposed mechanism of action of these compounds is an attack on the ability of endometrium (and endo) to grow, producing a shrinkage of the tissue. Recent evidence suggests that another mechanism of action at the molecular level is the suppression of tissue enzymes called MMPs, which are required for endo to implant and grow.[27]

The most extensively studied progestational agent for the treatment of endo is medroxyprogesterone. The drug was originally used orally for the treatment of endo, with doses ranging from 20 to 100 milligrams daily. (Published randomized studies are limited to 100 milligrams daily.) However, the depot (injectable) formulation has also been used, in a dose of 150 milligrams every three months. Side effects of medroxyprogesterone are multiple and varied. A common side effect is transient breakthrough bleeding, which occurs in 38 to 47 percent. This is generally well tolerated and, when necessary, can be adequately treated with supplemental estrogen or an increase in the progestogen dose. Other side effects include nausea (0 to 80 percent), breast tenderness (5 percent), fluid retention (50 percent), and depression (6 percent).[28] In contrast to danazol, all of the adverse effects mentioned here resolve upon discontinuation of the drugs. Norethindrone acetate also has been utilized as a treatment for endo. This drug has only been analyzed in a retrospective, uncontrolled trial of fifty-two women.[29] Each was treated initially with 5 milligrams daily, with increases of 2.5-milligram increments up to a maximum dose of 20 milligrams daily, until periods stopped. Side effects were similar to those seen with medroxyprogesterone.

Other progestational agents have also been used in the occasional study. These include lynestrenol, a gestagen used primarily in Europe. Levonorgestrel, the active ingredient of Norplant, also has been utilized recently, via an intrauterine device (IUD) delivery system.[30] The drug has been shown to effectively decrease vascular endothelial growth factor (VEGF), a chemical important in the development of new blood vessels. As endo requires a new blood supply following implantation in order to grow and develop, there is rationale for use of this drug in treating this disease.[31] It has been touted recently as a desirable treatment for rectovaginal endo, although evidence thus far is uncontrolled.[30]

Progestogens may adversely affect serum lipoprotein levels, the molecules in the blood linked to risk of atherosclerosis and heart disease. These drugs significantly decrease high-density lipoprotein (HDL), a change linked to an increased risk of coronary artery disease.[32] Data on medroxyprogesterone acetate are less clear, with studies demonstrating either no effect[33] or a slight decrease.[34] It is likely that there is a decrease in HDL with all these agents, but the magnitude is related to the specific progestogen and the dose administered. Whether alterations in serum lipoprotein levels for four to six months have any medical significance is unclear because there has been no long-term follow-up.

Although progestogens clearly affect endometriosis, there is limited information on exactly what they do to lesions. In the rhesus monkey, levonorgestrel has been shown to decrease endo implant size. In the human, a single randomized prospective trial demonstrated that 100 milligrams of medroxyprogesterone daily for six months pro-

"When I took Synarel and Lupron, I knew about the side effect of bone loss. I read somewhere, possibly in the Endometriosis Association newsletter, that bone loss may continue for up to an additional six months after the drug is no longer being taken. Concerned, I mentioned this to my doctor at my annual checkup and he said he'd do a bone scan, just to take a look. I honestly thought my results would be normal as I take calcium and do weight-bearing exercises three to four times per week. When my doctor read the results of the bone scan, he was amazed. I had the bone density of a sixty-five-year-old woman (I am twenty-nine). He thanked me profusely, telling me that he would never have ordered the bone scan if I hadn't brought up the subject."

—Elizabeth, California

duced complete resolution of implants in 50 percent of patients and a partial resolution in 13 percent, whereas corresponding figures for placebo were 12 percent and 6 percent, respectively.[35]

Placebo-controlled studies offer the best evidence as to the efficacy of pharmaceutical agents in the treatment of endo-associated pain. Only one such high-quality study exists where researchers evaluated the effect of medroxyprogesterone acetate, 100 milligrams a day for six months. The medication produced a significant and substantial improvement in pain scores while patients received the drug, as well as up to six months following discontinuation.[22] Randomized comparative trials suggest medroxyprogesterone to be comparable in efficacy to danazol; conversely, the progestogen, lynestrenol, performed less well than a GnRH agonist for all aspects of endo-associated pain.[36]

Progestogens have not been shown to be effective in improving fertility. A recent randomized trial showed medroxyprogesterone to be ineffective at enhancing fertility rates compared to placebo.[37] In a nonrandomized trial of women with early-stage disease who were treated with medroxyprogesterone, danazol, or observation (no treatment), the pregnancy rates over a thirty-month period were similar.[38] Another randomized study, including women with all stages of disease, similarly found no difference in pregnancy rates among these three treatments.[26]

In conclusion, progestogens appear to be of value in combating the physical manifestations of endo (at least temporarily), as well as the pain associated with the disease (at least temporarily). However, there is no evidence that progestogens can be used to improve fertility rates in women with endo-associated infertility.

Oral Contraceptives (Numerous Brands)

The combination of estrogen and progestogen for therapy of endo, the so-called pseudo-pregnancy regimen, has been utilized for more than forty years. The treatment was based on the early observation that pregnancy, with high levels of both hormones, produces a regression of the disease. Although we now know this not to be universally true, experimental data suggest some endo does indeed respond in this manner.[39] Interestingly, this finding directly conflicts with data from a rhesus monkey study demonstrating larger implants with considerable local growth following such a therapeutic approach.[40]

Combination oral contraceptive pills such as norethynodrel and mestranol, norethindrone acetate and ethinyl estradiol, lynestrenol and mestranol, and norgestrel plus ethinyl estradiol have all been used to treat endo. Side effects include those encountered with progestogens alone, as well as estrogenic- and androgenic-related effects. Estrogens may cause nausea, high blood pressure, blood clots, weight gain, and enlargement of the uterus. The progestogen portion of the pill may cause effects such as acne, hair loss, increased muscle mass, decreased breast size, breakthrough bleeding, and deepening of the voice.

In a comparative trial of birth control pills versus danazol, researchers found that 41 percent of the birth control pill group failed to complete their course of therapy due to side effects of the medication.[41] However, in that study, dosages generally involved more estrogen and progestogen than are found in modern contraceptive preparations. The oral contraceptives commonly prescribed today for combination therapy are most likely to produce a progestogen-dominant picture similar to that of progestogen alone (see the previous section on progestogens).

Today, oral contraceptives are the most commonly prescribed treatment for endo. Despite this, there are little data regarding mechanism of action. One recent investigation suggests that oral contraceptives suppress proliferation and enhance programmed cell death (apoptosis—see Glossary) in endometrial tissue, perhaps providing a clue for the action of these drugs.[42]

> "As a teenager I had menstrual pain and heavy bleeding, but have since had very mild symptoms after I first took the birth control pill for a year in my early twenties."
>
> —Nancy, Virginia

Numerous uncontrolled trials have evaluated pain relief, generally demonstrating improvement in 75 to 89 percent of women treated with this medication.[28] A recent randomized clinical trial compared cyclic low-dose oral contraceptives to a GnRH agonist and found no substantial difference in the degree of relief afforded these women by the two drugs, except that the GnRH agonist provided greater relief of dysmenorrhea.[43] An uncontrolled trial of oral contraceptives given continuously (no sugar pills, as are generally at the end of the pack) following failure of cyclic therapy suggested that this regimen may be superior, as 80 percent responded with pain relief.[44] However, no randomized trials have as yet assessed continuous administration.

Reports of pregnancy rates in women with endo-associated infertility treated with oral contraceptives are sparse and uncontrolled. None provide evidence of improvement of fertility by these medications.

In summary, oral contraceptives have been documented to improve endo-related pain symptoms to a degree comparable to other treatments and at a fraction of the cost. However, there are no data suggesting fertility-enhancing effects.

GnRH Agonists
Leuprolide (Lupron), Nafarelin (Synarel), Goserelin (Zoladex), Buserelin (Suprefact), Triptorelin (Decapeptyl), Deslorelin plus Ethinyl Estradiol (Libra), Histrelin (Supprelin)

Gonadotropin-releasing hormone agonists (GnRH agonists) are drugs similar in structure to the hormone GnRH. This hypothalamic hormone is responsible for stimulating the pituitary gland to secrete FSH and LH, two hormones necessary for normal ovarian function. The hormone is administered by the brain in pulses; the correct pulse results in stimulation of FSH and LH release. A pulse rate that is too fast or too slow results in a decrease in pituitary hormone secretion.

GnRH agonists are modified forms of GnRH that bind to the pituitary receptors and remain for a lengthy period. Thus, the pituitary identifies them as rapidly pulsatile GnRH. They initially stimulate FSH and LH secretion, then they bring about a shutdown (down regulation) of the pituitary and no resulting stimulation of the ovary. The result is a state of low estrogen similar to that of menopause, producing a lack of growth of the uterine lining and a cessation of menstrual periods. This may be how the drug works on endo, also—by preventing growth. Other possible mechanisms of action include altering the proteins in the body responsible for inhibiting cell attachment to and invasion of other tissues.[45]

The agonist can be given as a nasal spray, an injection just below the skin, or an injection deep in the muscle, depending upon the specific product. Frequency of administration ranges from twice daily to every three months. The side effects are those of having a low estrogen level, such as transient vaginal bleeding, hot flashes, vaginal dryness, decreased libido, breast tenderness, insomnia, depression, irritability, fatigue, headache, osteoporosis, and decreased skin elasticity. These are dose dependent.[46]

A modification of GnRH agonist treatment is to "add back" small amounts of hormone in a manner similar to that used in the treatment of postmenopausal women. The theory is that the requirement for estrogen is greater for the growth of endo than is needed by the brain (to prevent hot flashes), the bone (to prevent osteoporosis), and other tissues deprived of this hormone.[47] This theory seems to be true for pain symptoms, with estrogen-progestogen add-back therapy resulting in an equivalent rate of pain relief with far fewer side effects than GnRH agonist alone. Estrogen as a solitary add-back, however, is less effective and thus not advised.[48]

The effectiveness of GnRH agonists in the treatment of endo-associated pain has been demonstrated in both placebo-controlled and comparative randomized trials. The one placebo-controlled study demonstrated greater effectiveness of the drug at three months, at which time those in the placebo group still suffering from pain were allowed to opt out of the study.[49] In comparative trials, GnRH agonists and danazol were equally effective in relieving pain.[21, 50–64] As mentioned earlier, oral contraceptive treatment is nearly as effective as GnRH agonist treatment.[43] The length of relief from these medications is highly variable from study to study and has not been compared with other medications.

> "I would like to see the Association take a strong stand on the fact that no presently available medication can offer a 'cure.' Many women, myself included, have endured debilitating side effects, in addition to financial hardship, in order to pay for medication, in the belief that it was known to provide lasting benefit. In truth, the medication (partially) suppresses growth of endo tissue, but only as long as the medication is continued. When the medication stops, the endo continues. All I got from Lupron was six months of hell. Surgery eight months after Lupron revealed severe, deeply invasive disease—so what good was a medication that gave me mood swings and ate my bones? Choosing *not* to take Lupron or the other drugs is a valid choice."
>
> —*Susan, Texas*

While the studies just described randomize patients for initial therapy of endo-associated pain, one study has examined the value of GnRH agonist in patients who have tried a medical therapy already and failed to obtain relief. In this study women who had not obtained relief with oral contraceptives were treated with either GnRH agonist or placebo.[65] Those treated with GnRH agonist responded significantly better than those given placebo, with more than 80 percent experiencing pain relief in three months.

Several trials have addressed the efficacy of combined add-back therapy and GnRH agonist treatment during six-month treatment periods.[66-71] In general, pain was relieved as effectively with the combination as with GnRH agonist alone, and it significantly reduced the side effects of the GnRH agonist. The results were similar in three longer trials of approximately one year's duration.[72-74] It seems clear that add-back therapy can be added to GnRH agonist treatment without loss of efficacy but with a substantial reduction in the type of symptoms that result from low estrogen levels. This seems to be the case even when the add-back therapy is begun during the first month of treatment, suggesting that an interval without add-back therapy at the beginning of a treatment cycle is unnecessary.[71]

Treatment of endo-associated infertility with GnRH agonists has not proven to be of value however. Randomized trials have failed to show any improvement of pregnancy rate.[75]

In summary, GnRH agonists are an effective treatment for endo-associated pain, and although the side effects can be substantial, these can be minimized with estrogen-progestogen or progestogen-only add-back therapy. GnRH agonists with add-back therapy have been used in studies for up to twelve months. They may be able to be administered longer in a safe and effective manner if bone density scans are utilized perhaps every fifteen to eighteen months to monitor GnRH agonist–caused bone loss, although no data are available yet. However, the value of GnRH agonists in endo-associated infertility has not been demonstrated.

GnRH Antagonists
Abarelix-Depot, Cetrorelix (Cetrotide), Ganirelix (Antagon)

Like GnRH agonists, the class of drugs called GnRH antagonists are molecules similar to GnRH that cause the pituitary gland to stop producing hormones that stimulate the ovary. In response, the ovary ceases to make estrogen, just as with GnRH agonists. Unlike GnRH agonists, however, these drugs do not cause an initial stimulation of gonadotropin and ovarian hormone release.

Studies in animal models of endo have been quite promising,[86] and preliminary clinical trials suggest the drug is safe and efficacious. A recent investigation in women demonstrated a GnRH antagonist to improve the health-related quality of life in women with endo.[87] Clinical trials are currently ongoing to further validate the use of this med-

Unfortunately, Joe's company has changed to an HMO insurance plan. His plan doesn't cover the endo specialist who did his last surgery, so he sees the HMO doctor.

ication for endo, as questions must be answered regarding relative efficacy and rate of side effects compared to GnRH agonists.

Ethylnorgestrienone (Gestrinone)

Gestrinone is an antiprogestational hormone used extensively outside the United States for the treatment of endo. Its effects include androgenic, antiprogestogenic, and anti-estrogenic actions. The latter is not mediated by estrogen receptor binding.

This steroid has long been believed to act by counteracting progesterone in endo, so that estrogen cannot act on the tissue. Interestingly, these effects did not occur in experimental samples of endometriotic tissue.[76] Gestrinone may also inhibit ovarian hormone production.[77] Thus, the mechanism by which this drug works is still unclear.

Gestrinone is administered orally in doses of 2.5 to 10 milligrams weekly, on a schedule of daily, twice weekly, or three times weekly. Most side effects are mild and transient, but several—such as deepening of the voice, increased hair growth, and enlargement of the clitoris—are potentially irreversible.

Several randomized trials have assessed the ability of Gestrinone to decrease the amount of endo. The drug has been shown to reduce the amount of disease comparably to danazol,[78] and doses as low as 1.25 milligrams twice weekly can accomplish

These comments about support groups for endo were actually made by doctors at a California HMO meeting.

this.[79, 80] Comparative trials show Gestrinone to be roughly equivalent in pain relief to danazol[78] and GnRH agonists.[81] One study has even shown Gestrinone to be slightly more efficacious than GnRH agonist for relief of dysmenorrhea six months after discontinuation of medication.[81]

Finally, there is no evidence that Gestrinone can enhance fertility in women with endo-associated infertility.[82] Thus, clinical efficacy of Gestrinone appears to be similar to that of all the aforementioned medical treatments for endo.

Antiprogestins (Mifepristone) and Selective Progesterone Receptor Modulators (J867)

Apart from its role in pregnancy termination, mifepristone (RU486) may well prove to be of value in a wide variety of disorders, including endo. The drug is an anti-progesterone and antiglucocorticoid that can inhibit ovulation and disrupt endo. It can also decrease the number of estrogen and progesterone receptors in endo, making the tissue less responsive to these hormones.[83] Daily doses of the medication range from 50 to 100 milligrams, with side effects ranging from hot flashes to fatigue, nausea, and liver toxicity. No effect upon lipid profiles or bone mineral density have been reported.

The ability of mifepristone to produce a regression of endo has been variable and apparently depends upon duration of treatment. Trials of two months in rats[84] and three months in humans[85] failed to produce regression of disease. However, six months of therapy result in less visible disease in women.

Uncontrolled trials suggest possible efficacy for endo-associated pain, although the number of women studied is small.[85] No data have yet been collected regarding fertility enhancement.

Selective progesterone receptor modulators (SPRMs) are partial antagonists of progesterone, but also behave like progesterone in some tissues. This mixed agonist-antagonist effect may prove valuable if an SPRM can inhibit growth of endo while not producing other systemic effects of progesterone, such as breast tenderness, depression, and fluid retention. Early studies of the SPRM J867 have suggested efficacy in pain relief with minimal side effects.

Pentoxifylline (Trental)

Pentoxifylline is a drug that affects the immune system in a wide variety of ways, primarily by decreasing inflammation. Given the many immunologic abnormalities described in endo, this medication may seem like a rational choice to correct immune dysfunction. As it is not an inhibitor of ovulation, pentoxifylline has an advantage over most hormonal agents when attempting to treat endo-associated infertility: it can be administered throughout the time period of attempting conception. Doses have ranged from 400 to 1,200 milligrams daily. The drug is extremely well tolerated, with the major adverse effects being gastric (stomach) discomfort and dizziness. Both side effects are seen in few patients utilizing the recommended dose. Randomized trials evaluating the utility of this drug are currently under way.

Selective Estrogen Receptor Modulators (Raloxifene, Evista)

Selective estrogen receptor modulators (SERMs) are drugs that behave like estrogen in some tissues but actually combat estrogen in other tissues. Specific SERMs have been identified that do not cause growth of endometrium but act like an estrogen in bone, liver, and brain. Thus, the potential for these drugs is to inhibit the growth of endo without producing side effects of low estrogen elsewhere in the body. Initial studies proved to be uninspiring, but better-constructed studies are currently under way and may show promise.

Aromatase Inhibitors
Letrozole (Femara), Anastrozole (Arimidex), Exemestane (Aromasin), and Others

Endo appears to depend upon estrogen for growth and development. However, the estrogen does not have to come from the ovary! Recent investigation has shown that endo is capable of producing its own estrogen, due to the presence of an enzyme called aromatase.[88] This enzyme is not found in normal endometrium but is seen in endo. Aromatase inhibitors stop the enzyme from producing estrogen, thus preventing endo growth. Aromatase inhibitors have now been tested in rats with good success.[89] In addition, a case report of the use of one such aromatase inhibitor in a postmenopausal woman with severe endo suggests the potential value of this treatment in women.[88] However, substantial bone loss in this woman emphasizes the need for caution with this class of medications and reinforces the value of larger clinical trials to determine safety and efficacy. Such trials will soon be forthcoming.

TNF-Alpha Inhibitors

Tumor necrosis factor alpha (TNF-α) is a cytokine that appears to be overproduced in endo patients and may well be at least partially responsible for the influx of peritoneal macrophages known to occur in women with this disease. One therapeutic approach that has been considered is some type of blockade of this molecule. This has been attempted in the baboon, where a protein that strongly binds and inactivates TNF-α (TBP-1) was administered to menstrual endometrium before distributing the tissue in the abdomen.[90] In this scenario, endo development was inhibited. Additionally, baboons with endo were treated with TBP-1, GnRH antagonist, or placebo; significantly less endo was noted with TBP-1 and GnRH antagonist treatment. These studies suggest TBP-1 is effective in treating the physical manifestations of endo in the baboon and may be of value in the human. Clinical trials, however, have not yet been conducted.

Angiogenesis Inhibitors
Endostatin, Celecoxib (Celebrex), Rosiglitazone (Avandia), TNP-470, 2-Methoxyestradiol

The establishment of a new blood supply is essential for the survival and development of endo. This process, called angiogenesis, represents a potential target for drugs designed to stop the spread of this disease. Several factors that aid in the development of new blood vessels have been noted in endometrium and endo. The most prominently studied of these factors is vascular endothelial growth factor (VEGF), which is responsible for inducing early blood vessel growth. This molecule has been noted in endo lesions,[91] endo cysts of the ovary,[92] and the peritoneal fluid[93,94] of endo patients. (However, in the case of peritoneal fluid, it is unclear whether levels are the same as or increased

"I followed my doctor's recommendation and went on danazol. However, I had tried that course before and was literally knocked flat by the side effects. I asked my doctor if a smaller dose than 800 milligrams per day was better for someone of my size. I am five feet tall and weigh less than ninety pounds. He wasn't sure but was willing to try it. After one episode of breakthrough bleeding after two weeks on the danazol at 400 milligrams, my periods were stopped for nine months. The side effects were minimal. This may be of interest to teens and others who are small or may have had side effect problems."

—Susan, Wisconsin

"I happily renew my membership because of the work you all are doing. If it were not for information about an experimental study on [a drug], I would probably have had a hysterectomy. Instead I am now a joyful mother of an almost three-year-old daughter."

—Barbara, Massachusetts

over controls.) In any event, one logical therapeutic step would be to attempt inhibition of these new blood vessels as a way of deterring the development of endo. This has been attempted in the mouse, where several inhibitors of angiogenesis (endostatin, TNP-470, celecoxib, and rosiglitazone) reduced the number and size of lesions.[95] No human trials have yet been conducted with these or similar agents.

Matrix Metalloproteinase Inhibitors

Matrix metalloproteinases (MMPs) are enzymes that remodel tissue to facilitate attachment and growth of other tissues. MMPs are crucial to the development of endo, and inhibition of these enzymes might be effective in stopping its development. Only one study has been conducted to date: the MMP inhibitor ONO-4817 was used in mice to deter the development of experimental adenomyosis.[96] The value and practicality of this approach in endo remains to be tested.

Medical Therapy Following Surgery

The use of medical therapy for endo is not restricted to the use of medications as stand-alone agents. Frequently, physicians have used drugs in combination with surgical treatment of the disease. When this approach is utilized, the medical therapy may be administered either before or after surgery.

Only one randomized trial has studied the value of hormonal therapy before surgery.[97] In this study, women with advanced endo were treated either with three months of a GnRH agonist prior to surgery or with surgery alone. Surgery was noted to be easier, according to the surgeon, after treatment with the GnRH agonist (but not statistically significantly easier), but surgical outcome was not assessed in terms of symptom relief.

Numerous randomized trials have examined the use of medical therapy after surgery as a means of further reducing pain. Danazol was found not to enhance the results of surgery when administered for only three months,[98] but six months of use after surgery reduced pain versus placebo for at least six months following discontinuation of the drug.[100] High-dose medroxyprogesterone (100 milligrams per day) behaved similarly.[99]

Three randomized studies have examined the use of GnRH agonists after surgery. Three months of treatment did not enhance pain relief,[100] but six months of postoperative therapy significantly reduced pain scores and delayed recurrence of pain.[101, 102] The use of oral contraceptives for six months following surgery has been shown ineffective in improving the results of surgery.[103] Finally, a randomized trial compared use of a levonorgestrel-containing IUD after surgery versus surgery alone. This study found that the addition of the postsurgical IUD significantly reduced all forms of pelvic pain.[104]

One randomized clinical trial has examined the use of a single medical therapy after surgery versus two medical treatments in a row following surgery.[105] The researchers compared the use of six months of postoperative GnRH agonist therapy with six months of GnRH agonist followed by six months of danazol (100 milligrams per day). Twelve months following surgery (at the conclusion of danazol for one group, and after six months of no treatment for the other), there was significantly less pain in those treated with the two medical treatments in sequence.

Three studies have investigated the use of medical therapy after surgery for fertility enhancement, utilizing GnRH agonist[100, 102] and raloxifene,[106] a selective estrogen receptor modulator. None have demonstrated any enhancement of fertility in women with endo utilizing this approach.

Conclusions

Given the data seen in this chapter, a number of conclusions can be reached regarding treatment of endo symptoms with medical therapy. It appears that most established medical treatments are effective for the initial treatment of endo-associated pain, and all seem to be roughly equivalent in the degree of pain relief. Thus, for initial treatment, the choice should probably be based on the cost and side-effect profile of the drug being considered. However, only GnRH agonists have been proven effective after the failure of a prior medical hormonal therapy. It remains to be seen what the value is for the newer, investigational therapies; the answers will await upcoming efficacy and comparative trials.

The role of medical therapy after surgery is more difficult to assess. Clearly, six months (rather than three) of medroxyprogesterone, danazol, or GnRH agonist seem to be more effective at relieving pain than surgery alone. However, concern regarding the adequacy of surgery must raise caution. At least one retrospective trial has indicated that excision of endo results in greater pain relief than ablation of lesions, and it is unclear what approach and what degree of surgical skill were used in these trials. Further high-quality studies are needed to further examine this issue.

A more definitive and interesting answer surfaces when evaluating the value of medical therapy in the treatment of endo-associated infertility. Currently, five studies with six treatment arms have been published evaluating active medical treatment versus either placebo or no treatment.[25, 26, 37, 75, 82] The results of these studies clearly show that medical therapy—whether individual drugs or cumulative effects—does not result in an enhancement of fertility.

But wait! While some studies were placebo-controlled, others simply compared medication to no treatment. For this latter study design, follow-up of the patient was begun at the conclusion of therapy. Thus, women receiving no treatment began attempting to conceive immediately after the diagnostic laparoscopy, while those placed on drug therapy were not allowed to attempt conception until after the medication course was completed (generally six months). These studies were analyzed as if the time began at the conclusion of "treatment," but for the patient, the clock begins ticking at the time of diagnostic laparoscopy. The real question is not who gets pregnant faster after therapy is completed, but rather who gets pregnant faster from the time of diagnosis.

If we reanalyze the same data, with follow-up proceeding from the time of diagnosis instead of conclusion of treatment, a different conclusion emerges. Now medical therapy proves significantly detrimental to fertility. In essence, the interval spent on medical therapy has been wasted time, merely serving to prolong the infertility in a number of couples. Should we consider this? After all, a woman may want or need to be pregnant as rapidly as possible. Thus, the answer to the rigorous scientific question of the value of medical therapy in endo-associated infertility differs from the best response to the clinical question: Scientifically, medical therapy has no apparent effect upon fertility. Clinically, the use of medication appears to be harmful.

This is not to suggest that medical therapy is incapable of playing a role in the treatment of the infertile couple with endo. It is quite possible that there is a subgroup of infertile women who could be helped with drug therapy. However, this subgroup is thus far unidentified; advocates should focus future trials upon somehow looking at specific subgroups of endo patients and then randomizing them to drug versus no treatment. Until that time, it is clear that medical therapy plays no role in the treatment of endo-associated infertility.

This is an exciting time for both physicians and patients who desire better treatments for endo. For many years there has been little new on the medical treatment horizon, but this is about to change. Many new drugs are under development, and several show the promise of being able to directly attack endo while avoiding effects upon the remainder of the body. This new, specific, highly targeted approach is a direct result of our improved understanding of the disease process itself. It is hoped that as that knowledge is further enhanced, medical interventions will achieve even greater efficacy.

EDITOR'S NOTE See *The Endometriosis Sourcebook* for in-depth information on GnRH agonists and danazol, and watch the Endometriosis Association international newsletter for updates on new drugs as information becomes available. Women interested in possibly participating in new drug clinical trials should contact the Association; we alert many thousands about such trials each year.

MORE THAN YOU BARGAINED FOR: DO YOU KNOW WHAT'S IN YOUR MEDS?

Brenda W. Quinn

If you are a woman with endo, it may seem that you take more than your fair share of prescription and over-the-counter medications. But as you deal with the latest side effect, did you ever think that the problem may not be the *active* ingredients, but the *inactive* ones?

"I happen to be extremely allergic to dairy products and Provera is made with lactose, so I had to cope with various allergic reactions," wrote one member. As a result of her comment and those of other members, we got out the *Physicians' Desk Reference* and began looking up the ingredients of drugs often used by women with endo.

We were surprised to find a cornucopia of "fillers," some very complicated and some—like wax, table salt, black iron oxide—just plain odd. The majority of the fillers, though, were simple: lactose (milk sugar), starches, sugars, and dyes or colorings (see Figure 2.2).

Many people don't think twice about ingesting these ingredients. But it's been well documented by Association research that women with endo are often more sensitive to chemicals and have more allergies and asthma than the general population. In addition, some treatments for endo involve limiting or eliminating these very substances. So it's doubly important for us to know *all* of the ingredients in what we're taking, even if it's only our daily vitamin.

Your pharmacist receives very detailed information on every drug dispensed. He or she can easily copy it for you when you pick up your prescription. Many drug companies and pharmacies provide patient information inserts automatically, but if they don't, *ask for them and read them.*

Additionally, most libraries carry medical reference books that list drug ingredients. Some of the information is available online. The U.S. Food and Drug Administration has online information about inert ingredients (visit fda.gov/cder/drug). In Canada, go to hc-sc.gc.ca/hpb/drugs.dpd for information.

If you can't find the information you want, contact the drug's producer. Drug companies are not required to list inactive ingredients, but many do. Also, if you believe you have experienced side effects from any of these elements, report it to your doctor, the manufacturer, and your government drug administration. More and more studies are being done on the effects of these "inert" substances, and it's important to make your voice heard. In the United States, report adverse reactions to MedWatch at the FDA (phone 301-443-1240 or visit fda.gov/medwatch). You can also call the FDA with questions (888-463-6332). In Canada, consumers can contact Health Canada to report adverse reactions (phone 866-234-2345 or send E-mail to cadrmp@hc-sc.gc.ca).

FIGURE 2.2 Inert Ingredients (Additives) in Medications

Additives	Drugs Containing Additive* Partial List	Who Needs to Know	Conditions Caused by Additive** (Possible Reactions)
Lactose (milk sugar)	Aygestin, Benadryl, Celebrex, conjugated estrogens (generic of Premarin), Danocrine (danazol), Estratab, Evista (raloxifene), MS Contin, Norgesic, Ortho-Novum, Ortho Tricyclen, Oxycontin, Premarin, Provera, Toradol, Vioxx	Those who are allergic to milk or lactose intolerant	Diarrhea; cramping; bronchospasm
Starch (includes corn starch, pre-gelatinized starch)	Conjugated estrogens, Danocrine, Demerol, Ecotrin, Estratab, Excedrin, Mifeprex (mifepristone), Motrin, Norgesic, One-a-Day vitamins, Ortho-Novum, Ortho Tricyclen, Percocet, Provera, Tri-Norinyl, Tylenol, Vicodin, Xanax	Diabetics; those with allergies; those who are prone to have *Candida albicans* or other yeast problems	Digestive upset and allergic reactions in those sensitive to these ingredients
Sugars (includes cellulose, sucrose, dextrose, glycerin)	Aleve and Anaprox (naproxen sodium), Aygestin, conjugated estrogens, Darvocet, Demerol, Depo-Provera, Ecotrin, Estratab, Evista, Indocin, Lupron, Mifeprex, Motrin caplets, Norgesic, Premarin, Premarin vaginal cream, Provera, Toradol, Tylenol liquid, Tylenol Extra Strength, Vioxx	Diabetics; people who are prone to *Candida albicans* or other yeast problems	Digestive upset and allergic reactions in those sensitive to these ingredients
Benzalonium chloride	Synarel	Those sensitive to this chemical, especially those with asthma	Bronchospasm; cough; burning sensation; decreased lung function
Benzyl Alcohol	Premarin vaginal cream, Tylenol gel caps	Parents (Benzyl alcohol can be toxic to infants.)	Respiratory problems and death in newborns; in adults, contact dermatitis, nausea, fatigue, and fever

Ingredient	Products	Who Should Be Concerned	Effects
Dyes: FD & C Blue 2, Yellow 6, Green 5, or Red 7, 27, 28, and 40	Aleve, Anaprox, conjugated estrogens, Danocrine, Ecotrin, Estratab, Evista, Indocin, MS Contin, Norgesic, Ortho-Novum, Ortho Tricyclen, Oxycodone, Percocet, Ponstel, Premarin	Anyone sensitive to dyes or aspirin	Bronchospasm; gastrointestinal intolerance; contact dermatitis in adults; hyperactivity in children
Carnauba wax	Ecotrin, Estratab, Evista, Motrin caplets, Premarin, Excedrin	Consumers	With ingestion of large amounts, irritation of the digestive tract and nervous system
Talc	Aleve, Anaprox, EC-Naprosyn (naproxen sodium), Danocrine, Ecotrin, Estratab, MS Contin, Oxycodone, Premarin, Provera, Synthroid	Those concerned with the health risks of talc use	Several studies show external use of talcum powder increases risk of ovarian cancer (American Cancer Society website). The effects of oral ingestion may be different.
Calcium sulfate (also known as plaster of paris***)	Premarin	Consumers	Nontoxic, but large amounts can cause obstruction
Polyethylene glycol (a solvent—a substance that has the ability to dissolve)	Aleve, Anaprox, Depo-Provera, Ecotrin, Evista, Indocin, Miralax powder, Motrin caplets, Norgesic, Nulytely (bowel prep product, also known as GoLytely), Toradol	People facing surgery; those with certain intestinal diseases or blockage; those sensitive to this chemical	Skin rash; bloating; nausea; cramping; bronchospasm

*Source: Physicians' Desk Reference, 55th Ed., 2001.

**Sources: MEDLINEplus Drug Information; American Academy of Pediatrics Policy Statement; U.S. Occupational Safety and Health Administration Material Safety Data Sheets.

***Plaster of paris is a substance that is wet when applied but quite hard when dry. It is used as a building material, in sculpture, and in paleontology as a mold for fossils.

It's interesting to note that there are fewer additives in medications that are *not* taken orally, such as suppositories, creams, or even injections. You may want to discuss this with your doctor or pharmacist when deciding on treatment. Endo treatment doesn't have to be "one size fits all," and there are doctors who will customize your dosage and pharmacists who will compound your prescription. (See Chapter 11, "Menopause and Endometriosis.") Ask your pharmacy about the ingredients used in their preparations.

Figure 2.2 is by no means comprehensive but should give you a starting point for your own investigation. If a drug is not included in this table, do not assume it is free of potentially harmful inert ingredients. Prepare to be amazed, then do your homework so you know what you're taking!

3 Surgery and Endometriosis: Expanding Horizons

ENDO SURGERY . . . OR NOT?

Ellen Agger

When I woke from my third endometriosis surgery late last year, I didn't know what I would face. Had the doctor removed my uterus? My tubes? Ovaries? Most important, did she suspect ovarian cancer?

For a dozen years, I had successfully been able to control my endo symptoms with various "alternative" treatments—the latest symptoms of bloating, headaches, and muscular pain minimized by avoiding foods to which I had become sensitive. But then I discovered, through a routine pelvic ultrasound, a new, large mass on my right ovary. This was not the first such finding in my history with this disease. I decided to watch and wait.

This picture began to change by summer with further bloating and abdominal pressure. Unlike so many women with endo, I have never experienced much pain, although my endo is extensive. However, I had become increasingly concerned, particularly in light of new information from the Endometriosis Association, that what I had presumed was another ovarian endometrioma could in fact be ovarian cancer.

A move from the largest city in Canada to rural Nova Scotia meant not only a change of gynecologist, but a change in the relatively easy access I had had (never mind the waiting time) to a choice of sophisticated endo treatment options. I consulted my local gynecologist, who referred me to another gynecologist in the larger city nearby, one who had more experience operating through the laparoscope. My goal: to have less invasive laparoscopic surgery to remove and biopsy the mass on my right ovary. I needed to know what it was.

However, according to the second doctor, it wasn't going to be as simple as that. She was concerned about endo behind the uterus that might have penetrated the bowel; she found uterine fibroids, seen on previous ultrasounds, that may have been growing. She would have to do the surgery using a laparotomy, a major incision in my abdomen, a much more invasive surgery than I was seeking. And she felt it might be necessary to remove my uterus as well as one or both tubes and ovaries. This was not the news I expected at that first visit.

Difficult Questions

I had a number of difficult questions to answer before I could make any decisions:

- Was the endo worsening, or was I perhaps feeling an increase of symptoms because I was not sticking closely enough to my dietary regime?
- Were my symptoms bad enough to warrant major surgery? Would the scarring from this kind of surgery be worse than the symptoms themselves?
- What about my fears of ovarian cancer? If I chose not to have surgery, was I willing to live with the constant fear that I might in fact have early-stage, possibly treatable ovarian cancer that would later become untreatable and would kill me?
- Did I have any options to return to my previous gynecologist in my old city, who might be able to do this surgery through the laparoscope? What if he tried, then during surgery found he had to do a laparotomy, leaving me stranded a thousand miles away from home?
- Was I going to sign consent papers giving the gynecologist permission to remove my uterus and both tubes and ovaries if she deemed this necessary during the surgery?
- If I awoke from the surgery without my ovaries, suddenly thrust into surgical menopause, would I need to take estrogen immediately, or did I have other options? Could I spend time experimenting with herbal approaches to menopause symptom relief? Would my mother's severe osteoporosis put me at greater risk for developing it myself if I was suddenly, at age forty-seven, in menopause and chose not to take hormone replacement therapy?

What had started as a simple visit to my local gynecologist to ask about having a laparoscopy to make sure everything was OK had taken me down a much different road, one on which I was not yet prepared to travel.

Learning More

I needed more information to help me answer these questions and feel comfortable with my decisions. So I set out to learn about ovarian cancer, its symptoms, my chances of having it, treatment options. I consulted a naturopath about herbal hormone replacement options if I found myself in surgical menopause. I learned all I could about hormone replacement therapy so I could be as informed as possible if I needed it right after the surgery. Yes, I was exhausted from the stress of research and worry.

In Preparation

After vacillating for weeks, I finally decided to go ahead with the surgery. Since I didn't know how extensive it would be and exactly how long the recovery period would last, I planned to set up my house so I could live and work on the main floor during what might be a six-week recovery period. As I live alone, I arranged for help from friends during that time. None of this was easy.

I prepared for the worst-case scenario: total hysterectomy with removal of both tubes and both ovaries, plus a removal of a section of bowel if the endo had penetrated the bowel wall. I did not plan for the truly worst-case scenario: ovarian cancer. I realized I needed to protect myself psychologically and emotionally from what felt like "too much information." Instead, I identified local and Internet resources available to me for further investigation if and when I needed those.

I also prepared for the surgery by buying and using daily a set of audiotapes recommended by Mary Lou Ballweg and available through the Endometriosis Association. These *Surgical Support Tapes* included six tapes that claimed to reduce pain and promote healing after trauma. I arranged with my doctor and anesthesiologist to get their support so I could use the tapes during the surgery and in the recovery room. These tapes, I felt, made a world of difference, allowing me to use less pain medication than is typically used. I suspect they also speeded my recovery.

The Results of the Surgery

I do not have ovarian cancer. The endo did not involve my bowel. The doctor was able to leave my uterus intact, as I had clearly indicated was my preference. She removed both tubes, the entire left ovary (full of an endometrioma that hadn't been seen on the ultrasounds), and one-third of the right ovary along with its endometrioma. I am not in surgical menopause.

For five weeks, I devoted myself to healing, with the help of many friends, resting and sleeping when I needed to, going for daily walks of increasing distance over the weeks. I was able to get back to a limited schedule of computer work after two weeks, early perhaps for some, but manageable with the supports I had put in place.

I feel tip-top now, six months later. My energy is back to its normal high level, abdominal strength what it was. I was fit before the surgery, and I gradually increased my physical activity during the recovery period and was able soon to enjoy the winter snow with daily snowshoeing complementing yoga and long walks.

As I look back now, the experience is a fleeting shadow in my life, but at the time, it took an enormous amount of energy and focus to struggle with the many questions that at first seemed to have no clear answers. I discovered that only I could make the decision to have surgery, based on all the information I could gather—much of it speculating about the odds—coupled with my intuitive feelings about what was best for me. If I develop further problems with endo, my first approach will be, as always, to investigate alternative treatments. But the decision to have surgery at this time was the right one for me.

WHO'S WATCHING OVER YOUR SURGEON'S SHOULDER? SURGICAL REGULATION IS SURPRISINGLY LAX

Linda Duczman and Mary Lou Ballweg

When you fly (or look skyward to see a jet passing overhead), it's reassuring to think, if it occurs to you at all, that the pilot at the controls is licensed. The safety and welfare of air passengers and air travel is considered so important that governments oversee the process of licensing pilots. To become licensed, aspiring pilots must "fly" on flight simulators, accumulate a specified number of hours of flying time, and pass both written and oral exams. They must demonstrate proficiency at handling an aircraft during a test flight with a qualified government inspector or designated pilot examiner. The examiners who do the testing (the Federal Aviation Administration, or FAA, in the United States) are independent of pilots, airlines, and any person or organization that may have an interest in whether the pilot being tested gets a license or not.

Now, consider the surgeon at the controls of the complex array of equipment required to perform operative laparoscopy. The surgical profession is self-regulating; there is no FAA for surgeons. The government does not license surgeons to perform surgical procedures. A surgeon's ability to perform surgery, including operative laparoscopy, is supposed to be judged by other surgeons. For anyone contemplating having surgery, it's important to know that the medical system, as it exists today, does not provide consistent, objective scrutiny of a surgeon's capabilities by an independent third party (persons with nothing to gain or lose from the outcome of a situation or process).

How Self-Regulation, in Theory, Works

The current process of surgical self-regulation involves "credentialing" and "privileges." Both processes are typically undertaken through the hospital at which a surgeon wishes to do surgery. Credentialing involves determining whether the surgeon meets certain predetermined standards, including a medical degree as well as specific training. Sometimes specialty medical organizations set up credentials to allow their members to perform certain procedures. Privileging involves any process set up by an individual hospital to determine whether a physician can provide care to that hospital's patients.

These processes are inherently problematic. Obviously, if a hospital does not have surgeons on staff with appropriate "privileges," it will not be able to bring in the patients and funds to keep the hospital going. In addition, the surgeons who serve on the privileging and credentialing committees in hospitals often fear charges of restraint of trade (and lawsuits in this regard are not uncommon) if they fail to allow a surgeon to join the hospital staff. These and other reasons make the current "self-regulation" system patchy at best.

Endo at the Cutting Edge

Women with endometriosis are very much affected by these issues because surgical techniques for endo are, so to speak, "cutting edge." Most endo surgeries are conducted via laparoscopy, which, until the mid-1980s was used primarily for diagnosis, not actual surgical procedures through the laparoscope. All of that has changed—mostly for the better—since, at the Association's beginnings in the early 1980s, women were frequently undergoing major open abdominal surgery with all of its pain and long recovery. However, because the state of surgical regulation is less than perfect (to say the least!) and since the surgeries we undergo are usually with newer techniques, the issues about surgical regulation affect us directly.

Operative laparoscopy was not pioneered in medical schools but rather by top endo surgeons. As such, the techniques were considered suspect and too new to routinely teach as part of gynecologic training. Thus, there has not been, and to some degree still is not, a carefully developed program of training to ensure that gyns are trained in at least basic operative laparoscopy techniques in medical school itself. The fact that these techniques were so new meant that the surgical self-regulation system did not have the opportunity to catch up with the field. This was made all the more difficult by the natural controversies and issues of any evolving technology. (Of course, one could ask why the regulatory mechanisms weren't—and still aren't—*ahead* of the innovations so that patients can be protected while new techniques are being developed.)

Some of these problems came to light in 1995, about a decade after operative laparoscopy had been introduced to clinical practice, in a paper by Italian researchers Pier Crosignani, M.D., and Association Advisor Paolo Vercellini, M.D. In the paper, they reviewed data, comments, and proposals on the controversy as to whether laparoscopy or laparotomy was better at treating endometriosis.[1] (Since that time there has been something of a consensus that laparoscopy, *if performed by a skilled and experienced surgeon*, is better—the patient can often leave the hospital the same day and recover much more rapidly than with laparotomy. In short, it is much less invasive.)

Crosignani and Vercellini concluded in 1995 that laparoscopy had become the treatment of choice for minimal and mild endo lesions, for cutting out cysts, and when adhesions were not particularly dense. They also concluded that despite the information and opinions published up to that time, it was still uncertain whether laparoscopy or laparotomy was better for treatment of advanced disease. Some of the papers they looked at suggested inadequate reporting of complications associated with advanced laparoscopic procedures. Other papers pointed out that in evaluating successful laparoscopic surgery, too much attention was being paid to the kind of equipment used, rather than to the surgeon's skill and experience, his or her preference for technique, and proper patient selection. Still other papers noted that new surgical techniques and new applications of these techniques were often introduced in clinical practice without controlled comparison and before their safety was demonstrated.

Crosignani and Vercellini made it clear that surgery for severe endo tested a surgeon's skills and required high levels of expertise. But as one of the papers they reviewed stated, there were questions about how the "technically feasible" was separated from what was "therapeutically appropriate." In other words, just because it was possible to do something, did not mean it was good for the patient. The researchers made suggestions for the future training and preparation of laparoscopic surgeons—suggestions that are revealing for what they say about the preparation of laparoscopic surgeons:

> "First, this is one more letter of thanks for the wonderful flow of information and hope you provide with your hard work and dedication to us endo sufferers. Thanks to your organization of cooperation between the researchers, doctors, etc., us laymen can try to take control of this chronic illness with some dignity.
>
> "I'm writing from my hospital bed in frustration. I've just had my second laparoscopy. My surgeon removed a cyst and found a new batch of what he called multiple pinpoint lesions on my ovaries. He left them intact and untouched. . . . The medical team wanted me to see a psychiatrist because they believe these pinpoint lesions are incapable of causing the pain I complain about. I am furious that I'm not being taken seriously. From your article "Choosing a Laparoscopic Surgeon" in *The Endometriosis Sourcebook* and other sources, I know small lesions can be sources of pain."
>
> —Amy, Germany

- Trainee surgeons should be able to perform procedures at laparotomy before attempting the corresponding laparoscopic interventions and should be able to manage potential complications.
- Time spent working with expert surgeons in training centers should be lengthened.
- Continued monitoring (of practicing surgeons) could be partly ensured by requiring annual lists of procedures performed, with complications and postoperative results, countersigned by the highest-level administrators from the institution in which the surgeon worked.
- Weekend courses or those lasting a few days whose main purpose is "to obtain qualifications" should be limited.

There is no guarantee that any of the improvements the researchers suggested have been widely implemented. If you think you have a guarantee of competence and qualification because your prospective surgeon is credentialed and has surgical privileges at a hospital, you may want to take a closer look before letting him or her perform your surgery.

According to D. Alan Johns, M.D., director of the Gynecologic Laparoscopy Center at Harris Hospital in Fort Worth, Texas, few residency programs teach advanced laparoscopy and endoscopy. Johns says programs for ob-gyns provide less experience in surgery than do programs for any other surgical specialty. The short time spent in the operating room makes it almost impossible for someone in such a program to learn everything necessary to perform as an adequate surgeon, according to Johns, who has served on credentialing committees and is certified in laparoscopy and hysteroscopy by the Accreditation Council for Gynecologic Endoscopy. Johns has spoken on complications of operative laparoscopy at the World Congress on Endometriosis and at the annual meeting of the American Association of Gynecologic Laparoscopists.

The issue of limited surgical training and experience for residents in obstetrics and gynecology was the subject of the presidential address to the Society of Gynecologic Surgeons in 1997. "Too many residents have performed a limited number of vaginal or pelvic procedures by graduation. Some residents still sit for the basic board examination having completed one or two vaginal hysterectomies. Yet, the Resident Review Committee has modeled residency programs that deemphasize gynecologic surgery," said James G. Blythe, M.D., of Saint Louis, Missouri. Blythe traced this development back almost forty years to when teaching institutions fused the education and training for obstetrics and gynecology into a single department. Little by little, he said, attrition in the quality and training experience occurred, especially in gynecologic surgery.[2]

To address training needs, short courses to teach relevant laparoscopic skills have been developed. In 1998 researchers looked at one such course, comparing the basic laparoscopic surgical and suturing skills of trained surgeons and residents who had completed the two-and-one-half-day Yale Laparoscopic Skills and Suturing Program.[3] For two of four skills tested, they found that, following the training, residents' per-

Joe and Stella decide to pay themselves for a visit to the endo specialist who did his last surgery.

formance was the same as that of trained surgeons. For the other two skills, residents performed better on one, and the trained surgeons on the other. The study concluded that basic skills could be acquired with a high level of competence in a brief course, unrelated to prior surgical experience.

Credentialing for Laparoscopy Becomes an Issue

So, credentialing guarantees high-quality standards, right? Consider how it's determined that a surgeon's skills make him or her sufficiently qualified and competent to perform laparoscopic surgery. Tragedies—both in the United States and England—drew attention to the qualifications of surgeons performing laparoscopy. In 1992, following 7 deaths and 185 life-threatening complications resulting from laparoscopic gallbladder surgeries (performed by general surgeons, not gyn laparoscopists), New York became the first state in the United States to issue training guidelines in surgery. The New York State Health Department specified that "surgeons must perform at least 15 laparoscopies under supervision" before a hospital could allow them to perform the procedure independently. Two years later in England, the wife of a prominent citizen died following a laparoscopic hysterectomy. Her grief-stricken husband approached Parliament, asking about the experience and qualifications of the performing surgeon. An inquiry raised questions about the surgeon's competency that compelled the Royal Colleges of Surgery and Obstetrics and Gynaecology to develop recommendations for training and credentialing in operative laparoscopy.[4]

Following the deaths in New York, Ricardo Azziz, M.D., of the University of Alabama at Birmingham, discussed in a medical journal the "pressing and immediate problem" of training and credentialing laparoscopic surgeons.[5] He noted that university hospitals at the time were reluctant to undertake operative laparoscopy training, many considering the technique a gimmick rather than a surgical advance. Referring to New York's guidelines for surgical training, Azziz warned fellow surgeons that if responsible surgeons did not do what was necessary to assure quality training and credentialing, it was obvious that government might. Like most businesses, the medical business does not want government regulation (which may mean paperwork, bureaucracy, inspections, additional cost, etc.). Azziz advocated that the various medical societies encourage a structured training and credentialing process that those granting operating privileges at each hospital would enforce.

> "I am so grateful to you, for it is through the endo newsletters that I learned of Dr. X. After two surgeries I am now feeling *normal*. What a feeling!"
>
> —Helen, Illinois

"Credentialing a surgeon's skills, particularly when they have not been acquired in residency, can be a political and legal hot potato," Azziz noted. He suggested that "uniform and indiscriminate implementation of credentialing guidelines" would neutralize this issue. To simplify the process, he divided operative laparoscopy skills into three levels. In terms of dealing with endometriosis, the first skill level would qualify the surgeon to remove mild and moderate lesions and small cysts. The second skill level would allow the surgeon to excise large cysts and less severe adhesions. Only at the third level would a surgeon be allowed to perform advanced procedures like presacral neurectomy and large bowel resection. The profession listened to Azziz—sort of.

Professional Organizations Issue Guidelines

Ultimate responsibility for credentialing in the United States belongs to the medical staff of hospitals, with guidance provided by the Joint Commission on Accreditation of Healthcare Organizations (JCAHO). (There is more information later in this chapter on JCAHO and on credentialing in Canada.) As Azziz suggested, professional organizations have attempted to help surgeons document their qualifications for credentials. In 1992, a committee of the American Association of Gynecologic Laparoscopists (AAGL) issued its first guidelines for qualification of gynecologists requesting privileges to perform operative laparoscopic procedures:

- Each applicant must be a member in good standing of the hospital and department of obstetrics and gynecology.
- Each applicant should have extensive experience using the laparoscope and hysteroscope for diagnostic or sterilization procedures or both. Experience should include the use of video monitors to direct procedures in addition to operating through the laparoscope.
- Each applicant must have documented resident education and experience, usually obtained by a course in operative laparoscopy that has been approved for American Medical Association category 1 credits or American College of Obstetricians and Gynecologists (ACOG) continuing medical education credits. Training should include sessions of eight to ten hours that cover theory and review instruments and safety factors. Following this, a "hands-on" laboratory must be incorporated, with each participant having at least two hours of actual experience using the instruments on actual tissues.
- The applicant should observe live surgery by other surgeons. Following this training experience, each surgeon should be supervised in the use of these techniques, preferably in the hospital where privileges are requested. The supervisor should make recommendations to the department in writing.
- Gynecologic surgeons should restrict their activities to equipment with which they are qualified and procedures for which they are credentialed.[6]

AAGL guidelines also refer to Azziz's three-level measure of skills. Level 1 would be acquired in residency, Level 2 in practice and after an additional training program like that suggested by the AAGL, and Level 3 only after significant additional training:

- **Level 1**—Mild-to-moderate cutting and division of adhesions, small-to-moderate cysts, and mild-to-moderate endometriosis
- **Level 2**—Large cysts; severe adhesions
- **Level 3**—Innovative surgery, presacral neurectomy, colon resection, extensive pelvic sidewall dissection, dissection of an obliterated cul-de-sac

AAGL also started the Accreditation Council for Gynecologic Endoscopy (ACGE) to address the credentialing issue. To be certified by the ACGE, gynecologists are required to submit certified hospital lists of their advanced endoscopic cases (fifty laparoscopies and/or twenty hysteroscopies) and provide dictated operative notes on the procedures listed and pathologic reports. In questionable cases, further documentation is requested, including a discharge summary. ACGE reviews these materials. It also queries the National Practitioner Data Bank and asks applicants to demonstrate continuing education credits and good standing in the medical community by way of a letter of recommendation. (The National Practitioner Data Bank, established in 1990, collects information on adverse actions taken against health practitioners and malpractice payments made on their behalf. This information is made available to hospitals and other healthcare groups that review credentials of medical personnel. The data bank is maintained by the Health Resources and Services Administration, one of eight Public Health Service agencies within the U.S. Department of Health and Human Services.) According to Anthony Luciano, M.D., one of the founding members and current president of the ACGE, only those surgeons who fulfill the established ACGE criteria are certified by the council.

In Great Britain, a working party of the Royal College of Obstetrics and Gynaecology (RCOG) reviewed operative laparoscopy practices and recommended a classification of degrees of skill required similar to that proposed by Azziz:

1. Diagnostic laparoscopy
2. Minor procedures (including sterilization and coagulation of endometriosis AFS stage I)
3. More extensive procedures (including lasering or coagulation of endometriosis AFS stage II or III)
4. Advanced laparoscopy (including dissection of obliterated cul-de-sac and endometriosis AFS stage III and IV)

The group also suggested that the RCOG set up a Training and Certification Committee. It gave this committee the responsibility of identifying a panel of gynecologists experienced in performing and teaching laparoscopic and hysteroscopic techniques to supervise and oversee the training. They had also decided that any trainee found inept at the surgical skills training course would be advised not to proceed with a surgical career. Three national laboratory centers for training were established. After a surgeon complied with the training suggested, RCOG would issue a certificate of competence. But, as with training and credentialing efforts in the United States, implementation of this plan was delayed when it became difficult to review the qualifications of the prospective trainers.

Canada and Australia reported similar credentialing efforts and similar delays, "both qualification and political in nature." Most of Europe planned to follow RCOG recommendations; France and Switzerland were exceptions. Some French surgeons pioneered development of laparoscopic surgery, but unfortunately the majority of French surgeons did not learn the techniques. France established a formal education program for certifying surgeons, and Switzerland considered a requirement that a surgeon perform twenty supervised procedures before being given a "passport" to perform procedures alone. The World Health Organization (WHO) is planning regional training centers with European-based surgeons in developing countries.[7]

Credentialing in Practice

So many organizations; so many guidelines. What does it all mean? According to Dr. Johns, the various professional organizations have established recommendations for credentialing that are essentially meaningless. The guidelines are designed to be broad enough so that the vast majority of an organization's members will qualify, because if they don't, individuals who don't meet the guidelines will drop their membership in the professional organization. "There is no objective assessment of expertise," said Johns.

Dan C. Martin, M.D., of Memphis, Tennessee, is past president of the AAGL and editor of the *AAGL Manual of Endoscopy* as well as an Advisor to the Endometriosis Association. He points out that the various organizations' guidelines also don't always agree with one another. Moreover, none are validated, meaning there is no scientific proof they improve patient care.

A 1995 survey of 144 hospitals in the United States provides a snapshot of the current state of credentialing. The researchers divided the hospitals into four categories: university-affiliated, large medical centers, medium-sized centers, and small. Of the hospitals queried, 92 percent responded.

Consider that according to this survey, only half the hospitals have a written code of credentialing criteria! Three out of four have specific requirements for awarding surgical privileges. Less than half have a formal method for identifying surgical complications.[8] It appears that laparoscopic surgery has yet to achieve the "uniform and indiscriminate implementation of credentialing guidelines" that Azziz thought would cool the "hot potato" of credentialing.

"It's rare for an institution to deny privileges to perform laparoscopies," says Dr. Johns. He explains that in qualifying a surgeon for surgical privileges at a hospital, a "proctor" may watch a gynecologist, for example, perform a handful of cases. The proctor then writes a report on the surgeon's performance. But Johns, like many others, believes fear of lawsuits or charges that a proctor is attempting to stifle competition mean that the report seldom recommends against allowing a surgeon to operate. Another reviewer for this article notes, "While credentialing can often be too lax due to fear of lawsuits by the denied physician, the opposite can also occur: inadequate surgeons can attempt to limit competition in an area by making the credentialing process so onerous even a great surgeon cannot get credentialed. A common example is with urologists preventing gynecologists from performing urogynecologic procedures, despite being well trained and with experience. Money and monopoly speak loudly!"

One foolproof way to judge a surgeon's proficiency, according to Johns, would be to require the surgeon to supply unedited videotapes of five to ten complete treatments of difficult cases. "On video you can see everything that happens. It's almost the same as sitting in the operating room and watching," he says. Johns has proposed videotapes to the accreditation council, but the suggestion has been voted down. "Doctors are afraid of malpractice and lawyers getting hold of the tapes," he explains. And Association Advisor Kay Lie, M.D., of Toronto, Ontario, states that malpractice insurance companies recommend to surgeons that they not videotape their surgeries.

In an editorial for the *Journal of the American Association of Gynecologic Laparoscopists*, Dr. Luciano discusses credentials as one of several factors a hospital should

Survey of Hospital Requirements for Surgeons Doing Laparoscopic Surgery[7]

Requirement	% of Hospitals with Requirement
Credentialing by individual procedure, with surgeons required to take course in that procedure	65%*
Specific requirements for awarding privileges	75%
Systematic collection of credentialing criteria and availability in written form	50%
Formal method for identifying complications	<50%
Required animal laboratory/laser course	50/60%
Proctoring	85%
Proctoring for residents at university-based hospitals	<50%
Subdivision of cases according to difficulty (simple, moderate, advanced)	<50%
Categorization of laparoscopic-assisted vaginal hysterectomy and repair of ureter or bowel as advanced (opinion on other procedures varies widely)	90%

*University-based hospitals were the least likely to have this requirement!
Source: C. J. Levinson, "Credentialing in the United States," *Journal of the American Association of Gynecologic Laparoscopists* 2(4) Supp. (August 1995): p. S26.

consider in granting privileges for advanced endoscopic surgery. Luciano, of New Britain, Connecticut, is the editor of the journal as well as a past president of the AAGL. He argues that appropriate patient selection, professionalism, integrity, and honesty are also important, and these can only be assessed by professional colleagues and quality assurance and peer review committees.[9]

Luciano said that every hospital of which he is aware has a peer review system for assessing a surgeon's performance by reviewing his or her cases and complications. He believes careful consideration of many different measures is the best way to judge performance. "We are people, and people are not perfect," he reminds us. "Some days we do a better job than others."

Luciano also believes the profession, through mechanisms like the ACGE, can be self-regulating and does not want to see government get involved in credentialing. He fears the added bureaucracy and expense but recognizes that if doctors don't do a good job of credentialing on their own, government involvement is inevitable.

According to Luciano, at many hospitals (including his own) that do not have a formal credentialing program for advanced laparoscopic surgery, gynecologists can schedule these procedures even if they haven't had sufficient training. For the woman with endo, an insufficiently trained surgeon often does not remove enough disease, eventually making additional surgeries necessary.

Like Johns and Martin, Luciano is an advocate of videotape to assess qualification. While he recognizes that hospitals may not want to encourage videotaping of every procedure because of legal liability, Luciano believes it would be a useful tool for credentialing. He, too, suggests that women considering a surgeon ask if the surgeon would videotape her procedure and provide her with a copy.

"We're not looking for evidence of God's gift to surgery," says Johns of the credentialing process. According to Johns, credentialing is not about subjective things, like which surgeons are better than others. He says the process is merely designed to assess a basic level of skill: Are an individual's skills adequate or inadequate?

Luciano says sentiment within the medical profession is moving toward certification as a process for identifying providers with proper expertise and knowledge. He says some insurance companies and HMOs are now demanding certification before they will reimburse for certain kinds of care. The trend toward certification that began with ACGE, notes Luciano, is expanding to areas like bone densitometry and ultrasound.

In an editorial for the *AAGL Journal*, Luciano cites a report about a gyn endoscopic privileging program to demonstrate why proper credentialing is so important. Surgeons at an urban teaching hospital were invited to apply for advanced privileges based on their case lists. Forty-five surgeons applied. Only five qualified for advanced laparoscopy privileges, and five more for advanced hysteroscopy privileges. Intermediate privileges were granted to thirty-four in laparoscopy and seven in hysteroscopy; the rest qualified for only basic endoscopic procedures. "Yet, all forty-five believed they were advanced endoscopic surgeons," according to the editorial.[9]

> "One of my first doctors was a firm believer that I imagined everything. He was so sure of himself on the surgeries, that when all the same symptoms would come back (within four to five months), he would always say, 'That's nuts. I removed all of it; it can't come back.' He made me go through a complete upper-GI workup, just to prove he was right. Every single test came back fine! When I would finally convince him that I needed another surgery, he would always say, 'Fine, but we are not going to find anything. I removed it all last time!' After every surgery, there he was: 'Well, we found more; it has been growing.' I went through this three times with this man. I guess that was my fault for staying with him for so long."
>
> —Tara, Minnesota

Luciano believes that as women become more assertive, demanding more information regarding doctors' performance and expertise, a movement to assure that laparoscopic surgeons are qualified will be established.

Tips from Endo Surgeons on Choosing an Endo Surgeon

Dr. Martin believes the question of competency is nearly impossible to deal with and is an issue that extends well beyond surgeons. "How can you be sure you have a competent anything (plumber, electrician, etc.)?" he asks. Martin suggests that a prospective patient apply several measures to gauge laparoscopic competence: Did the individual make it through residency training? Is this person board-certified in ob-gyn? Is he or she board-certified in reproductive endocrinology? (This gives him or her three more years of experience, increasing the chances of being qualified.) Has he or she passed the certification process for this procedure in the doctor's hospital? Does he or she have a local or national reputation for this procedure?

Martin also suggests asking a prospective surgeon how long he or she has been performing laparoscopic procedures. If this is the doctor's first week, that's not the person you want performing this procedure, Martin says. Still, in the end, he reminds us, "There's no way to credential judgment."

Camran Nezhat, M.D., renowned pioneer laparoscopic surgeon and Association Advisor, Palo Alto, California, adds these tips: "As knowledge is power, an educated patient would benefit significantly by doing proper due diligence on the surgeon who is going to operate on her. Endometriosis is a specialty of its own. Not all gynecologists are specialists or interested in endometriosis surgery.

"The patient must ask the doctor many questions," he says, "and should find a surgeon who has done a lot of surgery for endometriosis and knows the disease very well, and only then have the operation.

"Put the doctor on the spot," Nezhat advises. "Talk to the doctor face to face, and videotape the conversation (tell the surgeon you don't want to forget anything). Look in his eyes. Ask the surgeon how many of his patients have died; ask him or her if it was your daughter or your sister, who would you want to do the surgery?

"Often patients go to a surgeon simply because their friends like him or her, because the surgeon is closer to their home or in their insurance plan, etc., and they ignore checking what is surgically best for them. What I mean is this: It is your body, and you only have one," Nezhat says.

Remember, the more procedures a surgeon has done laparoscopically, the more skilled generally. A study that looked at the risks, mistakes, and complications following introduction of laparoscopic gallbladder and appendix removal by one medical facility noted that there is a learning curve for the surgeon and the entire staff. Laparoscopic procedures take longer to perform at first. The surgeon, now working with a two-, rather than three-dimensional view, loses the direct tissue feeling of classic surgery and must be well trained in the indirect manipulation of instruments, as well as possible complications.[10]

Dr. Johns believes surgical skill is directly related to the number of surgeries a surgeon performs. Handling one case every two weeks or once a month is simply not enough to develop and maintain expertise. And yet, with lower insurance reimbursements and greater managed-care restrictions, many surgeons are reluctant to refer patients to more experienced surgeons. Johns estimates that of roughly one hundred ob-gyns practicing in his community, only four or five refer patients for surgery, preferring to attempt to handle the surgery on their own. Commenting on some endo patients who have finally been referred to him, Johns says, "By the time they come to me, I'm stuck with adhesions and a mess."

"Most surgeons don't refer because they don't want to refer; they think they can do it [laparoscopic surgery] as well as anybody else," says Dr. Luciano. "We have big egos; if we didn't, we wouldn't have become surgeons."

Johns suggests that a woman in search of a qualified laparoscopic surgeon ask nurses about the surgeons with whom they are familiar. He also offers a number of questions that could be asked of a prospective surgeon: Is there any other gynecologist in this area who has more experience than you do? (If the surgeon can answer that question honestly, it will be telling, he suggests.) Will you videotape my case? ("If the answer is no, I wouldn't go to that doctor," says Johns.) How many cases do you do in a week? In a year?

A surgeon who is doing fewer than one laparoscopic surgical procedure a week is not doing enough to keep up his or her skill, according to Luciano. Luciano, who is recognized as an expert and gets many referrals, says he averages 6 operations a week or about 250 each year. Of these, 50 percent are for endo-related infertility or pelvic pain. In addition to questions about how many procedures a surgeon has performed, Luciano suggests a woman ask a prospective surgeon the reasons for the surgeries—infertility, pelvic pain? He also advises questions about surgeons' results and whether or not they have written articles that have been published in medical journals.

You're the Consumer

In fall 2000, the American College of Surgeons (ACS) issued a statement to a task force for the National Summit on Medical Errors and Patient Safety Research.[11] The statement made several recommendations, including the development and testing of models, computer simulations, and other teaching and assessment tools to support the introduction of new technology to practicing surgeons. Another recommendation called for evidence on which to base clinical decisions when there is surgical controversy or when new technology is introduced. These are the kinds of issues you might think the existing credentialing process would have already settled.

Despite the medical organizations (from the AAGL to the ACS); despite the credentialing processes; despite the education, training, skill, and best intentions of most surgeons, there is no system to guarantee that one hundred percent of surgeons are competent. If you are searching for a competent and qualified surgeon, you, unfortunately, may not be able to rely on the surgical profession's self-regulation, as this article shows. The lack of consistent, objective, careful monitoring and evaluation means *you* must be both a vigilant and cautious consumer.

As consumers of surgical services, women with endo must recognize this reality. We must continue to ask prospective surgeons difficult questions. We must insist on answers. We must continue to demand that the hurdles in the way of an objective process for assessing the qualifications of laparoscopic surgeons be overcome.

Interested in reading more about the regulation of surgery? "Guiding the Knife" ("The surgeon's knife is a strong medicine. Why isn't it regulated like one?") was published in *The Economist* on May 4, 1991, but is, alas, still relevant. While not specific to endo, the article may be useful to those with a strong interest in this topic. Contact Association headquarters for a free copy.

Help in Choosing a Laparoscopic Surgeon

The Accreditation Council for Gynecologic Endoscopy (ACGE) maintains a list of members it has certified to perform laparoscopic and hysteroscopic procedures. To check whether a surgeon you are considering has qualified for ACGE certification, call 1-800-554-2245. (Remember that certification, while important, does not guarantee the surgeon is an endo expert, nor does the certification process make surgeons *prove* their skills.) On the website of the American Medical Association (AMA)—ama-assn.org—is a section called Doctor Finder, where you can search for physicians by specialty, name, or location. The site lists credentials such as education, certification, and affiliations and may include information about the physician's philosophy.

Also helpful are JCAHO's hospital performance reports. These reports are available online at jcaho.org. Generally a good surgeon won't be found operating at a poorly rated hospital. See the information following this for more on JCAHO.

And don't forget the Association's Healthcare Provider Registry, available to members. The Registry is a listing of healthcare providers who are members of the Associ-

Credentialing in Canada

Credentialing issues for advanced laparoscopic procedures in Canada are very much the same as in the United States, according to Togas Tulandi, M.D., a professor of obstetrics and gynecology and the Milton Leong Chair in Reproductive Medicine at McGill University in Montreal, Quebec, as well as an Association Advisor.

There is no Canadian equivalent of the ACGE, although Tulandi notes that several Canadian gyns have been accredited by ACGE. And Canada, like the United States, has no official board doing credentialing, Tulandi said. However, accreditation information on health institutions is available from the Canadian Council on Health Services Accreditation. Call 613-738-3800 or visit the council's website at cchsa.ca.

A more pressing issue in Canada is the overall shortage of doctors, according to Kay Lie, M.D., a Toronto endo specialist and Association Advisor. "If you are a good doctor or a bad doctor, you are paid the same," says Lie, who notes that many good Canadian doctors have relocated to the United States and its market-driven fee system, which means more money for doctors. "That means if you stay here, you are no good, right? Of course not! Not everyone practices medicine for the money," he says. Lie, like many ob-gyns who decide to specialize, no longer sees patients for obstetrics. That gives him the time to do complicated surgeries. Lie believes that the volume of surgeries a surgeon does has an impact on his or her level of skill.

According to Tulandi, medical residents are by and large well trained. He notes that there are fellowship programs, like the one at McGill, that provide opportunities to develop surgical skills. "Patients and other doctors know who to refer patients to," says Tulandi. He suggests that a woman looking for a competent surgeon talk with friends and doctors familiar with treating endo, and contact the Association. Tulandi is unaware of any movement demanding stricter credentialing guidelines in Canada.

ation, with background information supplied by the provider on his or her training, experience, and special approach, if any, to endo treatment. Of course, as with the other entities described in this article, we also have no way to verify the information, and sometimes the pages are not filled out completely (which, however, is useful information showing that the physician may not feel it important enough to supply the information). The Registry list for your area comes with the Contact List of some members in your area willing to share support and information.

Remember, as Drs. Lie and Tulandi note in the "Credentialing in Canada" sidebar above, collectively members of the Association have vast experience with gyn surgeons. You owe it to yourself to talk with members at your nearest support group. Or you can order a Contact List of other members in your area who have given permission for their names and numbers to be shared for just such conversations.

Like Tulandi, Lie recommends that patients learn as much as they can from word of mouth—through support groups and friends who have had surgery. He also thinks a patient must feel comfortable with the surgeon she has chosen.

Lie has his doubts about the value of some of the ways we ordinarily determine whether a surgeon is skilled or not. He notes that even doctors who are professors or who publish are not always the best practitioners. Academic credentials and published papers do not always guarantee good results for the patient. He noted that one can obtain a surgeon's CV (curriculum vitae or medical résumé), but there's no way to verify the training. When he was researching surgeons in a different discipline recently for a family member, he says, he found it was very difficult to obtain solid information on surgeons, "and I'm in the business!"

There is also the problem, he says, that too few doctors want to do endo surgery (because it can be so difficult and the reimbursement can be meager, especially in Canada). So, at least in Canada, if the patient asks too many questions, doctors don't take care of that patient, says Lie. Or they may practice defensive medicine, which can work against the patient—for instance, not surgically treating a lesion on the bowel (because it's riskier), which could leave the patient with the problems for which she sought the surgery. Lie advises that patients remember the human factor and establish a rapport with the surgeon to obtain the best results.

In his own practice, Lie says, he sees many difficult cases that other doctors don't want to do. That doesn't mean they are bad doctors, he explains. They are simply setting limits for themselves. Lie says that in consulting with patients he will often suggest they get second and third opinions. If they then decide they are comfortable with and want to return for treatment, he is more than happy to do their surgeries.

The Joint Commission on Accreditation of Healthcare Organizations

The American College of Obstetrians and Gynecologists (ACOG) says credentialing is a local matter to be decided by the hospital in which a procedure is to be performed. The Society of Obstetricians and Gynaecologists of Canada holds a similar position. To handle the matter of credentialing locally in the United States, hospitals depend on guidelines established by their accrediting organization, the Joint Commission on Accreditation of Healthcare Organizations (JCAHO).

JCAHO evaluates and accredits almost 19,000 healthcare organizations and programs in the United States, including most hospitals. (According to a spokesperson, the

"I had become debilitated. I was so run-down, I could hardly walk, could not ride in a car because the vibrations intensified the pain, was too weak to move, and had to quit my job. A full hysterectomy did away with my pain. . . . At thirty-five, I have my life back. I can walk again, run, play tennis, hike, do all the things I couldn't do for so many years. The first time after my hysterectomy that I went to a restaurant, I cried. I was so happy to be able to visit a restaurant!

"I have always suffered from allergies and now chemical sensitivities. Sinus infections, gastro problems, diarrhea, low-grade fever, general weakness, and fatigue. I still battle with some of these, but at least I no longer have pain in my pelvis or fever. If only I had been diagnosed with endo sooner and treated. I lost all those years to pelvic pain.

"I now run a support group for women. Our goal is to see to it that no woman suffers alone like many of us have. We provide hospital visits, phone support, a friendly shoulder to cry on, and an understanding of what a woman with endo is going through."

—*Nancy, Washington*

hospitals they accredit account for 96 percent of U.S. hospital beds.) JCAHO's hospital performance reports are available by individual hospital at the commission's website, jcaho.org. Also, if you have a complaint about a JCAHO-accredited healthcare organization, you can call JCAHO directly at 1-800-994-6610, between 8:30 and 5:00 CST, or E-mail complaint@jcaho.org. Complaints must be made in writing. You can also obtain limited information about past complaints through these contacts.

Independent and not-for-profit, JCAHO describes itself as the nation's predominant standards-setting and accrediting body in health care. Its stated mission is "to continuously improve the safety and quality of care provided to the public through the provision of health care accreditation and related services that support performance improvement in health care organizations." A hospital voluntarily chooses to be accredited by JCAHO. Those that don't are subject to inspection by the state in which they are located. JCAHO's standards are superseded by state laws.

Using our pilot's license analogy, does JCAHO wield the kind of independent, third-party authority for credentialing surgeons that FAA does for pilots? Do JCAHO and its guidelines assure Azziz's "uniform and indiscriminate implementation of credentialing guidelines"? Unfortunately, no. JCAHO defines the standards, but the hospital retains responsibility for credentialing.[8] The organization's 1997 initiative, "ORYX: The Next Evolution in Accreditation," was designed to integrate the use of outcomes and other performance measures into the accreditation process. Again, the responsibility to do so remains with the hospital. Every individual hospital has discretion over the specific information used to make decisions regarding appointments. It's hard to imagine how the process can meet Azziz's "uniform and indiscriminate" standard, given the thousands of hospitals and competitive pressures on hospitals to offer the newest techniques.

Moreover, the way JCAHO is governed seems to guarantee that only parties with vested interests are involved. To become a member of the board, you must be nominated by one of JCAHO's founding organizations. Nominations made by the American Hospital Association and the American Medical Association each fill seven seats on the board. The American College of Physicians, the American Society of Internal Medicine, and the American College of Surgeons get three seats each. The American Dental Association has one seat. One seat is filled with an at-large nurse representative. Even the six seats allocated to the public at large are filled with people nominated by a committee of the founding organizations. So, at least at this time, consumers probably cannot look to JCAHO for objective, third-party protection of their interests. (The organization did establish a Public Advisory Group in 1999, made up of representatives of patient groups to, hopefully, increase public involvement in the accreditation process.)

One could probably argue that those who work daily with a given surgeon have the best sense as to whether that person should be credentialed or not. But today's healthcare environment is competitive. Surgeons are business professionals and human beings, too. They respond to business interests, have personality conflicts, and will run the gamut with regard to skill. With hospitals retaining the responsibility to credential or not, where is the opportunity to create a comfortable distance between the surgeon seeking to be credentialed and those who make the decision whether to grant credentials?

SAFER TROCARS

Mary Lou Ballweg

A trocar is the device used in laparoscopic surgery to gain access to the abdomen. This instrument traditionally has a sharp blade at the tip, which cuts through the abdominal wall and often takes much force to be inserted.

A survey of 1,000 Association members found that 21.5 percent experienced one or more complications associated with trocars. Of these complications, 24 percent were major (approximately 60 percent due to internal injury to a blood vessel or organ from the trocar; approximately 30 percent due to hernias at the site of insertion). "Minor" complications included continued bleeding from the trocar site and excessive pain at the trocar insertion site.

A number of surgical equipment companies are working to develop safer trocars, but the concept has not caught on much yet. One company that has led the way, Inner-Dyne, has designed a safer alternative to the traditional trocar, called the Step system. This system relies on a needle that, upon insertion into the abdomen, leaves behind a woven plastic sleeve. Instead of cutting through the tissue, the surgeon dilates the sleeve, stretching open the tissue.

The Step system requires much less force to insert, stretches (rather than cuts) the surrounding tissue, and has a blunt end. This system thereby reduces postoperative pain and the most frequently occurring trocar-related injuries (abdominal wall bleeding, bowel and bladder injury, insertion point hernia, and organ penetration) associated with sharp trocars.

If you are facing a laparoscopic surgery, talk with your surgeon about trocar safety. It can help reduce the chance for injury during your surgery. Keep in touch with the Association, too. We will work to keep members abreast of developments in all areas of surgical safety.

ONE WOMAN'S STORY OF SUCCESS WITH HYSTERECTOMY

Marielle Saint-Louis

The surgery was coincidentally scheduled for my next period. I told the assisting resident the following morning it was the best period I ever had! Honestly, the still-attached catheter didn't matter.

Of course, the decision to finally have the hysterectomy was excruciating. Each month, the pain had been worsening, disrupting my life for ten to fourteen days each cycle. In addition, each cycle had been surreptitiously getting shorter while the pain portion remained the same. When not in pain, I spent my time catching up with things I had had to put off because of the pain, getting ahead in other areas before the pain started again, or even making amends for the way I had dealt with some matters when I was in pain. I just had to face it: I could not go on like this.

Earlier in the year, with all other avenues having offered only temporary relief in the past and following in-depth discussion with my gynaecologist, I reluctantly reached the conclusion that if I was going to have surgery yet another time, "everything must go," or almost everything. I signed the papers agreeing to this. However, with the knowledge my doctor would be away on maternity leave for the coming months, the surgery appeared in my mind merely as a distant event looming terrifyingly sometime in the future. It was distant in that I could still change my mind; it was terrifying in the thought, "What if this major surgery didn't help?" What if the pain still remained, as it had in my cousin's case? Let alone the ramifications of losing both ovaries and the subsequent complexities of hormone replacement therapy.

By September, I was doing a temporary work stint in Whitehorse, Yukon Territory, when I got the call from the gynaecologist's office back in Vancouver regarding the seventh and, hopefully, final laparoscopy I would ever have to go through. A week

Diagnosing Endo Without Surgery

One of the most exciting events at the VIII World Congress on Endometriosis was the announcement by Procrea BioSciences, Inc. that its diagnostic test, the first nonsurgical test for endo, was approved for use in the province of Quebec. The test, which requires both a blood draw and an endometrial biopsy, detects immune and biochemical markers in the blood and the endometrium, the inside lining of the uterus. (An endometrial biopsy is a microscopic examination of a sample of endometrial tissue.) The test, called the MetrioTest, is available in Canada and is expected to be available in the United States at an undetermined date. (Contact the Endometriosis Association for up-to-date information.)

A number of other research groups, including the Association's own research team at Vanderbilt University School of Medicine (in experiments directed by Grant Yeaman, Ph.D.), are also searching for less invasive tests for endo. It is expected that a nonsurgical diagnosis for endo would help shorten the long delay—now averaging nine to ten years—between the onset of symptoms and diagnosis so many girls and women currently face.

or so later, I drove the longitude of British Columbia for three days to get back home, the surgery and its implications all but forgotten in the beautiful Indian summer scenery.

The surgery was delayed by a few hours, not only because the woman ahead of me was also having a vaginal hysterectomy and had never had children, but also because my doctor took a break to breastfeed her newborn baby. At long last, they administered the anaesthetic. I was released from the hospital the following afternoon, with a prescription for painkillers I had needed much more in the months prior to the surgery! I never had it filled.

My recuperation period was mostly spent doing a lot of reading and going for short walks, going a little farther each time out. I was told to give myself six to eight weeks to recover before returning to work. Sure enough, attendance at a one-day workshop two and a half weeks following surgery had to be aborted by lunchtime. It was not so much due to any pain as to the extreme fatigue that overcame me.

Twenty-eight days after the surgery, I was appalled to wake up to pain, which lingered through a whole day of denial. I was devastated—this couldn't be happening. The next morning, the pain was gone, as if I had never had any.

I returned to work in the seventh week. By the end of the last afternoon of that week, I began to feel the familiar twinges of pain again. I added some crème de cacao to my hot chocolate that evening and slept soundly through the night. I woke up refreshed and pain free the next morning.

FIGURE 3.1 Treatment Results: Laparoscopy and Laparotomy

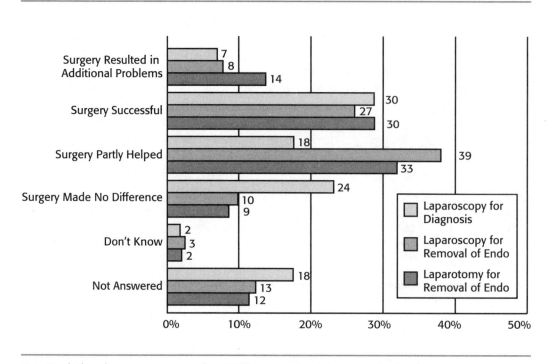

Note: Results based on survey responses from 3,711 women who underwent endo-related surgery.

The pain returned cyclically, as if on cue, every month for six months following the hysterectomy. My gynaecologist explained it as the prostaglandin pain pathways realigning themselves. To me, what it felt like was "phantom organ pain." But the fact that the length of time it lasted got shorter and shorter each month was good enough for me. It made me appreciate just how much I had been suffering and how grateful I was that the pain was no longer as bad.

Now, a whole year later, it's difficult to remember the pain. I suppose it is much like the memory of childbirth has been described to me. It used to be bitter for me to hear women talk like that when I suffered agonizing pain every month and had no children to show for it. I could never forget it because it happened too frequently. Now, just as it is for them, the pain is a faraway memory.

Moreover, my husband and I have been able to enjoy a much improved sex life! I now realize what an excellent prophylactic the pain had become. I was almost always in too much pain to have intercourse; hence, contraception had long been a nonissue.

FIGURE 3.2 Treatment Results: Other Surgeries

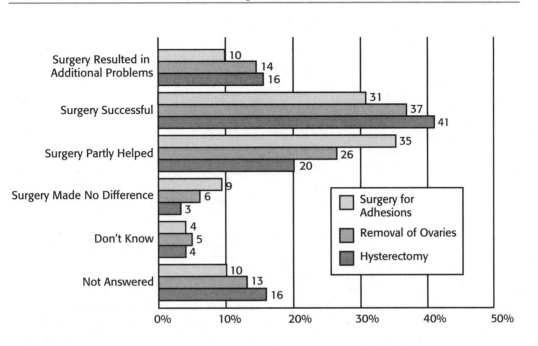

Note: Results based on survey responses from 3,711 women who underwent endo-related surgery.

In the Association's large Research Registry II, 3,711 women reported on their experiences with surgery. For comparison, see the figures on medical treatment in Chapter 2 and on alternative treatments in Chapter 4.

There was not much endo on my ovaries, and my doctor chose not to remove them so I thankfully have not had to face the dilemma of hormone replacement therapy. Who knows if this will cause a problem in the future? However, I have not been so pain free for such a long period of time in over twenty years. Feeling the way I do now, I wish I had had the hysterectomy five or ten years ago. This is not to say this is the solution for everyone.

To think of the time I wasted in suffering—this is infinitely less painful and way less messy besides!

EDITOR'S NOTE Marielle Saint-Louis had a good outcome with her surgery; however, women's experiences vary greatly, as seen in Figures 3.1 and 3.2.

PVC AND ME: NOT JUST ANOTHER SURGERY

Kim Collier

One would think that I would have been dreading the thought of facing another surgery for my endo. After all, it was my fourth laparoscopy in seven years. Yet there I was crossing off each day on the calendar in eager anticipation of January 19. What wasn't there to look forward to? After a year of unbearable pain, cramping, and bleeding, I finally would be getting some relief.

This is not to say I was without reservations about the procedure. I knew if certain precautions were not taken, this day of surgery could expose me to toxins. Unfortunately, the pledge "Do no harm" is not always honored by hospitals, and I knew I could be exposed to products that might endanger my health. Topping my list of concerns was the use of products made from polyvinyl chloride (PVC). Since my last surgery, I had learned a great deal about the negative health impacts tied to PVC plastic and had made a promise not to put myself at risk.

Three weeks before my surgery, I wrote down a list of concerns to discuss with my doctor. The conversation never happened. Between flying out of state for surgery, dealing with last-minute insurance problems, and coming down with the flu, I completely forgot to request PVC-free products during my procedure and stay at the hospital.

On January 19, I arrived at the surgery unit oblivious to this oversight. Instead, I was preoccupied with the normal preoperative rundown and all the gadgets and equipment surrounding me. I did not realize my error until I was in the operating room. As the anesthesiologist started my intravenous line, I watched drops of saline and sedative travel toward my hand. It was only as the cold drops entered my body and my eyelids grew heavier that I realized my surgery was going ahead using PVC products.

Immediate Threat

When I awoke in recovery, my thoughts immediately returned to those final seconds before I was put under. I stared at the IV in my hand and the liquid being channeled into it. Although still groggy, I knew the liquid was coming from an IV bag made of PVC plastic. I closed my eyes and cursed my forgetfulness. Where there is PVC in flexible medical products, there usually is the toxic additive DEHP [Di(2-ethylhexyl) phthalate]. Chances are good that I was exposed.

The source of the problem stems from the type of plastic used to make a good deal of today's disposable medical products—polyvinyl chloride (PVC). When most people think of PVC, they do not think of medical equipment. Instead, they envision the rigid pipes and tubing used by the construction industry. Yet PVC plastic plays an impor-

Fortunately, Joe is no longer alone with his endo-related pain.

tant role in the medical industry, accounting for as much as 25 percent of the total disposable plastic products used. PVC can be found in products such as IV bags and tubing, gloves, patient identification bracelets, and fluid collection devices.

To make PVC soft and flexible for use in medical applications, a toxic additive, or plasticizer, is used. The most common additive applied is DEHP. Because it is not chemically bonded to the plastic, DEHP can run off or "leach" from IV bags into the solutions they contain and directly into patients. (In fact, the chemotherapy drugs Taxol and Taxotere both come with warnings from the drug manufacturer against using PVC equipment for this reason.) The plasticizer has been associated with a number of health effects in humans and lab animals, including damage to the heart, liver, ovaries, testicles, lungs, and kidneys.

In July 2002, the U.S. Food and Drug Administration (FDA) distributed a Public Health Notification regarding PVC devices containing the plasticizer DEHP. The FDA acknowledged that DEHP can leach out of PVC plastic medical devices and that animal tests show DEHP affects the development of the male reproductive system and sperm. According to the notification, "Precautions should be taken to limit the exposure to the developing male to DEHP," and it recommends that healthcare providers consider using non-PVC/DEHP devices when high-risk procedures are to be performed on male newborns, pregnant women carrying male fetuses, and males in puberty.

The threat from DEHP to patients with chronic conditions like endo also is quite serious when one considers the health impacts from cumulative exposure. Granted, it is not as toxic as dioxin (the most toxic substance known to humans), but it still can wreak havoc in the body. Unfortunately, the individuals most at risk for impacts of DEHP are chronically ill people who are frequently hospitalized and/or receive regular intravenous treatments. Since women with endo undergo numerous procedures requiring IV hookups (sometimes as many as fifteen to twenty in a lifetime), we fall into a high-risk category for exposure. In my case, this was the fourteenth procedure (mostly endo- and immune-related) requiring an IV. The most recent laparoscopy only added to my body's toxic burden. As a woman whose immune and endocrine systems are already compromised, this is *not* the substance to which I wanted to be exposed.

Long-Term Threats

I wish I could say that this oversight only affects *my* health, but it does not. PVC offers a double whammy to women with endo and others who are chronically ill. The second and more far-reaching threat comes from PVC in the medical waste stream. When PVC is disposed of via incineration (burned at very high temperatures—the most common form of medical waste disposal at hospitals and treatment facilities around the world), dioxin is created. This is the very same group of toxins known to trigger endometriosis. In a landmark 1992 Association study, the dose of dioxin was also found to correlate with the severity of the disease in animals. (For background on the research linking dioxin to endo, see Chapter 14 and *The Endometriosis Sourcebook*.)

My surgery added to an already abundant dioxin waste stream. The disposable products used during my short stay went on to become medical waste. While incineration is not mandated for medical waste (the majority of it is similar to that found in the average household: cardboard, paper, cans, plastic bottles, etc.), most facilities choose to burn it for the sake of convenience. A critical problem lies with the medical waste specifically comprising PVC. Being the least recyclable plastic, PVC disposable medical products (gloves, IV bags, tubes, catheters, product packaging, etc.) account for 80 percent of the total chlorine being fed into medical waste incinerators.

PVC medical waste is usually incinerated right at the hospital or shipped to a neighboring community for processing. Because the plastic contains chlorine, a great deal of dioxin is generated and released into the air. (In fact, medical waste incineration is the third largest source of dioxin emissions to the air, according to the U.S. Environmental Protection Agency.) It then travels along wind currents and deposits itself on the ground and in the water, where it waits to enter the food chain (primarily through meat, fish, and dairy products). Once it does, girls and women like myself (as well as our families) are exposed to dioxin again and again, thus continuing the toxic legacy. I can only wonder if this additional exposure escalates the progression of our disease.

What Can You Do?

Sometimes women with endo say it is all they can do to make it through the day because of their pain. They feel they do not have the physical stamina or the emotional reserves to deal with overwhelming issues like DEHP and dioxin exposure. But there are a great many girls and women with endo who are ready to do what they can to safeguard their health and the health of those around them. For those people, there is plenty to do.

Speak Up

Every time a girl or woman with endo points out the role that hospitals play in exposing patients to these toxins—every time she chooses to do something about it—she is personally contributing to her health and the health of those around her. This is one area where women with endo can take very simple steps and make a great difference. And the best part about it is that we do not have to do it alone! The Endometriosis Association, through its participation in Health Care Without Harm, can be right by your side, so these steps remain simple and straightforward.

Request PVC-Free Products

Well before your surgery or test, request the use of PVC-free products. Don't assume that you will think logically during the days before your procedure; most women have plenty of other things on their minds like last-minute insurance hassles, final preoperative exams and tests, and time-sensitive chores and tasks. Make your request known to your doctor the date your procedure is first discussed. (Not all facilities stock these alternatives, so prior notification is needed.) Follow up later to make sure your request has been noted. Finally, on the day of the procedure, choose a trusted partner to verify that PVC-free products will be used.

Write to Your Hospital

Write a letter to the chief executive officer of your local hospital and to the person in charge of purchasing, and ask them to purchase PVC-free medical products. Hospitals value the feedback of patients—especially that of "regular customers." Voice your concerns about PVC, in particular about DEHP and dioxin exposure. (Again, the Association can help you.) You can also contact your hospital's patient advocacy group and ask them to send a letter on your behalf. There are many cost-competitive alternatives available to hospitals, including products and services offered through companies like B. Braun, Baxter Healthcare, Universal Health Services, and Tenet Healthcare.

Health Care Without Harm, an international coalition of several hundred organizations dedicated to environmentally responsible health care, has many excellent materials that you can use to help inform your doctors and hospitals about the risks of PVC and DEHP. For a list of PVC-free alternatives and other reports and materials to quote, visit noharm.org.

Contact Government Agencies

Petition the government agency that regulates the safety of medical products in your country. In Canada, this charge falls to the Health Protection Branch of Health Canada; in the United States, it falls to the Food and Drug Administration (FDA). Unfortunately, safety parameters are not always established for medical products. For example, the FDA has yet to set any limits on the "acceptable" amount of plasticizers that can be leached from medical devices. The agency, however, has issued limits related to food containers (plasticizers cannot account for more than 30 percent of the weight of a container). Sadly, PVC IV bags, blood bags, and tubing all contain more than 30 percent DEHP by weight. With over 5.5 million girls and women suffering from endo in North America (and millions more worldwide), we have the power of numbers and need to use it when approaching government agencies about health impacts related to PVC.

Support Environmental Groups

Participate in outreach initiatives with community-based environmental groups. Many groups around the world have adopted the elimination of PVC products as their call to action. As a woman whose health has been directly affected by the use of these products, lend your support to these groups. Speak with members of your community and the media about endometriosis and its devastating effects. Give a "face" to the pain that results from exposure to dioxin and other toxins.

For more information about PVC and the health threats related to DEHP and incineration, please contact the Environmental Coordinator at Association headquarters.

4 Immunotherapy: The Newest Treatment for Endometriosis

Mary Lou Ballweg

When the Endometriosis Association was just three years old, several members discovered something amazing: When they were treated for allergic symptoms resulting from a common yeast, *Candida albicans** (the yeast that causes vaginal yeast infections as well as intestinal and oral yeast infections), the endo symptoms also cleared up. We published a short notice in our newsletter in January 1984, asking if other members had had related experiences, and followed up with an excellent article by professional writer Laura Stevens (herself a woman with endo and *Candida albicans* problems) in September 1984. A fuller scientific explanation followed in an article by myself in the summer of 1985.

As always, members continued to respond with their experiences, which have always been a springboard for Association research and exploration. The feedback on *Candida albicans* and its expanding universe of related problems hasn't stopped since. In fact, looking back over the Association's history, it's fair to say that no other approach

---

*Pronounced Căn'-dĭ-dă al'-bĭ-căns. Physicians and researchers interested in the scientific literature on *Candida* can obtain a scientific review and an extensive bibliography by sending a large self-addressed, stamped envelope to the Association headquarters. Also see M. L. Ballweg, "Immunotherapy for Endometriosis: The Science Behind a Promising New Treatment," in Diamond & Osteen, eds., *Endometrium and Endometriosis* (Malden, MA: Blackwell Science), 1997.

FIGURE 4.1 Did the Alternative Approach Help?

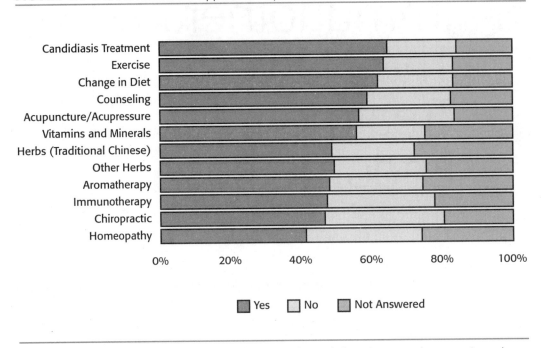

Note: Results based on survey responses from 2,293 women who used alternative approaches to treating endo.

For comparison, see the figures on medical treatment in Chapter 2 and on surgical treatment in Chapter 3.

to endo treatment has given as consistent and long-term positive results as has treatment for *Candida albicans* allergy/infection and its related problems. This was verified in research conducted in 1998, in which members stated that this treatment approach (called—though it's not a very clear name—"immunotherapy") was the most effective of all they had tried for their endo (see Figure 4.1).

The reason for these consistently positive reports may be that *Candida albicans* opens the door right into the intersection of the immune and endocrine systems, the very intersection where endometriosis sits. Candida turns out to be a marker, connector, and door opener, it seems, between the allergic-immune health problems seen in women with endo and their families on the one hand and the hormonal imbalances seen in these women on the other hand. *Candida albicans* may not be the instigator of these problems, although in some cases that is possible. More likely, *Candida albicans* in most cases is an opportunistic organism that capitalizes on an existing weakness in us and, simply by being itself, makes a bad situation worse.

The Allergy Connection

But we're getting ahead of ourselves here. The story really starts back in the early 1980s, when the Association established the world's largest research registry on endometriosis at the Medical College of Wisconsin. There, under the leadership of Karen Lamb, R.N., Ph.D., the detailed case histories of our members were analyzed for any clues to this mysterious disease. One of the most important discoveries to result from that analysis was that women with endo and their families have a statistically significant higher incidence of allergic diseases (hay fever, food sensitivities, eczema, etc.), and women with endo in addition have a statistically significant higher incidence of yeast infections. There was also a trend, although it did not reach statistical significance, toward greater incidence of chemical intolerances and asthma in women with endo. Chemical intolerances did reach statistical significance in the families.[1, 2]

Richard Mabray, M.D., a gynecologist in Victoria, Texas, also noted in the early 1980s that women with endo and their families were more likely to have allergies.[3] Recently, similar findings were observed in a Chinese study, and a Russian study found increased sensitivity to drugs in women with endo.[4, 5]

Well, "so what?" you might say. Allergies—or "just allergies," as they are so often referred to—are often not considered important in our society. Like endo itself, they can range from minor (sniffles and congestion during pollen season) to full-blown disability (such as severe multiple chemical sensitivity in which the affected person must remain primarily in a specially outfitted safe area such as a room or trailer) or even death (as in severe asthma or in anaphylactic shock in people severely allergic to peanuts or shrimp, for example). But allergies are a very clear signal that the immune system is not working correctly, and they damage the body. Add *Candida albicans* to the picture, and then allergies to one's own hormones, and a fairly sinister picture emerges.

What Is an Allergy?

A healthy immune system, according to *The Thorn in the Starfish*, an easy-to-read book on the immune system, "is the body's doctor, or personal physician that cures and protects us from a panoply of disease." And, as the book notes, "it is a system with the exquisitely specific virtuosity to recognize, molecule by molecule, virtually every antigen on earth."[6] (An antigen is any substance recognized by the immune system.) But, with allergy, this beautiful system doesn't work quite right.

When confronted by a germ or other foreign material that could pose a danger, the immune system in a healthy person, through a number of steps and pathways, confronts the invader and destroys it. One key way the immune system carries out this mission is by designing specific weapons, custom-made for that particular invader.

Two major types of cells are involved: B cells and T cells. Both types of cells carry receptor molecules on their surfaces. These receptors fit molecules of the invader just

Symptoms of *Candida Albicans* Allergy and Infection

Candida albicans problems, as described in this chapter, can present with a wide array of symptoms. Here are some of the common symptoms that *may* be caused by candida allergy and infection. This list comes from an excellent article by author Laura Stevens, which appears in the Association's first book, *Overcoming Endometriosis*. The list and additional information also appear in her book *The Complete Book of Allergy Control*. As Stevens notes, if you answer yes to several of these questions, your symptoms *may* be related to *Candida albicans*:

1. Do you have a history of yeast infections—oral, skin, vaginal, or intestinal?
2. Did your symptoms start or worsen after taking birth control pills, antibiotics, prednisone or cortisone-type drugs, or after repeated pregnancies?
3. Have you ever taken tetracycline for acne? Have you taken repeated rounds of antibiotics for recurrent bladder, ear, or other infections?
4. Do you suffer from:
   - other menstrual difficulties (such as spotting or excessive bleeding) with symptoms increasing right before or at the beginning of your menstrual period?
   - diminished sexual interest?
   - chronic constipation, diarrhea, rectal itching, spastic colon, or mucous colitis?
   - urgent or frequent urination?
   - chronic nasal congestion or other respiratory symptoms?
   - depression, irritability, and other mental symptoms?
   - headaches?
   - muscle aches?
   - multiple allergies?
   - an immune disorder such as multiple sclerosis, lupus, rheumatoid arthritis, or Crohn's disease?
5. Are you sensitive to molds or baker's and brewer's yeast? Do you feel worse on damp, windy days or in moldy environments?
6. Do you crave sweets, breads, or alcohol? Does eating refined carbohydrates exacerbate your symptoms or cause gas and bloating?
7. Does exposure to gas fumes, perfumes, insecticides, or tobacco cause symptoms?

as a lock and key fit together. When a B cell finds an invader, it produces "antibodies," which lock onto the invader. (There are five types of antibodies, called "immunoglobulins": IgG, IgM, IgD, IgA, IgE.) The antigens of the invader are then displayed on the surface of the B cell, which attracts a T-helper cell (called "helper" because it helps the B cell). Substances produced by the T cell, called cytokines, cause the B cell to multiply and then go on to produce many antibodies specially designed to lock onto matching antigens of the invader. T-suppressor cells shut off the immune response, which is important to prevent proliferation of B and T-helper cells and autoimmune diseases. The antibody-antigen complexes are then eliminated from the body by other immune mechanisms or by the liver or spleen.

This process of launching an immune attack is accompanied by inflammation. While this inflammatory response helps defend the body against infection, it also causes symptoms such as redness, warmth (and sometimes fever), swelling, pain, and loss of function. The reddening is due to increased blood flow to the site. Swelling or edema is caused by dilation and increased permeability of blood vessels in the area, which results in leakage of fluid from the blood vessels (allowing rapid access of the immune cells to the invader). Pain is caused by pressure of the swollen tissues on nerve endings and by the irritating chemicals released by the immune system. Heat is caused by enzyme activity in and around the infection due to the action of the body's immune system. In other words, the immune system's attack creates the symptoms as much or more so than the invader does.[7, 8] (For a detailed—and humorous—explanation, see "Understanding the Immune System's Role in Endometriosis" in Chapter 7.)

In an allergic or hypersensitivity reaction,* the immune response just described occurs after exposure to seemingly harmless substances—dust, animal dander, foods. Highly irritating substances such as histamine cause the sneezing, wheezing, itching, hay fever, asthma, intestinal disorders, eczema, fatigue, hives, and other miseries well known to allergy sufferers. The most common symptom, according to the American Allergy Association, is fatigue.[9] Other substances, including prostaglandins (familiar to women with endo as the substances that cause the severe cramping, increased pain, swelling, and other symptoms of dysmenorrhea), also are released during an allergic reaction and play a major and complex role.

Some people are more prone to allergies, a tendency that is strongly influenced by genetics. It is not understood why seemingly harmless substances such as grass pollen cause this reaction. Other substances, such as dust mite feces—ugh!—seem to my thinking anyway, to hardly qualify for a description of "harmless." IgE, the immunoglobulin involved in the best-known allergic reactions, is present in the blood of nonallergic individuals only in minute amounts. But in an allergic individual, it can be found in amounts sixty times higher than in nonallergic individuals.[11]

Why Allergies Are Not Regarded as Important

Perhaps we don't take allergies seriously because they are so common, similar to the attitude toward menstrual problems. It is estimated that one in every five or six people in the United States (and probably similar numbers in other industrialized countries)

---

*"Allergy" and "hypersensitivity" are used interchangeably. Both refer to "tissue damage caused by an overreaction of the body's immune system to antigens that are usually harmless to most people," according to the excellent resource, *Understanding Allergy, Sensitivity & Immunity*.[10]

So Joe prepares to go to yet another doctor, but this time it's different.

suffers from some type of allergy-related illness.[12] Yet other health problems—such as obesity, also all too common in the modern world—*are* taken seriously.

Allergy may not have always been so common. At the time of one of the first descriptions of hay fever (by a physician at the beginning of the Industrial Revolution, who described it in himself), it was apparently so unusual that he took several years to identify a dozen or more sufferers.[13] Now, not only are allergies very common, but the number of people with them is increasing. According to a report in *The Human Ecologist*, many studies have noted an increase over the past few decades. A study in Wales noted that the incidence of hay fever rose from 9 percent to 15 percent between 1973 and 1988. Increasing levels of sulfur and nitrogen oxides, ozone, combustion products, and other air pollution sources worsen asthma and other allergies by several pathways, the article notes.[14] Even worse, asthma deaths are rising, according to many sources.[15]

Allergic diseases cost society a bundle. It is estimated that over $3 billion per year is spent on direct costs of allergies, including the cost of physicians, hospitals, and drugs in the United States alone[16] and $6 billion per year for treatment of asthma-related illnesses.[17]

Another reason allergies may not be taken seriously is that they affect women disproportionately. More women than men report allergies of all types, and the onset of allergies has sometimes been noted to coincide with hormonal fluctuations, such as at adolescence or menopause. Menstrual asthma is a well-known entity, and allergies generally are said to worsen premenstrually.[18]

Yet another reason allergies are sometimes not accorded the respect they should be is that the field of allergy itself, the medical specialty, has bogged down for years in internal controversy and splinter groups, resulting in less respect from other medical societies. According to a former president of the American Academy of Allergy and Immunology, the divisiveness "prevents allergy and immunology from speaking with a single strong voice."[19] Moreover, allergy and immunology are complex and evolving fields without easy answers. As a newspaper article on the controversies notes, "Medicine, oriented to providing answers, often downplays diseases that don't offer them."[20]

The controversies start with the very definition of allergy. The first allergies understood in this century were the allergies involving the antibody IgE. Additional allergies and hypersensitivities have since been described through research, but some reactions are still not understood, including some food reactions. In the words of the authors of a comprehensive resource on food allergy and intolerance, "There has been a strong tendency for the conventional physician to say that if the mechanism is not understood then food allergy does not exist. . . . This is of course unacceptable."[21] Patients with food allergies have often been said to be neurotic.[22] Women with endo have seen similar thinking in endometriosis: If the mechanism by which endo causes pain is not understood, then the pain doesn't exist.[23]

"Today, I know what to do for my problem. I know not to reach for alcohol or drugs because of the pain. I watch my diet even though I crave sugar, alcohol, and other yeast-type foods, especially pizza, breads, cakes, pies, etc., or I'll pay for it later. . . . Don't give up. If one doctor looks at you like you have come from another planet, go to one who will listen. Read all you can in order to know what others have learned. It will save you money and a lot of heartache. Once you begin to help yourself, help others. Get involved with such groups as E.A."

—Carol, North Carolina

Other areas of controversy in allergy and immunology include testing and treatment approaches. Unfortunately, rather than prizing the free exchange of ideas and practices, the professional societies in the field attack those with whom they disagree with an almost religious fervor and have attempted in some cases to drive practitioners with opposing views out of practice.

In addition, the many manifestations of allergy, which can affect virtually any part of the body, fly in the face of modern, superspecialized medicine. At a conference on *Candida albicans*, Timothy Guilford, M.D., an ear, nose, and throat specialist in San Mateo, California, who treats candida problems, said, "Swelling, congestion, and outpouring of fluid—when that happens in the nose, we've been in the habit of calling that hay fever in the spring season and rhinitis the rest of the year. When that happens in the lung, you call it asthma. And when it happens in the gastrointestinal tract, you call it everything from food allergy to 'gas.'"[24] It has been difficult for modern medicine to look at biological processes wherever they occur in the body, not just the end organ affected.

Nor does the same allergen (a substance causing allergic reaction) cause the same reaction from person to person—understandably, since the problem in allergy, by definition, is the immune system of the person, not the allergen itself. A given individual will, however, tend to have the same symptoms from an allergen. This means the physician must focus more on the patient, less on disease agents such as germs, and less on high-tech tests, precisely the opposite direction of most of modern medicine. Allergy management can be hard work for physician and patient and may require both to become medical detectives, sleuthing out leads amidst confusing and sometimes changing reactions.

Health Consequences of Allergies

Clearly it is time for allergy to be accorded much greater respect, given its impact in terms of the number affected and the cost of these health problems. But a greater cost may be the damage to the health of those affected, among whom we can count women with endometriosis, especially women with family histories of endo. Moreover, these effects are not limited to the miseries directly caused by the allergies themselves. Allergies inhibit the immune system, making it less effective in carrying out its job of defending us.[25] Studies have found defects in the regulation of the immune system in allergic individuals.[26] In addition, immune cells in these individuals produce more prostaglandin E_2.[27]

Allergies are also very common in the medical histories of those who develop chronic fatigue immune dysfunction syndrome (CFIDS), another health risk for some women with endo.[28, 29] Some experts believe the allergic background is a factor in development of CFIDS.

There is also fear that the deranged immune system, reacting vigorously against seemingly harmless substances, is more at risk for reacting against cells of one's own body, which is what occurs in autoimmune disease. Rheumatoid arthritis, multiple sclerosis, and Hashimoto's thyroiditis are examples of autoimmune diseases in which immune cells attack the joints, the myelin sheaths of nerves, or the thyroid by making antibodies and T cells directed against those tissues. (When the body makes antibodies against its own cells, they are called autoantibodies.)

Some researchers studying endo have suggested that it may be an autoimmune disease. Autoantibodies have been detected in women with endo.[30–33] Women with endo have been found to have an increased T-helper to T-suppressor ratio in peritoneal fluid, meaning there are too many helpers and not enough suppressors.[34, 35] A decrease in T-suppressor cell activity in peripheral blood (the blood in general circulation) in women with mild disease has also been found, as well as a further drop in T-suppressor cell activity plus an increase in T-helper cell activity in women with severe disease.[36] Persons with autoimmune responses have also been found to have a depression in T-suppressor function; the cells normally slowing down the reactivity of the immune system to one's own tissues are not operating maximally.[37] For women and girls with endo, the danger of further health problems, including autoimmune disease, may be the best reason to take allergies seriously. (For information on preventing allergies and asthma, see Chapter 12.)

Candida Albicans and Allergy

The link between allergy and *Candida albicans* has been noted by a number of researchers. C. Orian Truss, M.D., the Birmingham, Alabama, allergist who rediscovered the importance of *Candida albicans* in chronic health problems in the 1960s, observed that *Candida albicans* is associated with and leads to allergies.[38] Others have found that candida is linked to some cases of allergic diseases, including hives, asthma, irritable bowel disease, and psoriasis, as reviewed in an article by George Kroker, M.D., an allergist in LaCrosse, Wisconsin.[39]

In fact, some of these patients are allergic to candida itself. Patients with asthma and atopic eczema have been shown to exhibit immediate skin reactivity* to *Candida albicans*, for instance.[40–44] Candida has been shown to have over 100 immunologically distinct antigens and thus is clearly capable of inducing allergic responses.[39, 45–47]

Allergy and candida together are a bad combination, as shown in important studies by Cornell University Medical College professor Steven Witkin, Ph.D. "I think the evidence is now very good that *Candida* can be involved in the induction of immunosuppression, especially in allergic individuals," Witkin says in William Crook, M.D.'s book *Chronic Fatigue Syndrome and the Yeast Connection*.[48] Witkin found that women with a history of stubborn vaginal yeast infections had an immune defect resulting in overproduction of prostaglandin E_2 (PGE_2). This is the same prostaglandin that has been found in women with primary dysmenorrhea and endo, and it clearly causes mischief in both. As the authors of *Understanding Allergy, Sensitivity & Immunity* note, "PGE_2 is one of the most active prostaglandins and a good example of how many ways one

---

*In testing for allergy, a common technique is to inject or scratch a tiny amount of a suspected allergen into the surface of the skin. If an inflammatory reaction occurs in the form of a small swollen area called a "wheal," the immune system is reacting to the substance with a classic IgE allergy reaction.

"I met, through the Association, a woman who had been diagnosed with endo and knew of the anti-candida diet. We talked at length about the diet, and since I was a long-time vaginal yeast sufferer, I decided to go on the diet, if not for the endo, then at least I might get some relief from the pain and burning that accompanies this candida problem.

"It has been approximately 6 months since I started the diet, and not only has it helped my candida problem—but my symptoms of endo have improved greatly! My periods are much less painful. I used to pass large blood clots, which I no longer experience. My premenstrual symptoms of pain, bloating, nausea have all but disappeared. I have been able to get through my periods with a few Advil, rather than half a dozen or so Percocet.

"At first, the diet was depressing. I felt worse before I felt better. I read this was because the yeast were dying off—so I hung in there. . . . I notice when I go off the diet, even for a while, my symptoms return—first the candida infections, then the painful periods."

—*Bernadette, Maine*

chemical can affect inflamed tissues. It dilates blood vessels, can make tissues more sensitive to pain, contributes to swelling by increasing blood vessel permeability and consequent seepage of fluid, and acts powerfully to heat inflamed tissues."

PGE_2, in other studies, has been found to inhibit the appropriate immune response to candida,[49, 50] as well as to stimulate candida to develop into its invasive hyphal form.[51] Witkin found that adding a prostaglandin inhibitor to a candida culture allowed patients' immune cells to respond more appropriately to candida.

Witkin's experiments also showed that PGE_2 levels in vaginal fluids correlated with the presence of IgE antibodies, the classic antibody of allergy, which Association Advisor Subbi Mathur, Ph.D., of the Medical University of South Carolina, had noted in vaginal candidiasis in the 1970s.[52] The key trigger for the overproduction of PGE_2 is the allergic response, via production of histamine, which triggers macrophages to produce it.[53] Witkin found that women without a history of recurrent vaginal candidiasis do not produce PGE_2 in response to *Candida albicans* but that their immune cells (peripheral blood mononuclear cells) could be induced to produce high levels of PGE_2 in response to candida if histamine was added to the culture. Histamine alone, in the absence of *Candida albicans*, had no effect. However, the peripheral blood mononuclear cells from women with recurrent vaginal candidiasis spontaneously produced PGE_2, and this response could be further stimulated by histamine alone or by *Candida albicans*. The combination of histamine and *Candida albicans* resulted in the highest levels of PGE_2.[54] While Witkin studied only women with stubborn vaginal *Candida albicans* problems, a number of other investigators have linked resistant candida problems to allergic reactions to *Candida albicans* in other sites as well as the vagina.[55–62]

Witkin summed up the candida allergy synergy in this way: "If *Candida albicans* is present at the time and location of an allergic response, the symptoms may be more severe due to the ability of *Candida* to synergize with histamine. Treatments aimed at eliminating residual *Candida*, inhibiting the synthesis of PGE_2 or preventing allergic responses in susceptible women will sometimes end the cycle of immune suppression and allow the person's immune system to prevent the future growth of *Candida*."[63]

A physician who has noted a frequent occurrence of *Candida albicans* and allergies in women with endo is gynecologist Pamela Morford, M.D., of Tucson, Arizona. Morford says, "I've found that people with endometriosis and pelvic pain frequently have a problem with yeast and allergies. And if I treat a patient with endometriosis using anti-candida therapy, she will more than likely lose her pelvic pain. . . . I won't say that the endometriosis goes away, yet I will say that the pain and the symptoms go away. . . . Endometriosis is an autoimmune disease of the pelvis, and in those people who are genetically predisposed to developing it, candida may interfere with the immune system functioning and allow the disease to become manifest. At least, that's my theory."

The Hormonal/Gyn Connection

If *Candida albicans*'s proven effects were only those related to allergy that have already been noted, it would clearly be serious enough for us all to consider keeping our allergies and candida in check. But its effects are even more insidious: It is also linked to hormonal disruption. Candida can bind and use our hormones, including estrogen, progesterone, and the adrenal gland hormone, corticosterone.[64–69]

Back when we were first writing about *Candida albicans* in the mid-1980s, science was just beginning to find hints of these hormonal links. But the links had long been suspected, since *Candida albicans* has always been noted to be affected by the hormonal status of its host. For instance, vaginal candidiasis is most common in women just before menstruation, during pregnancy, and during the use of oral contraceptives. Experiments with rats showed that *Candida albicans* thrives during estrous and that estrogen given after removal of the ovaries predisposed the animals to candida infection while progesterone did not. (Estrous is the cyclic period of sexual activity in mammals other than primates.) Estradiol, the most active estrogen, was shown to stimulate the transition of the yeast to the invasive hyphal form.[70, 71]

Not only does the host's hormonal status affect the impact of the yeast on the host, but the hormones act similarly in yeast. This fact, which stunned scientists when it was first discovered, indicates that messenger interactions have been strikingly preserved in organisms from yeast to human through the millennia of evolution. It also means that any disruption of these universal messenger systems seen in other species must serve as a warning for us.[72–74] A number of observers have noted that candida sensitivity or overgrowth and altered intestinal microorganisms may begin in humans or lab animals after exposure to such chemicals as formaldehyde, pesticides, and dioxin and related compounds.[75, 76] Indeed, in the dioxin-exposed monkeys made famous by the Association's groundbreaking study linking dioxin exposure and endo, monkeys with endo were found to have abnormal intestinal microflora and increased intestinal inflammation.[100] Also, experiments at Stanford found that yeast binds with an estrogen mimic, bisphenol A[77] (a plastic found in lab flasks and in many consumer products such as the jugs used to bottle drinking water).

Hormones and allergies also have been clearly linked, all the way back to 1947, when a researcher first noted that women could be allergic to their own hormones.[78] Other studies confirmed this.[79, 80] Dr. Richard Mabray found, in pioneering work in the 1980s, that women with endo had at least one immunoglobulin abnormality 76 percent of the time and that IgE levels were significantly increased.[81, 82] And Waukesha, Wisconsin, allergist Wayne Konetzki, M.D., has found in a study of his patients that women with endo are most likely to be allergic or sensitive to luteinizing hormone and estrogen, as well as *Candida albicans*, chemicals, and foods, but any combination of sensitivities is possible.[83] (Interestingly, he found that women with PMS were most likely to be allergic or sensitive to progesterone. Konetzki believes that the simplest form of hormonal allergies can be seen in primary dysmenorrhea.)

Perhaps even more insidiously, *Candida albicans* has been linked to a variety of autoimmune disorders, especially those involving our hormones. These disorders, called autoimmune endocrinopathies, include ovarian disorders, thyroid disorders, and adrenal disorders. Subbi Mathur, Ph.D., has been a courageous pioneer in her work in this area. Mathur found that antibodies to *Candida albicans* were also antibodies to ovary and to certain T-helper cells.[84] Another researcher has now confirmed these findings.[85] In other words, our immune system, in building antibodies to *Candida albicans*, may be building antibodies against our own ovarian tissue. Naturally, our reproductive system cannot work well if our immune system is trying to destroy parts of it. Some researchers think that because *Candida albicans* can bind with our hormones, the immune system in building antibodies to candida is building antibodies to our own hormones, which are bound to *Candida albicans*! Thus, the immune system becomes confused (and we may become confused, too!).

Other researchers found that anti-ovarian antibodies and autoimmune endocrine disease were associated with candidiasis in an interesting case involving two sisters,[86] and *Candida albicans* has been associated with thyroid and adrenal gland diseases in studies of chronic mucocutaneous candidiasis,[87-91] a disease in which an inherited immune defect specific to *Candida albicans* allows chronic candida infections. In addition, the clinicians working with women with endo and candida problems have noted the presence of thyroid antibodies (an autoimmune disease known as Hashimoto's thyroiditis) and other immune abnormalities and/or adrenal antibodies in some of these women.

Treatment

Case History of a Comprehensive Candida/Endo Treatment Program

Comprehending the full scope of a good candida/endo treatment program can be difficult. Such programs are new and include many steps. Furthermore, relatively few trained practitioners are available to guide a woman or girl through the steps. So, many who would benefit from the full candida treatment program never have the privilege of working with an experienced practitioner who can help them implement it in a way to turn around their health—not just their gyn health, but their general health as well. To help members understand what a good candida treatment program can entail (and because so many women have said they're interested in my story), I will share with you my candida treatment program.

In 1982, after all treatment options had been exhausted, I had a hysterectomy and removal of my remaining ovary. My "miracle" baby was six months old, and as the pain increased, I was anxious to avoid becoming bedridden again as I had in the past, for months on end, and miss out on the time with her. I'd gone without replacement hormones for eight and a half months after the surgery and had done quite well. But mid-1983, I began to have many symptoms, including ear infections for the first time in my life. By late 1984 I was miserable with frequent colds, sore throats, and infections (including five ear infections in two months in spring, some of which were treated with antibiotics, of course), severe reaction to certain chemicals and cigarette smoke; and eye irritations and pain.

Because we'd been following and writing about the positive results some Association members had received with treatment for *Candida albicans* allergy and overgrowth and its related problems, it wasn't too hard to see the parallels in my own case. Still, I was skeptical. When Richard Mabray, M.D., wrote us that women with endo and their families had a strong history of allergy, I jotted in the margin of the letter that this was not true in my family or my case. Little did I know! Like most in our society, I was unaware of the many manifestations of allergy and candida and had to learn through my own experience, unfortunately.

So, in early 1985, when I went to see allergist Wayne Konetzki, also a pioneer in candida-allergy-endocrine problems, I was in for a big surprise. Like many of the excellent practitioners in the specialty of environmental medicine, Konetzki starts with a very thorough history, in this case a long written questionnaire before my first appointment. He said it looked like I had so much going on that he wondered what to do first— where should we start? I said why not test for candida first, since that seems to be a problem for so many women with endo and seems to connect to so many of the other problems. So, still not believing candida would really turn out to be a problem for me, I had the dilute drop of candida put under my tongue and then went to read the interesting things on the bulletin board. (A typical way to test for allergies is to scratch or inject a tiny bit of the suspected allergen under the skin or to put a drop of the substance, very diluted, under the tongue. The patient then waits ten minutes, and a lab technician measures the swelling that takes place on the skin—called a "wheal"—or records reactions if the substance was placed under the tongue.)

Whammo! After being at the bulletin board for only a few minutes, I was so dizzy, headachy, and stuffy that I had to sit down! "What on earth had they given me?!" I wondered. I found it hard to believe a little bit of yeast that lives in everyone could make me so sick.

Then, almost as if by magic, the technician was able to lessen my symptoms with succeeding drops, a process called neutralization, although it took some attempts to find just the right dilution that told my immune system to stop the reaction. (Remember, it's the immune system that's causing the symptoms in allergy, not the substance itself—although for candida problems, which often are both an allergy and an infection, the allergic reactions and the symptoms caused directly by the organism are both occurring.) According to Sherry Rogers, M.D. (a physician in Syracuse, New York, who treats many patients with candida and chemical sensitivities), with these techniques you can turn the patient on and off like a light bulb! It certainly can be very convincing that a particular substance or organism is indeed a source of your problems when exposure to the substance under controlled circumstances reproduces all your symptoms and neutralization stops the symptoms.

If I had any lingering doubts that candida and related problems were key factors in my health, they were dispelled by the treatment program. Having misheard Konetzki when he was describing how to take ketoconazole (a powerful systemic antifungal) and nystatin (an antifungal that remains only in the gastrointestinal tract), I went home and started taking both at once. Perhaps my candida reaction had not been completely neutralized, and I was still a little fuzzy when he was telling me to take the ketoconazole first for three weeks and then go on to the nystatin. As any reader who has been through this knows, when a large amount of candida is killed quickly, it can cause a "die-off" reaction as yeast proteins are released in a person who is hypersensitive to yeast. (Fortunately, newer drugs used now, such as fluconazole or Diflucan, tend not to cause these die-off reactions.) The powerful combination of drugs apparently caused such a die-off, and at first I was very sick. As I became better and better, I had many opportunities to realize all over again that candida, allergies, and related problems are indeed important in my health. If I knowingly or unknowingly ate something yeasty or sugary, my symptoms flared up. After I tested very allergic to molds, typical of those who react to candida, I resisted the suggestion to remove houseplants from my bedroom. Finally, in desperation, I did, and lo and behold, the sore throat I had awakened with each morning was gone.

Hormonal problems often are part and parcel of candida, and unfortunately, I have not been spared these. For some years in the late 1980s, after going through the program just described, I enjoyed unprecedented health. Then, in summer 1990, joint pain and other problems led to an increase in my estrogen dose to a still-low 0.625 milligram per day. By November I was again experiencing endo symptoms. I had a surgery to remove endo that had likely been left at the time of my hysterectomy eight and a half years earlier. And I was found to have Hashimoto's thyroiditis, an autoimmune disease that is quite common in women with candida and endo problems. It turned out to be easy to treat with replacement thyroid, once we determined that the synthetic thyroid wasn't working and switched to natural. This step made a major difference in my health.

Also, I was found to have additional severe allergies. With the help of ELISA/ACT (see Resources in back of the book) lab tests, which can check up to a thousand foods and substances for delayed hypersensitivity reactions with one blood draw, I was able to gradually reduce the number of substances I react to from thirty-five to ten. I was also found to have low levels of the adrenal hormone DHEA, and supplementation of that has been crucial to my health. (See explanation later in this article.) As long as my hormone replacement stays stable and I avoid those things I'm allergic to and watch out for candida, I stay well.

While each case is somewhat different (as we've said before, there is no one-size-fits-all treatment approach for endo), my story illustrates much of the treatment program for candida and related problems. Not everyone will need all the elements described here, but some combination of the different parts of the program seems to have been helpful for many of our members. Moreover, this approach treats many of the symptoms women with endo experience that are not addressed with surgery and hormonal medications. Best of all, the treatment does no harm, as our late Advisor Arnold Kresch, M.D., of Palo Alto, California, said at the Association's fifteenth anniversary conference. Kresch implemented this treatment program into his gyn surgical practice after hearing Konetzki speak at the tenth anniversary conference and was amazed at the results. Deborah Metzger, M.D., Ph.D., another Association Advisor, merged her practice with Kresch's and continues the immune-enhancing work pioneered by both.

> "I suspected that I was suffering from *Candida albicans*—I was constantly plagued by thrush when I was in my teens and twenties. My doctor was very sympathetic to my request for antifungal treatment, and it was decided that I take Diflucan (fluconazole). The medication is used in conjunction with a change of diet—not the full anti-candida diet—I just do not eat sweets, cakes, or anything containing sugar. Within two weeks of starting this treatment, I can report virtually no pain, no PMT [premenstrual tension], no depression, no fatigue, and all this for six months so far. I can only suggest that anyone else who suffers in this way try this treatment."
>
> —Helen, from National Endometriosis Society newsletter, Great Britain

Allergy Testing and Treatment

Let's look in more detail at the three main parts of a candida–allergy–hormone balancing program. The first major component is allergy testing and desensitization. A

thorough history and allergy testing are used to identify what one is allergic to—*Candida albicans*, hormones, pollens, molds, foods, chemicals. A variety of techniques are used in allergy testing, and there is much infighting among allergists themselves over which techniques are best. Ignore this infighting—just be sure you're with a practitioner who "believes in" food and chemical sensitivities, since otherwise you won't be tested or treated for these, which are common in women with endo. In addition to foods and chemicals, women with endo also often test allergic to *Candida albicans*, luteinizing hormone, and estrogen, but any combination of sensitivities is possible, including sensitivity to molds, pollens, and progesterone.

Some women will be surprised to find they're allergic to *Candida albicans* because, like me, they may have no overt symptoms of candida overgrowth. In fact, because many of the symptoms are allergic in nature, only a small candida presence may be necessary to set off symptoms, just as with any other allergy. Other women, however, will have a long history of overt *Candida albicans* overgrowth (vaginal, intestinal, and less commonly, oral), or symptoms will worsen as the amount of yeast increases.

Avoidance

Standard allergy techniques are then used to treat the allergies—avoidance and desensitization. For food sensitivities and inhalant allergies,* including pollens, molds, dust, and chemicals, this includes avoidance of the offending substance as much as possible. One study found a highly significant response ($p < 0.000024$) in food-sensitive patients who avoided the foods that gave them reactions compared with patients following a placebo diet.[92] (See Glossary for explanation of p value.) Another double-blind, placebo-controlled study found that a yeast-free and sugar-free diet enhanced the effect of nystatin in reducing symptoms.[99] Yeast foods include baked goods and other products made with or by yeast (bread, bagels, pastries, pretzels, pizza, rolls, alcohol, B vitamins and selenium made from yeast, and pickled or fermented foods). Replace these food items with sourdough bread made with sourdough starter culture only (not commercial yeast), biscuits and muffins made from baking powder, vitamins and selenium made without yeast, and lots of vegetables and whole grains.

Sugar and other concentrated sweeteners are the other big category to avoid, including, of course, sugar itself in all forms, as well as honey, molasses, maple syrup, dextrose, and corn syrup. A research study found that candida growth and invasion in the intestines was about 200 times greater in mice fed a sugar solution (dextrose) than in mice that did not receive dextrose.[93] Sugary substances are big troublemakers for those with *Candida albicans* sensitivity, so do your best to skip the candy, sugary cereals, cookies, and soft drinks. Check out a good health food store, where you'll be amazed at the range of delicious snacks and whole-grain cereals and cookies you can substitute.

At least three studies have found that ingesting the substances eliminated on the candida diet was correlated with recurring vaginal yeast infections. Avoiding baked products with yeast may be helpful for women with endo anyway, since *Saccharomyces cerevisiae*, which is baker's yeast, and baked goods made with it have been found to contain estrogen. If you're sensitive to mold, you may also have to avoid foods that tend to have a high mold content, such as dried fruits, cheese, and frozen fruit juices. Substitute fresh fruits and other proteins and fats for cheese. Every practitioner will have adaptations of these guidelines based on the treatment approach taken by that practitioner and your own individual health problems, so be sure to check in with him or her. Also, don't forget to call on members of the Association who have been on the program and will have many helpful tips and suggestions.

This part of the program can be *very* difficult, especially at the beginning. Remember that yeast foods and sugary foods are the most important to avoid. As one article on the candida problem states, "Putting sugar into your body when you have a yeast infection is like throwing gasoline on a flame."[94] Avoiding yeast and sugar may be very difficult for a number of reasons. First, yeast and sugar foods may be a big part of your

---

*Inhalant allergies are those contacting us through our nose, mouth, throat, and lungs as we inhale.

diet, requiring major diet changes. Second, in a cruel twist of nature, one is often somewhat addicted to the foods one is allergic to! But it does get easier over time as the cravings diminish. Candida, in particular, seems to be able to create intense cravings for the very things that feed it. It may not be a coincidence, for instance, that pregnant women sometimes crave such things as pickles, vinegar foods, and ice cream. Pregnancy is one of the times of high susceptibility to candida growth.

When I had recovered from candida enough that I could reintroduce into my diet small amounts of foods that had been off limits for months, I decided to have a blueberry–cream cheese croissant (yum!). To my surprise, I found I no longer craved such a yeasty-sugary pastry as I would have when my candida was full-blown. Where in the past I'd trusted my body to tell me what it needed, I came to learn that my body included organisms such as candida, which—sneaky little devils—were able to send messages calling for just such confections. But the blessing of the anti-candida diet is "the complete loss of a 'sweet tooth,' which means that an ex-candida sufferer is far more likely to stay on a healthy diet without being attracted by sugar or junk foods, thus insuring a healthier future."[95]

Here are some tips to help you with the dietary part of the program:

- If possible, put the whole family on the same diet. It is a lot easier to avoid foods you should not eat if they are not in the house. You may find other members of the family feel better, too.
- "Controlled cheating" (allowing yourself a little of the forbidden food after a week of following the diet strictly, for example) or finding special treats that are OK on the diet can help. During the first weeks of the diet, it's very important not to cheat, if at all possible, but if you do, don't despair. Just pick yourself up and go on. It seems easier to follow the diet if you realize that at times you'll fail than to set yourself up for the impossible goal of perfection.
- Try to make an adventure out of the new program. A number of anti-candida cookbooks are available to help. When I was first on the antiyeast diet, a coworker shared a gourmet fish cookbook with me. Since I could no longer eat cheese, which had been a main source of protein (and fat!) in my diet, I found it very enjoyable to cook really great fish recipes. (Fish might not be the right thing for you—and all of us must avoid dioxin- and mercury-contaminated species—but the point is that the whole program will be more fun and more doable if you make an adventure out of it.)

Desensitization

In addition to avoidance, desensitization is a key allergy treatment technique. A number of names are used for this technique: mini-dose, low-dose, or neutralizing dose immunotherapy (or "immunotherapy" for short); provocative neutralization; and serial dilution end point titration. With dilute doses of the allergic substance, in oral drops or injections, the allergic response is reduced or eliminated over time. While desensitizing allergic reactions is a standard allergy management technique, used since the early 1900s, the way it works is still not completely understood. Much interest has arisen in a similar therapy in recent years for autoimmune disease.[96] As the patient improves, the correct neutralizing dose may change, so retesting may be needed, especially in the earlier stages of treatment.

This part of the program is extremely important. You will not be getting at the root of the problem if you do not include allergy management and desensitization in your treatment. (Hormone balancing, which will be covered shortly, also is critical to undoing the immune/endocrine derangement that can lead to so much damage.) A number of physicians have become attuned to the candida problem, but if all they do is prescribe an antifungal, they're doing very little more than physicians who prescribe antibiotics where underlying allergy is the real problem. This approach to medicine is called the "see a bug, give a drug" approach.

Gynecologists in particular may find it hard to believe that candida could be such a troublemaker or that specialists from fields other than gynecology could be so helpful to women with these problems. "As a gynecologist," says Dr. Mabray, "I found these stories difficult to believe because candida vaginitis was one of the most common problems I saw. Moreover, I was using nystatin orally and vaginally. And I did not see any of the dramatic results that were being described." Then he says he learned to put his patients on a diet low in sugar and other simple carbohydrates along with the nystatin. And he says, "I was absolutely astounded. Within two weeks I had several people calling to tell me what a genius I was because for the first time in a long time they felt really good."

Antifungal Treatment

The second part of the treatment program involves measures to reduce the population of candida. A range of antifungals is available. One that has been used for over forty years is nystatin, which is available in a number of forms but is most often taken orally for the types of candida problems described in this chapter. This treatment approach has been studied in a double-blind, randomized, placebo-controlled study (so the next time a physician tells you this approach has not been validated, point out this study).[99] Because very little of it is absorbed from the intestines, it is very nontoxic. The oral suspension of the drug is not recommended because of its high sugar content, and tablets usually are not recommended for this type of candida problem because they do not keep the mouth, throat, and esophagus yeast-free. The nystatin powder, mixed as needed with a half glass of water, does help keep these areas free of candida because the patient swishes the solution around in the mouth before swallowing. Some physicians also recommend nystatin enemas to remove the heavy load of candida that usually resides in the colon. Additional antifungals are available in European countries, and Miconazole, an antifungal that remains primarily in the gastrointestinal tract, is available in Canada.

Nystatin and Miconazole cannot reach other places where candida may be residing beyond the gastrointestinal tract. For these locations, systemic drugs are used, including ketoconazole, fluconazole, and itraconazole (brand names Nizoral, Diflucan, and Sporanox, respectively). These drugs, particularly Diflucan, have been very useful to candida patients in killing the yeast wherever it is and in lessening the rapid die-off reaction that sometimes made earlier antifungal treatment an ordeal.

All of the azole drugs, as they are called, have a potential for liver toxicity. Because of this, they are usually given only for short time periods, while nystatin is often given for months, even years when necessary. These drugs should not be taken during pregnancy, with cisapride, or with the antihistamines Hismanal or Seldane, as together they can cause irregular heartbeat or cardiac arrest. Check with your doctor about these or other antihistamines you may be using. The azole drugs can also lessen the effectiveness of birth control pills, so you may need to use another form of birth control while on them. (Many doctors who treat candida problems will suggest you stop the birth control pills anyway, as they tend to increase candida problems.)

Dr. Konetzki typically uses one of the azoles first to eliminate candida from the bladder, vagina, nasal and mouth passages, and other areas outside the intestines. Then he prescribes oral nystatin powder, ⅛ teaspoon in half a glass of water four times daily with food for at least three months. Then, if the patient is doing well, the dosage is slowly scaled back, although the patient will need to remain on the drug for at least nine months.*

In addition to these prescription antifungals, various nonprescription antifungals are sometimes used. They include caprylic acid under a variety of brand names; grapefruit seed extract (ParaMicrocidin, Paracan-144, Nutriotic); taheebo tea, which is also called pau d'arco or La Pacho, made from the bark of certain South American trees; garlic; and others.

Another important element in removing as much candida as possible and reestablishing intestinal health is supplementation with *Lactobacillus acidophilus* and *Bifidobacteria*. These "friendly" bacteria are normal inhabitants of the intestines and produce substances that may help keep candida in check and compete with candida and other organisms for nutrients and for attachment sites in our intestines; help detoxify the intestinal tract; and manufacture our B vitamins. When candida takes over, it tends to wipe out the competing bacteria, such as *Lactobacillus acidophilus*, so "reflorastation," restoration of our natural flora, is needed. Be sure to consult with your healthcare practitioner for recommendations on types of supplements and dosage, as well as other supportive therapies to help in the healing process. Quality really counts here, as some brands have been found to contain only *dead* bacteria.

---

*Free supplies of Diflucan are available for financially distressed patients in the United States. To obtain more information, call Pfizer, Inc. at 800-869-9979.

Hormone Balancing

The third major component of the treatment program is testing for hormone imbalances and correcting them. This whole area of candida treatment has evolved and seems to be leading practitioners more and more into the realm of autoimmune diseases. Testing can reveal an incorrect ratio of estrogen to progesterone; thyroid malfunction; and adrenal hormone imbalances, elevated levels of cortisone and reduced levels of testosterone and dehydroepiandrosterone (DHEA).

We are all familiar with ovarian supplementation in the form of estrogen and progesterone but less familiar with thyroid or adrenal supplementation. Dr. Konetzki, in a chapter he wrote for a medical textbook on endo, states, "If there is chronic fatigue associated with longstanding, severe endometriosis, then DHEA, cortisone and free and total testosterone levels need to be drawn and deficiencies corrected. In addition, evaluation of fatigue should include a thyroid evaluation including a T_3, T_4, and FTI (free thyroxine index). The recent trend to evaluate thyroid status with only a TSH level or a T_4 and a TSH is not appropriate here as people with chronic fatigue states tend to be deficient in DHEA which is necessary for efficient conversion of T_4 to T_3."[97] He notes in cases where one sees a low T_3 with a normal T_4 and TSH, DHEA should be replaced first and then the thyroid panel remeasured. The typical symptoms of thyroid deficiency (which can be due to the DHEA deficiency just described, underactive thyroid, or Hashimoto's thyroiditis) are fatigue, hair loss, sensitivity to cold, depression, poor memory, and menstrual disturbances.

Thyroiditis has been found in greater frequency in candida patients than in the general population. There is also a relationship among candida, thyroiditis, and mitral valve prolapse, a condition that has been noted in women with endo in the past.

Dr. Konetzki notes that testosterone plays a very important role in metabolism of carbohydrates, fats, and proteins and that without the proper level, our body does not have the energy needed "for each and every cell of the body to do its job." Natural testosterone is now available from compounding pharmacies, and synthetic forms also are available. Methyltestosterone has been linked in some cases to liver tumors, so some practitioners feel that natural testosterone may be better.

The adrenal hormones are more mysterious and unfamiliar to many of us, and indeed adrenal hormone testing and balancing are relatively new among the practitioners working in this area also. Here it is clearly important to have a practitioner with some experience work with you.

One of the most important adrenal hormones that frequently seems to be low when tested in women with endo and related candida problems is DHEA. Interestingly, DHEA appears to be critical in immune regulation. Women with lupus (an autoimmune disease for which women with endo are at greater risk) have abnormally low levels of DHEA. "How many autoimmune folks, of course, have elevated helper/suppressor T-cell ratios, way too many helper cells, not enough suppressor cells. DHEA will usually straighten that situation out," said Jonathan Wright, M.D., a Kent, Washington, physician at a medical meeting. "Over time it's quite reliable that the helper/suppressor T-cell count will settle on down toward normal and as it does that, of course, the autoimmune disease or the severe allergic disease symptoms become better."[98]

In addition, in a large study of 5,000 women at the University of California, San Diego, it was found that women who developed breast cancer had subnormal urinary excretion of DHEA breakdown products as long as nine years before development of the breast cancer, and the highest risk of cancer was linked with the lowest levels of DHEA. DHEA also appears to be very important after menopause; further research is occurring at this time.

Because DHEA is a natural substance and no drug company has a patent on it, it has not been widely promoted, but quality DHEA is available via prescription. According to Konetzki, the most desirable DHEA products are in micronized form. Taking DHEA to replace it in the body or bring it back to a normal level should not be confused with the large doses of hormones some body builders and athletes take (illegally). It is much like other hormones in which the body is deficient: Bringing the body back to a normal level may help it function normally; overdoing it or taking megadoses creates a pharmacologic or drug effect. DHEA has also proved useful, according to Dr. William Crook's book *The Yeast Connection and the Woman*, in people with chemical sensitivities, rheumatoid arthritis, lupus, chronic fatigue syndrome, ulcerative colitis, and Crohn's disease.

Conclusion

It is important to choose a knowledgeable physician to help you in a program such as the one described in this chapter. Many of the physicians experienced in this type of treatment are members of the American Academy of Environmental Medicine. See information on how to contact the academy in the Resources section at the back of the book. Also, be sure to talk to other women with endo in your area, as they may know of a helpful physician for a candida treatment program. Finally, you may wish to see the comments about working with physicians on this issue in the book by Dr. Crook, just mentioned.

It has been discouraging that the new clinical findings on candida initially met much skepticism from the medical community. This is not surprising, as our modern super-specialized medical system is very suspicious of syndromes that involve multisystem symptoms. In addition, much of the information about candida emerged, at least in North America, from clinical physicians (those actually treating and working with patients), rather than from medical schools. That also increased suspicion among some academic physicians. However, the charge that there is no scientific basis for this specialty is blatantly untrue. There is massive scientific literature on the subject, even in English, and even more in other languages.

Finally, there was disbelief related to the candida problem because it became a fad in the mid-1980s. This is unfortunate because it caused the clinical work on candida to be discredited. But just because something had the misfortune to become a fad does not mean that it is not useful to at least a segment of the population. Women with endo will be comforted and thrilled to discover that many of the physicians in this field are among the most innovative, open-minded, and gifted physicians they will ever have the privilege of meeting—physicians who truly make healing their mission and restore our faith in the ability to get better. Thank you to those wonderful physicians who have persisted in caring deeply about their patients and working with them to reach health.

Avoiding *Candida Albicans* Problems: Tips for Women with Endometriosis

Women with endo seem to be highly susceptible to problems with *Candida albicans*. Here are some tips to help you reduce or prevent these problems.

Take Allergies Seriously

As this chapter points out, allergies set you up for candida problems and probably set you up for more trouble from endo. Allergies may also be a key risk factor for chronic fatigue immune dysfunction syndrome; about 75 percent of chronic fatigue patients have a significant number of allergies. As Steven Witkin, Ph.D., says in his article on the effect of *Candida albicans* and histamine on PGE_2, regardless of whether or not you have had allergies previously, the presence of *Candida albicans* at the time and site of an immediate hypersensitivity response may exacerbate PGE_2 release.[101] Thus, avoiding allergic responses can help prevent this setup for trouble.

Avoid "Irrational Use of Antibiotics"

One leading mycologist (a scientist who studies fungi) describes the indiscriminate use of antibiotics as "irrational." Antibiotics "break the normal relations between intestinal microorganisms, activate the pathogenic bacteria and also break the vitamin metabolism," he writes.[102] In addition, some antibiotics interfere with a key component of the immune system.[103]

All too often antibiotics are prescribed when it is not known whether a bacterial infection is even present, versus a viral or a fungal infection. Since only bacteria are susceptible to antibiotics, if the infection is caused by a virus or a fungus or due to an allergic reaction, the antibiotics do not address the source of the problem. Some physicians have referred to our overuse of antibiotics, such as in children with ear infections or in women with urinary tract infections, as "promiscuous."

Moreover, even when an infection is present, antibiotics are not specific for the organism causing the infection. They wipe out the good bacteria we need, such as lactobacillus, along with the infectious ones. Then, without the lactobacillus that helps keep candida in check in the intestines, the candida is free to grow out of control. In addition, our overuse of antibiotics is leading to increasingly dangerous resistant bacteria. Already people have died of these new superinfections, which can kill even healthy people very quickly. The sudden death of Jim Henson, creator of the Muppets, is an example.

Be aware that antibiotics may also be present in meats because they are fed to animals in livestock production where crowded conditions cause quick disease transmission. According to an article in the *Canadian Family Physician* (May 1993), antibiotics in meat may cause reactions in sensitive patients. Antibiotic-free, hormone-free meat, eggs, and dairy are available in health food stores (and taste better, too!).

If you must take an antibiotic (and bacterial infection has been confirmed), use precautions such as taking *Lactobacillus acidophilus* with the antibiotic and watch your diet carefully while on the antibiotic so as not to feed the *Candida albicans*, making it even easier for it to go wild. As one Russian physician said, "In Russia, it is a maxim that one should never prescribe an antibiotic without giving a prescription for an antifungal medication to go along with it."[104]

Reevaluate Use of Birth Control Pills

If *Candida albicans* is a big problem for you, you may need to avoid birth control pills, which often exacerbate or bring on *Candida* problems. This, of course, is a tough decision because many women with endo rely on birth control pills to keep endo symptoms at bay. As always, do your homework, talk with other women with endo and your physician, and make your decision.

Don't Overuse Nonsteroidal Anti-Inflammatories (NSAIDs)

Frequent use of nonsteroidal anti-inflammatories has been shown to create a chronic state of hyperpermeability ("leaky gut syndrome") associated with inflammation, according to Leo Galland, M.D., who reviews the research literature in his excellent article, "Leaky Gut Syndrome."[105] As with the birth control pill issue, women with endo seem to be constantly forced to decide between the lesser of two evils. Galland writes that the only NSAID that does not increase small bowel permeability is nabumetone (Relafen).

Miscellaneous Dietary Hints

Here are some other tips for avoiding candida problems. (For the key dietary requirements for candida treatment programs, see the accompanying article.)

- **Balance essential fatty acids.** Essential fatty acids are the precursors to prostaglandins. The formation of prostaglandins is limited to some extent by the presence or absence of their fatty acid precursors in the body. (For more on this subject, see Chapter 5.) However, in brief, you can slow down the production of harmful prostaglandins, such as PGE_2, by reducing the presence of the essential fatty acid precursor arachidonic acid, which is found in abundance in dairy products and meats. On the other hand, you may want to try to increase levels of "good" prostaglandins (PGE_1, PGE_3, and PGI_3) by increased intake of the essential fatty acid precursors for the omega-3 essential fatty acids (which are found in fish oils, walnuts, and flaxseed oil) and the omega-6 essential fatty acids (found in evening primrose oil, borage oil, safflower oil, and seed and nut oils). These helpful prostaglandins can slow cholesterol formation and prevent inflammation and platelet aggregation (clotting).
- **Eat more magnesium-rich foods.** Many studies indicate magnesium deficiency in those with candida problems. The deficiency may be more than dietary, however, as Dr. Galland has found evidence of magnesium wasting in these patients. However, this indicates an even greater need for supplementation and good dietary sources, such as whole grain breads, cereals, nuts, beans, and seafoods.
- **Supplement *Lactobacillus acidophilus* and the *Bifidobacteria*.** These normal residents of our bowels and vagina help keep candida in check. You can do this by eating yogurt containing these organisms or taking nondairy-based supplements if you don't like yogurt or are avoiding or allergic to dairy. Look for yogurt that does not contain added sugar or honey. Check the ingredients on the yogurt container, which will indicate if the yogurt contains "live" or "active" cultures. Some supplements have been shown to have no live *Lactobacillus* in them, so look for a good-quality brand, and ask for recommendations from a knowledgeable healthcare practitioner or from a trusted health food store. Yogurt is also very easy to make at home.

Avoiding Vaginal *Candida Albicans* Problems

- **Avoid douching.** Studies have found that women who douche regularly have a higher incidence of *Candida albicans* in their vaginas. One study found that douching with plain water had no harmful effects, however.
- **Avoid use of chemicals, perfumed toilet paper, deodorant soaps, deodorant sprays, and other "feminine hygiene" products.** One physician, in a review article on vaginal candidiasis, wrote, "It is astounding how often I see inflammation of vulvar and perineal tissue caused by agents in deodorant soaps or perfumed or softened toilet paper. These agents are particularly noxious because they are being leached out of the undergarments as a woman moves and perspires during her working day."[106] If you have allergy tests indicating sensitivity to certain chemicals, don't forget to check soaps, shampoos, and other toiletries for these ingredients. It's amazing how many harsh chemicals can be found in these products. Natural food stores often offer milder, very pleasant alternatives. Detergent residues also can be a problem. Marjorie Crandall, Ph.D., a scientist who suffered for years from endo and candida problems, recommends that you not use fabric softeners. These also contain harsh chemicals.

- **Watch for other chemicals.** Chlorine in swimming pools, chlorinated disinfectants (one study found the vagina is highly susceptible to these), and spermicides all can cause vaginitis. Especially avoid spermicides with nonoxynol-9, an estrogenic chemical that increases the adhesion of *Candida albicans* to vaginal cells.
- **Watch what you wear.** Pantyhose, tight underwear made of synthetic fabrics, and other garments that keep the vulva moist set you up for *Candida albicans* to grow in the vulva area or vagina. Changing clothes after sweaty sports activities, drying thoroughly after showers and baths, and wearing 100 percent cotton underwear and loose, airy clothes whenever possible will help keep candida at bay. If your vulva is especially sensitive, you might want to try organic cotton underwear—that is, cotton grown without herbicides and pesticides and woven without harmful chemicals, dyes, or bleaches. Sources of organic cotton clothes are included in the Resources section at the back of the book.
- **Consider menstrual supply alternatives.** The vagina is an organ with a sensitive mucosal surface and is susceptible to chlorinated compounds, so tampons and sanitary pads containing traces of dioxin and other undesirable substances can be harmful. See *The Endometriosis Sourcebook* for alternatives. Clearly, women should avoid deodorant tampons and pads and talcum powder. (Talc has been linked to ovarian cancer.) These substances can also trigger allergic reactions, and as shown in research by Steven Witkin, Ph.D., any allergic response in the vagina increases the risk of candida invasion.

5 What You Eat Affects Your Endo

NUTRITION AND ENDOMETRIOSIS

Nancy Edwards Merrill

"Let your food be your medicine. Let your medicine be your food."
—Hippocrates

The notion that what we eat—or don't eat—affects how our bodies function seems as reasonable today as it was for Hippocrates 2,500 years ago. Perhaps it is even more pertinent today. After all, the diet of the industrialized world has changed both in what we *aren't* getting in our diets anymore (for example, vitamins and minerals stripped out in the milling of grains) and in what we *are* getting but don't want (such as pesticides, preservatives, hormones).

Diet has been linked to many diseases and "is a factor in five of the 10 leading causes of death in the United States."[1] Yet diet and nutrition can also be viewed as an essential part of a more holistic approach to disease—and to health.

Thus, it is not surprising that women with endo want advice on nutritional approaches that might help manage some of the disease symptoms. Many women with endo report benefits from improved nutrition in general and also from nutritional approaches geared specifically toward endo. In fact, in a survey of Association members, "change in diet" was reported as the third most effective alternative approach to treating endo (right after candidiasis/immunotherapy treatment and exercise), far more effective than traditional surgery and medical treatments. (For a chart with the data, see Figure 4.1 in Chapter 4.)

This chapter presents the nutritional strategies that seem most reasonable and promising for women with endo. Nutritional approaches to endo discussed here will focus on three mechanisms of action: anti-inflammatory, anti-estrogenic, and analgesic (pain-relieving).

No article, however, can provide a specific dietary plan for all women; each person is unique, and not every approach will be appropriate for every person. The best way to start implementing some of these strategies is to evaluate your present nutritional status and habits and then discuss your options with a knowledgeable health professional such as a registered dietitian (R.D.) or a nutritionist, nurse, or physician with nutritional training.

Anti-Inflammatory Nutritional Approaches

Nutritional approaches that seek to produce anti-inflammatory actions often target prostaglandins. These are hormone-like substances found in many of the body's tissues. They can exert both positive and negative influences on the body and are involved in dysmenorrhea (menstrual pain and related symptoms) and endometriosis.

Our bodies make prostaglandins from two essential fatty acids, linoleic acid and linolenic acid—called "essential" because our bodies cannot make them and must obtain them from food sources. Depending on their fatty acid precursor (starting point), prostaglandins fall into three different series. Linoleic acid is the precursor

FIGURE 5.1 Precursors for Prostaglandins

LA → GLA → DGLA → AA   LNA → SA → ETA → EPA

     ↓   ↓   ↓

    Series 1 Series 2   Series 3

for both series 1 and 2 prostaglandins; linolenic acid is the precursor for series 3 prostaglandins.

In the body, linoleic acid (LA) is changed into gamma linolenic acid (GLA), then to dihomogamma linolenic acid (DGLA), and finally to arachidonic acid (AA). As shown on the left in Figure 5.1, series 1 prostaglandins are made from dihomogamma linolenic acid (DGLA), and series 2 come from arachidonic acid (AA). The precursor for series 3 prostaglandins is linolenic acid (LNA). The body changes this essential fatty acid first to stearidonic acid (SA), then to eicosatetraenoic acid (ETA), and finally to eicosapentaenoic acid (EPA).[2] As shown on the right in Figure 5.1, series 3 prostaglandins are made from linolenic acid.

Prostaglandins have various functions in regulating cellular activity throughout the body.[2] Series 1 prostaglandins include PGE_1, the best-known "good guy" of the prostaglandins. PGE_1 has been shown to prevent inflammation, keep blood platelets from sticking together, open up blood vessels, slow down cholesterol production, help remove fluid from the body, improve nerve function, and aid T cell function.

PGE_1 is an important factor in pain relief because it prevents cell membranes from releasing arachidonic acid (which causes inflammation).[3] If less arachidonic acid is released, then less of the series 2 prostaglandins will be produced, including PGE_2, the best-known "bad guy" prostaglandin. PGE_2 causes inflammation, promotes platelet aggregation (clumping together or clotting), and induces the kidney to retain salt. Series 3 prostaglandins include PGE_3 and PGI_3, the other "good guys," which have platelet anti-aggregating (anticlotting) properties similar to those of PGE_1 and also are anti-inflammatory.

Prostaglandins and Endo

There has been a good deal of study on the role of prostaglandins (particularly the "bad guy" series 2 prostaglandins) in primary dysmenorrhea and endo. Prostaglandins themselves are quite short-lived, so researchers sometimes measure more stable metabolites of the prostaglandins. Much of the work has concentrated on PGE_2, PGF_{2a}, PGI_2 (measured through one of its metabolites, 6-keto PGF_{1a}), and a breakdown product of series 2 prostaglandins, thromboxane A_2 (TXA_2, which itself is measured through its metabolite TXB_2). Attempts to measure these four compounds in the peritoneal fluid

of women with and without endo have shown mixed results, with some studies show-ing higher levels in women with endo and some showing no significant difference between the groups.[4]

One study looked at levels of PGE_2, PGF_{2a}, TXB_2, and 6-keto-PGF_{1a} in women with endo and severe dysmenorrhea compared with levels of the same compounds in women with endo but without severe dysmenorrhea. The researchers found a signifi-cant direct correlation between the severity of dysmenorrhea and prostaglandin pro-duction in tissue taken from endometrial cysts. This supports the idea that increased series 2 prostaglandin production may be implicated in the pain of dysmenorrhea and endo.[5] Another study also found significantly higher PGE_2 levels in women with endo-related infertility than in women with infertility not due to endo (in this case, tubal obstruction).[6]

Diet and Prostaglandins

If series 2 prostaglandins are implicated in the pain of endo, then it is sensible to try to inhibit their actions. One strategy for bringing down levels of series 2 prostaglandins is to use prostaglandin synthetase inhibitors, such as ibuprofen (available in many brands), naproxen sodium (prescription names Anaprox, Naprosyn; over-the-counter brand Aleve), indomethacin, or tolfenamic acid. These drugs, however, work by inhibit-

---

Essential Fatty Acids (EFAs)

Sources of EFA which produce "good" (Series 1 or 3) prostaglandins:

> fish oils*—cod liver oil, salmon, mackerel
> evening primrose oil
> seed and nut oils, especially linseed, flaxseed, safflower oils; also soy, sunflower, and corn oils; walnuts

Sources of EFAs (and other conditions) that can produce "bad" (Series 2) prostaglandins or interfere with production of good prostaglandins:

meat and dairy products	aging
margarine	high alcohol intake
processed oils	high cholesterol diet
diabetes	stress-related hormones
deficiencies in vitamin B_6, zinc, magnesium, and calcium	

*To avoid the risk of vitamin A toxicity, do not take more than one teaspoon of fish oil per day.

---

ing the production of *all* prostaglandins, both the "good" (series 1 and 3) and the "bad" (series 2).

A more selective approach is to try to bring down only the levels of the series 2 prostaglandins. This is done by boosting the series 1 prostaglandins, particularly PGE_1, which blocks the production of series 2 prostaglandins from arachidonic acid.

If the body is not producing enough series 1 (and series 3) prostaglandins and thus there are insufficient levels, an imbalance between "good" (series 1 and 3) and "bad" (series 2) prostaglandins can occur. There are several possible reasons for insufficient series 1 prostaglandin production. One factor is that the modern North American diet contains little dihomogamma linolenic acid (DGLA) or gamma linolenic acid (GLA), so series 1 prostaglandins must be made from linoleic acid (LA) and go through the entire conversion process from LA to GLA to DGLA to series 1 prostaglandins. In addition, many factors can interfere with the conversion of linoleic acid to gamma linolenic acid. Diabetes, aging, and high alcohol intake interfere with this transformation, as do high cholesterol, stress-related hormones such as catecholamines and cortisol (see Glossary), and deficiencies or low intake or malabsorption of pyridoxine (vitamin B_6), zinc, magnesium, biotin, or calcium. High levels of trans fatty acids (abundant in margarine and processed oils) also interfere with the metabolism of essential fatty acids.

In contrast, the body can easily make series 2 prostaglandins, the so-called "bad guys," from dietary sources of arachidonic acid, particularly meat and dairy products, foods common in the typical Western diet.[3] Thus, it is vital to reduce consumption of meat and dairy products in order to decrease production of series 2 prostaglandins, and to eat more vegetables and fish oils. These guidelines are summarized below.

Evening Primrose Oil and Fish Oil

Increasing dietary intake of linoleic acid and gamma linolenic acid (GLA) helps increase levels of the "good" series 1 prostaglandins. Good sources of linoleic acid are seed and nut oils, especially safflower oil and evening primrose oil. Evening primrose oil is one of the few direct nutritional sources of gamma linolenic acid and is often recommended for helping to bring series 1 and series 2 prostaglandins back into balance. (The other main source of GLA is human milk.[2]) Taking gamma linolenic acid directly bypasses any problems in the more complex process of converting linoleic acid to gamma linolenic acid and also helps if you have difficulties with absorption.

Some studies have been done with series 3 prostaglandins, which are made from eicosapentaenoic acid, a product of linolenic acid, and which share some of the properties of the "good" series 1 prostaglandins. Eicosapentaenoic acid (EPA) is found in significant quantities in fish oil. In a study done to determine if fish oil might reduce the risk of colon cancer, fish oil reduced PGE_2 levels in the rectal mucosa of healthy subjects.[7] Studies involving the administration of EPA to patients with active rheumatoid arthritis showed an improvement of symptoms due to its anti-inflammatory effect, as well as a significant decrease in immune inflammatory factors.[8, 9]

Another study[10] examined the results of feeding fish oil to rabbits in which endometriosis had been surgically induced. In measurements of prostaglandins at twenty-eight and fifty-six days, concentrations of PGE_2 and PGF_{2a} ("bad guy" prostaglandins) in peritoneal fluid were significantly *lower* in the group given fish oil than in controls given olive oil. In addition, the researchers found that total endometrial implant diameter was smaller in the rabbits given fish oil than in controls.

A double-blind crossover study involving fish oil supplements given to adolescents with dysmenorrhea also showed beneficial results.[11] In the study, forty-two adolescents with dysmenorrhea were divided randomly into two groups of twenty-one girls. One group received daily omega-3 fish oil supplements for two months, followed by two months taking a placebo. The other group received a placebo for the first two months and the fish oil for the second two months. Eighteen symptoms associated with dysmenorrhea were assessed at the beginning of the study and every month thereafter.

After two months on the fish oil, both groups showed a marked reduction in menstrual symptoms. The girls also took fewer ibuprofen tablets during their periods while taking the fish oil than while taking placebo. While four of seven girls with severe dysmenorrhea reported no improvement from the fish oil, 68 percent of the girls overall rated the fish oil as at least moderately effective and moderately worthwhile, or better. The findings suggest that further research into the benefits of fish oil as well as evening primrose oil supplements is warranted. Another study found that a low-fat vegetarian diet was associated with reduced length of pain and intensity of pain during the period.[12] And a third study found that menstrual pain was associated with low intake of linolenic acid.[13]

Anti-Estrogenic Nutritional Approaches

Another dietary approach to managing endo symptoms is to try to lower estrogen levels in the body. One possible approach to lowering estrogen levels might be to try lowering body fat content in general, since fat cells are a source of estrogen in the body, and obese women have been found to have higher estrogen levels than lean women. Fat tissue converts androgens ("male" hormones produced in both men and women) into estrogens, accounting for roughly a third of the estrogen circulating in the blood of premenopausal women. It is the main source of estrogen in postmenopausal women. In addition, the fatter a woman is, the more she converts androgen into the most active form of estrogen, estradiol.[14] One well-known study, however, did not confirm an increased risk of endo based on weight.[15]

As is the case for many alternative therapies, there are few studies to prove effectiveness, especially for endo. But there are nutritional strategies that attempt to manipulate estrogen levels based on what is known of the functions of various vitamins and foods (B vitamins and soy, for example).

B Vitamins

The B complex vitamins, particularly vitamin B_6 (pyridoxine), are almost always recommended in diets for endo. The reason is the role of B vitamins in lowering estrogen levels. The liver depends on the B vitamins to create the enzymes needed to break down estradiol, the most active form of estrogen, into estriol, a form of estrogen that does not cause the tissue proliferation that estradiol does.[16, 17] Also of interest to women with endo, many of whom suffer from asthma and allergies, is the discovery of low levels of vitamin B_6 in adult asthmatics.[18]

The body is easily depleted of B vitamins by the overconsumption of sugar, white bread, and other refined carbohydrates, alcohol, and caffeine; stress; and courses of antibiotics. Thus, according to nutritionist Dian Mills, it makes sense to supplement with a 50-milligram yeast-free B vitamin complex, limit your intake of B-depleting foods, eat foods high in the B vitamins, and manage stress as best you can. The following sidebar lists foods rich in B vitamins, as well as foods and conditions that deplete B vita-

B Vitamins

Foods rich in B vitamins:

- meat, poultry, and fish, especially salmon—be aware that consumption of meats may increase levels of PGE_2 and be aware of possible dioxin contamination in fish.
- eggs and dairy—again be aware of PGE_2 levels.
- legumes: sunflower seeds, soybeans, chickpeas, navy beans, lentils, nuts, peanut butter
- brewer's yeast—do not use yeast products if you are susceptible to *candida* problems.
- whole grains
- brown rice

Foods and conditions that deplete B vitamins:

- refined carbohydrates
- caffeine
- alcohol
- stress
- sugar

Symptoms of B vitamin deficiency:

- poor memory, irritability, depression, inability to concentrate, especially with B_1 (thiamine) deficiency
- premenstrual tension, depression—B_6 (pyridoxine) deficiency
- cracks at the corners of mouth; reddish, fissured tongue; flaky areas around nose—B_2 (riboflavin) deficiency
- nervousness, digestive disturbances—B_2 deficiency
- paleness, fatigue, anemia—B_{12} deficiency

mins, and symptoms of a deficiency. If you decide to supplement vitamin B_6, however, seek professional advice regarding dosage, as high doses can cause severe nerve damage. Never take more than 200 milligrams daily unless your healthcare provider recommends it, says Mills, coauthor of *Endometriosis: A Key to Healing Through Nutrition*.

The Vegetarian Diet: To Bean or Not to Bean

Diet clearly has an effect on estrogen levels. It has been shown that a vegetarian diet is associated with decreased estrogen levels in women before and after menopause.[19] Vegetarian women excrete more estrogen in their feces due to the higher fiber level and have lower plasma levels of unconjugated estrogen than do women who eat meat.[20, 21] Fiber is needed to bind estrogen and is vital to estrogen balance. Fats in meats and dairy products are probably the culprits that raise estrogen levels in nonvegetarian women, although it may be that increased fiber intake is responsible for keeping estrogen levels low in vegetarian women.

Fiber also helps to keep the correct balance of *Bifidobacteria* in the intestines. You should try to maintain a three-to-one balance of *Bifidobacteria* to *Bacteroides* bacteria by consuming more fiber from fruits, vegetables, and whole-grain cereals and less processed, high-fat, high-sugar foods. Live yogurt or the use of fructooligosaccharides (see Glossary) and acidophilus can be an adjunct to vitamin and mineral supplementation. The use of the birth control pill, hormone and antibiotic treatments, and stress can disrupt intestinal flora, so maintaining the *Bifidobacteria* count and taking 30 grams of fiber daily is important to estrogen balance.

Although studies have not been done to show whether vegetarian women have a lower incidence of endo or fibroids, it has been shown that they have a lower incidence of breast cancer, which can also be an estrogen-dependent disease. One study notes that cruciferous vegetables (broccoli, brussels sprouts, cabbage) in the diet may help lower estrogen levels: "Cruciferous vegetables contain at least three unique compounds—indoles, dithiolthiones, and isothiocynates—which influence certain enzymes that rev up the body's detoxification system . . . [estrogen] is detoxified and ultimately excreted from the body."[22]

Dioxin and PCBs: Hormonally Active Chemicals in Our Diet

Studies indicate that hormonally active chemicals such as dioxin and PCBs can have profound immunological and reproductive effects, including acting like hormones (estrogen and others) in our bodies. Research sponsored by the Endometriosis Association showed that 79 percent of monkeys exposed to dioxin developed endometriosis, and the disease increased in severity in direct proportion to the amount of dioxin exposure. Most of the dioxin we encounter comes to us in our food.[23, 24]

Suggestions gleaned from toxicologists for limiting our dietary exposure to these chemicals include the following:

- Avoid contaminated fish (at the very least, follow state fish consumption guidelines).
- Eat lower on the food chain (more vegetables and grains, fewer animal products).
- Trim fat from meats and fish.
- Eat organically grown foods.
- Drink purified water.[25]
- Avoid eating the twelve fruits and vegetables that carry the most toxic pesticides (see Figure 5.2).

A 1994 report from the U.S. Environmental Protection Agency found that meats and cheeses are a major source of dioxin exposure in the United States today.[26] Figure 5.3

FIGURE 5.2 Shopping List: Eat Healthy and Reduce Risks from Pesticides

Rank	Instead of These (produce with most pesticides and most toxic pesticides)	Try These Substitutes*
1	Strawberries	Blueberries, raspberries, blackberries, oranges, grapefruit, U.S. cantaloupe, kiwi, watermelon
2 (tie)	Red peppers	Romaine lettuce, carrots, broccoli, brussels sprouts, asparagus, tomatoes
	Green peppers	Green peas, broccoli, romaine lettuce
2 (tie)	Spinach	Broccoli, brussels sprouts, romaine lettuce, asparagus
4	Cherries	Oranges, blueberries, raspberries, blackberries, grapefruit, U.S. cantaloupe, kiwi
5	Peaches	Nectarines, U.S. cantaloupe, watermelon, tangerines, oranges, red or pink grapefruit
6	Cantaloupe (Mexican)	U.S. cantaloupe or watermelon
7	Celery	Carrots, romaine lettuce, broccoli, radishes
8	Apples	Pears, oranges, grapefruit, cantaloupe, kiwi, watermelon, nectarines, bananas, tangerines, or any fruit not on the list of most contaminated foods
9	Apricots	Nectarines, U.S. cantaloupe, watermelon, tangerines, oranges, red or pink grapefruit
10	Green beans	Green peas, broccoli, cauliflower, brussels sprouts, potatoes, asparagus
11	Grapes (Chilean)	U.S. grapes
12	Cucumbers	Carrots, Romaine lettuce, broccoli, radishes, or any vegetable not on the list of most contaminated foods

*All the alternatives listed are good sources of most or all principal vitamins and nutrients found in the contaminated food.

Sources: Reprinted with the permission of Citizens for a Better Environment, 647 West Virginia St., Suite 305, Milwaukee, WI 53204, and Environmental Working Group, 1718 Connecticut Avenue, NW, Suite 600, Washington, DC, 20009.

shows the ten foods in the Food and Drug Administration's 1999 Total Diet Study found to be most contaminated with residues from persistent pesticides and dioxin. This table lists the persistent toxic chemicals in each of these foods.

Phytoestrogens

Phytoestrogens are weak, naturally occurring estrogens found in many plants such as soybeans and flaxseed. They possess both estrogenic and anti-estrogenic (agonist and antagonist) properties.[27] Phytoestrogens are similar to estradiol functionally and struc-

FIGURE 5.3 Top 10 Foods Most Contaminated with Persistent Toxic Chemicals

	Chlordane	DDE	DDT	Dieldrin	Dioxin	Endrin	Heptachlor	Hexachloro-benzene	Toxaphene
Butter	X	X	X	X	X		X	X	
Cantaloupe		X		X	X		X		X
Cucumbers/pickles	X	X		X		X	X		X
Meatloaf		X		X	X		X	X	
Peanuts		X		X				X	X
Popcorn	X			X					X
Radishes	X	X	X	X		X	X		X
Spinach		X	X	X			X		X
Summer squash	X	X		X		X		X	X
Winter squash	X	X		X		X		X	X

Sources: Pesticide Action Network North America and Commonweal, "Nowhere to Hide: Persistent Toxic Chemicals in the U.S. Food Supply" (March 2001); U.S. Food and Drug Administration, "Total Diet Study" (September 2000.); A. Schechter et al.,"Congener-Specific Levels of Dioxins and Dibenzofurans in U.S. Food and Estimated Daily Dioxin Toxic Equivalent Intake," *Environmental Health Perspectives* 102: pp. 962–966; U.S. Environmental Protection Agency, "Estimating Exposure to Dioxin-Like Compounds, Volume II: Properties, Sources, Occurrence and Background Exposures," U.S. EPA Office of Research and Development, EPA/600/6-88/005Cb, External Review Draft (1994).

turally but can block the action of the estradiol our body produces by locking onto estrogen receptor sites. This prevents the estradiol, a much stronger estrogen, from using the receptor site. One phytoestrogen, genistein, is only about 1/100,000 as strong as estradiol.

Phytoestrogens consist of a number of classes, including lignans, isoflavones, coumestans, and resorcylic acid lactones.[28] Oilseeds such as flaxseed contain the highest concentration of lignans. Isoflavones occur in high concentrations mainly in soybeans and soy products.[28] The major isoflavones are genistein and daidzein, both of which have weak estrogenic activity; however anti-estrogenic activity also has been noted.[28]

According to researchers at Bowman Gray School of Medicine, the "potential risks or benefits of phytoestrogens depend not only on dose and potency but also on duration and pattern of exposure."[27] They state, "The emerging impression is a balance of concern regarding possible risk of adverse effects to fetal-neonatal nervous and reproductive system development and adult reproductive endocrine function, as well as enthusiasm regarding potential benefit on risk of several chronic Western diseases (for example breast and prostate cancers, cardiovascular disease, and osteoporosis)."[27]

One group of researchers found no reports of phytoestrogens causing adverse affects in human infants, although they state that recent animal studies offer conflicting data. They warn that it may not be appropriate to extrapolate animal study results directly to humans, and they encourage human studies.[28]

Some studies show phytoestrogens can disrupt fertility in animals. A study involving female offspring of rats fed diets high in phytoestrogens showed they were unable to ovulate and reproduce.[29] Another study revealed a possible link between phytoestrogens and infertility in cheetahs fed a soy diet in zoos.[30] (More information on phytoestrogens can be found in Chapter 11.)

Analgesic and Multidimensional Nutritional Approaches: Vitamins and Minerals

In addition to the B vitamins, other vitamins and minerals possess anti-inflammatory and analgesic actions, and even a slight deficiency of some nutrients might affect estrogen excretion. Eric Thomas, M.D., of England notes, "Certain sub-clinical deficiencies of nutrients may be adversely affecting the body's ability to degrade excess production of [estradiol] . . . into [estriol], a form which the body can excrete."[31] Some of these important nutrients may include magnesium, calcium, selenium, vitamins E, A, and C, zinc, and iron.

Magnesium

Essential to many metabolic processes, adequate magnesium is necessary to relax smooth muscles[32] and may be an important preventative against miscarriage, muscle cramps, and painful uterine contractions.[33] One study reports magnesium deficiency to be common in premenstrual syndrome.[34] In addition, a physician has reported a possible connection between magnesium deficiency and mitral valve prolapse, a condition for which women with endo appear to be at risk. One Association member with mitral valve prolapse reported complete relief from chest pain as a result of taking a highly absorbable magnesium supplement.[35]

As noted in Chapter 4, "Immunotherapy: The Newest Treatment for Endometriosis," deficiencies in magnesium and vitamin B_6, which would trigger disruption of fatty acid metabolism, are also frequently found to accompany chronic candidiasis.[36] Magnesium deficiency also has been reported in many patients with asthma, multiple chemical sensitivity, and chronic fatigue.[37] Several double-blind studies involving asth-

---

Magnesium: Dietary Guidelines

Good dietary sources of magnesium:
- seed foods: nuts (especially almonds and cashews), seeds, whole grains, dried beans
- seafoods
- raw, green leafy vegetables

Foods that can impair magnesium absorption:
- soft drinks—carbonated soft drinks contain magnesium-binding phosphates
- alcohol
- caffeine
- foods with high levels of saturated fats: margarine, processed oils
- food preservatives and beef (both contain phosphorous)

Symptoms of magnesium deficiency:
- muscle weakness
- twitches, tremors, tics
- shaky hands
- muscle cramps
- irregular heartbeat, palpitations
- insomnia, irritability
- anxiety, panic attacks
- cold hands or feet
- premenstrual tension and cramps

---

matics with magnesium deficiency noted improvement in lung capacity and lung muscle strength after magnesium supplementation.

One study reported that women who had difficulty conceiving or a history of miscarriage with a subsequent inability to conceive were found to be profoundly and uniformly deficient in magnesium.[38] In the study, magnesium levels were successfully repleted after four months for six of twelve women using supplementation of magnesium. The six who did not replete were found to have low levels of a selenium-dependent enzyme; the six who did replete had normal levels of this enzyme.

Of the six women who had not had their magnesium level repleted, three were then given an oral magnesium supplement, and the other three were given magnesium with selenium (yeast free). After two months, the three treated with magnesium alone still had low magnesium and low enzyme levels; the three treated with the magnesium and selenium had normal magnesium and enzyme levels. The three women with low levels were then treated with the magnesium and selenium, and after two more months, their levels were normal, too. After successful repletion, all twelve of these women either carried a child to term or were more than six months pregnant at the time of the report.[38]

Magnesium deficiency is associated with an increased release of histamine (an immune suppressant and key element in allergic response*), altered metabolism of essential fatty acids (interferes with EPA formation, one of the "good" prostaglandin sources), altered reactivity to prostaglandin and, some theorize, increased prostaglandin formation.[39]

According to Stephen Davies, M.D., of England, magnesium deficiency is greatly underdiagnosed and often misdiagnosed as hypochondria. In part, this may be due to the wide variety of symptoms and their uncanny resemblance to many other conditions. Awareness of the existence of magnesium deficiency has lagged because of medical dependence on serum level testing, the least reliable test for this mineral, according to Davies.[38]

It is widely acknowledged that we do not get enough magnesium in our diet. Some even say we have a "negative balance" of magnesium in our modern Western diet, which is generally deficient in magnesium.[40] What magnesium we do get in our diet can be depleted by alcoholism, chronic stress, and a high intake of phosphorous, found in carbonated beverages, beef, and food preservatives.[40, 41] In addition, urinary excretion of magnesium is increased by high sodium in the diet and an excess of Vitamin D and dairy foods high in calcium.[41] Some cases of severe magnesium deficiency may not respond to oral supplementation until the level has been elevated first through IV therapy. The guidelines on page 119 list foods that are good dietary sources of magnesium, as well as foods that can impair the absorption of this important nutrient.

Oral Supplements**

Magnesium supplements vary widely in cost, solubility (whether they dissolve in the stomach easily), absorbability, and taste. Discuss with a knowledgeable healthcare practitioner which supplement is best for you. The following list provides a sampling of some magnesium supplements:

- **Magnesium chloride**—Dissolves in water; doesn't need stomach acid for solubility; may have a bad taste
- **Magnesium oxide**—Inorganic salt; relatively inexpensive; insoluble in alkali and thus relatively unavailable in the small intestine, the primary site of absorption

---

*Allergies are quite common in women with endo; refer to Chapter 4, "Immunotherapy: The Newest Treatment for Endometriosis," for more information on allergies, candida, and endo.

**Any supplementation probram you undertake should be under the supervision of a knowledgeable healthcare practitioner, but it is particularly important if you have kidney disease and are considering supplementing magnesium.

Calcium: Dietary Guidelines

Food sources of calcium:
- sardines and salmon (especially if you eat the soft little bones)
- milk and cheese
- dark leafy greens
- tofu and soy flour, and other soy products
- blackstrap molasses
- dried peas and beans
- broccoli

Conditions that accelerate calcium loss:
- high protein diet
- lack of exercise
- steroids (such as prednisone)
- excessive intake of sodium or caffeine
- menopausal hormonal changes (estrogen levels decrease)

- **Magnesium citrate**—Slightly better absorption than magnesium oxide (little difference, however, if taken with food)
- **Magnesium carbonate and sulfate**—Less soluble
- **Aminochelated magnesium**—Well tolerated; less diarrhea, better absorption than magnesium oxide and magnesium sulfate

Calcium

Calcium works closely with magnesium. Although many women eating a Western diet are more likely to suffer greater deficiencies in magnesium than calcium, calcium is especially important to women with endo because of its role in building and maintaining bone. As we know, the GnRH drugs used in endo treatment reduce bone mineral density, increasing the risk for osteoporosis. Calcium (and magnesium and other minerals) taken before and after GnRH treatment may help lessen this risk. Calcium taken *during* GnRH treatment will not be useful unless a source of estrogen is present (as may be with add-back; see Chapter 2).

Calcium Supplementation

Several types of calcium supplements are available, with differing concentrations of calcium. Calcium carbonate and calcium citrate contain about 40 percent calcium; calcium lactate contains 13 percent calcium; calcium gluconate contains 9 percent. Dolomite and bone meal should be avoided, since they may contain toxic heavy metals such as lead and cadmium.

If you supplement calcium, also supplement magnesium. You should maintain a calcium/magnesium ratio of about two to one (twice as much calcium as magnesium). Too much calcium in relation to magnesium can block magnesium absorption. Dosages above 2,500 milligrams per day should be monitored by a doctor. Check with a knowledgeable healthcare practitioner or a registered dietitian (R.D.) before starting any supplements. Too much calcium can also block absorption of zinc and iron.

As with most supplements, calcium should be taken with food. The presence of other vitamins and minerals (such as vitamin D and magnesium) aids in the absorption of calcium.

Selenium

As noted earlier, selenium (yeast free) in combination with magnesium proved helpful in one study in treating magnesium deficiency in women with a history of miscarriage and difficulty conceiving. In another report, selenium used in conjunction with vitamin E provided improvement in inflammation in some women with endometriosis.[42] Animal studies show that selenium may have an anti-inflammatory effect and may enhance the immune response.[32] Selenium is also important to thyroid function (as is DHEA; see the discussion of immunotherapy in Chapter 4) and is necessary for conversion of thyroid hormone T_4 to the more active form, T_3. Thus, thyroid tests that merely measure T_4 levels may not be sufficient in determining thyroid function and iodine uptake. A deficiency of selenium has been linked to a higher incidence of cancer, and one study reported that high dietary levels of selenium helped protect against the development of breast tumors in rats.[43]

Women and girls with endo are advised to take a yeast-free form of selenium,[32] due to our common yeast sensitivity. Selenium-rich foods include seafood, whole-grain cereal and bread products, kidney, and liver.

Vitamins E, C, and A

Vitamin E, C, and A are antioxidants. Vitamin E also has an analgesic effect (probably due to its inhibition of prostaglandin PGE_2 synthesis), and animal studies suggest it may have an anti-inflammatory action.[32] It has been shown to strengthen the immune system of animals; in rats, higher plasma levels of vitamin E correlated with enhanced immune response.[44] One study reports that vitamin E may be useful in treating fibrocystic breast disease and premenstrual syndrome.[45] Vitamin E taken orally and used topically has been shown to help keep scar tissue soft and flexible in burns and diabetic ulcerations.[16, 46] Research shows that vitamin E acts slowly and limits the degree and duration of inflammation; it is less effective in suppressing preexisting inflammation.[32]

Because vitamins E and A can accumulate in the liver to toxic levels, some experts advise obtaining these vitamins through food rather than supplements. If you want to take vitamins or any supplement, consult your physician, nutritionist, or dietitian.

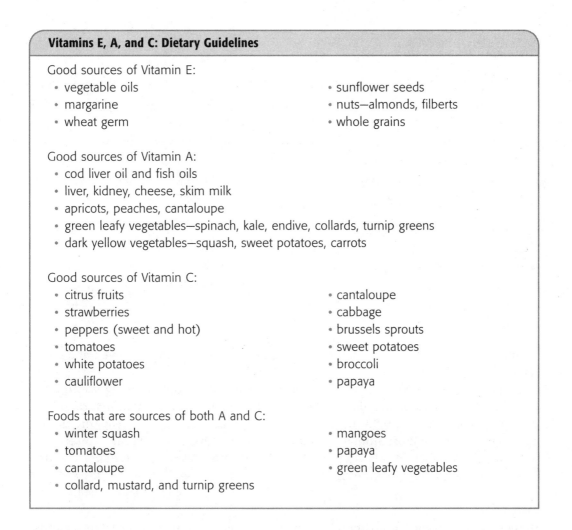

Vitamins E, A, and C: Dietary Guidelines

Good sources of Vitamin E:
- vegetable oils
- margarine
- wheat germ
- sunflower seeds
- nuts—almonds, filberts
- whole grains

Good sources of Vitamin A:
- cod liver oil and fish oils
- liver, kidney, cheese, skim milk
- apricots, peaches, cantaloupe
- green leafy vegetables—spinach, kale, endive, collards, turnip greens
- dark yellow vegetables—squash, sweet potatoes, carrots

Good sources of Vitamin C:
- citrus fruits
- strawberries
- peppers (sweet and hot)
- tomatoes
- white potatoes
- cauliflower
- cantaloupe
- cabbage
- brussels sprouts
- sweet potatoes
- broccoli
- papaya

Foods that are sources of both A and C:
- winter squash
- tomatoes
- cantaloupe
- collard, mustard, and turnip greens
- mangoes
- papaya
- green leafy vegetables

(Indeed, vitamin and mineral pills alone can never substitute for a balanced, nutritious diet. Fifteen to 25 percent of the U.S. population is said to eat no fruits or vegetables[47]— obviously anyone with endo who falls into that 15 to 25 percent could improve her health dramatically by adding these healthy foods to her diet.)

Besides being antioxidants like vitamin E, vitamins A and C also appear to boost our immune defenses against cancer.[48] Vitamin A seems to help keep our immune defenses functioning properly preoperatively and may help with faster recovery after surgery. In stress situations, large amounts of vitamin A are needed to stimulate immune responses weakened by that stress. Vitamin A has also been shown to decrease the size of breast cysts.[43] Vitamin A can be obtained from animal foods in a form that enters the bloodstream directly or as carotene or beta-carotene, which is converted into a useful form in the small intestine and requires zinc for this conversion. Use caution when

---

Zinc: Dietary Guidelines

Foods rich in zinc:

Meats and cheese
- chicken hearts
- liver
- turkey & chicken

- beef
- lamb
- Swiss & cheddar cheese

Legumes, nuts, and seeds
- pumpkin & sunflower seeds
- black-eyed peas, soybeans, chickpeas, lentils

- Brazil nuts, cashews, peanuts
- rolled oats

Conditions that deplete zinc:
- cigarette smoking
- alcohol
- birth control pills

- illness
- injury
- emotional trauma

---

supplementing, as excess vitamin A is not excreted, but stored in the liver, and could cause damage.

Vitamin C appears to act as a natural antihistamine,[49] making it highly useful to all with allergies, and can help reduce infection and promote healing. Vitamin C can affect the ability to digest food, fight the effects of stress, metabolize and detoxify drugs, and heal wounds. Unlike most animals, humans cannot manufacture vitamin C internally, so we need a diet rich in this vitamin. In addition, extra C is needed for smokers, diabetics, the elderly, allergy sufferers, and people under stress.[43]

Zinc

Studies show that zinc has an anti-inflammatory effect in rheumatoid arthritis patients, and in physiological concentrations it can cause approximately 40 percent inhibition of immunologically induced histamine and leukotriene release from basophils and mast cells,[32] key elements of an allergic reaction. Since allergic manifestations appear to be common in women with endo, dietary measures countering this tendency may be helpful. In other words, eat foods rich in zinc and avoid foods to which you are sensitive.

An article in *Internal Medicine* states that in rats, PGE_2 binds zinc and facilitates its transport across the intestinal mucosa.[50] (Because this can cause less zinc to be utilized, you may want to limit consumption of foods that are PGE_2 precursors, such as dairy and meats.) Experiments in humans indicate that iron intake can interfere with zinc absorption,[50] so zinc and iron, if necessary, should be taken at different times of the day. (See the discussion of iron in the next section of this article for further cautions.) Furthermore, zinc deficiency makes you more susceptible to bacterial and yeast infections—an important consideration for the many women with endo who suffer from candida problems.[51] Zinc can also be depleted by cigarettes, alcohol, oral contraceptives, illness, surgery, injury, and emotional trauma.[52] On the other hand, too much zinc can cause nausea, vomiting, fever, and diarrhea. Consult a knowledgeable healthcare provider before supplementing.

Iron

Iron is vital to the oxygenation of our bodies' tissues. A deficiency of iron can cause iron-deficiency anemia, which can appear as fatigue, paleness, headache, dizziness, and lowered immunity. However, some experts now warn against iron supplementation, as studies indicate a possible link between high iron stores and both heart disease and cancer.[52] A Finnish study published in 1992 in the American Heart Association journal, *Circulation* (volume 86) reported a link between serum ferritin (iron) levels above 200 and a doubled risk of heart disease. Two studies published in 1994 in the *International Journal of Cancer* (volume 56) suggested a link between high levels of circulating iron and cancer.[53]

For those who have frequent or chronic yeast infections, there is a further consideration. Candida needs iron for its growth, so the more iron we have stored in our bodies, the more we may be helping the candida grow! It also seems that candida has the ability to compete more effectively than you or me for available iron, perhaps contributing to iron deficiency. One study found a slightly increased risk for candida problems with increased iron intake, although the results were not statistically significant and other studies have had conflicting results.[54] In his book, *The Yeast Connection and the Woman*, the late William Crook, M.D., states that iron supplementation is not necessary unless the woman has lost a lot of blood during the menstrual period or has had heavy blood loss as a result of surgery.[55]

Elmer Cranton, M.D., president of the American College for Advancement in Medicine, states the case against iron supplementation even more strongly: "Iron is so potentially dangerous that I recommend blood testing before prescribing it for anyone."[56] He even recommends against eating iron-fortified foods "if you are an adult male or a woman past menopause." Premenopausal women should not supplement, he states, if they eat a good diet, have normal hemoglobin and other iron tests, and do not lose excessive amounts of blood during menstruation. Check with your doctor before supplementing iron.

Benefits of a Nutritional Approach

Dian Mills, nutritionist with the Institute for Optimum Nutrition in London and trustee of the SHE (Simply Holistic Endometriosis) Trust, reported on a double-blind study of

---

Tips for Eating a Healthful Diet

- Limit the amount of fat you eat, especially saturated fat. Most nutrition experts now recommend that fat make up no more than 30 percent of your total calories (with saturated fats being less than 10 percent).
- Increase the amount of fresh fruits and vegetables you eat (especially dark orange and green vegetables) to five or more servings a day. Eat crunchy cruciferous veggies several times weekly at least; these include cauliflower, broccoli, brussels sprouts, and cabbage.
- Increase your intake of whole grains, cereal, rice, legumes, nuts, and seeds. Eat six or more servings daily of grains, cereals, rice, potato, etc. (One serving is a slice of bread, one-half cup cooked pasta or rice, or a medium potato.) For possible modification to this tip, see the article "Insulin and Endometriosis," later in this chapter.
- Eat three to four calcium-rich foods each day, and also include magnesium-rich foods in your daily diet. If you supplement, maintain a two-to-one ratio of calcium to magnesium.
- Limit or avoid sugar, caffeine, soda, and alcohol intake. Avoid yeast products if you are sensitive to yeast.
- Cut back on meat and dairy; eat more protein-rich foods such as legumes (dried beans and peas), fish, and poultry. If you eat fish, choose the safest source possible, and cut off the fat to lessen toxin ingestion.
- Cut back on highly processed foods that rob your diet of vitamins and minerals. Use cold-processed rather than heat-processed oils.
- Buy or raise organic produce whenever possible to avoid pesticides, hormones, antibiotics, and preservatives. If you can't buy organic, minimize your consumption of pesticides by scrubbing or peeling produce (however, rinsing with water removes only about one-third of the pesticides on the surface of the fruit). Peeling can help reduce contamination but isn't practical for crops such as strawberries, celery, or peppers. Other fruits can be peeled but then lose valuable nutrients.

---

dietary supplements involving twenty women diagnosed with endo and eight women with no history of female complaints.[57] The women were matched in pairs according to deficiency symptoms, and each pair was randomly split into groups A and B. For a three-month period, group A received placebos composed of rice flour, while the women in group B received a nutritional supplement consisting of thiamine (100 milligrams of B_1), riboflavin (100 milligrams of B_2), pyridoxine (100 milligrams of B_6), magnesium aminochelate (300 milligrams), and zinc citrate (20 milligrams). Each woman assessed her overall condition on a scale of 1 to 5 at zero to three months. During the three-month trial period, the women in the placebo group showed no statistical change

- Another way to help minimize the amount of pesticides and toxins in your food is to avoid eating any of the foods that contain the *most* pesticides and the *most* *toxic* pesticides. See Figures 5.2 and 5.3, earlier in this chapter, for examples.
- Consult a registered dietitian or a physician with special training in nutrition for dietary and supplementation guidance. Supplementation must be individualized based on your diet, genetics, medical conditions, and other factors. What's right for you may not be the right balance for others. The quality of supplements, like the quality of food, must also be considered. Some supplements are of poor quality or even made with harmful additives, preservatives, coatings, and colorings.
- Remember that in their most natural, beneficial forms, vitamins and minerals aren't pills that we pop on our way out the door in the morning; they are vital nutrients best obtained in our food. Vitamins are organic compounds (thirteen altogether) found in food that perform many vital jobs in the body. Minerals are inorganic (carbon-free) elements in food; nineteen of the more than thirty-six known minerals are necessary to good health. While vitamin pills and mineral supplements can help provide the body with these necessary nutrients if there is a deficiency, they cannot substitute for a well-balanced diet that provides us with fiber, phytochemicals, and other components that supplements may lack. Think of supplements as complementary to a balanced diet, not as a substitute.
- Making the changes necessary to eat a nutritious diet usually requires a change in lifestyle—and that can be difficult at first. Once you begin to notice the positive effects of eating healthy foods, however, the changes become self-rewarding and easier to maintain.

Sources: Resources consulted include Elizabeth Somer, *Nutrition for Women: The Complete Guide* (New York: Henry Holt and Co., 1993); Citizens for a Better Environment and Environmental Working Group, *A Shopper's Guide to Pesticides in Produce* (Milwaukee, Wis.: Citizens for a Better Environment; Washington, D.C: Environmental Working Group).

in their symptoms, but the group receiving the supplement showed a 98 percent improvement in symptoms. The study suggests that nutritional supplements and/or improved nutrition may offer significant alleviation of some of the symptoms associated with endo.

No nutritional approach is likely to alleviate pelvic pain totally and/or immediately. Indeed, most who espouse any nutritional approach—whether to lower estrogen levels, decrease inflammation, or for analgesic action—recommend staying with the diet and supplements for at least four to six months.[16] Some women who try nutritional approaches, however, do report good results fairly quickly.

"In 1995 the doctor diagnosed me with endo. I was relieved; finally I had a name to put to this vicious pain that gripped my family for two generations. My feelings of elation were short-lived as the doctor explained that there was no cure. He gave me a pamphlet issued by the Association. There was no local chapter of the Association in Jamaica at that time. . . . My family migrated to the United States. . . . Two years later my world crumpled; I could not believe that the endo was back. . . .

"My sister sent me a book with an article on endo. It stated that persons with endo could get relief if they went on a vegetarian diet. . . . I was determined I would eat vegetables if this were the only way to get rid of the pain. I could not believe it; all my life I detested vegetables, and here I was eating lettuce. . . . After two weeks I added raw carrots. After a month I switched to cooked vegetables. I went to the local library and selected books on vegetarian diet. As I read, I tried various combinations of vegetables. I added fruits, carbohydrates, and fats. I ate each food item one at a time. I noted my reaction. Some reactions were quick, and some foods took a longer time to show the effect [they were] having on my body. My theory is that endo is a chronic allergy to food. . . .

"I am now pain free. I am on a strict vegetarian diet. . . . I am allergic to grains (wheat, potatoes, oats, rice, brown bread, white bread, barley, and corn). I cannot eat fats, drink milk or eat milk products, or eat food that has been processed (boxed, bagged, pasteurized, canned, or preserved). With this strict diet I have been pain free for three and a half years. Whenever I eat meat, I have pains on the side and top of my left leg and a tearing pain in my groin. Whenever I eat fats, the pain radiates from deep inside my left side and leaves me doubled over. Grains give a hypoglycemic reaction. They make me very sleepy after three hours. . . . I wrote this so that you may know that there is hope and that endo can be conquered."

—Rose Marie, South Carolina

A number of nutritional and other approaches may be recommended at the same time. Leo Galland, M.D., a New York City physician known for his work with patients with candida and other complex problems, says, "My own first line of therapy for patients with endometriosis is a low-fat diet; supplementation with a multivitamin, magnesium, and fish oils; and a program of aerobic exercise. If the patient is a good candidate for the yeast approach—which most are—I recommend a yeast-free diet along with oral nystatin and/or an imidazole antifungal."

As yet there is no proof that a healthful diet can prevent endo, nor is a nutritional approach meant to replace more traditional treatment options. At the very least, however, a healthful diet may contribute to better overall health, a stronger immune system, and an improved ability to handle stress and pain. In addition, taking charge with a healthful diet also means regaining some sense of control in a situation where women all too often feel an acute loss of control. Finally, nutritional strategies that seek to lower estrogen levels, decrease inflammation, and provide analgesic action may help relieve some of the devastating consequences of suffering with endo.

INSULIN AND ENDOMETRIOSIS

Lynn Castrodale

Another way to look at nutrition and endo has developed through research and clinical observation by John R. Mathias, M.D., a doctor of neurogastroenterology in Houston, Texas. Mathias discovered that women with endo have seizure activity of the fallopian tubes and gastrointestinal (GI) tract. Although the intestines normally have contractions at regular intervals, the seizure activity he refers to is actually spasms of the intestinal and fallopian tube walls. These seizures are caused by the body secreting too much insulin, resulting in excessive "bad" prostaglandins. According to Mathias and others such as Barry Sears, Ph.D., author of *The Zone*, today's average diet stimulates the secretion of too much insulin.[58, 59] This results in a "cascade of biochemical events" that causes diseases. These events and diseases involve protein synthesis, glucose transport, and prostaglandins. According to Mathias, endo is just one expression of this group of diseases.

Mathias believes that the key to regulating the production of prostaglandins is to control insulin. His advice is to decrease high-glycemic-index carbohydrates (foods that enter the bloodstream quickly and result in a rapid rise in blood sugar) in the diet because they cause the body to secrete too much insulin, leading to stored fats, increased triglycerides (see Glossary), and potentially diabetes.

HIGH GLYCEMIC CARBOHYDRATES: DECREASE USE

Potatoes	Corn	Pasta
Beets	Rice	Refined flours and foods
Bread	Fruit juices	Carrots

In contrast, low glycemic index carbohydrates are recommended. These include some fruits and many vegetables, especially green vegetables like spinach and broccoli.

Caffeine and tyramine (a stimulatory amino acid) contribute to the GI seizure problem. Mathias found that eliminating foods that contain these substances decreases seizure activity and symptoms of the gastrointestinal tract.

EXAMPLES OF CAFFEINE- AND TYRAMINE-CONTAINING FOODS

Coffee, tea, colas, etc.	Liquor, wine, beer
Flat beans (such as pea pods, fava beans, pinto beans, lima beans)	Chocolate
	Red meat
Figs, avocados	Soy
Bananas	Aged cheeses

To help create the "good" series 1 and 3 prostaglandins, Mathias suggests the daily use of omega-3 and omega-9 fatty acids. Omega-3 fatty acids, precursors of series 3 prostaglandins, are found in fish oil and flaxseed oil. Omega-9 is known as the regulator of insulin. Omega-9 fatty acids come from olive oil, canola oil, and peanut oil. These oils can be eaten frequently—in salad dressing, for example—and are recommended for cooking.

"After being on danazol for a total of twenty months and suffering almost every side effect possible, I had to search for an alternate form of treatment. I hoped to find a remedy that would really work, since the endo recurred twice while [I was] still on hormone treatment.

"I bought several books, did some research, and came up with the following combination of evening primrose oil and vitamins. I altered it a little to accommodate my arthritis as well as the endo. I also checked with a nutritionist at the hospital to make sure the amounts were within a safe limit. Here is what I take daily: multiple vitamin, vitamin C, calcium/magnesium/zinc, vitamin B$_6$, vitamin E, niacin, evening primrose oil. . . . It is suggested that the evening primrose be taken not all at once, but split and taken two or three times a day. . . .

"I've been following this schedule for four years now and have not had a recurrence of the endo. I still have some cramping and increase ibuprofen during the first three days of my period. The first two days involve a lot of heavy bleeding, and I have ovulation pain every few months. But all of that is minor compared with what I went through six years ago: constant pain, all month long, so bad that I wasn't able to eat or sleep. I'm five feet seven inches and was down to 100 pounds before the endo was finally diagnosed. I started the regimen with the approval of my physician, and he is thrilled that it has worked, especially after seeing the hormone therapy fail big time!

"My doctor is great, and I think of us as partners against this disease because he does care. We had a scare this July when I suddenly developed severe pain during ovulation and a large ovarian cyst was discovered. Dr C. was unable to remove it through the scope, so a full laparotomy was done, the second in five years. But there was only good news: it was not endo (a ruptured corpus luteum); he didn't see any endo; there were minimal adhesions from the previous surgery five years ago; and I was able to keep the ovary."

—Kathleen, New Hampshire

To summarize, Mathias suggests reducing high glycemic index carbohydrates, supplementing with omega-3 and omega-9 fatty acids, and omitting foods that stimulate the nervous system—foods that contain caffeine and the amino acid tyramine. (Some experts have remarked that this diet, with its low carbohydrate levels and low levels of refined sugars and starches, is similar to the *Candida albicans* diet; see Chapter 4, "Immunotherapy: The Newest Treatment for Endometriosis," for more details.) Although each person is biochemically unique, Mathias's theory is that controlling insulin may help prevent or control endo. Early reports from members of the Association who have tried Mathias's dietary approach to endo have been positive.

A POSITIVE OUTCOME FOR ME, AT LAST

Kelly Dobert

Having to undergo another surgery just a year after a total abdominal hysterectomy and removal of the tubes and ovaries, and discovering that I was again a stage 4 even without hormone replacement was devastating physically and emotionally. For two months after my last surgery, I had felt better than I'd ever remembered feeling, then pain returned. It took me months to handle that returning pain emotionally. My morale was at an all-time low. That's not easy for me to admit, but I know that you know what I mean by that. But after living with the pain of endometriosis for twenty-three years, I finally have a positive story and a massive reduction in pain. My quality of life is at an all-time high. What relief!

It all started with watching a TV interview of myself. I was disgusted with the weight gain, and menopause certainly hasn't helped that! I vowed to start dieting. I knew we collect dioxins and other toxins in our fat, and I was sure that I must have had enough fat on me to toxify a nation of Amazons (personal, self-deprecating comment on my part).

I'm a hungry person, and I *so* love food. I was starving on Weight Watchers, so I started the Suzanne Somers diet with a friend. (I hear the groans starting, but be patient.) If you are not familiar with this, basically it is food grouping. There are limitations, but it is something I could live with temporarily. It deals with how the digestive tract can digest foods properly, and I knew that my plumbing has kinks and doesn't function like a normal person's would. Unlike Atkins, Sommersizing allows carbs (whole grains only), but it also stresses good proteins, good fats. Anyway, I lost twenty pounds in six weeks and became "regular" without benefit of my previous mandatory Smooth Moves tea. That was most miraculous! My stomach wasn't bloated, I lost every bit of nausea that I had been dealing with for twenty-three years, and better yet, I was

"After reading your article about nutrition in the Endometriosis Association newsletter, I tried vitamins and saw favorable results within a month. Now after a year of continued usage, I am still virtually symptom free, with only minor pain and moderate bleeding during menstruation. . . . Like so many others, I was desperate for relief of the intolerable pain and tried this therapy as a last resort."

—Candy, North Carolina

eating healthier than ever. I buy organic when it's available and when I can afford it.

During this time, I noticed that the whole grains were really causing pain within twenty minutes of my consuming them. Whole-grain breads have more gluten, and it turns out that several members of my extended family are allergic to gluten. So I no longer eat bread of any kind, no rice, no potatoes, carrots, bananas, or other starchy veggies. I do eat a ton of other vegetables and fruits (by themselves). Basically, if it's processed, I don't touch it.

I had looked at, and tried, the candidiasis diet for a week and just couldn't stick with it. It was too difficult to maintain, I had no willpower for it, and I also had a family of hungry hippos who balked at my cleaning out the fridge. This diet works for all of us, and it's easy for me to do. Even my bread cravings are gone, though I do miss my pancakes on Sunday mornings. I am still losing weight, twenty-eight pounds so far. My husband has lost nearly sixty—which is not fair, by the way.

I feel great 95 percent of the time and am functioning at a level that I am not used to. My boss commented the other day about my stamina and energy level. Last year, I couldn't work more than four hours at a time without debilitating pain. Now I'm working regular eight- to nine-hour days, several times a week, and actually keeping up with the young whippersnappers. Freedom from pain, energy, *and* regularity? What more could I possibly want?!

If you are still skeptical about a change of diet helping to reduce pain (and I was the most skeptical of all), just ask yourself if you can try it for a few weeks. You have nothing to lose by trying, and you might be pleasantly surprised. My father used to say to me, "Talking to you is like talking to a wall." Well, after twenty-three years of walled-up pain, the grouting has crumbled, and I'm ready to listen and take action. I was awfully tired of waiting for somebody to fix me. So, to the Endometriosis Association, I say, "I'm sorry for taking so long to truly listen to what you were saying about diet and nutrition, and a big thank-you for continuing to say over and over again that it can and does make a difference." I'm a believer!

6 Endometriosis and Infertility

OPTIONS WHEN ENDO MAKES IT HARD TO GET PREGNANT

Elizabeth Dougherty

About a third of women with endometriosis experience infertility, and about a third of women with infertility have endometriosis. *Infertility* typically is defined as failing to become pregnant after one year of unprotected intercourse or two or more spontaneous pregnancy losses. Infertile individuals should consult an infertility specialist at one year—waiting longer is OK if you are younger, less if you're older.

You might be one of the 20 percent to 30 percent of women diagnosed with endo who had infertility as your only symptom,[1] or perhaps you'd like to preserve your fertility but alleviating pain is your current concern. You might plan never to have kids. Whatever your individual circumstances, your goals for parenthood may influence how you choose to treat your endo.

In this article, we'll look at practical strategies for preserving fertility and for getting pregnant. We'll also explore the link between infertility and endo and what researchers have discovered about this complicated and controversial area of study.

Why Infertility?

Why so many women with endo experience infertility is a complicated question that research is just beginning to answer. An association seems clear, but a causal relationship is more elusive. Does endo cause infertility, or does it coexist with or cause another condition that is the culprit? To add to the complexity, the severity of the disease also appears to influence fertility in different ways.

Our current definition of *endometriosis* might be one reason it's so difficult to understand the relationship between endo and fertility. Robert L. Barbieri, M.D., and Stacey

---

Biological Mechanisms That Might Link Endo and Infertility

Evidence suggests several possible biological mechanisms linking endo and infertility.

Distorted Pelvic Anatomy: Adhesions can distort pelvic anatomy and interfere with the mechanics of reproduction. For example, if adhesions block your fallopian tubes, the tubes can't pick up the egg, and/or sperm can't get into the tubes for fertilization. It's important to determine if your tubes are clear, so you don't waste your time with inappropriate treatments.

Abnormal Implantation: The lining of your uterus (the endometrium) is prepared to receive an embryo only a few days each cycle, creating a "window" of implantation approximately a week to ten days after you ovulate. During this time, the endometrium produces certain proteins called integrins. Bruce A. Lessey, M.D., Ph.D., from the University of North Carolina at Chapel Hill, found that some women with endo don't produce the beta-3 integrin, which is needed for the embryo to implant effectively in the uterus.[3] This finding suggests that a dysfunctional uterine lining may reduce fertility in some women with endo by impairing implantation. Further research is needed to determine the optimal use of beta-3 integrin testing and treatments of potential abnormalities.

Altered Peritoneal Fluid: Women with endo often have an increased volume of fluid in the pelvis. Within the peritoneal fluid are substances produced by the immune system, including macrophages and prostaglandins (see Glossary), which may create an environment that impairs egg, sperm, embryo, and fallopian tube functions.[4]

Altered Hormonal and Cell-Mediated Immunity: Elevated disease-fighting proteins produced by the immune system, including IgA and IgG antibodies and lymphocytes, found in the endometrium of women with endo also might affect its receptivity and ability to implant an embryo. Some women with endo also have increased autoantibodies—proteins the immune system produces in response to one's own cells or their components.[4] See Chapter 7 for more information.

Missmer from Harvard Medical School in Boston, Massachusetts, suggest that the disease we call endometriosis might actually represent "a constellation of many unique diseases that we cannot currently differentiate"[2]—some of which might reduce fertility.

Preserving Your Fertility

If you have endo and want to get pregnant in the future, evaluate your treatment options with this goal in mind. For example, the number of surgeries you have and

Endocrine and Ovulatory Abnormalities: Women with endo can also suffer from hormone and ovulation abnormalities that can reduce fertility. A complete evaluation can help uncover these problems so that you and your physician can address them. These conditions can be difficult to diagnose, but tests sometimes include serum progesterone levels, endometrial biopsy, and ultrasound of the ovary and endometrium. Examples of these conditions include the following:

- **Luteinized unruptured follicle syndrome**—A condition in which the follicle (a cyst-like structure on the ovary containing one developing egg, which is supposed to rupture at ovulation to release the egg) fails to release the egg
- **Luteal phase dysfunction**—A hormonal imbalance that affects the uterine lining, preventing even fertilized eggs from implanting
- **Abnormal follicular growth**—A condition in which the follicle does not grow or does not grow sufficiently
- **Premature or multiple luteinizing hormone surges**—Improper timing or number of surges in luteinizing hormone (a hormone produced by the pituitary gland involved in maturing of the egg)

Response to Environmental Contaminants: Exposure to environmental contaminants such as dioxin appears to affect fertility. For example, studies led by Canadian researcher Warren G. Foster, Ph.D., from McMaster University, Hamilton, Ontario, showed that in women with infertility, the levels of DDE (a form of DDT) were ninety times higher than in women who did conceive.[5] The United States banned DDT more than thirty years ago, but DDE remains in the soil and continues to enter the food chain. When ingested, DDE mimics estrogen.

what the surgeon does can affect your future fertility. Multiple surgeries put you at a greater risk for developing adhesions, which can cause anatomical problems, such as blocked fallopian tubes. Surgery on your ovaries, one of the most common sites for endo, can compromise the blood supply to the ovaries or reduce the volume of ovarian tissue.

Before surgery, tell your surgeon that preserving your fertility is a priority. Discuss what the surgeon can do to prevent adhesions. If you are having surgery to relieve pain but also want to preserve your fertility, you and your surgeon will need to balance these goals, for example, when deciding how extensively to remove endo and adhesions on your reproductive organs. Frankly discuss this trade-off, since your surgeon won't be able to ask you during the surgery. To reinforce your wishes, you may want to write instructions on your surgical consent forms, such as, "Do not remove reproductive organs unless necessary for lifesaving reasons."

Hormonal treatments, such as continuous birth control pills and GnRH agonists, that suppress your menstrual cycle can alleviate pain, but they don't improve fertility. When you're evaluating hormonal treatments, you and your physician should discuss their effect on future fertility. For example, progestin-based drugs administered by injection may suppress ovulation for many months even after they're discontinued.

Wanting to be a parent in the future is yet another great reason to take the best possible care of yourself, for example, by embracing good nutrition, exercising regularly, and not smoking. Also, try to limit your exposure to environmental contaminants such as dioxin that could affect fertility. The healthier you are, the better your chances of pregnancy (and the more involved in your child's life you can be). See Chapter 12, "Preventing Endometriosis: It May Be Possible!" to learn more about how you can maintain and possibly improve your health and the health of any child you may conceive in the future.

Trying to Become Pregnant

Pregnancy, of course, is a serious life choice. Your health is one of many factors to consider as you contemplate potential parenthood. Too often women feel pressured to try to become pregnant as soon as possible once they're diagnosed with endo. Remember that only you can decide when the time is right for you to become a parent and whether you want to become a parent via your own pregnancy or by another means, such as adoption.

If you decide you want to get pregnant, you can do several things to increase your chances for successfully conceiving. Keep in mind that about two-thirds of women with endo do not experience infertility. You don't know what will happen until you try to become pregnant. Here are some steps to help yourself in your journey to becoming a parent.

Clarify Your Goals
Start by having a frank and detailed discussion with your partner about your goals and expectations for the process of becoming a parent. Discuss the range of parenting options, such as pregnancy or adoption, and what options you would like to pursue. For example, do you want to look into adoption or foster parenting in parallel with trying to become pregnant? If you consider early on how far you're willing to go to get pregnant or adopt—in terms of emotions, time, money, and technology—the effort might ease decision making down the road.

Choose Your Physician

Work with a gynecologist who specializes in fertility treatments or a reproductive endocrinologist who can identify treatable problems early in the process. Too often women with infertility wish they had started working with a specialist—whose expertise might have helped them avoid inappropriate treatments or diagnose a problem—sooner than they did.

Be prepared, though, that a specialist will probably offer a range of treatment choices, which might seem overwhelming. You want a specialist who will walk you through your options without making you feel pressured and will encourage you to decide what's right for you on your timetable.

Ask about the physician's credentials, especially fellowships and board certifications.[6] Be aware that membership in professional societies typically indicates interest rather than training. Make sure you're comfortable with the physician's experience treating infertility *and* endo. When you're discussing pregnancy and birth rates, ask for comparisons with patients who are your age and have endo. The Association can help you find a physician in your area.

> "I feel that I was diagnosed too late, though I complained bitterly about very painful, heavy periods since my midteens. I think it's disgraceful that doctors aren't more interested in treating this disease before things get so out of hand. It may be too late for me, but I pray that the Association can make a difference for young girls just developing endo. I am thirty-six and too destroyed (physically and emotionally) to carry on the fight to preserve my 'fertility.' Keep up the good work."
>
> —Anne, New York

Know Your Insurance

Read your insurance documents, and research whether your state requires insurance companies to cover infertility treatments. In Canada check into what your province covers. Request and read your evidence of coverage to find out how your insurance company defines infertility and what, if any, infertility benefits your coverage includes. Some treatments might fall under your coverage for gynecological services. For example, if your diagnosis is endo, a test to check your fallopian tubes, called a hysterosalpingogram, might be a covered expense, but it might not be if your diagnosis is unexplained infertility. Also, discuss your policy coverage and limitations with your physicians.

Make a Plan

With your partner and physician, put together and document a plan. Take into account issues such as the severity of your endo, your age, other health issues, desired timetable, and health risks. Age is a consideration because fertility peaks in a woman's twenties and decreases after age thirty, with a significant decline starting around age thirty-five. Also, the rate of miscarriages increases with age.

Talk to your physician about what tests are appropriate and when. For example, you might list tests from least to most invasive and move forward to next steps based on test results. An "if/then" flow chart can be helpful. Discuss how aggressive you want to be with your treatments and your timetable and why.

Address Medication Issues

If you're trying to get pregnant, medical treatments for endo will not improve your odds of—and can actually delay—conception because they are contraceptive in nature. If you're using medical treatments for pain relief and need to stop so you can try to become pregnant, discuss with your physician how long you should wait before trying (to allow your body to recover from the effects of the medication) and how you can control your pain while you're trying to become pregnant.

Educate Yourself

Learn the intimate details of your own reproductive cycle by tracking and documenting your basal body temperature, cervical fluid consistency, and ovulation test results. Educate yourself about *timed intercourse*—having intercourse on the best cycle days for conception. Check out resources such as the American Society for Reproductive Medicine (a professional organization for fertility specialists) and Resolve, an infertility educational and support organization.

Try Expectant Management

The more severe your endo is, the more likely you are to have trouble conceiving. Women with mild endo, however, can also experience infertility. If you have mild to moderate endo, the first approach to getting pregnant is generally what is called "expectant management," which is careful medical observation as you try to get pregnant without drugs or surgical treatment. How long you try expectant management is a personal choice that might be influenced by factors such as your age. Typically, physicians suggest healthy couples try expectant management for a year. Generally, the older you are, the longer it might take to get pregnant.

Timing is key to conceiving. It's a myth that all women ovulate on day fourteen. Each woman's cycle is individual and can vary from month to month. That's why it's important to understand both the mechanics of conceiving as well as the details of your own cycle.[7] A positive ovulation test usually means you will ovulate in twenty-four to thirty-six hours. (An ovulation test typically involves urinating on a color-coded test strip. The surge of luteinizing hormone that occurs before ovulation triggers a positive result.) You want to anticipate ovulation because the peak days for conception are typically the two days before ovulation plus the day of ovulation. During your peak fertility days, your cervical fluid—the medium through which the sperm travels to reach the egg—often will resemble stretchy egg whites.

Tracking your basal body temperature also can provide useful information. To obtain your basal body temperature, take your temperature using a basal thermometer before getting out of bed at the same time each morning. Your temperature might dip slightly before you ovulate and then go up. It should stay up until the day or two before your period starts. Charts to track your basal temperature are available from physicians, books, and the Internet.

Talk to your physician about what you can do to enhance your fertility and what you should avoid. For example, most vaginal lubricants can impair sperm mobility.

Identifying and Treating Causes of Infertility

Just because you have endo doesn't mean you'll experience infertility. If you're having trouble getting pregnant or staying pregnant, the problem might not be your endo. The problem also might not be you; it's important to evaluate your partner's sperm early in the process. Work with your physician to rule out treatable problems other than endo.

Show your physician your temperature chart. If your temperature comes down earlier than the day or two before your period, you might have a progesterone deficiency. If your period starts fewer than twelve to fourteen days after ovulation, you might have a luteal phase defect, a hormonal imbalance that affects the uterine lining, preventing even fertilized eggs from implanting. Both of these problems can be treated with vaginal progesterone, but you need to identify that you have them.

Invest in a complete physical and evaluation for you and your partner—a process that you and your physician might break down into several stages. A semen analysis for your partner is an easy place to start; your gynecologist can even order the test. Simple blood tests for you, such as a complete blood count and thyroid panel, might show easily treatable problems that could affect fertility. Patients should ask their physicians about testing for anti-thyroid-stimulating-hormone antibodies and for the conversion of thyroid hormone T_4 to T_3. Women with endo have a higher incidence of hypothyroidism (insufficient thyroid hormone) and Hashimoto's thyroiditis (autoimmune thyroid disease), both of which can adversely affect fertility and pregnancy (see Chapter 12).

Other lab tests might include a postcoital test that evaluates the movement of sperm in your cervical mucus, an ovulation assessment, hormonal checks on different cycle days, and checks of insulin, prolactin, and androgen levels. More invasive, painful, and expensive tests include an endometrial biopsy and a hysterosalpingogram, a procedure to check the fallopian tubes. An ultrasound might show anatomical distortions caused by adhesions. If you're in your thirties or older, a test might be suggested to check the quality of your eggs.

TRIP OF A LIFETIME

Anonymous

Whatever else is severed away,
the hysterectomy
could not uproot and discard
whatever comes back and back brightly, happily, hardy,
and daily prolific in me.
Four months later, I am handed, I confidently take up
my baby nephew. The one startled into kicks of revelry
by the clasping, unclasping pudge
of his own luminous fingers and toes.
I hug his soft accepting self to myself, coo: *Come on
Champ, we're going on the trip of a lifetime.*
I swoop him away to the backyard.
We bounce down giggling into the weedy height
of unmown grass
that tickles. I seize a white hazy humorous glow
of finished unvanquished dandelion, present it to
his widening intent eyes, repeat gleefully: Dandelion, Dandelion as my
fingers crumble and disperse it into every direction,
he squeals and squeals
and flails his blur of perfect limbs.
Amputated, shorn of womb, I remain in on the creation,
the naming of names,
the unending infant laughter of God
sent forth floating seedlike
to all four corners, still catching and rounding the light,
joyfully bent on multiplying the Divine.

Considering Surgery

Should you have surgical treatment for your endo if you are trying to become pregnant? That's one of the most controversial and complicated questions a woman with endo and infertility might face. As discussed earlier, multiple surgeries put you at risk of developing adhesions that can distort pelvic anatomy, which potentially can interfere with the mechanics of conception. However, if you have pain or advanced endo is distorting your reproductive organs, surgery might alleviate your pain and/or restore pelvic anatomy.

If you have mild endo and no pain but infertility, having surgery becomes a murkier issue. The two randomized studies that looked at the effect of surgery versus no surgery on infertility in women with early-stage endo report conflicting results.

A collaborative group of Canadian researchers conducted a randomized study of women with stage 1 or 2 endo and more than one year of infertility.[8] The women had either a diagnostic laparoscopy (no treatment) or a surgical laparoscopy in which the surgeon destroyed endo lesions and cut adhesions. They were followed for thirty-six weeks after surgery. There was an absolute increase of 13 percent in probability of pregnancy within the thirty-six-week term of the study attributable to surgical treatment. That is, one in eight infertile women with minimal or mild endo should benefit from surgical destruction of endo lesions. However, another group or researchers conducting a similar study had conflicting results (the no-treatment group had a higher pregnancy rate). Obviously, more study is needed.

Association Advisor David L. Olive, M.D., and Elizabeth A. Pritts, M.D., from Madison, Wisconsin, combined the results of these two studies into a meta-analysis, which they said still favored surgical treatment, though "it is likely that the effect is small."[10] They concluded that the effect of surgery on early-stage, endo-associated infertility remains "unsettled."

Association Advisors Dan C. Martin, M.D., from Memphis, Tennessee, and David Adamson, M.D., from Palo Alto, California, both caution women with infertility, previously diagnosed endo, and no pain to consider carefully the risks of surgical complications, including adhesions, before having additional surgery. They both suggest weighing the risks and potential benefits of a laparoscopy against those of in vitro fertilization (IVF) if you've already ruled out treatable infertility problems, have a normal pelvic exam, and have tried assisted reproductive treatments discussed later, such as clomiphene citrate (Clomid or Serophene) with intrauterine insemination. Likewise, if you have advanced endo and have previously had surgery, IVF might be a better option than another surgery.[11] Not all endo or infertility experts agree with this position. More research is needed.

Considering Other Options

Only you can decide how long you are willing to try to become pregnant based on expectant management and timed intercourse. You may base your decision on factors such as the severity of your endo and your age. For example, if you're twenty-five years old with mild endo and have ruled out treatable fertility problems, you might choose to try to become pregnant by timing intercourse to ovulation for a year or even two. But if you're thirty-five, you might want to accelerate your timetable in seeking out more aggressive treatments. The combination of endo and age may decrease fertility more than either alone, according to Association Advisor Robert Schenken, M.D., of San Antonio, Texas.[11] If you have severe endo, you might also want to move to more aggressive steps sooner. You might decide that you're not comfortable with pursuing more aggressive medical treatments at all, as they have inherent physical risks and can be financially and emotionally taxing.

Controlled Ovarian Hyperstimulation

If you have not been able to conceive and decide to pursue more aggressive strategies, a common next step is controlled ovarian hyperstimulation combined with intrauterine insemination (IUI). With controlled ovarian hyperstimulation, you take drugs to increase the number of eggs you release. With intrauterine insemination, sperm are injected through the cervix into the uterus. Two randomized trials have shown this combination to increase fertility compared with no treatment for women with endo who have undamaged fallopian tubes.[12, 13]

Typically, you take clomiphene citrate tablets (Clomid or Serophene) for six days to induce ovarian hyperstimulation for three to a maximum of six cycles, per the American Society for Reproductive Medicine guidelines. The majority of pregnancies occur within two to four cycles of treatment. "In very young patients, with otherwise excellent prognosis, up to six cycles of hyperstimulation might occasionally be indicated," according to Dr. Adamson.[14] Injections of gonadotropins (Follistim, Gonal F, Pergonal, or Repronex) also can be used to induce ovarian hyperstimulation for a maximum of six cycles, but the risk of multiple births is higher.

Intrauterine insemination is timed to ovulation. The sperm can be processed in a way that selects those with the most normal structure and mobility, while removing white cells and infectious organisms. Intrauterine insemination also sidesteps cervical problems such as poor mucus. For example, the drugs used to induce ovarian hyperstimulation can adversely affect the quality of your cervical mucus, reducing the effectiveness of intercourse alone.

Clomiphene citrate is frequently prescribed for women who are having trouble conceiving—maybe too frequently and inappropriately, critics suggest. Before you take it, make sure you've ruled out other treatable problems for you and your partner. It's not going to work if your fallopian tubes are blocked or you have a hormonal deficiency, for instance.

Also, evaluate the risks of ovarian hyperstimulation. Ovarian cysts frequently develop, which could be harmless or could cause problems. Hyperstimulation syndrome, a rare but possible complication, could occur. With hyperstimulation syndrome, a woman develops a large number of cysts, and fluid accumulates in the abdomen, causing symptoms such as vomiting, diarrhea, and abdominal distention. Anecdotally, Association members have reported that clomiphene citrate and gonadotropins have made their endo symptoms worse.

Joe's health improves so much that he and Stella decide to adopt a baby.

Producing multiple eggs also puts you at a higher risk for multiple births: 5 to 10 percent of pregnancies induced with clomiphene citrate result in twins, and 25 percent of gonadotropin-induced pregnancies result in multiple fetuses. Multiple births increase risks for both the mother and the babies, including premature birth and low birth weights. Expect your physician to monitor your follicle development with ultrasound and blood tests to determine how many eggs you are releasing and whether you should attempt pregnancy that cycle.

There has been concern based on a 1992 report that the drugs used to induce ovarian hyperstimulation can increase the risk of ovarian cancer.[15] A more recent Danish study found no association between the use of fertility drugs and ovarian cancer.[16] If there is a risk, it may come from the increased ovulation rather than from the drugs themselves. The more you ovulate, the greater your risk for ovarian cancer. Conversely, pregnancy, breastfeeding, and oral contraceptives, all of which reduce ovulation, seem to protect against ovarian cancer. Women who have never been pregnant are at increased risk of ovarian cancer. Unfortunately, women with endo also are at a greater risk for certain cancers, including ovarian cancer (see Chapter 8).

Assisted Reproductive Technologies

Assisted reproductive technologies involve laboratory techniques performed outside of the body to assist in fertilization and implantation. They usually utilize ovulation induction through ovarian hyperstimulation, egg retrieval, and embryo transfer. The most common procedure is in vitro fertilization (IVF), where the egg and sperm are combined in a laboratory dish and the resulting embryo is transferred into a woman's uterus with a catheter. Other procedures include gamete intrafallopian transfer (GIFT), where a retrieved egg is immediately transferred with sperm to the fallopian tube, and zygote intrafallopian transfer (ZIFT), a hybrid of IVF and GIFT.

You might want to consider IVF under one or more of the following circumstances:

• Ovarian hyperstimulation with intrauterine insemination does not work.
• You have extensive endo that has blocked your fallopian tubes.
• You have damaged fallopian tubes.
• Previous surgeries haven't helped.
• You are older than thirty-five. (However, success rates decrease with age.)
• You have experienced infertility for more than three years.

IVF is an expensive procedure, with an elevated risk for multiple births, that often is not covered by insurance and does not have a guarantee of success. However, IVF might be the best or last option for women with advanced endo or a combination of the other factors just listed. To evaluate this option, discuss your particular situation and the risks involved with a fertility specialist.

The effect of endo on IVF success remains controversial.[10] No large randomized clinical trials address the effectiveness of IVF versus expectant management in women with endo. In one small study, twenty-one women with endo and infertility were randomly assigned to receive IVF or undergo expectant management.[17] None of the five women in the expectant management group became pregnant. Of the fifteen women who underwent IVF, five became pregnant. The numbers are too small, however, to draw any meaningful conclusions. Studies before 1989, when most eggs were retrieved laparoscopically, suggested that women with extensive endo had a lower IVF pregnancy rate. However, some recent studies with transvaginal egg retrieval have shown no difference.[10] Others have suggested a lower pregnancy rate.[18] A 1999 joint report by the Society for Assisted Reproductive Technology and the Centers for Disease Control does not show any differences in IVF pregnancy rates between those with and without endo. (The report is available at cdc.gov.)

Another study showed that the stage of endo does not appear to affect pregnancy outcomes, but it may have a slight effect on ovarian stimulation response, with women with milder-stage endo having better responses. Zev Rosenwaks, M.D., and Steven Spandorfer, M.D., of Cornell University, New York, conducted a retrospective study of 1,417 consecutive cycles in 872 patients with endometriosis undergoing IVF.[19] They found that endometriomas (cysts) might diminish pregnancy rates, so surgery to remove them before IVF should be considered.[19]

Women with advanced endo might improve their pregnancy rates and reduce miscarriages by undergoing treatment with a GnRH agonist before they undergo IVF. This is one of the only situations where medical treatment appears to have a useful role in treating infertility in women with endo. The length of treatment, however, remains controversial. Typically, GnRH agonists are administered for two to six weeks before ovarian stimulation with gonadotropins. In one randomized trial, women with severe endo either took gonadotropins alone to stimulate ovulation before IVF or were treated with GnRH agonists for six months and then took gonadotropins to stimulate ovulation. The women treated with GnRH agonists had a higher pregnancy rate.[20] While it's clear that using a GnRH agonist in any patient prior to IVF produces a higher pregnancy rate, the issue of whether two weeks is sufficient for women with endo or six months is required "remains unresolved," according to Drs. Olive and Pritts.[11]

Whether surgical treatment of the endo before starting IVF improves IVF results in women with endo is being analyzed in an Open Research Fund study funded by the Association. (The Open Research Fund, made possible through donations, currently funds twenty research studies in seven countries.)

Conclusion

"If you want to have children, do it soon." That's what the physicians said to me in 1989 when a laparoscopy revealed endo. Unmarried and twenty-four years old, I knew I wanted children someday, but certainly not then. Now, married and older, I worry my age or my endo could prevent me from becoming pregnant.

My oldest sister, Kathy, also diagnosed with severe endo, encourages me. I've learned from her years of struggles with infertility. However, her two sets of twins show me the rewards of what's possible. Like the majority of women with endo, my sister was able to become pregnant, albeit with some help.

Whether you want to become pregnant now, someday, or never, keep your personal goals for parenthood in mind as you decide how to treat your endo. If you want to

> "The decision to have a hysterectomy is difficult for everyone. It was hard for me for many reasons, including that I am single and always dreamed of having children. I looked into artificial insemination (which is not easy for a single woman, at least not in North Carolina), adoption as a single parent, having a fling to get pregnant . . . . I decided that at this time in my life, being a single parent was not the right choice. I also decided that I could not wait for the 'right man' to come along so I could try to get pregnant to start enjoying my life. However, I could not enjoy my life in constant pain and stress. I decided that adoption at some future time was a very valid option for me, that for me being a mother is important, not being pregnant."
>
> —*Deborah, North Carolina*

become pregnant, make a plan, choose a good physician, and educate yourself before embarking on the journey. If you are in the subgroup of women with endo who have infertility, explore your treatment options with your partner and physician, and evaluate what the right steps are for your individual situation. Only you can decide how far to pursue pregnancy.

Many women who experience infertility describe the process of trying to become pregnant as an emotional and physical roller coaster. At any point, you might decide not to pursue additional treatments. Also, remember that you don't need to be pregnant to become a parent. Being a foster parent or adopting a child both offer rewarding options, or you might find that there are other ways you can enjoy children without giving birth.

THREE STORIES OF ENDOMETRIOSIS AND INFERTILITY

Judy, Marg Fundarek, and Lori Price

Judy's Story

I was thirty-two years old when I learned that I had endo. Even though I had always had painful periods, I had never been to a doctor about the pain; I guess I had accepted that pain is a woman's lot. But when I couldn't get pregnant, I knew something had to be wrong.

My doctor wanted to perform a laparotomy to remove as much disease as possible, but from talking to other women, I had learned of a surgeon who could do the same procedure through the laparoscope. I changed doctors and underwent the less invasive surgery. After the laparoscopy, this doctor prescribed Lupron for four months. After these two interventions I was supposed to be very fertile—but nothing happened.

We were offered in vitro fertilization (IVF) but decided against it because of the fertility drugs. I have a cousin in England who developed cancer of the uterus after taking fertility drugs. She had a hysterectomy, but it didn't resolve her problems, and she died during subsequent surgery. She underwent a great deal of pain. At that point in time, I didn't know that fertility drugs can also make endo worse, something I have since learned from other women.

We began to look into adoption, and it was while we were being evaluated as potential parents that I learned I was pregnant. This was eighteen months after I had discontinued the Lupron, so in my opinion it would be a real stretch to attribute this pregnancy to the drug. My pregnancy was pretty normal, and my daughter was born at term: eight pounds, ten ounces. I breastfed her for two years. My periods returned at the end of the first year. They were still painful, but I think I coped better. Your focus is totally different when you have a baby. Unlike at work, at home you can lie down if you need to.

My allergies had always been a problem, but they worsened after my daughter was born. By the time my daughter was two years old, I was really sick. I started having attacks of breathlessness, almost like asthma, frighteningly often. My general practitioner put me on an inhaler and then, when I got one cold after another, on erythromycin. But this antibiotic is based on a synthetic mold, and it actually triggered worse symptoms.

I like my family physician, but his treatments were not helping. Because I had seen family members improve after consulting a naturopath, I decided to pursue this route. I was diagnosed with candida. I began an allergy desensitization program, followed the "yeast diet," and went to an acupuncturist for TENS treatments (electrical stimulation of acupuncture trigger points). These did help the painful periods. I also took large doses of vitamin C and acidophilus, and I quit smoking. Six months later I was much better, with less pain and greatly reduced allergy symptoms. I stopped using the inhaler. And I was pregnant. My son was also born at term: nine pounds, four ounces.

I think we need to be cautious about all the treatments we pursue, including alternative treatments. There simply hasn't been enough long-term research to ensure our safety or the safety of our children. If I could pass on one piece of advice to other women in the same boat, it would be this: *Think it through.* Think how you will feel later, as well as now. Talk to other women who have been there before you. You need to make a decision today that you can live with tomorrow, five years from now, and also much later in your life. Of course, that's what makes these kinds of decisions so difficult.

Marg Fundarek's Story

Before I was diagnosed with endo, I remember feeling that achieving a pregnancy might be difficult. I have always had cramping during my period, although relief was generally

> "I had six months of Zoladex injections. . . . I asked if I should use barrier methods of contraception but was assured that I could not fall pregnant. After the final Zoladex injection, a blood test showed, to my joy, that I was pregnant. At four months, a scan showed problems, and a week later, the foetus had died. I had to wait, in great distress, for an 'evacuation' of my womb. At no time was I warned of any dangers of getting pregnant so soon after treatment. Please—whatever the doctors say—use some sort of barrier contraception, and avoid the grief and distress that I suffered."
>
> —*Rossana, England*

147

just an aspirin away. My mother also experienced discomfort with her period, so I came to believe that my pain was normal.

But the diagnosis of severe endo—after trying for six months to get pregnant and undergoing a laparoscopy, D&C, and hysterosalpingogram—was still a shock. Extensive adhesions had glued my ovaries to each other, and they, in turn, were stuck behind my uterus. My tubes appeared to be blocked. On my doctor's recommendation, and feeling that it probably represented our only chance for a pregnancy, my husband and I signed up for an IVF program.

While we waited, I was put on Lupron Depot for six months to treat the endo. The hot flashes, mood swings, and weight gain were the hardest side effects with which I had to contend. I would go from hysterical laughter to tears at the drop of a hat. Flannel nightgowns gave way to nudity in the middle of winter. Joint aches made me feel a hundred years old.

Following this treatment, a surgeon at the IVF clinic performed another laparoscopy, an endometrial biopsy, and another hysterosalpingogram. My tubes were now open. He suggested we try Clomid and timed intercourse for two cycles. No luck. He then suggested ovulation induction, so that my ovaries would produce as many follicles as possible, thereby increasing the number of eggs released close to the tube openings.

The Clomid and Pergonal put me on new emotional roller coasters. I felt a loss of my femininity, helpless, and my self-esteem plunged. There was no success after one induction cycle. We signed up for IVF at a private clinic, as the funded clinic had a three-year waiting list at that time. More Clomid, more Pergonal, and the daily blood work that was so hard to bear with my tiny veins. Each day at the clinic, I saw the familiar faces of women going through the same ordeal of blood tests, ultrasounds, and injections; hopes and fears soared and plummeted continuously. I have often described the effects of fertility drugs to other women as awful PMS, multiplied a hundred times. Four of my ova were retrieved, and two embryos were transferred, but still no pregnancy. The resulting menstrual period was incredibly painful. I vomited and had to be taken to the hospital in an ambulance.

I insisted that the surgeon do a laparotomy to remove my adhesions and try to restore my reproductive organs to as normal a state as possible. After the surgery, he prescribed danazol for my endo. I could endure the side effects of the medication for only three months: I became severely depressed and often thought of suicide. I also gained more weight. Only at our insistence did the doctor reluctantly agree that I could stop taking the drug.

I developed abdominal and leg pains five months later. Ultrasound revealed my right ovary had an endometrioma, which continued to grow and cause increasing pain each month. I was uncomfortable most of the time. Meanwhile, our turn came up for a second IVF attempt, this time partially funded. We postponed it for several months, as we couldn't rationalize attempting a pregnancy while I was taking painkillers, though the doctors said it would not make any difference. We felt as if they just wanted us to take our turn and be done with it. I had two shots of Lupron to try to shrink the endometrioma,* then, months later, I had a laparoscopy. I believe the surgeon ended up draining the cyst instead of removing it, because after one pain-free month, the cyst filled up, and the pain returned.

We were losing the battle against endo and time, and decided to go ahead with the second IVF attempt. My forearms were black and blue from a nurse slapping them to raise my veins during blood tests. The cyst caused problems during the vaginal ovum retrieval; the doctor had to do a laparoscopy to retrieve a lone egg. Miraculously, it fertilized and was transferred to my uterus. Again, no pregnancy. The ensuing period resulted in another trip to Emergency.

Six months later, I tearfully phoned a doctor who specializes in endo. I told him that the pain was unbearable now and that I was missing a lot of work. I needed stronger and stronger painkillers, which offered only sporadic relief. Ultrasound revealed a cyst on each ovary. The right one grew to the size of a large grapefruit before I had my second laparotomy. During the three hours in the operating room, this surgeon removed my right ovary and tube and the two large cysts; another surgeon removed my appendix and cut out a nodule of endo from my bowel. The pain was gone immediately. My husband and I were elated and looked forward to pain-free days and years ahead.

Unfortunately, however, the fertility drugs had done their job well. Along with their success in stimulating my ovaries, they had also kicked the endo into high gear. The cysts returned, and so did the pain. I remember that after I had taken the five rounds of fertility drugs, my original surgeon remarked to us that "taking fertility drugs with endometriosis present is like throwing gasoline onto a fire." My husband had to resist throttling him at that moment. It's unconscionable that we were not informed of this risk before I took the drugs. I can't say that such knowledge would have dissuaded us from trying fertility drugs the first time, as we were desperate for a baby then. But I'm not sure we would have opted to expose me to these drugs on four additional occasions.

Reflecting back to my life five years ago, I realize I had been one of the "lucky" women with endo who have extensive disease but virtually no pain. Now I find myself in a different situation. Two laparotomies and five laparoscopies later, I'm still enduring cyst and pain problems. I'm thirty-eight, childless, and overweight. Thankfully, I'm still happily married, with my sense of humor intact.

I'm not yet prepared to undergo a hysterectomy and an oophorectomy, although I have come very close at times. I do want to warn other women with endo to carefully consider the possible consequences of fertility drugs. I know how all-consuming the quest for a child can be. I also know that I sincerely would not want another woman with endo to end up suffering any more than she already has. Please, take care.

---

*Editor's note: Medications are generally considered ineffective for endometriomas.

Lori Price's Story

> "I read many letters in your newsletter from women in physical pain. I always feel isolated because I have stage 3 endo but no pain at all (physically). Emotionally, however, I am a wreck. I can't have a baby. I have been through ten or fifteen fertility tests. . . . I feel that there is no hope. I hate those fertility drugs. Actually, Clomid was the reason that my endo was found. *Only* when I took Clomid did I have terrible endo pain and massive rectal bleeding. But when I stopping taking Clomid, the pain went away. . . . I cry and cry at how unfair life is. I am anxious to try IVF, but I am worried that Pergonal, like Clomid, will make my endo grow out of control. And that would not be the best situation for trying to conceive."
>
> —*Marianne, Japan*

I had a laparotomy at twenty-two because of severe abdominal pain. That is when I learned I had endo. A year later I had a laparoscopy and a D&C, and three years later I underwent laser surgery through the laparoscope. All three surgeries were for pain, and on all three occasions, a large amount of disease and adhesions were removed. I constantly suffer from severe abdominal pain, although I have had several pain-free periods in the last eight months.

Because of the fatigue and the unpredictability of the pain, I am unable to hold a full-time job outside my home. I do day care at home, which allows me to operate on my own schedule. It also gives me a chance to surround myself with children, an activity that is important to me because I desperately wish to have my own children. My work gives me an outlet for these emotions.

When my husband and I were ready to start a family, I asked my gynaecologist how I would know when I was pregnant. I was already experiencing many of the symptoms of pregnancy: nausea, bloating, sore breasts, and six- to nine-month spans without menstruating. My gynaecologist gave me a three-month prescription of Clomid, as well as Provera to start my periods. I began keeping a basal body temperature chart. After several months I found I no longer needed the Provera: I was menstruating again, on a thirty-four-day cycle. I continued to take the Clomid for a year, without results. I underwent a hysterosalpingogram, which indicated that my tubes were clear, and a twenty-one-day progesterone test, which confirmed that indeed I was ovulating.

I consulted a fertility specialist, who increased the Clomid. We didn't really see that we had a choice, because I was not ovulating on my own. The cost of the drug is minimal, considering the magnitude of our wish to have children. I have not experienced side effects other than the usual PMS symptoms of fatigue, moodiness, the ongoing breast tenderness, and abdominal pain.

I do find the process frustrating. Being told that I should be able to conceive and continually being disappointed is disturbing. I am also frustrated by the people who tell me not to think about it. It's difficult not to think about what's going on in your body when you are required to take your temperature even before you can turn off the alarm or visit the washroom each morning.

The options beyond Clomid have not been defined for us. We have considered IVF, but because of the risks associated with the drugs involved, we will not pursue that avenue at this point. If we are unable to conceive our own children, we will adopt.

Experiencing infertility has given me insight into the meaning of terms such as *maternal instinct* and *biological clock*. Wanting a child that you cannot have leaves behind a definite emptiness and a very real ache.

EDITOR'S NOTE These three stories originally appeared in the newsletter of the Infertility Awareness Association of Canada.

EARLY MENOPAUSE

Clara Klein

They told me long ago I wouldn't, I couldn't
Conceive
Anything more than a fantasy.
And fantasies I've had.
What would it be like?
To carry a growing life inside me,
Fruit of a wondrous union of love
Between my husband and me.
But I found my husband too late.
I was already on my way
Through that door that would close
Off all dreams of carrying on
The cycle of life.
Hope that not all was in vain
And lessons that were learned
Would be passed on
To found a greater knowledge
For the next generation.
To extend and improve
Upon the continuum.
But it won't.
Why do all souls wish a material proof
Of their being?
For the fear that
That which can be felt but not touched
Is not real.
Is who I am and how I am not enough?
If not a child,
A book?
An invention?
A discovery?
Must you remember my name?
Society will forget over time.
Even children
Will forget
Over generations.

EARLY MENOPAUSE *(continued)*

So I feign noble
And congratulate myself
On not adding to the problem
Of too many people
In a too-confused world.
I will take care of children
Already here.
I will teach
Those I can.
And our love is real enough
To my husband and me.
Yet a grief creeps upon me.
Six weeks, seven weeks I wait.
Anticipation
Is killed by familiarity.
The old problem.
It is not a new beginning
That delays me
But an end.
One cycle comes slowly
To a stop
And another
Never had a chance.
I can't close
This door softly.
It is slammed
Shut.

Vital New Information on Endometriosis

7 The Immune System: Part and Parcel of Endo

UNDERSTANDING THE IMMUNE SYSTEM'S ROLE IN ENDOMETRIOSIS

Grace I. Migaki, M.D./Ph.D. Candidate
Introduction by Mary Lou Ballweg

Introduction

Ever since Association Advisors Leila Adamian, M.D., of Russia, and Paul Dmowski, M.D., Ph.D., of the Institute for the Study and Treatment of Endometriosis, Chicago, published research on certain immune abnormalities in women with endo in the late 1970s and early 1980s, it's been clear that the immune system plays a pivotal role in endo. A flurry of research in the mid- to late 1980s demonstrated that almost every immune cell studied in women with endo was malfunctioning in some way. These studies triggered a lot of excitement that our field was on the brink of understanding this complex disease.

Alas, the more researchers studied, the more complex it all got. To make matters worse, the field of endo has rarely attracted the immunologists it has greatly needed (who were busy in the 1980s and 1990s with the new worldwide epidemic of AIDS). Struggling in a field that is daunting even to those trained in it and hampered by a lack of research funding as well as a lack of interest by some physicians who specialize in endo, most of these early researchers abandoned the pursuit of the immunological

Research Shows Risk for Autoimmune Diseases in Endo

Due to the Association's work starting in 1980 with our first research registry, which showed that immune dysfunction is somehow part of endo, our ongoing question has been "Why?" Now a new Association study,* carried out in collaboration with the National Institutes of Health (a great privilege in itself!), shows what many of us already knew or suspected: Women with endo are at high risk for certain autoimmune diseases.

Association research had shown links between endo and allergies and other signs of immune dysfunction. This data spurred members to push for further research to determine what other diseases are more common in those with endo. A research team from the Endometriosis Association, the National Institute of Child Health and Human Development, and the School of Public Health and Health Services at George Washington University, Washington, D.C., analyzed a survey of 3,680 members of the Association who had endo. They found certain patterns of illness among these women:

- Twenty percent had more than one other disease.
- Up to 31 percent of those with coexisting diseases had also been diagnosed with either fibromyalgia or chronic fatigue syndrome, and some of these had other autoimmune or endocrine disease.
- Chronic fatigue syndrome was more than a hundred times more common than in the female U.S. population generally.

*N. Sinaii, S. D. Cleary, M. L. Ballweg, L. K. Nieman, P. Stratton, "High Rates of Autoimmune and Endocrine Disorders, Fibromyalgia, Chronic Fatigue Syndrome and Atopic Diseases Among Women with Endometriosis: A Survey Analysis," *Human Reproduction* 17(10) (2002): pp. 2,715–2,724.

understanding of endo. The Association has been able to fill the void a little since 1994, when we began our research program at Dartmouth Medical School and, more recently, at Vanderbilt University School of Medicine.

It's true the immune system is complex, especially in endo. But that's the disease we have, so, like it or not, all of us with endo and working in the field will have to grapple with understanding it. Moreover, once you get into it, the immune system is utterly fascinating and gives one a whole new sense of wonder and appreciation for creation!

Also, there's a wonderful incentive for learning all we can about endo from the immune side. It seems that quite possibly, endo is more treatable from the immune side. Candidiasis (immunotherapy) treatment, for instance, has been rated by members of the Association as the most effective treatment of all. In addition to candidia-

- Hypothyroidism was seven times more common.
- Fibromyalgia was twice as common.
- The autoimmune inflammatory diseases, systemic lupus erythematosus, Sjögren's syndrome, rheumatoid arthritis, and multiple sclerosis occurred more frequently. (The earlier a girl or woman had pelvic endo symptoms, the higher the risk for lupus, Sjögren's, rheumatoid arthritis, and chronic fatigue syndrome.)
- Allergies and allergic conditions such as asthma and eczema were higher: 61 percent of the endo sufferers had allergies, compared with 18 percent of the U.S. general population, and 12 percent had asthma, compared with 5 percent. If a woman had endo plus an endocrine disease (such as hypothyroidism), the figure for allergies rose to 72 percent, and to 88 percent if she had endo plus fibromyalgia or chronic fatigue syndrome.
- Two-thirds reported they had family members with diagnosed or suspected endo, confirming research that suggested there is a familial tendency. (Remember that this does not necessarily mean that endo is genetic. Families share environment and behaviors as well as genes.)

"These findings suggest a strong association between endometriosis and autoimmune disorders," said lead investigator Ninet Sinaii from the National Institute of Child Health and Human Development. "Healthcare professionals may need to consider these disorders when evaluating their patients for endometriosis."

The Association and the NIH are continuing these studies, including studies of autoimmune diseases in the families of women with endo. Watch the Association newsletter for additional information in the future.

sis treatment, other efforts to treat endo from the immune side are being studied. To understand the research in our field (and more coming in the future), one has to take at least a crash course in immunology, which this chapter provides. See the Glossary at the back of the book for definitions of unfamiliar words.

A Crash Course in Endo Immunology

What is the connection between our immune systems and this pain-in-the-neck disease, endometriosis? Not only is the continuing search for such links and, hopefully, for a cure stemming from such knowledge what is keeping me employed, I also join you in an earnest desire for the swift discovery of a miracle cure. In any case, until that day, it can't hurt to become familiar with some of the immunological aspects of this disease.

So put on your thinking caps, get comfy with your favorite pillow and heating pad, and get ready to learn! Take your time, and don't be intimidated. Let's start with some basics, and from there we will turn to specific characteristics of endo that lead us to believe that our immune systems are key players in the game of endo.

Self and Nonself

Why do we even have an immune system? Protection! Your immune system exists for the sole purpose of protecting you against the various insults of our world. From those ubiquitous "germs" your mother saw everywhere to the more tangible viruses (like the flu and the common cold) and bacteria (yep, that's right: food poisoning), the array of challenges your immune system must conquer is truly astounding.

How does your immune system manage to recognize and react against each and every offense? The answer lies in the remarkable ability of your immune system to distinguish between that which belongs (self) and that which most certainly does *not* belong (nonself).

An important and confounding breakdown of this ability to distinguish between self and nonself can lead to auto- (self-) immunity, a condition with which you may be familiar. The inability to mount a destructive offense against things that definitely belong (that is, self) is called "tolerance." Tolerance is, as Martha Stewart would say, a good thing; it permits our immune system to run freely throughout our body, defending its territory with whatever armaments it sees fit to use, without having to worry about making a mistake by attacking some component of self. In effect, our bodies have developed a way to avoid "friendly fire" accidents.

When you are immunodeficient, your body may be able to make the required distinction between self and nonself but may lack the ability to respond appropriately to the insult. For example, AIDS (acquired immunodeficiency syndrome) is a disease characterized by an immune system that is so crippled by the war against the human immunodeficiency virus (HIV) that it is unable to defend the patient against things such as the common cold, other viral insults, bacterial invaders, and so on. It is actually these "secondary" infections that end up being the most detrimental to the patient as they further ravage an already weakened system.

Another important duty performed by your immune system is that of "cleanup." Your immune system includes cells that are specialized for such duties and, in normal situations, recognize when a tissue or cell—even though it is your own—is out of place. Does this remind you of endometriosis? Well, before we discuss that idea, let's think about the answer to this question: What *is* my immune system anyway?

FIGURE 7.1 Monocytes Mature into Macrophages

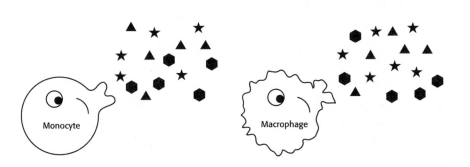

Immune System Components

A remarkable group of cells, called hematopoietic stem cells, reside in your bone marrow and are able to differentiate, or develop into any number of types of cells (see Figure 7.1). These cells mature into red blood cells (erythrocytes) and white blood cells (leukocytes).

The leukocytes are the soldiers in our immune system army. They can be divided into three broad categories: lymphocytes, granulocytes, and antigen-presenting cells (APCs). Early in a pregnancy, the population of lymphocytes divides into two distinct camps in the developing embryo. One group migrates to the **t**hymus gland (a small gland located between the heart and the base of the throat) to mature and are therefore referred to as T lymphocytes, or just T cells. The second group remains behind in the **b**one marrow to mature and are thus referred to as B lymphocytes, or B cells.

These cellular elements work in concert with some very basic defense mechanisms to protect us against infection. Our skin, our mucous membranes, our tears, our sweat (even earwax protects us in some way), and a variety of organs specialized for certain immune functions work with our immune system "soldiers" to battle the myriad and ever-present enemies that accost our systems every day.

In spite of all these armaments, we are still vulnerable to many things; hence the existence of normal bacterial populations in our bodies. Like cleverly disguised assassins, these "friendly" bacteria compete with enemy bacteria for nutrients and resources. In addition, they secrete poisons and acid to prevent the growth of disease-causing bacteria and fungi.

Despite these defenses, tiny organisms are still able to get into our bodies. Two basic ways in which our immune system deals with such invaders are by producing and secreting chemical substances that are lethal to bacteria and by actually consuming the enemy, a strange, bacterial cannibalism called phagocytosis. (*Phago* means eat, and *cyto* means cell—"cell eating.") Phagocytosis is the specialty of two cell types, the macrophage (*macro* meaning big, *phage* meaning eat—"big eater") and the neutrophil. The neutrophil is the major white blood cell in the blood. Within its body, it carries "bags" called granules that contain bacteria-killing chemicals.

Phagocytosis starts with cells called monocytes. Monocytes circulate in our blood and migrate into our tissues, where they develop into macrophages. Macrophages are present throughout our bodies and are especially concentrated in areas like our lungs, livers, and spleens.

Phagocytosis begins when a germ sticks to the surface of the neutrophils or monocytes. Our neutrophil and monocyte soldiers wear uniforms that are partially composed of carbohydrates, and it is believed that these carbohydrates are sticky to bacterial cells. Once the ill-fated offender is stuck, the neutrophil or macrophage gradually begins to surround the enemy with its cellular membrane until it completely encloses the prisoner in a vessel called a vacuole or phagosome. In less than a minute, the granules containing the lethal agents fuse with the vacuole, empty their contents, and kill off the captured foe.

A variety of systems exist to aid and enhance the process of phagocytosis. One such system is the complement (C') system, a group of twenty-odd proteins that work in concert in three ways:

1. Killing invaders independently
2. Killing invaders in conjunction with neutrophils and macrophages
3. Dealing with offenders via acute inflammatory reactions

To kill invaders independently, a series of the C' proteins bind to the enemy cell and eventually work together to form a structure called a "membrane attack complex" (MAC). This MAC is essentially a hole in the enemy's cell membrane, which allows water and salts to fill the enemy cell until it eventually explodes, a process called cell lysis. (To remember this, think, "Too many Big Macs may make you explode.")

C' has two ways of working with our neutrophils and macrophages. First, C' proteins can coat the surface of an invader, providing "handles" that the neutrophils and macrophages recognize and grab, thus adhering the offender to their surfaces and initiating the first step in phagocytosis. Second, one of these special C' proteins acts as a potent chemotactic agent. Chemotaxis is the process by which a cell is directionally attracted to a site or location of infection. For example, the chemicals that comprise the odor of freshly baked bread lure us right to the kitchen, so these chemicals could be envisioned as *chemotactic* agents, or attracting agents, for hungry (or not so hungry) humans!

Some cells in our immune system do not consume offenders but are nonetheless effective killers as well. Aptly named and highly effective, natural killer (NK) cells are able to kill virally infected cells before the virus is able to reproduce. Large, special proteins appear on the surfaces of all virally infected cells, and an NK cell can recognize and bind to them, thus bringing itself closer to its unwitting victim. The NK cell then releases the contents of its granules into the space between it and the infected cell. The granules contain proteins that bind the infected cell and form a structure similar to the C' MAC, which then induces cell death. Importantly, NK cells also can recognize and kill certain cancer cells and other abnormal cells as well.

> "I also had a horrendous problem with fluid retention, a recurring and constant vaginal yeast and thrush problem, off-and-on urinary tract infections, and many colds and viruses."
>
> —Deborah, Pennsylvania

How do we know that our immune systems are working? The answer might surprise you. People tend to blame the terrible aches, pains, and fevers of an infection upon the offending bacteria or virus. That assumption is correct in an indirect way, but often the body's immune system itself causes such symptoms. For example, immune cells can release certain substances that produce fevers. Often the products and the actions of your immune cells are what causes the various signs and symptoms of disease. Inflammation is another great example and will be discussed later in this article.

Endometriosis and the Immune System

Now let's turn to endometriosis. Endo is now considered by many to be a systemic disease characterized by alterations in the immune system. Immunological defects have been noted in even the mildest forms of the disease. I've struggled in trying to settle on a clear, simple way in which to present this material, and I hope that the method I selected will prove to be easy to digest (sorry about the reference to the GI problems we all know and love), interesting, and, yes, fun.

Endo is basically defined as the implantation and growth of tissue similar to that which normally lines the inside of your uterus, in areas other than the inside of the uterus. Usually this means somewhere in the pelvis, perhaps on an ovary or on the bowels, but it can also mean on a lung and even on the brain. Why do only some of us "fortunate" women end up with this disease? Obviously there is something, or many things, in us that make us different from our endo-free friends. It is these differences in our immune systems and immune responses that I describe in the remainder of this article. (For simplicity, this article doesn't address how endometrial tissue finds its way to places other than inside the uterus. The question of what causes endometriosis confounds the scientific community to this day, and several theories exist.) However, whatever the underlying cause(s) of endo, it's very obvious that the immune system is a key player.

Endometriosis has been described as many things from an autoimmune disease with overactive immune activity to a disease of weakened immunity. It's important to keep in mind that endo is truly a fascinating and unique disease because it can actually be characterized by aspects of *both* types of problems and more. Thus, when someone talks about "boosting" her immune system, you'll soon learn that in many ways our immune systems are already in overdrive and that any improper or unnecessary "boosting" may actually lead to more problems.

So, let's take a look at our favorite fictitious endo sister—we'll call her Jane—and her lucky endo-free friend, Sally. Let's take this one step further and say that both Sally and Jane experience retrograde menstruation (backward flow of menstrual tissue), but only Jane actually ended up with endometriosis.

Natural Killer Cells Weakened in Endometriosis

In a person with endometriosis, scientists say the body's NK cells "exhibit decreased cytotoxicity." Using my example and some more colorful language, we could state this as a newspaper headline: "Jane's Trained Assassins Turn Raging War into Candlelight Vigil." What image does that headline bring to your mind? Well, try to picture this: We all have cells in our immune system that are basically trained killers. Their job is to take care of the enemy in the most definitive way. It's no wonder, then, that they are called natural killer cells (NK cells). Sally's NK cells (like the first one pictured in Figure 7.2) are marching about her body, taking care of business and eliminating any "undesirables" they encounter; Jane's, on the other hand, are there and marching, but that seems to be about all they're doing (lazy slackers!). They look like the one in the middle of Figure 7.2.

Try to picture this: Endometrial tissue flows back through Sally and Jane's fallopian tubes and into their abdominal cavities. In Sally's body, her NK cells, along with other members of her immune system army, recognize this presence as improper, wrong, something that is *not* to be tolerated. Sally's NK cells and other members of her defenses work together to eliminate this tissue, leaving Sally free of endo and healthy. Jane's NK assassins and immune system soldiers, in contrast, are ineffective in eliminating this misplaced tissue. Jane's NK cells may not recognize the need to go to work. Perhaps they are weakened or ineffective killers for some reason, or perhaps Jane's endometrial cells are resistant to the NK cell armaments (and, well, there's always the possibility that they're simply conscientious objectors, but they certainly aren't being very conscientious to us endo gals!). Any one or all of these possibilities may contribute to Jane's unfortunate diagnosis.

Jane's Immune System Soldiers Are a Bit "Confused"

Sally's monocytes, when confronted with the errant endometrial tissue, respond by suppressing, or inhibiting, the growth of the endometrial cells. By inhibiting the proliferation (growth) of the endometrial cells, Sally's monocytes are able to help keep Sally endo free.

FIGURE 7.2 NK Cells and Endo

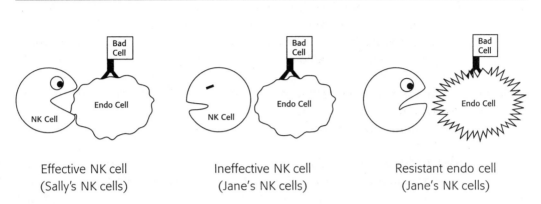

Effective NK cell
(Sally's NK cells)

Ineffective NK cell
(Jane's NK cells)

Resistant endo cell
(Jane's NK cells)

Jane's mixed-up little monocytes, however, do not respond to the confrontation appropriately at all. In fact, they don't even intimidate those misplaced endometrial cells one tiny bit. Endo-Jane's mixed-up monocytes actually respond by stimulating (encouraging) the proliferation of the endometrial tissue! Whether these cells are simply confused or blatantly traitorous, Jane's monocytes do her no favors in behaving in such a deplorable manner.

Jane's Antibody Factories Are Out of Control

An antibody is one of our immune system's most ingenious inventions. This tiny little molecule is indispensable to our immune armies. It works together with other defense mechanisms, is capable of recognizing our sly enemies, and actually tags undesirables and invaders with a kind of "red flag" so that the rest of our body knows to beware. Antibodies, also called immunoglobulins, are proteins capable of activating the complement (C′) system, described earlier. They also can stimulate other immune cells/soldiers and can bind to and mark unlucky targets.

The structure of the antibody is what endows this protein with its versatility. An antibody can be divided into three main components: two arms and a stem. An antibody is shaped like a Y. The arms of the Y—specifically, the tips of the arms—recognize and bind to invaders. The stem or foot of the Y communicates with the rest of the immune system. The arms can distinguish among billions of unique enemies, each sometimes different from the last by only an infinitesimal degree, each different from components of our *own* body by only the palest of shadows.

Without becoming mired in the various distinctions among the immunoglobulin classes, let's address some general aspects of antibody- or immunoglobulin-mediated immune responses. B lymphocytes manufacture, display, and secrete antibodies; they are, in effect, antibody factories. (Remember, **B** cell is related to **b**one marrow and, now, anti**b**ody.) Each B cell produces millions of a single type of antibody (millions of "clones"—remember Dolly, the famous sheep?). Each antibody recognizes a single, specific foreign factor, an antigen. (Very simply, an antigen is anything that is recognized by the immune system and is capable of eliciting an immune response.)

Antibodies can exist in cell-surface forms—that is, bound to the surface of a B cell—or as soluble proteins, floating free within our plasma and other fluids, where they can recognize and bind foreign particles and foreign invaders. Once their variable regions bind an antigen, their constant region, the stem of the Y, remains freely accessible. Special features of the stem enable it to communicate with our complement system, our phagocytic cells, and much more. Communicating through this stem, the bound antibody is able to stimulate the appropriate actions to deal with a particular offender, be it through a C′ MAC, phagocytosis, or some other distinct immunological defense.

Sally's immune system recognizes the refluxed endometrial tissue as being her own but out of place. Thus, her B cell antibody factories are not thrown into action upon encountering this normal but geographically confused tissue. Jane's antibody factories, however, are hyperactive and wired (imagine a hummingbird on caffeine). Whereas Sally's antibody factories roam purposely through her body, dutifully differentiating between self and nonself, generating the necessary antibodies when appropriate, Jane's antibody factories encounter this misplaced endometrial tissue and say, "Hey! I have nothing better to do than to pump out millions of antibodies against this tissue!" Does this remind you of the zillions of allergies many of us have, with our immune systems making antibodies to everything from pollen to, according to some scientists, progesterone? Well, it should, because that is *exactly* what is going on.

No one knows for certain whether Jane's antibody factories don't bother to make the required distinction between self and nonself, whether they actually are unable to make the distinction, or whether there is something unique about Jane's refluxed endometrial tissue that makes it appear to be foreign. But we do know that Jane's antibody factories produce antibodies against the endometrial tissue, so-called anti-endometrial antibodies, shown on the attack in the second part of Figure 7.3. Moreover, Jane's antibody factories go one step further and actually make antibodies against the various pieces of her endometrial cells.

"I am a thirty-one-year-old married woman who has suffered with endo for over eighteen years. I got my period when I was thirteen, and my life changed. I thought I had a very low pain tolerance as I had been told. The same year I came down with mononucleosis and missed my eighth-grade graduation. Throughout my school years, my nickname was "Sickie." I always had chronic stomach problems, flulike symptoms, upper respiratory infections, bladder infections, migraines, and allergies. Also, severe menstrual cramps.

". . . I had to quit my job due to the everyday debilitating pain. I am never pain free. . . . I am allergic to estrogen, progesterone, LH hormone, and candida."

—*Jeannie, California*

FIGURE 7.3 Antibody Factories

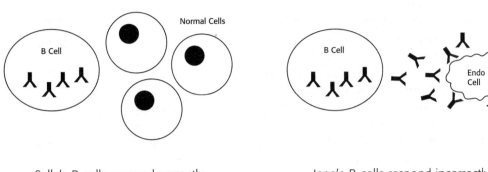

Sally's B cells respond correctly
to stray endometrial tissue

Jane's B cells respond incorrectly,
making matters worse.

In taking this bold step, Jane's antibody factories have now introduced the element of autoimmunity into Jane's already overloaded immunological résumé. Remember, auto ("self") immunity is reactivity against self. By producing antibodies against her own endometrial cells, Jane's antibody factory has unwittingly produced proteins that react against, in a nutshell, Jane!

This scenario brings up another important aspect of endo immunology. Many endo patients suffer from various allergies. Surveys performed by the Association and others have demonstrated that endo patients seem to be more likely to suffer from some sort of allergy than people without endo. Although the research surrounding this issue is in its infancy, it is possible that Jane's hyperreactive antibody factories react to many things, from foods to pollens and pets.

Allergic reactions can be characterized by a variety of symptoms, from the familiar runny nose and itchy eyes to the less familiar stomach cramping, diarrhea, and muscle aches. The symptoms all depend on the type of allergy a person experiences. Despite the wide array of symptoms, I'm sure most readers have experienced more than one of them, and it's likely that many of your symptoms have confounded more than one physician. It's important to realize that there may be logical explanations for your complaints. However, identifying the causes may require an exploration beyond what basic gynecology is used to pursuing. As we know so well, most of the doctors treating endo address only the gyn or pelvic parts of the disease, ignoring the immune aspects. To change this basic approach to treatment of endo, we, and our physicians, will need to understand the endo immunology that follows (and more that science has not yet diccovered).

OK, each of your cells is made up of innumerable components. There are the pieces of the cell membrane, the proteins and molecules inside your cells, and the machinery required to keep that cell—not only that cell, but *you*—alive and well. Since it makes no sense at all to have our immune systems attacking the components of our own cells, normal immune systems are trained to ignore these things and accept them as necessary, normal, and important pieces of each and every one of us. In some, but not all endo patients, the B cell antibody factories malfunction and actually produce antibodies against these very things.

Some women with endo have been diagnosed with antiphospholipid antibodies (phospholipids being one of the building blocks of your cell membranes), anti-DNA antibodies (DNA being the very building blocks of *you*, the instructions for everything from that annoying cowlick to your big brown eyes), and the list goes on. This unfortunate situation—one in which our antibody factories end up producing antibodies to things that do belong, to self—is one of the most significant reasons that people may consider endometriosis to be a type of autoimmune disease.

The existence of antibodies against multiple parts of their own bodies suggests that some patients with endo exhibit "polyclonal B cell activation." This means that the immune systems of such patients are always on. This constant production of antibodies against self-tissue can lead to chronic inflammation and all the "fun" that goes with it. Since these antibodies are found in a soluble form—that is, free-floating in the blood serum or in fluid that may collect in the pelvic cavity—this brings us to another point.

Jane's Humoral Immunity Is Way out of Whack

We've already seen how one component of Jane's humoral immunity differs from Sally's. Now let's turn to another important difference. Remember our complement (C′) systems? Our C′ system consists of twenty-odd soluble proteins. Jane's C′ system appears to be a bit off-kilter—nothing quite as blatant as the production of immune weapons (antibodies) against her very self, but something a bit subtler. Researchers have found that the refluxed endometrial tissue from patients like Jane produces much more C3 protein than a number of other tissues.

So, in our comparison, let's take a look at endometrial tissue from Jane's uterus and Sally's uterus and at the refluxed endometrial tissue from both women as well. Although the two samples of endometrium and the sample of Sally's refluxed endometrial tissue may produce some levels of this C′ protein, the sample of refluxed endometrial tissue from Jane produces a much higher quantity of the C3 protein than those other tissues.

What does this mean? Well, C3 can be broken into different parts. One of these C3 parts actually recruits and activates other immune system soldiers (cells). Since one of the most common findings in endo patients is a whole host of immune cells accumulating in the pelvic cavity, it is important to look at how and why these soldiers end up congregating there. Something must be attracting or recruiting the soldiers to this site, and that little portion of the C3 molecule may be one of the key players in this

> ### Basic Immune Abnormalities Observed in Endo Patients
>
> - **High levels of activated macrophages in peritoneal fluid**—The high level of activated macrophages results in high levels of inflammatory cytokines, which may produce a chronic inflammatory state in the pelvis.
> - **Natural killer cells exhibit decreased cytotoxicity**—NK cells from endo patients fail to eliminate misplaced endometrial tissue.
> - **Monocytes exhibit aberrant reactivity**—Monocytes stimulate proliferation of endometrial tissue instead of suppressing growth of misplaced endometrium.
> - **Polyclonal B cell activation**—Some endo patients exhibit multiple autoantibodies, antibodies that are directed against self-antigens such as endometrial cells or cellular components.
> - **Humoral immunity abnormalities**—In addition to autoantibodies, there appear to be abnormalities in the C′ systems of endo patients. For example, abnormal production of the C′ protein C3 may result in the attraction and activation of unnecessarily high numbers of immune cell soldiers.
> - **Cell-mediated immunity abnormalities**—Immune cells from endo patients may respond to immune challenges with inappropriate armaments and with incorrect instructions for other cells.

activity. However, it's not the only thing that can attract or recruit immune system soldiers. Other proteins can act as very potent chemotactic agents. This brings us to yet another difference between Jane and Sally.

Jane's Cell-Mediated Immunity May Not Be Playing with a Full Deck

In the doctor's office, in your lab results, and during the ever-popular evening drama "ER," you may have noticed references to a blood test called a CBC. A CBC, or complete blood count, is a profile of the cellular elements in your blood. The CBC counts two major populations: your red blood cells (RBCs, or erythrocytes) and your white blood cells (WBCs, immune cells, or leukocytes). Your WBC count is further divided into the various types of immune cells. The relative numbers of each type of cell can often yield important information about one's immune system and immune function.

These numbers frequently do not vary between people with and without endo. That is, Jane's CBC and Sally's CBC might actually look very similar, both within normal ranges. However, the function and activities of these cells may differ drastically.

We've already discussed a couple aspects of cell-mediated immunity. As the name implies, this term refers to the immune system defenses that are controlled or performed by the cellular elements, the soldiers, of our immune systems. We looked at differences between Jane and Sally's trained assassins, the NK cells, and between the responses of Jane and Sally's monocytes to refluxed endometrial tissue (inhibition versus stimulation of endometrial cell growth). Jane and Sally's monocytes and macrophages actually differ in other significant ways as well; in fact, some believe that the monocyte and macrophage soldiers play a key role in this disease.

The cells of our immune systems can produce a wide range of immunologically active substances. Think of them as an array of weaponry produced by our immune cell soldiers. We call these substances cytokines, and they are produced by a wide array of cells, both immune and nonimmune. Cytokines include the interferons (abbreviated IFN); the interleukins (*inter* meaning between, *leuk* meaning "white" cells, abbreviated IL), substances that form a basis of communication among our immune cell soldiers; and the tumor necrosis factors (abbreviated TNF). Each of these cytokines acts as a type of message to other cells and serves specific functions in waging war against invaders, tumors, and misplaced tissue.

Our soldiers generally produce cytokines once the soldiers are "activated." In other words, once our soldiers encounter something that prompts them to take action, to turn on and become active, they assess the situation and produce the weapon or weapons appropriate for that particular encounter. These weapons can consist of many things, and one type of weaponry that may be used is cytokines. Once produced, the cytokines can directly attack the intended target, but they also act as important forms of communication among our soldiers. Some cytokines may indicate to a macrophage that it is to consume an invader; others may recruit or attract additional soldiers to the battlefront.

Monocytes and macrophages can produce and release multiple types of cytokines. Sally's monocytes and macrophages behave in a well-trained and appropriate manner. When they encounter bacteria, they respond by producing and secreting instructions and weapons specifically designed to deal with bacterial invasion. These instructions are sent to each other and to other cell soldiers in our bodies, and the outcome is the swift and efficient end to the unfortunate bacterial invader. Be it a bacteria or virus or even a tumor, Sally's soldiers know exactly how to get the job done.

Jane's soldiers are sorely confused, perhaps even operating a few eggs shy of a dozen. I tend to think of them as high-strung, overreactive, hypersensitive Nervous Nellies. (Nice, huh? and I wonder why my immune system doesn't like me.) What in the world would give me such a less-than-flattering view of my monocytes and macrophages? Well, whereas Sally's soldiers respond with an appropriate profile and level of weapons and instructions, Jane's soldiers appear to have some sort of defect that makes them respond with levels of cytokines that far exceed any need.

Think more is better? Remind me to send you all my laundry, my bills, and those carpenter ants that are holding their annual jamboree on my deck. An overload of cytokines means that Jane's body is in a (nearly) continuous state of active defense. This may account for many of the chronic symptoms associated with endo, including low-grade fevers and chronic fatigue.

Jane's monocytes produce high levels of tumor necrosis factor alpha (TNF-α), inter-leukin 8 (IL-8), and interleukin 6 (IL-6). TNF-α is capable of promoting or stimulating the growth of endometrial tissue, is a strong chemoattractant for monocytes, and can play a major role in inducing and maintaining inflammation and inflammatory reactions. In other words, just as our immune system produces a fever when battling infection, our immune system may actually be *causing* some of the symptoms associated with endo.

IL-8 is also a chemoattractant to monocytes and acts to attract neutrophils as well. In addition, IL-8 may contribute to the growth of blood vessels in the endo tissue. To survive, the tissue must establish a blood supply for itself, a process called angiogenesis. Thus, the instructive agents for angiogenesis must be present in order for endometriosis to occur. And IL-6 is a protein flag that tells B cells to produce antibodies, so it may play an important role in the generation of all those nasty and abnormal antibodies we discussed earlier.

In addition, the array of cytokines produced by Jane's monocytes, macrophages, and various other cells does not lend itself neatly to categorization. As in our example with Sally's soldiers and the bacterial invasion, we might see that Jane's soldiers produce some of the cytokines appropriate for the situation. But we might just as easily see her soldiers throwing out instructions for killing virally infected cells, for killing parasites, for making an apple pie—just about anything. As a result, the immediate situation is not remedied, and the other soldiers in her army remain confused and addled by the overwhelming jumble of conflicting and inappropriate instructions.

Another type of confused or abnormal soldier in Jane's army that we haven't really talked about yet is the T lymphocyte, or T cell (described earlier under "Immune System Components"). We can divide our T cells according to the types of proteins they display on their surfaces. For example, one of the most common ways to divide T cells into distinct populations is based on whether or not a T cell displays a protein called CD8 or a protein called CD4 on its surfaces. Think of these proteins as a type of name tag, an identifying flag or sign on the surface of the cell that permits us to identify it.

We can also divide T cells functionally based on their ability to affect an immune response by helping or suppressing certain processes, or by their own ability to produce a "cytotoxic" (*cyto* for cell, *toxic* for poisonous) response. Although the divisions are not absolute, CD4+ T cells (that is, T cells that display a CD4 molecule on their surface) are generally associated with helper functions, while CD8+ cells (T cells that carry a CD8 molecule on their membranes) are associated with suppresser or cytotoxic functions.

However, we now know that a CD4 cell can be either a traditional helper or an instigator (inflammatory), so a different type of functional categorization can be made according to the profile of cytokines produced by a given T cell. T cells that generally produce IL-2, IFN-gamma, and TNF-β are called TH1 cells or inflammatory CD4 cells. T cells that produce IL-4, IL-5, IL-9, IL-10, and IL-13 are called TH2 or helper CD4 T cells. (Although traditionally, and for our purposes, scientists know that both CD4 and CD8 cells can exhibit TH1 or TH2 cytokine profiles.) Whether or not a specific type of cell will be activated—and, thus, what cytokines will be produced—depends upon the situation, environment, and offender. For example, Sally's macrophages, upon ingesting bacteria, can produce IL-12, which, in turn, drives the differentiation of T cells toward the TH1 type—the type of cytokines that can activate macrophages to kill the unfortunate prisoners harbored in their vacuoles. In contrast, the cytokines produced by the TH2 cells activate B cells to produce antibody.

Immune responses may be categorized by whether or not our soldiers produce TH1-type or TH2-type cytokine profiles (although this designation is not as clear cut as was initially believed, so these types of divisions are not used as frequently these days). In Jane's case, if we were to sample the fluid that collects in her pelvic cavity (peritoneal fluid), we would see that all types of cytokines are being produced and that they are being released in massive quantities. Again, this is an example where "boosting" Jane's immune response is not an appropriate goal; her system is already on overdrive in this sense. However, some researchers have shown that despite these high levels of instructive activating agents, T cells from endo patients exhibit a diminished reactivity. Thus, it is possible that if you could selectively boost the appropriate reactivity of a lethargic or unresponsive T cell, this strengthening of the immune system might be appropriate. Unfortunately, attaining such a specific and delicate goal is very difficult.

Putting It All Together

Sally and Jane both experience retrograde menstruation, resulting in the presence of endometrial tissue in their pelvic cavities. Sally's immune system responds with the efficient and appropriate actions necessary not only to prevent the growth of this tissue, but to destroy and eliminate it as well. Sally's B cell antibody factories circulate in her body and, when they come upon this tissue, recognize it as being part of Sally and stand aside to permit other soldiers in Sally's immune army to respond. As shown in the first half of Figure 7.4, Sally's monocytes produce a variety of cytokines when they encounter this tissue. They suppress the growth of the endometrial tissue and produce

FIGURE 7.4 Monocyte Responses to Endo Cells

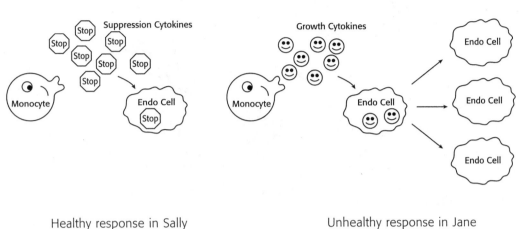

Healthy response in Sally   Unhealthy response in Jane

instructions for her trained assassins, the NK cells, and another set of killers, her cytotoxic T cells, that tell these cells to eliminate this tissue from its inappropriate location. Sally's killer cells then follow these instructions appropriately and destroy the refluxed tissue. In addition, her monocytes differentiate into macrophages and, in this form, work together with her trained killer cells to eliminate the misplaced endometrial cells.

In Jane's case, unfortunately, the endometrial tissue ends up implanting and growing in her pelvic cavity. Whereas Sally's B cell antibody factories recognized that it would be inappropriate to produce antibodies to the refluxed tissue, so they stood aside to permit Sally's soldiers to go to work, Jane's antibody factories did nothing of the sort. Jane's antibody factories, upon encountering the refluxed tissue, became activated and responded by producing antibodies against the endometrial cells and, in some cases, against the actual components of the cells themselves.

Additionally, instead of producing cytokines that suppress the growth of the endometrial cells, Jane's monocytes actually send out signals stimulating the endometrial cells to set up camp and grow (see the second part of Figure 7.4). In addition, Jane's assassins—her NK cells and cytotoxic T cells—and macrophages do not work together to eliminate the offending tissue.

Why? No one really knows for sure, and more than one thing undoubtedly contributes to the abnormal behavior of her immune cell soldiers. Perhaps her soldiers are confused by the overwhelming volume and mixed-up content of the cytokine instructions produced by her monocyte soldiers. Perhaps they understand what they are sup-

FIGURE 7.5 Jane's Endometrial Cells May Be Exceptionally Resistant.

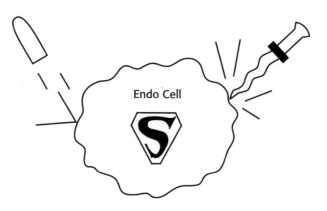

Jane's endometrial cells may be exceptionally resistant.

posed to do but simply can't respond for some reason. Perhaps they simply don't see anything wrong at all, or perhaps Jane's endometrial cells are exceptionally hardy and resistant to the attacks from Jane's immune army. Perhaps Jane's immune cells have been damaged by radiation or dioxins, agents known to damage the immune system. Perhaps genetic predisposition is a factor. Whatever the reason, the result is the frustrating and infuriating generation of the disease endometriosis.

As if the pelvic pain, expensive medications, and prospect of multiple surgeries weren't enough, many of us have had to deal with yet another aspect of endo, infertility. Even the infertility associated with endometriosis may be related to immunological abnormalities. Multiple scientists have speculated on the involvement of the immune system in endo-related infertility. It is possible that the high levels of cytokines in the fluid of an endo patient's pelvis are toxic to sperm. Perhaps all those activated immune cells and the high levels of cytokines damage the ovary and/or the eggs. It is also possible that the antibodies produced against the endometrial cells and/or their cellular components cause the immune system to react against the blastocyst or the endometrium, thereby preventing implantation or causing the process to proceed abnormally. The list goes on, but it is easy to see that there are multiple steps at which an aberrant immune system may interfere.

Our immune system plays a critical role in maintaining some semblance of order in a normal, healthy uterus as well. All these immune cell soldiers and the cytokine messengers I just described are present within the normal endometrial lining of the uterus and play critical roles in functions of the uterus, including menstruation and pregnancy. These cell soldiers must maintain perfectly clear communication among themselves and the other cells present in the uterus via the cytokine messages to prevent and control infections. At the same time, however, they must also be able to nurture a developing embryo.

To become pregnant, a woman's endometrium must check out the fertilized embryo and give it the big OK and accept it. But here's the catch: The embryo is partially *foreign* to the mother (remember that other half? that male half?). Accepting something foreign is quite a feat for a system designed specifically to reject such things!

Scientists are only beginning to learn how the immune system of the female reproductive tract works. We do know that our hormones (estrogen and progesterone) give instructions to our reproductive tract immune cells. We also know that these hormones regulate the cytokine messengers. Thus, in the endometrium, our hormones and our immune system must coordinate their activities perfectly, acting like a finely tuned orchestra, to provide clear instructions for the nonimmune endometrial cells. Such instructions might include directions as to when to proliferate and when to secrete other hormones in anticipation of a pregnancy, and if pregnancy does not occur, they must act together to signal the endometrial cells to die at the onset of menstruation.

The future of research in endo immunology is wide open. Promising studies have already been published that look at treating endo with immune-modulating medications. It is possible that even current medications such as the GnRH agonists and danazol mediate some of their effects through the immune system.

Although there is much, much more to this immune-endo tale, I hope that this article serves as an understandable and enjoyable introduction to the role of the immune system in endo. There is so much more out there to learn, and I do hope that you will look at new findings and the research reports in the Endometriosis Association's newsletters with only curiosity and enthusiasm, not with fear or frustration. Good luck to you!

THE PROBLEMS WITH PERFUME

Lyse M. Tremblay

Perfume, a mixture of natural oils, aroma chemicals, and solvents in an alcohol base, appears to be causing adverse reactions in an increasing number of individuals, according to the U.S. Food and Drug Administration (FDA). The FDA acknowledges that these reactions may involve the immune system and be of a neurotoxic nature.[1] Perfumes are found not only in perfume proper but also in men's colognes, cosmetic products, scented mail, hygienic products, drugs, detergents, plastics, industrial greases, oils, solvents, furniture waxes, tires, inks, kitty litter, and other household products.[2, 3]

Reactions to Perfume

Reactions resulting from perfume exposure can range from headaches and sinus pain all the way to anaphylactic shock, seizures, and even death,[21] depending on the specific perfume mixture and on the sensitivity of the individual. Other common health complaints associated with perfume include nausea, dizziness, inability to concentrate, mood changes, depression, lethargy, restlessness, irritability, and anger.[4]

More specifically, perfume can provoke a recurrence of symptoms in those suffering from multiple chemical sensitivities (MCS)[5] and can result in a substantial drop (18 to 59 percent) in the results of pulmonary function tests of asthmatics.[6]

Why Is the Problem Growing?

The reason for the increase in reactions appears to be twofold. First, populations are becoming more sensitive as a result of increased pollution in the air, water, and food. Second, the shift toward stronger-fragrance products and toward the use of a higher proportion of aroma chemicals (synthetic ingredients derived from petrochemicals) as opposed to essential oils is increasing the chemical load.

Aroma chemicals, being substantially cheaper than essential oils (for example, $10 per pound for synthetic versus $10,000 per pound for essential oil ingredients), can represent up to 95 percent of a fragrance's composition. However, according to the National Academy of Sciences, 84 percent of these ingredients have minimal or no toxicity data. Where toxicity data does exist, the results indicate cause for concern.[7, 8] Here are a few examples:

- Musk ambrette can damage the central and peripheral nervous system in exposed laboratory animals.[9, 10]
- Linalool can produce ataxic gait (defective muscular coordination), respiratory disturbances, and depression in test animals.[11]
- Cychlohexanol can, when inhaled, cause, among other things, a narcotic effect intermediate between benzene and chloroform.[11]

- Toluene is toxic and can produce headaches, nausea, and narcosis (a stuporous state). Yet, according to the EPA, it was detected in every fragrance sample collected for a 1991 report.
- Musk AETT, which was widely used between 1955 and 1976 both as a fragrance ingredient and as a masking fragrance in so-called unscented products, was voluntarily withdrawn in 1977 when tests showed that it caused permanent brain damage in lab animals. Furthermore, according to Peter Spencer, who conducted the study, similar properties exist in many other widely used aromatic hydrocarbons, and they should also be tested for possible chronic neurotoxic properties.[9, 10, 20]
- Phthalates, a large family of industrial chemicals that are linked to birth defects, are ingredients in perfumes and fragrances, as well as many other cosmetics. *Not Too Pretty*, a report by the Environmental Working Group, shows that toxic phthalates were found in 100 percent of the fragrances tested and 72 percent of all cosmetic products tested (for details, visit Not TooPretty.org).

It was also found in 1989 that out of 2,983 chemicals used in the fragrance industry, the National Institute of Occupational Safety and Health (NIOSH) recognized 884 as toxic substances capable of causing cancer, birth defects, central nervous system disorders, skin and eye irritations, allergic reactions, and chemical sensitivites.[12] In addition, a number of chemicals found in fragrances (for example, toluene, methylene chloride, and benzyl chloride) are designated as hazardous waste disposal chemicals.[13]

Further complicating the issue is the fact that one fragrance can contain up to 600 separate ingredients. Exposure to one or several of these ingredients may not be problematic, but exposure to the combination may result in serious problems.

Essential Oils

Essential oils are not exempt from the list of potentially problematic ingredients in perfumes. Bergamot oil, for instance, is a strong sensitizer of the same order as formaldehyde. In spite of this, its use in perfumes appears to be increasing. According to one FDA official, civet, galbanum, patchouli oil, and asafetida can also cause adverse reactions in hypersensitive individuals.[14, 15]

Conclusion

An article published in *Green Alternatives* in 1992 quotes Dr. John Bailey of the FDA as saying, "The fragrance and cosmetic industry is the least regulated industry. There is no pre-clearing of chemicals with any agency." That being the case, it behooves us to protect ourselves from potential harm.

It is encouraging to note, however, that public awareness is growing. For instance, the University of Minnesota School of Social Work, as well as several schools, churches, and public transit authorities in the Halifax-Dartmouth area of Canada, have either banned perfumes outright or requested that people refrain from wearing fragrances while on their premises.[16, 17] As more and more people become disabled from MCS[18] and the incidence of asthma (31 percent increase in the last decade alone)[19] and allergies continues to climb, it is only a matter of time before the right to breathe fresh air becomes not merely desirable but a necessity.

EDITOR'S NOTE If you have visited our offices or attended our conferences, you will have noticed that we strive to make all places where we meet "fragrance free." This is because many of the ingredients in scents are toxic or produce allergic reactions, and women with endo are particularly prone to allergies and chemical sensitivities.

8 Endometriosis and Cancer: What Is the Connection?

Linda Duczman and Mary Lou Ballweg

This chapter was first published as an article in the Association's newsletter, after which the following letter came to the Association:

Thank you for saving my life.

It is with the deepest of gratitude that I am writing to thank you for saving my life. . . .

I chose to deal with my symptoms with a holistic approach, trying diet and a short-term bout with acupuncture, all of which alleviated some symptoms but really didn't address the problem. When that didn't work, I simply denied my symptoms and told myself that come January I would find a new doctor and deal with the issue then. However, when January rolled around, I found myself denying symptoms and procrastinating the inevitable simply because I didn't want to go through the hassle of finding a new doctor, surgery, etc.

So, I decided I could live with the pain for another few months, at least until June or so and then venture into this process once again. With that decision made, I didn't worry about it until I received your newsletter in January on Endometriosis and Cancer. After reading this newsletter and identifying with 90 percent of the risk factors, I got frightened and scheduled an appointment with a new doctor the very next week.

During that initial gynecological exam, my doctor detected a lump in my left breast, which turned out to be cancer. The tumor was quite large and the doctors were quite concerned that this cancer was invasive. The biopsy showed it at the earliest of stages (stage 0), but due to the size of the tumor (3 × 4 centimeters), the doctors were concerned that underneath the cancer may be invasive and could have spread to the lymph nodes.

As it turned out, now at the age of thirty-seven, I have had a mastectomy on my left breast and the cancer was non-invasive and did not spread to the lymph nodes, which meant I would not have to undergo chemo or radiation. Three surgeons were shocked that this cancer was non-invasive due to the size of the tumor, and I know in my heart if I had waited until June to go to the doctor, I might not be here today. In fact, the operative report stated that there were several enlarged lymph nodes, which caused great concern for the surgeon, and that the cancer had just begun to start turning invasive. However, the pathology reports showed everything was fine.

God bless you and the work you do, Mary Lou; you are an angel to me. I pray that my letter may encourage other women with endo to address their health and not ignore their symptoms. It's not only about endo anymore—it could be life threatening. One thing I've learned in years of suffering with this illness is that I don't like to face it when it creeps in again. With your help, I've learned I dare not ignore it! Thank you again and all your colleagues who helped in the writing of that article—the timing was nothing short of divine.

—Maria, Florida

Introduction

Cancer is a word that strikes terror in our hearts. We don't want to think about it. We almost don't want to know about it. In past decades, people wouldn't even say the word—it was the "big *C*."

From the beginning of the Association, we were aware that some experts considered endometriosis itself to be a "benign cancer." We were also aware of a few women in whom cancer tragically arose from their endo. Endo itself transforming into cancer is covered more extensively in our first book, *Overcoming Endometriosis*. This possibility has always been noted in our popular yellow brochure, despite a number of doctors telling us we should remove it because it would scare women. Our response has been that not disseminating this information is tantamount to sentencing some women with endo to death. Without this knowledge, we may assume all our symptoms are endo and not get early diagnosis or care for cancer. Or we may not do all we can to improve our health and counteract the risk.

But we didn't get serious about looking at the possible links between endo and cancer until our dioxin discoveries in 1992 (see Part 3). When we learned that dioxin, a toxic environmental pollutant, was strongly associated with development of endo, we knew we would have to research and learn more about cancer in women with endo (and in their families, because families tend to share environmental exposures). Because dioxin has always been considered one of the most powerful cancer-causing agents known, it was logical that if some of our members had endo due to dioxin exposure, they might also be susceptible to cancer.

During the same time (1992 to 1999), additional research was showing a higher cancer risk in women with endo. And we were becoming more aware of women with endo who had cancer and were sometimes dying from it. We asked Association Advisor Dan Martin, M.D., to tackle this tough topic at our fifteenth anniversary conference in 1995. We also asked him to lead a brainstorming session on the topic at the sixth World Congress on Endo in 1998.

Finally, we decided to look at the experience of cancer in women with endo and their families. In 1998 we surveyed our North American members about many aspects of their health, including cancer. If we'd ever had any doubts that cancer was a serious risk for women with endo and their families, this data wiped those doubts away!

We are surrounded by cancer-causing agents in our society. While none of us wants to think about cancer, we cannot protect ourselves and our families if we are ignorant. With action on our part, we may be able to counteract the risks, make better treatment decisions, and focus research attention on this topic.

This important article is dedicated to Beth Thompson and Joan Moultrie, whose stories are told in sidebars later in this article, as well as to our brothers, Victor S. Duczman, who died at forty from pancreatic cancer, and Peter W. Ballweg, who died at forty-one from brain cancer.

Cancer Risks in Women with Endometriosis

Suppose thieves are targeting your neighborhood and authorities can identify a pattern: a day and time they typically strike, their usual method of entry. Wouldn't you want to know? Wouldn't you appreciate the opportunity to be extra vigilant? We are writing this chapter in the hope that awareness of risk for specific cancers will give women with endo the incentive to manage the risk factors within their control, remain alert to subtle changes in their health, and make certain that the healthcare professionals on whom we depend are especially watchful with regard to these cancers.

It has long been documented that endometriosis can transform and become cancerous.[1] However, in addition to cancerous transformation, recent and compelling evidence suggests that having endo itself increases the risk of developing cancer beyond the sites of the endo. Since cancer is, after heart disease, the second leading cause of death in the United States, women with endo deserve the chance to study this issue more closely and to do everything possible to protect themselves.

In a brochure distributed by the Gilda Radner Familial Ovarian Cancer Registry, Radner's husband, actor Gene Wilder, writes that had the comedian known her mother's and grandmother's ovarian cancer deaths put her at special risk, Radner might be alive today. Increased awareness of risk is by no means a cancer cure, nor does it make a cancer diagnosis inevitable. However (as airlines caution their passengers, "In the unlikely event . . ."), identifying and detecting many cancers at their earliest, most treatable stages seems to offer the best chance for survival.

First, we'll take a look at the ways cancer and endo are similar. Then we'll review the most important studies showing the risks for certain cancers in women with endo. After discussing risk issues generally related to endo and cancer, we'll look at each of the four cancers most linked to endo: breast cancer, ovarian cancer, non-Hodgkin's lymphoma, and melanoma. For each, we'll examine incidence and general information about the cancer, symptoms, risks, and family links. Finally, we'll look at ways to reduce our risk of cancer and, hopefully, prevent it.

To understand how endometriosis and cancer could be linked, a brief review of characteristics shared by the two may help. *Cancer* is the name applied to well over 100 different diseases. The U.S. National Cancer Institute describes cancer as a group of diseases that occur when cells become abnormal and divide without order or control. This cell division results in more cells than the body needs; the extra tissue sometimes forms tumors.

Cancer cells not only grow and divide out of control but can also metastasize—that is, invade other organs and move to new areas. These cells pass along to their descendants the inability to control growth. If this invasive growth cannot be stopped, the cells eventually overwhelm the organs to which they have spread and disrupt their normal functions.[2] Author Sandra Steingraber paints a vivid picture of this destruction in her book *Living Downstream: An Ecologist Looks at Cancer and the Environment*: "Cancer cells are dancers deaf to the choreographer. They are builders in flagrant violation of zoning ordinances and architectural blueprints. They are defiant, disobedient, and in the view of many cancer biologists, almost purposeful in the ways they disrupt cellular biochemistry."[3]

Parallels Between Endo and Cancer

Endo: The "Benign Cancer"

Endometriosis has been called "benign cancer." Not unlike cancer cells, endo cells have established themselves in the wrong place. In both cancer and endo, invasive cells grow unrestrained to overwhelm the cells in the site where they become implanted and cause disease, scarring, and pain.

Natural Killer Cells

Another link between cancer and endo is an important cancer-fighting immune cell called the natural killer, or NK, cell. (See Chapter 7 for background on NK cells.). Based on a number of important studies, NK cells are less active in women with endo. When

NK cells are less active, there is a higher risk of tumor progression and distant metastasis. Italian researchers report that a number of studies relate increased levels of sex hormones and decreased activity of natural killer cells. The researchers suggest that the immune systems of women with endo are responding to some stimulus in the progression of neoplastic (tumor-forming) disease. They hypothesize that the body's immune and endocrine systems play a similar pathogenic role in both endo and formation of tumors.[4, 5]

Japanese researchers found, after treatment of endo, that both the number and percentage of natural killer cells increased to normal.[6, 7] Other researchers "postulated the existence of a substance in the serum of endometriosis patients that suppressed NK cell activity, perhaps intended to allow the continued growth of ectopic endometrial cells [endometriosis], much in the same fashion as occurs with cancer patients."[8]

Oncogenes

All cancers are the result of genetic mutations. However, only a few cancers are the direct result of mutations inherited from our parents. Most cancers are the result of genetic mutations that occur *after* we are born.

The p53 tumor suppressor gene is a brake for cell growth. Mutation of this gene can result in a variety of cancers, depending largely on the person's exposure to cancer-causing substances. Researchers have identified abnormalities of the p53 tumor suppressor gene as possibly contributing to the malignant transformation of borderline tumors, endometriosis, and other precursor lesions into ovarian cancer. They found that these abnormalities occurred relatively early in the tumor progression process.[9]

Studies demonstrate that both the inside lining of the uterus (endometrium) and endometriosis often have high levels of proteins encoded with oncogenes. Oncogenes are potentially cancer-inducing genes. Under normal conditions, these genes play a role in growth and proliferation of cells. But they can be altered by cancer-causing substances, causing cells to grow uncontrollably.

One such oncogene, named *ras*, encourages cell growth. Alterations in the way *ras* genes are activated, or the way the p53 tumor suppressor gene is inactivated, are very common in cancers of the uterus and ovaries. Knowing this, researchers looked for structural mutations of these genes. They analyzed biopsy specimens taken during surgery from ten patients with severe ovarian, cul-de-sac, or rectovaginal septum endo. They could find no mutations to account for the abnormal growth or infiltrating behavior of these cases of severe and progressive endo. However, they suggested more study to investigate whether the abnormalities were in the way *ras* and p53 function, rather than how they are structured.[10] While we know p53 plays a role in cancer by not suppressing the out-of-control growth of cancer cells, the role it plays in the growth and infiltration of endo is still unclear.

Angiogenesis

Angiogenesis is one more characteristic common to both endo and tumors. Angiogenesis is the growth of new blood vessels to supply the blood that endo and cancer tissues need to survive. Angiogenesis is induced by immune reactions, among other things.[11-13]

Loss of Heterozygosity

Research by Doctors Eric Thomas and Jan Campbell identified a critical difference between the normal tissue lining the inside of the uterus (endometrium) and endo. Their study examined how the growth of endo is controlled at the molecular level. Examining highly pure endometriosis from fresh and preserved samples, they looked for areas of molecular genetic damage. The study found the type of damage common in tissue in which control of proliferation is breaking down (such as in a malignant tumor). This damage is called "loss of heterozygosity" (LOH).

Thomas, a professor of obstetrics and gynecology at Southhampton University, England, concluded that the fact that LOH is common in endo but not in endometrium strongly suggests that endometriosis has suffered molecular genetic damage during its presumed journey from the uterus to the pelvic cavity. He also notes that molecular genetic studies have shown that in a number of cases, endometrioid cancer of the ovary has evolved from endo.[14]

The possibility of endo as a precursor to ovarian cancer has been debated in research literature since 1925.[15] Thomas and his research group believe they've found the first molecular evidence that at least some endo may be premalignant. They say these findings support microscopic studies showing that malignant transformation of endo may be a source of endometrioid and clear cell ovarian carcinomas. They examined fourteen cases of endo in patients who also had ovarian cancer. In the four cases where carcinoma occurred with the endo and five of seven where carcinoma was next to the endo, they found common genetic lesions, which led them to conclude that the cells shared a common lineage. In addition, a p53 gene was found in one case of endo next to carcinoma.[14]

In a 1980 analysis of the literature, researchers had already determined that, although the occurrence is rare, endo can transform into cancer. They also admitted the difficulty of proving this without a doubt. The cancer may have destroyed the endo from which it originated. Documentation of the cases then available for study was not as complete as they would have liked. And, the researchers were not certain that a large enough tissue sampling had been taken to show the endo transitioning into cancer in some cases.

Even though they believe that cancer developing from endo is rare, the researchers cautioned gynecologists to watch for it whenever a patient with known endo undergoes an unexpected change. They also suggested greater care in decisions about estrogen replacement therapy. This was based on the observation that some patients

---

Joan Robin Moultrie's Story

Joan Moultrie was one of the three founding members of the New Zealand Endometriosis Foundation. As a registered nurse who specialized in oncology, a speaker and trainer on endo, and a Trust Board member of the Foundation, Joan's life was dedicated to dealing with cancer and endo. It is ironic that it was those two things that eventually ended her life.

Joan had surgery for a massive endometrioma. The cyst ruptured when it was removed and spilled into her pelvic cavity. The lab report later showed that it was malignant. She had unsuccessful chemotherapy and further surgery; however, by that stage, the cancer was no longer confined to the pelvis. She had further complications and, after a fierce struggle, died.

Joan's paper on endometriosis, "The Internal Thorn," is used extensively as a resource by doctors and women with endo in New Zealand. She conducted seminars and training sessions throughout New Zealand. Joan summarized her dedication when, as part of an international panel at the Endometriosis Association's fifteenth anniversary conference in Milwaukee in 1995, she stated, "As long as there is a need, we will continue to support the growing numbers who ask for our help and contribute to the understanding of endometriosis internationally."

She strongly believed in the importance of patient education and the responsibility of a patient to make informed decisions about her own care. She believed in learning to manage oneself physically, emotionally, and spiritually. She was a devoted wife to Ian; loving mother to Linda, Ross, and Fiona; and an adoring Nan to Evelyn, as well as a nurse, educator, and activist. She is sorely missed by all those who knew her.

---

experienced hyperplasia (excessive growth of cells) before developing cancer in endo or tissue adjacent to it. Cancer in other patients may have been affected by an excess of estrogen from within their bodies or from outside sources, according to the researchers.[16] Almost twenty years after this study, with even more (and less circumstantial) evidence, the "benign cancer" is beginning to look less benign.

A 1990 study helps put the seriousness of cancer arising from endo into perspective. Researchers identified 205 cases of malignant tumors arising in endo. The ovary was the primary site in 165 cases (80 percent). In 44 cases (21 percent), the tumors occurred outside of the ovary. (In 4 cases, two sites were affected.) The average age was forty-six, and the most common symptoms before cancer diagnosis were abdominal and/or pelvic pain, vaginal bleeding, and a pelvic mass. In most cases the tumors were low grade and confined to the site of origin. When they had not spread beyond the pelvis, the tumors could often be controlled completely by radiation therapy. Follow-up was reported in eighty-six patients. In fifty-seven of these patients, the tumor was confined to the ovary; in eleven, it was confined to the site of origin outside of the

Beth Thompson's Story

"What are you going to do with a diagnosis?" asked Beth Harris Thompson. The question was purely rhetorical. A creative woman by nature and profession, she was doing with her most recent cancer diagnosis what she had done with her endo diagnosis more than a decade ago—taking action.

With three large cancerous masses growing inside her, Beth described herself as "way too alive to be dying." She was in another round of chemotherapy and looking for a surgeon "to cut these things out of me." She was also talking to the Association about her cancer. Perhaps cautioning us to find out all we can about our families' medical histories. Perhaps motivating us to overcome the stigma and reluctance to connect these two diseases.

"With endo, as with cancer, you don't look sick," said Beth, then forty-two. When she showered, dressed, and went out, people could not tell by looking at her how precarious her health was. "They tell you you look good," she said.

But Beth knew all too well that things were not necessarily what they seemed. By sixteen, the first menstrual periods, which are normally milestones in a young girl's physical development, brought Beth only bleeding and pain so severe she often had to leave school in a wheelchair.

At thirty, when the surgery intended to remedy an ovarian cyst became a hysterectomy, leaving her with one-fourth of her right ovary, she learned that she had endo. "I had a cyst and went in to have an ovary removed. When they did the hysterectomy, my stepmother was horrified. She called my father—she thought we had a lawsuit," Beth recalled.

Surgery revealed a nine-pound fibroid on the back wall of her uterus and chocolate cysts on her ovaries. "They left the quarter ovary for hormones," she explained. "I was thirty, and I was so sick; I was sure I had cancer and they were not getting to it. I thought I was dying and they were not telling me what it was. The hysterectomy was a relief. I thought this was all taken care of," she remembered.

During a routine physical two or three years after the surgery, Beth was told her ovary had regenerated into a "nice healthy ovary." She soon learned "that was not the case," and that, too, was soon removed. She still had endo. Two laparotomies and three laparoscopies followed.

Beth joined the Association in 1990 and, upon moving from Chicago to California, helped organize an Association support group in San Diego. Beth knew how disruptive endo pain could be, professionally and personally. She said she was grateful for having been able to work more than some women with endo were able, holding down jobs and maintaining relationships. A graphic artist who once ran her own company, Beth worked most recently as a book editor. She said she was fortunate to have had good insurance and employers who allowed her time off when she was sick or recovering from surgery.

Beth put her tremendous creative energies to work for the Association with creation of an outdoor billboard advertising campaign designed to help women in minority communities become more aware of endo. Beth learned that many women in these communities who were suffering from endo were mistaking it for the better-known PMS and not receiving appropriate treatment. Working with a young Hispanic communications student, she created a billboard advertising campaign designed to address this problem with the slogan: "It's not necessarily PMS."

Beth twice secured donation of ten outdoor billboards, for two months each, so that the campaign could run in Milwaukee just before the Association's fifteenth anniversary conference. The increased visibility for endo, at that critical time, proved most effective.

In January 1997, Beth was diagnosed with what was suspected to be ovarian remnant syndrome and a possibly malignant pelvic mass. Surgery to remove what she describes as an "eggplant" found cancer cells. After that, she was in and out of chemotherapy. She had two additional surgeries in 1997.

At the time she was diagnosed with endo, Beth knew her mother had died of cancer that had begun in her breast when she was in her early forties. It was then that Beth also learned that her mother, with whom she hadn't lived since she was a young child, had had her own share of "female problems." "In the fifties," she said, "who talked about 'em?" Her mother's medical history included several miscarriages and uterine cancer, which went into remission for several years and eventually reappeared in her spine and liver.

Beth encouraged women with endo to keep in contact with the Association. She also suggested that they check to make certain that their doctors are well aware of the Association and its work. When her cancer was first diagnosed, Beth wondered if other women with endo were also developing cancer. She called the Endometriosis Association for information and had been reading the literature that suggested a connection between endo and cancer. More tired in her final days, Beth continued to reach out, continued to look for answers, and continued to hope. Beth Harris Thompson eventually lost her heroic battle with cancer. In celebration of her life and fight, friends and family donated generously to the Association.

ovary; and in eighteen, it had spread throughout the peritoneal cavity. Five-year survival in each of these situations was ovary only, 65 percent; outside of the ovary, 100 percent; and spread in peritoneal cavity, 10 percent. The authors of this study concluded, "The actual frequency of malignancy arising in endometriosis may be higher than reported."[17]

Endo and Cancer: On an Enzyme Level

Some researchers speculate that the growth of tumors and endo may share common processes at an enzyme level. They note that the same proteolytic enzymes (enzymes that break down a substance into simpler compounds) known as matrix metalloproteinases (MMPs) are involved in both metastatic tumor invasion and establishment and growth of endo.

Experimenting with mice, the researchers found that estrogen-associated MMP expression promoted development of endometriosis. Suppressing the enzymes with progesterone provided a significant degree of protection. Unfortunately, dioxin was able to stop the protection provided by progesterone.[18] The research team will be investigating this further as part of the Endometriosis Association Research Program at Vanderbilt University School of Medicine.

Apoptosis

Apoptosis is the normal death of cells, which is necessary to help rid the body of diseased and redundant cells. In cancer, apoptosis is decreased, resulting in excessive proliferation of cells. An important study by Howard Gebel, Ph.D., suggests that apoptosis is also decreased in endometrial cells in women with endometriosis and may contribute to development of endo.[19]

Increasing Cause for Concern: The Brinton, Vercellini, Hornstein, and Association Studies

Four key studies have recently alerted those concerned about endo that the risk related to cancer is not just for transformation of endo into cancer. Rather, the larger concern is that endo itself creates a greater risk for cancer in the body gererally.

The Brinton Study

National Institutes of Health scientist Louise Brinton, Ph.D., and other scientists, conducted one of the most important studies of endo and cancer ever done.[20] Brinton's study, "Cancer Risk After a Hospital Discharge Diagnosis of Endometriosis," found a significant number of cancers in women diagnosed with endo. According to the authors, prior investigation of the potential cancer risk associated with endo has been limited.

To evaluate this risk, Brinton turned to Sweden, where a nationwide patient registry could be linked with a central cancer registry. The study compared cancer rates of women with endo with those of the entire female population of Sweden. A total of 20,686 patients who were diagnosed with endo between 1969 and 1983 were entered in the study. This represents 216,851 person-years of follow-up. Average follow-up was 11.4 years; average age at entry into the study was 38.8; average age of cancer diagnosis was 52.3.

In this population of women, researchers would have expected 623 cancers. Instead, there were 738 cancers, with significant elevations for breast cancer (approximately one-fifth higher), ovarian cancer (nearly a twofold excess), and hematopoietic cancers (malignancies of the blood-forming organs, especially bone marrow and lymph nodes), specifically non-Hodgkin's lymphoma (almost 50 percent higher). On a more positive note, a slightly reduced risk was observed for cervical cancer, and no association was observed for cancer of the endometrium.

Risk was examined by follow-up period (one to two years, three to four years, five to nine years, and so on). Breast cancers were observed during all but the first time period and did not appear to decrease or increase with longer follow-up. As with breast cancer, ovarian cancer risk was elevated for all time periods except the first. However, risk increased significantly for subjects followed for ten years or longer. Risk for lymphatic and hematopoietic cancers—in particular, non-Hodgkin's lymphoma—was elevated across all follow-up time periods with no evidence of an increasing or decreasing trend.

Age at first hospital admission (under forty versus forty and older) did not appear to affect the risk of breast or ovarian cancer. However, greater risk for cancers of the lymph and blood (like non-Hodgkin's lymphoma) was restricted to patients who were older than forty at first admission.

Gynecologic surgery, particularly removal of the ovaries, influences breast cancer risk, usually lowering it in most studies. Attempts were made to control for this factor. Unfortunately, there were significantly elevated risks of breast cancer in women with endo who had their ovaries and in those who did not.

For 8,934 patients studied, endo was the only diagnosis in their first inpatient record. Whether endo was the exclusive diagnosis or patients had other conditions as well appeared to make little difference in overall cancer risk or in risk for breast cancer or cancer of the uterus. The study also referenced other research linking menstrual irregularities, lack of vigorous physical activity, childlessness, and delayed pregnancy as shared risk factors, which may help to explain the elevated breast cancer risk.

A diagnosis of infertility seemed to accompany the majority of ovarian cancers. Women who had ovarian endo appeared to account for the largest proportion of ovarian cancers. Only limited information was available on the types of ovarian cancer.

The study reported that the elevated risk of hematopoietic cancers among women with endo—in particular, non-Hodgkin's lymphoma—was especially unexpected. The authors note that other studies have shown that women with endo have impaired immune systems, and defective immune function has been linked to certain cancers. The study also suggests shared environmental factors as a possible link between non-Hodgkin's lymphoma and endo. It notes that the well-recognized immune-impairing agent dioxin is associated with both diseases. (Dioxin is discussed more fully later in this chapter.)

When evaluating Brinton's findings, it's important to keep in mind that in being cautious, the study may have underreported the incidence of cancer in women with endo. First, some patients with cancer were eliminated up front. The study removed from its calculations 181 patients who died during hospitalization and 514 with a recorded malignancy before a diagnosis of endo. For the main analysis, 19,751 person-years representing the first year of patient follow-up and 54 cases of cancer detected during that same time frame also were eliminated, to minimize any impact of selection bias.

So, to avoid the possibility of counting any cancers that may appear to have predated an endo diagnosis or that may have otherwise been possibly unrelated to the endo, the study data omitted a substantial number of actual cancers. As women with endo well know (see data reported in Chapter 13), endo diagnosis is delayed an average nine to ten years, even in recent years in North America. Thus, eliminating the data before diagnosis may not be valid, as the women likely had endo for years before diagnosis.

A second reason for possible underreporting is related to the difficulty of diagnosing endo and the fact that hospitals delivering data to the Swedish Inpatient Register did not provide the data at the same levels throughout the study period. (Sixty percent of hospitals provided data in 1969, 75 percent in 1978, and 85 percent by the end of 1983.) As a result, the registry itself may have recorded fewer diagnosed cases of endo than actually existed in the population.

When the records were unclear as to whether ovaries had been removed, person-years and reproductive cancers were not counted beyond the first gyn operation. Again, in the interests of erring on the conservative side, the researchers did not count some patients and cancers.

Finally, the women whose cases were entered into the study were diagnosed at any time between 1969 and 1983, but follow-up continued only until 1989. This may have provided insufficient time for many cancers to appear. In fact, the average follow-up (11.4 years) is not even long enough to cover the time (13.5 years) from average age of entry into the study (38.8) until average age of cancer diagnosis (52.3). This is not meant as a criticism of the Brinton study, which is an extremely important and groundbreaking study. Rather, these concerns show that the study may significantly underreport the true incidence of cancer in women with endo, and more study and long-term follow-up are needed. (We urge readers to become and stay part of the Association for the long term so that these long-term studies can be done!)

Are Endo and Cancer Related?

- Both are abnormal growth of tissue.
- Both have the ability to invade other tissues and organs.
- Natural killer cells, important cancer-fighting immune cells, typically have reduced activity in both cancer and endo. Defective immune function has been linked to both.
- Certain oncogenes (tumor genes that can be activated by cancer-causing substances) may be common in both endo and cancer.
- They both share an ability to develop a network of blood vessels to provide a blood supply and nourishment (angiogenesis) to support their growth.
- Cells in both endometriosis and cancerous tumors display loss of heterozygosity (that is, molecular damage on the genetic level, leaving cells without a normal, functioning tumor suppressor).
- Matrix metalloproteinases (MMPs) are involved in both cancer invasion and endo.
- Some research has suggested that in both cancer and endo, defective apoptosis (a process by which a damaged cell destroys itself) may be at work.
- Risk factors for endo, such as exposure to dioxin, related chemicals, and radiation, are also risk factors for certain cancers.
- Lifestyle changes that may reduce risk for the cancers to which women with endo are most susceptible also reduce the symptoms of endo. These changes include reducing estrogen and its effects by cutting back on dietary fat, reducing alcohol consumption, exercising to reduce fat and estrogen, avoiding chemical exposures, and adding antioxidants (vitamins C, A, and E) to the diet.
- Three of the four cancers that research found were risks for women with endo and their families (breast, non-Hodgkin's lymphoma, and melanoma) all appear to be on the rise, just as endo itself appears to be on the rise.
- Hormonal factors seem to be clearly involved in endo and in at least two of the cancers (ovarian and breast) found in women with endo and their families.
- Endo and the cancers related to it appear to have a familial pattern of development in some instances.
- Endo and ovarian cancer both sometimes register positive on the CA-125 ovarian cancer test. In fact, CA-125 is not a very useful tool for ovarian cancer detection in women with endo, because it frequently registers positive for ovarian cancer, even when there is no cancer.
- Infertility, a common problem in endo, is a risk factor for both ovarian cancer and breast cancer. However, whether it is a predisposing factor or a symptom is not entirely clear.

The Vercellini Study

Paolo Vercellini, M.D., is an Association Advisor and well-known endo expert who conducts research in Milan, Italy. His study "Endometriosis and Ovarian Cancer" examined the records of women undergoing surgical treatment for ovarian cancer at two teaching hospitals to evaluate the frequency of endo in this population.[21] Of the 556 cases of ovarian cancer, 52.2 percent of the patients were premenopausal, and 47.8 percent postmenopausal when the cancer was diagnosed.

In as many as one-fourth of all the women diagnosed with ovarian cancer, endo was present. Endo was present in "only" 3.6 percent to 5.6 percent of those with serous, mucinous, and miscellaneous ovarian cancers but was present in an astounding 26.3 percent, 21.1 percent, and 22.2 percent, respectively, in endometrioid, clear cell, and mixed subtype ovarian cancers. The greater frequency of endo observed in the endometrioid, clear cell, and mixed ovarian cancers occurred regardless of age, pregnancy and childbirth history, menopausal status, and stage of ovarian cancer.

In attempting to interpret their findings, the researchers admit a straightforward conclusion is difficult. Direct histological proof (as seen under a microscope) of transition from endo to cancer is complicated by the possibility of cancer destroying the endometriosis from which it may have arisen, and by the wide sampling and multiple sections required to demonstrate the transition of endo into cancer. They also warn that the situation is difficult to interpret when endo is found next to, but not continuous with, a cancer.

The Hornstein Study

A 1997 study by Association Advisor Mark Hornstein, M.D., of Harvard Medical School, "Association Between Endometriosis, Dysplastic Naevi and History of Melanoma in Women of Reproductive Age," found that women with endo are at greater risk of developing dysplastic nevi, moles that can be precursors to melanoma, a deadly skin cancer.[22] Sixty-six women with endo and thirty-five controls were surveyed and physically examined. An association was found between dysplastic nevi and endo in younger women of reproductive age (age thirty-two or younger).

Women with endo were also more likely to have a family history of melanoma (29 percent for women with endo versus 10 percent for the control group). The researchers suggested gynecologists and dermatologists may both find this information useful in the evaluation and care of young women.

The Endometriosis Association Study

In 1998 the Association surveyed 10,000 North American women with endo. We particularly looked at the histories of cancer to determine if indeed these women had a greater risk as had been found in earlier studies, including the Brinton, Vercellini, and Hornstein studies. We also wanted to see if their families shared that risk. Unfortunately, the data confirmed, once again, the risk of cancer for women with endo. In addition, we found increased risk of cancer in the families. (Some of this data was presented by Farr Nezhat, M.D., and Mary Lou Ballweg at the 1999 annual meeting of the American Association of Gynecologic Laparoscopists. Dr. Nezhat is a well-known endo surgeon and expert, as well as a gynecologic oncologist.[23])

This data shows that women with endo and their families have a heightened risk of breast cancer, melanoma, and ovarian cancer (see Figure 8.1). There's also a greater risk of non-Hodgkin's lymphoma in their families. Of the women with endo, 9.8 percent had one or more family members with melanoma (compared with 0.01 percent in the general population), 26.9 percent had one or more family members with breast cancer (0.1 percent in the general population), and 8.5 percent had one or more family members with ovarian cancer (0.04 percent in the general population). Interestingly, first-degree relatives (parents, siblings, and children) were most likely to be affected by melanoma and non-Hodgkin's lymphoma, while second-degree (grandparents, aunts and uncles, nieces and nephews) maternal and paternal relatives were most likely to be affected by ovarian cancer and maternal relatives by breast cancer (see Figures 8.2, 8.3, 8.4, and 8.5). The Endometriosis Association is continuing to study these patterns, now in partnership with the National Institutes of Health. Follow our newsletter for updates as they become available. Because many of the women with endo in the study are young (in their teens, twenties, and thirties), it is believed that

FIGURE 8.1 Cancer in Women with Endo and Their Families: The Endometriosis Association Study

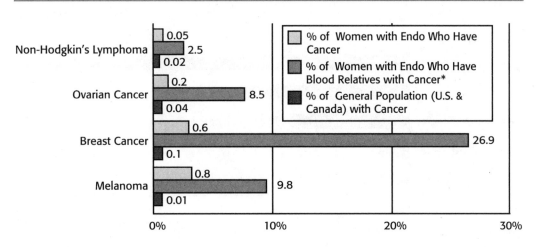

*This number is the percentage of women with endo who have family members with a particular cancer, *not* the percentage of family members with that cancer.

Note: Percentages for women with endo are based on survey responses from 3,999 women. Percentages for general population are based on national data for 301 million people.

FIGURE 8.2 Non-Hodgkin's Lymphoma Occurrence in Family by Relationship

(Percentages do not equal 100 because only the largest degree categories are shown)

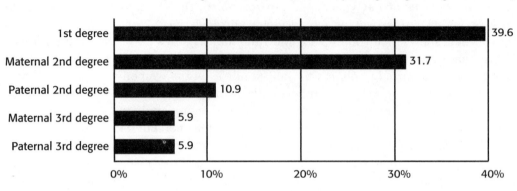

Maternal: Mother's side of family
Paternal: Father's side of family
1st-degree relative: Parents, siblings, children
2nd-degree relative: Grandparents, aunts/uncles, nieces/nephews
3rd-degree relative: First cousins

Note: Number of cases = 101

FIGURE 8.3 Melanoma Occurrence in Family by Relationship

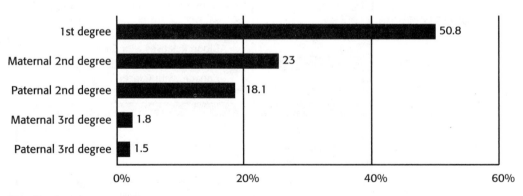

Note: Number of cases = 392

FIGURE 8.4 Ovarian Cancer Occurrence in Family by Relationship

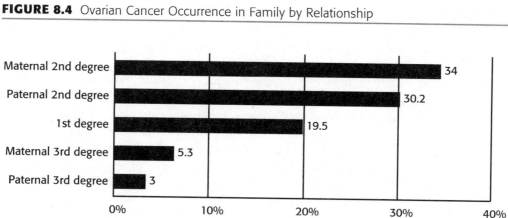

Note: Number of cases = 338

FIGURE 8.5 Breast Cancer Occurrence in Family by Relationship

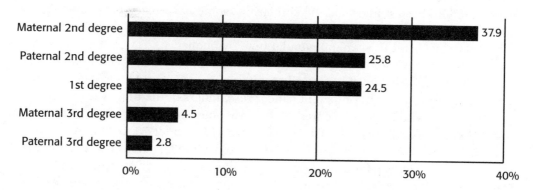

Note: Number of cases = 1,077

over time they may face the same risks seen in their families and in the Brinton study, since most cancers are more prevalent in older age groups.

In the Brinton study, the average age of cancer diagnosis was fifty-two. Unfortunately, the average age of cancer diagnosis in women with endo in the Association's study was substantially younger than in the general population. For instance, the average age of ovarian cancer diagnosis is fifty-two; in this population of North American women with endo and ovarian cancer, the mean age was thirty-four. Breast cancer in the general population is most often diagnosed in middle-aged and older women. In women with endo, the average age of diagnosis was only thirty-nine.

We are continuing to study the data and general incidence of several other cancers. We do not yet know if some other cancers (prostate cancer, for example) may also be a greater risk in the families of women with endo.

Thinking About Risk and Cancer Vigilance

Supported by other research, the Brinton, Vercellini, Hornstein, and Endometriosis Association studies encourage serious thinking about "risk." The increased cancer incidence noted in these studies and the similarities some have noted between endo and cancer suggest that women with endo may have a potent, additional risk factor at least as critical as age is for the general population of women.

It's helpful to have some kind of benchmark, or it may feel that we are all doomed to cancer. A 1981 study by Peto and Doll provides perspective and hope. They reported that the consensus among competent cancer researchers of the time was that 80 to 90 percent of cancer could be prevented. Using available cancer registry data, they concluded that in most parts of the United States in 1970, about 75 to 80 percent of the cases of cancer in both sexes might have been avoidable. They arrived at this figure by comparing the incidence for each separate type of cancer in a given area with the lowest reliable incidence recorded elsewhere in the world where comparison data had been collected. In other words, unavoidable cancers represent only 20 percent of cancers.[24]

In sorting out the best approach to cancer protection, the individual—especially a woman whose health is already compromised by endo—would seem wise to weigh all available information in light of her own situation. To help you do that, we'll examine the general concept of cancer risk; discuss the cancers cited in the Brinton, Vercellini, Hornstein, and Association studies, their symptoms, and special implications for women with endo; and review factors that affect cancer risk, including family history, lifestyle, and environmental carcinogens. Finally, we'll suggest things you can do to reduce your own risk.

In discussing breast cancer risk, *Dr. Susan Love's Breast Book* provides a useful way to think about risk and risk factors in general. What the author (and numerous other

Jane's Story: Melanoma

"I wish I had been smarter earlier in my life with melanoma and endo," says Jane Senkbeil of Wisconsin, thinking back on what she might have done differently and what might have been. "So much has had to be self-education," she adds.

Jane, now fifty-two, had been a lifeguard when she was younger. She saw a clear connection when she developed melanoma. Red hair runs in her family, and she has a reddish complexion and high color ("I burn easily"), but she did not know of the possible connection between endo and melanoma. She identified suspicious moles on her back, thanks to an article about melanoma that she read in *Good Housekeeping*.

Jane, who suffered endo symptoms from her teenage years, didn't have full-blown endo problems until after the birth of her third child. In a two-step vaginal hysterectomy, her uterus was removed, then she had a second surgery, an abdominal oophorectomy that included removal of her appendix (which was filled with endo). "That was at the end of the long road of trying to figure out what was wrong with me," she explains. Jane had progesterone therapy and is now taking estrogen and feeling better than ever.

There is no history of melanoma in Jane's family. Her parents smoked, and she smoked for a short time during college. She is not certain if her mother, who died of cancer at age fifty-three (when Jane was twenty-nine), had endo. She knows her mother did have difficulty with her second pregnancy, the one that produced Jane. Her mother's cancer was the result of a radioactive dye used to diagnose an angioma (similar to an aneurysm).

Jane remembers doctors brushing off her complaints about endo pain by saying, "'I guess that's the way your body works.' 'If *your* body worked this way, you'd fix it,' I thought," she said, "and I started asking around."

Although her daughter doesn't appear to have endo, Jane realizes it's a possibility. "I pay a lot closer attention to my daughter now," says Jane. "I encourage her to ask more questions."

sources) makes clear is that when trying to use risk factors to determine your personal risk, there are neither easy answers nor cut-and-dried rules.

Dr. Love defines breast cancer as a "multifactorial disease" whose many causes interact in ways not completely understood. She warns against over- or underestimating risk, whether your health history includes a specific risk factor or not. Being a woman is risk enough, she contends. When assessing your personal risk, Dr. Love suggests you consider your age in combination with other factors such as the incidence of cancer within your ethnic group and socioeconomic class. In the general population of women, about 80 percent of breast cancer cases occur in women over fifty.

Cancer is not all alike. As we discussed earlier, the word *cancer* is used to label over 100 different diseases. Epithelial ovarian cancer, for instance, occurs as one of three major variations—serous, mucinous, and endometrioid. Researchers have found a specific genetic mutation (PTEN mutation) in endometrioid ovarian tumors but no similar mutations among serous or clear cell tumors. From this they conclude that the different subtypes of ovarian cancer have distinctly different developmental pathways.[25] Recent studies of epithelial ovarian cancer cite a combination of genetic, environmental, hormonal, and viral factors as directly or indirectly related to development of the disease.[26] In other words, when it comes to ovarian cancer, for example, endo may increase your risk for some types but not necessarily others. Similar patterns of genetic mutation, as yet undiscovered, may exist for other cancers as well.

A small (in two fertility clinics) pilot study points out the importance of understanding risk. The study aimed to evaluate the level of ovarian cancer risk that infertility patients are willing to accept related to their psychological status and knowledge of ovarian cancer. The majority (67 percent) of subjects said they were aware of a potential increased ovarian cancer risk related to fertility treatment. However, 62 percent said they did not know whether treatment for ovarian cancer was curative, and only 24 percent realized this type of cancer cannot usually be cured. The researchers conclude that only a minority accurately understood that death is the expected outcome of ovarian cancer, even though the majority of patients seemed to find a modest increase in risk in relation to fertility treatment acceptable.[27]

The term *high risk* is emotionally charged. Assessing risk is complicated. And, of course, what may trigger development of a certain cancer in a particular person is not clear. That's why full understanding of potential risk and likely outcomes is so critical.

Risk Factors

Beverly Zakarian, cofounder of CAN ACT, the first activist cancer-patient organization, reminds us in her book, *The Activist Cancer Patient: How to Take Charge of Your Treatment*, that cancer is different in different people. Having an oncogene for a particular cancer does not mean getting that cancer is inevitable. Even in families with recognized hereditary forms of cancer, any one person in that family may never develop the disease or may develop a cancer unrelated to the genetic predisposition.[28] Risk and actually getting cancer are not synonymous; however it's good to be alert to risk. It's even better to use risk as an impetus to take the best possible care of yourself.

A Family "Connection"

When thinking about the cancer and family connection, author Sandra Steingraber reminds us, "Families share environments as well as chromosomes . . . our genes work in communion with substances streaming in from the larger ecological world. What runs in families does not necessarily run in blood." She cites a study of cancer among adoptees, which correlated cancer within their adoptive families rather than their biological ones. If the adoptive parents had died of cancer before the age of fifty, the mortality rate of the adoptees was five times higher.

Hormones, the Environment, and Cancer Risk

In *The Politics of Cancer*, Samuel Epstein, M.D., cites studies showing how abnormalities or excesses in sex hormones in both experimental animals and humans can be cancer causing. This evidence included a study by the U.S. National Cancer Institute (NCI), which linked Premarin, prescribed for estrogen replacement therapy, with ovarian cancer. He also notes that DES, which was once used in estrogen replacement therapy, has been incriminated as one possible cause of ovarian cancer.[29]

Dr. Love notes that a 1984 study of women who took DES while pregnant showed a slight increase in breast cancer among these women, which may be related to increased exposure to external estrogen. A slight increase in a rare form of vaginal cancer also has been noted in their daughters. The daughters of these women are just now approaching the age at which breast cancer is most common, so we may begin to see if any additional risk was passed along to them. A large follow-up study of DES mothers, daughters, and sons is currently under way at NCI.

The possible impact of environmental estrogens was raised by Devra Lee Davis, Ph.D., and her colleagues in the early 1990s. Davis was previously a senior advisor to the U.S. Assistant Secretary of Health and is now an epidemiologist at the World Resources Institute in Washington, D.C. Challenging conventional thinking, she and her colleagues contended that increased exposure to estrogen might explain the trend toward greater mortality from lung, breast, and prostate cancer in people older than forty-five; drastic increases in several major countries in brain and other nervous system cancers among people older than seventy-five; and increased incidence in the United States of brain cancer among the young. They identified the possible culprit as increasing environmental levels of fat-soluble synthetic chemicals such as dioxin and PCBs, which mimic or amplify the physiological effects of estrogen (xenoestrogens).[30]

These xenoestrogens are turning up in places where you'd least expect them. A 1995 study examined twenty different brands of food in cans coated on the inside with plastic. Researchers found that when food from these cans was tested with an estrogen screen, it showed estrogenic activity. Since estrogen is a factor in a number of cancers, an estrogenic substance in our food is obviously a concern. In another part of the experiment, when water that had been autoclaved in empty cans (autoclaving involves heating under high pressure to sterilize, as these foods would be in processing) was added to human breast-cancer cell lines in a lab, it increased proliferation of the cells as much as 70 percent of the effect of estrogen. The plastic monomer bisphenol A was found in the liquid of preserved vegetables from the cans, as well as in water autoclaved in the cans. The bisphenol A is thought to cause the hormonal activity measured.[31]

Estrogenic canned food is a good example of the problem as Davis described it at the 1997 World Conference on Breast Cancer. She explained that direct cause and effect

Diane's Story: Breast Cancer

Diane of Oregon gets frustrated and angry when she hears advice about healthful eating and exercise to prevent breast cancer. A vegetarian for roughly twenty-five years, she has always exercised—in other words, she has "walked the walk," as they say. And yet she developed breast cancer five years ago at age forty-two and endo before that. Diane's two sisters are not health conscious, she says, but they have not developed these diseases. (Her mother had breast cancer at age seventy, and several great-aunts have had cancer.) Diane believes there is a breast cancer epidemic that can probably be traced to pesticides coupled with a genetic susceptibility to the disease.

Today Diane eats strictly organic food and uses herbs. She is a firm believer in an annual mammogram. Her own cancer was discovered by mammogram. The malignancy, which was confined to the breast, was found in a microcalcification that could not be felt. She says the mammogram revealed eight or ten dots that could barely be seen; three doctors examined her but could feel no lumps. She had a biopsy, had surgery, and refused tamoxifen—her concern for blood clots and liver damage, as possible side effects, made the drug unacceptable to her.

Diane's first mammogram was at the insistence of her gynecologist at age thirty-seven or thirty-eight. She has follow-ups annually. She does not believe breast self-exam, which she said she tried after her surgery, is useful. "After I went through all of this, I tried to check myself, but with all the scar tissue, I would always feel something and freak out. Endo is a miserable disease, but nothing compared to breast cancer. It's like living with an ax over your head. When you're still in your forties, it's really a lot to handle."

Diane, who says she has a high tolerance for pain, once missed a lot of work due to the pain from her endo. Today endo is no longer a problem, and she describes herself as cured. Diagnosed at thirty-three via laparoscopy, she had surgery in 1985 and another in 1989, in which an ovary was removed. She credits acupuncture with helping control her pain and allowing her to delay the second surgery for eighteen months, just in time for the surgical revolution (from laparotomy to laparoscopy) then under way. Diane credits the delay with helping her keep her uterus (which would have been more readily removed with earlier surgical techniques).

A medical-legal researcher/analyst by profession, Diane is now writing a book about people given a short time to live. Her interviews with those who have gone through life-threatening experiences have convinced her that healing is spiritual and must come from inside a person. She says many of the people have changed careers, some have gotten into the arts, and they are surviving, despite fatal diagnoses.

One thought she has found particularly helpful: "If after a few years you can't recognize yourself, the work (inner healing) has been deep enough." Diane is happy to say that she no longer recognizes herself. After years of waking up with nightmares, with fear running through her life, she now believes she is healed and will make it.

between environmental estrogens and human cancer is difficult to establish because people are unaware of the different chemicals to which they are exposed. (For example, who would think they were getting a good dose of estrogen in canned peas?) Screening chemicals for safety is left entirely up to manufacturers.[32]

A study by Mary Wolff, Ph.D., which has been disputed, found significantly higher levels of DDE, a by-product of the pesticide DDT, in the blood samples of women who developed breast cancer. The study suggests, but does not prove, that toxic residues, especially DDE, are strongly associated with breast cancer risk.[33] DDE is a widespread contaminant of animal food products, which we absorb when we eat foods such as red meat and dairy products. The study proposes that once in our bodies, DDE may bind with receptors that allow it to modify cell regulation and may interfere with steroid and sex hormone metabolism. The possibility that low-level environmental contamination with organochlorine residues may be a breast cancer risk prompted the National Institutes of Health to research the causes of high risk for breast cancer on Long Island (the study is still in process) and on Cape Cod (the Massachusetts Breast Cancer Coalition is in the second phase of this study).

Two Canadian studies presented at the 1999 World Conference on Breast Cancer found evidence of links between pesticides and breast cancer. A study of tissue samples from more than 400 women who underwent breast biopsies, some with and some without breast cancer, showed that mirex, a now-banned pesticide, was linked to higher breast cancer rates in women who had given birth but not breastfed. The study is apparently the largest of its kind ever done. The other study showed that women with high DDT exposure have breast cancer that is more aggressive—that is, faster spreading.[34, 35]

The search for proof that certain organochlorines cause cancer continues, reminding us that they can be the source of other health problems. Another organochlorine, the fungicide HCB (no longer produced commercially but once used on grain and field crops in the United States and now produced as a by-product of chlorinated solvents, pesticides, and other chlorinated compounds) was studied to assess its connection with breast cancer. Although HCB is found almost everywhere (air, soil, water, and plants), researchers could not link it to increased breast cancer risk. They did, however, point out that, like other organochlorines, HCB can act as an "environmental estrogen" to lower sperm count, decrease the duration of lactation, and make preterm births and birth defects more frequent.[36]

Cancers Linked to Endo

The cancers that research has most strongly linked to endo are breast cancer, ovarian cancer, non-Hodgkin's lymphoma, and melanoma. Let's look at each of these in terms of their symptoms, risk factors, and implications for women with endo.

Breast Cancer

Breast cancer accounts for nearly 30 percent of all newly diagnosed cancers among women in the United States. The rate of breast cancer has been increasing worldwide; by the year 2000, annual incidence was expected to reach 1 million women.[37] Twenty-two percent of all breast cancer cases are diagnosed in women under the age of fifty.[38] According to the National Cancer Institute pamphlet "Understanding Breast Changes: A Health Guide for All Women," a woman's chance of developing breast cancer rises from 1 in 2,525 by age thirty to 1 in 10 by age eighty.[39]

Symptoms of Breast Cancer

Breast cancer does not usually cause pain, nor is pain necessarily a sign of cancer, but breast cancer can be painful when it invades the chest wall or triggers inflammation or swelling of lymph nodes in the breast. A breast lump you can feel may or may not be malignant. Of the four dominant kinds of breast lumps, three are benign.[40] The American Cancer Society recommends you take note of lumps, thickening, or swelling of the breast, dimpling, skin irritation, distortion, nipple retraction, or nipple discharge.

Risks Specific to Breast Cancer

Estrogen exposure is identified as the single greatest risk factor for development of breast cancer. This may help to explain why breast cancer risk increases among women with the longest lifetime exposure to estrogen—those who start their periods early or experience late menopause, and women who never bear children. (Simple estrogen exposure is probably not the whole story, however, since estrogen skyrockets in pregnancy, as does progesterone.)

Stimulated by estrogen, breast cells proliferate rapidly, although how estrogen actually causes breast cancer is not known.[40] Normal cell growth is thought to be controlled by oncogenes, which promote growth. Researchers have discovered other genes, tumor suppressor genes, which constrain growth. Breast cancer is thought to result from both activation of an oncogene and failure of a tumor suppressor gene to activate.[40]

Breast cancer can be thought of in three categories: sporadic, genetic, and polygenic. Most breast cancer (70 percent) is sporadic, meaning there is no family history of breast cancer. Genetic cases of breast cancer account for about 5 percent of all cases. The BRCA1 gene, which is also thought to be linked to ovarian cancer, is usually at fault in genetic cases. Risk for both breast and ovarian cancer linked to BRCA1 can be as high as 80 percent by age eighty, and the cancers often occur at a young age. Polygenic breast cancer (13 percent of all breast cancer) occurs when there is a family history but no single dominant gene to account for it. In polygenic breast cancer, there may be a gene, for example, that makes a woman more susceptible to a diet high in fats or a gene that predisposes a woman to early menstruation or late menopause.

Family lifestyle and values also affect breast cancer risk. In families that encourage later childbirth (into the thirties), women may face higher risk because later childbearing has been implicated in breast cancer risk. Obviously, this is not a "genetic" pattern, but it may appear to be a "family" cancer pattern.

But is it the childbearing alone that is actually protective? The results of several 1995 studies indicate that breastfeeding also protects against breast cancer, reducing risk by as much as 30 percent. Breastfeeding delays menstruation (by signaling your hypothalamus to inhibit release of estrogen, progesterone, and other hormones that trigger the menstrual cycle), so it lowers your estrogen exposure. Breastfeeding also reduces the levels of built-up carcinogens in the breast; the longer you breastfeed, the lower those levels fall. This, however, is good news/bad news in itself, since the carcinogens pass from you to your baby through the breast milk.[41]

As with endo, this supposed risk factor may be related to the documented passage of toxic chemicals from the mother to the baby, thereby lessening her risk (while increasing the baby's health risks). Earlier childbearing may mean earlier removal of these toxins from the mother's body, resulting in less years of exposure for her. Those who bear children later may also give birth to fewer children, lessening this toxin-dumping effect. As we have learned with endo, there may be a lot more to the "delayed childbearing" idea than meets the eye.

Hormones and Breast Cancer

In terms of hormonal risk and breast cancer, Dr. Love again notes wide gaps in our understanding. In general, the longer a woman menstruates, the higher her risk. Early removal of the ovaries, without hormone therapy,[42] reduces breast cancer risk. But, as with tamoxifen (a drug discussed later), this "protection" may come at a price—in this case, perhaps increased risk for heart disease and osteoporosis.

Use of birth control pills, specifically long-term use, appears to increase breast cancer incidence by about 3.3 percent per year of use. Women who took the estrogen DES during the 1940s to 1960s are showing a slight increase in breast cancer. Women taking postmenopausal estrogen and progesterone replacement (in the form of progestin, synthetic progesterone) also show higher incidences of breast cancer.[42]

The formulas for birth control pills and hormone replacement have changed over time, so it is hard to compare use of earlier formulations with today's formulations. Long-term use of the early estrogen-only hormone replacement therapy was linked to increased cases of uterine cancer, so synthetic progesterone was added to balance the estrogen.[43] A 1989 Swedish study found an increased risk of breast cancer in women who used estrogen over the long term following menopause. There was a 10 percent greater risk of developing breast cancer that grew to 70 percent, the longer treatment continued (more than nine years). The researchers noted that their findings were consistent with those of two previous cohort studies and several case control studies. Risk increased with long-term use among women who used estrogen with no progestins added, those who used the two in combination, and those who switched from estrogen alone to an estrogen/progestin combination.[44]

In addition to how long the treatments were used, the Swedish study looked at risk according to type of estrogen used. Most of the women in the study (56 percent) were taking estradiol, and its use seemed to create a higher risk than estrogens overall—with risk doubling after six years of treatment. The study found no association between breast cancer and use of the weaker estrogen, estriol, or conjugated estrogens (Premarin, Ogen) commonly used in the United States. The researchers noted that their negative findings on conjugated estrogen were at odds with previous U.S. studies. They attributed this to less use of conjugated estrogens among the women in their study (only 20 percent of treatment periods). Also, their dose of 0.625 milligram was about half the dose used by women in the U.S. studies (1.25 milligrams).[44]

According to an editorial review of the Swedish study, although this study found estrogen plus progestin more likely to cause cancer than estrogen alone, a 1983 study found less risk of breast cancer among women who used the combination than among women who used estrogen alone or among those who did not receive hormone therapy.[45] Other studies point out that risks and benefits for hormone replacement versus no hormone replacement must be carefully balanced.[46, 47] (See the section on cancer prevention later in this chapter and in Chapter 11, "Menopause and Endometriosis," for more information.)

Another hormone that may have an important relationship to breast cancer is DHEA. For a discussion of this hormone, see Chapter 4.

Race or Ethnicity

The National Black Women's Health Project cites the National Cancer Institute when it warns that while breast cancer is higher in white women overall, incidence is higher in African-American women under age forty. A higher mortality rate for African-American women than white women is attributed to diagnosis at a later stage of the disease.[48]

Alcohol

Consumption of alcohol has also been associated with breast cancer. Compared with women who never drink, those who consume one drink or more a day may increase their risk 50 percent. Why does alcohol appear to increase risk? Among the theories is that it may weaken the immune system, leaving it less able to defend our bodies against other noxious agents.[49] Two drinks of alcohol a day have been shown to raise estrogen levels (higher estrogen levels being linked with greater breast cancer risk). However, studies also indicate that moderate use of alcohol (one to two drinks per day)[50] protects against heart disease, which for the "average" woman is a greater threat than breast cancer.[51]

Another source noted that nutritional deficiencies are associated with or made worse by consuming alcohol in excess, which affects the body's ability to fight off cancer. When our bodies lack essential vitamins and minerals (such as vitamin A and beta-carotene—needed for normal tissue growth—and antioxidants, such as carotenoids and

> ### G's Story: Ovarian Cancer
>
> Ovarian cancer, the disease that usually strikes "older" women, struck G when she was nineteen. Today, as both a medical student and a woman with endo, G is well aware that endo is relatively new to the scientific literature and still not considered a terribly "serious" disease. "Nobody dies [from endo], it's not communicable, it's not killing small children, it's quiet, chronic, and female," she explains. She says no one wants to make a connection between cancer and any other condition for fear of panic. "There is a real unwillingness to make a link," she admits.

vitamin C, which help trap free radicals), then substances originating outside our bodies can trigger damage. This damage can then induce chromosomal damage, disruption of enzymes as well as the body's metabolism, and abnormal cellular changes in target organs.[37]

Pregnancy

Sources generally agree that women who have never been pregnant seem to be at greater risk for breast cancer than women who have given birth. This pattern may suggest that pregnancy prevents cancer, but women who have never been pregnant appear to be less at risk than women whose first pregnancy occurred after age thirty. Dr. Love discusses the aggressiveness of cancer in young women and cites two studies in which young women who developed breast cancer had higher mortality if they were pregnant within the preceding four years. Risk was highest immediately following a pregnancy. Dr. Love concludes that the aggressiveness of cancer may be less related to age than to changes in the immune system that prevent the body from rejecting a fetus and to the hormonal changes of pregnancy.[42]

Ovarian Cancer

According to the U.S. National Report Card, incidence of ovarian cancer continued to fall 0.6 percent in 1990 to 1995, as it had during 1973 to 1990.[52] Most women who develop ovarian cancer will die from it. While incidence of ovarian cancer is lower than that of other gynecologic cancers, it accounts for 50 percent of all deaths from gynecologic cancer. Of those diagnosed with ovarian cancer, only half are still alive five years later.[53, 54]

As to its cause, M. Steven Piver, M.D., chief of the Department of Gynecologic Oncology at Roswell Park Cancer Institute, says researchers think ovulation may damage the surface of our ovaries. The body usually repairs this injury as it would any other injury. However, the greater the number of ovulations, the greater the damage, and the greater the chances that eventually the damage will go unrepaired, resulting in abnormal cell division and ovarian cancer.[55]

Women who ovulate less frequently enjoy some protection against ovarian cancer. In fact, use of oral contraceptives for five years or longer appears to reduce ovarian cancer risk by as much as 40 percent.[40] Removal of the ovaries or tubal ligation also lessens risk.

Ovarian cancer occurs as either epithelial or nonepithelial tumors. The majority are epithelial. Rare but not unheard of in women under thirty-five, ovarian cancer in the general population occurs most frequently in women ages fifty-five to fifty-nine.

A 1992 study concluded that ovarian endo increases the risk for ovarian cancer, especially in postmenopausal women. Eleven (26 percent) of the women in the study with endometrioid ovarian cancer had laboratory evidence of endo next to the cancer. Eight of the eleven (73 percent) were postmenopausal. Only three of the premenopausal patients (27 percent) had laboratory evidence of endo adjacent to the cancer. The study's authors did not indicate whether the postmenopausal patients were taking replacement hormones.[56]

A number of other studies also have found an association between ovarian cancer and endo. One of the most interesting is a recent Japanese study, which concluded that a type of ovarian endo with atypical cells possesses precancerous potential. The researchers described atypical ovarian endo as cells that, when examined in the lab, showed epithelial stratification, tufting, crowding of glands, and nuclear enlargement. (Although these pathology terms are beyond the scope of a lay audience, we include them here for the many doctors and researchers reading this. Remember that the word *atypical* also is used to describe endo that does not look like classical "chocolate"-colored or "powderburn" endo through the laparoscope. That's not what's being described here.) The researchers recommend that "extended examination and close long-term follow-up are required" when a woman with endo has these atypical cells. Of course, this requires that biopsies and careful lab work follow removal of ovarian endo.[57]

Symptoms of Ovarian Cancer

Like many cancers, ovarian cancer can be present without symptoms in its earliest stages and may later mimic other, less serious illnesses. Early detection often requires us to be alert to unusual pain. This is especially critical for women with endo, who may routinely attribute any pain to endo. Dr. Piver cautions that subtle symptoms are often present in stage I and II ovarian cancer—for example, bloating that causes clothes to no longer fit as well as they once did, back pain, and fatigue.[55]

If you are living with endo, many potential symptoms of ovarian cancer may be familiar: constipation, flatulence, water retention, pain, abdominal swelling, a frequent need to urinate, nausea, and abdominal discomfort, symptoms that can be part and parcel of endo.[49] What, then, is the warning for women with endo that an ovarian cancer is present when it is? We hope to answer that question by following closely the women with endo who develop ovarian cancer. (Readers' suggestions and ideas are always welcome!)

Presence of a palpable abdominal mass increases the chances of cancer. In women with such a mass, when examination, tumor marker assessment, and gray-scale ultrasound are suspicious, 77 percent of premenopausal and 83 percent of postmenopausal women have had malignant tumors.[46]

Risks Specific to Ovarian Cancer

The five-year relative survival rate for all stages of ovarian cancer is 50 percent. If the cancer is diagnosed and treated early, the rate is 95 percent, but only about 25 percent of cases are detected at the localized stage. Five-year relative survival rates for women with regional and distant disease are 79 percent and 28 percent, respectively.[58]

Three case control studies in a review of twelve that examined the causes, incidence, and distribution of ovarian cancer looked specifically at use of fertility drugs. Of the 2,238 women in these three studies, 711 had invasive ovarian cancer, and 31 of those had used fertility drugs. The study's report did not specify the drugs involved, dosage, or length and type of treatment. Among the women who were diagnosed as infertile and who had received fertility drugs, the risk for invasive epithelial ovarian cancer was almost three times greater than for women with no history of infertility.[26]

Some physicians have theorized that infertility itself may express a common underlying phenomenon associated with ovarian cancer. However, the studies also found that infertile women who had never taken fertility drugs had no increased risk. Also, infertile women who took the drugs and became pregnant did not have a significant increased risk. But significantly increased risk was associated with use of fertility drugs among infertile women who never became pregnant.[59] The American Society for Reproductive Medicine also reports that some researchers have found an increase in borderline ovarian cancer in women who used injectable gonadotrophins, ovulation-stimulating hormones.[60] However, the results of a number of studies conflict with these findings. For example, a Danish study found that women who took fertility drugs had no increased risk for ovarian cancer, regardless of whether they had children.[61]

A history of menstrual problems, infertility, bearing no or few children, a high-fat diet, early onset of periods and late menopause, and previous experience with breast, rectal, or intestinal cancers appear to increase ovarian cancer risk, as does exposure to asbestos and talc in the genital area.[58] Whether the use of talc—often found in baby and body powders—causes cancer is in dispute. A 1982 Harvard Medical School study[62] found an increased risk, but a 1988 Stanford University study[63] found no increase. Asbestos is a known cancer-causing agent; talc particles are similar to asbestos. Until 1976, when manufacturers initiated guidelines on permissible levels, asbestos was an ingredient in some talcum powders. Why might talc applied to the genital area or on sanitary napkins cause cancer? The theory is that the particles travel to the ovary through the cervix, the uterus, and fallopian tubes with toxic effect on the ovary.[55] (The *Physicians' Desk Reference* lists talc as an ingredient in danazol. We do not know if this oral ingestion has the same effect as body powder.)

Fertility Treatment and Cancer

A 1993 article in *Health*[64] and the book *Gilda's Disease* cite the Whittemore study, which connects the use of fertility drugs—specifically, ovulation-inducing drugs—to a tripling of ovarian cancer risk. In her study, Whittemore notes that the only other large-scale study of fertility drugs and cancer, a 1987 Israeli study, found no cancer connection but failed to track women into their fifties, when these cancers are most likely to develop. While the study was not considered conclusive, the National Institutes of Health launched an investigation into the risks, and the FDA suggested fertility drug manufacturers add the potential risk of ovarian cancer to their labels.[59]

A 1995 booklet, "Ovulation Drugs: A Guide for Patients," available from the American Society for Reproductive Medicine (formerly the American Fertility Society), does not emphasize a possible connection between ovulation-inducing drugs and cancer in a table that describes seven commonly used drugs. The table charts each drug's generic name, brand name(s), form, and most common side effects. Typical side effects listed include hot flashes, headache, mood swings, and incidence of multiple births. At the end of the pamphlet, there is a brief discussion of ovarian cancer and fertility drugs in a paragraph under the heading "Long-Term Risks of Ovulation Drugs." It mentions that several studies have connected ovulation-inducing drugs, such as clomiphene (Clomid) and hMG, (human menopausal gonadotropin, such as Humegon and Pergonal) with increased risk of ovarian cancer.

Admitting that the data suggests a greater risk for ovarian cancer among infertile women, many of whom have taken fertility drugs, the brochure also says it is unclear which drugs, if any, might increase that risk. The brochure also cautions women to "weigh the unproven risks against clear benefits of ovulation-inducing agents."[65] Neither the "unproven risks" nor the "clear benefits" are defined. More research is obviously needed.

Deciding to pursue fertility treatment is an emotion-charged and highly personal decision. Women contemplating such a decision would do well to review carefully the research (as limited as it is) in light of their other personal risk factors.

Race or Ethnicity

Caucasian women of northern European descent living in industrialized countries appear to be at increased risk for ovarian cancer.[58]

Family History

A family history of ovarian cancer is by far the most significant known risk factor for the disease. Having one close relative with ovarian cancer increases a woman's risk of developing ovarian cancer by nearly three times. Having additional family members with breast or ovarian cancer increases the risk even further. It is important to understand that most women with risk factors for ovarian cancer will never actually get ovarian cancer. Even with significant risk factors such as family history, the overall chances of getting ovarian cancer are still small.[58]

BRCA1 gene mutations occur in 80 percent of families with multiple cases of ovarian cancer, but the abnormal gene by itself will not result in the cancer. It appears to require some environmental trigger, such as use of talc, never having been pregnant, a high-fat diet, or other factors, to actually cause disease.[42]

Non-Hodgkin's Lymphoma

Lymphomas are cancers of the immune system. In 1990, 5 percent of all new cancer cases were lymphomas, and 83 percent of these were the non-Hodgkin's type, which is the seventh most common cancer overall. By the time non-Hodgkin's lymphomas (NHLs) are diagnosed, they have usually formed solid tumors.

Lymphomas are divided into two distinct groups: Hodgkin's and non-Hodgkin's. According to the Leukemia Society, non-Hodgkin's lymphomas usually begin in the lymph nodes, but 20 percent start in other sites, such as the lungs, liver, and gastrointestinal tract. Most consist of malignant B cells, but T cells also can become malignant. The progress of non-Hodgkin's lymphomas is far less predictable than that of Hodgkin's disease and may affect cells in different organs simultaneously.[66]

The disease (of which Jacqueline Kennedy Onassis died) usually affects younger people—the average age of patients is forty-two—and occurs 50 percent more frequently in males than females. However, Association members who already had been diagnosed with NHL at the time of our large 1998 survey were an average age of thirty-six at diagnosis.

Incidence has been increasing in recent times. Higher incidence in males begins at a young age, raising questions about occupational exposure to carcinogens as a cause.[40] Lymphatic cancers tend to occur in clusters in precise geographical locations.[2]

The booklet "What You Need to Know About Non-Hodgkin's Lymphomas," available from the National Cancer Institute, estimates that as little as thirty years ago, few people survived this disease. Today almost half survive, due to improved treatment with chemotherapy and radiation.

Symptoms of Non-Hodgkin's Lymphoma

The National Cancer Institute identifies a painless swelling of the lymph nodes in the neck, underarm, or groin as the most common symptom of this disease. Other symptoms include night sweats, fevers, tiredness, weight loss, itching, and reddened patches on the skin. Low-grade non-Hodgkin's lymphomas may be so free of notable symptoms that they are first diagnosed during a routine physical. Enlargement of lymph nodes is often combined with liver or spleen enlargement. One-third of these cancers present with a metastatic tumor in the tonsils or throat, tear glands, salivary glands, gastrointestinal tract, the bones, skin, or central nervous system.[40]

Risks Specific to Non-Hodgkin's Lymphoma

The immune systems of people who develop non-Hodgkin's lymphomas experience chronic antigenic stimulation, such as chronic exposure to certain viruses, bacteria, or toxic substances.* Such reactions are typical of organ transplant patients and those with immunodeficiency diseases. This stimulation can make it difficult for the body to control tumor-inducing infections.[37] Non-Hodgkin's lymphoma can be a complication of HIV/AIDS.[67]

Those with autoimmune diseases, in which the immune system attacks one's own body, are also said to be at greater risk for non-Hodgkin's lymphoma. Unfortunately, women with endo are at risk for certain autoimmune diseases—perhaps a clue to understanding our risk for endo as well as NHL.

People who receive immunosuppressive drugs (such as adrenal corticosteroids, which help prevent transplant patients from rejecting a new organ, for example) have thirty-two times more risk of developing non-Hodgkin's lymphoma.[49] Those exposed to excessive radiation (such as the survivors of the atomic bomb in Hiroshima and those who have undergone aggressive radiotherapy) also appear to be at increased risk of developing the disease.[42] Although the evidence is not conclusive, individuals with occupational exposures to chemicals (evidence pointing to phenoxy herbicide exposure is growing) also appear to be at greater risk.[37]

A Swedish study reported significantly increased risk for non-Hodgkin's lymphoma due to exposure to herbicides, especially Roundup, and fungicides. The use of Roundup, reportedly the world's most widely used herbicide, is said to be rapidly increasing because of its compatibility with genetically engineered crops. Monsanto, the company that formerly produced PCBs, developed genetically engineered crops that are resistant to Roundup, which it also makes, leading to greater use of the herbicide on these crops. The researchers noted that, while confirming the results of other studies that reported increased risk for NHL after exposure to phenoxy acetic acid herbicides, this study found the risk restricted to exposure within two decades of diagnosis.[68]

The study also found increased risk associated with exposure to glass wool (insulating material, a form of fiberglass) and fungicides. They conclude that this study supports the idea that chemical agents play a role as a cause of NHL. They suggest that since many of these pesticides have been used only since World War II, this increased recent use may explain the recent increase in NHL noted in many countries. They also note that immunosuppression is an established risk factor for NHL and that pesticides such as the phenoxy acetic acids and chlorophenols are reported to have an immunotoxic effect.[68]

---

*An antigen is any substance recognized by the immune system. Chronic stimulation means that the body is constantly activated against real or perceived "enemies." For more on allergies and endo, see Chapter 4, "Immunotherapy: The Newest Treatment for Endometriosis."

While exposure to certain chemicals seems to increase risk, the connection is not yet conclusive. Steingraber, in her book *Living Downstream: An Ecologist Looks at Cancer and the Environment*,[3] cites studies by the National Cancer Institute pointing to a connection between phenoxy herbicides (namely 2,4-D, sold as Ded-Weed, Lawn-Keep, Weedone, Plantgard, Miracle, and Demise) and non-Hodgkin's lymphoma in people involved in agriculture, as well as in the general population. She also notes that an Institute of Medicine study of Vietnam veterans exposed to herbicides (Agent Orange, a mixture of dichlorophenoxy acetic acid, 2,4-D, and the dioxin-contaminated trichlorophenoxyacetic acid, 2,4,5-T) concluded that there was a positive correlation between their exposure and non-Hodgkin's lymphoma. The herbicide 2,4-D, which also contains dioxin and has been linked to tumors in rats and identified as a possible cause of non-Hodgkin's lymphoma in human beings, is a widely used weed killer in gardens.

Family History

As discussed earlier, there is evidence of an increased incidence of lymphoma in the families of patients with immunologic disorders.

Melanoma

The most dangerous skin cancer is melanoma, a cancer that develops from a type of mole called a dysplastic nevus. The incidence of melanoma is increasing around the world.[37] Melanocytes are cells in the lower region of our epidermis, the outer layer of our skin. These cells produce a dark pigment called melanin, which contributes to skin color and can become abnormal, dividing too often and growing without control or order.

Melanoma can be cured by surgery if discovered when it is thin, before the tumor has grown downward from the skin surface. Otherwise, it can invade and destroy the surrounding healthy skin, spread through the bloodstream and lymphatic system, and become deadly. It is believed to be triggered by ultraviolet waves in sunlight.[70]

Melanoma affects white-skinned people almost exclusively, except for a form unrelated to sun exposure. Thirty-five percent of all cases are diagnosed in people younger than forty-five, and occurrences peak among people in their fifties in the general population. In women with endo and melanoma in the Association study, the average age of diagnosis was only thirty-two.

Risks Specific to Melanoma

People at greatest risk for melanoma have sun-sensitive skin that freckles easily, a history of spending a good deal of time in the sun, an abundance of moles (common, or "funny looking"—dysplastic nevi), a family or personal history of the common skin cancers (squamous and basal cell), or a family or personal history of melanoma. People taking immunosuppressive drugs or who have immune-system-related health problems also appear to be at increased risk. The most common forms of melanoma are

Joe's life has taken a decided turn for the better, but there are still some struggles.

associated with heavy, intermittent sun exposure—the kind a person who normally spends her days indoors would get on vacations and weekends.

Many dermatologists advise against tanning with the "artificial sunlight" of tanning salons.[69] This light emits UV-A rays, a wavelength linked to skin aging and non-melanoma skin cancers. It also will not give you an effective base tan that protects you from burning outdoors. Combined with the UV-B rays from natural sunlight, it may trigger melanoma.

Moles are a risk factor for melanoma, no matter what your skin type. What kind of moles should you be alert to? Suspicious moles—dysplastic nevi—are asymmetrical (one half is unlike the other), have irregular or ragged borders, have color that varies (shades of tan, brown, black or even red, blue, and white), have a diameter greater than six millimeters (about one-quarter inch, the size of a pencil eraser), or are growing or changing.[70]

Reducing Our Risks

Now that we have examined the concept of risk, studied in detail the key research linking endo and cancer, and reviewed factors that may affect risk in breast cancer, ovarian cancer, non-Hodgkin's lymphoma, and melanoma, we'll look at ways to *reduce* our risk. Interestingly, much of what helps improve health when one has endo also seems to have some effect related to cancer, perhaps indicating again that the two disease processes are similar. It's nice to know that the same health-improving steps you take can accomplish so many health goals at once.

Diet and Cancer

Diet, a word once almost synonymous with swimsuits, calories, and deprivation, is taking on new meaning. New research on nutrition is expanding our appreciation of the role diet plays in health overall. From the cup of antioxidant-rich blueberries to the bowl of fat-laden premium ice cream, we are beginning to understand that the foods we choose to consume can help us tip the scales to prevent cancer or promote it. Is diet the only factor? Hardly! But it is critical, and it is something we control.

Chapter 5 discusses how nutrition can help manage the symptoms of endo. A good endo diet and a good cancer prevention diet often overlap. For example, since estrogen plays a critical role in both endo and cancer, the article suggests ways to control estrogen levels—increasing dietary fiber, consuming adequate levels of B vitamins, and limiting dietary fat.

The American Institute for Cancer Research estimates that as many as 375,000 cases of cancer, at current cancer rates, could be prevented each year in the United States through healthful dietary choices. Our understanding of diet and nutrition and how they relate to our health is constantly changing. The 1998 controversy over Dr. Bob Arnot's bestselling book *The Breast Cancer Prevention Diet* reminds us that research is ongoing and experts will disagree. Among the recommendations Arnot makes is that women eat more soy, fish oil, and flaxseed oil. He also suggests we eat less of foods that cause the largest increase in blood sugar, since this raises triglyceride levels, and high triglyceride levels appear to increase the risk of breast cancer. The foods to avoid include white bread, potatoes, instant rice, and parsnips.[71] An American Cancer Society spokeswoman, Joann Schellenback, notes that much of the nutritional material in Arnot's book is highly speculative and that the society believes no one diet can prevent breast cancer. She also says there is no body of scientific evidence to support the idea that breast cancer can be prevented by diet.[72]

Obviously, the debates on cancer will continue for decades. Powerful forces will continue to argue, making it harder for us all to sort out the issues. The bottom line is we all know that more healthful living will pay off in better health. We probably need to ignore the political battles and not use them as an excuse to eat processed, additive-laden foods, skip exercise, and so on.

Fat in Our Diet

An association between breast cancer and dietary fat was first suggested in 1942. High-fat diets appear to increase the biologically active form of the hormone prolactin, which stimulates breast growth and possibly growth of latent abnormal cells to form tumors. Fats also affect digestion. For instance, compared with vegetarians, people on high-fat diets appear to reabsorb more estrogen. These people would have a greater cancer risk because increased levels of estrogen in the bloodstream may promote cancer. Fats also increase exposure to such chemical hormones as DDT, PCBs, and dioxin. Estrogen exposure is further increased because fat cells produce estrogens. Fat also affects the body's level of prostaglandins, substances well known to women with endo.

High levels of trans fatty acids, found in margarine and processed oils, make it difficult for the body to metabolize the essential fatty acids that are the precursors of the "good" prostaglandins. In fact, a study has found that women with high levels of trans fatty acids in the body have a 40 percent greater risk of breast cancer.[73] In general, populations at low risk for developing breast cancer (people who live in Japan and other Asian nations or in underdeveloped countries) eat diets higher in the precursors for the "good" prostaglandins. (For more on this topic, see Chapter 5.)

Of course, not all the research literature agrees on the issue of dietary fat either. Andrew Weil, M.D., reports that Japanese doctors think higher consumption of soy products, instead of a lower-fat diet, explains the lower rates of breast and other gynecologic cancers among Japanese women in Japan versus Japanese women who move to America. Soybeans and products made from them contain well-known phytoestrogens that are acknowledged to affect hormonal levels in some animals. Weil reports that Japanese women in menopause complain less of hot flashes, which he thinks may also be attributed to the protective phytoestrogens contained in soy foods. As Weil explains, soy phytoestrogens might attach to the estrogen receptors of cells without activating them, thereby decreasing estrogen exposure.[75] (See Chapter 11 for additional information on phytoestrogens.)

A high-fat diet also contributes to production of estradiol, a principal estrogen that fuels breast tumors. High-fat diets tend to be lower in fiber, which helps reduce estrogen levels by trapping it in the digestive tract and removing it from the body. Neal Barnard, M.D., argues for a diet of 15 percent fat—well below the 30 percent suggested by the National Cancer Institute.[76]

Protein in Our Diet

Researchers are examining the role of dietary protein in breast and other cancers. Amino acids from protein are turned into neurotransmitters, which control hormone levels. A high-protein diet might alter the level of neurotransmitters. This could increase or decrease the levels of prolactin, estrogen, and progesterone and possibly increase vulnerability to breast cancer.[49]

A study of 35,156 healthy Iowa women, ages fifty-five to sixty-nine, suggests that a diet high in fat and protein in older women puts them at increased risk for non-Hodgkin's lymphoma, one of the cancers for which women with endo and their families seem to be at higher risk. The women in the Iowa study filled out questionnaires in 1986 and were followed for seven years. While the researchers did not consider their results conclusive, they said that higher risk appeared to correlate with higher intakes of animal fat, saturated fat, monounsaturated fat (such as olive oil), and red meat (especially hamburger). The researchers also found a decreased risk correlated with greater consumption of fruits.[77]

Weight and Breast Cancer

Compared with their lean counterparts, obese women appear to have a higher incidence of postmenopausal breast cancer.[40] High caloric intake during childhood is associated with early puberty and consequently an increase in total lifetime estrogen exposure. In fat tissue, a precursor molecule may be converted into estrogen, raising estrogen exposure. Studies of young girls have found correlations among exercise, later menstruation, and changes in frequency of ovulation. (For more on this subject, see Chapter 12 on preventing endo.) Since late onset of menstruation has been identified as a protective factor related to breast cancer, Dr. Love notes that this is a significant finding. However, she also notes that other studies discount obesity at a young age as a contributing factor to breast cancer risk. Some researchers even report that being lean at a young age can be a risk factor.[42] As usual, only more research will resolve the issue.

Vitamins in Our Diet

Another issue is vitamins as cancer protectors. Researchers from the Center for Cancer Causation and Prevention, AMC Cancer Research Center in Denver, Colorado, hypothesized in an editorial in *Nutrition* that insufficient consumption of vitamin A during adolescence, when young girls' breasts are developing, may put girls at greater lifelong risk for cancer. The researchers point to epidemiological studies (the study of health and disease in populations; in this case the widely known Nurse's Health Study) to suggest that when women with the lowest intake of vitamin A from food were given a vitamin A supplement, their incidence of breast cancer was reduced.[78]

Beta-carotene, found in yellow and dark green vegetables, is also believed to fight cancer by neutralizing "free radicals," which can attack cells and cause cancer. Beta-carotene also increases the number of natural killer cells and T-helper cells, which help direct immune response.[79]

Other researchers report more new findings regarding breast cancer and the protective value of vitamin D, a nutrient made by the skin when it is exposed to sunlight. According to their report, vitamin D (also found in fish oil, egg yolk, and liver) may lower breast cancer risk 30 percent to 40 percent or more.[80] They say that as little as ten to fifteen minutes of sunlight daily, without sunscreen, could be enough to generate this protective effect. Other research would seem to support this theory.[81-83] This same study looked at the therapeutic use of vitamin D compounds in treating breast cancer and found they may induce apoptosis ("cell suicide," which causes a genetically

Roberta's Story: Cancerous Transformation of Endometriosis

"Endometriosis. What's that? Are we talking cancer here, or what?" Roberta Innarella of New Jersey remembers asking when she was diagnosed in 1978 at age twenty-seven. Her doctor reassured her that endo was not cancer, and in fact cancer was something that she did not have to worry about. So Roberta describes the results of the 1997 endo surgery that found a malignant transformation of an endometrioma (cyst) into endometrial carcinoma as "a shock."

Roberta's history of surgeries and hormone treatment will sound familiar to anyone with endo. Until she began reading about the disease, she had considered the pain, cramping, and diarrhea that accompanied her periods since she was a teenager as normal. "Didn't everyone have that?" Then came that first surgery (a chocolate cyst had ruptured, and she was full of scar tissue and adhesions). Her left ovary and fallopian tube were removed, and she recalls the doctor telling her the best thing she could do for herself was to get pregnant. When she finally did attempt to conceive, she had no problems.

Roberta switched doctors and some years later began to have abnormal bleeding, which she attributed to an IUD. The doctor told her he didn't think the IUD was her problem. Roberta had no intention of having more children and asked him not to "patch her up," depending upon what he found. Surgery uncovered endo on her uterus. Her right side (ovary and tube) had migrated behind the uterus and stuck to the left side. A hysterectomy was performed (the remaining ovary, tube, and uterus removed). Roberta was given estrogen shots in recovery and started on a combined estrogen/progesterone treatment, which she followed for eight years with no problems. The estrogen dosage was 1.25 milligrams. She cannot remember the progesterone dosage, and since she didn't have a uterus, the progesterone was discontinued after two months.

In 1994 Roberta reported pain during a manual exam that was part of her annual checkup. An ultrasound was done. Finally, an endometrioma on the left side of the bowel, where the left ovary had stuck, was removed and a bowel resection performed. Three months later, Roberta resumed estrogen at half the previous dosage.

By early 1995, her symptoms were back. "I waited a while," said Roberta. "I wondered, 'Is this just in my head?'" When the pain got too bad, she called her doctor, who told her not even to come into the office, but go directly to the hospital. Something was there, and Roberta was referred to a colorectal surgeon. There were more tests, and she was taken off of estrogen as the doctors debated whether the problem was the intestine wrapped around itself, adhesions, or another endometrioma. They put her back on estrogen and continued to monitor the situation with ultrasound, once a month for three months, then every three months.

By fall 1997, even as she followed the doctors' directions, things got worse, and Roberta complained louder. "They asked me if it was interfering with my lifestyle," she said. "I told them, 'I almost passed out at work the other day.' So surgery was performed. I came close to a colostomy. They removed eight inches of the large intestine, part of the rectum, and part of the vaginal cuff." The surgeon also reported that he took care of some endo on the bowel and told Roberta he never wanted her on estrogen again. "Never, ever!" Then came the biopsy and the cancer discovery.

Although she understands the reluctance to do unnecessary surgery, now Roberta wonders why it took three years for this last operation. She wonders if surgery a year earlier would have taken care of the problem before malignant transformation of the endo (which she had no idea was even possible) had occurred.

According to Roberta, her family has autoimmune problems "big-time." Her niece has had two endo surgeries, but until recently, there was no cancer in her family. Not long ago, both her father and brother had precancerous lesions removed from their noses. Her mother had developed a lymphoma in her stomach. A nephew had a cancerous growth removed from his lung.

Roberta continues to smoke, even as she reads more about natural health and nutrition. She's thinking of seeing a nutritionist and has included various anticancer supplements in her diet. She exercises, as she did before, and continues to work full-time. She suffers side effects from the radiation treatments that followed the surgery; as well as some vaginal dryness. She takes progesterone and Megace (intended to keep more cells from becoming cancerous).

"When they say cancer, they say five years," she explains. When she asked about her case being discharged, she was told, "After five years we lose track of you." Roberta remembers when women were told having a baby would cure endo, when having a hysterectomy would cure endo. "You put your faith in them [doctors]." When she received the good news that there was no cancer at her last check, Roberta was a bit more cautious. "And now you have x-ray vision," she responded.

damaged cell to destroy itself) in aggressive, late-stage tumors that appear to be estrogen independent.[80]

Environmental Carcinogens, Cancer, and Endo

In his book *The Politics of Cancer*, Samuel Epstein, M.D., proposes that the spectrum of diseases we know as cancer may have common features and related causes. In attempting to explain the last century's dramatic increase in cancer death rates, Epstein believes evidence points to neither genetic changes in the population nor aging. Instead, he says, epidemiological studies implicate environmental factors for 70 to 90 percent of all cancers. Epstein claims, "Informed consensus has gradually developed that most cancer is environmental in origin and is therefore preventable.[29] His book includes an informative discussion of carcinogens in the environment, including a list of the substances regulated as recognized carcinogens and suggestions for eliminating them from the environment. He also suggests how to limit your own exposure to a wide range of carcinogens in food additives, pesticides, cosmetics, and other sources.

A discussion of chemical carcinogens in R. Grant Steen's book *A Conspiracy of Cells: The Basic Science of Cancer* reminds us that the "informed consensus" Epstein envisioned is still under debate. Steen argues that eliminating carcinogens from the environment is probably impractical. He notes that stable, indirect-acting chemical carcinogens can exist in the environment for long periods. At some point they can be activated and become carcinogenic; this activation depends upon the individual's makeup, including sex, age, diet, and genetics. He does not appear overly concerned about carcinogens in the environment and suggests that if they raise cancer death rates by less than one in a million, the risk to society is acceptable.[40]

A study appearing in *The New England Journal of Medicine* argues against exposure to DDT and PCBs increasing the risk of breast cancer. While suggesting that there are many good environmental reasons to avoid release of DDT and PCBs, the study authors do not believe prevention of breast cancer is one of them.[84]

The researchers measured the plasma levels of DDE (a by-product of DDT) and PCBs among 240 women who gave blood samples in 1989 and 1990 and subsequently developed breast cancer. The median age of the women studied was fifty-nine (in a range of forty-three to sixty-nine). Each patient was matched with a control (by year of birth, menopausal status at time of blood sample, and so on) who did not develop cancer. The researchers found no evidence of a positive association between high levels of plasma DDE or PCBs and a risk of breast cancer.

However, they did note that DDE and PCBs are highly lipophilic—meaning they have an affinity for fats, don't break down, and undergo lifelong sequestration in human fat tissue. They are among the most stable biologic markers of exposure known. (Thus, studies based on *blood* samples may not reflect true risks; fat samples may be necessary.) The researchers note that epidemiologic data regarding a possible relation of organochlorines with breast cancer are limited.

The researchers did not rule out prebirth or childhood exposure to DDT and PCBs as an increased risk. However, they pointed out that these chemicals were introduced into the environment in the 1940s and 1950s. Thus, early exposure to them cannot explain the increased incidence of breast cancer in their study, which was greatest in postmenopausal women who would have been adults by the time those compounds were most widely used.

While this study found no association between breast cancer risk and exposure to DDE and PCBs, the report refused to rule out other pesticides or environmental contaminants in association with breast cancer.[84] Other experts note that this study doesn't definitely rule out DDE or PCBs either. In other words, more research is needed.

In 1994, the U.S. President's Cancer Panel again heard increasingly from critics (including Epstein) that as cancer is becoming more common, a search for unknown environmental factors should be undertaken. A former director of the National Institute of Environmental Health Sciences, David P. Rall, M.D., Ph.D., suggested a need for better data on levels of pollutants. He argued that most of the chemicals people are exposed to have either been inadequately tested or not tested at all.[85]

Figures gathered in response to the Emergency Planning and Community Right-to-Know Act (EPCRA), passed by the U.S. Congress in 1986, put the environmental pollution problem in perspective. The data for southeast Chicago, one of the most heavily contaminated areas in the country, indicated that releases or transfers into that area's air, water, or land in 1993 included 11,337,550 pounds of carcinogens, 43,439,901 pounds of developmental toxins, 441,503 pounds of genetic toxins, and 76,332,085 pounds of chronic toxins (those which can cause adverse effects, other than cancer, after long-term exposure, such as damage to the kidney, lungs, or liver).[86]

In his 1993 paper, "Environmental Pollutants as Unrecognized Causes of Breast Cancer," Epstein called attention to atrazine, one of the most heavily used herbicides in the world. This chlorinated herbicide has been identified as one of the most common carcinogenic pollutants in European and U.S. lakes and rivers. It exerts a hormonal effect on the hypothalamic-pituitary-gonadal axis. In lab studies, atrazine has induced both breast and reproductive tumors in rats and has been incriminated in human ovarian cancers and those of the lymphatic and hematopoietic (blood-forming) systems, such as non-Hodgkin's lymphoma. Epstein also points out that living near hazardous-waste sites has been associated with major increased risks of breast and other cancers.[87]

Ovarian Plus Gynecologic Cancer Prevention Quarterly noted in 1994 that stories about carcinogens like atrazine were conspicuously absent from general U.S. media reports. It pointed to a 1989 article in the *Scandinavian Journal of Work, Environment, and Health*, which carried news of an Italian study showing that women exposed to triazine herbicides, such as atrazine, demonstrated a two- to threefold risk of epithelial ovarian cancer as compared with unexposed women.[88]

A study appearing in *Science* raised another red flag for women with endo. In examining environmental factors as causes of cancer, the researchers noted that, dose for

Barb's Story: Non-Hodgkin's Lymphoma

Barb of Illinois had read that if you have a lump for three months that doesn't go away, it should be biopsied, but it took two years before she could find a doctor who would do a biopsy. He identified a non-Hodgkin's lymphoma in her pelvis.

"They told me that I was a nervous woman," she recalled, when she raised questions about the small growth that was found incidentally while checking for adenomyosis with an MRI scan. Although the lump continued to grow, she said a series of doctors would do nothing. "By the end, you could see it; it showed through my bathing suit. It was unbelievable and scary."

Barb describes two years of very low energy. "They didn't get the fact that I was feeling very, very sick. They diagnosed me with MS and other things."

"It's a good thing that I had the endo experience," she recalls. "I had been told that there was nothing wrong with me so many times [with the endo], I wouldn't believe it. The scenario [for identifying the cancer] was exactly the same as I'd been going through for twenty years [with endo]."

Having seen several well-respected physicians, Barb says she has lost faith in the medical community. Diagnosed with endo at twenty-one, Barb has two sisters who also have endo. She had a hysterectomy in 1995 (for adenomyosis). She says the radiation used to treat her lymphoma destroyed her ovaries, and when they started growing large cysts, she had them removed as well. At forty, she is now taking hormone replacement and feeling better.

While not specifically non-Hodgkin's lymphoma, there is a strong history of cancer on Barb's father's side of the family (including her father, her brother, four uncles, and four cousins who have died of cancer), so she was aware of her own increased risk.

"There are some positive things going on," Barb adds. Her lymphoma, although incurable, was caught at a localized stage, and there has been no sign of disease for two years. Her blood counts are perfect, her strength and endurance are good, and she is feeling healthy. "We have to wait and see where it pops up next," she says. She hopes that by the time that happens, better, more effective ways to treat non-Hodgkin's lymphoma will have been developed. In the meantime, she encourages her two healthy, athletic daughters, who have not yet started their periods, and hopes they will not have to go through what she has.

What would she recommend to other women with endo who may not be feeling well and suspect something more serious could be wrong? "Trust your gut. If you think it's wrong, it's wrong."

dose, women are inherently more susceptible to certain carcinogens than men. In addition, immune problems, preexisting disease, and nutritional deficiencies can increase a person's susceptibility to carcinogens.[89]

Dioxin

A chemical of extreme concern, for both cancer and endo, is the organochlorine dioxin, described as the most potent carcinogen ever tested. For a fuller discussion of dioxin, including reports of research linking it to endo and discussions of ways to minimize your exposure, check *The Endometriosis Sourcebook* and two other chapters in this book: Chapter 12, "Preventing Endometriosis: It May Be Possible!" and the article "Why Endometriosis Is an Environmental Issue" in Chapter 14.

Dioxin is an unintended chemical by-product of industrial processes that involve chlorine and processes that burn chlorine with organic matter. Acting as a key or switch for certain genes, dioxin can cause genetic damage that results in cell proliferation, mutations, or cancer.[90] In the preface to her book *Dying from Dioxin*, Lois Marie Gibbs explains that dioxin is so prevalent in the environment that even if you do not live near an obvious source of contamination, you cannot avoid exposure. She notes that largely through diet, average people—men, women, boys, and girls—accumulate levels of dioxin significant enough to damage their health.

The challenge, of course, is establishing a link between dioxin and cancer. Dioxin-contaminated Agent Orange was used as a defoliant during the Vietnam War. With veterans reporting a variety of health problems, including their own cancers and birth defects in their children, several studies, surrounded by much controversy, examined the health of Vietnam veterans following the war (and continue to do so). These included a U.S. Centers for Disease Control and Prevention (CDC) "selected cancers" study and a Department of Veteran Affairs (VA) study that looked specifically at Vietnam vets and non-Hodgkin's lymphoma (NHL). The selected-cancers study noted a 50 percent higher incidence of non-Hodgkin's lymphoma in vets, which may have been connected to dioxin exposure.[91]

In contrast, the VA study did not find a higher incidence of non-Hodgkin's lymphoma in Vietnam veterans. The researchers noted that their results were at odds with other studies[92] linking NHL and occupational (largely agricultural) exposure to phenoxy herbicides. They attributed that to the fact that the men in their study were younger than those in other studies, and the follow-up period may have been too short for NHL to develop.

One of the occupational studies that the VA study referenced found a sixfold increased risk of NHL in farmers exposed to phenoxy acetic acid herbicides (2,4-D) more than twenty days per year. Researchers suggested that the herbicide-NHL connection was plausible because dioxin is a potent animal carcinogen that appears to harm the immune system.[93]

Marilyn Fingerhut and her colleagues at the U.S. National Institute for Occupational Safety and Health (NIOSH) spent thirteen years examining the effects of on-the-job exposure to dioxin among 5,172 men working in the chemical industry in twelve U.S. plants. The workers studied were divided into a high-exposure group (one year or more of potential daily exposure) and a low-exposure group (less than a year).[94] An article in *Science* following publication of the study noted that the men in the "low" exposure group were exposed to dioxin levels 90 times higher than that to which the general population is exposed. The high-exposure group received doses an estimated 500 times higher.[95]

The NIOSH researchers noted cancer deaths were significantly greater than expected among high-exposure workers with twenty years or more of latency (see Glossary). They also noted this group had a 46 percent increase in all cancers combined and a 42 percent increase in respiratory cancers. They were surprised to find a small but significant increase in deaths from all cancers—15 percent higher—among both high- and low-exposure groups. The researchers concluded that their findings supported a causative link between exposure to dioxin and development of cancer.[94]

Another interesting study on dioxin looked at the effect of exposure during pregnancy on breast cancer. Pregnant rats were exposed to small amounts of dioxin on the fifteenth day of pregnancy in this study done in England. When the female offspring were seven weeks old, their mammary glands had developed an unusually high number of "terminal end buds," which are the places where breast cancers develop. (Four studies have found a correlation between the number of terminal end buds and susceptibility to breast cancer.) When the young rats and a control group of rats were exposed to a known carcinogen, the rats that had been exposed to dioxin before birth developed many more breast cancers.[96]

Dioxin may be responsible for 12 percent of the cancers in industrialized countries, according to a study by German scientists.[97] (That would be 120,000 cancers each year in the United States, as calculated by *Rachel's Environmental and Health Weekly News*.[98])

A large study looked at cancer mortality in a historical cohort study of 21,900 men and women in thirty-six groups exposed to phenoxy herbicides, chlorophenols, and dioxins in twelve countries. In a subgroup of 13,800 workers exposed to phenoxy herbicides contaminated with dioxin, there was a statistically significant number of deaths from all neoplasms. All deaths occurred ten years or more after first exposure. Death from non-Hodgkin's lymphoma was slightly higher than expected and increased with time from first exposure. Surprisingly, the highest risk was seen in workers with less than one year of exposure.[99]

Cause-and-Effect Links

The 1993 Greenpeace report "Chlorine: Human Health and the Environment" was endorsed by a panel of distinguished scientists in Canada and the United States as "an excellent public presentation of the growing body of evidence that links low-level organochlorine contamination of the environment to the risk of breast cancer in women." The report suggests a new standard of "proof" to replace the old "evidence beyond a doubt of a cause-effect link between individual chemicals and disease." Although the report acknowledges that not every organochlorine contributes to cancer, it argues that many that don't cause cancer have other harmful effects on people and wildlife. It also proposes that the "Precautionary Principle"—that public and private interests should act to *prevent* harm—be the basis for evaluating scientific information and forming public policy. This would place the burden of proof on polluters. As it now stands, rather than polluters being forced to prove a chemical is harmless, the public must prove that the chemical causes harm. (For more discussion of the Precautionary Principle, see Chapter 14.)

Self-interest further complicates risk assessment and efforts to pinpoint cancer causes. As far back as 1964, the World Health Organization concluded that environmental influences could be responsible for as much as 80 percent of all cancer, a suggestion that remains controversial.

A Harvard Center for Cancer Prevention study attributed only 2 percent of all U.S. cancer deaths to "environmental pollution" (air pollution and hormonally active organochlorines). A critique of this work points out that the study downplays "environmental" risk in part by how it defines pollution. The author says that adding what the study describes as "additional" environmental factors alone (occupational exposure, radiation, food additives, and contaminants) could raise the 2 percent figure to 10 percent. The Harvard study also fails to address synergies between immune systems damaged by environmental pollutants and the estrogenic chemicals we now consume in our food.[100]

Those who doubt the results of the Harvard study note that major donors to the Harvard School of Public Health (the parent organization for the Center for Cancer Prevention) include chemical manufacturers such as DuPont, Dow, Monsanto, Union Carbide, Procter and Gamble, Novartis, and Eastman Chemical.[100] A spokesperson for the Harvard School of Public Health confirmed that these companies are donors to the school. In responding to the suggested conflict of interest, however, he said that donations from these companies do not go directly or indirectly to the Center for Cancer Prevention and would not have given these companies influence over the center or the study.[101]

Cancer Prevention

Given the conflicting evidence and opinion, what can individuals do to reduce their cancer risks? In *Cancer and Vitamin C*, Ewan Cameron and Linus Pauling, Ph.D., discuss the importance of nutritional and environmental factors in causing cancer. They blame what they label a cancer pandemic on our long exposure to an intense bombardment of carcinogens from an increasingly polluted environment. They believe that the damage done by a single weakly carcinogenic additive or environmental chemical may be small, but their combined effects extremely harmful. The book documents their numerous clinical trials that involved supplementing cancer patients (many in the final stages of disease) with high doses of vitamin C. At a minimum, they report improved quality of life for patients with the most advanced cases, improved survival for many patients, and complete remission for some.

By way of cancer prevention, they advocate first reducing carcinogens in the environment and second adopting measures to render humans more resistant to cancer. They recommend supporting government efforts to identify carcinogens and ban them. And—you've heard it before—they also recommend a diet with a minimum of 250 milligrams of vitamin C daily. They note that most people may need as much as 1 to 10 grams (1,000 to 10,000 milligrams) for the best health. They also advocate adequate intake of vitamins A and E, the B vitamins, and minerals. The antioxidants in particular (vitamins C, A, E, and others) are directly involved in preventing cells in the body from becoming cancerous. So mother did know best—eat your fruits and vegetables!

The suggested diet includes green, yellow, and red vegetables and low sugar intake. Their suggested daily regime includes eating breakfast, not eating between meals, and not overeating. (Women with endo who are hypoglycemic should, of course, eat small amounts of food more frequently in light of their special needs.) They suggest avoidance of foods and soft drinks that may contain carcinogenic dyes and other additives, moderate alcohol intake, an absolute ban on smoking, regular daily exercise, and seven to eight hours of sleep each night.[2]

Neutralizing Your Breast Cancer Risk

The second edition of *Dr. Susan Love's Breast Book* informs readers that not enough was known about prevention when the first edition was published to create a separate prevention chapter. Signaling progress, the 1995 edition does contain a chapter that discusses risk factors and prevention. The chapter advises women to reduce fat in the diet, obesity, and use of estrogens at menopause. It also suggests that women who intend to have children shift back to giving birth for the first time at an earlier age.

One "prevention" approach that has received much press is the drug tamoxifen. Evidence had suggested tamoxifen may prevent breast cancer. A study was undertaken, even though this synthetic antiestrogen was known to cause cancers of the liver and endometrium. Critics of the approach have asked how it can make sense to take a drug to prevent one cancer while risking others. Defenders of the tamoxifen study proceeded in the hope that in the long term, the drug would prevent more disease than it caused.[85] Women with endo should note that tamoxifen can also contribute to the growth and development of endometriosis, so is not appropriate for us.[46]

By how much could breast cancer be reduced if women were able to alter their exposure to specific risks, such as a high-fat diet? The text *Breast Diseases* suggests that it's unlikely women could alter exposure to all the factors believed to contribute to breast cancer, particularly those that are hormonally related. However, using numerous studies, the authors determined the percentage of risk attributable to various environmental and lifestyle factors:[102]

- High-fat diet: 26 percent
- Age twenty-five or older at first birth: 17 percent
- Obesity: 12 percent
- Estrogen replacement therapy: 8 percent

Of course, some women living with endo must grapple with infertility, which raises a serious question about an individual's ability to "control" that particular cancer risk. And even if we could, the decision whether to have children is a life choice, not a disease preventative. Most recently, we must factor into the decision to bear children our knowledge that we pass chemicals like dioxin and PCBs as well as medications into our children during pregnancy and breastfeeding.[105] In addition, there is increasing concern over the environmental impact of an ever-growing human population worldwide, now at six billion.

Another study reported that women in their reproductive years who participated in four or more hours of exercise each week demonstrated a decreased breast cancer risk. The effectiveness of exercise in preventing breast cancer for women has not been fully studied, although it is anticipated such a program would help women beyond their reproductive years, as well.[103]

Any woman could benefit from cutting back on consumption of animal fats and eating a low-fat diet overall. This may be especially important for teen and preteen daughters. Evidence suggests much of the damage that increases risk may occur early in life.

The Breast Book speculates that rather than the food, the cause of cancer may be the hormones, pesticides, and other carcinogens that we consume along with our food. This includes hormones in beef, mercury in fish, and the pesticides sprayed on our vegetables.[42] Even grains are treated with strong pesticides to protect against weevils and fungal damage.[104] In his newsletter, *Natural Health*, Andrew Weil, M.D., notes that the residues of estrogenic hormones given to animals to promote growth often remain in our meat, poultry, and dairy products as xenoestrogens. A good deal of information is available, even in the popular press, about ways to decrease the risk of these exposures. These suggestions include eating less red meat, washing fruits and vegetables more thoroughly, buying organic produce, and adopting a more vegetarian diet.

Breastfeeding results in a reduction of the toxins stored in the fat in the breast, but it's certainly a matter of grave concern to know these toxins are going directly into the baby. The 1991 Institute of Medicine report "Nutrition During Lactation" recommends against breastfeeding if the woman has experienced heavy exposure to pesticides, heavy metals, or other contaminants.[106] Because the concentration of dioxin in breast milk decreases as it is eliminated through nursing, another option for nursing moth-

Kathryn's Story: Melanoma

Like many women with endo, Kathryn Fitzner of Georgia had suffered endo symptoms since she was a teenager but was not diagnosed until she was in her late twenties. Also like many women with endo, she had difficulty getting pregnant and a history of surgeries (twelve or thirteen, she estimates), including removal of an ovary.

In 1992, while recovering from a laparotomy, she developed what she thought would prove to be endo in her nose. "I noticed this cyst in my right nostril, and the doctor gave me cortisone injections, but it didn't clear up. I had heard in my support group about women having endo on nerves, and I just knew that that was what they were going to find." But it wasn't endo, it was cancer—spindle cell melanoma.

Kathryn says there is no history of cancer in her family, but there is red hair. Her own hair is blond, and she has hazel eyes. "I don't have freckles, but I sunburn and am prone to have spots," she explains.

She took note of the Association article on red hair and melanoma. And, searching her mind for causes of the cancer, she remembers spending childhood summers on the beach in Savannah, Georgia, blistering once or twice and then getting really dark. She also remembers the paper mills, which were giving off dioxin, within fifteen miles of where she played. "The smell was so awful," she recalls. "I know I was exposed to that kind of poison."

Her right nostril and part of her face had to be removed to her ear; a skin graft was done, then she underwent a cheek implant and five surgeries to rebuild her nose. Kathryn says she was able to get disability benefits when she had the cancer, but not with the endo. "And the endo was more disabling, more chronic," she says. She received no radiation or chemotherapy, and six years past the diagnosis is doing well. "I was so tuned into my body, I think I just caught this [the cancer] in time, because of the endo," she says.

She thinks the possibility of cancer is something everyone has to be aware of. Kathryn describes endo as "one step away" from cancer because of the way it behaves in the body. "I would love to see the numbers on [women who have endo] and cancer."

ers is to pump and discard milk between feedings. Not only will the baby be getting somewhat safer breast milk, but the mother will also be lessening her own dioxin stores. Gibbs, in *Dying From Dioxin*, cites one study in which the dioxin level in the milk of a mother exposed at her workplace dropped from 14 parts per million at the start of nursing to 4 parts per million one year later.[90] For additional, important ideas on this topic, see Chapter 12, "Preventing Endometriosis: It May Be Possible!"

Melanoma Risk

A word about melanoma: *New Age* magazine reported a warning from researchers who addressed the American Association for the Advancement of Science. While sunscreens offer sunburn protection, they do not prevent melanoma. Keep in mind that the biggest risk factors for melanoma are fair skin, blond or reddish hair, and a tendency to develop moles. Your best protection is to avoid sun exposure beyond a few minutes a day. When you're out in the sun, wear protective clothing.

Reducing Ovarian Cancer Risk

Awareness of the increased risk of ovarian cancer in women with endo changes the approach to treatment for ovarian endo. If you find your practitioners unprepared for questions on this topic, help them by sharing the Brinton and Vercellini studies (contact the Association for free copies) and this chapter. Because our field has been dominated by fertility experts, whose focus is pregnancy and conservation of ovarian tissue, that orientation has shaped endo treatment for many years. A shift toward treatment based on the long-term health of the woman herself, as well as any offspring she may have, will take many years.

Farr Nezhat, M.D., is a well-known endo surgeon and gynecologic oncologist in New York City. He is also the only gyn oncologist specializing in both endo and cancer. Nezhat recommends that if a cyst persists for two to three menstrual cycles, then it must be biopsied. In fact, every persistent cyst should be biopsied, he notes, and (except for a functional cyst) has to be completely removed. Dr. Nezhat says if a woman with endo has a tendency to form cysts, he and his brothers Drs. Camran Nezhat, in Palo Alto, California, and Ceana Nezhat, in Atlanta, Georgia, recommend regular exams and oral contraceptives to suppress cyst formation. He notes that women who've taken oral contraceptives are at less risk for ovarian cancer; fewer cysts are formed when women take oral contraceptives.

Another important protective measure for women with endo is to discuss with your surgeon ways to prevent cells from spilling into the abdomen any time an ovarian cyst is to be removed. Dan C. Martin, M.D., reports on three medical papers showing significant ill effects when ovarian cancer is spilled at laparoscopy.[107–109] To minimize the risk of spill in case a cyst turns out to be cancerous, Martin suggests bagging (in which the cyst to be removed is secured in a bag with alis clamps or temporary sutures to maintain an airtight seal at both laparoscopy and laparotomy). He believes this approach is prudent, even if the risk of opening an ovarian cancer while treating endo is small.[46]

Ceil Sinnex, founder and president of the *Ovarian Plus International Gynecologic Cancer Prevention Quarterly*, stresses, "If a woman ever receives a recommendation for gynecologic surgery and there is a suspicion it is cancer, she should insist on getting a referral to a gynecologic oncologist." Given the difficulties of recognizing and removing endo, an endo expert surgeon and a gyn oncologist together may be best able to handle such a situation.

Daniel Tsin, M.D., Mt. Sinai Hospital of Queens, Astoria, New York, treats many women with endo. He is concerned that we lose valuable opportunities to identify ovarian cancer in its early, most treatable stages when the possibility of malignancy is not explored during endo laparoscopy and laparotomy. These opportunities are lost because physicians and patients are not thinking of endo and cancer. According to Tsin, clinical evidence shows that 80 percent of malignant transformations of endo occur in the ovary.[110]

Speaking at the World Congress of Gynecologic Endoscopy in 1997, Tsin told his peers, "Endometriosis is a multifactorial disease of more than one entity, until better understanding of the pathogenesis is acquired. We should consider all factors during the decision making process for the treatment of severe endometriosis, including the rare but dangerous factor of malignant transformation."

With malignant potential in mind, Dr. Tsin suggests that women older than forty past childbearing with severe endo of the ovaries and a family history of ovarian cancer have their ovaries and as much endo as possible removed. (Some endo experts argue that as much endo as possible should be removed in all women with endo.) In women younger than forty, he suggests a microscopic diagnosis during surgery be done.

Well aware that most patients prefer the most conservative treatment possible and that definitions of *conservative* may vary, Tsin advocates removal rather than just destruction of endo cysts in order to preserve tissue, which can then be checked for cancer. When cysts are removed, the walls as well as the contents must be examined. "Two-thirds of the ovarian cancer found is beyond cure," according to Tsin. "Here we have a great opportunity to diagnose early, why are we going to lose it?"[111]

Tsin therefore recommends that all women having surgery for endo cysts make sure that the cysts are tested for cancer—even if cancer is not suspected. "Since endo may have a malignant potential," says Tsin, "the microscopic evaluation must rule out cancer in all cases." Be sure to tell your surgeon before surgery that you wish to have a biopsy (frozen section) performed if you have an endo cyst.

If cancer cells exist in the ovaries—even if no symptoms of ovarian cancer have appeared—removing the ovaries does not totally rule out the chance that ovarian cancer will develop in later years. Cancerous cells could have metastasized to other parts of the body, causing ovarian cancer to develop even after the ovaries have been removed. But the chance of this happening is quite small; one study says 1.8 percent.[111]

Reduced ovarian cancer risk is associated with an increased number of pregnancies, deliveries, use of oral contraceptives, tubal ligation, and longer duration of breastfeeding (all associated with lack of ovulation). Hysterectomy also decreases the general risk of ovarian cancer—in this case, by half. This is good news for women with ovarian endo, although it further complicates decisions about treatment.[46] The National Women's Health Network information packet "Ovarian Cancer/Ovarian Cysts," the Gilda Radner Familial Ovarian Cancer Registry, and other sources recommend preventive removal of the ovaries for high-risk women (women who have two or more close relatives—sisters or mother—with a history of ovarian cancer) who have reached the age of thirty-five or have completed childbearing.[58] For those under thirty-five with a family history, Dr. Farr Nezhat suggests oral contraceptives.

Women at special risk should alert their doctors about their risks when undergoing checkups. Those at special risk include women with a family history; who are age fifty-two to fifty-nine; with endo or a history of menstrual problems; with physician-diagnosed infertility; who have never had children; or who have previously had breast, rectal, or intestinal cancer.[49] High cholesterol levels also are a risk; a study found that women with high cholesterol levels are more than three times as likely to get ovarian cancer as those with the lowest levels.[112]

To date, there are no simple, reliable screening tests for ovarian cancer, although screening for the CA-125 antigen following an abnormal ultrasound improves diagnosis. These tests are likely to be positive when a woman has metastatic disease. However, since CA-125 is typically elevated in endo (possibly another hint of the relation between endo and cancer, rather than mere coincidence), its value for screening for ovarian cancer in women with endo may be very limited. An article in *The Female Patient* suggests that CA-125, vaginal ultrasound, and a properly done pelvic exam together can be very sensitive to ovarian cancer.[113] (For more on the subject, see "Demand a Thorough Pelvic Exam," later in this chapter in the discussion of cancer prevention methods.)

In 1998, the British medical journal *The Lancet* published research findings from Boston's Brigham and Women's Hospital reporting that women who use acetaminophen as a painkiller appear to cut their ovarian cancer risk in half. Because this is the first study of its kind, more research will be undertaken. Use of the painkiller, which is believed to depress ovary-stimulating hormones, is not currently recommended specifically for this purpose. Another study of women regularly using acetaminophen for menstrual pain indicates that those women have lower levels of gonadotropin and estradiol than those using other pain medications or no medications, factors associated with lower risk of ovarian cancer.[114]

Genetic Testing

Genetic testing for cancer is becoming increasingly available. Women in whom the BRCA-1 and BRCA-2 mutations are found have a greatly increased chance of developing ovarian and breast cancer. BRCA-1 and BRCA-2 are most commonly found in women of Ashkenazi (Eastern European) Jewish ancestry, as well as women from Iceland. These women may want to consider genetic testing.

If you are seriously considering this step (insurance does not usually cover the cost, which ranges from $250 to $2,000, depending on the extent of the tests), weigh the potential value of any results carefully. Remember that cancer is not a single disease. In low-risk families, carefully researching your family health history and more carefully monitoring any suspicious changes in your own health may prove just as useful as genetic tests in protecting you from further illness. In high-risk families, these tests may well save lives.

Over the years the Association has been saddened by the news of members who have died of cancers. They have often been young women, and their cancers seemed wholly unlikely given their ages, their personal histories, and what is known about these cancers. There have always been nagging questions: Are these cancers just coincidence? Would these women have developed them even if they didn't have endo? At the very least, the studies by Brinton, Vercellini, Hornstein, the Association, and others should raise this important issue.

Perhaps it is time to become better informed, to compile a family health history, to change your diet or your lifestyle, to become personally or politically active regarding cancer risks that concern you and your community. Perhaps, in a roundabout way, having endo can even benefit us because we are already aware of our bodies and committed to our health. As Kathryn Fitzner, who was diagnosed with melanoma, says, "I was so tuned into my body, I think I just caught this [cancer] in time, because of the endo."

The Potential of Cancer Prevention

No one knows better than a woman living with endo that good health is not a "given." No one has a greater stake in our good health than we do. The more knowledgeable we become, the more we take responsibility for our own health and well-being, the better we'll do with our health, sometimes even being able to prevent health problems. The American Institute for Cancer Research estimates that dietary guidelines alone can achieve the following dramatic impact:

- Eating right, plus staying physically active and maintaining a healthy weight, can cut cancer risk by 30 to 40 percent.
- Recommended dietary choices, coupled with not smoking, have the potential to reduce cancer risk by 60 to 70 percent.
- A simple change, such as eating the recommended five servings of fruits and vegetables each day, could by itself reduce cancer rates more than 20 percent.
- As many as 375,000 cases of cancer, at current cancer rates, could be prevented each year in this nation through healthful dietary choices.

So here's a suggestion: Make a pact with an endo friend or set up a friendly competition in your support group to help each other make your diets more healthful by making certain changes, one by one, together. Keep records and see how you all do over a month or two with each change. Encourage each other. And let us know at the Association; we'd love to share your successes with others.

Things You Can Do to Decrease Your Cancer Risk

Based on what we do know about cancer and cancer prevention, we can suggest a number of measures women with endo can take to protect themselves.

Start Young

Throughout *The Breast Book*, Dr. Love refers to how a young woman may be more susceptible to carcinogens, whether the source is dietary fat or alcohol consumption, in the time between her first period and first pregnancy, when the breast has not yet gone through its complete hormonal development.[42] Eating to fuel our bodies with adequate protein, fiber, complex carbohydrates, and the essential micronutrients that promote normal tissue growth and keep us healthy will be important throughout life. Why not build a strong foundation when we are young, before (hopefully) any damage to our bodies is done? Women beyond that stage of life can't turn back the clock, but we can inform our daughters and other young women concerning their potential vulnerability.

Consume Less (or No) Alcohol

Various studies link alcohol consumption with breast cancer, although as with diet, the greatest damage may occur when we're young. Alcohol consumption appears to slightly increase cancer risk for all women, although the increase is not quite so dramatic for women already at high risk.[42]

Avoid Milk and Milk Products from Cows Given BGH

The study "Circulating Concentrations of Insulin-Like Growth Factor-1 and Risk of Breast Cancer," published in the prestigious medical journal *The Lancet*, links the growth factor with breast cancer. (This growth factor has also been linked to endo.) Premenopausal women fifty years or younger with the highest levels of IGF-1 in their blood appear to have a sevenfold increased breast cancer risk.[115]

Dairy cows injected with the genetically engineered bovine growth hormone produce milk with elevated levels of IGF-1, which is passed along to consumers. The body would naturally break this hormone down in the stomach, but casein, a protein present in the milk, prevents such breakdown.[116]

A commentary on the study, published in the same issue of *The Lancet*, suggests that work showing IGF-1 is critical for cell survival and maintenance of transformed cells may explain the cancer connection. Apoptosis ("cell suicide," which causes a genetically damaged cell to destroy itself) can be prevented by factors from outside the cell. IGF-1 appears to be one of the most abundant and potent of such factors. IGF-1 also promotes the growth of more cells and local tissue in our organs, promotes cell survival, and amplifies the action of hormones like gonadotropins.[117] Generally, natural food stores are a reliable source of milk produced without BGH. They also encourage consumers to learn about nutrition and the food they eat.

Alert Your Healthcare Providers to Your Family History and Risk

When you visit your general practitioner and other healthcare providers, be sure they know about your family history and risk as a woman with endo. Ask your healthcare providers to help you monitor your risks over time. They may be aware of new research or other studies that affect your risk for certain cancers.

Get to Know Your Body and What's "Normal" for You

Faithfully perform breast self-exam or feel your breasts throughout the month (as you shower or bathe), so that you know which lumps have been there for years and when something new has developed. With estimates that 90 percent of breast lumps are discovered first by patients, monthly breast self-exam is recommended as a convenient, no-cost way to detect most cancerous lumps at an early, treatable stage. *The Informed Woman's Guide to Breast Health: Breast Changes That Are Not Cancer* by Kerry Anne McGinn outlines a three-step approach to breast health, beginning with breast self-exam. Her book contains a thorough description (including illustrations) of breast self-exam. McGinn suggests that each exam include visual inspection for bulges, increased blood vessels, and dimpled or reddened areas; palpation of the entire breast, under the armpits, along the collarbone, and beneath the nipples; and reporting of any changes to a medical professional.

Even though breast cancer is rare in the very young, McGinn recommends starting breast self-exam early, so any suspect changes will be immediately obvious. She also recommends a professional breast exam every two to three years for women under forty, annually for women over forty. At a minimum she suggests this exam include a history of risk factors and past problems at your first visit, questioning about your current breast concerns, visual inspection under good light (both sitting and standing) with arms down and raised, and careful palpation of all breast tissue, including in the armpits, along the collarbone, and beneath the nipples.

In contrast, Dr. Love, in her book, is concerned that self-exam is too rigid and may make some women anxious and alienate them from their breasts. She suggests feeling your breasts (for example, in the shower) as part of getting comfortable with your body. She stresses that our breasts feel different throughout the month and that being well acquainted with them gives a woman an integrated sense of her own body. She also believes women get a sense of power from knowing what's normal for them and what's not and encourages women to be active in their own care. Her description of what you will feel as you examine your breasts is very helpful—and not at all scary![42]

Demand a Thorough Pelvic Exam

Similarly, a thorough bimanual pelvic exam is important in the early detection of ovarian tumors. As described by Ezra Greenspan, M.D., clinical professor of oncology at Mt. Sinai Hospital in New York City, such an exam (after the patient has eliminated all feces) would include the following:

- Simultaneous insertion by the physician of one finger in the vagina and another in the rectum. To the patient, it will feel as if the rectum is being stretched by the posterior finger. (According to Greenspan, "old-fashioned" exams through the vagina only may not be deep or high enough to rule out any abnormal pelvic mass.)
- During the exam, the top side of the abdomen must be felt with the flat side of the examiner's other hand.

When the records of 150 patients with tumors of the ovary or fallopian tubes were reviewed, a bimanual (using two hands) pelvic exam was found to have missed only 10 percent of tumors smaller than 10 centimeters in diameter.[118]

If at High Risk, Get a Transvaginal Ultrasound Screening

Dr. Piver, the Buffalo, New York, gynecologic oncologist, recommends an annual or semiannual screening with transvaginal ultrasonography for women with a family history of ovarian cancer and for those with suggestive symptoms like bloating, pelvic discomfort, abdominal expansion, and presence of a pelvic mass.[119] Women with endo experiencing such symptoms should seriously consider this type of screening. Many women with endo experience these symptoms with their cycles or due to allergies, especially food allergies. Either way, competent medical help is recommended.

Any type of pelvic mass must be explored. Even if you've had many prior endo cysts, you cannot just assume you have another cyst. We have lost members in this way, because they or their doctors thought they had another endo cyst, based on symptoms, so they delayed treatment. Only later did they find ovarian cancer leading to death.

Sleep in the Dark

Studies also seem to indicate that estrogen levels can be moderated (and breast cancer susceptibility therefore reduced) by resting at night in a sufficiently dark environment. As reported in *Science News*, bright lights are thought to curb the brain's production of melatonin, a regulator of estrogen production.[120] Ben Franklin's expression "Early to bed, early to rise makes a man healthy, wealthy, and wise" might not be just for men! (This may be a worthwhile suggestion for moderating the influence of estrogen in endo, too.)

Eliminate the Use of Talc

Don't use talc—for yourself or your children. If you want to use baby powder, cornstarch is considered a safe alternative.

Filter Your Shower Water

The Centers for Disease Control and Prevention called a conference in 1993 to examine environmental pollutants and the high incidence of breast cancer on Long Island.

Among the potential risks discussed was exposure to chlorine gases inhaled during hot showers. Taking cooler showers, running an exhaust fan, or cracking a window might help you control this potential source of chemical exposure.[42] Excellent shower filters that remove the chlorine are also available from sources such as the Seventh Generation catalog and others (see Resources at the back of the book). Decreasing chlorine levels in shower water also can reduce skin irritation for those with sensitive skin.

Don't Use Herbicides and Pesticides

Consider changing how you live, where you live, and what you eat, to avoid exposure to pollutants. Limit your exposure to pesticides and herbicides. Don't use them at home or work! There are many natural alternatives. Help educate your neighbors and your community about the dangers. Keep your children off and away from lawns and playgrounds where pesticides and herbicides have been used. (Isn't that a shame? Letting children be able to play and be healthy should be more important than how lawns look!) Be especially vigilant when you are pregnant.

When it comes to chemical and industrial pollutants like xenoestrogens, Dr. Weil, in *Natural Health* magazine, goes so far as to recommend that women with higher risks even consider moving away from badly contaminated localities. If that is not possible, he suggests limiting consumption of flesh foods from animals raised with hormones, filtering drinking water, and eating organic produce and soy-based foods, especially as alternative protein sources. Only by eating organic foods (or growing your own without pesticides and herbicides) can one avoid these chemicals in food, including the higher residues of pesticides that may occur in genetically engineered foods. (In the United States, genetically engineered foods do not have to be labeled, so one cannot avoid them except by eating certified organic foods.) Many processed foods also contain artificial colors and flavors that have been shown to cause cancer in animals.

Also, CancerOption.com suggests that people "minimize microwave heating of foods in soft plastic containers. The use of microwave heating with plastic containers can release [toxins] from the container or wrapping of the food. Some of these toxins are considered xenoestrogens."[121]

Drink Plenty of Purified Water

Water helps dilute and flush some toxins from our bodies, so be sure to drink the recommended six to eight twelve-ounce glasses daily. When you can, choose purified water, and drink from glass containers.

Breastfeeding: A Thorny Issue

Breastfeeding lowers your chemical exposure over time and reduces the level of toxins built up in the breast. However, these toxins do pass from you to your baby.

Limit Sun Exposure

Since sun exposure is a known risk factor for melanoma, avoid excessive exposure. Covering the skin and wearing hats is more effective than sunscreen, which does not protect against melanoma. In particular, take precautions to avoid sunburn. Remember to take these precautions for your children, too!

Exercise

Rose Frisch, Ph.D., of Harvard School of Public Health, found in a study of 5,400 female college graduates that those who had been athletes in college or trained regularly had about half the risk of developing breast cancer as nonathletes. Nonathletes also had higher rates of cancers of the uterus, ovary, cervix, and vagina.[122]

Limit Radiation Exposure

It is generally agreed that radiation exposure is a breast cancer risk, but it's not clear what this means for exposure related to our medical care. Since certain types of radiation have also been linked to endo in U.S. Air Force studies (see *The Endometriosis Sourcebook*), limiting radiation may deliver a double benefit. Susan Love, M.D., believes the value of diagnostic chest x-rays (to detect pneumonia, for example) and of mammograms far outweighs the danger of exposure to low-level radiation from up-to-date mammograms or necessary x-ray procedures.[42] In terms of breast x-rays (mammograms), *McGinn's Breast Health Guide* says there is no evidence that exposure to the low-dose radiation of mammography has ever caused cancer. At the same time, mammography can often detect a lump too small to feel, a stage at which, if cancerous, it can almost always be cured with minimal treatment.

The Complete Book of Cancer Prevention suggests avoiding routine x-ray screening unless the information provided will definitely affect your treatment or prognosis.[49] Radiation can cause the electrons in the exposed atoms to be ejected in the process of ionization and form free radicals. It can also interact with the cell nucleus to create protons or other charged particles. In either case, damage to cells results. For example, some women treated with radiation for inflammation of the breast following childbirth later developed breast cancer.[40]

Looking well beyond mammography, John W. Gofman, M.D., Ph.D., blames as much as 75 percent of current breast cancer on earlier radiation for a broad range of medical conditions. His book, *Preventing Breast Cancer: The Story of a Major, Proven, Preventable Cause of this Disease*, is a thorough discussion of the relationship between breast cancer and ionizing radiation from medical sources. Gofman builds a strong case for the role the "average" person has to play to eliminate what he argues is one of the most serious, preventable causes of breast cancer (for example, questioning suggested x-ray procedures and forming community watchdog organizations to make sure that radiation doses in facilities in your community are adequately measured).[123]

In 1997 a National Institutes of Health consensus panel released a controversial report that recommended insurance coverage of breast cancer screening for women in their forties but did not recommend routine screening for all women in their forties. The National Women's Health Network lauded this decision, saying the data does not support the need for screening for all women in their forties. The network also reminded women not to let the screening controversy dissuade them from getting mammograms when needed for diagnostic purposes (when there is a lump, change in breast appearance, or nipple discharge). The group further reminded women that even with screening, a thorough and careful clinical exam is critical, since mammograms can miss tumors. (Mammography misses 25 percent of the tumors in women under fifty years of age and 10 percent of those in women over fifty.)

The National Women's Health Network also recommended that women check to see that board-certified radiologists are reading their mammograms. The network pointed out that good screening is especially important for African-American women, who are diagnosed with breast cancer seven years younger, on average, than white women.[38]

As you weigh the potential benefits of mammography versus clinical exam for yourself, you may want to consider the findings of another recent study that looked at a group of women screened for breast cancer every two years over a ten-year period. The researchers found that one-third of these women had a false positive result that required additional evaluation (outpatient appointments, diagnostic mammograms, ultrasound exams, biopsies, and even a hospitalization) when no breast cancer was present. False positives were defined as mammograms or clinical exams that were interpreted as indeterminate (not definite), aroused suspicion of cancer, or prompted recommendations for further workup in women in whom breast cancer was not diagnosed within the next year. The study found that the more times you are screened, the more likely a false positive result is.[124] As in many things medical, there appears to be no single, always successful approach, which makes the need to be well-informed advocates for our own health all the more critical.

When Planning a Hysterectomy, Ask About Getting All the Endo Out

If having a hysterectomy (with or without removal of the ovaries, which may be followed by hormone replacement now or in the future), think through the importance of removing all the endo that's feasible to remove. Endo left behind can become cancerous; it's not clear at this time how often that happens. In other words, even when having a hysterectomy, a surgery that is performed by many gyns, you may still need an endo expert!

Some members of the Association have gone without hormone replacement for some months after hysterectomy and removal of the ovaries to give any residual endo time to quiet down (though it may never completely die out). Researchers who studied endo that transformed into cancer state, "Consideration must also be given to bilateral oophorectomy (removal of both ovaries) at the time of abdominal surgery in patients with significant endometriosis who are approaching the menopause, especially in those with ovarian endometriosis."[17]

Before Taking Hormone Replacement, Review All Your Options

Before menopause, a woman's ovaries produce three forms of estrogen—estradiol, estrone, and estriol—along with progesterone and testosterone. Many estrogen replacement preparations contain unopposed estradiol (not accompanied by the counterbalancing estrogens, estrone and estriol, or by testosterone and progesterone). Research has shown that an excess of estradiol may be a trigger for female cancers, as this hormone encourages cell growth. Mixtures of hormones tailored for your individual needs are now available; consult a physician specializing in natural hormone replacement. (For more on this topic, see Chapter 11, "Menopause and Endometriosis.")

In addition, if you've had a hysterectomy and removal of the ovaries and are taking estrogen, consider adding progesterone to counteract the continuous effect of estrogen on any endo that may have been left behind. Research indicates that progesterone may prevent or inhibit transformation of endometrial tissue into cancer. If you have candidiasis or have trouble tolerating progesterone, you may be allergic to it, as many women with endo are. An environmental medicine specialist can help desensitize you to it, if needed.

Some women with endo seem to tolerate bioidentical, compounded progesterone (same molecular structure as progesterone made by our bodies) better than synthetic, which is not identical to a woman's own but has some of the effects of progesterone. You may need to experiment before you find what's best for you. Remember that menopause (either surgical or natural) does not mean you can stop being vigilant about your health!

In the past, it was not felt that women with endo who had their ovaries and uterus removed needed progesterone, because they no longer had their uterus, which is most at risk for estrogen stimulation. It was also believed that removal of the uterus and ovaries nearly always caused any remaining endo to die out. We now know that estrogen can also cause the reactivation of endo left behind. (Moreover, some endo can be microscopic, so even if your surgeon says he or she "got it all," there are no guarantees that it's true.) In addition, any remaining endo has to be considered at risk for malignancy, just as the uterus would be. Based on this newer information, it may be wise to use progesterone any time estrogen is used. However, more research is needed and is being conducted by the Endometriosis Association and others.

Finally, remember that another option is to not use hormones. One expert reviewer of this article, immunologist Aristo Vojdani, Ph.D., believes strongly that women with endo reaching natural menopause should not use replacement hormones. (He makes

Micronutrients, Vitamins, and Cancer Prevention

There is some evidence that micronutrients can act as antioxidants, modifying the activity of potent carcinogens. These nutrients include beta-carotene and vitamins C and E.[40] Bioflavonoids (vitamin-like substances, also known as vitamin P), which occur naturally in cruciferous vegetables (cabbage, broccoli, brussels sprouts, and cauliflower), and plant estrogens (contained in soy products) may offer some breast cancer protection, along with relief of menopausal symptoms.[42]

Deficiency in the trace mineral selenium has been associated with higher incidence of cancer, and one study reported that higher levels of selenium in the diet helped protect against the development of breast tumors in rats. Seafood, brazil nuts, whole-grain cereal and bread products, kidney, and liver are rich in selenium.[74]

A study of the protective value of vitamin D on breast cancer risk reported that for women living in areas of high solar radiation, exposure to sunlight and intake of vitamin D in the diet were associated with a 25 to 65 percent reduction in risk of breast cancer. Women living in regions of low and medium solar radiation who reported sun exposure in the course of recreation and work also seemed to benefit from lower risk, but protection was not significant. The researchers admitted that the small number of breast cancer cases in their study made it difficult to predict meaningful trends of decreased risk with increasing exposure.[83]

Interest and research is growing in the use of nutrients and phytochemicals to improve the effectiveness of cancer treatment and improve patients' quality of life, as well as to prevent the onset of cancer. A discussion of such nutrients and phytochemicals was presented by Corey Resnick, N.D., of Integrated Therapeutics, a supplement company, at the thirty-third annual meeting of the American Academy of Environmental Medicine. Among the natural substances with anticancer activity noted were raspberries, walnuts, cruciferous vegetables, tomatoes, turmeric, and fish and fish oils (especially salmon, mackerel, and sardine). Thanks to Dr. Resnick for his work in drawing the following information together.[125]

Selenium

Sources of selenium include seafood, whole grains, and nutritional and brewer's yeast.[126] A deficiency in selenium is associated with increased breast and skin cancers. In a study of 1,300 patients, supplementation with 200 micrograms of selenium per day was associated with a 50 percent drop in cancer mortality and a 41 percent drop in incidence.[127] The strongest associations between selenium levels in the blood and cancer were found in breast and gastrointestinal cancers, and a synergistic effect was achieved with vitamin E in breast cancer prevention.

Glutathione (GSH)

Glutathione is one of the most widely distributed and important antioxidants in nature and the chief thiol (sulfur-bearing) molecule in most cells. Glutathione induced apoptosis (cell death by self-destruction) in human cancer cells in the lab without damaging healthy cells. Adequate amounts of intracellular GSH are needed for normal function of the p53 tumor suppresser protein (dysfunction is found in more than 50 percent of cancers). The best sources include dark green leafy vegetables, fresh fruit, and lightly cooked fish, poultry, and beef.[128]

Calcium D-Glucarate

Calcium D-glucarate increases elimination of carcinogens, toxins, and steroid hormones via glucuronidation. Glucuronidation is a reaction that eliminates toxins from the body and detoxifies many chemical carcinogens (nitrosamines, polycyclic aromatic hydrocarbons, aromatic amines) and steroid hormones (estrogen). Calcium D-glucarate decreases estradiol levels in animal models. This micronutrient occurs in low levels in broccoli, potatoes, oranges, and other fruits and vegetables.

Beta-Carotene

Beta-carotene, found in green and orange fruits and vegetables from spinach to mango,[128] demonstrates chemo-preventive properties in epidemiological and case-controlled studies:

- It inhibits mutations, malignant transformation, and tumor formation.
- It enhances immune function.
- Intake has been inversely correlated (the greater the intake, the lower the occurrence) with risk for breast and skin cancers, among others.

Natural and synthetic beta-carotene differ structurally and in antioxidant activity. Negative trials on beta-carotene used only the synthetic form. Foods linked to lung cancer prevention contain the natural form only.

Coenzyme Q10 (Ubiquinone)

Coenzyme Q10, or ubiquinone, is a cellular antioxidant found in all tissues of the body and is often deficient in cancer. It is especially active in cell membranes. It enhances the antioxidant function of vitamin E. Food sources include heart and liver.[128]

(Sidebar continues on next page)

Micronutrients, Vitamins, and Cancer Prevention *(continued)*

Administration of coenzyme Q10 brought about partial and complete remission of breast cancer in some patients in two small studies. A Danish Nutritional Intervention in Cancer protocol (ANICA) for "high-risk" breast cancer patients includes coenzyme Q10, vitamins C and E, beta-carotene, selenium, and essential fatty acids.

Coenzyme Q10 is commonly used by practitioners treating candida problems. Because these are so prevalent in women with endo, we may have a special need for coenzyme Q10.

Catechin

Catechin is a green tea polyphenol (another bioflavonoid and antioxidant, immune stimulant, and protector of DNA).[128] Green tea intake is associated with reduced risk of cancers of the stomach, colon, pancreas, and esophagus as well as improved prognosis for breast cancer. Catechin shows synergistic effect with curcumin (in the spice turmeric) and has the following effects:

- Reduction of aberrant hyperproliferation in certain cells
- Increased enzyme and antioxidant activity observed in skin
- Increased activity of antioxidant enzymes
- Inhibition of mutagenesis (see Glossary) and carcinogenesis
- Apoptosis (see Glossary)

Genistein

Genistein is one of two major isoflavones, a class of phytoestrogens that occurs in soybeans and soy products. Soy products containing genistein reduce cancer incidence, latency, and tumor numbers in animal models. The following effects have been attributed to genistein:

- Inhibition of DNA synthesis in estrogen-dependent cancer cells
- Induction of cell cycle arrest in breast cancer, melanoma, and leukemia cells
- Induction of apoptosis in breast and prostate cancer
- Inhibition of growth of melanoma in mice

---

an exception for women going through surgical menopause.) Since women with endo are clearly prone to unregulated cell growth, Vojdani says they should not use hormones that promote cell growth. Natural alternatives may be helpful to these women, he notes.

Helping Teens with Endo: Background for Parents, Doctors, and Friends

TEEN ENDO: AN OVERVIEW

Mary Lou Ballweg

The teen years are sensitive years for all, girls and boys. There probably isn't anyone who can remember no trauma from those extremely important developmental years. Now add to that a chronic, painful, stigmatized disease such as endometriosis. A disease that can keep a teen out of school, sometimes for long periods of time. A disease that can keep her from participating in extracurricular activities, including sports, theater, dance, and all the other fun things that teenagers so enjoy and need. A disease that can be virtually impossible to explain to others—particularly when undiagnosed. A disease that will be chalked up to "psychosomatic" problems by some because they lack awareness about endo. Add all that together, and one can understand why endo is very challenging for those with it, particularly teenagers.

Perhaps the biggest hurdle is getting diagnosed in the first place. "Teens don't get endo, do they?" We've heard this question all too often. Unfortunately, teens *do* get endo. We have been aware of this fact since the earliest days of the Association, and we often hear from teens with endo and from women whose symptoms began in their teen years. Indeed, our data research registry shows that two-thirds of the women with

"I am writing to you on behalf of my twelve-year-old daughter, who wishes to join the Association. . . . She has had a laparoscopy to suggest the diagnosis of minimal endo. . . . She has had to give up most of the things she loves the most, horseback riding and dance classes. She has gone from being a leader at school to just struggling to get to school. She misses on average a day a week and can no longer tolerate the bus ride to and from school, which means two twenty-mile round trips per day for us. I have been able to quite successfully educate her teachers about her condition and why she can't always participate, but she still feels that some of them are getting annoyed with her because she so often feels unwell. . . . She is a wonderful young woman with good decision-making qualities and a strong sense of self. I would hate to have all that eroded away by endo and its constant interruptions in her life. Nothing wears away quicker at self-image than having others disbelieve that you are experiencing what you say you are experiencing."

—*Kathleen, Saskatchewan*

endo listed in the registry reported that their pelvic symptoms first appeared before the age of twenty. (Thirty-eight percent of the women had symptoms first appear before age fifteen, while 28 percent reported symptoms first appearing between the ages of fifteen and nineteen.) For more data on teen endo, see Chapter 13.

As awareness of endo among teens grows, more teens contact the Endometriosis Association for support and information. The sobering question posed by thirteen-year-old Jessica—"Am I going to die?"—reflects the heartbreaking fears and desperate need for information that many teens face. Often, however, before the teen is even in a position to ask these questions, it is a major challenge first to recognize that certain symptoms are not normal, report these symptoms *and* be believed, and then receive a diagnosis. (No, Jessica, endo doesn't kill you, but it often alters our lives and dreams in major ways.)

Because there is no cure for endo, it is vital that it be diagnosed and treated in its early stages. This provides the best opportunity to prevent the progression of the disease and to help maintain fertility options, control pain, and improve the youngster's quality of life. It is crucial that teens know the symptoms of the disease and that they are taken seriously when they do report symptoms to parents, doctors, or school nurses. Once the disease has been diagnosed, it is equally important that teens have access to reliable information and support.

This section of our book has been developed to provide reliable information to teens and those who love and care for them. It has been shockingly difficult to develop this information. In the process, we became acutely aware how little is really known about endo in preteens, teens, and women in their early twenties. Very little research has been devoted to this subject.

Many physicians are uncomfortable treating this age group. Pediatricians, who typically treat children well into their teens, generally are not comfortable treating gyn problems. Gynecologists are generally uncomfortable treating teens and preteens with a disease that's difficult to treat even in adults. With teens, they can feel their hands are tied because the medications and surgical treatments used in adult women have not been well studied (or studied at all) in teens. There is very little guidance and no consensus on the best approach to take in treating teens. Because these youngsters are minors, there are parental issues to deal with, too. And teens appear to have some of the most difficult symptoms of all to treat—unrelenting, sometimes severe pain and sometimes prolonged bleeding.

In this section, we first learn about teen endo and programs to help these young women. Then we hear from a number of parents of teens with endo. As one mother writes, "Make no mistake, endo affects the entire family!" This is followed by a section especially for teens themselves.

We view these chapters as a starting point. Please share your own perspectives and send them to us. Together we will learn what best helps teens with endo. Together we make a difference for teens and ourselves!

TEENS: THE OVERLOOKED ENDO PATIENTS

Ann Beckmann

Jennie R. was only three days into her freshman year of high school when she found herself doubled over with pain during field hockey practice. "To have it happen *then* was horrible," says Jennie, whose condition was first thought to be appendicitis. The pain became worse before doctors determined fourteen-year-old Jennie had an ovarian cyst that ruptured. The pain became excruciating by the time she had her first laparoscopy. "They found half a cup of fluid from the first cyst and a second cyst," she describes.

Another laparoscopy, birth control pills, then Lupron and Motrin have been part of Jennie's experience with endo. She may have missed forty-five days of school her freshman year, but Jennie, who just turned fifteen, managed to complete her studies with the rest of her classmates. She's especially excited about having another go at field hockey.

Adolescents are a significant but often overlooked part of the endo patient population. "From the earliest days of the Endometriosis Association, we were aware that many women with endo started with symptoms in their teens," says Mary Lou Ballweg, president and executive director of the Endometriosis Association.

Marc Laufer, M.D., chief of pediatric and adolescent gynecology at Children's Hospital in Boston, says he saw the need for more emotional support for teenagers with endo some years ago: "Often they'd been to a lot of pediatricians, and it took a while

A year or so later . . .

before they were referred to a gynecologist. They'd be frustrated because nobody believed them when they'd explain their pain. So many times, teenage girls in recovery after a laparoscopy break down and cry and say, 'Finally, somebody believes me.'"

Paula Higgins, former president of the Boston Association Chapter and former coordinator of the Chapter's teen program, says what teens want most is positive feedback on how to help themselves: "They don't want this to become a big part of their lives. They want to be independent, not go running to someone for help."

Laufer is particularly sensitive to how teenagers with endo fear they'll have to forgo some of the peak experiences of their adolescence. "It's enough to go through adolescence without the added burden of pain," he says.

The first research to focus on the incidence of endo among teenagers was that of Fallon's 1946 study suggesting that endo likely begins soon after the first period and should be treated early to avoid the potential for infertility and incapacitating pain.[1] Donald Chatman, M.D., an Association Advisor who practices in Chicago, reported in 1976 that teenagers accounted for 8.5 percent of a series of endo patients.[2] In 1982 he reported a 65 percent incidence rate of endo in forty-three consecutive diagnostic laparoscopies for symptomatic black teens who complained of disabling pelvic pain and/or abnormal vaginal bleeding.[3] Dr. Chatman states, "Although the true incidence of endometriosis is not known, there is no medical reason to assume that teenagers and/or blacks should be immune to the disease." Furthermore, he asserts, "Our data clearly indicate that the disease is common in teenagers who have severe pelvic pain of a cyclic nature." Harvard researchers Goldstein, Cholnoky, and Emans found endo in 47 percent of girls aged ten and a half to nineteen years undergoing laparoscopy for chronic pelvic pain.[4] In 1990 they reported a 45 percent prevalence rate of endo in 282 adolescent females with chronic pelvic pain seen from 1974 to 1983.[5]

Early diagnosis is a big advantage, Laufer says, but the lack of awareness on the part of health practitioners continues to be a deterrent. "A lot of us in the medical profession have been taught that endometriosis only occurs when women are in their twenties and thirties," says Laufer, who lectures on teen endo for schools and healthcare providers.

Parents need information, too, according to Higgins. "A mom might ask, 'Why does my kid have to go on birth control pills? Why doesn't the surgery cure it?'" Parents may be inclined to dismiss the girl's reports, perhaps due to the natural desire of parents that nothing be wrong with their child. Others may be uncomfortable with the nature of the symptoms, which strike at the heart of the transition parents and children must make as children grow into sexually mature adults. Some parents feel the girl is exaggerating or confused, yet it has been the Association's experience that while some teens may exaggerate in other areas of their lives, they do not exaggerate menstrual or pelvic symptoms. Their realm of experience is too limited to even know about these symptoms (little background is given in menstrual education classes—something the Association is working to change), and discussing these symptoms with adults is the last thing these girls want to do.

Young Jennie R. says one of her best friends was diagnosed with endo just a few months ago. When Jennie's pal complained about pain to her own dad, the father's response was, "I don't want to hear about it right now." Jennie says, "I feel really lucky because my mom is always there for me when I have pain."

When she reflects on what she has been through, Jennie says she's actually happy she developed ovarian cysts. "It's the best thing, really, because otherwise I'd never have known. I'd just like to get the point across that if somebody's going through pain, it's important to be diagnosed at this age rather than later on. You shouldn't let it go, because it can just get worse. Let people know if you're having pain. Don't keep it inside," Jennie urges.

Sixteen-year-old Alyssa complained of pain when she was just fourteen. Because she'd had a kidney transplant at

> "Although I had endo as a young woman, one bout of birth control pills for six months and pregnancy brought me to a tolerable pain level. My daughter, however, started to suffer terribly at age sixteen. Now at [age twenty-two], after dropping out of school, undergoing two surgeries and two bouts of Lupron, she is still not out of the water. Without the Association, both my daughter and I would surely be in a mental institution."
>
> *—Alida, Connecticut*

> "My fourteen-year-old daughter lived two full years in constant pain and horrible bleeding, unable to go to school most of the two years. She has had eight surgeries in four years. We found . . . Dr. G, but we had to travel from Montana to Boston for major surgeries."
>
> —*Nancy, Montana*

age seven, Alyssa and her family figured it must be the kidney acting up. Laufer diagnosed her endo and recommended the Boston Chapter's teen program to Alyssa and her mom.

"I didn't really want to get into a support group* when I was diagnosed, but my mom said I really should do it. Now just knowing that other people know what I'm going through helps, or if I'm having a bad day, just talking to someone helps. When I was on Lupron and having hot flashes, it was great to know there was someone to talk to about what's wrong. The newsletter gives me ideas, too. I had ongoing headaches for two years, for instance. I never knew that had anything to do with endo," Alyssa says.

Jennie, like Alyssa, was reluctant to join a support group at first. "I didn't want to go, but I found it really gives me good ideas. I've learned about vitamins, exercising, trying to relax, aromatherapy. I've been doing aerobics every day for the last six months. It's so weird that something bad has to happen to open your eyes to stuff," Jennie says.

After the first year of the teen program, Boston Chapter's Higgins polled the thirty teens who were participating to see how the program fit their needs. All found the program helpful. Most preferred to attend monthly endo support group meetings outside their schools. "They'd rather meet at a hospital so their classmates aren't talking about them. They don't want to be labeled with anything," Higgins says.

The teens unanimously agreed that they wanted to receive a newsletter, telephone contact with other teens at the time of their diagnosis, and that they'd like to act as contact people for those newly diagnosed with endo. More than half expressed interest in a "big sister" with endo (now called our Mentor program, in which a teen is paired with an older teen or young woman with endo to help her through her endo experiences).

Although the Boston program operates with a slim pocketbook, Higgins and Donna Wolfe (president of the Boston chapter after Higgins) have no doubts about the value of their chapter's pioneer efforts with teens. "When a fourteen-year-old sends you a Christmas card saying, 'Thanks for being there,' you know it's worth it," says Higgins.

The Boston Chapter and Laufer won an award from the North American Society of Pediatric and Adolescent Gynecology for a scientific poster on teen endo. "It's all part of teaching other doctors and nurses how to interact with these kids," says Phaedra Thomas, R.N., B.S.N., a nurse associated with the program. The poster explained how the program works, as well as the results of the program.

---

*For information on support groups in your area, contact the Association.

A larger-scale network of teens with endo spurs Alyssa's enthusiasm. "I would love for it to be like that. I want to help others. One day it really clicked for me. I've decided I want to become a doctor. Getting involved in this helps me understand other people better—other people and their pain," Alyssa says.

"MY WORST FEARS ARE CONFIRMED: MY YOUNG DAUGHTER HAS ENDO"

Suzanne Rohrer

It's four in the morning, and I am suddenly awakened by the muffled sound of some-one sobbing in the dark. I instantly sit up and discover my fourteen-year-old daugh-ter—her small body shaking, her teeth chattering, and fright reflected in her wide eyes. As I pull her into our warm bed, I reassure myself that it's probably just a bad night-mare. As she warms up and relaxes a little, she tells me that it feels like someone is stabbing her in her stomach and her lower back. I instinctively reach over the side of my bed and bring up my ever-present heating pad that has always offered me so much needed comfort. I do all I can that night to calm her and alleviate her pain with Advil and a mother's caress. I don't get any sleep the rest of the night as my mind agonizes and I pray for my daughter.

Every month, as her menstrual cycle continues, the pain continues to worsen and last longer. My worst fears are confirmed; my young daughter has endometriosis. This disease with such a long, clumsy name will not be life ending, but most definitely life altering. I know. I suffer with the same condition and did so at a very young age. In one of life's very cruel ironies, our five years of infertility were erased with her birth. Now I discover to my heartbreak and disbelief that the disease that forever changed my life was passed on to my miracle child.

I calm myself with the belief that at least the doctors and public are much more aware and educated about this disease than they were when I was going through this twenty years ago. To my dismay and astonishment, I will discover that such hope in the education of the medical establishment and public was oftentimes way too optimistic.

What is it like to be a young victim of endo? The foremost problem the young girl has to endure is the unrelenting pain each month of every year. It usually begins a day or two before her period and continues through the first few days of heavy bleeding. As the disease progresses, it captures more and more days in its relentless grip. The pain is often described as stabbing and burning, and it continues for hours and days at a time, robbing her of sleep; all too frequently depriving her of participation in the normal activities teenagers enjoy. It often causes skepticism and criticism among her friends, teachers, family, and doctors and if left undiagnosed or misdiagnosed, results in her questioning her own validity and worth. As if that is not enough to endure during the highs and lows of adolescence, this disease can and often does affect her future as a fertile woman. She most likely will be subjected to not just one surgery but many as the endo continues to be "fed" with each menstrual cycle. She will be the scientific equivalent of a guinea pig as she continues down the road of drugs, chemicals, lasers, and scalpels in an attempt to lessen the pain, to slow down the disease, and to keep her options open concerning motherhood.

This endo is a chronic disease affecting her entire physical, mental, and emotional well-being and sometimes, as was my case, begins with what many call a celebration of "womanhood." She will be "welcomed" into this celebration with what the medical establishment refers to as periodic pain or dysmenorrhea. She will quickly learn to pronounce long, difficult words in an attempt to explain or validate her suffering. As a young woman in today's society, she may even be subjected to various psychological tests and have to look up the word *hypochondriac*. She will encounter various types of prejudice among her friends and schoolmates about her pain—all at a time when they mean so much to how she perceives herself, now and in the future. She might be led into the dark world of drug and alcohol abuse, beginning with prescribed pain pills to lessen the pain *if* she can get someone to take her pain seriously. And, worst of all, there is no sure cure for endo as of now, only stopgap measures to slow it down.

As bleak as her future may seem, it doesn't have to be this way. As a friend, parent, grandparent, aunt, uncle, cousin, teacher, principal, or school nurse, your education about endo and your understanding of how it can affect her will have long-lasting results. Her suffering is not outwardly obvious—she has no casts on any of her limbs, no obvious deformities, and no well-known "war" on her disease to find its cause and bring about its cure. She needs nonjudgmental care, concern, and support each and every month for many days at a time, for many years, and often for a lifetime. She needs a circle of support among her friends, family, and the medical establishment as she travels the medical road of drugs, chemicals, and surgery. She needs doctors, nurses, and researchers who can offer her, and the millions like her, hope for the future.

> "My daughter was recently diagnosed with endo after spending the last three to four years trying to find a doctor who would take her pain seriously. She is just nineteen and was told over and over, 'It's just menstrual cramps.' Even though I was there with her trying to convince the doctors this wasn't 'just menstrual cramps,' we still were basically ignored and treated like crazy women. The medical profession's ignorance of this disease angers me terribly, and if we can help change this and get the information to women before they wind up in my daughter's extreme condition, we would be more than happy to help. If you could also include fifty of your free brochures, we will make sure that they are made available at our doctor's office. It is obvious this information needs to get out to women urgently."
>
> —Linda, Michigan

She doesn't need to be made to feel like a freak; she doesn't need to be overly fretted about; nor does she need to be ignored. She wants to feel well, both physically and mentally. She wants to be a normal teenager. Maybe in the not-so-distant future, she might want to decide if motherhood is for her. However, statistically, at this time, this decision quite possibly will be taken out of her hands because of her disease.

She is not asking too much for a girl of her age, but it's not going to be easy for her. You can help with emotional and physical support. If you know of a teenager who exhibits extreme physical pain during her menstrual cycle, then you must insist that her complaints be taken seriously and take her to a qualified gynecologist.

You can help by educating yourself about the disease and ways to cope with it and last, but by no means least, financially supporting the international Endometriosis Association. The Association is the only group in the world focused on finding a cause and a cure for this life-changing disease. It was started by a few women in Wisconsin who vowed that no other woman would have to go through this pain alone and without information. The Association has many local support groups all over the world staffed by helpful volunteers who just happen to understand what it is all about because they have experienced the trials and tribulations of endo themselves. The local support groups hold meetings and host speakers from varied backgrounds and specialties, all of them offering recommendations and education about dealing with endo. Members share information on treatments, support and coping tips, and their experiences with local physicians, and they are tied into the educational and informational network of the overall Association. Please learn all you can about this frustrating disease and help us in the Association help others with whatever means you can—emotional, physical, and/or financial. After all, if *we* don't help our girls, who will?

SUGGESTIONS FROM THE PARENTS OF A TEEN WITH ENDO

Lori and Steve Schott

Doctors, whether they are general practitioners, pediatricians, or ob-gyn specialists, need to learn that young girls *do* get endometriosis. They should have pamphlets in their offices and, by screening their patients, determine a diagnosis much, much sooner. Our family practitioner said point-blank to our daughter, after her first confirming lap, that she had never heard of a twelve- or thirteen-year-old having endo. Doctors need to know that the average diagnosis takes over nine years, and they are perpetuating this problem by denying that young girls *do* have endo. When a young girl presents with endo symptoms, it is their duty to speak to the parents and educate them about the illness. We had never even heard of endo until our daughter's

THREE A.M.:
FOR MY MOTHER

Jean Wiswesser

I am suffering.
It is deep and
THROBBING and
n e v e r—e n d i n g . . .
I lie on my bed and hurt like hell
inside my pelvis (my heart).

I don't want to be this woman anymore,
so I let my head fall upon my shoulder,
pull my arms into myself, under my chin and
curl my legs up toward my chest.
I was genderless (painless) once
within your womb.

I was a baby
without these heavy, swollen breasts,
without these cystic ovaries,
wretched moods, numb thighs, or
cramping uterus.

I laid in this same position
only twenty-three years smaller
surrounded by your safe body
and peacefully slept
while your strong heart pumped life into me.

I just want to rest (die).
It is three A.M. when you hear the ring.
"Mommy, I hurt."
And on the other end of the cord you speak
gently, calmly, soothingly till
my bed becomes a womb
and your strong heart pumps life into me again,
so that I may go on living.

laparoscopy. We frantically got online, researching and teaching ourselves everything we could find. Doctors should all have the Association video *Teens Speak Out on Endometriosis* to let the patients get a grip on what they are dealing with.

Doctors treating adolescents need to understand they are still dealing with a child—in many cases, a child with an adult disease. You can't talk to or treat a twelve-year-old the same way you would a thirty-year-old. These kids are scared. Just when their bodies are beginning to develop, they have to deal with very adult problems. Unless absolutely necessary, a pelvic exam should be held off until some conservative treatments, like nonsteroidal anti-inflammatories or birth control pills, prove ineffective. If a pelvic exam is necessary, the examining doctor needs to go very slowly and let the young girl know exactly what the doctor is doing and what to expect. The girl's mother, older sister, female nurse, or other trusted adult should be present.

Doctors, above all else, need to be sympathetic and not tell a girl to live with the pain. Period pain should never stop a girl's daily activities or make her leave school. Doctors should never tell a girl that she needs counseling because stress is causing her endo.

Understand that endo is not just a gyn issue, and treat it accordingly. Have a team of other specialists who will help treat your young girls. Examples of people to include are environmental medicine specialists, nutritionists, acupuncturists, counselors, and endocrinologists.

Another opinion strictly from our own experience is that the doctor should recommend going on a modified candida diet to try and stop candida from taking over (see Chapter 4). We'd even suggest going as far as working with a nutritionist to get supplements and build the girl's immune system to be as strong as humanly possible. Avoid sugars, wheat, mold, and other exposures that trigger symptoms. Too many of our girls and women suffer bowel problems and are just blankly told they have irritable bowel syndrome.

Please tell doctors to stop telling girls to get pregnant and their endo will go away! Please stop telling people that a hysterectomy will cure their endo!

Most important, doctors need to tell a patient when they don't know things or can no longer treat a patient because

> "'Don't be a baby, honey; all girls get cramps. Take two aspirin and go back to class,' the nurse at my high school told me when I was bent over double in tears. . . . Over the years I learned to put the pain off and to eliminate mention of it to my doctors. . . . As strange as it seems, part of me actually believed that lack of acknowledgment would make my problems just disappear. That seemed to be what those around me—including teachers and doctors—believed, too.
>
> I'm not a baby. I'm not a hypochondriac. I am an endometriosis sufferer. It took six years to find out. Looking back, I wish I had been a more aggressive patient. I should never have allowed myself to believe these occurrences were all in my head. . . . Please don't fall asleep at the wheel like I did. Problems like endo do not just go away. Don't listen to the people who tell you to go away. Be persistent. Listen to your body. It knows what it's talking about."
>
> —Rachel, Pennsylvania

of lack of endo expertise. We, and so many others, would have so much respect for them! The doctor needs to tell the family he or she will help them find someone who does have some answers. We have experienced doctor after doctor who, when they can no longer help our daughter, tell her she is nuts and she needs pain management and counseling. The doctor needs to admit he or she is human and support these young patients through a very difficult time. One example would be for the doctor to give families the Association information, so they can begin to sort through this mysterious and baffling disease and get support from people who have the knowledge and can sympathize with what this family is going through. Make no mistake, endo affects the entire family!

WHEN ENDO IS A FAMILY AFFAIR

P. Fay Campbell, M.S.Ed.

Parenthood is probably never what you think it will be. But Suzanne and Steve, of Wisconsin, had additional surprises that came with parenting their only child, Alisa.

Alisa, now fifteen, had problems with her periods since they began at age ten. They would last eight or nine days and were unusually heavy. But at age fourteen, when she began having rectal bleeding with her periods, lots of gastrointestinal problems, and severe pain, she, Suzanne, and Steve embarked on a thirteen-month medical odyssey, which included Alisa's three colonoscopies, three endoscopies for gastrointestinal problems, a laparoscopy, countless doctors, and lots and lots of research. "On a scale of one to ten, her pain was very often an eight," explained Suzanne.

Six months after the symptoms began, the family spent a week at a children's hospital. Suzanne suspected endo and questioned physicians. They were told that Alisa's problems were probably gastrointestinal and that she was too young for endo. Worse yet, Alisa felt guilty about being in pain and experiencing pain with the examinations. She hadn't experienced pelvic exams like that before, and she thought it was her fault if anything hurt. As for the "probably" diagnosis, when your child is in pain, "probably" just isn't good enough. Suzanne and Steve were frustrated and angry.

So Steve went to a medical school library, and Suzanne went online. Everything they found pointed to endo. They wanted the best for their daughter, so they took her to a world-famous clinic, where they saw another gastroenterologist and two more gynecologists. Those doctors thought she "probably" had endo, but they didn't want to "put her through a laparoscopy." More frustration. More anger.

They finally found a physician in their area who was tuned in to endo. Ten months into the odyssey, he did the long-awaited laparoscopy. She had adhesions connecting her colon to the abdominal wall and endo near the rectum! The surgeon removed what he could find.

"But to be honest," explained Suzanne, "she didn't feel that great after the surgery. We'd hoped that this would cure it, and it just didn't. So even though the doctor didn't 'believe' in the yeast connection,* Alisa started on the diet. She also began seeing a traditional Chinese medicine doctor who does acupressure."** Alisa started to feel better.

"We had all been doing our research. We talked to people at the Endometriosis Association. I kept detailed records of the doctors we saw and the treatments tried, and now we have an amazing document. We network with other parents and teens. Steve is corresponding with a father whose daughter has endo. We can talk to each other about all of this, but it's more helpful to talk to other people who are going through the same thing. We share suggestions and tell each other what has worked for our daughter. I can't tell you how helpful the Association has been in all this. I don't know where we'd be without that support."

Lately Alisa's pain is not higher than a 5 on a scale of 1 to 10. The family knows they might not be done with endo problems, but because of the knowledge and support they've found, they feel better able to deal with it now. Suzanne's pride in her daughter bubbles to the surface when she talks about Alisa: "She is a 4.0 grade point average, is president of her class, and just got the lead role of Maria in *Sound of Music*. We explained the situation to her school so she could have a more flexible schedule. We stay in touch with her teachers via E-mail."

Asked what they have learned and what they would suggest to other parents who have teens with endo, Suzanne's answer was very clear: "You've got to trust your own instincts, and you've got to do your own research. You have to realize that doctors may not all know as much as you hope they know. It's really helpful to network with other parents and get the school involved." She stated that you know your child better than a physician does, and you need to find what works for her.

> "As I read the latest newsletter [on teens and endo], my daughter was just starting her second period. My own endo was resolved when she was born twelve years ago this month, and I'm nearing menopause now, so my worries about myself are few. I met my husband about the time I joined the Association, and as a result of my membership, got the *best* medical care and Hannah as a result. The newsletter shockingly crystallized all my current fears for Hannah, however. When she asked me during her first period what cramps felt like, I almost had an anxiety attack thinking about what the future holds and how little I can help if she actually does have endo. She's so young to have to explain how life changing the disease really is. I just sent a donation. Please use it for teen outreach."
>
> —*Paula, New Hampshire*

---

*See Chapter 4, "Immunotherapy: The Newest Treatment for Endometriosis."

**See *The Endometriosis Sourcebook*, Chapter 7, "Traditional Chinese Medicine and the Treatment of Endometriosis."

TIPS FOR PARENTS

Mary Lou Ballweg and Grace Janik, M.D.

While coping with the sadness, anger, frustration, fear, and other emotions a parent feels when a daughter has endo is never easy, here are some tips that will ease the load somewhat. Write us with any suggestions you have, and we'll share them in our newsletter and perhaps in a future book.

- **Get a handle on your own feelings.** As Suzanne Rohrer says in her article in this chapter, "'My Worst Fears Are Confirmed: My Young Daughter Has Endo,'" you will feel that your worst fears are being confirmed if your daughter, niece, or young person you care about develops symptoms of endo. You will have your own intense frustration and anger at those who will not understand or help. While it's fine to share your frustration, briefly, with the girl, remember that she will look to you for an example of healthy ways to deal with those feelings, and she will want to know you are an advocate for her. Obviously, you will be better able to do this if you have processed your own fears.
- **Understand that there is no quick fix for endo.** Hard as it can be to accept—and this is particularly true for parents and relatives who have not themselves experienced endo—there is no magical doctor or quick fix for endo. While researching and looking for good medical care for your youngster, resist the temptation to throw all your faith and hope in the medical establishment. This is not a disease that the average gyn is comfortable treating even in adult women, never mind preteens and teenagers. Ideally, you should consult an endo specialist. More than likely, there will not be one single doctor who can address your concerns; rather, you will need a combination of physicians, lifestyle changes, treatments, and coping skills.
- **A good "bedside manner" and gentle pelvic exams are essential.** These requirements are even more important for teens and young women than older women. Finding a knowledgeable physician, comfortable with treating teens in particular, who also has a compassionate bedside manner is like finding gold! When you find such a person, please share with others in the Association. Talk with other members for leads on finding these wonderful healthcare practitioners.
- **Prepare your daughter for that first pelvic exam.** In fact, as Lori and Steve Schott suggest in their article, "Suggestions from the Parents of a Teen with Endo," you might even delay that first pelvic exam as long as possible. A number of resources are available to prepare your daughter for that first exam. If you have not already purchased your daughter resources such as *Changing Bodies, Changing Lives* (by Ruth Bell, an author of *Our Bodies, Ourselves*), do so. Your daughter, even more than others her age, desperately needs lots of information about the changes she is going through. Unfortunately, even good books such as *Changing Bodies* have erroneous or little information specifically on endo, however.
- **Bear in mind that reduced pain and better functioning can be attained by improving overall health.** Work with your youngster to improve her diet and nutrition as much as pos-

sible. Exercise if at all possible, particularly during those times when she is not in pain. Clean up the environment around her, particularly if she has allergies, as so many of us with endo do. Encourage her to get enough rest. And keep up with the information and resources being constantly developed by the Association.

- **Get your daughter or loved youngster in contact with others her age.** Girls in this age group are extremely sensitive to their peers and will feel immensely reassured if they are aware that others their age also have this disease. They will be even more comforted if they can talk with others. One good place to start is by sharing *Teens Speak Out on Endometriosis*, the Association's award-winning video, with your loved young one.
- **Work with your young one and healthcare practitioners to obtain as much pain relief as possible.** Pain is spirit shattering. Your daughter is just developing her sense of herself and needs to be able to continue that critical developmental work at this stage. Don't forget alternatives such as acupuncture, physical therapy, and other approaches, too—there are lots of options to try. See *The Endometriosis Sourcebook* and the Association's international newsletters for more information. Suicide can be a risk among members of this age group with unrelenting pain.
- **Suggest that your daughter's doctor develop a pain management plan.** Have your daughter use a 1 to 10 scale to describe her level of pain. With the doctor, write down what to do at each level of pain. At each visit, review what has been working at what levels of pain and what has not been working. Refine the plan to continue to provide relief or at least the hope that, as you work together, relief is possible. Paying attention to her symptoms will help her feel that you and the doctor are really there for her, care about her, and will work with her to obtain relief from the symptoms.
- **Change healthcare providers when necessary.** Understand that endo is not just a gyn issue. A team of other specialists may help control endo symptoms.
- **Be aware that endo will affect the self-esteem of your daughter.** Do all possible to help build up her self-esteem and help her be aware of her positive points. Perhaps together you can develop a big poster of all the best things about her that she can turn to during times of pain and sadness.
- **Sign up for a family membership so your young person will receive** *TeenSource*, **the Association's quarterly teen newsletter.** There's also a Teen Correspondence Network of teen Association members. See the membership form at the back of this book.

The following tips are from Grace Janik, M.D., a Milwaukee, Wisconsin, endo specialist who treats teens with the disease:

- **Get a referral to a specialist.** You need to see a specialist to diagnose and treat teen endometriosis. Some pediatricians are uncomfortable with gyn problems and are unaware, generally, of what is being done in the adult endo world.

> "It feels like I'm an old lady trapped inside a little girl's body."
>
> —Ally, fourteen years old, Ohio

- **The kids feel better if they know there are lots of kids who have this problem.** Otherwise, they feel like freaks and can have problems with body image.
- **Fertility issues are important to teenagers, but adults have to talk about this issue very carefully.** Teens can get the idea they should test their fertility—which is probably not what you want.
- **Bear in mind that the time frame for teenagers is very different than for adults.** Six months seems like forever to teens. They may not stay in compliance with their medication or treatment schedule if they don't see results right away. They will need frequent reinforcement and encouragement.
- **Teens also go into denial easily.** Psychological denial is denying that there really is anything wrong. Parents and others who do not have endo may want to talk to other adults—in Association groups or through our contact list, for instance—to better understand denial.

Resources for and About Teen Endo

To obtain the following items, contact the Endometriosis Association (see Resources at the end of this book):

- *Teens Speak Out on Endometriosis*—In this documentary-style video, ten teens and friends describe their experiences with the disease. A very powerful film, the Association's *Teens Speak Out on Endometriosis* won a prestigious award at the WorldFest-Houston International Film and Video Festival, the world's largest film festival.
- *TeenSource* newsletter—This newsletter for teenagers with endo is published quarterly by the Association. Topics cover a wide range of issues, including coping with endo at school, nutrition for teens with endo, managing pain as a teen with endo, profiles of teens who have successfully come to terms with endo and have tips for other teens, and many more topics.
- **Brochures for teens**—An older-teen brochure is available for teens between the ages of thirteen and twenty-one, and a young-teen and preteen brochure is available for girls aged ten to twelve. These brochures are available in quantity to physicians' offices and schools.
- **Parents Correspondence Network and Teen Contact Network**—These two Association networks provide a list of parents and teens dealing with endo who are interested in sharing support and information. Also available is a Mentor Program, which pairs a teen who has endo with an older teen or young woman who has more experience with endo. This is especially helpful in families where there is no prior experience with endo.
- **Teen Outreach Program**—Schools may obtain a free copy of the Association's award-winning video, *Teens Speak Out on Endometriosis*, as well as a complete teaching unit on the subject of endo in teens, by writing to us on school letterhead and requesting the Teen Outreach Program school kit (available while funding lasts).

HUMOR: APPOINTMENT WITH THE GYNAECOLOGIST

I was due later that week for an appointment with the gynaecologist when early one morning I received a call from his office to say that I had been rescheduled at 9:30 A.M. It was around 8:45 A.M. already. The trip to his office usually took about thirty-five minutes so I didn't have any time to spare.

As most women do, I like to take a little extra effort over hygiene when making such visits, but this time I wasn't going to be able to make the full effort. So I rushed upstairs, threw off my dressing gown, wet the washcloth I found near the sink and gave myself a wash in "that area" in front of the sink. I threw the washcloth in the clothes basket, donned some clothes, hopped in the car, and raced to my appointment.

He called me in. Knowing the procedure as I'm sure you all do, I hopped up on the table and pretended I was in Hawaii. I was a little surprised when he said,

"My . . . we have taken a little extra effort this morning, haven't we?" but I didn't respond.

At 8:30 that evening, my 18-year-old daughter was fixing to go to a school dance when she called down from the bathroom,

"Mum, where's my washcloth?"

I called back for her to get another. She responded back, "No, I need the one that was here by the sink. I had all my glitter and sparkles in it. . . ."

EDITOR'S NOTE This article is reprinted by permission from *Tall Girls Inc., Newsletter* (Australia) of March 1999.

10 We Are Strong! A Chapter Especially for Teens and Young Women

EDITOR'S NOTE There are a number of different ways you can find other girls who under-stand what it's like to live with endo. You can join the Association's Teen Contact Network, which will put you in touch with teens from all over; contact your nearest Association support group; or join an online teens-with-endo group. Contact headquarters to sign up!

GETTING EVEN WITH ENDO

Lauren Gottschalk

When I was just starting middle school, I read a book about a group of girlfriends who could not wait to grow up. They dragged their mothers to the department store to buy bras and eagerly tried on maxi pads, imagining how wonderful it would be to get their periods. In health class, we saw twenty-year-old filmstrips about all the wonderful changes that would soon take place, and we saw giddy young teenagers talking about how excited they were to need their first box of tampons. All the girls I saw got their periods, smiled, jumped up and down a few times, and continued life as usual. My health teacher, who always wore bright neon outfits in all one color, explained to us that cramps were "normal" and that menstruation was not an acceptable excuse for missing school, work, or other activities.

Out of all the books, the teen magazines, the filmstrips, and the health classes, I never heard the word *endometriosis*. No one ever told us about this chronic disease, which affects more than five million women of all ages in the United States alone and millions more worldwide. I suppose it wasn't mentioned because myth says that endo is a "career woman's disease," so my classmates and I were "'too young" to have endo. On average, it takes a woman nine years to be diagnosed with endo. Why so long? When a teenager experiences menstrual pain, she is usually handed painkillers and told to stop complaining. If she seems genuine, she may be prescribed birth control pills. Some teens are told that their endo symptoms are symptoms of a sexually transmitted infection, even if they are not sexually active. Despite obvious factual evidence to the contrary, the myth persists that endometriosis is not found in teenagers.

> "Hi, my name is Tracy, I am sixteen and have recently been diagnosed with endometriosis. It has literally taken over my life; the pain is excruciating, and they will be putting me on Lupron this week. I often find that it is extremely beneficial to talk to others, but yet, no one I know really knows what it is like. If you could get me information on the support group [in my area], I would appreciate it greatly. Thanks so much for all your time, effort, and concern."
>
> —*Tracy, New York*

So how exactly is that fifty-cent word pronounced, and what does it mean? It's pronounced end-oh-mee-tree-oh-sis, but it's often simply called "endo." Every month, a woman builds up a lining of tissue inside her uterus to prepare for pregnancy. The body produces hormones, which tell the body to shed the tissue if pregnancy does not occur. That's the part they told you in health class; now here's the part that they didn't. In women with endo, that kind of tissue is also found outside the uterus. It is often found on the uterus, the fallopian tubes, the abdomen, the ovaries, the colon, and sometimes even the lungs. The tissue also responds to the body's hormones and bleeds, but because of its location, it can't leave the body. This causes internal bleeding, which leads to pain, formation of scar tissue, and many other complications, often including infertility.

In this summer before my freshman year at Brandeis University, I am an intern at the Endometriosis Association. I took the job because it was there, it paid, and I figured it would look better than a fast-food job on my résumé. I knew a bit about the disease, and I took home lots of brochures. Before long, I knew what I was talking about.

When I told people about my great new job, I got a lot of blank stares and even more questions like, "So what does that first word mean?" After a week or two, I lost count of how many people I explained endo to, and I stopped counting the "eews" that often followed. I was glad to inform people, but I was disappointed in the reactions I received. As the summer goes on, I am learning that my experience is not unique. I've seen more than one heartbreaking letter from a teenager who can't get anyone (even her parents or doctor) to believe that she is sick. In extreme cases, there have been suicides from girls who just could not take the physical pain of endo and the emotional pain of feeling so alone.

That even well-educated people (both male and female) who had no problem discussing other less-than-charming topics candidly would comment on how gross they thought the female reproductive system to be, even with such a serious disease, shocked me. Maybe it shouldn't have. By then I had watched enough television to realize that one of the very few taboos left in our society is women's health, especially having to do with anything "down there."

I realized that in many ways, whenever someone said, "That's disgusting," they were really saying, "I'm really glad that's not my problem," and, "It's too bad that people have that disease, but it doesn't affect me directly, so I don't care." The people that I talked to weren't insensitive or bad people. They included some of the most giving people I know.

First, I was disappointed in a society and in individuals that would refuse to acknowledge the extent of, or attempt to help with, a problem affecting so much of the population. Then I got mad at the frequency with which endo victims are misdiagnosed, told to "grin and bear it," or ignored altogether.

Now I'm getting even. Whether or not it's pretty and whether or not it fits neatly into a filmstrip, endo is a real disease, and it affects real people. Many of the people I work with and some of my teenage friends have been dealing with endo for years and may well keep dealing with it for the rest of their lives. It won't go away if everyone who has it ignores it (not that some of them can), but it will continue to inflict pain on a growing population of girls and women if it is not stopped. Research is being done to find a cure, and slowly the public and the medical community are being educated.

People get upset because they don't want to hear about endo, but I'm telling them anyway. They may ignore me, and they may forget what I have to say, but someday, when someone they care about is suffering, maybe they'll remember and will help that someone get the proper diagnosis and treatment she deserves. And maybe by then, no one will be embarrassed to talk about it anymore.

TRYING TO DO TWO THINGS AT ONCE: COPING WITH ENDO AND SCHOOL

Crystal Grotberg

Colleen is a senior in high school in Michigan. She enjoys music and softball, and recently she went to homecoming with her best friend, Angie. Unlike many of her friends, Colleen also has endo. It was diagnosed when she was a sophomore (after many years of symptoms), so her life can get a little complicated at times, compared with others she knows from school.

Dealing with endo and school at the same time can be a lot to handle. It doesn't simply disrupt one part of our lives. Sometimes it interferes with almost everything—attendance, concentration, social life, dating, physical activities, and self-confidence.

As Colleen describes, "I am absent a lot more than normal, which causes me to have to play catch-up all the time. I do well in school, but it takes me more time and effort because of the time I miss. I can't eat much when I'm at school because I run the risk of having to run to the bathroom! I don't think I look too good most of the time—it's just hard to look good when you feel so bad! It is hard for me to participate in all the extra high school activities that I would like to. I do a lot, but the endo does slow me down, and I can't do as much as my friends do."

Colleen's sister, Gwen, knows all too well what Colleen is going through. She was diagnosed with endo during her senior year in high school, though her problems began nearly seven years before. "When I was in school," says Gwen, "my body was at the point where I hurt every day, all over. I couldn't take the [pain] medicine I had while in school. If I did, I couldn't remember the day. I felt angry in school because there were so many people that didn't understand. They either thought it was a big joke or thought I was lying. I had two or three teachers who really understood, and then there were those who just got upset when I had to get up and run to the bathroom because I had started bleeding again or needed to go home and lie down because my body wouldn't last any longer."

For many of us, the stories of Colleen and Gwen are familiar. We know how hard it can be to miss a lot of school because of pain or surgery; we have been angry with friends or teachers who don't understand why we can't keep up all the time; we have been frustrated while stuck at home sick when we'd rather be out having fun with our friends. How can we make sure we are able to succeed at school despite endo?

Frequent Absences

Gwen and Colleen's mother, Linda, looks back over the years her daughters have dealt with endo and recalls, "The main problems they have had were caused by being absent so much. Once they got to middle and high school, it was so much harder to catch up on time missed in class. It's not just the bookwork, but the lectures and class discussions that are impossible to make up. It is also very difficult to listen and learn in class when you are in pain a lot of the time."

So how can we keep up? To help her deal with the time she misses, Colleen relies on the people around her who understand endo. "I can usually find someone in the class to fill me in, or I go to my teachers, who have been wonderful and supportive. Without them, it would be impossible!" She also emphasizes the importance of informing others about endo.

People are usually more willing to help us when they understand what is going on inside our bodies. You can help by giving them information. The Endometriosis Association has brochures that help explain what endo is, as well as some of the problems it causes.

"Let your teachers know that you will probably miss more than usual, but that you are serious about keeping up with school," advises Colleen. "Don't be embarrassed about it! It could happen to anyone! Tell your teachers and the school administration what is going on. Let them know what to expect while you are in school. The more your teachers know, the more they can support you."

If you are not comfortable explaining things to teachers or administration, ask your parent(s) or doctor to help you. Linda reminds parents of those with endo, "[We must] support and help our daughters with their schooling. Know that it is going to be a struggle sometimes. Stay in touch with the school and her teachers. Keep them informed of your daughter's health condition. Let them know how they can help. Let them know what to expect as far as absences, problems concentrating because of pain, the possibility of having to dash for the rest room in case of nausea or surprise bleeding. We can't expect teachers to understand and help if we don't let them know what to expect, and we as parents know better than anyone else how endo is affecting our daughter."

Both Colleen and Gwen have been helped and supported by their mother and are happier because of it. "Involve your parents!" recommends Colleen. "They can also speak for you at school. Sometimes a parent can make more headway with them than you can. Parents are wonderful for fighting for your rights at school."

> "I am seventeen years old and was diagnosed with endometriosis [when] I had a laparoscopy to see what was causing all the pain. The doctor removed what he could of the endo and put me on a birth control pill. Unfortunately I never had any relief. Another problem is that I am an athlete and have played field hockey for four years on the high school varsity team. I had hopes of playing next year in college. I am asking for your help. I would like information about what to do over the next few years so when the time comes I will be able to have children."
>
> —*Renee, New Jersey*

When Friends Don't Understand

When Gwen's endo got really bad, it was difficult for her friends to adjust and understand how she felt. "All these students had known me for years, and all of a sudden, *boom*, I'm a totally different person. No more parties, no more late nights on the weekends, no more movies (I can't sit through them), no more dancing, no more anything."

Gwen didn't want to lose her friends, but she couldn't just make the endo go away, either. She soon found out that explaining what was happening to her and being honest with her friends helped them adjust to her new behaviors. Try not to expect them to understand what is happening to you right away. As we know from experience, endo isn't always easy to comprehend, so give your friends a little while to take it all in.

Gwen found that not everyone could accept the changes, but those who did have since become some of her closest and dearest friends. "Ignore those that don't care, because they will go away," advises Gwen. "The ones that do care will come to you. They will be the ones that ask questions and cry with you, talk with you, laugh with you, and be there for you. Those are the ones that will be by your side whenever you need them."

We know who our truest friends are. Some of us might be like Gwen, who declares that her family is her best friend. For others, our closest friend might be someone we've known for years, our neighbor, or the person we are dating. Whoever it is, be sure to let that person know what you need most! Explain to him or her how you feel. If you know what would help you, let the person know that, too. The people who love us want to help us but many times aren't sure what they can do. They will appreciate your suggestions. Who knows—the problems of endo might even bring you closer together!

"Being around my friends and family helps the most. They are always there to listen, to let me cry on their shoulders when the pain hurts too much, to rub my back, or to just be there with me. I think the best part is that they comfort me and lift me up when I feel like giving up," remarks Colleen.

Being There for Each Other

Colleen, Gwen, and Linda have grown to know how to help each other during hard times. Colleen says, "With my sister [Gwen], when she is in bad pain, I play with her hair, rub her back, or something just to try and relax her, and she does the same for me. I know it is hard for my mom to watch us sick and in pain. But we really try to use humor as much as we can. There is nothing that will make you feel better, if only for a few minutes, than laughing with the people you love."

"We try very hard to end each day on a good note, no matter how rough the day has been. There is always something to be thankful for, so we find that something, hug each other, and remind each other how very much we love each other," tells Linda. "I know it sounds simple, but in this crazy world, especially when you are dealing with an illness like endo, sometimes the simple things mean the most."

Looking back on her life at school, Gwen remembers how important it was to know her body's limits. Her advice is, "Don't push yourself if it will make the endo worse. Know when your body is done and you need your rest. Take your time, and make sure that you have a lot of moral support and caring at your side! Keep your hopes up, don't give up—we are all here for you. Remember there are millions of us out there, and we will fight for each other for as long as it takes!"

FIGHT FOR YOUR RIGHT TO EAT RIGHT!

Brenda W. Quinn

There are lots of good reasons for eating healthfully. But did you know that eating well can help your endo symptoms? According to an Association survey of 4,000 women with endo, 62 percent reported improvement after a change in diet. In addition, 56 percent were helped by vitamins and minerals. Think about it: More than half of these women with endo felt better simply as a result of changing their eating habits and/or taking vitamin supplements. Could this work for you? Read on and find out!

Prostaglandins

How can what you eat affect your hormones? To understand how your food connects with your cramps, you need to know about prostaglandins, which are hormone-like substances found in the body's tissues. Prostaglandins are formed in our bodies from two essential fatty acids, linoleic acid and linolenic acid. (These are called "essential" because our body cannot make them and must obtain them from food sources.) Prostaglandins regulate the smooth muscles in the uterus, the intestines, and other tissues. Some prostaglandins are "good" in that they prevent inflammation (swelling and, thus, pain) and the release of too many "bad" prostaglandins. But if there is an overabundance of the "bad" prostaglandins, the uterus can contract too strongly and cause a lot of pain. This imbalance of "bad" substances also contributes to the gastrointestinal symptoms (diarrhea, nausea, etc.) that many women and girls with endo experience.

What's to Blame?

Fast foods are usually loaded with the bad fatty acids that contribute to the overproduction of "bad" prostaglandins. High levels of trans fatty acids (bad—boo, hiss), which are plentiful in margarine and other processed oils, also interfere with the body's processing of essential fatty acids (good—we *want* these guys). And according to an article in *Nutrition Alert*, 35 percent—more than a third—of the calo-

> "People need to realize that extreme pain is not normal. There are too many myths out there that need to be broken. Too many people out there are suffering when maybe there is something to alleviate their pain and symptoms. I know I am extremely lucky at the moment to be pain free. Maybe this will allow me to help others. Whether it's fundraising to pay for gift memberships or distributing brochures, I would love to become involved."
>
> —*Evangeline, eighteen years old, Delaware*

When Jeremy's problems continue, his parents are forced to take him to a doctor.

rie intake of people under the age of nineteen is fat. If you want a shock, take a look at the fat grams chart the next time you visit a fast-food place. Never mind the french fries, you'll be amazed at how much fat is in a sandwich, burger, or milkshake!

The *Candida* Connection

Sugar—which accounts for about 15 percent of the calorie intake of people under the age of nineteen—is another problem. The Association has for a long time reported a connection between endo and *Candida albicans*. Many women and girls with endo are susceptible to *Candida albicans*, a type of yeast infection and allergy usually affecting the intestines and sometimes the vagina, bladder, and other parts of the body. Over the years, a number of members have written that when they were treated for allergic reactions resulting from candida, their endo symptoms *also* cleared up!

"Putting sugar into your body when you have a yeast infection is like throwing gasoline on a flame," states one article on the candida problem. Yeast products—like bagels, pastries, and pizza—and sugar in all forms are big troublemakers for women with *Candida albicans*. So the "comfort foods" that we crave—yeasty foods, candy, sugary cereals, cookies, and soft drinks—may actually make those with endo who have problems with candida feel *worse*. For more on *Candida albicans*, see Chapter 4.

So, What Can I Do About It?

Even if you don't do the grocery shopping at your house, there are changes you can make in your eating habits.

Change Your Oil

It's not realistic (or healthy) to think we can eliminate fats and oils from our diets. But the *kind* of oil we eat can make a big difference. Some of the oils that help increase the level of "good" prostaglandins are seed and nut oils like safflower and sunflower oils. These are especially nutritious if they haven't been heated—if used in salad dressing, for instance.

Another option is supplementing your diet with fish oil, evening primrose oil, or flaxseed oil. One study of adolescents with painful periods showed a marked reduction in menstrual symptoms for those who received a daily omega-3 fish oil supplement for two months. Doctors in both the United States and Britain have studied and recommended evening primrose oil to relieve endo symptoms, as well as PMS. Check with your doctor, pharmacist, or dietician for dosage recommendations. Staff at your health food store can also help you choose the best supplement for you.

Eat at Home

Believe it or not, eating at home with other family members—even your little brother—is better for you than eating out. One recent study of 16,000 boys and girls between the ages of nine and fourteen found that those who ate at home less consumed more soft drinks and more fried foods than those who ate at home with other family members. More frequent family dinners were associated with higher intakes of fiber, calcium, iron, and other vitamins (the good stuff), as well as lower intake of the unhealthful saturated fats, according to dietician Karen Collins, R.D. When you have to be away from home, try packing your own food, including fresh fruit and veggies for snacks. You'll feel better and look better, too.

"I have just gone through this entire website [the Association website, EndometriosisAssn .org] and have developed a better understanding of this unfortunate disease. I was not even aware that this was a disease. I am eighteen years old, and I have experienced very severe menstrual cramps from the moment I got my first period at fourteen years of age. During menstruation my cramps are so severe that it drains all my energy from me. There have been many occasions on which I had to leave school because of the severe pain. My body begins to feel very shaky; I can hardly walk or keep my eyes open. Many times I find myself hovering over the toilet because of nausea and/or diarrhea and/or constipation. I also sometimes experience menstrual migraines. I'm not very sure whether I do have this disease, but I do hope that with this letter you will be able to help."

—Maria, eighteen years old, Ontario

Skip the Soda and Bone Up

A recent study in Boston concluded that girls who regularly drink soda—cola drinks in particular—and are physically active are *five times* more likely to fracture bones than those who do not drink it. Researchers are not sure why. Some think that phosphorus, a common ingredient in soda, depletes calcium from the bones. Others believe young people are drinking soda instead of more nutritious beverages like milk. (*Caution:* Organic milk is a safer choice, to avoid dioxins. For more on the dioxin-endo connection, see Part 3 in this book.)

According to *Our Daughters' Health: Practical and Invaluable Advice for Raising Confident Girls Ages 6–16*, by Sharon L. Roan, 85 percent of girls are not getting enough calcium. The body's ability to build bone stops in the early twenties, and girls who don't consume enough calcium may have 10 percent less bone mass by early adulthood and have a greater risk of developing osteoporosis. Osteoporosis is a disease in which the bones become thin and porous and can break easily. Women and girls with endo have additional reasons to be concerned about their bones. One is the long-term use of GnRH drugs used to treat endo (sold under the brands Zoladex, Synarel, Lupron), which without add-back estrogen replacement, can result in loss of bone density, which in turn can lead to osteoporosis. So teens with endo who have taken GnRH drugs really need to be aware of their need for calcium.

If you don't like milk or are allergic to it, a number of other foods are calcium rich: almonds; salmon or sardines; greens such as arugula, turnip greens, and kale; yogurt; broccoli; and part-skim mozzarella cheese.

Go Natural, and Take Your Vitamins

Eating more fresh fruit, vegetables, and fish will help regulate the prostaglandins in your body. Eating organic foods will help keep down the amount of dioxins and other chemicals in your body. Organic foods are foods certified by their producers to have been grown without toxic chemicals and without hormones in the livestock feed in the case of meats, chicken, and eggs. Organic food is available at health food stores. Many mainstream grocery stores now have an organic food section as well.

For those who don't get all the needed nutrition in the food they eat—or for the "junk food junkie"—a yeast-free vitamin and mineral supplement makes sense. The body is easily depleted of B vitamins, for instance, by the consumption of sugar and other refined carbohydrates, alcohol, caffeine, stress, or antibiotic use. But the B vitamins

> "I was thirteen when I was diagnosed with endo, but I had the cramps basically when my period started. I think my story is pretty typical for teens who have endo, but I think my endo has spread to a couple other places that it shouldn't have so early (i.e. bladder, intestines, and possibly *inside* the intestines). Sometimes it is really hard for me to deal with, but it is something I have to live with and try to work around. I would love to talk to other girls, because I know how hard it is to deal with, especially since my friends can't really understand because they aren't going through it."
>
> —*Debra, sixteen years old, Connecticut*

are especially important for women with endo because they lower estrogen levels. (Estrogen is a female hormone that can be a trigger for endo.) Magnesium, a mineral, may help relax smooth muscles like those in the uterus that cause cramps. Vitamins A, C, and D appear to help the immune system. You get the idea. Ask a healthcare professional for advice. Overuse of some vitamins can cause toxic reactions. (For more on nutrition and endo, see Chapter 5.)

The Best Reason

Member Heather Sloat may have the best reason for healthful eating. She wrote this when she was fifteen. "I am on a different diet and can't have sugar, wheat, or yeast. Talk about a big change. It's so hard to avoid the food when it's all around you. Especially when you're a teen involved in an active youth group that is always doing something. *The diet is hard, but if it works, it will be well worth it.*"

EDITOR'S NOTE This article originally appeared in the Association's *TeenSource* newsletter for teens with endo.

TEEN TO TEEN: TIPS FROM A YOUNG WOMAN WITH ENDO

Cindy Rice

EDITOR'S NOTE In this article, we bring you advice from a teen with endo. Cindy has worked hard with her doctors to treat her endo, and we thought she had some valuable tips for other young women. She made endometriosis the subject of her high school independent study program and assertively sought the medical help she needed. Here Cindy shares with us some simple, but potentially powerful coping techniques:

- **Support groups**—It is often good to speak with others who have endo. Remember, even though you may have different symptoms, your feelings may be the same. The Endometriosis Association can help you find or start a support group in your area.
- **Friends**—Often, for teenagers, friends are the biggest help. Good friends are people with whom you can talk, confide, and laugh. Caiti was my female friend who was willing to hold my hand and be there for me, no matter how bad things got. She often helped me to laugh about bad experiences with doctors or drug side effects such as hot flashes.

- **Family**—Friends are important, but most teens live with their families or others who care about them. Talk to your family, and listen to your family. One of my family members noticed my depression because I stopped cleaning my room. (I usually have a neat room. During the bouts of depression, it would turn into a sty.) I have an older sister, who helped me to understand the medications I was on. She also told me how I should be treated in a doctor's office and what I could expect. If relationships are difficult in your family, talk with a teacher, pastor, or other adult in whom you can trust.

- **Counseling**—It may be necessary to seek professional counseling if the emotional pain that can result from this disease becomes overwhelming. I now believe that I would have benefited from seeing a psychiatrist. I must also stress that I was not aware that I needed help for much of my depression. It is important to recognize when to ask for help.

  [**Editor's note:** If you decide to choose a professional counselor, be certain that he or she understands endo. Unfortunately, many mental health professionals do not yet understand the physical and emotional complexities of endo. Please contact the Association for help on this.]

- **Religion**—Many people find that turning to God or spiritual faith gives them the strength needed to fight this battle. Although teens are not always certain of their beliefs, if you do have a religious or spiritual faith, it may help you through the difficult times.

- **Inner Support**—You must believe in yourself. You need to know what is good for you and trust yourself. If you do not think that your care is adequate, you have to tell someone. But remember, it is almost impossible to cope alone.

- **Research**—Research and learn about the disease. Knowledge is important, but always be careful. Don't believe everything you read. Fact-check information with reputable sources like the Association. Ask questions about your care. It is best for you to know all options. As a teenager, you should ask questions about short- and long-term side effects when a drug is prescribed for you. Remember, the books written by Mary Lou Ballweg and the Endometriosis Association are excellent sources of information.

- **Hobbies**—Hobbies can help you to heal. What I mean by this is that you need something to take your mind off the disease. I carried around a sketchbook. My drawings were by no means works of art, but they did allow me to express my feelings. Now I express myself through music, photography, and occasional essays. You need an emotional outlet to help you express your feelings to yourself.

- **Exercise**—Exercise works wonders. I had problems with bouncing exercises such as running. For anyone with the same problem, I recommend walking, swimming, dancing, and weightlifting. These can help you to recover from surgeries faster, possibly reduce your chances of needing surgery, and reduce stress. It *is* much easier to handle a problem with a clear mind after exercising.

Pain causes emotional responses. When not dealt with, those responses can cause everything from anxiety to depression, which in turn can make you feel worse. You need to cope and deal with those emotions as well as the disease. If you have your mind, body, and spirit standing behind you, you can conquer anything that comes along.

BIG SISTER/MENTOR PROGRAM: PROVIDING FRIENDSHIP AND SUPPORT

Christel B. Wendelberger

Sitting comfortably in an Ann Arbor, Michigan, coffee shop and bookstore, Bryce, age nineteen, and Caitlin, twenty-three, share stories about their lives and laugh about their common experiences. Watching them talk and smile, the casual observer would never know that many of those experiences were filled with the pain and loneliness of endometriosis, or that two calls to the Association led to this first-time meeting.

In fact, Bryce and Caitlin are participants in the Association Mentor Program, a project that helps to establish supportive relationships between individual teens and women with endo. Their first meeting took place many months after Bryce's mother read about the Mentor Program in the Association's international newsletter and placed a call to the Association.

Bryce had been suffering with debilitating pelvic pain for a long time. After months of illness and a string of frustrating visits to doctors who could find nothing wrong, a CAT scan finally showed a large mass in Bryce's pelvis. Fearing the worst, doctors scheduled an emergency surgery that led to the removal of the mass and her left ovary. A diagnosis of endo was immediately made.

"I had never even heard of endo," Bryce says. "I had not a clue—didn't even know it existed. My mom found the Mentor Program and asked me if I wanted to sign up." Bryce joined the program and was paired with Caitlin. Caitlin had recently responded to a notice in the Association newsletter seeking Mentors. "I called the Association saying I was interested in the program because I was nineteen when endo started wreaking havoc in my life," said Caitlin, "and I have a peer counseling background, so it seemed like I could help."

Diagnosed with endo about four years ago, Caitlin has had extensive experience with the disease. She had always had extreme pain with her periods, but early in her college career, things took a drastic turn for the worse. "Over the course of a month, I went from having pain three or four days a month to every day of the month. I was having more and more trouble engaging as a student and ended up taking a leave from school," Caitlin explains.

"I'm eighteen years old and diagnosed with endo. I guess the pain started when I was thirteen. Just before I was diagnosed, I was experiencing chronic, severe pain—anywhere from aching to stabbing to burning. At times I was in so much pain that I would actually curl up and cry. Along with the pain I felt lightheaded, sick to my stomach, dizzy, and weak. As I learned more about my condition, my feelings went from confused, scared, to just plain depressed. My doctor says I have until my midtwenties to have kids—I'll still be in college. How can I possibly afford kids until after college? My whole life, I've always wanted children of my own. Why did this happen to me? I lie in bed at night, thinking or wishing I could someday feel my baby moving in my body. Now that might never happen. I might never get to feel that miracle."

—Michelle, Wisconsin

After two additional leaves from school, three surgeries, Lupron, hormones, and a series of nerve blocks, Caitlin has a deep personal understanding of endo and its toll. Yet despite her illness, she will soon graduate as a philosophy major from Williams College in Massachusetts. A self-described "doer and overachiever," she has sought to use her downtime constructively and give meaning to her personal suffering. "I have always enjoyed being there for people. I have been through this particular experience [endometriosis], and having an opportunity to share that with someone was very appealing to me," Caitlin explains.

After receiving some initial information about Bryce from the Association, Caitlin sent her an introductory letter. By this time, Bryce was back in school at the University of Michigan and enjoying her freshman year. Knowing that Bryce was doing well and not wanting to emphasize endo in her life, Caitlin's first letter described her own experience with the disease. Caitlin's description of the frequency and severity of her endo was initially difficult for Bryce to hear about.

"I have to admit that her first letter kind of scared me," Bryce says. But it was also clear to her that she had found in Caitlin someone who truly understood the pain of their shared disease. "My mom can be very understanding, but it's nice to talk to someone who really knows what the pain is like," Bryce explains. The relationship between the two young women grew through a series of phone calls and E-mails. Learning that Caitlin was still working through her studies at school and planning a future despite medical disruptions, Bryce soon began to take inspiration rather than fear from hearing of her mentor's experience.

"This disease is not fun, and it's hard to deal with, but it can be done. After hearing about Caitlin's experiences, it proved to me I could do it," says Bryce. "I just started college. I have my whole life in front of me. I'm majoring in engineering, and that's what I want to do with my life. I'm not going to let this disease get in the way of my dreams," she states.

When Bryce and Caitlin met in person at the coffee shop, the connection between them was immediate. Bryce now struggles to express her feelings during that initial meeting: "When we finally met, it was the weirdest feeling . . . we could just talk. It's hard to explain, but in her eyes I could just tell that she understood. It was just special. I can't explain it."

For Caitlin the visit was equally joyful. What struck her most, she says, was "the fact that it was largely a meeting between two normal people who had this thing in common. We giggled and talked. We talked about how you deal with it [endo] at school, etc. We talked about serious things, but it was light. To look at somebody who was smiling and going through this horrible thing and getting through it was heartening."

Both young women are back in school now, working toward their personal goals and dreams, separated by hundreds of miles. Busy with school and other activities, they won't have an opportunity to see each other often. But a strong bond exists between them, and phone calls, letters, and E-mail messages on difficult days will surely offer comfort and support for years to come.

As a result of her very positive experience, Bryce encourages other teens with endo to get involved in the Association's Mentor Program. "It's not like this big commitment. You don't have to write and call them all the time. But when you need them, they are there for you," she says.

EDITOR'S NOTE To learn more about the Family/Teen Membership and the Mentor Program, contact the Association at (414) 355-2200 or EndometriosisAssn.org.

11 Menopause and Endometriosis

Ellen Agger

Introduction

Will your endo symptoms resolve with menopause? Should you use hormone replacement therapy, or will it reactivate the endo? Are there other, safer ways to treat bothersome menopause symptoms? Even if the endo implants don't recur, what other health problems should you be aware of? There are no easy answers to these questions and few guideposts for the generation of endo-knowledgeable baby boomer women now entering menopause. The more we talk about our experiences in menopause, the more research will be done specific to our needs, and the sooner those guideposts will be available to us.

Although few studies have looked at the experience of women with endo in menopause, menopause in general is the focus of increasing medical study. To date, these studies have mostly been done on middle-class, Caucasian women in the United States and Western Europe.[1] Many look at healthy women or women with a particular health problem, such as osteoporosis or heart disease. We're not sure what these studies mean for women with endo and women with endo who are not middle-class and Caucasian. But we do know that endo is not easy to study. And we now know that it's not "simply" a disease of the reproductive system but involves the immune system and other systems in the body in a complex dance that is expressed differently in each woman at different times in her life and is not well understood.

The study results referred to in this chapter may or may not apply to you. When evaluating their usefulness, you will need to understand your own experiences and make choices that make sense to you. Develop a critical eye when reading about results of studies in the media. Talk with other women with endo. Consult your healthcare providers—your doctor, naturopath, acupuncturist—whomever you work with to help you look after your health. Consider how you approach looking after yourself and how you make decisions about treatment.

Finally, as you enter your postmenopausal years, you may find that endo no longer plays a central part in your health and life (although that's not the experience for all women with endo; read on). But it's critical that you not stop thinking of yourself as a woman with healthcare needs and health risks. Endo pain may be gone, and fertility may no longer be an issue, but you may face other health problems related to immune system dysfunction—allergies, autoimmune diseases, cancers. Learn as much as you can, and continue to look after yourself.

Menopause: What's It All About?

Women in the developed world will now spend more than one-third of their lives in their postmenopausal years.[1] The average age at which women reach menopause (defined as one year since your last period) is fifty-one, and most women enter menopause somewhere between forty-five and fifty-five. Smokers may reach menopause earlier than other women; family history may play a part; women who have not had children may reach it earlier; and we don't know what's "normal" for women with endo.

As you move through menopause, some of your hormone levels will be shifting—including the three types of estrogen (estradiol, estrone, and estriol, the most potent of which is estradiol), progesterone, testosterone, DHEA (dehydroepiandrosterone, a hormone the body converts into estrogen and testosterone), and cortisol. During perimenopause (the time around menopause), the ovaries begin to produce less estrogen; in fact, estrogen levels fluctuate, much as they did during puberty. This fluctuation usually lasts between three and six years—up to ten years for some women. Menstrual periods become erratic (sometimes coming more closely together, other times farther apart). Flow may change, with some women experiencing flooding. Bone density drops rapidly in the first five years after menopause, then bone loss slows down.

The ovaries continue to produce testosterone, an androgen, after menopause. Androgens are the hormone responsible for what we usually consider male characteristics. Testosterone, understood to be largely responsible for changes in sexual function and energy in menopausal women, decreases by 50 percent by the fourth or fifth post-menopausal year (although the levels may remain the same or even increase before that).[2] The production of two other androgens, DHEA and androstenedione, also slows down, although this may be due to aging rather than menopause.[3]

In menopause, the adrenal glands and fat cells become a major source of estrogen production; an enzyme called aromatase converts two types of androgens into estrogens. Thus, in natural and surgical menopause, the body continues to produce estrogen, although much less than before. This may be important for women with endo. Aromatase is present in at least some endo implants, especially in the cul-de-sac, the abdominal wall, and in ovarian cysts (also known as endometriomas).

Surgical menopause is a completely different story from natural menopause. Whereas in natural menopause, hormonal changes may occur over years, in surgical menopause, these hormonal changes occur within a day or two after removal of the ovaries. Even when the ovaries are kept, in rare cases they can stop functioning right after hysterectomy if the surgery has permanently cut off their blood supply. Menopause symptoms are usually more intense than in natural menopause. The estradiol concentration in the blood drops from a premenopausal level of 100 to 300 picograms per milliliter to just 5 to 15 picograms per milliliter.[4] As well, there is a sudden decline in certain androgen levels, which may account for the loss of sex drive some women experience.

Will you experience the menopause symptoms listed in the sidebar on page 279? You may experience none of these, some, or many. Menopause may be a breeze for you or a very difficult time. One interesting study looked at menopause symptoms in one of the largest and most diverse groups of women studied in the United States (16,000 women, age forty-five to sixty).[5] It found that lifestyle factors, race, ethnicity, and socioeconomic status affected women's experience of menopause symptoms. For example, women in the study who were poor, smoked, didn't get enough exercise, and were overweight were more likely to experience more menopause symptoms. Genetics and health problems like endo also play a role in how women perceive and experience menopause.

As many as 25 percent of women in natural menopause report having no bothersome signs of menopause,[6] while about 10 to 20 percent seek medical help for severe discomfort.[7] Some women feel better than before—this may especially be true for women who have suffered a great deal of pain with endo, whether they are in natural or surgical menopause. And for some, sex may finally be better (or even possible now). As with the experience with endo before menopause, we see a huge variation in how women with endo experience this time of transition.

Does Menopause "Cure" Endo? Recurrence and New Endo in Menopause

The good news is that it appears that many women with endo do experience the end of endo symptoms, especially pelvic symptoms, with menopause. However, the Association has heard from many women who have experienced continued problems with endo after either natural or surgical menopause. This is bad news.

Natural Menopause

Remember that endo implants, if they have not been removed surgically, may still exist, but the symptoms may no longer be a problem. There are only a few studies in the medical literature about recurrence of endo lesions in menopause (or about appearance of new endo lesions—it may be hard to tell the difference). We now understand that the lesions of endo depend on estrogen for their growth. It seems reasonable, therefore, to conclude that the lesions would no longer be stimulated when the ovaries produce less estrogen in menopause and monthly bleeding stops. However, smaller amounts of estrogen are still being produced. We don't yet know how large a factor this might be in women who experience continued endo growth and symptoms. Nor do we know what role the immune system, exposure to environmental toxins, diet, lifestyle choices, weight, and other factors play in endo after menopause.

So what *do* we know about the incidence of endo symptoms in natural menopause? According to data collected from 4,000 of the Endometriosis Association's members, only 100 had reached natural menopause. Of these, only 2.5 percent still experienced problems with endo after menopause. While the small percentage is hopeful, this is unfortunately too small a group from which to draw broad conclusions.

Another source also estimates that 2 to 5 percent of postmenopausal women have endo, including women up to age seventy-six.[8] A third source shows that an estimated 2 to 4 percent of postmenopausal women treated at one institution were diagnosed with endo for the first time during surgery for other problems—42 percent had not been using hormone replacement therapy (HRT).[9] This could contradict the belief that endo needs premenopausal levels of estrogen and/or added estrogens, such as HRT, to thrive.

The real question to ask may be, Is endo uncommon in menopause, or is it not commonly diagnosed in menopause? In fact, endo as a source of complaints may be underdiagnosed in postmenopausal women, as many physicians don't expect it and therefore don't consider it as a possibility. More research is clearly needed.

Surgical Menopause

Women who have had their ovaries removed may find that, in spite of the challenges of being thrown suddenly into menopause, they have finally seen the end of excruciating pelvic pain and other symptoms of endo. However, this is not always the case. In fact, women are still too frequently told that removal of the ovaries (and, hence, the main source of estrogen) will "cure" their endo, even if all visible endo is not removed at the time of surgery.

We know differently. The Association's data show that endo symptoms continued in 35.7 percent of 731 women who had undergone surgical menopause. This number

---

Common Menopause Symptoms

- Hot flashes and night sweats
- Difficulty sleeping
- Vaginal dryness
- Mood swings, depression, irritability, and anxiety
- Forgetfulness and difficulty concentrating
- Palpitations (rapid heartbeats)
- Bladder control problems (irritable bladder, loss of urine with coughing or running)
- Decreased sex drive
- Fatigue

---

is similar to that found in an earlier Association study. (See *The Endometriosis Sourcebook* for more on hysterectomy and removal of ovaries and on the earlier study.)

In another study of postmenopausal women with chronic pelvic pain, endo was found during laparoscopy in 37 percent of sixty-five women whose uterus and ovaries had been removed.[10] As well, new endo was found in 13 percent (three cases), but these may represent endo undiagnosed at the first surgery. The incidence of endo was more common in women who had used estrogen replacement therapy (ERT) after their initial surgery.

This number of endo cases is higher than those found in another study of 138 women with endo who had had hysterectomies.[11] This study found that 10 percent of the women who had their ovaries removed along with their uterus had recurrent endo symptoms. Interesting to note was the fact that all these women had been given HRT after removal of their ovaries. However, the authors suggested there might be a selection bias in this study toward recurrence because those who were treated at this particular facility had already had unsuccessful medical or surgical treatment elsewhere. In other words, these were women who had severe symptoms that were difficult to treat.

Andrew Prentice, M.D., a U.K. endo expert, writes in a clinical review on endo that even if both ovaries and fallopian tubes are removed, "not all of the endometrial tissue implanted outside the uterus will be removed from some patients and thus symptoms may persist."[12]

The Clinical Practice Guidelines on Hysterectomy prepared by the Society of Obstetricians and Gynaecologists of Canada advise physicians to discuss the effects of removing both ovaries with their patients before surgery, including the issue of symptom recurrence if ovaries are left intact.[13] The guidelines also state, "Women who have recurrent symptoms after hysterectomy and castration are likely to have persistent disease, most often involving the bowel." This was also observed in the Association's analysis

"I had a hysterectomy for endo when I was thirty. My ovaries were left intact. I am forty-seven now and am experiencing menopause. I am taking an estrogen supplement (Premarin) that has caused my endo symptoms to reappear. The doctors have told me that not all the endo was removed with that surgery years ago and the estrogen has reactivated it. I need the estrogen to function in my job and daily life. Do you have any information regarding menopause and endo?"

—*Val, British Columbia*

in the mid-1980s of data from its Research Registry. The study found that the majority of women in surgical menopause with continuing endo symptoms had bowel and/or bladder problems. This is most likely because gynecologists lack the skill or inclination to remove endo involving the bladder, ureters, or bowel!

Endo can also be stimulated by ovarian tissue left behind during surgery. If a small piece (or multiple pieces) of ovary is left behind at the time of surgery, it can grow and produce enough estrogen to reactivate endo. This is known as ovarian remnant syndrome. The majority of these remnants are located behind the peritoneum and often adhere to pelvic sidewall structures, including the ureter, vessels in the lower abdomen, and base of the bladder, making identification and removal challenging.[14]

David Redwine, M.D., an endo surgery pioneer and Association Advisor in Bend, Oregon, has studied endo after castration and has found that women can continue to have endo symptoms with or without estrogen therapy.[15] In his study of seventy-five castrated women who did not have ovarian remnant syndrome, 33 percent had intestinal involvement. He suggests, "Invasive disease of the uterosacral ligaments or intestinal tract is more likely to remain symptomatic following castration with retention of disease" [in other words, if the disease is not fully excised, or cut away]. He strongly recommends removal of invasive peritoneal and intestinal endo at the time the ovaries are removed. He also states that while a literature review shows that most women experience reduced symptoms after castration even if some endo lesions are left, "there is no scientific evidence that endometriosis [lesions are] physically destroyed by either removal of the ovaries or menopausal levels of E2 [estradiol]. . . . In fact, abundant clinical evidence supports the ability of symptomatic endometriosis to exist after menopause without estrogen replacement therapy."

Kelly L. Molpus, M.D., in Omaha, Nebraska, notes in a review article on endo in menopause that the ovary is the most common site of postmenopausal implants and adhesions.[16] Another source estimates that approximately 75 percent of "clinically significant lesions" involve the ovaries and bowel.[17]

The endo experts consulted in preparing this chapter agreed on one point: the importance of excising all visible endo, even when removing the ovaries. However, Camran Nezhat, M.D., the Association Advisor who helped pioneer the use of laparoscopic surgery for endo in the 1980s, cautioned that while it is possible to remove all *visible* endo, microscopic endo can be left behind and continue to cause symptoms. Nezhat, located in Palo Alto, California, stresses the importance of taking a patient's

Factors That May Promote Recurrence of Endo Symptoms in Menopause

- **Incomplete surgical removal of endo**—Removal of endo may be incomplete because its location makes it difficult to remove, because the treating physician lacks the necessary skill, or both. As well, many physicians still do not appreciate or agree with the belief that it is important to cut out all visible endo tissue whenever possible.
- **Use of HRT**—Hormone replacement therapy (HRT) is particularly likely to cause problems if it uses unopposed estrogen, that is, estrogen used without the modifying effects of progestin or progesterone. The type and dose of estrogen will also have an impact.
- **Other sources of endogenous estrogens**—These sources include fat cells converting the androgens androstenedione and testosterone into estrone and estradiol, respectively, as well as estrogen-producing tumors.
- **Obesity**—Obesity could contribute to a recurrence of endo symptoms due to the fact that a higher level of androgens is stored in and converted into estrogen within fat cells, as well as higher circulating levels of estradiol and estrone.[18] This is another area for more research.
- **An immune reaction**—The Association has heard from women who have had reactivation of pain so severe as to force them to bed after severe allergic reactions to food and other substances.

complaints of continued pain seriously and not thinking it's "all in her head." He is concerned that women who still suffer from pain are labeled unfairly, and he emphasizes the importance of seeing a physician with extensive experience treating endo on a daily basis, who can offer thoughtful evaluation and treatment.

If You Experience Endo Symptoms in Menopause

If you experience familiar or new endo symptoms that concern you, or if you develop new health problems, *don't assume it can't be endo.* Seek medical help. Because of widely held beliefs in the medical community that endo "dies out" after menopause, you may need to insist on further investigation. Be stubborn if you are worried! As always, try to find a gyn who has experience in treating endo. If you see a general surgeon for bowel pain, be aware that he or she may look for bowel cancer and may not consider endo (or the gastrointestinal problems of those with endo) as a possibility. Make sure the surgeon or gyn knows about your history with endo. Insist on a rectovaginal bimanual exam; not all doctors do this routinely. If there is tenderness, you may have endo; if not, the pain may be caused by adhesions from previous surgeries and old endo, according to one endo expert, Harry Reich, M.D., in Shavertown, Pennsylvania.

Signs and Symptoms That May Mean a Recurrence of Endo

If you notice any of the following signs or symptoms or have other health problems that concern you, seek medical advice. Be aware that some of these are common with endo but may also be caused by other health problems:

- Pain in your abdomen or pelvic area (the most common presenting symptom in postmenopausal women with a history of endo)
- Gastrointestinal (GI) or urinary symptoms: bloating, intermittent cramping, diarrhea, constipation, rectal pain or bleeding, painful or frequent urination, or blood in the urine
- Bowel obstruction (possibly including vomiting, crampy pain, diarrhea, a rigid and tender abdomen, and distention of the abdomen, depending on where the blockage is and what is causing it) or complete urinary retention—seek *immediate* medical attention for these

Treatment Options for Peri- and Postmenopausal Endo

Little information is available in the medical literature that addresses the question of treatment of endo in perimenopause and postmenopause. If you need treatment, look for a doctor who has extensive clinical experience treating endo.

When considering treatments for postmenopausal endo, Camran Nezhat, quoted earlier, believes that treating every patient individually is important, as do most endo experts. He believes endo does not behave the same in all women. He takes a thorough history, looking at the behavior of the endo in that particular woman and the type and extent of surgeries she has had. He assesses how sensitive she might be to estrogen and then develops an individualized approach to care. Nezhat may give estrogen for menopausal symptoms and may add testosterone (or use it alone) for its androgenic effects (based on the experience with danazol for endo). He considers that testosterone has a positive effect on breast tissue (based on his clinical observations of a lower incidence of breast cancer in women who use testosterone with estrogen) and has observed that it can help improve energy levels and sex drive.

Medical therapy is even less understood in postmenopausal women with endo than in those with perimenopausal endo. Side effects of danazol increase the risk of problems in women with severe high blood pressure, congestive heart failure, or impaired kidney function.[16] This reminds us that we might be dealing not only with endo in menopause, but also with age-related medical problems that must be considered as well. Progestin in low-dose continuous or cyclic administration is an accepted form of therapy.[19] Oral contraceptive use in postmenopausal women has not been evaluated and should be avoided, Molpus notes. Not everyone agrees on this last statement. Some endo experts believe the risks of oral contraceptives may be worthwhile in selected women.

Some endo experts do not prescribe GnRH agonists in menopausal women, as they put a woman into pseudomenopause, which is not required, since she's already in menopause. Others think they may be helpful, but Molpus suggests, "It is possible that postmenopausal women have a reduced capacity to recover from loss of bone mineral content," even with add-back therapy, the addition of hormones to prevent bone loss.

> "I'm a survivor of this dreadful disease. It's been seven years . . . since my hysterectomy, removal of ovaries, and a colostomy . . . I'm also on estrogen replacement therapy. I've since developed a thyroid problem, underactive thyroid."
>
> *—Lorrl, Ontario*

Serdar Bulun, M.D., a Chicago, Illinois, reproductive endocrinologist, has done clinical work with women with severe postmenopausal endo. He has used aromatase inhibitors to prevent the conversion of androgens into estrogens by fat, bone, skin, and other cells.[20] Of some concern is the bone loss that accompanies their use, although it appears that this loss may be temporary. It may also be that bone loss does not occur in all women. Bulun considers that postmenopausal women in natural menopause—and not on HRT—with severe endo make so much estrogen that it keeps their bone mass high to begin with. This is an area where further clinical study is needed. (For more on aromatase inhibitors, see the article "Medical Treatments for Endometriosis" in Chapter 2.)

Unless there are medical or other reasons not to do this, some endo experts suggest that the procedure of choice in postmenopausal women is "definitive" surgery. This means the complete removal of all visible endo, the uterus, tubes, ovaries, and adhesions (when possible). This is a contentious issue. Although a number of endo experts consulted during the preparation of this chapter emphasized the importance of cutting out all visible endo, not all agreed that the ovaries must also be removed, even in menopause. Reich, a pioneer laparoscopic surgeon, is one of these. He maintains that the ovaries do not need to be removed to effectively treat severe endo *if* all the visible endo is *thoroughly* excised and careful surgical technique is used to prevent adhesions during healing.

In women who have already been castrated and continue to experience endo symptoms, surgery can be done to confirm that endo tissue is still present, to rule out cancer, and to remove all visible endo. If prior surgeries have not included removal of ovaries, Molpus suggests it's reasonable at this time to do so. The ovaries are a likely location of endo implants, along with the bowel, which must also be treated, and, of course, the ovaries are contributing to the estrogen levels that feed the endo. However, some women still choose not to have their ovaries removed (they may prefer their own hormones rather than synthetic), even at this time, but prefer instead to have all remaining endo excised.

Since so little is really known about the safety and effectiveness of these treatments for peri- and postmenopausal endo, it may also be a time to consider other approaches to control endo symptoms, such as acupuncture, homeopathy, diet, and herbal treatments. While they have also not been the subject of much scientific study, we do know that some women with premenopausal endo have used them quite successfully to reduce endo symptoms.

> "I've had four major surgeries since I turned fifty, and I've had seven Lupron shots. I'm not the only one with this problem. Is anything being done for my age group?"
>
> —*Barbara, Tennessee*

So, should you worry about endo problems continuing in menopause? Hopefully, endo will no longer cause the same symptoms as in earlier years. You may be relieved to see the end of your periods and ovulation, if those were painful times. But, as always, listen to your body, and talk with your healthcare providers if you have any concerns about recurrence. As you enter a new phase of your life, you may find better health than before, or you may experience a new raft of problems associated with menopause or with endo, particularly related to your immune system. Remember that if you do experience problems, it's not "all in your head." Share your experiences with other women, especially through the Endometriosis Association, so we can learn what truly happens to women with endo in menopause.

Menopause Symptom Reduction and Disease Prevention

If symptoms such as hot flashes, vaginal dryness, and mood swings are affecting your quality of life, especially during perimenopause and the first few years after natural menopause, you may choose to treat them. But treatment is only necessary if these conditions are interfering with your life. The choice is yours.

These symptoms, as mentioned earlier, are usually more dramatic in women who have had their ovaries removed. Some women do get through this period with the help of nonhormonal therapies and remedies, but many choose hormone replacement therapy (HRT) because the sudden drop in hormone levels after surgery causes such discomfort. Physicians usually recommend HRT to reduce severe surgical menopause symptoms and prevent bone loss.

Many women also want to address ways to reduce their risk of osteoporosis, heart disease, certain cancers, and cognitive decline (a reduction of the ability to perceive, think, and remember) as they age. Some choose to look at ways they can prevent these long-term health problems through lifestyle changes such as diet and exercise, supplementation with calcium and other bone-building minerals, and/or use of medications. The challenge for each of us is to assess the ever-changing information that's available on how we can best prevent or reduce diseases more common after menopause and make informed decisions based on what is known now. Keep reading. Keep sharing. Keep learning.

Hormone Replacement Therapy

The question of whether or not hormone replacement therapy is a safe and helpful option for women with endo is of great concern to many women. Unfortunately, we cannot simply look to the medical literature for guidance. Studies on HRT are contradictory, hard to follow, and usually not specific to women with endo. Yet every day, clinical decisions are made and advice given based on studies with serious limitations. If you are searching for a way through the maze of contradictory findings, particularly those you read or hear about in the popular media, you are not alone!

The first large, randomized, controlled trial on HRT was the Heart and Stroke Estrogen-progestin Replacement Study (HERS).[21] It involved 2,700 women with heart disease and found that HRT was not effective in preventing further coronary heart disease in women in natural menopause.

The second was the Women's Health Initiative (WHI), which studied 27,000 healthy women using either the combined continuous HRT preparation called Prempro—conjugated equine estrogen (Premarin) combined with medroxyprogesterone acetate (Provera)—or Premarin alone (in women who had had hysterectomies).[22] Note that only one specific type of HRT was studied, and the same dose was given to all participants, no matter what their individual hormone levels or needs were. In 2002 the combined HRT part of this study was cancelled early when researchers concluded that health risks (increases in breast cancer, heart attack, blood clots, and stroke) exceeded benefits (reduction of hip fractures and colorectal cancer) after an average of 5.2 years of HRT. The trial had been hoping to see reduction of coronary heart disease and osteoporosis with this type of HRT, the most commonly prescribed in the United States and Canada. It did *not* look at the use of HRT for control of menopausal symptoms.

At the time of this writing, women in natural menopause are being advised to use HRT for short-term relief (no longer than four or five years) for severe menopausal symptoms only and to consider other approaches to prevent chronic disease. Further recommendations from this large trial (and from the estrogen-only part of the trial) are expected. In fact, the cancellation of this particular trial and the uproar that followed in the media remind us that our understanding of the implications of taking powerful hormones is constantly changing.

It's also important to remember that, given the lack of study of HRT use in women with endo, we don't know what any of these findings mean for the individual woman with endo, whether she's in natural or surgical menopause. Nor do we know the long-term effects of lower doses of these hormones, of bioidentical hormones (more on these shortly), or of other combinations of HRT, such as estrogen-androgen therapy. Continue to evaluate new information carefully as it becomes available, and stay in touch with the Association, which will continue to monitor and report on this and all other topics related to endo.

Risks and Benefits of HRT

Although physicians might be expected—and are bound ethically—to present both the benefits and risks of HRT, this does not always happen. Many women remain unconvinced about adverse reactions and long-term safety of HRT and are concerned it might reactivate their endo. When speaking with your doctor about HRT, be sure to ask how it can help reduce bothersome menopausal symptoms, but also discuss the risks that we now know more about. If you are considering using HRT for relief of menopausal symptoms, you may only need to use it for the period of time in which these symptoms are severe.

Estrogen has also been shown to be effective in preventing bone loss, one risk factor for fractures. However, "most available data are on risk factors for spine or hip fractures in Caucasian women aged 65 and older," say the authors of the International Position Paper on Women's Health in Menopause.[1] "Predicting risk in younger women and other ethnic groups is less accurate." (See the following section on osteoporosis for more information.)

Does estrogen prevent other chronic diseases? As mentioned earlier, the only randomized, controlled study (the WHI study) to look at the risks of heart disease and stroke in healthy women found an increased risk with use of Premarin and Provera over five years in women with a uterus. However, if you have a family history of heart disease or are at risk (for example, if you have diabetes, smoke, or are overweight), speak with your doctor about what you can do to reduce your chances of developing heart disease, the leading cause of death in women over sixty-five.

A number of studies have looked at the effects of HRT, if any, on the development and progression of Alzheimer's disease. A well-designed study reported in *The Journal of the American Medical Association* found that estrogen use, especially for longer than ten years, reduced risk of Alzheimer's disease.[47] This remains an area of ongoing study.

What about cancer? Of specific concern to women with endo are breast and ovarian cancer, non-Hodgkin's lymphoma, melanoma, and transformation of endo into cancer (see Chapter 8). Estrogen and progestin were found, in the WHI study, to increase breast cancer risk. However, some physicians are cautious in their assessment of these findings. Andrew M. Kaunitz, M.D., a co-principal investigator at the University of Florida's Jacksonville site of the WHI study, notes, "The increased risk of breast cancer in estrogen-progestin users in the WHI study is small . . . and only marginally achieved statistical significance."[23] There was no observed abrupt increase in breast cancer diagnosis after four years of HRT use, but the risk increased slowly over time. Many commentators have pointed out that the absolute risk to an individual woman is small. Kaunitz says, "For every 10,000 women taking HRT for one year, we would anticipate eight additional cases of breast cancer." Or, among 100 women using HRT for ten years, one additional woman would be diagnosed with breast cancer.

Another physician quoted in this same article, John F. Randolph Jr., M.D., of Ann Arbor, Michigan, says, "Biologically, it is most plausible that any [cancer-promoting action of HRT] is small but cumulative—just not apparent until after several years. Therefore, it would be most appropriate to use HRT for specific indications and for the shortest time possible."[23]

If you are considering using HRT to reduce menopausal symptoms, you need to think through the risks and benefits *for you*. If you decide to use it, you should see your doctor yearly to assess the pros and cons of continuing its use. You may need to taper off HRT gradually to see if your symptoms recur and then decide if you will continue using it. As well, there are a number of ways your doctor can tailor HRT to your particular needs.

HRT: "I'll Have the Usual, Please"

Most of the hormones commonly prescribed during menopause in North America are synthetic or derived from animals. In the United States, 90 percent of women are prescribed conjugated equine estrogen (Premarin), made from the urine of pregnant mares. However, many other types of estrogen are available. Progestin, such as Provera, is added to oppose the effects of estrogen on endometrial tissues (by making the estrogen receptors less sensitive to the effects of estrogen); it is given to women with an intact uterus to prevent thickening of the uterine lining, which can lead to endometrial cancer.

> "Natural menopause (Hallelujah!) rendered my endo a death blow. I am now fifty-six. . . . Hot flashes were the worst and could occur fifty to a hundred times a day. Migraines increased in number and intensity and did not let up post-menopause."
>
> —*Polly, Massachusetts*

Typically, Premarin is given in a dose of 0.625 milligram and Provera in a dose of 2.5 or 5 milligrams. One study looked at the use of lower doses and found that 0.3 milligram of Premarin, as well as 0.3 milligram of Premarin given with 1.5 milligrams of Provera, were found to relieve hot flashes and night sweats. In addition, the lower doses maintained skeletal health, produced fewer adverse side effects, and produced "favorable lipid profiles," in contrast to the WHI study findings, which showed poor lipid profiles.[24] (See Chapter 2 for more information on lipid profiles.) Kaunitz, quoted earlier, considers "lower dose" estrogen therapy to mean 0.3 milligram daily of conjugated equine or esterified estrogens, 0.5 milligram daily of oral estradiol, or 0.025 to 0.0375 milligram of transdermal estradiol patches.[23]

Anthony Luciano, M.D., of New Britain, Connecticut, notes, "Dose varies from patient to patient according to the severity of symptoms and the woman's ability to absorb and/or metabolize hormones."[23] Smokers may need the "typical" dose; obese women or women who consume a moderate amount of alcohol may need lower doses, he adds. He also suggests that taking HRT at bedtime lets a woman take advantage of the hypnotic (calming) effects of micronized progesterone (if used) and minimizes night sweats. If you do choose to use HRT, ask about lower doses and about the best time to take the medication.

The one-size-fits-all approach of typical HRT prescribing is of concern to some women and their healthcare providers, especially women with endo who know about the risk of worsened endo symptoms. Says one author in an article on tailoring hormone therapy to patients' needs, "Although the majority of postmenopausal women may respond to generic and traditional hormone regimens, each woman's hormonal need is actually as individual to her as her own thumbprint."[25]

Another Approach: Bioidentical Hormones

Although not all physicians are familiar with them, some women with endo have explored the option of using bioidentical hormones (sometimes referred to as "natural hormones") for HRT. Unlike the synthetic and animal-derived hormones, these have exactly the same chemical structure as the hormones that women's bodies produce. They include the three estrogens (estradiol, estriol, and estrone), DHEA, and micronized progesterone and testosterone. (Micronized means the medication is broken into tiny particles to improve absorption.) Bioidentical hormones come in various forms: skin patches, oral capsules, suppositories, gels, and cream. (Note that some preparations—including micronized progesterone—use peanut or soy oil as a base, so ask about this if you have allergies.) Bioidentical progesterone is also available over the counter in the United States (not in Canada) as progesterone cream and through prescription as tablets, capsules, or cream in the United States and Canada. For more information on progesterone creams, see the section titled "Other Approaches to Treating Symptoms of Menopause," later in this chapter.

Why consider bioidentical hormones for HRT? According to pharmacist Marla Ahlgrimm, R.Ph., an Association Advisor and co-author of *The HRT Solution*, bioidentical hormones have a different biological effect than synthetic or animal-derived hormones. They fit exactly, like a key in a lock, into the hormone receptors, making the hormones readily available within the body and better able to be broken down and eliminated.[26] Research by Joel Hargrove, M.D., and Kevin Osteen, Ph.D., an Association Advisor and director of the Endometriosis Association Research Program at Vanderbilt University School of Medicine, has shown advantages to using these natural sex steroids, including a reduction of adverse side effects so common with synthetic and animal-derived hormones.[27] As a result, some women are better able to tolerate bioidentical hormones, although their long-term effects still have to be studied thoroughly.

Ahlgrimm points out that the results of the WHI study, mentioned earlier, cannot be applied to women using bioidentical HRT. "We have known for years that synthetic preparations cause undesirable side effects, often worse than the symptoms they are supposedly meant to manage," she says.[28]

Your doctor may already be prescribing bioidentical estrogens (such as Estrace, Vivelle, Climara, and Estraderm patches) and micronized progesterone (Prometrium and Crinone vaginal gel), although he or she may be unaware that these are bioidentical hormones. If these are not effective or produce unwanted side effects, your doctor can customize the prescription (see the next section for an example) through a compounding pharmacy. Many such pharmacies can ship the preparation to you, so you don't have to have one close to where you live. (**Note:** Prometrium should never be taken by women with an allergy to peanuts.)

Measuring and Balancing Hormone Levels and Types

Two keys to successful HRT use are in getting the right balance of estrogen to progestin or progesterone (if you use it) and including testosterone or DHEA as needed. An important step in finding the right balance is measuring the hormone levels in the blood or saliva,[29] although current blood tests cannot accurately measure testosterone levels in the lower ranges of normal for women.[30] Saliva tests can be done at home, are more affordable than blood tests, and better measure "free" or active hormones in your body, says Ahlgrimm.

She stresses that measuring hormone levels is extremely important and helpful, no matter what kind of hormones you are taking. This information helps your doctor customize your prescription. She adds, "Timing is everything," and advises that repeat testing should be done at the same time of day (preferably in the morning) and month (in the second half of the cycle, when progesterone is being produced, if you still have your ovaries).

You will need to work closely with your doctor to find a balanced preparation that relieves menopause symptoms with the fewest unwanted side effects and without causing a flare-up of endo symptoms. The aim should be to minimize the levels of estrogen by finding the appropriate type(s) of estrogen, the lowest dose required, and the best method of delivery for *you*.

You can use lower doses by choosing creams, gels, or patches, which are absorbed through the skin or vaginal tissues. These avoid the higher doses needed when taking oral estrogen, which must first pass through and be broken down by the liver. For example, estriol, a weak estrogen, can be used in a cream or vaginal suppository just two to three times a week to help manage hot flashes, sleep disturbances, urinary tract infections, and vaginal dryness. It can be taken without progesterone because it has no effect on the uterine lining and little effect on breast tissue when used in low doses.[29] (Note that vaginal estrogen creams and estriol may not protect against heart disease or bone loss.[29]) In clinical trials, estrogen creams, patches, and silicone estradiol-releasing vagi-

Working with Your Doctor to Find the Right Bioidentical Hormone Regime for You

Marla Ahlgrimm, R.Ph., a pioneer in developing compounded hormonal preparations, offers the following pointers, based on over twenty years of working with physicians and women using bioidentical hormone therapy:

- First, find out if your doctor is familiar with prescribing bioidentical hormones.
- Ask to have your hormone levels measured through saliva or blood tests. (A number of compounding pharmacies and other sources can help interpret the results if needed.)
- Try one of the standard prescriptions for bioidentical hormones (listed earlier in this chapter, in the section "Another Approach: Bioidentical Hormones"). Assess the effects, measure your hormone levels, and adjust the dose as needed for symptom relief or osteoporosis prevention.
- If this is unsuccessful, ask your doctor to customize the prescription through a compounding pharmacy. Try different types of hormones, doses, and method of delivery until you get the desired results.
- Measure your hormone levels regularly, and adjust your HRT as needed. Be consistent with the timing of the testing.

nal rings appear to be better than systemic estrogen for relieving these symptoms and avoiding high levels of circulating estrogen in the blood.[1]

Should Women with Endo in Natural Menopause Use HRT?

Many Association members have written that they have experienced a worsening or reactivation of their endo symptoms when they have used HRT, particularly estrogen. One member writes, "I am forty-seven now and am experiencing menopause. I am taking an estrogen supplement (Premarin) that has caused my endo symptoms to reappear. The doctors have told me that not all the endo was removed with that surgery years ago [uterus removed but ovaries left intact], and the estrogen has reactivated it." In the prescribing information for U.S. physicians for Premarin, the list of general precautions says, "Endometriosis may be exacerbated with administration of estrogen therapy."

What do endo experts say? Not surprisingly, they vary in their approach to using estrogen, progestin or progesterone, testosterone, and DHEA in women with endo. Robert Franklin, M.D., a well-known surgeon and Association Advisor in Houston, Texas, who has treated women with endo for many years, thinks there is a critical point where additional estrogen, through HRT, stimulates endo to grow, even fifteen to twenty years into menopause. Franklin looks at each woman's quality of life and advises using estrogen as needed to control severe menopause symptoms. He starts with a low dose, monitors menopause symptoms, and adjusts the dose to find the point where menopause symptoms are controlled but endo does not flare up. If larger doses of estrogen are needed, he adds progestin or an androgen (usually danazol in peri-menopausal women), although he finds many women do not tolerate the side effects of progestin well. Another good option for women whose endo symptoms flare up with systemic estrogen, he says, is to use estrogen vaginally (cream or ring) for menopause symptoms that impair a woman's sex life (for example, vaginal dryness).

Dr. Redwine, quoted earlier, says women with endo whose menopause symptoms are bothersome should go ahead and try HRT: "If [endo] symptoms are destined to increase, they will usually do so within three months if the patient is on an adequate dose of estrogen [enough to control menopause symptoms]." He goes on to say that the right dose can be measured by symptom relief and blood levels of estradiol.

In Atlanta, Georgia, Association Advisor Mark Perloe, M.D., points out that endo is not the same disease in every woman, nor is it necessarily the same throughout a woman's lifetime. While some women will experience endo symptoms with estrogen use, others will not. He advises all his menopausal patients to use HRT because of the risk of osteoporosis and to treat significant menopause symptoms. If endo does become symptomatic, he prescribes micronized progesterone to moderate the effects of the estrogen. Unlike synthetic progestins, he notes, natural (or bioidentical) progesterone has positive effects on blood lipids—important to reduce risk of heart attack.

Deborah Metzger, M.D., Ph.D., a San Jose, California, endo expert and Association Advisor, notes the complexity of how endo responds in each woman, depending on its location and the state of the woman's immune system. She points out that women with endo do not have a normally functioning immune system and aims treatment of endo at restoring good immune system functioning through a variety of methods after the endo is completely removed surgically. (For more information on these methods, see Chapter 4, "Immunotherapy: The Newest Treatment for Endometriosis.") She has seen many women in her practice whose endo worsens with age; when their immune system is challenged with extreme stress, an accident, infection, or surgery; and under certain hormonal circumstances, including perimenopause. At this time, she sees an increase in allergies, asthma, and other immune system dysfunctions. Metzger favors bioidentical hormones as the preferred source of estrogen and usually adds progesterone. It is most important, she says, to work with each woman individually.

Another physician who regularly treats women with endo, Association Advisor David Olive, M.D., of Madison, Wisconsin, says that in his clinical experience, endo

> "What kind of research is being done for women who have gone through menopause by natural method or hysterectomy? After having a complete hysterectomy and being on estrogen for fourteen years, I then had to go through a bilateral urethral reimplantation and bilateral ureterolysis operation because of active endo at age sixty-three."
>
> —Rita, Ohio

As time goes on, Joe tries to help Jeremy as best he can.

pain does seem to resolve in most women after menopause. However, he adds, those who do have recurrence are most often taking unopposed estrogen.

Another HRT option, which needs more research, is DHEA. This hormone may help women who are not tolerating estrogen in their HRT, says Scott Stamper, R.Ph., senior pharmacist at Madison Pharmacy Associates in Madison, Wisconsin.[31] An Italian study also concluded that DHEA acts similarly to estrogen-progestin HRT and "should be considered an effective hormone replacement treatment."[32]

So make your decision about whether to use HRT based on your own health status, the severity of your menopause symptoms and previous problems with endo, your lifestyle, and your preferred approach to personal health care. Sound familiar? This is what we have become used to doing when making decisions about treating endo—and menopause decisions are no different.

Surgical Menopause and HRT Use

Will HRT use (especially estrogen) cause endo symptoms to recur after castration? Let's look first at the medical literature. There are only a few studies of HRT use in women following removal of their tubes and ovaries or their uterus, tubes, and ovaries. Most are retrospective studies that have not standardized diagnoses and follow-up evaluation. As well, most of these older studies used types of HRT no longer in general use.

One of the few prospective, randomized trials to look at the risk of recurrence of endo related to HRT in women with endo who had had their ovaries removed was published in 2002.[33] In that study, 115 women were given estradiol patches and micronized progesterone, while the other 57 were not given HRT. There was a low recurrence rate (2.3 percent) of endo overall.

Unfortunately, this study was too small to draw definitive conclusions. Three conditions led to a much higher recurrence rate: previous severe peritoneal involvement (defined as deep endo or firm adhesion areas, both at least three centimeters in diameter), removal of the uterus but not the ovaries, and "subtotal" hysterectomy (leaving the cervix rather than removing the entire uterus). The recurrence rate in cases of severe peritoneal involvement was 9.1 percent (compared with 1.2 percent for those without such involvement). The women who had subtotal hysterectomies and removal of the tubes and ovaries or just removal of the tubes and ovaries had a recurrence rate of 22.2 percent (2 out of 9 women). In contrast, those who had their complete uterus, tubes, and ovaries removed had a recurrence rate of 1.9 percent (2 out of 106). "In both situations [severe peritoneal involvement and uterus but not ovaries removed], a number of endometriotic implants can persist, which could be reactivated/stimulated by HRT," the report concluded.

Another retrospective, case-controlled study of 100 women found that persistence of endo after castration tended to be more common in women who had used estrogen replacement.[10] And in another article on management of endo in women older than forty, the authors state, "Retrospective studies show that estrogen replacement therapy after hysterectomy and bilateral oophorectomy was associated with a low rate (less than 10%) of recurrence of endometriosis."[14]

Many Association members who have gone through surgical menopause have voiced their concern about HRT. One woman writes, "I'm thirty-six years old, and I had my hysterectomy in 1992. Since I was young, my surgical menopause was severe, and my doctor convinced me taking replacement estrogen (Premarin) immediately after surgery was safe and would not affect my endo. As you can probably guess, she was wrong." This woman tried another type of estrogen, then went off estrogen for six months at a time, several times, "but I was miserable, and the 'natural' remedies did not help my menopausal symptoms at all."

She then started using a compounded, bioidentical estrogen, Tri-Est (a mixture of all three types of estrogen, each individualized for that patient). "My whole life has changed. My pain has been dramatically reduced, and for the first time in over five years, I have stopped taking morphine for pain. Plus the Tri-Est has been able to control my

> "I do not take supplemental hormones but found during menopause that Remi-femin (black cohosh), a health store product, reduced not only hot flashes but abdominal pain for me. Wish I'd found it years before I did."
>
> —*Joyce, California*

menopausal symptoms without any problems. I'm also taking yoga, which has been really helpful with my adhesions left over from surgery."

Another woman, in contrast, found she was unable to use Tri-Est because of side effects. A third found Premarin worked best for her. And as another member reminds us, "It's all trial and error—whatever makes you feel better."

A number of physicians who specialize in treating endo find the use of combined estrogen and progestin (or micronized progesterone) is helpful for many women with endo who are in surgical menopause, although some find the side effects of progestin difficult to tolerate. Ahlgrimm, the pharmacist quoted earlier, supports this view and advises that micronized progesterone, with fewer side effects than progestin, should always be used along with estrogen to make the estrogen receptors (in the endo and other tissues) less sensitive to the effects of the estrogen. For women with bowel endo left behind at hysterectomy, says Dan Martin, M.D., progesterone should be added to the estrogen, *if* HRT is used, to decrease the chance of keeping the endo active.

Dr. Metzger, quoted earlier, says combined bioidentical estrogen and progesterone can be used to alleviate severe menopause symptoms and prevent bone loss. However, she also feels it's important that women be informed about other ways to maintain health. If a woman chooses to use HRT and develops problems that are typical of a classic allergic response (such as an increase in pain, headaches, spaciness, irritability, and mind fog), Metzger uses desensitization therapy to desensitize the woman to those hormones, then finds she can usually use HRT successfully. Wayne Konetzki, M.D., an Association Advisor from Waukesha, Wisconsin, and other environmental medicine specialists pioneered these techniques, which have helped many with endo. For information on doctors in your area who use these techniques, contact the Association or the American Academy of Environmental Medicine (see Resources at the end of this book). Chapter 4 provides more information on these techniques.

Another option for women in surgical menopause is to consider combined estrogen-androgen therapy. Randomized, double-blind, crossover trials in Montreal, Quebec, "demonstrated that estrogen-androgen replacement therapy significantly improves energy levels and an overall sense of well-being among surgically menopausal women with respect to estrogen alone. In addition, estrogen-androgen therapy significantly enhanced sexual desire, sexual arousal, and frequencies of coitus and orgasm."[34] Testosterone was given in small enough doses to decrease the risk of unwanted side effects, such as excessive hair growth. No definitive studies have been done in women with endo using this particular hormone therapy, but you may want to explore this option further with your doctor.

Finding the right combination of hormones can be challenging. One woman writes, "I'm a thirty-eight-year-old [Association] member who underwent total abdominal hysterectomy/oophorectomy five years ago for severe endo. I held off HRT for six months after surgery and then tried taking unopposed estrogen. I wasn't able to do this without experiencing recurring pelvic pain, so I agreed to take a low dose of Prempro daily.

If You Decide to Use HRT in Perimenopause or Menopause

There are a number of important steps to take if you decide to use HRT. They include the following:

- Investigate bioidentical hormones to see if they may be an option for you.
- Consider using HRT for only two or three years if you are in natural menopause, to get you over the hump as your body adjusts to its new hormonal state. If you are in surgical menopause, most experts agree you probably need HRT until the time of natural menopause because of the greater risks for osteoporosis, heart disease, and other health problems due to surgical menopause.
- Ask about testosterone to help protect against osteoporosis, for an increased sense of well-being, and to boost your sex drive and energy levels if needed. (Taking it in the morning may help.)
- Try to find the lowest dose of HRT that will give you symptom relief while not reactivating your endo.
- Closely monitor your endo symptoms, and speak with your doctor or other healthcare practitioners if you think you are having a recurrence of symptoms.
- Look at all your choices for ways to prevent heart disease and osteoporosis.

Last month, I decided, with doctor's supervision, to try unopposed estrogen again (hate side effects from the Provera), and within two and a half weeks, pelvic pain had returned. Very frustrating. Now I'm on FemHRT, another combination of estrogen and progestogen [progestin], and I'm virtually without libido (wasn't great on the Prempro, either). So doc wants me to give Estratest a try—thinks the testosterone will work as well as synthetic progesterone in suppressing endo and will boost energy and libido."

In summary, if you decide to use HRT after surgical menopause, monitor your symptoms and work closely with your doctor to find the right hormone therapy for you. And stop the therapy if you experience any recurrence of endo symptoms.

Other Approaches to Treating Symptoms of Menopause

Women with endo have long treated their endo symptoms with a variety of approaches, ranging from immunotherapy and botanical remedies to acupuncture and diet changes. Some want to take this approach to bothersome menopause symptoms. Not surprisingly, there has been little scientific study on the effectiveness and safety of short- or long-term use of many of the popular remedies, and no studies have specifically looked at use of these approaches in perimenopausal and menopausal women with endo.

While women often look beyond conventional medicine for other ways to relieve menopause (and endo) symptoms, Canadian naturopath Lois Hare, N.D., in Berwick, Nova Scotia, suggests it's helpful to look at the larger health picture. When a woman

Nonhormonal Ways to Deal with Menopause Symptoms

If you experience troublesome symptoms related to menopause, see if these nonhormonal measures give you relief. Most can't hurt, and many will help your overall health and well-being.

Hot Flashes and Night Sweats

- Identify and minimize triggers such as caffeine, alcohol, spicy foods, and heat.
- Sleep in a cool room, and use fans during the day.
- Wear clothing made of natural, breathable materials.
- Practice deep, slow abdominal breathing (six to eight breaths per minute) when you feel a hot flash coming on.
- Do some kind of exercise for thirty minutes a day.
- Try vitamin E (800 to 2,000 International Units a day) with selenium.
- Give acupuncture a try.
- See *The Endometriosis Sourcebook* for additional ideas.

Insomnia

- Keep the bedroom cool, and wear light clothing, especially before and at bedtime to ease hot flashes (often responsible for wakefulness during the night).
- Have a bedtime routine that prepares you for sleep.
- Do not exercise after 6:00 P.M.
- Avoid alcohol after 6:00 P.M.
- Avoid reliance on sleeping pills.
- Exercise daily.
- Avoid caffeine and alcohol in the evening.
- Take a warm shower or bath before bedtime.

Mood Swings and Anxiety

- Invoke the "relaxation response," and use deep, slow abdominal breathing.
- Avoid tranquilizers.
- Exercise in the mornings and do yoga.
- Take time for self-nurturing activities.
- Have available comfort items: hot tea, favorite pictures, stuffed animals, etc.

Vaginal Dryness and Pain with Intercourse

- Use one of the over-the-counter vaginal lubricants or saliva, or try one of the many herbal approaches to nourish the vaginal tissues.[41]
- Try an estrogen cream or estradiol-releasing silicone vaginal ring. These avoid high levels of circulating estrogens.[1]
- Regular sexual activity helps reduce vaginal dryness. Be gentle and go slow until well lubricated.

comes to see her, Hare explains, she comes not as a woman with an endo history alone, but as a woman with a complex health picture and set of needs. Hare aims to put the body back into balance, seeking not only to find relief of endo and menopause symptoms, but also to improve the functioning of other parts of the body, like the immune system, liver, ovaries, and pituitary and adrenal glands.

Hare suggests that the safest way to start treating menopause symptoms is with lifestyle changes—including diet, exercise, stress reduction, changes in living environment, getting family support—and learning as much as you can about menopause. If these are not effective, a full menu of other approaches is available, especially if you are in surgical menopause and find that lifestyle changes aren't enough. We'll examine just a few here.

Herbs and Botanicals

Herbs (the leaves and stems of plants) and other botanicals (foods or supplements derived from any part of the plant) are perhaps the most frequently used nonhormonal remedies for menopausal symptoms. It's important to realize that even though these may be "natural," they can have powerful effects in the body and can interact with medications you may be taking, sometimes with serious consequences. When buying and using these remedies, consider the following issues:

- Possible mislabeling of ingredients because they aren't regulated in the way drugs are
- Possible adverse reactions (such as hypersensitivity or toxic effects on the liver)
- Quality of the product (its strength, purity, whether raw materials are properly identified, whether the product is pesticide free)
- Quality control in manufacturing

Although many herbs have been used successfully and safely for hundreds of years in different cultures, be wary of the many claims made in the advertising of herbal remedies. These usually have not been backed up by scientific evidence. A systematic review of scientific and lay literature on alternative treatments for menopausal symptoms offers this caution: "Because herbal medicines are legally classified as foods in North America, only limited scientific literature is required or available on their action, safety, and interactions with other drugs. While some herbs might be pharmacologically and clinically effective, they are not necessarily free from toxicity and side effects nor can we be sure that they will not interact with prescription medications. . . . Because of the reputed estrogen-like activity of some herbs, menopausal women might be exposing themselves to unpredictable amounts of unopposed estrogen."[35]

If you go this route, tune in to and observe your body's responses, and work closely, if you can, with a practitioner qualified in using botanical therapies to choose, monitor, and fine-tune your remedies. Also, be sure to let all your healthcare providers know about the various treatments you are using. A quick look at a few of the remedies com-

Learn More About Specific Herbs

The following sources offer information on herbs:
- American Herbal Pharmacopoeia (herbal-ahp.org)
- American Herbal Products Association's *Botanical Safety Handbook*
- *The Complete German Commission E Monographs*
- European Scientific Cooperative on Phytotherapy (ESCOP)
- *Herbs: Everyday Reference for Health Professionals* (Canadian Pharmacists Association and Canadian Medical Association)
- Natural Medicines Comprehensive Database (in print and electronic format)
- *New Menopausal Years: The Wise Woman Way* (Alternative Approaches for Women 30–90), by Susan S. Weed (New York: Ash Tree Publishing, 2002)
- *PDR® for Herbal Medicines™*, 2nd edition (Thomson PDR, in cooperation with PhytoPharm, US Institute for Phytopharmaceuticals, Inc., 2000)

monly taken for menopausal symptoms will give you an idea of what we know (or don't know) about their effects or cautions for women with endo:

- **Black cohosh (*Cimicifuga racemosa*)**—This herb has traditionally been used to reduce menopausal symptoms and is "particularly valuable when estrogen replacement therapy is either inappropriate or unwanted."[36] Randomized, controlled and uncontrolled studies of black cohosh have shown that it is effective in reducing hot flashes, headaches, palpitations, and anxiety. Some studies have described its effects as estrogenic,[37] although others have not. It may be taken long-term within the recommended dosage, but one source recommends that it not be taken for longer than six months because data from longer studies is lacking.[36] It should not be taken with HRT.[38]

- **Chasteberry (*Vitex agnus-castus*, also known as chastetree, Monk's pepper, Indian spice, sage tree hemp, tree wild pepper, and vitex)**—"This herb is used primarily to normalize hormone levels in women and thereby treat the array of symptoms arising from hormonal imbalance," says one source.[36] It has been recommended for vaginal dryness, low libido, and depression. Although many herbalists give chasteberry to treat menopause symptoms, its effects have not been scientifically investigated. It is slow acting and may take two to three months or longer to show effects; side effects are rare. Chasteberry should not be taken with HRT.

- **Dong quai (*Angelica sinensis*)**—Traditional Chinese medicine practitioners never give dong quai alone but modify its effects by combining it with other herbs or roots. Although dong quai is reported to relieve some menopause symptoms, studies have not shown this to be the case when it is used by itself. It should not be used with blood-thinning medications like warfarin. If you're interested in using dong quai, consider consulting a traditional Chinese medicine practitioner to ensure it is the best remedy for you to use and that you are using it correctly. (For more on traditional Chinese medicine, see *The Endometriosis Sourcebook*.)

Other commonly recommended botanicals for relief of menopausal symptoms include angelica, blue cohosh, chamomile, damiana, evening primrose, ginseng, licorice, motherwort, red clover, and saw palmetto, among others. However, we don't know much about the use of these botanicals in women with endo. As with all treatments, do as much research as you can before using them, listen to your body, and discontinue use if you have any concerns.

Phytoestrogens

Phytoestrogens are plant substances—found in many foods—that produce an estrogenic effect in the body. Soy (containing isoflavones), flaxseed and linseed (containing lignins), and red clover (an herb) are several that have been studied, although not extensively. Soy is increasingly being marketed as a menopause remedy, both in food form and as pills. Some studies on soy have used soy protein, and others have used extracted isoflavones, the plant estrogens that are among soy's active ingredients. A review of an article on soy's effects on menopausal symptoms, heart disease, breast cancer, and osteoporosis says studies have shown that soy is "probably no better than a sugar pill" for relieving hot flashes, night sweats, and other menopause symptoms:[39] "Only two North American studies have found a slight benefit [for hot flashes and other menopause symptoms] from soy or soy isoflavones," although it can lower cholesterol levels and reduce the risk of heart disease if you eat enough of it. We'll have to wait for results of ongoing studies on the impact of soy or its isoflavones on bone and breast health and on the safety of using extracted isoflavones.

One review of the scientific and lay literature on alternative treatments says phytoestrogens are only 2 percent as potent as estradiol.[35] However, the authors go on to say, in postmenopausal women, "Isoflavanoids can occupy more estrogen receptor sites, and since they have some estrogenic activity, they increase total estrogens in these women."

The use of soy by women with endo is controversial. Some women with endo have a sensitivity to soy. The Association headquarters has received some reports that soy flares up endo symptoms for some women with endo and may worsen digestive problems. If you choose to eat soy products (such as tofu, tempeh, miso, soy nuts, and processed products made from soy), observe your own responses. Discontinue use if you have endo or digestive symptoms or generally feel unwell.

Wild Yam and Natural Progesterone Creams

You may be familiar with topical wild yam cream, marketed as a progesterone supplement. Claims have been made that it converts into progesterone and that it can help menopause symptoms and premenstrual syndrome, as well as help prevent osteoporosis. Ahlgrimm explains that while these creams may have an endocrine effect on the body, wild yam cannot be converted into progesterone in the body. She cautions that women with endo need to know exactly which hormones—and at what doses—they are exposing themselves to, and we can't know that when using wild yam creams.

Transdermal progesterone creams and gels are sold as cosmetics in the United States (but not in Canada) and do contain progesterone. Ahlgrimm advises that if you use these, you should read the labels carefully and choose creams in the therapeutic range of 2 to 3 percent progesterone (one such cream is Pro-Gest). Saliva testing can help determine your level of progesterone if you are using progesterone cream. The creams are better absorbed than oral progesterone, so progesterone levels may be higher than when using the oral form.[40]

Dioscorea, an herbal tincture made from wild yam, can also be used under the direction of a naturopath or herbalist for endocrine imbalances and to ease menopause symptoms.[41] Like wild yam cream, it has an effect on many tissues in the body, including the brain. Again, the concern is that it's hard to know what effects it has in the body and what dose is appropriate.

Women who use these over-the-counter products have reported both improvement and worsening of endo symptoms, says Ahlgrimm. If you are going to try them, understand that advertising claims may be false or exaggerated and that self-prescribing may be unwise. Work with your physician or naturopath to closely monitor the effects on your menopause and endo symptoms, test regularly to assess your hormone levels, and discontinue use if you experience negative effects.

Chronic Disease in Menopause

Besides thinking about our endo, we need to be aware of other chronic diseases that become more common when women enter menopause. Two that deserve particular attention are osteoporosis and cardiovascular disease.

Osteoporosis

When we enter menopause, our risk of developing osteoporosis rises. Women who enter menopause with lower bone density (for whatever reason) are at greater risk. A number of risk factors for osteoporosis apply to all women, but some of them are particularly relevant for women with endo:

- Strong family history of osteoporosis
- Prolonged use of cortisone or prednisone used for inflammation and autoimmune diseases (to which women with endo are susceptible)

- Amenorrhea (missed periods)
- Early or surgical menopause (before age forty-five)
- Decreased estrogen levels[42]

We can add to this list a number of other factors related to endo:

- Hormonal treatments (such as GnRH agonist therapy) that purposely reduce estrogen levels
- Hormone imbalances, including problems with progesterone (a bone-stimulating hormone)
- Sensitivity to progesterone, as observed by environmental medicine specialists
- The documented increased risk for thyroid problems in women with endo (hypothyroidism and Hashimoto's thyroiditis)[43]
- Gastrointestinal problems that could lead to poor absorption of bone-building minerals and other nutrients
- Severe allergic disease, which increases body acidity, resulting in minerals being pulled from the bones to balance blood pH

One position paper on menopause says, "Lifestyle changes have been shown to improve bone density in young women and to prevent fractures in older women."[1] The authors recommend that women stop smoking; avoid extreme weight loss; do weight-bearing, muscle-building, and balance exercises; avoid sedatives and excess alcohol and caffeine; correct visual impairments; and make the home "fall proof."

Research has shown that estrogen therapy is useful in reducing bone loss and fractures in natural and surgical menopause. A low dose (0.3 milligram) will offer bone protection while reducing other risks, including a reactivation of endo, and is better tolerated than higher doses.[1] If you have low bone density, it is very important that you get follow-up bone density studies to make sure that the dose of estrogen is appropriate. As well, recent data suggests that starting HRT after age sixty may offer bone-conserving benefits while reducing the risk of breast cancer by starting HRT later.[44] Be aware that you must use estrogen for the long term to continue preserving bone.

Hormone therapy is now commonly used as add-back therapy in premenopausal women who use GnRH agonists (the agonists put them into a "pseudomenopause"). Because women using the agonists can lose up to 6 percent of bone mineral density in the first six months of use, estrogen is added (usually with progestin or progesterone) to reduce this bone loss and allow the use of the therapy for longer than six months. We don't know at this time if repeated use of GnRH agonists will result in women entering menopause with below-average bone density. We also don't know if add-back therapy successfully prevents bone loss; some studies show that it doesn't completely.

One author suggests a baseline bone density test before starting GnRH therapy to determine whether you have high or low bone density to start.[45] Some experts suggest all women get a baseline bone density test at the start of menopause or even earlier. A density in the low normal range or below might indicate a greater risk of long-term bone loss with use of GnRH agonists, so you should be monitored carefully. A urine test (NTx) can also determine the rate of bone breakdown, which can help you and your doctor adjust your dose and type of HRT, or lead you to consider it, to prevent further bone loss. (For more on GnRH agonists and bone loss, see *The Endometriosis Sourcebook*.)

In addition, there are some other ways to prevent or treat osteoporosis:

- Get adequate minerals and vitamins daily in your diet and through supplements. You need 1,000 to 1,500 milligrams of calcium from diet and supplements, 200 to 600 milligrams of magnesium from supplements, 400 to 800 International Units (IU) of vitamin D from supplements if you don't get ten to fifteen minutes of daily exposure to the sun without sunscreen (possible in Canada only in the summer months), and 90 micrograms of vitamin K from salad and other greens or from supplements.
- Make lifestyle changes (noted earlier in the section "Other Approaches to Treating Symptoms of Menopause").
- Add testosterone to your HRT (to slow the rate of bone deterioration and build new bone).
- Use one of the various osteoporosis medications such as bisphosphonates, calcitonin, and selective estrogen receptor modulators (SERMs) like raloxifene. Note that studies have not been done using these in women with endo for prevention of osteoporosis. However, at the time of this writing, the National Institutes of Health is conducting a study on raloxifene for the treatment of endo. Consult your doctor for more information on these options.

Cardiovascular Disease

Another concern after menopause is cardiovascular disease. Healthy women are now being advised not to use HRT as a primary prevention for coronary heart disease. Women with endo, along with all women, are advised to use a lifestyle approach (such as eating a heart-healthy diet, stopping smoking, getting enough cardiovascular exercise, maintaining a healthy weight) and to control blood pressure, cholesterol, and diabetes. Consult your doctor about your particular risks for cardiovascular disease and what you can do to prevent or treat it.

Sexuality in Menopause

Sexuality is a difficult area for many to talk about. It's complex, involving not only the physical responses that can change in menopause but also relationship issues, health problems, attitudes toward sexuality, personality, and stress. Studies on sexuality in menopause for women in general have resulted in diverse conclusions. For many women with endo, menopause can bring relief of endo pain, including pain with intercourse, although this is not always the case, especially for women in surgical menopause.

We do know that androgens, particularly those produced by the ovaries, play an important role in women's sexuality. While many women who have had their ovaries removed experience satisfying sexual lives, others report a worsening of sexual function, libido, orgasmic response, and psychological well-being.

If you are concerned about changes in your sexual response and think they may be hormonally based, speak with your doctor about the option of using estrogen/androgen therapy. (However, androgens have not been approved for treatment of sexual dysfunction, according to a 2002 article on female androgen insufficiency.[30]) One article on using natural sex steroids for hormone therapy suggests that micronized testosterone or DHEA may be preferred because, unlike the methyltestosterone commonly prescribed, it does not have an adverse effect on blood lipids.[27] As well, your body may respond differently depending on the method of delivery (pill, injection, or patch) and dose. Once again, more long-term study is needed.

DHEA, although popular in recent years as an over-the-counter preparation, also has not been well studied yet. Some researchers are concerned about findings that it may raise lipids in the blood, make women more insulin resistant (see Chapter 5), and be a potent source of estrogen. This particularly rings alarm bells for women with endo, even though it looks like DHEA might increase bone density and enhance libido and sexual responsiveness.[46] Clearly, more research is needed.

If you use any of these hormonal therapies, be sure you are monitored closely and regularly. A good physician will check hormone levels before prescribing these therapies and adjust the dose for maximum safety and comfort. Some gynecologists, reproductive endocrinologists, and environmental medicine specialists are skilled in this area.

Making It Through Menopause

This time of transition can be easy or challenging. On a personal note, I started getting perimenopausal symptoms—dripping hot flashes, sleep-discouraging night sweats, wild mood swings—shortly before I began this chapter ("How timely," I thought more than once). I watched my symptoms change over the course of four months, in response to a mixed herbal remedy suggested by my naturopath and, when that stopped working well, acupuncture treatments from an experienced practitioner. My symptoms have settled down, but because of my own risk factors for osteoporosis (including a mother severely affected by the disease), I'm now looking for the best ways *for me* to keep my bones strong so they will carry me into old age healthy and fit.

After months of poring through medical literature and reading dozens of letters from Association members, I wish I had found clearer answers and easy fixes for my own health challenges. Clearly, much more research is needed on women's experience with endo in menopause (not just on menopausal endo). The Endometriosis Association is keen to learn more about how you experience and handle menopause. Each of us is unique, but together our stories can make a difference.

12 Preventing Endometriosis: It May Be Possible!

Mary Lou Ballweg

Introduction

It's impossible, I believe, to suffer from endometriosis or see it close up in family or friends without praying and hoping it will never afflict those we love. Of course, this applies most of all to our "miracle" children, if we are fortunate enough to have them! As one of those lucky enough to have a child after being told I never would because of endo, I started thinking about how to prevent this disease even before my bundle of joy was born. And, indeed, with an immense amount of attention to our family's health, she has been able to enjoy a mostly normal childhood and youth despite having the whole range of problems that we see in women and girls who have endo or seem likely to develop it.

In this chapter, we share with readers what we in the Association have learned through the years that may help us prevent this miserable disease. Science has not yet addressed prevention of endo (indeed, there's only one article on prevention of endo in the medical literature, by French physician Alain Audebert, M.D.[1]). However, *outside* the endo literature, there is a lot of scientific information we can draw on and apply to endo if we look at the big picture of the disease. We hope that pulling these thoughts together will trigger interest in this important topic, just as some of our other groundbreaking articles have pushed the field forward.

When the Association hosted a brainstorming session on prevention of the disease at the VI World Congress on Endometriosis, we found few in the medical field were interested. Only one doctor attended that session, and he wanted to focus on early diagnosis. We couldn't get him to understand that, while we consider early diagnosis extremely important, we want to completely *prevent* the disease! Unlike the medical establishment, however, women with endo have definitely been interested in preventing endo and its related diseases in our daughters, and also in preventing the related diseases in our sons. So, knowing we are once again venturing into new territory, we share here what we can and invite readers to continue telling us about their experiences and ideas on this important topic. (To contact us, see Resources at the back of the book.)

An Ounce of Prevention Is Worth a Pound of Cure

Besides possibly preventing endo, there are other reasons to pursue optimal health for our families. Research has now clearly shown that we with endo and our families are at greater risk for certain cancers (see Chapter 8) and autoimmune inflammatory diseases.[2]

Each of these cancers and autoimmune diseases has repercussions for us and our families that we are far from understanding. For instance, one study found that 45 percent of the sons of mothers with lupus have forms of learning disabilities like dyslexia and mathematical difficulties, as well as stuttering, attention deficit disorder with hyperactivity, delayed speech, and autism.[3] And anecdotal reports and a preliminary review of the Association's data have raised disturbing concerns about the possible risk of birth defects in the children of women with endo. (We are studying this topic; stay in touch for news.) If we can prevent the disease processes involving endo, we may also be able to reduce our risk for these other health problems and all their repercussions.

Even if we cannot prevent endo in some cases, we may be able to delay it or slow it down. Think how many women with endo go to great lengths to "buy time" with various treatments—for instance, taking a GnRH agonist to delay having yet another surgery or to hopefully get to a point they'll be able to attempt pregnancy. By helping our children achieve the best possible health, we can probably delay the onset, lessen the severity, or slow the progression of endo. So, let's not despair. Let's look this beast endo straight in the eyes and stand up to it!

Most Diseases Don't Start Overnight

One of the most important concepts in health and disease is that neither happens instantaneously. We all know there are certain risk factors for diseases such as heart disease (family history, elevated cholesterol, being overweight, etc.). There are also risk factors for endo, although they are not well understood. Numerous immune and hormonal abnormalities have been identified. Many of these abnormalities are thought to be in place before the development of obvious signs of the disease, such as pain. If we can interrupt these abnormalities or prevent them in the first place, we might not go on to develop the full-blown disease.

Risk Factors for Endometriosis

- Family history of the disease
- Environmental exposures
- Family and personal history of allergy and other inflammatory diseases
- Short menstrual cycles (less than twenty-seven to twenty-eight days), early start to periods (twelve or younger), painful periods, long and heavy bleeding with periods (five to eight days)
- Red-hair gene
- Miscellaneous: anatomic obstructions that prevent menstrual flow (rare), IUD use, certain surgical and medical procedures, poorly timed abdominal surgery

---

Risk Factors for Endo

Are certain girls and women at high risk for endo? Unfortunately, it seems so. Here are some of the known risk factors.

Family History of the Disease

Not only are you five to nine times more likely to develop endo if you have close family members with it, but your disease is likely to be more severe[4] and the symptoms more likely to begin at a younger age.[5] There may be genetic factors that increase susceptibility. However, remember that just because families have endo does not mean it is necessarily genetic—families share environments as well as genes. As with many cancers, combined genetic and environmental influences may be important. As Dr. Audebert states in his article on prevention of endo, "It is likely that endometriosis is a common polygenic [involving many genes]/multifactorial disease caused by an interaction between genes as well as the environment."[1]

Environmental Exposures, Including Endocrine Disruptors and Radiation

Certain environmental exposures are known risk factors. Those that have raised concern are endocrine disruptors, including dioxin, and certain forms of radiation.

In 1992 the Endometriosis Association discovered a link between endo and dioxins, very toxic pollutants that disrupt our hormones and immune system and cause cancer (see Part 3 of this book and *The Endometriosis Sourcebook*). Since that time, tremendous scientific interest has unearthed many aspects of this link. While it may be a while before we understand all the mechanisms by which dioxin can lead to endo, it seems clear at this time that the link is solid.

> "There's only one thing worse than having severe endometriosis yourself. That's having a daughter with it."
>
> —Sue, Wisconsin

Another environmental factor, radiation, was identified in 1991 as a potential risk factor for endo. In a U.S. Air Force study, endometriosis developed spontaneously in 53 percent of monkeys in a study group during a seventeen-year period after radiation exposure.[6] The work on radiation is still preliminary, but enough has been done to warrant caution about x-rays and other sources of radiation if we are serious about preventing endo and related diseases in our children and families.

Family and Personal History of Allergy and Other Inflammatory Diseases

The Association's research, starting in 1980, and that of others has repeatedly shown the prevalence of allergic and inflammatory diseases in women with endo.[2, 8-16] Moreover, endo itself is an inflammatory disease. As Association Advisor Jacques Donnez, M.D., Ph.D., of Belgium, and his colleagues wrote, "Endometriosis is a multifactorial disease associated with a general inflammatory response in the peritoneal cavity."[7] This is a risk factor that you and your family can do much to lessen. It might seem surprising, but the same immune system cells and inflammatory reactions are involved in allergic diseases and endo. For some women, this immune dysfunction includes low resistance to infections and severe problems with the yeast *Candida albicans*. Intestinal problems also tend to be part of this allergic/inflammatory state.

Menstrual Risk Factors

Possible risk factors associated with menstruation include cycles that are shorter than average (less than twenty-seven to twenty-eight days) and start at twelve years old or younger, and periods that are painful and involve long and heavy bleeding (five to eight days). It's hard to know if these are true risk factors or actually a reflection of the disease already in place at the time these factors were noted in various studies. In any case, these conditions have been noted repeatedly in women with endo.[17-24]

Red-Hair Gene

Harvard scientist Rose Frisch, Ph.D., a world authority on the subject, says people with the red-hair gene (which includes those with natural red, strawberry blond, or auburn hair) have a somewhat different biochemistry, with more allergies and longer menstrual bleeding time.[25, 26] According to the group Redheads International, one in twenty people carries the red-hair gene. This is one risk factor that you truly can't do anything about. (See Chapter 13, "Research Reveals Disease Is Starting Younger, Diagnosis Is Delayed," for the Association's data showing greater risk for endo in those with the red-hair gene.)

Miscellaneous Factors

Anatomic Obstructions That Prevent Menstrual Flow

A number of rare abnormalities such as a narrowed or completely blocked cervix, a malformed or absent cervix, absence of the vagina, or a completely blocking hymen have been linked to the development of endo.[27, 28] However, these abnormalities are so rare that they are unlikely to affect your daughter. Treatment to correct the abnormality is advised. Robert Franklin, M.D., a prominent endo specialist, suggests that girls or women with very small openings of the cervix can be treated with progesterone to help soften up the cervix.

IUD Use

IUDs have been associated with a greater risk for endo. IUDs set up an inflammatory state and also are considered to increase the amount of menstrual flow.[29, 30]

Certain Surgical and Medical Procedures

Some surgical and medical procedures may contribute to developing endo. Surgical transplantation of endometrium (the inside lining of the uterus) is a proven cause of endo, as with episiotomy and laparotomy scars, including cesarean section scars.[31-33] A number of other surgical procedures, including tubal ligation, have been linked to development of endo (although the disease could have been present and undiagnosed before the tubal ligation).[34] Cone biopsy, in which a tissue sample is taken from the cervix, also has been linked to development of endo on the cervix.[35] Operative hysteroscopy (see Glossary) is another procedure that has been potentially linked to developing endo.[36] Endometrial ablation, in which the endometrial lining is destroyed, usually for excessive bleeding, has been shown to spread endometrial tissue into the pelvis.[37]

Time of Surgery

Finally, timing of abdominal surgery may also be a factor. In women who already have endo, a higher recurrence rate of the disease was found in those who had surgery near the end of the menstrual cycle (days twenty-two to twenty-eight) than in those who had surgery earlier in their cycle. While this study was carried out in women with proven endo, there may be reason to believe that having surgery early in the cycle for those at risk for endo would be better than later in the cycle.[38]

Many aspects of Colette's history are similar to the medical histories of others who go on to develop severe endo. For instance, the colic, low resistance to infection,[39] yeast problems, bowel problems,[40] and allergies are often heard in the histories of women with endo (see Chapter 4). Other events often heard in the early medical histories of women with endo include repeated ear infections, thrush as a baby (oral candidiasis), and diaper rash. Mononucleosis is typically seen in those with yeast problems as well as chronic fatigue immune dysfunction syndrome (CFIDS).[8] The onset of severe pain, heavy flow, and symptoms from the first period on is a classic experience in those who go on to severe endo or, more likely, already have it.

Reducing the Risk for Endo

Twenty-two years ago, when Colette was born, no one knew, of course, that all these factors were related to endo. But looking at similar histories today, we can see many areas where families may be able to reduce risks for endo. Based on the known risk factors, there are a number of principles that may help us prevent or delay endo or reduce the severity of the disease in at-risk families:

- Reduce inflammation.
- Reduce toxic exposures.
- Improve overall health.
- Delay puberty and menarche (the first period).
- Don't use an IUD.
- Avoid—if possible—cesarean section, episiotomy, possibly tubal ligation, cone biopsy, hysteroscopy, and endometrial ablation.

The remainder of this chapter explores ways to apply these principles.

Only the Best for Baby: Preconception Planning

Some women have decided not to have children, fearing they'd pass on endo and all its related diseases, not only to daughters but also, in the case of related diseases, to sons. If you do want to consider having a child, you can start your prevention plan before birth. While we can't change our genetic susceptibility to the disease, we can change and reduce many risks related to endo. This starts even before your baby is conceived with what's called "preconception planning," a concept that may be better known in the United Kingdom than in North America.

Preconception planning means the parents-to-be prepare for their coming child by getting into the best health possible. This concept has developed because of growing awareness that any condition that affects the health of prospective parents before conception, or the mother during pregnancy, may make it harder to become pregnant and may harm the health of the future child. You are your baby's first environment; just as a mother bird, you will want to prepare the best nest for your little one. You can be a good mother even before conception!

Here are several suggestions for parents-to-be and endo families.

Typical Profile of a Girl or Woman with High Risk for Severe Endo

Over the years, we have heard thousands of histories of women with endo. There are clearly some patterns! Here's the medical history for Colette, a young Toronto woman with severe endo:

Childhood Illnesses
Severe infant colic
Pneumonia twice before age two
Repeated bouts of tonsillitis and strep throat
Bladder infections
Kidney infections
Anemia
Mononucleosis
Allergies, including hay fever

Age Thirteen: First Period
From the beginning, acute pain with periods, sometimes severe enough to cause fainting
Heavy flow, nausea and vomiting, disturbed bowel function during period and sometimes before, painful urination, and difficulty voiding
Symptoms treated with painkillers and oral contraceptives (The oral contraceptives, according to Colette, regulated her cycles and minimized the flow but were associated with migraines.)

Age Twenty
Pain with sex, low-back pain, chronic pelvic pain
Recurrent yeast infections
All the period symptoms she's had since age thirteen

Age Twenty-Two
Diagnosed with endo

Eat Right

Practice the best possible nutrition for years before conception. Some research shows that nutritional deficiencies have impact for generations.[41] For more information, see the book *Endometriosis: A Key to Healing Through Nutrition* (details are in the Resources section in the back of the book).

Reduce Toxic Exposures

The most harmful chemicals build up in our bodies our entire lives. If you think you will want children some day, *now* is the time to eat healthfully, breathe healthfully, clean healthfully (no chlorine bleaches and other harsh cleaners), and keep a healthful yard (no pesticides or herbicides). Some day we hope to know how to remove these toxins from our bodies—one of the Association's Advisors is working on this very difficult problem—but currently this is not known. And the effects of exposure during prenatal development are permanent and irreversible.[42]

The most toxic endocrine-disrupting chemicals (chemicals such as dioxins, including PCBs and furans, that act like hormones) tend to build up in the body. Because of this, the Michigan Medical Society advised that children and anyone who ever plans to have children, male or female, should eat no Great Lakes fish.

Pesticides and herbicides especially need to be avoided. "If we design a compound to be toxic to an insect cell, why does it surprise us when we find out that the same compound is toxic to a human cell?" asks Lou Guillette, Ph.D., a scientist who studies hormonally active chemicals, in the book *Hormone Deception*. "We've always thought the issue was mass—that these things could be toxic to an insect without having significant effects in a much larger human. But how big is an embryo?"

Maternal and paternal exposure to pesticides, maternal exposure to paints (so let Dad paint the nursery), and paternal exposure to solvents and petroleum products have been linked to childhood leukemia.[43] Solvents are substances capable of dissolving or dispersing one or more other substances; some examples are benzene, carbon tetrachloride, trichloroethylene (an anesthetic), toluene (used in nail polishes), perchloroethylene (degreaser used in dry cleaning and by mechanics), and volatile petroleum distillate.

If you or your spouse smoke, you must stop now. Cigarette smoke contains over 4,000 chemicals, including dioxins and other cancer-causing agents and poisons. In addition, cigarette smoke reduces fertility.[44] Granted, these and other lifestyle changes take time. It isn't always easy to change. Make gradual changes if needed. That's why it pays to start as far in advance of conception as possible.

It's also important to limit your exposure to radiation, including x-rays and radon. In addition to the U.S. Air Force studies showing radiation might be a risk for developing endo,[45] radiation also harms sperm. So the father-to-be should avoid x-rays and radon during the time you are trying to conceive. (Radon is a naturally occurring radioactive gas present in some basements and soil. Have your home tested.)

Have Your Thyroid Checked

If you are a woman with endo, get your thyroid checked by sensitive testing techniques; if you have thyroid disease, get treated. (Environmental medicine doctors are experienced with these tests and treatment.) Why? Women with endo are at risk for autoimmune thyroid disease (Hashimoto's thyroiditis) and hypothyroidism (low thyroid hormone).[2] Thyroid disease will reduce your fertility. The children of low-thyroid mothers have been shown to be more likely to have lower IQs (even when the thyroid problem is so mild in the mother that she may not have symptoms).[46] Also, they are at greater risk for birth defects, especially cleft lip or palate, extra fingers, and heart problems,[47] and may be more sensitive to sex hormones[48, 49]—exactly what you don't want! Moreover, PCBs, a type of dioxin that has been linked to endo, have been shown to decrease thyroid levels and decrease IQ after prenatal exposure.[50, 51] Alteration in the mother's thyroid status is thought to alter development of the reproductive tract in the fetus.[44]

> "I have a two-year-old little girl, and her future may have endo in it. I think of her going through the severe pain constantly as I do. This thought chills my blood. It's for my daughter, and her generation, that makes me dedicated to the work we're doing now."
>
> —*Brenda, Ontario*

Get Dental Work Over With

Some preconception planning advisors suggest getting dental work done well in advance of attempting to conceive because some dental materials are potentially toxic. Avoid mercury amalgam fillings because mercury is highly toxic, especially for the developing brain.

Get Control over Candida and Allergies

The most important step for women with endo is to get *Candida albicans*, allergies, and asthma under control! Getting candida under control before attempting pregnancy may also increase your fertility, according to healthcare practitioners who work with women with endo. We have also heard reports from members that they finally were able to become pregnant after this type of treatment (see Chapter 4).

Lactobacillus, the friendly bacteria found in yogurt with live cultures or in supplements, was probably part of your program to control candida and build a strong immune system before pregnancy. It should continue to be part of your program when you're pregnant. Finnish researchers gave mothers Lactobacillus while pregnant, and their babies received it in the first two months of life. These babies had only half as many allergic disorders as a control group.[63]

If you suspect you have allergies or if you have asthma (allergists believe that almost all asthma is rooted in allergy),[52] get tested and desensitized before pregnancy. (More on this later in this chapter.) According to the book *For Tomorrow's Children: A Manual for Future Parents*, food allergies can lead to poor absorption that may mean the parent-to-be has nutritional deficiencies. Also, "allergies in either prospective parent seem to lead to allergies in their offspring, which can seriously impair development." The same book also notes, "People who work in the field of food allergy believe that a baby will be less liable to become allergic if the mother, during pregnancy, does not eat the substances to which she reacts. It would, therefore, seem wise to detect and eliminate incriminated foods or environmental factors prior to pregnancy."[53] In addition, you'll have a more comfortable pregnancy.

> **Before and During Pregnancy: Steps to Help Prevent Endo in Your Child**
>
> • Practice the best possible nutrition for years before conception.
> • Reduce toxic exposures.
> • Get your thyroid checked.
> • Get dental work done well in advance of conception.
> • Get *Candida albicans*, allergies, and asthma under control.
> • Reduce the risk of passing on your allergies.

You will need to start on this process of getting candida, allergies, and asthma under control at least six months before attempting pregnancy—more would be even better. To sweeten the whole deal, *your* health and quality of life will improve immeasurably.

These efforts might also help you avoid pregnancy-induced high blood pressure (also called toxemia of pregnancy and preeclampsia). Richard Mabray, M.D., a gynecologist from Victoria, Texas, and an environmental medicine specialist, has published amazing studies showing severe complications of pregnancy that may be related to prostaglandins. Dr. Mabray found higher hospital admissions for preeclampsia and eclampsia just after high mold and pollen season.[16, 54] A study done by midwives from Yale School of Nursing-Midwifery Program found a 5.3 percent preeclampsia rate in women with endo. This study was conducted with Endometriosis Association members and is reviewed in *The Endometriosis Sourcebook*.[55] Another intriguing research finding showed that babies born in late winter and spring were more likely to develop pollen allergies than if they were born at other times of the year. It is believed that the undeveloped immune system of the newborn may make the baby more susceptible to the allergens the baby is exposed to in early infancy.[56, 57]

During Pregnancy: Reduce the Risk of Passing on Your Allergies

A child born into a family with allergic respiratory disease has a risk of developing asthma or rhinitis (inflammation of the mucous membranes of the nose, causing swelling; runny nose; and sometimes, inflamed sinuses) or asthma that is up to 200 times greater than that for a child born into a nonallergic household, said James E. Shira, M.D., at a pediatric program presented by the University of Colorado School of Medicine, Denver.[58] Dr. Shira also noted that since 87 percent of children who develop an allergic disorder before age ten have at least one immediate relative who is allergic, prevention should begin in pregnancy and during breastfeeding by "having the mother follow a balanced diet without excesses."

Research shows that a woman can reduce the risk of her child developing allergies if during pregnancy she avoids the substances to which *she* is allergic.[59] Eat as widely varied a diet as possible; too much of one food can sensitize the developing baby.[60] If you have allergies yourself, do everything possible to control them during this time. This is not the time to indulge in ice cream if you're allergic to milk or to hang out in the park during hay fever season. Work with your allergist or environmental medicine specialist.

Your aim? As healthy a pregnancy as you can humanly manage! Not only will a healthy pregnancy lead to a healthier baby, but studies also show that premature babies[61] and babies born by cesarean section[62] have a greater risk for asthma. While we certainly don't have complete control over prematurity or problems that lead to cesarean section, a healthy pregnancy is more likely to produce a full-term baby and a vaginal birth. For this and many other reasons, you want to find the best obstetrician and/or midwife you can. This may very well not be your endo doctor, since endo specialists often don't do obstetrical work, so they can specialize in endo and related work. You will find there is so much you want to learn when you're pregnant—it's a very exciting time—that if you can get a head start before pregnancy, you will do a lot better.

Now is also the time to search for a pediatrician who can help you prevent endo and related health problems in your precious child. Ask the doctors who have especially helped you—perhaps an environmental medicine doctor but, in any case, a physician who is willing to work with an informed patient.

Behold, a Miracle Child Is Born!

You can't believe it! How could you and your husband have produced the absolutely most precious baby ever born? It's a very joyous and exciting time—but also filled with worries you didn't even know human beings could have. Among those worries, uppermost may be how to keep this baby from ever having to follow in your footsteps healthwise.

Breastfeeding Pros and Cons

Among the most important things you can do to reduce allergic disease, according to many sources, is breastfeeding.[64] Breastfeeding was found to reduce a child's likelihood of developing asthma in a study of 3,000 children exclusively breastfed during the first four months of life.[65] However, another study of 1,000 children who were exclusively breastfed in infancy found the risk of asthma was greater in those whose mothers have asthma, and the risk increased the longer the duration of breastfeeding.[65] Breastfed children were less likely than bottle-fed infants to develop lower respiratory tract infections in the first year of life. These infections increase risk for asthma later.[66] Breastfeeding was also found to reduce development of allergic eczema in children.[64]

It's important that the mother be aware of what she is eating when breastfeeding. Sensitivities can develop in the baby based on the mother's diet. Dr. James Shira noted the example of a week-old breastfed baby with hives and nasal blockage whose mother was eating a dozen eggs a week. Both parents had hay fever. The baby tested allergic to eggs; the hives and nasal stuffiness cleared when the mother eliminated eggs from her diet. Other research has found that cow's milk antibodies can persist in the breast milk of some mothers up to a week after drinking cow's milk, causing colic in their babies.[67] The mothers need not be allergic themselves to secrete allergens in their breast milk. Since dairy is one of the most common allergies in women with endo, consider this problem if your baby has colic or allergic signs. Other sources suggest also eliminating egg, peanuts and peanut products, fish, and soy.[67–69]

Another interesting study found that an excess of linoleic acid (omega-6) or a deficiency of linolenic acid (omega-3) in the breastfeeding mother's diet also could increase the risk for allergic diseases. There is presumably an even higher risk for formula-fed babies, because formulas contain primarily linoleic acid. (Soy contains 7 percent linolenic acid and 51 percent linoleic acid, according to the authors of *Allergies: Disease in Disguise*.[70]) For more on this important topic, see the section of this chapter entitled "Your Growing Child: Healthy Steps for the Endo Family."

Unfortunately, despite all the evidence on the benefits of breastfeeding, especially in families with allergic disease, women with endo have some major concerns. First, since our immune system abnormalities are so prominent, how do we know that women with endo are making breast milk that contains the immune protective elements that breast milk generally does? Research, please! With endo now affecting a conservatively estimated 89 million girls and women in the world, it's time we found out! The defective immunity in women with endo could possibly be exacerbating the situation.

The other major concern we have is that we are keenly aware that our bodies have stores of dioxins in our fat tissues, which are released during breastfeeding (as well as during pregnancy). These toxins built up over a lifetime, starting when we were embryos ourselves. Besides being potent cancer-causing chemicals, dioxins have been strongly linked to the development of endometriosis. They act both as hormones in the body, confusing and misdirecting the delicate interplay of our own hormones, and as immune system toxicants.

Exposure of newborns to dioxins in breast milk has been shown to cause the shriveling of lymph tissues; exposure of pregnant women can result in stillbirth.[71] In fact, dioxins are so toxic that it took the U.S. Environmental Protection Agency over 2,000 pages just to summarize the known effects of this pollutant, which has often been called the most toxic chemical known.[72] Toxicologists agree that these compounds are even more toxic to the developing embryo and the newborn than to adults.

The amount of toxin passed along in breast milk can be staggering. In the dioxin-exposed rhesus monkey colony the Association studied, the mother monkeys passed on to their offspring more dioxin per kilogram of weight than they themselves had been exposed to. (And the levels they had been exposed to as adults, when they were far less vulnerable to dioxin's effects than a newborn, caused the development of endo so severe that it killed some of them. See Part 3 in this book and Chapter 14 of *The Endometriosis Sourcebook* for more information.) In addition, some work has shown that the amount of dioxin in breast milk diminishes but can still be high even after breastfeeding quite a number of children—and, of course, being careful not to have new exposures during that time.[73]

One reassuring, though preliminary, Japanese study found that women who were breastfed as infants were less likely to have endo. The researchers speculated that there might be protective effects in breastfeeding that outweigh the risks of dioxin exposure.[74] The researchers did not study the mother's endo status.

So far, no one knows how to remove these dangerous toxins from our fat cells. An Association Advisor in Japan is researching this issue. We hope, based on his work and ours, to have information on fat detoxification in the next several years.

Leo Galland, M.D., in his excellent book *The Four Pillars of Healing*, writes, "The high levels of organochlorines [dioxin, PCBs, etc.] found in human milk raise frightening questions about the safety of breastfeeding. I urge my patients not to lose weight while breastfeeding, but to eat heartily. Weight loss releases organochlorines stored in body fat, which travel into the blood and from there into breast milk. Lose weight *after* weaning, *not* before."[75]

Pumping your milk between feedings will also help remove more dioxins. The body compensates by producing more milk, so the infant still gets plenty. Perhaps continuing to pump your milk after you've stopped breastfeeding is another way to remove more toxins. And if, for some reason, you decide not to breastfeed or the baby is unable to breastfeed, you may still want to "pump and dump" your breast milk as a way to remove toxins from your body, an idea suggested by Drs. Needleman and Landrigan

> "Hello! I'm writing for some insight. My miracle baby girl Brianna was born four months ago. I want to try and prevent endo from debilitating her life, if she does in fact have it, or will get it. I want to know if any surveys (of endo patients) have been done regarding two things: (1) How many women with endo were breastfed, and for how long? (2) How many women with endo wore disposable diapers, or cloth diapers? Dioxins have been shown to be linked to endo, but I'm not sure if disposable diapers are a cause for concern. I'm wondering whether I should switch to cloth. Also, I'm exclusively breastfeeding and I'm wondering if this will help her in the future. I can't believe how much I'm concerned! People say, 'Don't worry, just enjoy her,' but if I can do *anything* to lessen her chances *now*, why not?!!"
>
> —*Kelly, Pennsylvania*

in *Raising Children Toxic Free*. Some might consider such steps drastic. Perhaps only those who've suffered the years of pain and life-destroying aspects of endo and its related diseases can appreciate why women with endo would be willing to go to such lengths to protect our children.

Since miscarriage may be, unfortunately, a fairly common experience for women with endo, here's a tip that could remove some toxins from your body, possibly reduce your risk of breast cancer, and better prepare you for the next pregnancy: After a late miscarriage, pump your milk for as long as possible. There is milk in the breast from the fifth or sixth month of pregnancy, but according to La Leche League, you'll do better if you rent a special pump for premature delivery from the Medela (medela.com) or Ameda (ameda.com) companies. La Leche League (1-800-LALECHE; lalecheleague .org) can advise you.

It is appalling that we even need to think about these horrible scenarios rather than the joy of giving life and nurturing our baby. Thoughts about how these chemicals have stolen from us these beautiful opportunities (or at least an opportunity to enjoy breast-feeding our baby without these fears), as well as the fears for our baby, are what motivate so many women with endo to fight the pollution permeating our world.

Philosophically speaking, *might* it be better for future generations if our toxin-laden current generations in the developed world skip breastfeeding so that our children and their children can start life with a less toxic load? We do not know the answers! Perhaps making that sacrifice (because breastfeeding is a beautiful experience that should be a woman's, and a baby's, right) will buy us time—the time to find out how to remove dioxins from our bodies and time to stop the pollution and toxic trespassing of our bodies and those of our babies.

Formula-Feeding Pros and Cons

There are, of course, also many questions about formulas. Are they organic? Are they well balanced, nutritious, and, importantly, the right formula for an allergy-prone baby? And what about the plastic bottles used to feed the formula to baby? Made of polycarbonate, baby bottles have been shown to leach bisphenol A, an estrogenic substance. Tempered glass bottles are an obvious alternative.[76]

According to the authors of *Understanding Allergy, Sensitivity, and Immunity*, "Some pediatricians recommend a rotation diet of formulas with a milk, soy, or meat base in an effort to prevent or minimize adverse reactions in severely allergic children. Rotating the formulas avoids exposing a child to an overwhelming quantity of any one potentially allergenic food, and the level of each allergen is thus kept within tolerable limits."[60]

In a review of twenty-six studies analyzing the value of prevention for allergies, fourteen studies linked the development of allergic disease to early ingestion of cow's milk or mixed feeding in early infancy.[58] To prevent allergies, the infant should be breastfed exclusively for at least six and preferably nine months, according to the researchers.

Infancy: Steps to Help Prevent Endo in Your Child

- Weigh the pros and cons of breastfeeding.
- Weigh the pros and cons of formula feeding.
- Use great caution in introducing solid foods.
- Watch what is used on and around your baby.

The child should not be fed foods that may trigger allergy—particularly milk, egg, wheat, citrus, legumes, tomato, and artificially colored foods—during the first year of life. Other sources add soy and peanut to this list. In fact, the American Academy of Pediatrics guidelines for allergy-prone families suggests no peanuts until the child is three years old.[58, 68]

Solid Foods

When it is time to introduce solid foods, most allergy-sensitive pediatricians suggest introducing only one food at a time. It is also beneficial to continue breastfeeding while introducing solid foods to the baby, as maternal antibodies can continue to protect against some infections, and continued breastfeeding during and after introduction of wheat and gluten grains has been shown to protect against celiac disease.[77] (Celiac disease is a condition in which the body cannot digest gluten, the protein that is part of most grains, resulting in abdominal swelling, vomiting, diarrhea, muscle wasting, and fatigue. Intolerance of milk and dairy products can also occur in celiac disease.)

The *Mother's Almanac* states, "Any new food, including each type of cereal, must be served daily for five days to test for allergic reaction—perhaps a milk rash or the heaves or possibly even extreme dislike, which may signify a potential allergy. An allergy generally disappears if the problem food is stopped and then introduced again at one [year], but if you continue it without stopping, it usually gets worse. It takes nearly a year for a child to sample all the permitted food, but it's impossible to isolate a problem food if it's served in a jumble."[78] While these measures may not always prevent allergies completely, they can give the immune system time to mature and delay or reduce allergic reactions even if they aren't prevented.

Eczema also has been linked to the introduction of solid foods too early. In a large New Zealand study, infants who received four or more different types of solid food before the age of four months were almost three times more likely to develop chronic or recurrent eczema than infants who were not exposed to early solid feeding.[79]

Products Used on Baby's Skin

While we're focusing on what's going into the baby at the top end, let's not forget baby's bottom. Any chlorine-bleached product, including disposable diapers, contains traces of dioxin. And if you use cloth diapers, don't forget that you don't want to use chlorine bleach in washing them. (A diaper wash service will almost inevitably use chlorine bleaches.) Check your health food store or environmentally friendly product catalogs for alternatives. Finally, skip baby powders that use talc, which has been linked to ovarian cancer. Cornstarch is an alternative.

In fact, environmentally aware parents will find themselves looking with new awareness at everything used on and around their baby. We instinctively know to keep baby's room extra clean (without using harsh chemicals!). Research has shown that reducing the dust concentrations of allergens from cat, dog, and dust mites reduced development of allergy to these substances in allergy-prone babies (babies in which both parents had a history of allergy).[80]

Just because products are labeled for baby does not mean that the manufacturer has used any extra care in being sure the product really is safe for baby. Lynn Lawson, in her very interesting book, *Staying Well in a Toxic World*, notes that researchers at Loyola University Medical Center found that some of the chemicals in shampoos, powders, and other baby products were at least "moderately toxic" to animals. "A newborn baby more readily absorbs chemicals placed on its skin than does an adult," says Dr. George Lambert. The researchers suggest avoiding perfumes and additives and using only bland, simple products, and sparingly. A clean washcloth and warm water are often all that is needed, according to Lawson's sources.[81]

Beyond Infancy

If, in spite of your best efforts, your child does suffer from allergies, asthma, or related diseases, don't give up. Work with your child, family, and healthcare providers to mitigate those allergies.

Finding the right healthcare providers for a child with these problems can be as problematic as finding the right healthcare providers for you! According to the bestselling book *The Mother's Almanac II: Your Child from Six to Twelve*, "Your main difficulty may be in finding a good allergist, or a pediatrician with more than cursory knowledge in this field. The search, however, is worth it. So many children bring so much havoc on themselves and their families, all because of an egg or an orange."[82]

The section on allergies in *The Mother's Almanac II* offers more ideas for helping the allergic child, including a long list of symptoms of allergies in children. Another excellent source is *The Complete Book of Allergy Control*, in which Laura J. Stevens, who struggled with endo herself, describes the serious behavioral and other problems of her sons due to allergies. And there's the classic on the subject, *Is This Your Child's World?* by Doris Rapp, M.D.

Don't forget so-called hidden or delayed hypersensitivity allergies, which can trigger reactions up to seventy-two hours after exposure. Only certain kinds of testing, including ELISA-ACT tests (available from ELISA/ACT Biotechnologies, Inc.—see Resources), can detect this type of allergy, which unfortunately, seems prevalent in women with endo and thus, presumably, in their families, too.

Elimination of allergy triggers will reduce the allergic reactions and the inflammation that is part of those reactions. It will also help prevent the development of more allergies and asthma.[83] Many of us with endo and allergies have experienced a "spreading" effect of more allergies and more inflammatory problems over time. Even if your child has "only" a few allergies, treat allergic disease as the serious health problem it is. After all, if a system as critical to our health and survival as the immune system, which protects us from cancer and many other diseases, isn't working right, that's serious.

Depending on your child's allergies, you can take many steps that will make a difference. For example, you can use dust-mite-proof bed coverings and HEPA vacuum cleaners and air cleaners, avoid carpeting if your child is allergic to dust, avoid problem foods, and allow no tobacco smoke in your home or near your child. (Actually, due to the 4,000 chemicals, including dioxin, in cigarette smoke, you and your children must steer clear of it whether or not your family is allergic to tobacco smoke.) Parental smoking was found to be a significant risk factor for increasing the possibility of childhood allergies.[84] Your child's allergist will have many more ideas on how to change your child's environment to help lessen allergic reactions.

Also consider having your child desensitized to the things to which he or she reacts. Many allergy medications simply treat symptoms, rather than getting to the root of the problem. For the best opportunity for great health for your child (and yourself!), you want to address the immune system itself. Allergy desensitization, along with avoidance of triggers and other measures, can actually teach the immune system to react normally to things that used to trigger an allergic reaction. "Provocative neutralization," used by environmental medicine specialists, seems to have a good effect in women with endo (see Chapter 4). While we have the data to back up that statement in women with endo, we unfortunately do not have the data, only reports to the Association, that the same approach has worked well for the children of women with endo.

Keep in mind, as Laura Stevens writes in *The Complete Book of Allergy Control*, that "allergic reactions in children are not limited to asthma, hay fever, and rashes. Stomachaches, headaches, leg pains, and dizziness often have an allergic origin. Behavior problems, including temper tantrums, hyperactivity, violence, fatigue, depression, and Dr. Jekyll–Mr. Hyde personality changes, also may be allergic reactions. The same goes for learning disabilities. Children with pale, washed-out complexions, who are always tired or overactive, and have dark, puffy circles under their eyes should be checked for allergy."[85]

Besides helping your child develop normally, feel happy, and be able to enjoy life, there's another important reason to get those allergies diagnosed and modified early. That is, children with early development of allergies are more likely to develop asthma,

> "Since I have a compromised immune system, is it possible that as my son was developing in utero he acquired my immune system and that is why he is so allergic?"
>
> —*Suki, California*

eczema, and hay fever later.[83, 86] And, as we know, they're at greater risk for endo and related diseases. In the Association's joint study with the U.S. National Institutes of Health, those with allergic disease (allergies, asthma, eczema) were most likely to develop thyroid diseases, chronic fatigue immune dysfunction syndrome (CFIDS), and fibromyalgia.[2] But the good news is allergy treatment can prevent development of asthma, and perhaps the many measures described here can prevent or lessen the severity of all the allergic diseases.

It's especially important to prevent development of asthma in children, as asthma has reached epidemic levels in developed countries. Asthma deaths also are increasing. From 1980 to 1989, rates for asthma as the cause of death increased 54 percent for females, 23 percent for males.[87] Asthma has been strongly linked to air pollution. An important study reported in *The Lancet* found that children who played the most active sports in high-ozone areas developed the most asthma.[88] (Some public health officials recommend that children and adults with allergies and asthma stay indoors on high-ozone days.) Other asthma triggers are allergies of all kinds (including allergies to foods, pollens and molds, animal dander, dust mites, feather pillows), cigarette smoke, perfumes and fragrances (see the article "The Problems with Perfume" in Chapter 7), polyvinyl chloride (PVC—see the article "Why Endometriosis Is an Environmental Issue" in Chapter 14), and various chemicals, including household cleaning products, paint, hairsprays, and other substances.

According to an important study of over 8,000 children, asthma cases could drop nearly 40 percent in youngsters under age six if susceptible children did not have furry or feathered pets or other allergy triggers in their homes.[89] Other research studied 3,754 newborns in Norway. Those with PVC on the surfaces of their environment (from flooring and wall coverings) were at significantly greater risk of developing asthma symptoms than children in an environment free of PVC.[90]

Antibiotics in the first two years of life also have been associated with asthma, as well as with hay fever.[91] As women who have *Candida albicans* problems know, antibiotic use can trigger changes in intestinal organisms, leading to candidiasis and more allergies. Frequently antibiotics are used when allergies are the real underlying problem, setting the stage for candidiasis. So discuss any proposed antibiotic use carefully with your pediatrician.

Food allergies are all too common in endo and seem, according to early reports, to affect some of our children, too. Dub Howard, M.D., is an Association Advisor and infertility expert from Dallas, Texas. In his many years in practice, he has noted a history of "irritable bowel symptoms" in women with endo, dating back to before their periods. Marc Laufer, M.D., an authority on teens with endo, practices in Boston, Massachusetts. Dr. Laufer has actually diagnosed endo in girls who had pelvic pain thought to be gastrointestinal who had not yet had their first periods.[92] Other teens and families have told us similar stories of stomach and intestinal distress before menstruation started. Just as in adult women with endo, intestinal problems can be linked in these girls to food allergies and/or *Candida albicans* problems.

Women with endo who are susceptible to *Candida albicans* problems need to keep that susceptibility in mind for their child. As the late well-known pediatrician and author of *The Yeast Connection*, William Crook, M.D., said, "Women with chronic health problems, including allergies and *Candida*-related problems, often have children with similar problems."[93] Keep this in mind, too, when your little girl enters puberty, which will happen a lot faster than you can imagine! As another famous physician and candida pioneer, C. Orian Truss, M.D., wrote in his book *The Missing Diagnosis*, "A girl who enters puberty with chronic allergy, and particularly with an established yeast infection, is almost sure to have much trouble with her menstrual cycle."[94]

Allergies go hand in hand with candida problems, but they aren't the only manifestation. Diaper rash can also be due to candida—the irritating substances made by the yeast are what causes the sometimes intense red rash for the poor baby. Candida also is the cause of oral thrush in babies. Again, the absence of lactobacillus has been shown to be a key factor in making children susceptible to candida problems.[95]

Be sure to involve your child in the process of allergy management from the youngest age possible. This will help them understand that, after all, it's their body. It will also hopefully make them a partner in this program, rather than treating it as something to rebel against. Explain the health problem at a level the child can understand, and make a game out of finding the triggers for their reactions. Involve the whole family, and if at all possible, have the whole family eat the same diet as the child. This will help the child feel supported and less deprived. (Face it, could *you* really stay on the candida diet if your family were eating your favorite sugary foods in front of you?)

Your Growing Child: Healthy Steps for the Endo Family

The measures described in the following paragraphs may help you and your family to stay as healthy as possible by avoiding many of the risk factors associated with endo.

Use Purified Water

Use purified water for all your cooking, food washing, and drinking. Alas, our tap water carries many toxins, from plastic and medicinal residues (including hormonal preparations) to pesticide residues. The least expensive way to purify your water over the long run is to install a high-quality water purifier in your home. Bottled water isn't well regulated, and most of it comes in plastic, adding toxins directly from the bottle itself to the water. Be sure to do your homework to find the type of purification unit that can remove lead, pesticides, and other toxins. These are usually systems that use several methods of purification. (You may need to take mineral supplements, as purifiers tend to remove essential minerals.)

Watch the Omega-6/Omega-3 Balance

As your baby all too quickly grows out of infancy, vigilantly watch the balance between omega-6 and omega-3 fatty acids in your child's diet. This balance directly affects whether your child's body veers toward an inflammatory state or not. The fatty acids in our diets are the precursors to prostaglandins. Prostaglandins are key regulators of inflammation and are very much involved in endo and in allergies.[96-98] A number of studies have shown menstrual pain is reduced with omega-3.[97-99] The pro-inflammatory prostaglandins derived from omega-6 fatty acids are associated with severity of painful periods in endo,[96] and the inflammatory environment they create may be a key element in allowing the development of endo.

The omega-6 essential fatty acids, which produce the prostaglandins *promoting* inflammation, are abundant in our modern diet: dairy products, meat, eggs, margarine, vegetable oils. Omega-3 fatty acids used to be ample in meat, according to some sources. But as factory-style farming took over and farm animals were no longer fed seeds containing omega-3 fatty acids and chickens could no longer roam and eat bugs (which are rich in omega-3 fatty acids), omega-3 no longer occurred in the meat. More healthful organic meats and omega-3 eggs are now available from organic food stores.

Processed oils are an especially serious problem, resulting when processing methods turn the oils into trans fatty acids. These are not only useless to us but actually harm us in many ways, including blocking out natural healthful fat so it cannot function. Trans fatty acids are found in fried foods, margarine, vegetable oil, shortening, packaged and baked goods, french fries, crackers, and chips. (Check packages; they'll say "hydrogenated" or "partially hydrogenated.") Trans fatty acids were found to be associated with asthma, allergic rhinitis, and eczema in an important study in ten countries in Europe. The study also found that increased trans fatty acids in infants have been associated with changes in fatty acid composition of plasma lipids—changes similar to those seen in allergic diseases.[100]

While you're making all these changes for your child or children, remember you're benefiting yourself, too. For example, cutting down on trans fats may reduce your risk of breast cancer, one of the cancers for which women with endo are at higher risk. Women with high levels of trans fatty acids in the body have about a 40 percent higher risk of getting breast cancer.[101]

The U.S. Food and Drug Administration is issuing new rules to require labeling of trans fat in foods. Ideally, it would go further and forbid any food to contain more than a minuscule amount of trans fat, as some European governments have done.

The omega-3 essential fatty acids, which produce the prostaglandins *countering* inflammation, are far less available today in the typical Western diet: flax, walnut, pumpkin, soy, canola, evening primrose oil, borage oil, and fish, especially wild-caught salmon, mackerel, cod, and sardines. Even some of these sources, such as soy, have far more omega-6 essential fatty acids than omega-3. Bottom line? Eat a diet high in omega-3 and low in omega-6.

Soy, though it contains omega-3 fatty acids, may be problematic because it and flaxseed are phytoestrogens—that is, they contain weak, natural estrogens. Anecdotal reports from women with endo seem to show soy causes problems for some. Research has not yet clarified whether soy and other phytoestrogens are, on balance, good for women with endo (and those prone to endo) or not.[44] Moreover, most of the nonorganic soy products now available are from genetically modified soy, which also may be problematic for women with endo. More on genetically modified foods in the section "Eat Organic." See Chapter 5 for more information, and stay tuned to Association reports.

Substituting omega-3 for omega-6 essential fatty acids in the diet reduces inflammation in the body.[60] How to do this? Simply reduce the amount of omega-6 fatty acids, especially red meat and dairy, and increase fish and cold-pressed, unrefined oils (especially flax, walnut, and canola) and other omega-3 foods, such as walnuts, pumpkin seeds (they are a great snack for kids), and possibly soy. Grind up flax seeds (which have a delicious, nutty flavor) fresh in a small coffee grinder, and use the ground seeds immediately on cereals and salads.

> "I fit the pattern of so many other women. I had suffered with endo since puberty (only relieved by being on the pill), had intestinal symptoms since that time, have allergies and asthma (I also have a son with asthma and allergy), had several bouts with mono as a teen, two labors which were both extremely long because of being dysfunctional (in spite of both being induced), I was exhausted all the time and my heating pad was my closest friend, had a low-grade fever for six months and plain ibuprofen did more for my pain than narcotics. Prostaglandin relief!!"
>
> —*Nancy, New York*

An interesting study of allergies in Iceland and Sweden, both populated by Scandinavian people, showed that food and inhalant allergies occurred much more frequently in Sweden. The researchers cited the fact that the Icelandic population consumes large amounts of fish and cod liver oil, omega-3 fatty acids helpful in reducing asthma and allergy symptoms. They also noted that Icelandic homes had better ventilation because they are heated by geothermal heat systems and windows are regularly kept open for ventilation. The Swedish homes, by contrast, are heated by fossil fuels such as oil and gas.[102, 103] (While fish are a great source of healthy omega-3, be careful to avoid contaminated fish, which contain lots of dioxins! Follow the fish advisories in your area.)

Endo researchers have also found, amazingly, that survival of endometrial cells (from the inside lining of the uterus) from women with and without endo was significantly reduced when there was more omega-3 present in cell cultures.[104] This beneficial effect may mean that high levels of omega-3 in the tissues could help prevent development of endo.

Use Supplements Wisely

With the help of a knowledgeable nutritionist, naturopath, or environmental medicine doctor, develop a profile of needed vitamins and minerals based on your child's health problems and risks. Consider supplementing omega-3, especially if your child will not eat the foods in which it is abundant or if he or she is allergic to these foods. Purifying water may remove minerals, so you may need to supplement them. In addition, minerals are great buffering agents and can help rectify the acid-alkaline imbalance in allergic individuals. (For more on supplements, see Chapter 5, "What You Eat Affects Your Endo.")

Vitamin C, a powerful antihistamine, strengthens the immune system and has been found to sharply reduce asthma attacks.[105, 106] (For information on histamine, see Chapter 7, "The Immune System: Part and Parcel of Endo.") Magnesium is especially important for those with allergies and asthma. One study found that magnesium deficiency occurred in most individuals with asthma, multiple chemical sensitivity, and chronic fatigue syndrome.[107] Lactobacillus is especially important for the allergic child or adult.

Eat Organic

If I could do only one thing for my child to ensure his or her future health, it would be to feed him or her organic, whole (meaning unrefined, unprocessed) foods—food grown without pesticides and herbicides. Besides being much safer, these foods taste sooooo much better; this is how to raise a child who loves fruits and vegetables! Many whole foods and fibrous vegetables—especially cabbage, cauliflower, broccoli, and brussels sprouts—contain lignins, a type of fiber that helps remove excess estrogens from the body.[108] This is exactly what you want for your child! This ability to remove excess estrogens also is linked to the role of these vegetables in reducing cancer risk (see Chapter 8).

Whole foods also help one avoid the unhealthy jumps in blood sugar caused by refined foods. For more information on eating to balance blood sugar levels, see Barry Sears's book *The Zone* and *The 40-30-30 Fat Burning Nutrition Book* by Joyce and Gene Daoust. Eating organic whole foods, prepared in a healthful way, will also go far in eliminating trans fatty acids from your diet.

Does this mean your child can never have cookies, cake, or candy? Of course not! But if you provide three highly nutritious meals each day and healthful snacks (nuts, fruit), there won't be much appetite left for the sweets.

If you make family dinner an important priority in your house, not only will you have the peace of mind that you feed your children well, but you'll also find that the camaraderie and time together bonds your family. Involve your child in planning and preparing some meals, too. That gives the child a sense of control. If you start when

---

Childhood: Steps to Help Prevent Endo in Your Child

- Manage allergies and asthma.
- Watch out for *Candida albicans*!
- Use purified water.
- Watch the omega-6/omega-3 balance.
- Consider supplements.
- Reduce toxic exposures:
  - Eat organic to avoid toxins in food.
  - Avoid herbicides.
  - Keep the PVC out of your child's life.
- Delay puberty and menstrual periods:
  - Avoid endocrine disruptors.
  - Avoid hair products utilizing estrogen.
  - Watch out for hormones, pesticides/herbicides, phthalates, and too much overall fat or bad fat in the diet.
  - Exercise.
  - Watch out for cosmetics, fragrances, and nail polishes.
- Get active (as in "activist")!

---

the child is very young, you'll find it much easier. It's much more difficult by adolescence. After all, "adolescents believe they are special, and that they are not subject to natural laws, such as growing old or getting pregnant."[109]

Organic foods also help you avoid genetically modified foods, foods that have had genes from other, often unrelated, organisms inserted into them. For the allergic, this is a nightmare beyond our wildest dreams. How can you possibly know that the reason you're reacting to that tomato you had at lunch is because it has *fish* genes in it?[110]

Fatal Harvest: The Tragedy of Industrial Agriculture is a powerful and sobering look at the health and environmental damage caused by our current methods of growing food. According to the authors, the genetic engineering of food creates three hazards for the allergic: "First, it may increase the levels of allergy-causing proteins already found in the plant to the point where they prompt strong human allergenic response. Second, genetic engineering can transfer allergens from foods to which people know they are allergic to foods that they think are safe. . . . There is yet a third allergy risk associated with [genetically engineered] foods. These foods could be creating thousands of different and new allergic responses. Each genetic 'cassette' [which includes the gene, a bacteria to get the gene into the foreign cells, a virus to promote the invasion, and an antibiotic marker system] being engineered into foods produces a number of novel proteins that have never been part of the human diet, some of which could create an allergic response in some consumers."[110] Increased antibiotic resistance due to the antibiotic marker system is also a risk.

Due to the political power of the huge agricultural corporations, genetically modified food does not have to be labeled in the United States or Canada, two of the few developed nations that do not require labeling.[110] (The Centre for Science in the Public Interest, a nonprofit health advocacy group dedicated to education and pressing for changes in government and corporate policies, is pushing for this labeling. See the Resources section for contact information.) The majority of processed foods contain some genetically engineered ingredients, another reason to avoid them. Soy, corn, potatoes, squash, canola oil, cottonseed oil, papaya, and tomatoes are most commonly affected, but the food biotechnology companies have their eye on the entire food market.

Sometimes people say they can't afford to eat organic, and of course those in the lowest socioeconomic level can't. But I believe we really can't afford to eat any other way and that it's well worth making sacrifices in other parts of our lives to be able to feed ourselves and our families nutritious, pesticide-free food. Either we pay now for high-quality food that can nourish us and protect our health, or we pay later in the form of serious health problems, lost productivity, medical bills, pain, suffering, and heartache. In addition, our world, our environment, suffers. Eliminate the fad foods from your family's diet (sodas, chips, fast food, candy, doughnuts, etc.), and you'll save enough to buy the best. Some people can grow organic vegetables themselves in their yard, window box, or container garden or at a community garden. In addition, gardening is a continuous living lesson for children. Many poorer neighborhoods have community gardens or access to farmers' markets; these may be a source of organic vegetables, too.

Reduce Toxic Exposures

The things you did before conception, during pregnancy, and during your child's infancy apply all the way through his or her childhood, adolescence, and teen years. A good resource on hormonally active chemicals and how to avoid them is *Hormone Deception* by D. Lindsey Berkson (see Resources). Here are the most important steps to get you started.

Eat Right

Since food is the primary exposure to dioxins for most of us, eating organic is key. Another way to greatly reduce exposure to dioxins in food is to eat lower on the food chain. That means more vegetables, grains, and fruits and less animal products.

Stay Away from Pesticides

Avoid pesticides and herbicides. Check that the parks, school grounds, and playgrounds where your child plays have not been sprayed. Many parents take precautions with

very young children, but all children, even teens, may be susceptible. *Clinical Pediatrics* reports the case of a high school runner who had estrogen-like effects from exposure to commonly used herbicides.[III] She experienced four episodes of breakthrough bleeding that lasted two to three days. On all four occasions, the breakthrough bleeding occurred following a track meet where an herbicide (glycophosphate) had been used in or around the track stadium. At five track meets where no pesticides were used, no abnormal bleeding occurred. The study notes, "Most individuals are not cognizant of the potential harmful effects from pesticide use and indiscriminately apply them in parks, schools, movie theatres, restaurants, etc." The young woman described in the article, now in college, continues to have breakthrough bleeding, especially following cross-country meets held on golf courses, "where pesticides are commonly used." A teammate also is experiencing breakthrough bleeding after meets at golf courses.

There is also a significant association between cancer risk and childhood exposure to pesticides, solvents, and petroleum products, according to other studies.[43] Children who have been exposed to pesticides around the home and professional extermination methods within the home are three to seven times more likely to develop non-Hodgkin's lymphoma than children who have not been exposed to pesticides, according to a UCLA study. Interestingly, the child's risk for lymphoma was similar for pesticide exposure to the mother during pregnancy and direct exposure after birth.[112] Since non-Hodgkin's lymphoma is one of the cancers for which women with endo and their families are at special risk, we need to be especially vigilant about these exposures.

Pesticides have also been linked to immune abnormalities—in fact, some of the same immune abnormalities seen in endo. "These immunological changes may account for the frequent infections, asthma, and allergies commonly seen in children exposed to pesticides," notes a report in *The Human Ecologist* about a study on pesticide exposure in children.[113]

Avoid PVC

Keep PVC and other endocrine disruptors out of your child's life. Avoid PVC plumbing, shoes, rain gear, shower curtains, flooring, and toys. Dental sealants, used to seal children's teeth from decay-causing bacteria, typically contain an endocrine disruptor called bisphenol A. Bisphenol A is a plastic resin that is estrogenic. "I would be concerned about the possibility of high levels of this chemical getting into a child. And until we learn more about its biological effects, as a parent I would therefore err on the side of caution" when it comes to using dental sealants, said Frederick S. vom Saal, Ph.D., a scientist who has studied endocrine disruptors.[114, 115]

Delay Puberty and Menarche

Especially for our girls, we should do what we can to delay puberty (including development of breasts and pubic hair) and menarche (first menstrual period). This last idea might be the most controversial. People say we shouldn't interfere with nature, and I agree! But interfere with nature we have—big time!—by destroying the environment and our own health in the process.

When I was growing up, all seventh-grade girls (ages twelve to thirteen) were shown films about menstruation. In recent years, schools have had to start showing these films in fifth grade (ages ten to eleven), and that's not early enough for some of the girls. One hundred fifty years ago, girls' first periods occurred between ages fifteen and a half to seventeen. Since then, the age has been dropping worldwide to about thirteen and even younger now for some.[116]

A recent, important study of 17,077 girls across the United States found alarming results. A significant number of girls are now starting their periods even earlier: at age eleven, 28 percent of the African-American girls and 13 percent of the white girls; at age twelve, 62 percent of the African-American girls and 35 percent of the white girls. But especially alarming was the finding that 48 percent of African-American girls had either breast or pubic hair development by age eight (15 percent of the white girls had one or both by age eight). Medical textbooks say these hormonally triggered events occur between eleven and twelve, on average. Even more horrifying is that at age three, 3 percent of African-American girls and 1 percent of white girls are showing breast and/or pubic hair development, with these levels increasing to 27 percent of African-

American girls and 7 percent of white girls at age seven. Seven! An age when children are beginning to learn their multiplication tables and to jump rope should not be the age they start to worry whether or not to wear a bra![117, 118] A British study found similar trends. In a study of 14,000 children, Professor Jean Golding found that one in six girls showed early signs of puberty by eight years old. More boys (one in fourteen) were also showing signs of puberty by eight.[119]

What has caused the shift to earlier puberty and earlier menarche? No one knows for sure, but experts tend to place the blame on sugary, higher-fat diets, hormonally active compounds in that fat, and less physical activity among kids. There is an epidemic of obesity among children and adults, which has already manifested itself in a skyrocketing increase in diabetes in children.[120]

Another question is why African-American children tend to reach puberty before their white counterparts in the United States. While African-American children in the United States are now more likely to enter puberty earlier than white children, girls in Africa have normal or late menarche, depending on nutritional conditions.[121] Also, a 1944 study showed no differences in age of puberty between black and white Americans.[122] A number of studies give some clues as to why African-American children may be entering puberty sooner now. Some blame hair products manufactured for African-Americans, containing estrogen (yes, actual estrogen!) or placenta.[123] It is also widely acknowledged that many more African-Americans live in contaminated environments with more exposure to hormonally active chemicals. Similar studies of girls in the 1970s and 1980s—which analyzed the relationship between sexual maturity, blood pressure, and lipid levels—found African-American girls taller, heavier, and maturing earlier than white girls of the same age.[124-127] These findings again point to diets with more saturated fats and fats laden with toxins.

So the reason more nine-year-old girls are having to cope with periods (including pain and endo for some of them), developed breasts, and older boys' confusing attentions is that we've interfered with nature. The call to delay puberty and menarche is really a call to go back to a more natural, healthy childhood, which can lead to a more natural time for puberty and menarche, when the child is more emotionally mature and better able to handle sexual maturity. Besides, do we really want to steal childhood from our children? Let them experience the joy and abandon of a child's body for as long as nature really intended.

There are even more important reasons why we need to push the clock back on puberty and menarche. Early menarche increases the risk for endo, breast cancer, and ovarian cancer.[24, 128-132] In fact, there's a 50 percent greater risk of breast cancer if a girl starts menstruating before the age of eleven, compared with after age thirteen.[133-136]

Exposure to estrogen also causes shrinkage of the thymus, the organ just under the breastbone that produces our immune cells, and suppression of cell-mediated immunity, part of the immune system that is defective in women with endo. Estrogen also appears to increase antibody production, a key component of allergy.[137] Early-maturing girls are slightly shorter and significantly heavier in adult life, according to research on 16,000 white women.[138] Such women were found to be 30 percent more fat at age thirty than those with late menarche, increasing risk for breast cancer, diabetes, and heart disease. There are also other risks. Diana Zuckerman of the U.S. National Center for Policy Research for Women and Families states that girls who start to menstruate earlier "tend to begin dating and having sexual intercourse younger than their classmates," experience "more psychological stress," and drink and smoke more frequently.[139]

Leslie T. Dunn, director of the Teel Institute in Kansas City, which does research into child development, says, "The worries [about weight and appearance] we used to hear from fifteen- and sixteen-year-olds, we're now hearing from eight-year-olds, and they don't have the emotional tools to handle the stress and anxiety." Some preliminary research also found that early puberty may increase the risk for sexual abuse of girls.[140]

Diet

So how do we help our child enjoy a full childhood—and delay puberty and menarche to more normal times? First, watch your child's diet. We've already covered some of the key issues related to diet and, yes, those concerns must continue all the way through childhood and beyond. We simply weren't designed for fast food, 200 pounds of sugar a year (the average sugar consumed per person in the United States![141]), or mashed, smashed, slurried, and dried processed foods without an ounce of natural nutrition left in them!

One of the most important points running through all the research on age of puberty and menarche is that heavier girls will generally begin sexual development and periods earlier. Girls must reach a certain percentage of body fat to begin and maintain menstruation.[143, 144] Fat cells produce estrogen.

A *New York Times* article quotes Dr. Jaak Janssens, a Belgian expert on hormonal factors in cancer, as saying, "High calorie diets that are low in fruits and vegetables can induce puberty at an earlier age and facilitate estrogen action on the highly susceptible target organ of the breast."[145] In fact, the fat consumed by a child may be even more important a risk than the fat consumed by an adult. And Dr. Karin Michels, clinical epidemiologist at Harvard Medical School, states, "Just as heart disease has its origins in childhood, breast cancer is not just an adult disease."[145] Michels notes, "Evidence is accumulating, though the research is still in its very early phases, that the periods before and soon after birth, childhood and early adolescence are much more important to breast cancer risk than had been appreciated." In the same article, Dr. Malcolm Pike, described as a hormone researcher at the University of Southern California, Los Angeles, states, "We could get rid of 85 percent of American breast cancer by starting with 10-year-olds, keeping them on a low-fat, high-fiber diet, exercising them heavily and keeping them slim."

Dietary Problems and Solutions

Problem	Solution
Hormones in meat (especially beef) and milk	Eat organically certified meat and milk (or, as some have done, go vegetarian or skip red meat).
Pesticides, herbicides in food	Eat organic food from your own garden, farmers' market (ask lots of questions to be sure it is organic), or a growing number of supermarket chains and retail stores.
Phthalates in food	Don't store foods (including breast milk or formula for baby) in plastics.
PCBs, DDE (breakdown product of DDT, the notorious pesticide), dioxin, hormonally active chemicals in food	Avoid contaminated fish (follow government fish advisories and and other environmental group guidelines), meats, dairy, eggs. Safest solution is to go organic.
Saturated fats	Avoid fast foods, fried foods, processed oils; use good fats instead.
Too much overall fat, especially bad fats, in the diet; not enough fiber (which helps remove estrogens)[142]	Substitute vegetables and fruit; reduce bad fats; reduce refined, processed foods, which often have lots of hidden fats and raise blood sugar quickly (see "Insulin and Endometriosis" in Chapter 5).

Animal fats (along with trans fats) have been found to be most detrimental. Whether this is because of the fat itself or because animal fats are most likely to carry toxic chemicals is not yet sorted out. According to Dian Mills, author of *Endometriosis: A Key to Healing Through Nutrition* and the only specialized endo nutritionist in the world, animal fats stimulate certain bacteria in the intestines, which can produce estrogen as well as break down certain estrogen linkages, thereby freeing more estrogen to be reabsorbed into the body.[142] *Bifidobacteria*, used by so many with endo to help counter *Candia albicans* problems, are also helpful because they encourage estrogen clearance by inhibiting an enzyme that breaks these linkages.[146-148] While vegetarian diets, with their reduced total fat and higher fiber levels,[149, 150] have been found to decrease estrogen levels in pre- and postmenopausal women,[151-153] this effect was not clear in adolescent girls.[154]

Even more amazing in our growing understanding of fat is recent research showing that fat cells actually produce some cytokines, immune cells that are involved in inflammation and endo. Among these are TNF-α and IL-6 (see Chapter 7, "The Immune System: Part and Parcel of Endo").[155, 156] So keeping down the fat should also help keep down inflammation.

Exercise

Another way to achieve the goal of allowing our children, especially girls, to have all the years of childhood they should is to encourage more exercise. Studies by Harvard Medical School's Rose Frisch, Ph.D., considered a world authority on fat, fertility, and menstruation, show clearly that girls will not start their periods until they reach at least 17 percent (and most had 24 percent) body fat.[143]

One important way to keep body fat low is to exercise. Frisch showed that, in college-age swimmers and runners, each year of training they'd had before their first menstrual period had delayed the first period by five months. These athletes started menstruation, on average, at age fifteen, rather than the average of twelve years and seven months for the general population, Frisch found.

Exercise once was the mainstay of children, from wiggle-worm babies and toddlers to grade school children running all through recess and lunch hour. Now, TV, computer games, and other electronic activities; fear of crime in cities and on playgrounds; cars for teens (remember when teens walked, biked, and rode the bus everywhere?) all tend to keep our kids sitting and inactive in a way never before seen in human history.

So provide your young ones with daily opportunities for exercise: running, swinging (the backyard swing set is a favorite childhood memory of many adults), biking, gardening, lawn chores and housekeeping (make sure no detrimental chemicals are used), sports. Plan active family vacations with hiking, biking, skiing, and other sports your family enjoys. These activities will become treasured family-building times as well as memories. Team sports are especially good for girls because they can develop teamwork experience as well as physical skills. Of course, make sure these activities take place in areas with the cleanest air possible. Running in polluted air is not going to be helpful to your young one.

In addition, as most people know, exercise is important in maintaining heart health, building strong bones, reducing the risk of diabetes, reducing stress, and improving sleep. In young women, exercise has been shown to improve self-esteem and academic performance.[158]

Reduction of Toxic Exposures

Alain Audebert, M.D., in his article "How to Prevent Endometriosis?" states, "Indeed, every effort should be engaged in order to reduce pollution and to avoid exposure to

Boys

Boys are also entering puberty earlier, but not quite so dramatically earlier as girls. Again, African-Americans were more likely to start puberty earlier, with 21 percent of black boys developing pubic hair between their ninth and tenth birthdays. (The average age is twelve in white boys and Mexican-Americans and eleven in blacks.) But as with girls, some boys are beginning puberty as young as eight.[157]

pollutants carrying a potential risk of favorising endometriosis."[1] As readers may know, the pollutants "favorising" endo include the notorious dioxin family, made up of the dioxins themselves, PCBs, and furans.

An interesting study showing the link between these chemicals and early puberty highlights the amazing power of these toxins. Scientists measured PCBs and DDE (a breakdown product of the pesticide DDT, another known hormone disruptor) in the blood and breast milk of hundreds of pregnant women in North Carolina, as well as in the fetal blood from umbilical cords after birth. They then monitored the development of 600 of the children. Girls with the highest prebirth exposures to the chemicals entered puberty eleven months earlier than girls with lower exposures. One of the factors that makes this study particularly interesting is that the women in the study were exposed to PCBs and DDE from normal diet and environmental sources—like most of us—rather than industrial accidents or other abnormally high exposures. Those with the earliest menarche were daughters of mothers with the highest estimated blood levels of PCBs during pregnancy who had also nursed their infant daughters, giving them both prenatal and breast milk exposures. The study also found that boys exposed to DDE and girls exposed to PCBs were heavier than their unexposed peers at age fourteen.[159]

Another study found that girls exposed to relatively high levels of the fire retardant PBB (polybrominated biphenyl) in their mother's wombs—due to an accidental food contamination in Michigan—began menarche up to a year earlier than those exposed to lower levels. Those who had both prenatal and breast milk exposures began menstruation the earliest.[160] Many other studies in animals and humans have also found that prebirth exposure to endocrine disruptors speeded up sexual development.[161]

In Puerto Rico, girls between the ages of one and three years old began developing breasts and cysts on their ovaries in the 1970s and 1980s. After two decades of frustration among Puerto Rican doctors, a study by a pediatric endocrinologist found that the girls developing breasts as babies had higher levels of phthalates in their blood. Phthalates are toxic chemicals used to add flexibility to plastics and to dissolve other ingredients. They have been shown to damage lungs, liver, and kidneys and to harm the developing testicles of offspring.[162, 163] Diet is the probable source of the phthalates for these babies. Phthalates have been found in baby food and formulas.[163]

Preventing Endo

A Daughter's Story

When I was a baby, I drove my parents crazy with my colicky shrieks. I got a yeast infection that spread all the way down my thighs to my knees. As I grew older, my parents noticed that I would go bonkers after eating sugary foods. Around age three and a half, I started learning how to read and then forgot. Bright yet spacey is how I could be described, then and now. I had all kinds of allergies. As connections between endometriosis and my immune problems began to be better understood, my parents became concerned about my health problems and feared I might get endo like my mom.

My parents put me on the candida diet (no sugar, no yeasty or pickled foods), as well as nystatin prescribed by my doctor to help control my chronic yeast problem. They enrolled me in karate and soccer to keep me active. As a family, we ate a diet heavy in organic fruits and vegetables, whole grains, beans, poultry, and fish. I started taking supplements to help strengthen my immune system. The diet helped to some extent with my hyperactivity and spaciness. However, keeping a kid off sugar is not easy. I must say I did cheat—binging on massive amounts of candy when given the opportunity. To this day, sugar makes me behave as though I am drunk or high; afterwards I crash and often go to sleep.

I was almost fourteen when the much-awaited (and feared) period arrived so lightly and so painlessly I hardly realized I had gotten it. Future periods were accompanied by some cramps but never requiring more than one or two days of ibuprofen. I found that exercise and diet could help lessen the pain, and it has slowly decreased.

When I was sixteen, I was struck with terrible depression. I thought this might be normal for a teenager, but it would not go away. I decided that it was not OK or normal for me to be crying uncontrollably every single day when overall I felt that my life was great in every respect. I went to my environmental doctor, who tested my hormone levels over my monthly cycle. We found that my hormone cycles were off by a lot. I was able to see that the problem had been increasing from just a week per month to the whole month long! He gave me hormone supplements for a few days a month, and the problem cleared up immediately! A few months later I went off the supplements and have been fine ever since. I can't think of how many other girls would have just been put on Prozac and told to stop being a baby for something hormone related!

I still have allergies, mild asthma, and crazy sugar highs at the age of twenty. But I find that if I take good care of myself, I am repaid a thousandfold in positive self-image, learned discipline, clarity of thought, and a nearly pain-free existence. I eat a largely vegetarian diet, exercise five times a week, take my supplements, and get seven to nine hours of sleep a night.

A Mother's Story

She was a big, beautiful baby, eight and a quarter pounds, every mother's dream come true, but especially for an endo woman. Of course I wanted to breastfeed her and tried mightily. But her tummy seemed swollen all the time, and her crying could only be eased when Dad would carry her on his head, putting pressure on her poor little tummy. It still hurts to remember that at her six-week checkup we found she had lost a pound and that she had to be given formula. Only later did I learn that she and I were both allergic to dairy products and a lot of other things, and she was probably reacting to these things in my milk. And I learned that women who'd been exposed to toxic pesticides (as I had, but we didn't understand anything about it at the time) sometimes had more difficulty breastfeeding. So, with formula, my gaunt and unhappy-looking little elf turned into a giggly imp with three chins! Except, that is, when she was fed oatmeal, which would result in violent projectile vomiting and leave her so limp and white as to be terrifying. I wish I'd known more about allergies in those days!

Ear infections, diaper rash, severe yeast infections lasting over a year, and a persistent swollen lymph gland were signs things still weren't all right. At eighteen months she developed terrible "diaper rash," with redness so severe on her inner thighs she potty-trained herself in three weeks (it must have felt terrible to have a wet diaper on). The pediatrician gave us various medications, and the rash went away eventually.

Then, at almost four years old, things finally clicked. I'd gotten diagnosed with candidiasis and realized that was what my little one had, too. She and I both went through the rest of her childhood seeing an environmental medicine doctor, sometimes on antifungal drugs, always working around our allergies, and following the candida diet. (We were lucky that the small school she attended did not have a lunch program, as then I was able to send a healthful lunch, within diet restrictions, without her having to feel "different.") This treatment made such a big difference. With the exception of the usual childhood illnesses and severe growing pains in her legs at times, she turned into the healthy, gifted child she was meant to be.

As she began her periods, our wonderful environmental medicine doctor tested and watched her hormone levels. When her luteal phase started shortening, indicating problems with progesterone, he worked with hormone desensitizing and progesterone to get her cycles straightened out. Throughout college, he's been a great supporter in reminding her and working with her to take her health seriously, something many college students don't do. Thanks to him, her dad, and mostly to her own good sense, she has escaped the ravages of endo so far. We pray and hope it continues!

(Sidebar continues on next page)

Preventing Endo *(continued)*

A Father's Story

This was my first try at being a dad, so everything was new to me. Without the help from a dedicated mom, our doctors, and info from the Endo Association, I would have guessed that all our daughter's early problems were just typical troubles of all babies. Fortunately, we all grew together, learning about candida allergies, hormonal irregularities, and other health problems that related to her mom's and her endo.

I was more than a bit skeptical of the early measures we took to strengthen my daughter's health, especially when she was a tot. Part of me just did not want to believe the health issues we were learning about because I wanted so badly for her and our lives to be healthy and normal. I resisted making the lifestyle changes that it took to get our girl healthy. Changing our diets to eliminate all the junk and processed food was hard by itself. Later we would eliminate wheat, rice, dairy, and lots of other foods for long periods of time. But what seemed so difficult at first ended up being something of a new food adventure as we learned to cook and eat foods that did not cause reactions. It was amazing how set we were in our old ways of eating and how unhealthy much of it was.

Another side of the process was learning about all the chemicals that we surround ourselves with in our homes and workplaces and how they adversely affect us. It is impossible to avoid all of them, but we learned to do without most. It is unbelievable how much we falsely assume that the chemicals in the world around us are safe for us without ever giving it a second thought. We trust that the corporations and the government have been vigilant watchdogs to protect us from harm, but nothing could be further from the truth.

The payoff in all of this was working together as a family and watching our daughter grow more and more healthy and strong. The extra benefit was that it taught us all more about nutrition, exercise, the immune system, and a great deal about the body's needs. The lifestyle changes to raise a healthy daughter and get ourselves more healthy was in the end much less difficult than I had feared.

Take charge! If you really care about your children, family, and all those around you, then commit yourself to this life-changing process. You won't be disappointed.

—From a proud and healthy father

Frustrated that the same things that happened to him are now happening to his nephew, and concerned for his son, Joe decides to get active.

Unfortunately, women of childbearing age had significantly higher levels of a phthalate that is a reproductive and developmental toxin than any other group. The young women were exposed to phthalates in fragrances, fingernail polish, dyes, and plastics such as those in some food wraps.[164] So don't buy your sweet daughter perfumes, nail polish, and makeup kits, and don't let her play with yours. (By the way, what are *you* doing with those toxins in your house? Make a bold step for health: Out with them! These substances are classified as hazardous waste by my municipality and must be taken to the local hazardous waste facility. Check the rules in your community. There are now some safer alternatives available in some health food stores.)

Get Active (as in "Activist")!

Obviously, to really reduce the toxic exposures for our children and ourselves, we must get active. How is it that these toxins have proliferated all over the world, trespassing into the bodies of all of us, without our permission and often without our knowledge?

Join the Endometriosis Association, Health Care Without Harm, Collaborative for Health and the Environment, and other organizations fighting to bring sanity to our modern world of chemicals (see Resources and Chapter 14). Urge the FDA and other governmental bodies to regulate phthalates in cosmetics, perfumes, and personal care products. Help us get PVCs banned from medical use and from building materials, as they have been in some parts of Europe.

Together we make a difference. Together we can prevent endo!

P A R T

3

RESEARCH LEADS
THE ENDO MOVEMENT
IN NEW DIRECTIONS

13 Research Reveals Disease Is Starting Younger, Diagnosis Is Delayed

Mary Lou Ballweg

It's an axiom in medicine and science that data speaks louder than anything else. The Endometriosis Association's reputation and credibility were built rapidly in the early 1980s on gathering the largest data research registry ever and publishing extensively from it. And it was data again that gave the Association a loud voice at the VI World Congress on Endometriosis. In a nutshell, here's how we've updated endo knowledge, using our two big data registries:

- From 1980 to 1986, we collected data from 3,020 women—data that make up the contents of Registry I.
- In 1998 we conducted our North American Member Survey, mailing 10,000 questionnaires to North American Association members. The data in the first 4,000 questionnaires returned became Registry II.
- The results described in this chapter come from a combination of Registries I and II.

We first identified long delays in diagnosis as a major problem for women and girls with endo in the early 1980s. We also documented the chronic nature of the disease and the high rate of return of symptoms following treatments. While it is now widely accepted that endo currently doesn't have a real cure, at the time this concept was new. I vividly remember discussing our findings with a world leader on endo, who maintained that the reason our data showed the disease returned after the women were on danazol was that they were so afraid of it coming back that they imagined the symptoms were back!

Has there been any progress in the intervening years? The short answer is yes. Now, there is much more tendency to listen to women with endo and to realize that we can learn so much by going to where the disease resides, which, after all, is in the patient. In addition, it is now widely accepted, due to years of hard work on our part, that diagnosis is greatly delayed. As you can imagine, there is a long way to go, particularly in countries where the patient's voice is not yet very strong.

Pain: The Most Common Symptom

While it is now somewhat accepted (at least in countries where patients have made their voices heard) that pain is the most prevalent symptom of endo, that was not the case in the early 1980s. Then, because the disease was noticed by almost no one except infertility specialists, infertility was often viewed as the most common—and most important—symptom of endo. In looking at the symptoms experienced by the 4,000 U.S. and Canadian women in this data analysis, we found essentially the same pattern of pain and symptoms as in our first data registry from the early 1980s. As shown in Figure 13.1, 96 percent of the women in Registry II experienced pain. More specifically, 95 percent experienced pain at the time of the menstrual period, 83 percent at ovulation, and 75 percent at other times as well.

FIGURE 13.1 Symptoms Experienced

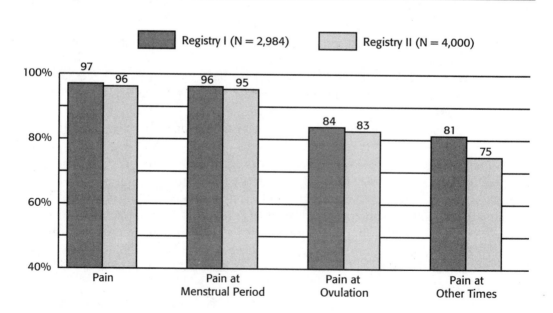

Pain at the time of the menstrual period was particularly a problem for those whose pelvic symptoms started early. Among those whose symptoms started before age fifteen, 99 percent reported pain at the time of the menstrual period. Of those whose symptoms started before age twenty, 98 percent reported pain during their periods. Conclusion: We obviously need to pay better attention to girls with menstrual pain.

Pain at the time of ovulation was surprisingly high (considering it's been given little attention) and especially a problem for those whose pelvic symptoms started before age twenty. The same was true for pain at other times in the menstrual cycle, again being highest in those experiencing their first pelvic symptoms before age twenty. When asked how bad the pain was, seven out of ten respondents ranked it between moderate and severe (see Figure 13.2). Another one-fifth said the pain could swing from mild to severe. As detailed in Figure 13.3, severe pain was particularly significant in those who began their first pelvic symptoms before age fifteen.

Endo's Many Symptoms

Besides pain, our first data registry identified many other symptoms of endo, and still more were added with the second registry (see Figure 13.4). Of these, many symp-

FIGURE 13.2 Severity of Pain

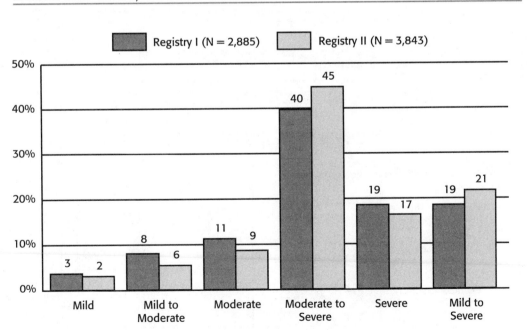

FIGURE 13.3 Age of First Symptoms for Women Reporting Severe Pain

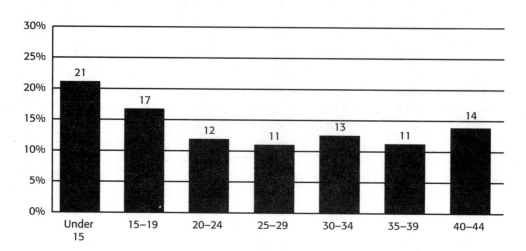

Note: Percentages based on survey responses from 4,000 women with endo.

FIGURE 13.4 Endo Symptoms Reported

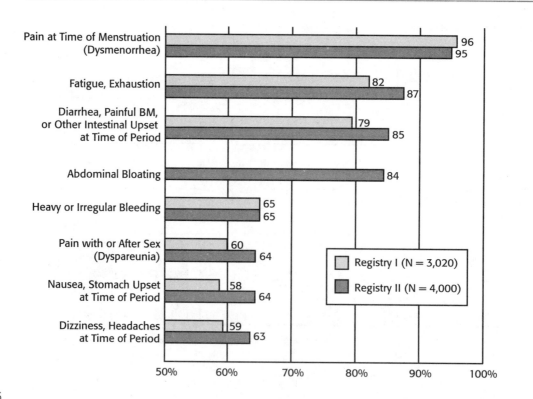

FIGURE 13.4 Endo Symptoms Reported *(continued)*

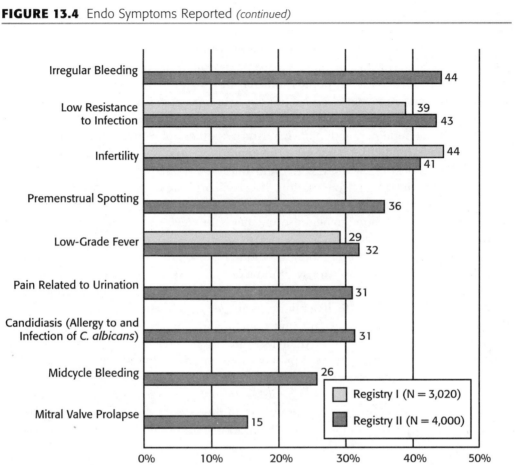

toms—especially fatigue, gastrointestinal problems, abdominal bloating, and a range of allergic diseases—are still not widely recognized as part of endo. In both registries, women identified "fatigue, exhaustion, low energy" as the second most common symptom after menstrual pain: 87 percent in Registry II and 82 percent in Registry I.

Following fatigue, 85 percent of women in Registry II experience "diarrhea, painful bowel movements, or other intestinal upset at time of period," and 84 percent experience abdominal bloating, a symptom that can be indicative of severe allergies, especially, it seems, to foods and hormones. Almost two-thirds experience heavy or irregular bleeding, pain with or after sex, nausea and stomach upset at the time of the period, and dizziness and headaches at the time of the period.

As we found in our first data registry, women with endo are prone to allergies. In Registry II, 57 percent of respondents reported allergies, particularly to pollens, dust, grasses, cigarette smoke, perfumes and fragrances, trees, foods, and cleaning products. Figure 13.5 details the types of allergies reported.

Using numbers from the American Academy of Allergy and Immunology, we compared the incidence of certain allergic diseases in women with endo from our 1998 registry with that of the general population. As shown in Figure 13.6, 41 percent of the women with endo reported allergies to pollen, compared with 13 percent in the general population. Of the women with endo, 14 percent reported asthma, while only 6 percent in the general population have it. And 17 percent of women with endo reported eczema,* compared with 6 percent of the general population. Other allergies also are very likely significant in women with endo, but it has been difficult to obtain numbers by category for the general population. It was also interesting to find that the age of appearance of these allergies tended to be the mid- to late teen years, except for chemical allergies, which tended to begin somewhat later. (See Figure 13.7 for a breakdown by type of allergy.)

We have long felt that researchers should look at the mechanism of allergy related to endo. In addition, because the symptoms of endo so often improve when allergies are addressed, the data suggest we should take allergies more seriously in girls and treat them early on with effective allergy management.

Pain with or after sex was significantly greater in women whose first pelvic symptoms started before age twenty-five. The women whose first symptoms started after twenty-four were less likely to have pain with sex, statistically significant for all groups after twenty-four. Conclusion: Failure to diagnose and help adolescent girls and young women with the early symptoms is more likely to doom them to pain with sex later.

Other symptoms significantly more likely in those whose first symptoms occurred before age twenty-five included pain related to urination and heavy bleeding. Heavy bleeding was particularly pronounced as a significant symptom in those whose first pelvic symptoms occurred before age fifteen. There was still an effect in those whose first symptoms occurred before twenty, but then it dropped off. There was a similar pattern for midcycle bleeding: Those whose first pelvic symptoms started before age fifteen were most likely to experience this symptom, and there was also an increasing likelihood of significance in those whose first symptoms started before age twenty. The same pattern appeared in nausea and stomach upset at the time of the period, with an age-related incidence. The younger the person was when she first experienced pelvic symptoms, the greater the likelihood of experiencing *this* symptom. And there was an increasing likelihood of *not* experiencing this symptom, the older the woman was when she first experienced pelvic endo symptoms. Exactly the same pattern occurred with the symptom of "diarrhea, painful bowel movements, or other intestinal upset" at the time of the period.

---

*Eczema is an inflammatory condition of the skin characterized by redness and itching. It can be due to allergy or other conditions.

FIGURE 13.5 Allergic Diseases in Women with Endo

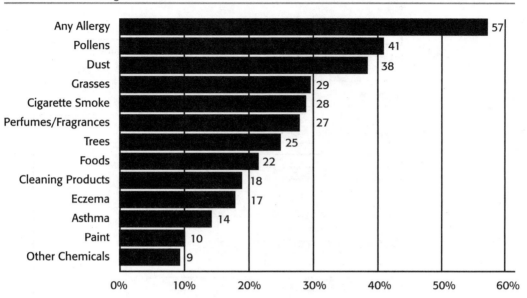

Note: Percentages based on survey responses from 4,000 women with endo.

FIGURE 13.6 Allergic Diseases: General Population Versus Women with Endo

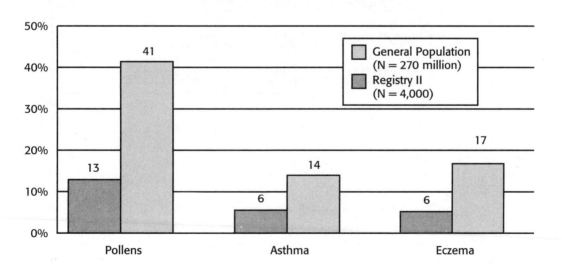

FIGURE 13.7 Allergic Diseases: Age of Symptoms Versus Age of Diagnosis

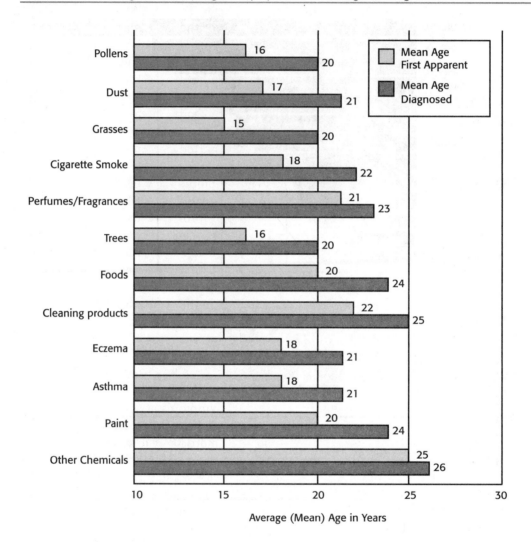

Average (Mean) Age in Years

Note: Based on responses from 4,000 women with endo.

The same pattern occurred with dizziness and headaches at the time of the period or pain. And this pattern, with a little variation among those age thirty-five to thirty-nine at the time of their first symptoms, occurred with the symptoms of fatigue, exhaustion, and low energy. Abdominal bloating was a big problem, and significant compared to other groups, for those whose first pelvic symptoms occurred before twenty years.

It's important to point out that most of these symptoms were common across the age spectrum—meaning the age of first pelvic symptoms, not the age now—but were the highest recorded in those whose pelvic symptoms started very young. There was a similar pattern for low resistance to infection and low-grade fever. (Overall, this symptom didn't affect as many as other symptoms did in all the age groups. But when it did, it was more likely in those who had their first pelvic symptoms very young.)

As to location of pain, those whose symptoms started before age twenty-five were more likely to report pain in the area of both ovaries than those whose first symptoms occurred later. The same was true for pain in the area of the uterus and mid-pelvis (a symptom particularly pronounced for those under twenty). Low-back pain was another defining characteristic of those whose first symptoms began before twenty-five versus those whose first symptoms began after twenty-five. The younger group was significantly more likely to have low-back pain. Pain in the rectum also was more likely to occur in those whose first symptoms began before twenty-five. These strong patterns provide diagnostic tools for earlier diagnosis of the disease in teens and preteens.

Those who were youngest at the time of their first pelvic symptoms were also most likely to be disabled by symptoms at some time—not necessarily at the time of the first symptoms, although they could be. Those with first symptoms before age twenty-five were significantly more likely to be disabled at times than those with their first symptoms later. The number of young women having to drop out of college due to endo appears, anecdotally, to our staff at headquarters to be increasing, a trend that is heartbreaking.

The younger the girl or woman was when symptoms first started (before twenty), the less likely she was to ever become pregnant.

> "What the newsletter does for me is keep me up-to-date, introduces me to other women and their experiences (which keeps me aware of what to look for in myself), and serves as a regular reminder of how important it is to stick to my diet, exercise, and lower-stress lifestyle. I did extensive research in medical libraries after my surgery, but I found the EA newsletter to be the most comprehensive and best source of information on the subject. You create order, focus, and useful information out of overwhelming and complex sources of research and data."
>
> —*Nancy, Virginia*

Red Hair and Endo

The red-hair gene (which includes those with natural red, auburn, or strawberry blond hair) has been linked to endo, so we asked respondents about their natural hair color. (Some respondents must have thought this was not a serious question because they didn't answer it!) Interestingly, the results were statistically significant, with 7.3 percent of the respondents reporting red, auburn, or strawberry blond hair, compared with 5 percent of women in the general U.S. population. (Numbers for the general population are from the Aveda Institute and Redheads International.)

The United States has a higher percentage of individuals with red-hair gene than many parts of the world, which weighs in with only 2 percent having the gene. The highest proportion of redheads is in Scotland—at 11 percent, according to a National Library of Medicine Resource. However, according to Redheads International, one in twenty people carries the red-hair gene. Rose Frisch, Ph.D., a Harvard scientist who is an expert on the subject, notes that red hair is correlated with a longer menstrual bleeding time.

Age of First Pelvic Symptoms

Compared with our first data registry, our 1998 data showed a huge jump in those who experienced their first symptoms before the age of fifteen. The proportion leaped from 15 percent in the 1980s to 38 percent in the 1998 registry (see Figure 13.8). Fully two-thirds of those responding to the 1998 survey had experienced their first pelvic symptoms before the age of twenty!

This huge jump confirmed for us what we have been perceiving for some years at headquarters: The disease is starting younger and, unfortunately, seems to be more severe in these girls than was seen among those whose symptoms started young in the baby boom generation. Recent studies done in the United States indicate the age of the first menstrual period is earlier than in the past. With the age of menarche (the first period) earlier, it may be that endo is also moving to earlier ages.

"Being a member of the Endometriosis Association and receiving the newsletter has been so helpful to me. Being a nurse researcher myself, I find that in the newsletter you maintain the delicate balance of providing the latest scientific research and techniques, as well as providing emotional support for each of us—something not all self-help organizations are able to do. Many thanks."

—*Carol, Illinois*

Disability Due to Endo

In Registry II, 79 percent of the women reported that they were sometimes unable to carry on their normal work, including housework, due to endo. (Respondents were asked to exclude time lost due to surgery.) As shown in Figure 13.9, this percentage is slightly larger than the 75 percent reporting disability due to endo in the first registry.

FIGURE 13.8 Age of First Pelvic Symptoms

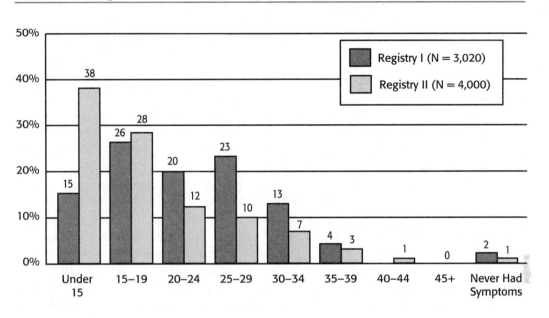

FIGURE 13.9 Are You Sometimes Unable to Carry on Normal Work?

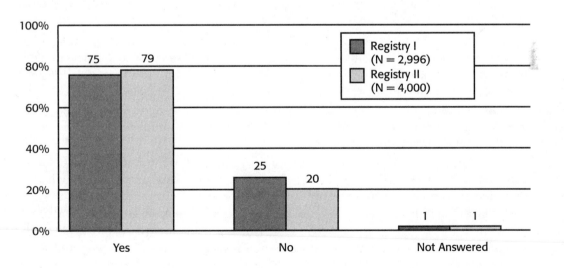

According to the 1998 data, a quarter of the women were incapacitated between two and six days a month, and 35 percent for one to two days a month.

Diagnosis

We first identified long delays in diagnosis as a major problem for women and girls with endo in the early 1980s. Of the 4,000 women in the 1998 sample, 96 percent have been diagnosed with endo, most by laparoscopy or laparotomy (major abdominal surgery). Of these, 64 percent had been diagnosed in the 1990s.

When they first sought help for their symptoms, 65 percent of the women specifically visited a doctor to discuss the symptoms. Another 19 percent brought up the symptoms when visiting a doctor about something else. Most of the women (70 percent) visited ob/gyns when they first sought help, while 19 percent first visited family or general practitioners. Because of the long delay in diagnosis so many women with endo experience, we had expected to find most had not first visited gyns. We were surprised that almost three-fourths indeed had visited gyns first.

When they first experienced endo symptoms, 58 percent of the women thought their symptoms were normal. Another 40 percent did not think their symptoms were normal, but only 23 percent suspected they had endo. Those who did suspect they had endo typically had learned about it through the media, from a friend or relative, at the library or through their own research, or from a brochure or pamphlet. (These percentages add to more than 100 because some women learned about the disease from a number of sources.)

When the women who thought they had endo suggested it to their doctors, about equal numbers of the doctors agreed and suggested a laparoscopy or a specialist (22 percent) as told the women it wasn't endo (21 percent). Equal numbers of doctors (13 percent in each case) either ignored the women or agreed and gave the women a prescription. Of the patients who received a prescription before diagnosis, 26 percent were given prescriptions for birth control pills. In addition, 20 percent were given nonsteroidal anti-inflammatory drugs.

Often, women with endo have to visit a doctor several times before they obtain a diagnosis or referral. In the 1998 study, 47 percent of the women reported they had to see a doctor five times or more before being diagnosed or referred. Those with the earliest onset of symptoms had to see the most doctors to reach diagnosis. The average was 4.20 doctors for those whose pelvic symptoms started before fifteen years old, compared with 3.85 doctors for those whose symptoms started between fifteen and nineteen years and "only" 2.64 doctors for those whose symptoms started at thirty to thirty-four years old—the age at which doctors traditionally think of endo as occurring. For a detailed breakdown, see Figure 13.10.

FIGURE 13.10 Younger Patients See More Doctors Before Endo Is Diagnosed

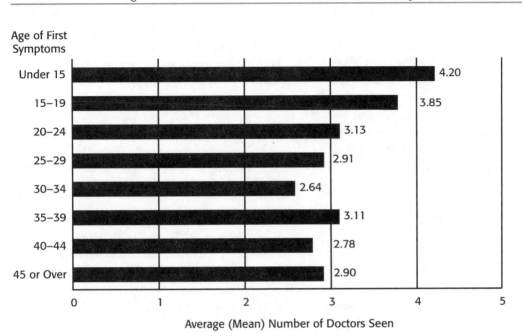

Note: Based on responses from 4,000 women with endo.

Overall, the delay between onset of symptoms and actual diagnosis of the disease was a whopping 9.28 years. Part of the delay was that the girl/woman took 4.67 years, on average, to report her symptoms to a doctor. Part of it was that the doctors, on average, took 4.61 years to diagnose the disease.

The averages in the Association data compare unfavorably with average diagnostic delays in Australia and Great Britain. In Australia, the average onset of symptoms is almost twenty-three years old, and the time to diagnosis is 6.1 years. The diagnostic delay is 6.8 years in Great Britain. Why the difference? The survey, conducted by the Australian-based Endometriosis Association (Victoria), found a diagnostic delay of 8.3 years in those who first reported symptoms at fifteen to nineteen years old. In the British survey, conducted by the National Endometriosis Society, 62 percent of the respondents had their first symptoms by age twenty-five, while in our group, 66 percent had their first symptoms by age twenty. It is *very* difficult for a young girl to get help. In our group, 38 percent of the respondents were *under* fifteen years old at the time of their first pelvic symptoms. It's not hard to see why eleven- to fourteen-year-olds have difficulty reporting their symptoms to a doctor or getting diagnosed. Obviously, we need to explore why the disease is starting so young in the United States and

"As a woman with endo, I have tried to become as informed as possible, primarily through the Association newsletters and medical journal articles, in seeking treatment options. Even though I felt myself to be well informed, most of my experiences with physicians have been frustrating due to their lack of knowledge about the disease, unwillingness to listen, and focus on infertility as the major, often only, symptom of the disease. Physicians have referred to my symptoms as unusual. I would then read newsletters and find that they are most usual, almost classic. Women are saying we have pain, chronic fatigue, gastrointestinal disturbances, and painful intercourse, in addition to endometrial lesions, and the doctors are saying no, no, no, the problem with endometriosis is infertility. It is unfortunate that many physicians in this field have lost the inquisitiveness of the scientist and are not using the symptoms as clues to understand the pathway and origin and ultimately the cure for this disease.

"As frustrating as all this may be as a patient, I found myself even more frustrated as a first-year medical student listening to a guest lecturer, an infertility specialist, tell 150 future physicians that pregnancy is a cure for endo, and that GnRH agonists are wonder drugs that obliterate the disease. No mention of the side effects of these drugs was made.

"I want you to know how very grateful I am for your strength, courage, and thoroughness in trying to combat this disease and all the political and social problems strongly attached to it. You and the organization have been a great source of strength for me.

"I wonder if it would also be possible to target future physicians directly. To make them aware that political and social issues can distort scientific method and block the advancement of medical knowledge and in the process increase the suffering of the same patients that they are trying to help."

—*Susan, New York*

Canada! (Unfortunately, this trend now appears, at least anecdotally, to be occurring in other parts of the world.)

Another compelling reason to push for earlier diagnosis is that those who had taken a long time to be diagnosed were more likely to end up with a hysterectomy. In the Association's Registry II, those who had a hysterectomy had taken 11.3 years to be diagnosed, while those who did not have a hysterectomy had taken 8.7 years to be diagnosed (see Figure 13.11). A parallel situation occurs in data previously reported from the National Endometriosis Society in Great Britain.

To understand the length of time to diagnosis, it may help to look at doctors' responses to women's complaints. Of the women in Registry II, 56 percent said they felt doctors they saw about their symptoms did not take their symptoms seriously

FIGURE 13.11 Delay in Diagnosis

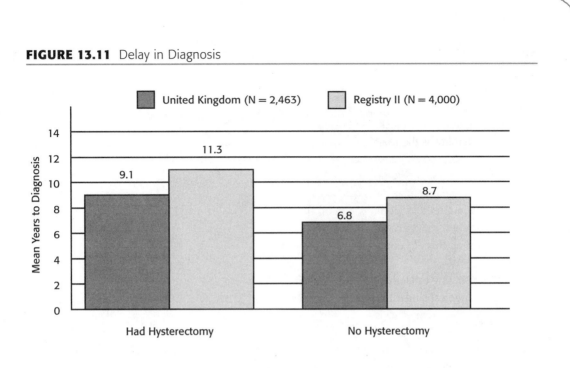

FIGURE 13.12 How Seriously Did Doctors Take Your Symptoms?

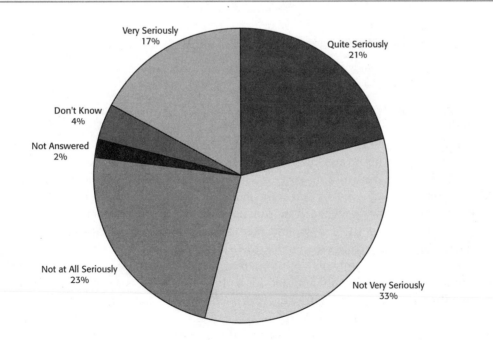

Note: Percentages based on survey responses from 4,000 women with endo.

FIGURE 13.13 Were You Ever Told There Was "Nothing Wrong"?

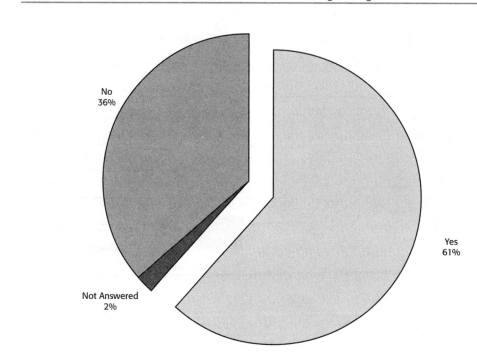

No
36%

Yes
61%

Not Answered
2%

Note: Percentages based on survey responses from 4,000 women with endo.

(answering "not at all seriously" or "not very seriously"). However, as shown in Figure 13.12, verdicts on the helpfulness of doctors were divided.

A matter of concern is that 97 percent of the women saw a gynecologist with regard to their symptoms. This is shocking; we can't blame the lack of diagnosis on other specialties. At the same time, the majority of those diagnosed were diagnosed by a gynecologist. From the data, it seems that some gyns are good at diagnosing endo, and some definitely are not. How do we teach those who are not—or at least teach them to refer?

Of the 4,000 women, 61 percent said that when they consulted a doctor, they were told that nothing was wrong (see Figure 13.13). In and of itself, it's not so surprising that women were told there was nothing wrong. We hear that frequently because the symptoms of endo have been dismissed for so long. But what is most shocking in the survey is that, as detailed in Figure 13.14, gyns more often than anyone else were the ones saying the symptoms were normal—69 percent! Is there something in the training of gyns in North America that influences them to think women's symptoms are to be ignored, that it's normal to have pain, or teaches them to be dismissive of patients?

FIGURE 13.14 Who Said Nothing Was Wrong?

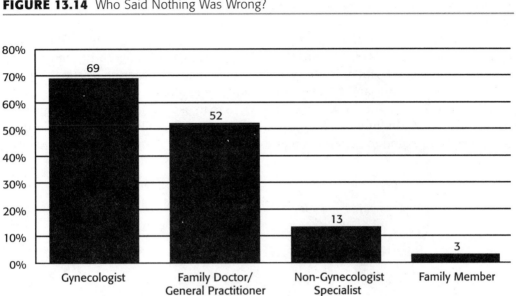

Note: Percentages based on survey responses from 2,448 women with endo who reported being told nothing was wrong.

FIGURE 13.15 Time Elapsed Before a Definite Diagnosis

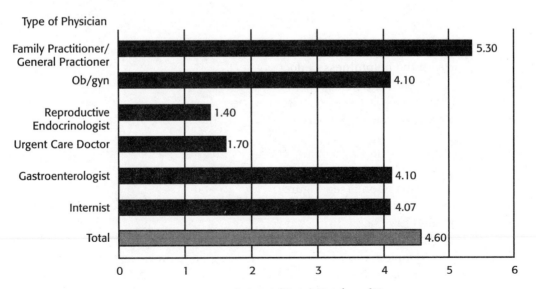

In what other business can one so readily insult one's customers and apparently get away with it?

The practitioners consulted by women with endo differed in terms of how long they took to reach a diagnosis (see Figure 13.15). It took gyns, on average, 4.10 years to diagnose endo, compared with only 1.40 years for reproductive endocrinologists, 1.70 years for urgent care doctors, and 5.30 years for family practitioners/general practitioners.

The Association invites researchers everywhere to use our data research registry to track leads, check out hunches, find patients and patients' families with particular medical backgrounds, and in general, to get excited about the many keys to endo that lie in this data.

14 Endometriosis Goes Public

WHY ENDOMETRIOSIS IS AN ENVIRONMENTAL ISSUE

Lynn Castrodale

The following information applies to you whether you are female or male, a construction worker, a homemaker, a factory worker, an accountant, a lawyer, a nurse, a librarian, a scientist, or a pastor. It applies to moms, dads, grandmothers, teenagers, students, and retirees. It applies to people on all continents, even people in the Arctic regions. If you live on Planet Earth, you may want to know the following because it affects your life and is worthy of your attention.

There is a struggle going on—a struggle between sustainability and the degradation of our environment. Toxic chemicals are building up in our bodies and the environment. These chemicals are causing terrible harm and disease. The good news is that we have the choice to fight for sustainability and against persistent toxic chemicals in order to protect ourselves and future generations.

The purpose of this chapter is to describe the "big picture" of health risks from toxic chemicals in the environment. Scientific research has established the link between endometriosis and environmental toxins. This article will explain how our health and the environment are inseparable, how persistent toxic chemicals are related to endo and other diseases, and how to empower yourself to take action.

The Real Definition of Environment

The spirit of the old saying "You are what you eat" should no longer be restricted to food. Perhaps the more contemporary way to state it is, "You are the environment, and the environment is you." The word *environment* does not just mean the forests, lakes, and oceans; it includes our cities, our backyards, our homes, and our bodies. From the air we breathe to the clothes we wear and the furniture we sit on—all are part of the environment.

Our bodies reflect the state of the environment around us. Our health and the health of our world are intertwined. When the planet and its environment are diseased with toxic chemicals, our individual bodies become diseased and sick. When we eat contaminated food or live in a toxic building, we are polluting our most important environment, ourselves. We require clean air, water, and food to keep ourselves and our families healthy.

J. P. Myers, Ph.D., coauthor of *Our Stolen Future*, a powerful book about endocrine-disrupting chemicals, made the following statement in a presentation to the United Nations Commission on the Status of Women: "Throughout human evolution we have always had a refuge from our mistakes. Early on, if we depleted the game in one valley we moved to the next. As we polluted one river course, there was always another . . . and if the pollution wiped out one clan or one township, well, in the grand scheme of things, there were always other people somewhere else. No pollutants affected everyone. This is now changed irrevocably and fundamentally. There is no next valley waiting to be filled. There is no watershed completely lacking of pollutants. None."

The waste that we produce today will be in tomorrow's water, air, and soil. Toxic chemicals that are created in factories and incinerators end up in our food and drinking water. Toxins that we unknowingly breathe or ingest must be processed by our bodies and can overload our systems. No one is immune to our toxic environment, and our immune systems pay dearly.

It is worth mentioning that many people have the notion that "environmentalists" are confrontational extremists who hug trees. But if you care about your home and the town you live in, you could be considered an environmentalist. Planting a garden, trimming dead branches off a tree, recycling aluminum cans, giving your old clothes to the Salvation Army—these are all examples of caring about the world you live in. If you care about yourself and your surroundings, then it is important to take positive actions to protect and nurture them. If we acknowledge that we all play a part in caring for our health and our environment, then we can each accept the awesome responsibility of protecting our health and planet from threats like toxic chemicals.

Our Bodies Are Absorbing Harmful Chemicals

Of the thousands of manufactured chemicals in our world (experts estimate there are over 88,000), very few have been tested for health effects on adults, even fewer for health effects on children. Every baby born on the planet today has "persistent toxic chemicals" in his or her body. One thing that makes these chemicals so dangerous to human health is that they accumulate in our bodies (starting before birth and continuing throughout life) and resist breakdown. These persistent toxic chemicals are among the most threatening to human life and our natural environment.

Using state-of-the-art blood testing, researchers find that all of us, no matter where or how we live, have a minimum of 200 detectable manufactured chemicals in our blood.[1] And although some are worse for our health than others, we really do not know how these chemicals will affect us today or twenty years from now. We do not know which ones interact with each other to cause potentially larger effects than they do individually. Human beings, at present, lack the scientific ability and resources to test them together to uncover their synergistic chemical reactions. Yet these chemicals continue to intermingle in our bodies.

This is especially frightening for the parents of children of this era, as exposures to toxic chemicals can affect a child's development. "A growing body of evidence is raising concerns that exposure to toxic chemicals may harm children and developing babies far more than adults," according to Bill Moyers's report "Trade Secrets" on PBS.[2] Infants and children breathe more rapidly and inhale more pollutants per pound of body weight than do adults. They also eat more food and drink more water, milk, and juice per unit of body weight than most adults.[3] Until recently, safety testing and regulation of environmental substances has not been taking this difference into account. The U.S. Environmental Protection Agency (EPA) first began taking children's biological differences into account in 1996. Before then, it was assumed that children were just miniature adults, an assumption that is scientifically invalid.[4]

How the Environment Fits into the Endometriosis Puzzle

It has been established that endo is a disease related to environmental toxins. In fact, it is one of the first diseases (outside of cancers) to be linked to persistent organic pollutants like dioxin in humans. Since 1992, research findings have been showing that dioxins and polychlorinated biphenyls (PCBs) can cause the development of endo. This has shifted the previous perception of endo from an unexplained gyn disease to a disease that is most likely triggered or worsened by the environment in which we live. In addition, it may be possible that endo is just one part of a larger disease family resulting from exposure to these chemicals.

Scientific evidence implicates dioxins, PCBs, and many other chemicals in disrupting the immune and endocrine (hormonal) systems. We already know that endo is a disease of the immune and endocrine systems. Now an important study shows that the prevalence of other hormonal or immune disorders is higher in women with endo than in the general female population. These diseases include hypothyroidism, fibromyalgia, chronic fatigue immune dysfunction syndrome (CFIDS), rheumatoid arthritis, lupus, Sjögren's syndrome, and multiple sclerosis.[5] (For details, see Chapter 7.)

Moving beyond endo to view the big picture of diseases plaguing our society today, it is important to know that dioxin and other environmental toxins have also been linked to childhood cancers (at least preliminarily), attention deficit disorder, reproductive cancers, Parkinson's disease, chronic fatigue immune dysfunction syndrome (CFIDS), diabetes, and asthma. As we watch scientific evidence link more and more diseases to environmental toxins, we have to ask ourselves if this is why health issues are escalating out of control in our society. It is too early to know for sure which diseases are linked to which toxins or how the diseases themselves are related, but it is never too early to educate ourselves on the key toxins.

Dioxins and PCBs

Dioxins are a class of seventy-five chemicals with similar properties that are known to be the most toxic chemicals ever produced. Dioxins are the by-products of industrial processes that involve chlorine or the burning or incineration of chlorinated material with organic matter. The most toxic form of dioxin is 2,3,7,8-tetrachlorodibenzo-p-dioxin (TCDD), a known carcinogen. This was the type of dioxin fed to rhesus monkeys in the groundbreaking study that first linked dioxin to endo. Monkeys that ingested TCDD in amounts as small as five parts per trillion developed the disease.[6]

According to the U.S. EPA, the average American adult has enough dioxin in his or her body today to cause adverse health effects. Some have even more. For example, people living near a vinyl plant in Louisiana were found to have an average combined dioxin level of 68 parts per trillion. Four people tested showed levels of 150 parts per trillion, and several girls in the area developed endo as teenagers.[7]

The top three sources of dioxin are municipal waste incineration, backyard burn barrels (individuals burning their trash in their yards), and medical waste incineration.[8] Other sources include chemical and vinyl (PVC, or polyvinyl chloride plastic) manufacturing, metal smelting, and pulp and paper bleaching. Dioxin emissions from smokestacks and discharge pipes travel long distances in the atmosphere via air currents. After the dioxin falls to the ground, it is often consumed by livestock that graze on the dioxin-contaminated crops or soil. Dioxin is fat soluble and accumulates in the tissues of the animals. The higher an animal is on the food chain, the more dioxin it will accumulate. Therefore, animal products that we eat, such as beef, dairy, chicken, pork, fish, and eggs, are regularly contaminated with dioxin. The EPA estimates that over 95 percent of human exposure to dioxin is through our food. People who live near incinerators or manufacturing plants, such as the vinyl plant in Louisiana mentioned previously, are unfortunately exposed to additional dioxin through air, soil, and possibly water.

Certain types of PCBs behave similarly to dioxin in the environment and our bodies. PCBs are a group of nonflammable chemicals that were used as insulation and/or coolants in electrical transformers, as well as lubricants, hydraulic fluids, cutting oils, liquid seals, and in carbonless paper. In the United States, they were widely used between 1929 and 1977. Because PCBs are incredibly persistent chemicals, it can take 20 to 160 years for them to completely break down. Unfortunately, companies that manufactured PCBs for industrial use dumped millions of pounds of these toxins directly into rivers and lakes before the U.S. government banned them. They are now found in the body fat of almost every living creature on our planet and are especially concentrated in fish from polluted waterways.

Endocrine-Disrupting Chemicals

Certain types of dioxins and PCBs, in addition to many other types of chemicals, are known to be endocrine disruptors. The endocrine system is a complex system of glands (such as the thyroid, pituitary gland, and ovaries) and hormones that regulate activities such as reproduction in human beings and animals. Hormones are biochemical messengers secreted by endocrine glands into the bloodstream to control and direct the function of specific organs. Nearly all animals, including mammals, fish, amphibians, reptiles, birds, and invertebrates, have endocrine systems.

> "My research so far has led me to believe that PCBs or dioxins have played a part in my endo. I have contacted the EPA and am waiting to see if they feel water and/or soil testing needs to be done in my area. I live on an old naval air station."
>
> —*Shannon, Florida*

"Endocrine disruptors" are substances that mimic hormones, fooling the body into overresponding, responding at inappropriate times, or blocking the effects of a natural hormone. Endocrine disruptors "may directly stimulate or inhibit the endocrine system, causing overproduction or underproduction" of the body's hormones.[9] They can mimic estrogen, block progesterone, or affect testosterone levels. Many chemicals are known endocrine disruptors, and more are being discovered every year. Many of them are in pesticides, detergents, cosmetics, and the plastics used to package food. Through the air we breathe, the water and food we consume, and the substances that touch our skin, our bodies are regularly exposed to endocrine-disrupting chemicals.

Endocrine disruptors can have negative effects on the female reproductive system, including increased risk of breast cancer, early puberty, altered menstruation, decreased fertility, increased miscarriages, and early menopause.[10] For males, it has been found that exposure in the womb to a compound present in common plastics causes abnormality in the adult male prostate.[11] A group of common chemicals called phthalates can "damage the developing testes [testicles] of animal offspring and cause malformations of the penis and other parts of the reproductive tract."[12]

Endocrine disruptors and other persistent chemicals do not necessarily cause health effects overnight. There is often a long time lag between exposure and the health problem, which adds to our confusion about cause and effect. Exposure in the womb may not manifest in health problems until the child becomes an adult.

Finally, Jeremy's parents agree something is wrong.

Toxicity of a chemical may not be scientifically proven until years after it is spread throughout the environment (and our bodies). Take the scientific history of lead poisoning, for example. In 1975 it was considered harmless for a tenth of a liter of human blood to contain thirty-nine micrograms of lead. Today we know that thirty-nine micrograms can cause severe brain damage in children. Many scientists believe that *any* amount of lead can damage the central nervous system and reduce IQ. However, the lead industry still hires scientists to dispute these conclusions.[13] Fortunately, society has been made aware of the danger of lead exposure. This is not yet the case for dioxin and many endocrine-disrupting chemicals.

Protecting Health or Profits?

While people generally have had faith in governments and corporations to protect us from harm and injustice, today it is clear these institutions are not living up to that

expectation. One example close to the hearts of women with endo, given the link between dioxin and endo, is the EPA's report on the sources and health effects of dioxin commonly referred to as the Dioxin Reassessment. The following history shows how long people have been waiting for the U.S. government to complete a key report meant to protect human health.

In 1977 animal studies first indicated that dioxin causes cancer. In 1985 the U.S. EPA published the first Dioxin Risk Assessment, which was a scientific review of the health effects of dioxin. This assessment prompted the establishment of an "acceptable" daily dose of dioxin of 0.006 picogram (a picogram is one trillionth of a gram) per kilogram of body weight per day. (The assumption regarding "acceptable daily doses" is that small amounts of chemicals are safe as long as they do not exceed a certain daily amount. The same dose is set for all people, regardless of whether they are sick or healthy, young or old.)

In the late 1980s, dioxin-producing industries claimed that the established daily dose was too low and that higher levels, like those set in some other countries at that time, were more appropriate. These industries requested that the EPA do a reassessment of the 1985 Dioxin Risk Assessment, expecting an increase in the acceptable dose. By 1990 the chlorine industry had succeeded in persuading the EPA to undertake a formal reassessment of dioxin, and in 1994 the EPA released the first Draft Reassessment. This document revealed that our environment is full of dioxin, dioxin has accumulated in our bodies, and any additional exposure is too much. Findings included the following:

- The data strengthen the conclusion that dioxin causes cancer in people. The EPA found that dioxin is the most important cancer-causing chemical for the general population and that the average adult has a risk factor of 1 in 100 of getting cancer from dioxin exposure. EPA's "acceptable" risk level for cancer is 1 in 1 million.
- Noncancer health problems may have even more impact on public health than the cancer-causing effects of dioxin because they are passed down from generation to generation. (In addition to being carcinogenic, there is evidence of dioxin's immunotoxicity, developmental toxicity, reproductive toxicity, and endocrine disruption.) Endometriosis is just one example of a noncancer health problem.
- Suppression of the immune system and other health effects of dioxin were found to occur "at or near levels to which people in the general population are exposed."[14]

Realizing that the eventual release of the final Dioxin Reassessment would eliminate any doubt about the danger of dioxin and may precipitate federal regulations to reduce dioxin production and exposure, the dioxin-producing industries have campaigned to stop the final report from being issued. They have succeeded in blocking its release for over seven years. (At the time of this writing, the final report has still not been issued.) Meanwhile, the evidence regarding the serious health problems associated with dioxin exposure continues to accumulate, while the U.S. government still has not taken action to protect the public's health.[15]

Currently, the profits of industry and a "business as usual" attitude appear to come before the health of living beings. Just like the tobacco industry, chemical industries are paying experts to downplay the toxicity of chemicals and confuse the issues. Vinyl, or polyvinyl chloride (PVC) plastic, is known to create dioxin throughout its life cycle— during the manufacturing process and when burned or incinerated. In addition, many more toxic chemicals, including lead, cadmium, and phthalates, are added to raw PVC to stabilize or plasticize it for use in a wide range of consumer products.[16, 17] According to a comprehensive public television documentary by highly regarded journalist Bill Moyers, the industry has been aware of many toxic health effects from vinyl production but has worked to keep them secret from the public and government agencies.[18, 19]

Precautionary Principle

While powerful corporations and others with vested interests spend money to defend their harmful chemicals and shroud the emerging science in a veil of uncertainty, we are all taking part in uncontrolled scientific experiments that risk our fundamental rights to healthy lives. The current system of regulating chemicals forces the public to "prove harm" *after* the chemicals are on the market and in the environment. By the time scientists are able to prove harm, it is too late—harm has already occurred in those exposed. Once released into the environment, damaging chemicals are impossible to recall.

The current reactive, rather than proactive, system of monitoring chemical health effects has several inadequacies:[20]

- Millions of people have to become sick before regulators can begin to prove harm.
- The current system fails to take into account the cumulative effects of thousands of small, supposedly safe exposures to that chemical.
- There is no way to account for the fact that all living creatures are subject to *multiple* exposures of many different environmental contaminants.
- The "prove harm" regulatory system bases its determinations on what current science alone can prove—often industry-sponsored science—omitting many essential human values such as personal philosophies, religion, and other values (such as not feeding babies contaminated milk or formula). Currently, the right to pollute outweighs the right to be born without toxins in your body.

Taking proactive, precautionary actions when developing potentially toxic chemicals is one solution to this problem. The 1998 Wingspread Statement on the Precautionary Principle was drawn up by top scientists and experts in this field, who discussed their concerns and defined the Precautionary Principle. Key components of the principle include "upholding the basic right of each individual and future generations to a healthy, life-sustaining environment" and "placing responsibility on originators of potentially dangerous activities to thoroughly study and minimize risks." When there is credible evidence that a substance will cause harm to public health or the environment, policy changes should be made, even if the magnitude of the harm in not fully proven.[21]

This brings us to the discussion of "environmental justice" and how it relates to endometriosis. Just as the past and present neglect toward women in diagnosing and treating endo is sometimes a result of inequality issues between women and men in our society, environmental injustice springs from inequality among races, socioeconomic groups, and developing and developed nations. Waste incinerators are often strategically placed in poorer communities,

> "Endometriosis is in itself an unknown; it is becoming an epidemic of our time, our global situation. It is an opportunity for women to take on a power incomparable to anything in our recent history. It is a chance to tend to our larger body, the planet, recognizing the alignment of her fertility with our own."
>
> —Sarah, California

Things You Can Do Every Day to Help Yourself and the Environment

- You can improve the environment and your health through your purchasing practices. Everyday items such as detergent, toilet paper, and toothbrushes with "greener" ingredients or materials are available. Support companies that make environmentally safe and healthy products by buying their products. Find these products at ecomall.com and other websites, as well as at your local natural or health food stores.
- Certain plastics (especially PVC) can leach toxic chemicals into food. Be especially careful to avoid letting plastic wrap touch food, and do not cook in plastic containers. Glass, ceramic, and stainless steel are preferable materials in most cases.
- Choose cosmetics, shampoos, and personal care products without harsh chemicals and phthalates. For more information on phthalates in cosmetics, visit nottoopretty.com.
- Request the use of PVC-free products for medical procedures involving IV bags, including laparoscopies. See noharm.org or aaa.dk/pvc for information on alternatives to PVC medical devices.
- Avoid chlorine and chlorine-based products (such as PVC plastic) because they can create and possibly contain dioxin. Replace chlorine-bleached materials such as paper, tampons, and coffee filters with unbleached or non-chlorine-bleached alternatives.
- Contact manufacturers to ask what materials are used in their products. Tell them they should disclose materials and ingredients on the package. If it is made with PVC (polyvinyl chloride plastic, or vinyl, marked with the number 3 inside the recycle symbol), ask for PVC-free alternatives. See greenpeaceusa.org for more information.
- Dioxin and many persistent toxins build up in meats and other animal products, particularly in the fatty portions. To minimize PCB and dioxin consumption, eat low-fat meats and dairy products, preferably certified organic ones. Cut nonorganic meats and dairy products out of your diet whenever possible (or altogether).
- Fish are the main sources of PCBs in food, especially fish caught in contaminated lakes or rivers. Avoid eating contaminated fish and game (such as ducks). Call your

local health department to find out about any fishing advisories, and obey them. Remember to peel vegetables and fruit, because PCBs and pesticides concentrate in the lipid, or fatty, layer of their skins.

- Avoid pesticides and herbicides, indoors and out, because they are toxic to adults, children, and pets. Try organic pest control, integrated pest management, and home remedies (for example, jalapeño pepper bug spray to repel ants). For more information, see beyondpesticides.org or panna.org.
- If you like to garden, consider growing your own organic food.
- Recycling is an important way of improving our environment. Plastics marked with numbers 1 (PETE) and 2 (HDPE) are the most commonly recycled. PVC (numbered 3) is not recycled, even if they pick it up at your curb, and can contaminate batches of other plastics. This is another good reason to avoid PVC. Plastics marked 6 (PS) and 7 are often not recyclable, either.
- Avoid plastics that leach suspected endocrine disruptors. These include plastics numbered 3 (PVC), 6 (PS), and 7 (PC or "other").
- Avoid using electrical devices and appliances, including old fluorescent lighting fixtures, TVs, and refrigerators, that were made before 1979. These items may leak small amounts of PCBs into the air when they get hot during operation.
- PCBs can be rapidly absorbed through the skin. Do not disturb or handle dirt near hazardous waste sites or in areas where there was a transformer fire. Prevent or limit skin contact with the shore soil and water in contaminated areas.
- For gifts and holidays, consider buying environmentally friendly products and services for your family members and friends.
- Raise your children, nieces and nephews, and/or grandchildren to respect the environment and other people. Many educational books and videos deal with the subject of the environment. Your actions are usually the best teacher. For more information on children's environmental health, visit iceh.org and partnersforchildren.org.
- Be aware that some product marketers are trying to "greenwash" the public by using slogans such as "all natural." Reading labels and ingredient lists is more trustworthy than reading just the marketing slogans. (Be aware that some products have undisclosed chemical ingredients.)

pesticides that are banned in the United States are exported to developing countries, and "company towns" housing toxic industries exploit and poison the workers and their families who are too poor or dependent on the jobs to move away. Their rights are ignored in the name of profit, "progress," and economic growth.

Historically, the environmental justice movement has been made up of many important groups, especially human rights leaders, community-based activists, and labor unions. Peter Montague, editor of *Rachel's Environmental and Health Weekly News*, believes that there is a new, powerful group of "people whose health has been affected by multiple chemical sensitivities, birth defects, breast cancer, endometriosis, lymphoma, diabetes, chronic fatigue, veterans affected by Agent Orange and Gulf War Syndrome, and many others"[22] now becoming part of the environmental justice movement.

Creating Change and Healing

Future generations depend on those living today to leave them with a safe and healthy environment. How do we, as people whose health has been compromised by environmental toxins, create change for ourselves and for future generations? The key is to become empowered advocates for our health and the health of others. Women and girls with endo can empower themselves and go from being victims to being part of the solution.

Victims don't heal anything, just as caterpillars don't fly. The caterpillar must go through a process of transformation before it emerges as a weightless butterfly. For a woman with a disease who feels incapable or insignificant, becoming empowered can truly be a metamorphosis. A period of fear, anger, and feelings of being overwhelmed may be a necessary stage of this transformation, much like the cocoon stage for the caterpillar. Emerging from the cocoon as an advocate for yourself and the environment, you can help your situation (and that of many others) immensely.

If you are learning to be assertive with your healthcare providers—partnering with them instead of expecting them to "fix" you, for example—then you are halfway there. You may no longer accept the inequalities of our current world, and you fight for your rights, whether they are women's rights, minority rights, healthcare rights, or something else. Take the same approach to the environment, and watch the empowered person you have become accomplish substantial and significant change. Remember, every small action that you take to help the environment counts.

If the human mind can produce new technology that is dangerous and destructive, it can also use its ingenuity to create technology, products, and inventions that are safe and empowering. Use your own creative talents, whether as architect, investor, consumer, scientist, cook, parent, or nurse to create healthy, environmentally friendly

ALIVE/TO TESTIFY

Wanna Wright

I's got to reach out to keep 'em alive
din you can teach 'em to testify
'bout de air an de waters
dat's killin us daughtus.

So pleas don't dis me caus my ribbon's pink
I wears it to make my sistas think
(more soft)
bout breakin' down barriers, bout choosin life
(more oft)
bout early detection—maybe even da knife.

We got problems you don't know
we sheddin layers, we tryin to grow
to trust—to believe—to claim our power
to save lives lost hour after hour

we hafta save lives one at a time
we's got to catch up—we's behind
so save us a place, we's on our way
gettin stronga ev'ry day by day.

we makin it known, makin it unda'stood
soon no toxins/Dioxins allowed in da Hood
but first we got to stay alive—
Then we will stand—(with you) to testify.

contributions to our world. Using your creativity toward this goal will help heal the planet, not to mention your own health.

The most important victory we can influence with our actions is a "climate of opinion" change. This battle is not fought in the complicated political and regulatory arena only. "Climate of opinion" is a concept illustrating that social acceptability of inequalities can change.[23] At one time in history (only one hundred years ago), it was understood and accepted that women were not allowed to vote. The suffrage movement succeeded in securing this right for women. Today, our society would not consider going back in time and revoking a woman's right to vote. It is unthinkable. The civil rights movement is another example. We will not go backward and segregate the races again—that would be absurd.

The issue of toxic chemicals will be another example someday. When all of us speak out and educate others about the unacceptable health hazards of persistent toxic chemicals, public opinion will change. The new climate of opinion will evolve on this vital issue, just as it has evolved with others. The health and rights of humans and all other forms of life will finally outweigh the rights of toxic polluters. They will be held accountable, and destructive products, such as PVC plastic, will be completely replaced with alternatives that have been proven safe for our health and the environment. It is only a matter of time until we free ourselves from the hold that these toxic chemicals have over our lives, and we will be able to look back and know that we helped make it happen.

The right to live freely in a clean environment is a part of our collective civil rights movement affecting all races, ages, sexes, and nationalities. The fact that these toxins spread around the globe makes this a *worldwide* issue. Cumulative actions by people around the planet can force the cleanup of contaminated areas, the replacement of toxic chemicals with safer alternatives, and the phaseout of persistent toxic chemicals altogether. Together we make a difference!

Join with Others to Make a Difference!

A number of wonderful organizations sponsor worthy efforts. Consider joining in!

- Get involved in an environmental campaign through the Endometriosis Association (visit EndometriosisAssn.org or call 414-355-2200) or a local environmental group.
- Support the Center for Health, Environment and Justice (CHEJ), and get involved when you can. For more details about their campaigns, go to chej.org.
- Become a member of the Collaborative on Health and the Environment (CHE). CHE is a network of health-affected groups and patients, physicians, scientists, environmental health advocates, concerned citizens, and funders interested in working together to improve environmental health. For more information, visit cheforhealth.org.
- For updated information on endocrine-disrupting chemicals, visit ourstolenfuture.org.
- Get a free subscription to *Rachel's Environmental and Health Weekly News*. Go to rachel.org for more details.
- Support organized boycotts against foods or products that are proven to be unsafe.
- Support legislation that will increase research on environmental health issues, such as endocrine disruption.
- If you live in the United States, find out what companies are polluting your area by going to scorecard.org and entering your zip code.

ENDOMETRIOSIS WALK FOR AWARENESS: OUR MOVEMENT GOES PUBLIC

Mary Lou Ballweg

EDITOR'S NOTE This speech was given on the steps of the Lincoln Memorial in Washington, D.C., on the occasion of the first Endometriosis Walk for Awareness, March 2000. The walk came about through the hard work of Karen Blackwell and Kim Collier of Connecticut; Kelly Dobert, New York; Tammy Wilshire, Pennsylvania; and Lynn Witwer, Washington, D.C., and the Endometriosis Association. The walk is now held in communities around the world, focused during March, Endometriosis Awareness Month.

Thank you to each and every one of you for helping raise awareness of endometriosis today by being part of this walk and Endometriosis Awareness Week. You are helping make history today. Thank you.

But this walk is only a beginning. There are so many more to reach—at this very moment there are teens and even younger girls crunched up in agony on couches and bathroom floors, wondering how they are going to make it through the pain today. There are women and men in emotional agony because they could not make love last night due to endometriosis, wondering how their relationship can make it. There are others in emergency rooms being treated, all too often, with disdain and insensitivity. There are mothers and fathers, and brothers and sisters wondering how they can help, what is happening to their loved one. There are women and men crying, with tears in their eyes or in their hearts, because they long for children, and they long for children without passing on this scourge. Even now, women and families are reeling with the shock and pain of a cancer diagnosis—cancers that we now know occur more frequently in those with endo and their families.

Not long ago, the Endometriosis Association's European Representative and I decided we had to estimate how many women and girls with endo there are worldwide. People keep asking us, and while there are no truly accurate numbers available because of widespread underdiagnosis, we decided to make the best, most conservative estimate possible. After working through the process, we came up with a number so huge we decided we could not talk about it much because no one would believe us. Or they would do what some media people do when I tell them the large number of women with endo: "Well," they say, "if so many women have it, then it must be normal." (They don't say that about heart disease, or prostate cancer or enlargement, which affect so many millions of men after a certain age.) The number of women and girls with endo in the world—based on a very conservative estimate—is 89 million. Eighty-nine million!

I invite every one of you in range of our words here today to help reach out and heal the pain among those millions. It is a monumental task. But not as monumental as it was twenty years ago, when we began the Endometriosis Association, the first organization for women with this disease in the world. At that time, people wouldn't even talk about the disease. Doctors told me—and these are direct quotes—"A group for women with endometriosis? The next thing you know, they'll have a group for people with fallen arches," and another doctor said, "That's like starting a group for people with halitosis [bad breath]."

"I have endo, and I believe it could have been caused by the dioxin levels in the river one mile from where I grew up being eighty times the state-allowed limit. I didn't have contact with this river directly, but the dioxin was also pumped into the air by the local chemical plant, and the air levels cannot be measured. I may qualify for testing in the spring to see how much dioxin is in my system, but until then, I'm trying to inform myself as much as possible, as well as provide information to local environmental groups on the link between endo and dioxin."

—Rachel, Michigan

Women themselves, those with endo, often would not talk about it or let people know they had it. Endo was routinely dismissed. My friends and colleagues were furious at me for "throwing away" a wonderful career for something they had never heard of. There was almost no research occurring on the disease, there was no body of lay literature available, and not even a medical textbook devoted to the disease except one small, outdated one. And there certainly was no support available for women and girls with the disease—no support groups, no contact networks, no way to even check out that what you were feeling and going through was similar to others' experiences. This event today could only have been a wonderful fantasy at that time.

When I think of how much has been accomplished in twenty years, it's almost unbelievable. Think of how much could have been accomplished, where we would be today, if this work could have started forty or even eighty years ago, when Dr. John Sampson first named the disease. That was impossible, given the world's attitudes about women's pain.

But now we no longer have a choice. Endometriosis is an epidemic, and as data presented by the Association at the sixth World Congress on Endometriosis so clearly showed, it is starting younger and is more severe and more debilitating by the generation. I fear what we will see in the next generation, in those girls who are just now being born. Sometimes I fear that these future generations will not even be able to fight as effectively as we can now. Even now we hear from families every week whose girls have to drop out of college or miss high school or be home-schooled, and from women who cannot work at all or cannot work to their best potential.

Our cause, our movement, is not just about us but about the future of our children, our children's children, their children, and the world. This is not a struggle that can be won individually. Changing attitudes that are thousands of years old, helping millions who as yet have no name for their pain, standing up to the powerful polluters whose pain and death-causing chemicals are destroying our world—this takes a unified, powerful, movement.

You and I and hundreds of thousands of others are called to this mission. Vow today that you, for the rest of your life, will be part of stopping this life-destroying disease.

We stand here today in front of the Lincoln Memorial, a memorial to a man who helped end slavery for African-Americans, one of the causes—affirmative action and civil rights—that I was devoted to in my life and career before endo. It is only in recent years that I have understood that another kind of slavery is being imposed on us and our children. The Association made its breakthrough research discoveries, starting in 1992, on how chemicals such as dioxins act like hormones in our bodies and poison our immune systems. These chemicals and this disease steal from us the profound joys of womanhood that prior generations enjoyed, the ability to live life without pain, the ability to dream of a life without pain for our children. These new life-destroying chains are often imposed on us and our children before we are even born. Like Theo Colborn, Ph.D., the author of *Our Stolen Future* (a book everyone needs to read), I believe our window of opportunity is not open very wide. Those alive now must act before the damage to our world, ourselves, and our children, daughters and sons, is irreversible.

Let's take our inspiration from Abraham Lincoln and the thousands of women who worked as abolitionists in the last century to end the slavery of African-Americans. Let's take our inspiration today from the beautiful *hope* alive in us and end this new slavery enveloping humans.

"AS I MARCHED, I COULD HEAR VOICES"

Maria Herth Schulz, R.N.

As our taxi takes us from Arlington, Virginia, across the cobblestones into Washington, D.C., my skin suddenly erupts in goose bumps. Already my emotions are stirring. I sense the spirits of all who have come here before me, taking their places in history, from colonial times to present-day groups who have come to Washington for so many important reasons. It occurs to me that women with endometriosis are about to take their own steps into history, today, as we begin our walk, our journey, toward recognition.

Last night I met my friend Lisa. We had originally met on an endo support group list on the Internet and have been corresponding and telephoning for months. She is

such a blessing to me. We have both been through so much with our endo, as have so many others. We are simply single voices in a chorus of pain and suffering. We bring here our hope for the future.

As the taxi arrives near the Lincoln Memorial, I have knots in my stomach. I am so excited and already so emotional. As we sign in and begin to connect names with faces, I see the person whom I have longed to meet for so long: Mary Lou Ballweg, President of the Endometriosis Association. You see, Mary Lou is my personal hero.

I have been a member of the Association for ten years. Though I had never met her personally, through newsletters I have felt a kinship with her. I deeply admire this woman who was able to accomplish so much in her life, despite her own personal battle with endo. Mary Lou has increased funding and recognition and touched so many lives worldwide, and she never let anything stand in the way of her fight for all women with endo. I myself owe her a huge debt of thanks, for it was through her that I finally found the medical care I needed to begin living again.

I was actually close to suicide in 1996. I felt imprisoned by my pain. Not being able to even take a step without pain, not knowing where to turn, I turned to Mary Lou. I spoke with her on the phone, and she gave me the strength and information to begin my search for better medical care. Reflecting on the obstacles that Mary Lou had overcome gave me courage. I was able not only to locate a doctor who released me from "my prison of pain" but also to fight a protracted battle (and win!) with an insurance company that was refusing to pay for the care I had received—the only care for endo that was ever successful for me. One of my personal goals for attending the walk was to briefly tell Mary Lou how much I admire and appreciate her work. I was so thankful to accomplish that goal.

Then, it was time for the march. After inspiring speeches, we began. Some of us were a little slow, hampered by pain, recent surgeries, problems with ambulation, or even joyfully slowed by the tiny steps of our miracle children who had come to us through birth or adoption.

As I marched, I could hear voices. The voices of the women in support groups, women on the Internet, late at night, asking other women, "Will I ever get pregnant? Will I ever be normal? Will I ever have sex without pain? Will I ever be able to pursue my career? . . ." Voices of women pleading with their doctors to end their pain, even pleading with doctors to *believe* their pain. I realized that these women whose voices I heard were there with us in spirit. We were carrying the banner of their pain with us as we marched.

Other voices joined in. Voices from the nearby memorials to our soldiers who had fought so bravely for the United States of America and lost their lives in the process. All the voices became entangled and built in their intensity, on this hallowed ground, where decades of marches had taken place: marches for equal rights, marches to raise awareness, marches to end war. A chorus of people who were willing to speak out and place their very lives on the line to help others, to end suffering, to end inequality, and above all, to make a difference.

And then the voices faded. From behind me, I heard a single voice: Mary Lou's voice. She was speaking to a woman and offering advice and comfort, probably just one incidence of thousands of times that she has done so to help another woman with endo. As she and the woman passed me, I felt certain that I followed the footsteps of a true American hero.

I would like to salute not only Mary Lou but all the women on the Endo Walk committee, who worked so hard to make it a success. You, too, are my heroes. You have helped us take our first steps on the journey to raise awareness, to salute the women who struggle every day with their pain, and to educate the medical community to provide better treatment, so we may help endo sisters of the future. We are a voice united now, thanks to you. And together, we *will* make a difference. I hope that one day, we will march celebrating the cure for endometriosis. Thank you from the bottom of my heart.

Appendix

© WRITTEN BY MARYLOU BALLWEG
ILLUSTRATED BY MERI LAU

In *Overcoming Endometriosis*, we met Joe, a young man whose dreams were shattered by a mysterious disease called endometriosis. Joe went through a lot of frustrating experiences not unlike that of millions of women with endometriosis.

Joe is a typical young man in his twenties. He has all the realistic dreams of a young man—the perfect life, perfect wife, perfect job, perfect house, perfect family, perfect body. There's just one problem . . .

Thousands upon thousands of letters received at the Association headquarters describe how numerous doctors, mental health people, and husbands of women with endometriosis do not understand that pain with sex is a real physical problem.

Note: When we conducted our first analysis of 365 case histories of women with endometriosis, we were horrified to find a percentage of the women had been given tranquilizers for symptoms and told it would take care of their problems!

A couple of years later, Joe's health, on the birth control pills, has improved tremendously. He's been promoted at work and his former pain with sex and the problems between Stella and him because of it have been alleviated.

A year later . . .

Joe is put on a female hormone to treat the disease. He is told "the side effects are well tolerated by most patients." But privately, he agonizes over his development of breasts.

Fortunately, the breasts Joe developed as a side effect of the female hormone go away after the drug is stopped. But by then the disease is back. Major abdominal surgery is the next step.

Joe has to go to part-time work because he's sick so much, tired, and prone to lots of illnesses.

Note: Have you noticed any preventive testectomies being done?

Note: The most tragic stories heard by the Association are those of women who've gone all the way to the end of the road to hysterectomy and removal of the ovaries but still have endometriosis! It defies reason to remove the ovaries one day in order to remove the hormonal stimulation of stray endometrial tissue and then give the woman hormones the next day. A better approach is waiting three to nine months to give stray endometrial tissue a chance to die out and then go on hormone replacement.

Joe had been assured by his doctor that sex would be better than ever after the removal of his testicles just as women often are assured that sex will be better than ever after the removal of their uterus and ovaries.

A week later . . .

TRH: testosterone replacement hormone

Joe's health rebounds. He's doing great at work. He even has time again for a social life. It appears his bad experiences with endo are going to become just a memory.

Unfortunately, the doubled dose of TRH has some consequences.

Finally, Joe finds some real hope.

Joe learns of an endo specialist from his support group and gains the confidence to pursue better treatment.

Glossary

Acupuncture: Puncture with long, fine needles; an ancient Oriental system of therapy (to redirect or stimulate *qi*, or life energy).

Add-back therapy: The addition of estrogen and progesterone in an effort to replace those hormones suppressed by GnRH drugs.

Adenomyosis: Disease characterized by growth of the endometrium into the walls of the uterus.

Adhesions: Bands of scar tissue sometimes formed due to endo or abdominal surgery, potentially causing inflammation, blockage, and pain.

Addiction: Compulsive, uncontrollable dependence on a substance.

Adrenal glands: Two glands positioned on top of the kidneys. They produce adrenal hormones, including *cortisol* (also called hydrocortisone), which is involved in providing energy in the body, preventing low blood sugar, and other functions; *adrenaline* (also called epinephrine), which acts as a heart stimulant and blood vessel constrictor; *testosterone*, a hormone involved in sex drive and food and energy metabolism; and dehydroepiandrosterone (*DHEA*), an important hormone which is the precursor for other hormones and involved in immune regulation. The adrenal glands are under the direction of the pituitary gland.

Adrenaline: See definition for adrenal glands.

AFS staging system: "The revised staging criteria of the American Society for Reproductive Medicine are based on the location of implants, presence of superficial or deep endometriosis, and presence of filmy or dense adhesions. Endometriosis may be classified as stage 1 (minimal), 2 (mild), 3 (moderate), or 4 (severe). . . . However, observer variability is high in the evaluation of endometriosis, and a more useful method for staging the disease is being sought." In addition, the system is not validated. Definition from *The Merck Manual of Diagnosis and Therapy, Seventeenth Edition.*

Agent Orange: A defoliant mixture of two phenoxyherbicides, one of which contained dioxin, TCDD.

Agonist: A drug or other substance that can bind with a receptor to produce a reaction similar to another substance. An estrogen agonist, for example, acts like estrogen and has similar effects.

Allergen: A substance causing allergic reaction.

Allergy and hypersensitivity: Used interchangeably. Refers to tissue damage caused by an overreaction of the body's immune system to antigens that are usually harmless to most people.

Analgesic: A drug to relieve pain.

Androgen: Male sex hormones that promote the development and maintenance of the male sex characteristics.

Angiogenesis: Growth of new blood vessels to supply the blood that endo and cancer tissues need.

Antagonist: A drug or other substance that exerts an opposite action to that of another or competes for the same receptor sites. An estrogen antagonist, for example, blocks estrogen.

Antibodies: Various proteins in the blood that are generated in reaction to antigens, which they neutralize, and which produce immunity against certain microorganisms or their toxins.

Antigen: Any substance that, when introduced into the body, is recognized by the immune system.

Antigen-presenting cell (APC): B cells, macrophages, and various other body cells that "present" antigens in a form that T cells can recognize.

Antiglucocorticoids: Agents that act against any of the hormones of the adrenal cortex that promote mobilization of fat and amino acids.

Antioxidants: Compounds in the body or in nutrients that slow or prevent the effects of harmful substances called free radicals by converting these free radicals into water and oxygen. Free radicals are highly reactive substances found in air pollution, tobacco smoke, pesticides, foods, and ultraviolet sunlight that are manufactured during normal body processes; they damage cell membranes and result in tissue damage associated with heart disease, cancer, arthritis, premature aging, and other conditions. Antioxidants help slow or prevent these processes and may play a role in the immune system. [Adapted from *Nutri-tion for Women* by Elizabeth Somer (New York: Henry Holt and Co., 1993).]

Apoptosis: "Cell suicide," a process by which a genetically damaged cell destroys itself.

Aromatase: Enzyme that converts adrenal hormones into estrogen in fat and in endo cells.

Asthma: Chronic respiratory disease, often arising from allergies, accompanied by labored breathing, chest constriction, and coughing.

Atopic: Allergic diseases that have a hereditary component including allergies, asthma, atopic eczema, etc.

Autism: A developmental disorder characterized by extreme withdrawal and an abnormal absorption in fantasy, accompanied by delusion, hallucination, and inability to communicate verbally or otherwise relate to people.

Autoantibodies: Antibodies that the body makes against its own cells.

Autoimmune disease: One caused by autoantibodies or lymphocytes that attack one's own tissues or cells.

Autoimmune endocrinopathy: A disease in which parts of the endocrine system are attacked by the body's own immune system.

Autoimmunity: A disease state that results when the immune system mistakenly attacks the body's own tissues. Rheumatoid arthritis and lupus are examples of autoimmune diseases.

B cells: Immune cells that produce antibodies.

B lymphocytes; B cells: Small white blood cells crucial to the immune defenses. They are derived from bone marrow and produce antibodies.

Bagging: Enclosing a cyst being removed in a secured bag to maintain an airtight seal during surgery to minimize the risk of spill in case the cyst turns out to be cancerous.

Bilateral: Occurring or appearing on two sides.

Bilateral salpingo-oophorectomy: Removal of both ovaries and fallopian tubes.

Biochemistry: The chemistry of living organisms and life processes.

Bioidentical hormones: Hormones produced by compounding pharmacies that have an identical chemical structure to those made by the body.

Blastocyst: Early stage of embryo development during which implantation in the wall of the uterus usually occurs.

Borderline tumors: Also referred to as "low malignancy potential tumor." A type of tumor (usually associated with ovarian tumors) which rarely metastasizes or is invasive.

Candidiasis: A condition of allergy to and infection with *Candida albicans*.

Carcinogen: A cancer-causing agent.

Carcinoma: General name for tumors arising in the skin and the linings of organs such as the lungs or uterus (also called epithelial tissues).

Case control studies: A retrospective scientific study in which a group of patients with a particular disease is compared with a control group of persons who have not developed that medical problem.

Castration: The surgical removal of the ovaries or testicles.

Catalyst: A substance that influences the rate of a chemical reaction.

Catecholamines: Any of various compounds that are secretions, or by-products of secretions, of the medulla (inmost portion) of the adrenal gland and affect the sympathetic nervous system.

Cell-mediated immunity: Immune protection provided by the direct action of immune cells (versus humoral immunity).

Chemotaxis/chemotactic agent/chemoattractant: A chemical that attracts cells to a specific location. Chemotaxis is the movement of cells to that location in response to the attracting chemical.

Chronic Fatigue Syndrome; Chronic Fatigue Immune Dysfunction Syndrome (CFIDS): A condition characterized by disabling fatigue, accompanied by a constellation of symptoms, including muscle pain, multi-joint pain without swelling, painful swelling of lymph glands in the neck and armpits, sore throat, headache, impaired memory or concentration, unrefreshing sleep, and weakness and discomfort following exertion.

Chronic mucocutaneous candidiasis: A progressive disease in which an inherited defect of the immune system (the cell-mediated immune system) only to *Candida albicans* allows invasion of *Candida*, causing chronic *Candida* and viral infections followed by the development of autoantibodies against organs or substances of the endocrine system. Associated diseases can include diabetes, Addison's disease (a disease of complete failure of the adrenal glands), hypothyroidism, and pernicious anemia.

Chronic toxins: Poisons that can cause adverse effects other than cancer, after long-term exposure, i.e., damage to kidneys, lungs, or liver.

Clear cell: A type of cell that does not take on a color when stained for microscopic examination. The principle cell found in kidney (renal) cancer, occasionally found in ovarian cancer.

Clomiphene: A fertility treatment drug used to stimulate ovulation. Marketed under the trade name Clomid.

Coagulation: Clotting; the process of changing a liquid into a solid, especially of the blood. This term is frequently used instead of desiccation (the drying of tissue with cellular destruction, which is the effect of using a bipolar or thermal coagulator).

Coitus: Sexual intercourse.

Colostomy: Surgical creation of an opening in the abdominal wall for drainage of bowel contents. In temporary colostomy the opening is closed after healing of the cut parts of the intestines and the person returns to normal bowel movements. In permanent colostomy the person uses a bag at the site of the surgical opening or uses a pad over the opening and needs a bag only at the time of bowel movement. (Permanent colostomy is not used for endometriosis of the bowel.)

Complement (C′) system: A complex series of blood proteins whose action "complements" the work of antibodies. Complement destroys bacteria, produces inflammation, and regulates immune reactions.

Complete blood count (CBC): A blood test that counts the number of white blood cells, red blood cells, and various white blood cell subsets in blood. The test also looks at the amount of hemoglobin in blood and can be used to look for anemia.

Cortisol: See definition for adrenal glands.

Credentials: A predetermined set of standards, such as licensure or certification, establishing that a person or institution has achieved professional recognition in a specific field of health care.

Cross-reaction: The reaction between an antigen and an antibody that was generated against a different antigen.

Cul-de-sac obliteration: Extensive adhesions in the cul-de-sac uniting the cervix or the lower part of the uterus to the rectum.

Cul-de-sac: The space between the back of the uterus and the rectum that forms a pouch.

Cytokines: Powerful chemical substances secreted by immune cells.

Cytotoxic T cell, suppressor T cell: A subset of T lymphocytes that can kill body cells infected by viruses or transformed by cancer; counteract stimulatory effect of helper T cells, shut things down.

DDT: (dichlorodiphenyltrichloroethane) A long-lasting chlorinated hydrocarbon insecticide. Federal restrictions were placed on the synthetic pesticide DDT in 1972 by the Environmental Protection Agency (EPA). DDT has been shown to adversely affect the immune and reproductive systems in humans and animals.

Defoliant: A chemical spray that strips growing plants of their leaves.

DES: Diethylstilbestrol, a synthetic estrogen, was given to pregnant women between 1941 and 1971 to prevent miscarriage. Subsequent research showed that the drug did not prevent miscarriage. DES has since been linked to breast cancer in the mothers, pregnancy complications and a rare form of vaginal cancer in exposed daughters, and fertility problems in both daughters and sons.

Detoxification: The removal of a poison or its effects from a patient.

DHEA: See definition for adrenal glands.

Dioxin: TCDD (2,3,7,8-tetrachlorodibenzo-p-dioxin), the most toxic of a group of chemicals prevalent in the environment from herbicides, industrial wastes, and other sources; dioxin is a toxic chemical by-product of pesticide manufacturing, bleached pulp and paper products, and hazardous waste burning.

Dysbiosis: Imbalance of intestinal microorganisms such as occurs in candidiasis.

Dysmenorrhea: Pain in conjunction with menstruation. When severe, can also cause nausea, vomiting, dizziness, and painful/frequent bowel movements.

Ecosystem: All living and nonliving things that support a chain of life events within a particular area.

Ectopic: Out of place. Said of an organ not in the proper position, or of a pregnancy occurring elsewhere than in the cavity of the uterus.

Eczema: An inflammatory condition of the skin characterized by redness, itching, and oozing lesions which become scaly, crusty, or hardened.

Embryo: Any organism in the earliest stages of development.

Endocrine system: System of glands and other structures that controls hormones; includes thyroid, pituitary, parathyroid, adrenal glands, ovaries and testes, pancreas, pineal body, and paraganglia.

Endocrinopathy: Disease of the endocrine system.

Endometrioid: A type of cancerous tumor found outside the uterus (i.e., ovary), but closely resembling cancers found in the lining of the uterus.

Endometrioma: A cyst, a mass containing endometrial tissue, usually on the ovary. Sometimes called a "chocolate cyst" because of its color.

Endometrium, endometrial: Tissue that lines the inside of the uterus and builds up and sheds each month in the menstrual cycle.

Endoscopy: The visualization of the interior of organs and cavities of the body with illuminated optic instruments such as a laparoscope.

Enzymes: Proteins produced in a cell that are capable of causing or speeding up reactions in the body.

Epidemiological studies: The study of health and disease events in populations.

Epithelial: Referring to the tissue covering internal and external organs of the body.

Erythrocytes: Red blood cells.

Essential fatty acids: Two fatty acids (linoleic acid and linolenic acid) that the body requires and cannot make from other substances so they must be supplied in our food.

Estriol: A weak form of estrogen found in high concentration in urine.

Estrogen: A hormone produced by both sexes, however primarily a female sex hormone responsible for such sex characteristics as breast and genital development, and body hair and fat distribution. In the menstrual cycle, prepares the body for fertilization, implantation, and nourishment of the egg.

Et al: The abbreviation for *et alia*, a Latin phrase meaning "and others." Used, for example, in listings of research papers to show that there were other researchers besides the names listed.

Etiology: The study of all factors that may be involved in the development of a disease; the cause of a disease.

Fecundity: Fertility.

Fibromyalgia: A syndrome characterized by muscle tenderness, soreness, and pain, sleep disturbance, stiffness, and fatigue. Certain spots called trigger points are painful when pressed and may include sites in the back, shoulders, arms, hands, knees, hips, thighs, legs, and feet.

Five-year survival rates: The number of people living five years after diagnosis without a reoccurrence of cancer.

Flatulence: Intestinal gas.

Flora: The various bacterial and other microscopic forms of life inhabiting the body.

Follicle: A cyst-like structure on the ovary containing a developing egg.

Follicular phase: Part of the ovulation process when the egg is still in the follicle (days 1–14 of a 28-day cycle: day 1 is the first day of the period).

Free radicals: Unstable oxygen molecules created during metabolism.

Fructooligosaccharides: Nondigestible, short-chain fructose compounds utilized almost exclusively by the *Bifidobacteria* in our intestinal tract. Fructooligosaccharides are widely distributed in vegetables and grains and some fruits; they are also available in supplement form.

Fungus, fungi: A group of organisms including yeasts, molds, mildews, smuts, and rusts.

Furans: A group of 135 chemical pollutants with a structure similar to dioxins, with similar toxic and biological effects on animals, and often found in conjunction with dioxins.

Gastroenterologist: A physician who specializes in diseases affecting the gastrointestinal tract.

Gastroenterology: Medical specialty concerned with the stomach and intestines, and the diseases especially affecting them.

Gastrointestinal: Relating to the stomach and intestines.

Genetic mutation: A physical or biochemical change in hereditary material (chromosomes, genes).

Genetic: Referring to or concerned with genesis, origin or generation. Related or belonging to birth or reproduction. Inherited. Congenital. Any disease involving the generative organs. A drug or agent that affects the generative organs.

Glands: Any organ in the body that secretes a substance used elsewhere in the body. Hormones, saliva, and blood components are produced by glands.

Gluten: The elastic protein part of certain grains such as wheat.

Granules: A small, grain-like body.

Granulocytes: White blood cells filled with granules containing potent chemicals that allow the cells to digest microorganisms or to produce inflammatory reactions. Neutrophils, eosinophils, and basophils are examples.

Hashimoto's thyroiditis: An autoimmune disease in which the immune system attacks the thyroid and thyroid hormone.

Helper T cell: A subset of T cells that typically carry the CD4 marker and are essential for turning on antibody production, activating cytotoxic T cells, and initiating many other immune responses. Helper T cells "help" the immune response in various ways.

Hematopoietic stem cells: (he-ma-to-poi-ET-ik) Bone marrow cells that are capable of developing into various types of cells.

Hematopoietic system: System in body that forms blood or blood cells.

Heterozygosity: In context, loss of heterozygosity = damage to DNA.

Histamine: A substance found in all body tissues, with the highest concentration being in the lungs. Histamine dilates small blood vessels; contracts smooth muscles; induces increased gastric secretion; and accelerates heart rate. Excess amounts of histamine are released during allergic reactions or shock.

Histological: What tissue structures look like under a microscope.

hMG: Human menopausal gonadotropin, such as the Humegon and Pergonal brands.

HMO: Health Maintenance Organization. A type of group healthcare practice that provides basic and supplemental health maintenance and treatment services to voluntary enrollees who prepay a fixed periodic fee that is set without regard to the amount or kind of services received.

Humoral immunity: Immune protection provided by soluble factors such as antibodies, which circulate in the body's fluids, or "humors," primarily serum and lymph.

Hypha, hyphal: Threadlike filaments that make up the body or the mycelium of a fungus.

Hypoglycemia, Hypoglycemic: Pertaining to or resembling a state of low blood sugar level.

Hypothalamic-pituitary-gonadal axis: A series of hormonal signals. The hypothalamus releases GnRH (gonadotropin releasing hormone), which signals the pituitary to release FSH (follicle stimulating hormone), which signals the ovaries to produce estrogen and then progesterone, which signals the hypothalamus to produce GnRH, repeating the cycle.

Hypothyroidism: A disease in which there is decreased production of thyroid hormone. Symptoms can include weight gain, sluggishness, fatigue, dry skin, thinning hair, low body temperature, gastrointestinal disturbances including constipation, arthritis, inability to tolerate heat and cold, and depression.

Hysterectomy: Surgical removal of the uterus.

Hysteroscopy: A procedure in which a scope (called a hysteroscope) thin enough to fit through the cervix with minimal or no dilation, is inserted through the cervix into the uterus. The inside of the uterus is filled (distended) with a liquid or a gas (carbon dioxide) so the surgeon can see inside. Diagnostic hysteroscopy and simple operative hysteroscopy are usually done in an office setting. More complex operative hysteroscopy is done in an operating room.

Immunodeficient: An inability to mount an adequate immune response upon challenge.

Immunoglobulin: A family of large protein molecules; antibodies.

Immunosuppressive: Something that decreases or stalls a response from the immune system.

Incidence: The number of times an event occurs.

Interferons (IFN): Cytokines that can induce cells to resist viral replication; they "interfere" with viral infections.

Interleukins (IL): A generic term for cytokines produced by leukocytes.

Irritable bowel syndrome: A poorly understood, loosely defined bowel problem characterized by irregular and uncoordinated contractions of the intestines.

Laparoscopy: A surgical procedure, generally done on an outpatient basis under general anesthesia. A small incision is made near the naval, and a lighted, thin tube is inserted, through which the surgeon can view organs in the abdomen. Additional small incisions may be made to introduce other instruments into the abdomen for removing endo growths and adhesions or performing other surgical procedures. A diagnostic laparoscopy is a laparoscopy done to diagnose the problem. An operative laparoscopy means that surgical procedures are carried out during the laparoscopy. Most endo specialists now do operative laparoscopies at the time of first diagnosis.

Laparotomy: Major surgery done through a large incision in the abdominal wall.

Latency: A state of inactivity or dormancy. In cancer, a state in which there are no outward signs of the disease, though tests indicate the disease is still present in an inactive state.

Lesions: In endo, "lesions" describes the patches, colonies, or growths of endometrial tissue outside the uterus. In general, lesions refer to any pathological disturbance such as an injury, infection, or a tumor.

Leukocytes: All white blood cells; our immune cells.

Lupus (systemic lupus erythematosus): An inflammatory disease, generally occurring in young women, which causes deterioration of the connective tissues and may attack soft internal organs as well as bones and muscles. Symptoms vary widely but may include fever, rash, abdominal pains, weakness, fatigue, and pains in joints and muscles.

Luteinizing hormone: A hormone produced by the pituitary gland that stimulates the production of estrogen by the ovary and is involved in the maturing of the egg at ovulation.

Lymph: A thin watery fluid that contains mainly blood cells and emulsified fats and is filtered through the lymph nodes and pumped throughout the body via the lymphatic system. This system is responsible for protecting and maintaining the internal fluid level of the body.

Lymphatic: Forming lymph fluid.

Lymphocytes: Small white blood cells produced in the lymphoid organs and paramount in our immune defenses.

Lymphoma: Tumors that begin in the lymph or lymphatic system.

Lysis: To cut, break up, divide, separate surgically.

Macrophages: Immune cells that destroy bacteria and other foreign material by surrounding them and gobbling them up.

Mammary glands: Glands located in the central part of the breast which allow for the passage of milk into the nipple.

Megace: A drug given to patients with advanced breast or endometrial cancer.

Melatonin: A hormone that helps regulate estrogen production.

Membrane attack complex (MAC): A structure formed by complement proteins that forms a hole in the cell membrane. This allows fluid to pour into the cell causing it to swell and lyse.

Meniere's disease: A sometimes disabling disorder of the ear, causing hearing loss, dizziness, and ringing in the ear (tinnitus).

Menopause: Cessation of menstruation, measured as one year since a woman's last period.

Metabolism: The chemical processes of a living organism that result in energy production, growth, elimination of wastes, and other bodily functions related to distribution of nutrients after digestion.

Metabolite: Any product of metabolism.

Metastasis: The spread of cancer to other areas of the body.

Mitral valve prolapse: A defect in which a valve on the left side of the heart flaps up instead of closing tightly, allowing some blood to backflow.

Monocyte: A large phagocytic white blood cell which, when it enters tissue, develops into a macrophage.

Mucinous: A type of tumor made up of cells that produce mucin, the chief ingredient in mucus.

Mucous membranes: The membranes that line all those passages by which the internal parts of the body communicate with the exterior, and are continuous with the skin at the various openings of the surface of the body. They are described as lining the two tracts—the gastro-pulmonary (gastrointestinal tract and the lungs) and the genito-urinary (the vagina and urethra).

Mucus/mucosal: The clear, sticky secretion of the mucous membranes; relating to the mucous membranes.

Multifactorial: The result of the combined effect of several factors.

Multiple sclerosis (MS): A chronic disease, generally occurring in young adults characterized by hardening patches scattered randomly throughout the brain and spinal cord interfering with the nerves of those areas. Can cause visual disturbances, balance impairment, unsteady walk, loss of bladder and bowel control, and paralysis.

Mutagenesis: The occurrence of genetic mutation.

Myofascial: A muscle and the connective tissues (tendons, ligaments, etc.) surrounding it.

Natural killer cells: Large, granule-filled lymphocytes that take on tumor cells and infected body cells. They are known as "natural" killers because they attack without first having to recognize specific antigens.

Naturopath, N.D.: Naturopathic doctor; one who practices naturopathy, a system of medicine stressing maintenance of health and prevention of disease using a variety of methods to help the body heal itself, i.e., nutrition, exercise, massage, acupuncture, etc.

Neoplasms: Tumors.

Neoplastic: Tumor-forming.

Neutrophil: A white blood cell that is an abundant and important phagocyte.

Non-Hodgkin's lymphoma: Cancer affecting the lymph tissue; mainly found in patients over 50 who are immunosuppressed.

Nonsteroidal anti-inflammatory drugs (NSAIDs): Pain medications that work by inhibiting prostaglandins, and that include ibuprofen and naproxen sodium (both nonprescription) and ketoralac tromethamine (Toradol) by prescription.

Nucleus: The central controlling body within a living cell, usually round, containing genetic codes for maintaining life systems of an organism and for issuing commands for growth and reproduction.

Oncogene: A potentially cancer-inducing gene. Under normal conditions such genes play a role in the growth and proliferation of cells, but, when altered in some way by a cancer-causing agent such as radiation, a carcinogenic chemical, or an oncogenic virus, they may cause the cell to be transformed to a malignant state.

Oophorectomy: Surgical removal of the ovaries.

Opioid: A synthetic narcotic that acts like an opiate (a narcotic derived from opium) but is not derived from opium.

Organic: Organic foods are grown without the use of chemical pesticides and fertilizers, genetically engineered ingredients, or sewage sludge.

Organochlorine: A chemical compound produced by combining chlorine with organic substances, usually petrochemicals.

Osteoporosis: A disease of the bones in which the bones become thin and porous.

Outcomes: Evidence-based medicine; evaluating the results of various treatments like surgical techniques, or drugs.

Ovarian remnant syndrome: The presence of ovarian tissue in the pelvis after the ovaries have been removed; more common when adhesions and inflammation made the surgery difficult.

***p* value:** A number used to determine the significance of a statistical test. The smaller the *p* value, the greater the significance. A *p* value less than .05 means the test was significant.

Palpation: Feeling with fingers and hands.

Pandemic: Epidemic on a global basis.

Pathogenic: Disease-causing.

Pathophysiology: Derangement or alteration of function seen in disease.

PCBs (Polychlorinated biphenyls): A group of nonflammable chemicals that were widely used as coolants in electrical transformers, industrial lubricants, hydraulic fluids, and in "carbonless paper" from 1929 until they were banned in 1979. Some PCBs persist in the environment for more than 100 years.

Perimenopause: The time around menopause, which can be a few years before and a year after menopause.

Perineal: Pertaining to the area between the vulva and the anus in the female (and between the scrotum and the anus in the male).

Peritoneal cavity: The internal abdomen; the abdominal cavity.

Peritoneum (peritoneal): The thin membrane covering the walls of the abdomen and pelvis and the organs contained within them.

Person years: A unit of measurement equal to one year of a human life. Example: two years of one person's life and three years of another person's life equals five person years.

Phagocytosis: The process by which microbes or other cells and foreign particles are ingested by large white blood cells called phagocytes.

Phagosome: See vacuole.

Phthalates: Chemical compounds in plastics. Some have estrogenic activity. Some are cancer-causing. Phthalates used in IV bags, tubing, and dialysis equipment have been shown to leach out of the material into solutions and patients.

Physiological (concentrations): Relating to physiology, the physical and chemical processes involved in the functioning of living organisms.

Phytoestrogens: Weak, naturally-occurring estrogenic compounds found in some plants such as flaxseed and soybeans.

Pituitary gland: A small gland at the base of the brain that secretes, regulates, and stores a number of hormones that affect the thyroid, ovaries, and adrenal glands as well as other parts of the body.

Polyendocrinopathy: A disease of a number of parts of the endocrine system.

Polygenic breast cancer: A cancer caused by many genes.

Preeclampsia: A metabolic disturbance of late pregnancy characterized by high blood pressure, edema, and excess protein in the urine.

Premarin: Conjugated horse estrogens.

Presacral neurectomy: A procedure severing the nerves at the back of the pelvis to help provide pain relief.

Primary dysmenorrhea: Painful periods and other symptoms due to an imbalance in prostaglandins.

Privileges: Authority granted to a physician by a hospital governing board to provide care to the hospital's patients. Clinical privileges are limited to the individual's professional license, experience, and competence.

Proctoring: Supervised experience with expert colleagues; rare outside of medical school.

Progesterone: A hormone that prepares the uterus for reception of the fertilized egg.

Proliferation: Rapid and repeated reproduction of new parts, as by cell division.

Prostaglandins: Substances found in semen, menstrual fluid, and various body tissues. They stimulate contraction and relaxation of the uterus and other smooth muscles. They also can lower blood pressure and affect the action of certain hormones.

Proteolytic enzymes: Enzymes that break a substance down into simpler compounds.

Provera: Synthetic form of the hormone progesterone.

Randomized: Random selection; a method for choosing patients or subjects for a research study in which all members of a particular group have an equal chance of being selected; selection by chance.

Rectovaginal bimanual exam: Simultaneous insertion by the physician of one finger in the vagina and another in the rectum.

Red blood cell (RBC): Also called an erythrocyte. Disk-shaped cells with concave faces, responsible for transporting the oxygen bound to its iron-containing core through the body.

Relative survival rate: The rate of survival after eliminating all other causes of death except cancer.

Resection: Excision (removal by cutting) of a portion of an organ or other structure.

Residency: After graduating from medical school, a physician goes into postgraduate clinical training. The first year is called internship. After the internship year, the second, third, and fourth years of postgraduate training are called residency. The length of residency varies according to specialty. If additional training occurs, it is referred to as a fellowship.

Retrograde menstruation: A backward flow of menstrual fluid into the pelvic region.

Rheumatoid arthritis: An autoimmune disease in which the immune system attacks the joints. Symptoms may include fatigue, weakness, poor appetite, low-grade fever, anemia, morning stiffness, joint pain or tenderness, and swelling of at least two joints.

Sciatica: An inflammation of the sciatic nerve, usually marked by pain and tenderness along the course of the nerve through the thigh and leg.

Sclerotic: Hard, indurated, or hardening.

Selection bias: A tendency toward a certain outcome in a study created by the way subjects are selected to be a part of the experiment. Example: I want to survey 100 people to find out their favorite brand of ketchup, so I ask people as they are leaving XYZ grocery store. However, XYZ grocery store only carries its own brand of ketchup. If a shopper really likes UVW brand of ketchup best, chances are he won't shop at XYZ grocery. Therefore, the outcome of the study will be *biased* toward XYZ brand.

Serous: A type of ovarian tumor containing cells that produce or contain serum, the clear liquid found in blood.

Serotonin: A naturally occurring derivative of tryptophan (an amino acid essential for normal growth in infants and for nitrogen balance in adults), which constricts blood vessels.

Serum: The watery component of blood.

Sjögren's Syndrome: An autoimmune disorder in which deficient moisture production can affect the eyes, salivary glands in the mouth, and other mucous membranes. Abnormal dryness can lead to damage to the eyes, dental disorders, lung, and other problems.

Steroidal: Adjective for steroid. Any of a group of molecules based on a common structure that includes the sex hormones (estrogens, testosterone, progestins), cholesterol, bile acids, and many other biologically active compounds.

Substance P: A material made by the body that acts to stimulate dilation and constriction of intestinal and other smooth muscles.

Systemic: Pertaining to the body as a whole.

T lymphocytes; T cells: Small white blood cells that orchestrate and/or directly participate in the immune defenses. They are processed in the thymus and secrete lymphokines.

Talc: A component in some baby, body, or dusting powders whose molecular structure is similar to asbestos.

Tamoxofen: A drug used in the treatment of advanced breast cancer patients whose tumors are estrogen-dependent.

TENS (Transcutaneous electrical nerve stimulation): A method of pain control by the application of electric impulses to the nerve endings through the use of electrodes that are placed on the skin and attached to a stimulator.

Testosterone: See definition for adrenal glands.

TH1 cells: T cells that generally produce IL-2, IFN-g, and TNF-b, historically called inflammatory (CD4) T cells.

TH2 cells: T cells that generally produce IL-4, IL-5, IL-9, IL-10, and IL-13, historically called helper (CD4) T cells.

Thyroid: An endocrine gland situated at the front of the neck that secretes hormones that increase the rate of metabolism; affect body temperature; regulate protein, fat, and carbohydrate catabolism in all cells (catabolism is a complex metabolic process in which energy is liberated for use in work, energy storage, or heat production); maintain growth hormone secretion and skeletal maturation, heart rate, force, and output; promote central nervous system development; stimulate synthesis of many enzymes; and are necessary for muscle tone and vigor. The thyroid gland is under the direction of the pituitary gland.

Thyroxine: Hormone that influences metabolic rate.

Tolerance: A state of nonresponsiveness to a particular antigen or group of antigens.

Toxemia of pregnancy: See definition for preeclampsia.

Transdermal: Absorbed through the skin.

Triglycerides: Fat compounds that make up most animal and vegetable fats and are the principal fats in the blood.

Tumor necrosis factor (TNF): A cytokine made by macrophages and T cells.

Tumor progression: Advancing development of a tumor.

Tumor suppressor gene: Normal gene that controls cell growth. In a "loss of function" mutation both genes in the tumor suppressor gene pair are damaged and the cell becomes cancerous. The normal p53 gene is a tumor suppressor gene that tells a cell when to turn off. When both p53 genes are mutated, control of cell division is lost, because the cells' "off switch" no longer operates.

Urethra: A small tube that drains urine from the bladder to the outside of the body. The opening of the urethra is above the vagina and below the clitoris.

Ureterolysis: Removal of part of a ureter.

Urologist: A medical specialist dealing with the urinary system (bladder, kidneys, ureter, urethra, etc.).

Vacuole: Also called a *phagosome*. A phagocytic vesicle that contains ingested material.

Vaginal cuff: The top of the vagina which is sewn shut after a hysterectomy and removal of the cervix.

Vaginitis: Inflammation of the vagina.

Vulva: The region of the external female genital organs, including the labia (the inner and outer lips around the opening of the vagina and urethra), mons pubis (the slight elevation caused by a pad of fatty tissue over the pubic bone just above the clitoris), clitoris (the small sensitive organ that swells during sexual arousal, just above the urethra), and opening of the urethra and the vagina. (The urethra is a small tube that drains urine from the bladder to the outside of the body.)

Vulval, vulvar: Relating to the vulva.

White blood cell (WBC): See leukocyte.

Xenoestrogens: Foreign estrogens; estrogens not produced by the body.

(Definitions for immunological terms were compiled with the aid of the National Cancer Institute publication: *Understanding the Immune System*, publication No. 92-529; revised October 1991.)

Resources

Following is a list of resources that may prove useful to readers. The information included is current as of our printing. If you have difficulty contacting any of these organizations, you may want to get in touch with a national self-help clearinghouse or call directory assistance in the cities in which these groups are based. For additional resources, see *The Endometriosis Sourcebook*, available from the Endometriosis Association.

For All Aspects of Endometriosis

Endometriosis Association
International Headquarters
8585 N. 76th Place
Milwaukee, WI 53223-2600, U.S.A.
Telephone: 414-355-2200; 1-800-992-3636 (in North America)
Fax: 414-355-6065
E-mail: endo@EndometriosisAssn.org
Website: EndometriosisAssn.org

Contact us—we're here to help! We also invite you to join and be part of our mission to cure and prevent this disease.

A wide variety of informative, accurate, and highly acclaimed literature on endo and related health problems is available to you through the Association. Resources include our second book, *The Endometriosis Sourcebook*, almost 500 pages of authoritative information on endo (now in its seventh printing), and our first book, *Overcoming Endometriosis*, now in its tenth printing:

Ballweg, Mary Lou, and the Endometriosis Association. *The Endometriosis Sourcebook*. Chicago: Contemporary Books, 1995. The definitive endometriosis guide for the nonmedical professional. It is available from the Association for $14.95 U.S. or $23 Canadian, plus shipping and handling ($2.50 U.S. or $9.25 Canadian) or from your local or online bookstore.

Ballweg, Mary Lou, and the Endometriosis Association. *Overcoming Endometriosis.* New York: Congdon and Weed, 1987. An anthology of acclaimed articles, fact sheets, research reviews, and the "Joe with Endo" cartoon series.

The Association also has available educational video and audio recordings of speeches by leading experts on the disease, as well as booklets, kits, and newsletters. For a free information packet, including our "Materials to Help You" catalog, call, write, fax, or E-mail the Association.

If you have not been diagnosed with endo but wonder if you might have it, you can order the Association's Diagnostic Kit, "How Can I Tell if I Have Endometriosis?" Send $4.75 U.S. or $7 Canadian, plus $2.25 U.S. or $7 Canadian for shipping and handling charges. Also take the "Killer Cramps" screening test on the last page of this book.

To become a member of the Association, fill out the membership form on the last page of this book.

For Women with Endometriosis Outside the United States

Contact Endometriosis Association International Headquarters (see first page of this section for address). The Association has affiliated groups in dozens of countries, and more are being added all the time. Don't suffer alone—contact us!

For Women with Endometriosis in the British Isles

The National Endometriosis Society
50 Westminster Palace Gardens, Artillery Row
London SWIP IRL, England
Telephone: 020 7222 2781
Fax: 020 7222 2786
Helpline: 0808 808 2227
Website: endo.org.uk
E-mail: nes@endo.org.uk

The SHE Trust (Simply Holistic Endometriosis)
Red Hall Lodge Offices
Red Hall Drive
Bracebridge Heath, Lincoln
Lincs LN4 2JT, England
Telephone/Fax: 0870 774 3665
Website: shetrust.org.uk
E-mail: shetrust@shetrust.org.uk

For Women with Endometriosis in Australia

Endometriosis Association (Victoria) Inc.
28 Warrandyte Road
Ringwood, Victoria 3134, Australia
Telephone: 61 3 9879 2199 (outside Victoria); 1 800 069 697 (within Victoria)
Fax: 61 3 9879 6519
E-mail: info@endometriosis.org.au
Website: endometriosis.org.au

For Women with Endometriosis in New Zealand

New Zealand Endometriosis Foundation Inc.
P.O. Box 1683
Palmerston North 5301
Telephone/Fax: 64 (0)6 359 2613
E-mail: nzendo@xtra.co.nz
Website: nzendo.co.nz

Organizations

Listings are in the United States unless otherwise indicated.

For Help with Environmental Medicine and Allergies

Allergy and Asthma Network
Mothers of Asthmatics, Inc.
3554 Chain Bridge Road, Suite 200
Fairfax, VA 22030-2709
Telephone: 800-878-4403 (U.S. only); 703-641-9595 (outside of U.S.)

American Academy of Environmental Medicine
7701 East Kellogg, Suite 625
Wichita, KS 67207
Telephone: 316-684-5500
Fax: 316-684-5709
E-mail: administrator@aaem.com
Website: aaem.com

The American Environmental Health Foundation (AEHF)
8345 Walnut Hill Lane, Suite 225
Dallas, TX 75231

Telephone: 800-428-2343 (U.S. only); 214-361-9515 (outside of U.S.)
Fax: 214-361-2534
E-mail: aehf@aehf.com
Website: aehf.com

For General Women's Health Issues

The National Women's Health Network
514 Tenth Street, N.W., Suite 400
Washington, DC 20004
Telephone: 202-347-1140 (admin.); 202-628-7814 (health)
Fax: 202-347-1168
Website: womenshealthnetwork.org

Healthfinder
healthfinder.org

For Help with Adhesions

The International Pelvic Pain Society
Women's Medical Plaza, Suite 402
2006 Brookwood Medical Center Drive
Birmingham, AL 35209
Telephone: 205-877-2950
Fax: 205-877-2973
Website: pelvicpain.org

International Adhesions Society
6757 Arapaho Road, Suite 711
PMB 238
Dallas, TX 75248
Telephone: 972-931-5596
Fax: 972-931-5476
Website: adhesions.org

For Environmental Health and Activism Information

Birth Defects Research for Children, Inc.
930 Woodcock Road, Suite 225
Orlando, FL 32803
Telephone: 407-895-0802
Website: birthdefects.org

Center for Health, Environment and Justice (CHEJ)
P.O. Box 6806
Falls Church, VA 22040
Telephone: 703-237-2249
E-mail: chej@chej.org
Website: chej.org

Center for Science in the Public Interest
1875 Connecticut Avenue, NW, Suite 300
Washington, DC 20009
Telephone: 202-332-9110
Fax: 202-265-4954
E-mail: cspi@cspinet.org
Website: cspinet.org

Chemical Injury Information Network
P.O. Box 301
White Sulphur Springs, MT 59645
Telephone: 406-547-2255
Fax: 406-547-2455
Website: ciin.org

The Collaborative on Health and the Environment
c/o Commonweal
P.O. Box 316
Bolinas, CA 94924
E-mail: info@cheforhealth.org
Website: cheforhealth.org

Coming Clean
P.O. Box 8743
Missoula, MT 59807
Website: chemicalbodyburden.org
E-mail: info@comeclean.org

Co-op America
1612 K Street, NW, Suite 600
Washington, DC 20006
Telephone: 202-872-5307; 800-58-GREEN (U.S. only)
Fax: 202-331-8166
Website: coopamerica.com

The Green Guide Institute
Prince Street Station
P.O. Box 567
New York, NY 10012
Telephone: 212-598-4910
Fax: 212-410-0184
Website: thegreenguide.com

Health Care Without Harm
1755 South Street, NW, Suite 6B
Washington, DC 20009
Telephone: 202-234-0091
Fax: 202-234-9121
E-mail: info@hcwh.org
Website: noharm.org

Healthy Building Network (HBN)
Institute for Local Self-Reliance
2425 18th Street, NW
Washington, DC 20009-2096
Telephone: 202-232-4108
Fax: 202-332-0463
E-mail: info@healthybuilding.net
Website: healthybuilding.net

Human Ecology Action League, Inc.
P.O. Box 29629
Atlanta, GA 30359
Telephone: 404-248-1898
Fax: 404-248-0162
E-mail: HEALNatnl@aol.com

Women's Environment and Development Organization (WEDO)
355 Lexington Avenue, 3rd Floor
New York, NY 10017-6603
Telephone: 212-973-0325
Fax: 212-973-0335
E-mail: wedo@wedo.org
Website: wedo.org

Women's Network on Health and the Environment
517 College Street, Suite 233
Toronto, ON M6G 4A2 Canada
Telephone: 416-928-0880
Fax: 416-928-9640
Website: web.net/~wnhe

For Information on Pesticides

Beyond Pesticides
National Coalition Against the Misuse of Pesticides
701 E. Street, SE, Suite 200
Washington, DC 20003
Telephone: 202-543-5450
Fax: 202-543-4791
E-mail: info@beyondpesticides.org
Website: beyondpesticides.org

Pesticide Action Network North America
49 Powell Street, Suite 500
San Francisco, CA 94102
Telephone: 415-981-1771
Fax: 415-981-1991
Website: panna.org
E-mail: panna@panna.org
Pesticide database: pesticideinfo.org

For Information About Cancer
General—All Cancers

American Cancer Society
Telephone: 800-ACS-2345 (U.S. only)

The American Association for Cancer Research
615 Chestnut Street, 17th Floor
Philadelphia, PA 19106-4404
Telephone: 215-440-9300
Fax: 215-440-9313
Website: aacr.org

Cancer Prevention Coalition
University of Illinois at Chicago, School of Public Health
2121 West Taylor Street

Mail Code 922
Chicago, IL 60612
Telephone: 312-996-2297
Website: preventcancer.com
E-mail: Epstein@uic.edu

Center for Advancement in Cancer Education
300 E. Lancaster Avenue, Suite 100
Wynnewood, PA 19096
Telephone: 610-642-4810
Fax: 610-896-6339
Website: beatcancer.org
medicine-mail: caceinfo@aol.com

Centers for Disease Control and Prevention (CDC)
Website: cdc.gov/publications.htm

International Cancer Information Services
Website: cis.nci.nih.gov/resources/intlist.htm

International Union Against Cancer (UICC)
Website: uicc.org

Myriad Corporation
Website: myriad.com
A for-profit corporation with an informative website on genetic testing.

National Cancer Institute
9000 Rockville Pike
Building 82, Room 103B
Bethesda, MD 20892
Telephone: 301-496-4000
Website: chid.nih.gov/ncichid/ (Cancer Patient Education Database)
Website: cancer.gov (Live Help Online)

Oncolink
University of Pennsylvania
Website: oncolink.upenn.edu

Women's Cancer Network
Website: wcn.org

The Women's Cancer Resource Center
4604 Chicago Avenue South
Minneapolis, MN 55407
Telephone: 612-822-4846; 877-892-6742 (U.S. and Canada)
E-mail: wcrc@mr.net
Website: givingvoice.org

World Research Foundation
41 Bell Rock Plaza
Sedona, AZ 86351
Telephone: 928-284-3300
Fax: 928-284-3530
E-mail: sross@wrf.org
Website: wrf.org

Breast Cancer

In an extensive appendix, *Dr. Susan Love's Breast Book* (listed under "Books") includes a thorough listing of regional support organizations for cancer and breast cancer patients.

The Breast Cancer Fund
2107 O'Farrell Street
San Francisco, CA 94115
Telephone: 415-346-8223
Fax: 415-346-2975
E-mail: info@breastcancerfund.org
Website: breastcancerfund.org

Breast Cancer Society of Canada
401 St. Clair Street
Point Edward, ON, Canada N7V 1P2
Telephone: 519-336-0746; 800-567-8767 (within Canada only)
Fax: 519-336-5725
Website: bcsc.ca
E-mail: bcsc@bcsc.ca

Cancer Information Service (Canada)—Ontario Region Only
Telephone: 888-939-3333 (within Canada only); 905-387-1153

National Alliance of Breast Cancer Organizations (NABCO)
9 East 37th Street, 10th Floor

New York, NY 10016
Telephone: 888-80-NABCO (in U.S. only); 212-889-0606
Fax: 212-689-1213
E-mail: nabcoinfo@aol.com
Website: nabco.org

National Breast Cancer Coalition
1707 L Street, NW
Suite 1060, Washington, DC 20036
Telephone: 202-296-7477
Fax: 202-265-6854
Website: stopbreastcancer.org

Susan G. Komen Breast Cancer Foundation
5005 LBJ Freeway, Suite 250
Dallas, TX 75244
Telephone: 972-855-1600
Fax: 972-855-1605
Website: komen.org

Y-ME National Breast Cancer Organization
212 W. Van Buren Street
Chicago, IL 60607
Telephone: 800-221-2141 (toll-free hotline 8:00 a.m. to 5:00 p.m., CST (U.S. and
Canada)
Telephone: 800-221-2141 (24-hour counseling and support) (U.S. and Canada)
Spanish hotline: 800-986-9505

Ovarian Cancer

Gilda Radner Familial Ovarian Cancer Registry
Roswell Park Cancer Institute
Elm and Carlton Streets
Buffalo, NY 14263
Telephone 800-OVARIAN; 1-800-682-7426 (U.S. only)
E-mail: gradner@roswellpark.org
Website: ovariancancer.com

Gynecologic Cancer Foundation
401 North Michigan Avenue
Chicago, IL 60611
Telephone: 800-444-4441 (U.S. only); 312-644-6610 (outside U.S.)

Fax: 312-673-6959
E-mail: gcf@sba.com
Website: wcn.org/gcf/

National Ovarian Cancer Coalition
500 Spanish River Boulevard, Suite 14
Boca Raton, FL 33431
Telephone: 888-OVARIAN (U.S. and Canada); (561) 393-0005
Fax: 561-393-7275
E-mail: noccnat@bellsouth.net
Website: ovarian.org

Ovar'coming Together
Kelly Allen, Executive Director
3050 North Meridian St.
Indianapolis, IN 46208
Telephone: 317-250-OVAR
Fax: 317-925-6673
Website: ovarian-cancer.org

Ovarian Cancer National Alliance
910 17th Street, NW, Suite 413
Washington, DC 20006
Telephone: 202-331-1332
Fax: 202-331-2292
E-mail: ocna@ovariancancer.org
Website: ovariancancer.org

The Ovarian Cancer Research Fund, Inc.
One Pennsylvania Plaza, Suite 1610
New York, NY 10119-0165
Telephone: 212-268-1002; toll-free: 800-873-9569
E-mail: info@ocrf.org
Website: ocrf.org

Ovarian Plus International: Gynecologic Cancer Prevention Quarterly
P.O. Box 2831
Springfield, VA 22152-0831
Telephone: 703-644-3162
E-mail: csinnex@yahoo.com
Website: monitor.net/ovarian

Society of Gynecologic Oncologists
401 North Michigan Avenue
Chicago, IL 60611
Telephone: 312-644-6610
Fax: 312-673-6959
E-mail: sgo@sba.com
Website: sgo.org

Ovarian and Breast Cancer

SHARE, Self Help for Women with Breast or Ovarian Cancer
1501 Broadway, Suite 1720
New York, NY 10036
Telephone: 866-891-2392 (toll-free); 212-719-0364
Spanish Hotline: 212-719-4454 (breast); 212-719-1204 (ovarian)
Telephone: 212-719-2943 (Education Wellness)
Fax: 212-869-3431
Website: sharecancersupport.org

Non-Hodgkin's Lymphoma

Leukemia and Lymphoma Society
1311 Mamaroneck Avenue, 3rd Floor
White Plains, NY 10605
Telephone: 800-955-4LSA (toll-free, U.S. and Canada); 914-949-5213
Fax: 914-949-6691
E-mail: infocenter@leukemia-lymphoma.org
Website: leukemia-lymphoma.org

Lymphoma Foundation of America
814 North Garfield Street
Arlington, VA 22201
Telephone: 703-875-9800; patient hotline: 703-525-2076
Fax: 703-527-4056
Website: lymphomahelp.org

Melanoma

Melanoma Education Foundation
P.O. Box 2023
Peabody, MA 01960
Telephone: 978-535-3080
Fax: 978-535-5602

E-mail: MEF@skincheck.org
Website: skincheck.com

Melanoma Patients Information Page
E-mail: admin@mpip.org
Website: mpip.org

Melanoma Research Foundation
23704-5 El Toro Road, #206
Lake Forest, CA 92630
Phone/Fax: 1-800-MRF-1290
E-mail: mrf@melanoma.org
Website: melanoma.org

The Skin Cancer Foundation
245 Fifth Avenue, Suite 1403
New York, NY 10016
Telephone: 800-SKIN-490 (toll-free, U.S. and Canada); 212-725-5751
E-mail: info@skincancer.org
Website: skincancer.org

Products and Services

Delayed Hypersensitivity Testing

ELISA/ACT Biotechnologies, Inc.
14 Pidgeon Hill Drive, Suite 300
Sterling, VA 20165
Telephone: 800-553-5472
Fax: 703-450-7064

Testing for Toxins in Body Fat, Blood, and Urine

Accu-Chem Laboratories
990 North Bowser Road, Suite 800–880
Richardson, TX 75081
Telephone: 800-451-0116 (toll-free, U.S. and Canada); 972-234-5577
Fax: 972-234-5707
E-mail: accuchem@accuchem.com

Environmentally Friendly Products

Shower filters that remove the chlorine from your water are available from several sources. Check with your local natural foods store. Even if they do not stock this item, they may be able to order for you. You might also want to try the following catalog retailers:

Seventh Generation, Inc.
212 Battery St., Suite A
Burlington, VT 05401-5281
Telephone: 802-658-3773; toll-free: 800-456-1191
Fax: 802-658-1771
Website: seventhgeneration. com

Gaiam, Inc.
316 Interlocken Blvd.
Broomfield, CO 80021
Telephone: 303-222-3600
Fax: 303-222-3700

Compounding Pharmacies

The International Academy for Compounding Pharmacies (IACP)
P.O. Box 1365
Sugar Land, TX 77487
Telephone: 800-927-4227 (U.S. only); 281-933-8400
Fax: 281-495-0602
E-mail: iacpinfo@iacprx.org
Website: iacprx.org

Products for People with Allergies

The Dasun Company
P.O. Box 668
Escondido, CA 92033
Telephone: 800-433-8929; 619-480-8929
Fax: 619-746-8865

Janice Corporation
198 Route 46
Budd Lake, NJ 07828
Telephone: 800/JANICES (U.S. and Canada); 973-691-5459
Fax: 201-691-5459

Miller Paint Company
317 S.E. Grand Avenue
Portland, OR 97214
Telephone: 503-233-4491
Fax: 503-233-7463
Website: millerpaint.com

National Allergy Supply, Inc.
1620-D Satellite Boulevard
P.O. Box 1658
Duluth, GA 30096
Telephone: 800-522-1448 (U.S. and Canada)
Website: nationalallergy.com

Products for People with Cancer

The Cancer Club
Telephone: 800-586-9062 (U.S. and Canada)
Website: cancerclub.com

LifeCare Concepts
New York City
Telephone: 800-401-2233
Website: cancerresources.com

Books

Ahlgrimm, Marla, R.Ph., John M. Kells, and Christine Macgenn. *The HRT Solution: Optimizing Your Hormone Potential.* Madison, WI: Avery Penquin Putnam, 1999.

American Institute for Cancer Research. *Food, Nutrition and the Prevention of Cancer: A Global Perspective.* Washington, DC: American Institute for Cancer Research, 1997. This 660-page report is available from the American Institute for Cancer Research (call 1-800-843-8114 or visit aicr.org on the Web).

Austin, Steven, N.D., and Cathy Hitchcock, M.S.W. *Breast Cancer: What You Should Know (but May Not Be Told) About Prevention, Diagnosis, and Treatment.* Rocklin, CA: Prima Publishing, 1994.

Bateson-Koch, Carolee, D.C., N.D. *Allergies: Disease in Disguise.* Burnaby, BC: Alive Books, 1994. (This book is listed with reservation, since it contains some errors, but in general will be helpful.)

Berkson, D. Lindsey. *Hormone Deception.* Chicago: Contemporary Books, 2000.

Colborn, Theo, Ph.D., Dianne Dumanoski, and John Peterson Myers, Ph.D. *Our Stolen Future.* New York: Penguin Books, 1996. A related website is available at ourstolenfuture.org. The book is available from the Endometriosis Association.

Crook, William G., M.D. *The Yeast Connection and the Woman.* Jackson, TN: Professional Books, 1995.

Crook, William G., M.D., and Laura Stevens. *Solving the Puzzle of Your Hard-to-Raise Child.* New York: Random House, 1987.

Dadd, Debra Lynn. *Nontoxic, Natural and Earthwise.* Los Angeles: Jeremy P. Tarcher, Inc., 1990.

Daoust, Joyce, and Gene Daoust. *The 40-30-30 Fat Burning Nutrition* Book. Del Mar, CA: Wharton Publishing, 1996.

Desowitz, R. *The Thorn in the Starfish: The Immune System and How It Works.* New York: W. W. Norton, 1988.

Epstein, Samuel, M.D., and David Steinman. *The Breast Cancer Prevention Program.* New York: Macmillan, 1997.

Falcone, Ron. *Natural Medicine for Breast Cancer.* New York: Dell Books, 1997.

Frähm, Anne E., with David J. Frähm. *A Cancer Battle Plan: Six Strategies for Beating Cancer from a Recovered "Hopeless Case."* New York: Tarcher/Putnam, 1992.

Galland, Leo, M.D. *The Four Pillars of Healing.* New York: Random House, 1997.

Gibbs, Lois Marie, and the Citizens Clearinghouse for Hazardous Waste (now the Center for Health, Environment and Justice). *Dying from Dioxin.* Boston: South End Press, 1995.

Joneja, Janice Vickerstaff, Ph.D., and Leonard Bielory, M.D. *Understanding Allergy, Sensitivity, and Immunity.* New Brunswick, NJ: Rutgers University Press, 1990.

Kenet, Barney J., and Patricia Lawler. *Saving Your Skin.* New York: Four Walls Eight Windows, 1998.

Kimball, Andrew, ed. *Fatal Harvest: The Tragedy of Industrial Agriculture.* Washington: Foundation for Deep Ecology and Island Press, 2002.

Lawson, Lynn. *Staying Well in a Toxic World.* Evanston, IL: Lynnword Press, 1993.

Love, Susan M., M.D., with Karen Lindsey. *Dr. Susan Love's Breast Book.* Cambridge, MA: Perseus Book Group, 2000.

McGinn, Kerry Anne, R.N., B.S.N., O.C.N. *The Informed Woman's Guide to Breast Health, Breast Changes That Are Not Cancer.* Palo Alto, CA.: Bull Publishing Company, 2001.

Mills, Dian Shepperson, M.A., and Michael Vernon, Ph.D. *Endometriosis: A Key to Healing Through Nutrition.* Boston: Element Books Limited, 1999. This book is available from the Endometriosis Association.

Needleman, Herbert L., M.D., and Philip J. Landrigan, M.D. *Raising Children Toxic Free.* New York: Farrar, Straus and Giroux, 1994.

Pitchford, Paul. *Healing with Whole Foods: Oriental Traditions and Modern Nutrition.* Berkeley, CA.: North Atlantic Books, 2000.

Piver, M. Steven, M.D. *Gilda's Disease: Sharing Personal Experiences and a Medical Perspective on Ovarian Cancer.* Amherst, MA: Prometheus Books, 1996.

Poole, Catherine M., with DuPont Guerry IV, M.D. *Melanoma Prevention, Detection and Treatment.* New Haven, CT.: Yale University Press, 1998.

Rapp, Doris J., M.D. *Is This Your Child's World?* New York: Bantam Books, 1996.

Rogers, Sherry A., M.D. *The E.I. Syndrome: An Rx for Environmental Illness.* Syracuse, NY: Prestige Publishing, 1986.

Sears, Barry, Ph.D. *The Zone.* New York: Harper Collins, 1995.

Smith, Gregory White, and Steven Naifeh. *Making Miracles Happen.* Boston: Little, Brown and Company, 1997.

Steingraber, Sandra. *Living Downstream: An Ecologist Looks at Cancer and the Environment.* Cambridge, MA.: Perseus Publishing, 1997.

Stevens, Laura. *The Complete Book of Allergy Control.* New York: Macmillan Publishing Co., 1983.

Tilberis, Liz. *No Time to Die.* Boston: Little, Brown and Company, 1998.

Truss, C. Orian, M.D. *The Missing Diagnosis.* Birmingham, AL.: The Missing Diagnosis, Inc., 1983.

Turiel, Judith Steinberg. *Beyond Second Opinions.* Berkeley: University of California Press, 1998.

Booklets, Magazines, and Newsletters

Allergy Alert. P.O. Box 31065, Seattle, WA 98103; phone 206-547-1814.

Allergy Hotline. Hotline Printing and Publishing, P.O. Box 161132, Altamont Springs, FL 32616.

Conversations! The Newsletter for Those Fighting Ovarian Cancer. c/o Cindy Melancon, P.O. Box 7948, Amarillo, TX 79114-7948; phone 806-355-2565; fax 806-467-9757; E-mail CHMelancon@aol.com.

Crandall, Marjorie, Ph.D. *How to Prevent Yeast Infections.* Yeast Consulting Services, P.O. Box 11157, Torrance, CA 90510-1157; phone 310-375-1073.

Create a Dust-Free Bedroom. 9000 Rockville Pike, Bldg. 31, No. 7A50, Bethesda, MD 20892.

Greater Boston Physicians for Social Responsibility. *In Harm's Way: Toxic Threats to Child Development.* Cambridge, MA: Greater Boston Physicians for Social Responsibility, 2000.

Mastering Food Allergies. 2615 N. 4th St., #616, Coeur d'Alene, ID 83814. For information about newsletter, send a long SASE.

National Cancer Institute (NCI). "Taking Time: Support for People with Cancer and the People Who Care About Them" and "Understanding Breast Changes: A Health Guide for All Women" (1988).

National Cancer Institute (NCI). "What You Need to Know About Non-Hodgkin's Lymphoma" (June 1999). To order copies of this free booklet in the United States, call 800-4-CANCER, or access the NCI online at www.cancer.gov.

NEEDS/National Ecological and Environmental Delivery System, 527 Charles Avenue 12A, Syracuse, NY 13209; phone 800-634-1380.

Schindler, L. "Understanding the Immune System." Bethesda, MD: National Institutes of Health, 1993.

Schindler, L. "The Immune System—How It Works." Bethesda, MD: National Institutes of Health, 1992.

Audio and Video Recordings

Helfand, Judith, and Daniel B. Gold. *Blue Vinyl* (2002). Videocassette. Order from Toxic Comedy Pictures, P.O. Box 1084, Harriman, NY 10926; 845-774-7335 (toll-free, 800-343-5540); or visit bluevinyl.org and myhouseisyourhouse.org.

Mabray, Richard, Arnold Kresch, and Wayne Konetzki. *Immune Therapy for Endometriosis: The Newest Treatment Frontier*, Tape #103, Endometriosis Association 15th Anniversary Conference Audiotapes. Milwaukee, WI: Endometriosis Association, 1995. Audiotape. Available from Association headquarters.

Rea, William, M.D. *The Relationship of Endometriosis and Chemicals*, Tape #205, Endometriosis Association 20th Anniversary Conference Audiotapes. Milwaukee, WI: Endometriosis Association, 2001. Audiotape. Available from Association headquarters.

Zukerman, Francine, and Martha Butterfield, producers. *Exposure: Environmental Links to Breast Cancer*. Unapiz/Miramar, 1998. Videotape. Order from Unapiz/Miramar, 206-284-4700 or miramarupx.com.

References

Chapter 1

1. G. Arason and A. Luciano, "Laparoscopy Versus Laparotomy in the Treatment of Endometriosis," in *Endometriosis: Advanced Management and Surgical Techniques*, edited by C. R. Nezhat, G. S. Berger, F. R. Nezhat, et al. (New York: Springer-Verlag, 1994), pp. 201–206.

2. C. Cleeland, "Pain and Its Treatment in Outpatients with Metastatic Cancer," *New England Journal of Medicine* 330 (1994): pp. 592–596.

3. D. Redwine, "Treatment of Endometriosis-Associated Pain," *Infertility and Reproductive Medicine Clinics of North America* 3(3) (1992).

4. A. Lipman, "Undertreatment of Pain," *Fibromyalgia Network* (April 2002).

5. M. Brown, "Finding the Help You Need: Is Anybody Out There?" *Pain Community News* (Summer 2002).

6. M. Y. Dawood, "Prostaglandin Metabolites in Peritoneal Fluid in Women with and Without Endometriosis," in *Endometrium and Endometriosis*, edited by M. Diamond and K. Osteen (Malden, MA: Blackwell Science, 2002).

7. L. Muzzi, "Correlation Between Endometriosis-Associated Dysmenorrhea and the Presence of Typical or Atypical Lesions," *Fertility and Sterility* 68(1).

8. S. Badawy, L. Marshall, A. Garbal, et. al., "The Concentration of 13, 14-dihydro-15 Keto Prostaglandin F Alpha and Prostaglandin E in Peritoneal Fluid of Infertile Patients with and Without Endometriosis," *Fertility and Sterility* 38 (1982): pp. 166–170.

9. B. Basbaum and M. Bushnell, "Pain: Basic Mechanisms," in *Pain: An Updated Review*, edited by Maria Adele Giamberardino (Seattle, WA: IASP, 2002).

10. A. Copperman and D. Olive, "Pathogenesis of Pelvic Pain in Endometriosis," in *Endometriosis: Advanced Management and Surgical Technique*, edited by C. R. Nezhat, G. S. Berger, F. R. Nezhat, et al. (New York: Springer-Verlag, 1995).

11. D. Stoval, "Endometriosis-Associated Pelvic Pain: Evidence for an Association Between the State of Disease and a History of Chronic Pelvic Pain," *Fertility and Sterility* 68(1).

12. N. Petersen and D. Redwine, "Psycho-Social Issues for Women with Endometriosis," *Women's Health Forum* (May 1993).

13. C. Avery, "The Stigma of Chronic Pain," in *The Endometriosis Sourcebook*, edited by Mary Lou Ballweg (Chicago: Contemporary Books, 1995).

14. N. Sinaii, S. Cleary, M. L. Ballweg, L. Nieman, P. Stratton, et al., "Autoimmune Inflammatory

Diseases, Endocrine Disorders, Fibromyalgia and Chronic Fatigue Syndrome, and Atopic Diseases Among Women with Endometriosis: A Survey Analysis," *Human Reproduction* 17(10) (2002): pp. 2715–2724.

15. K. Armitage, L. Schneiderman, R. Bass, et al., "Response of Physicians to Medical Complaints in Men and Women," *Journal of the American Medical Association* 241 (1979): pp. 2,186–2,187.

16. K. Brune, "Non-Opioid (Antipyretic) Analgesics," in *Pain: An Updated Review*, edited by Maria Adele Giamberardino (Seattle: IASP Press, 2002).

17. N. Wartik, "Hurting More, Helped Less," *New York Times* (June 23, 2002).

18. S. Spitz, "Diagnostic Dilemma: Learning to Look and Listen," *Science for the People* (July/August 1997).

19. E. Catalano, *The Chronic Pain Control Workbook* (Oakland, CA: New Harbinger Press, 1987).

20. P. Doyle-Gordon, "Pain Medications for Endometriosis," Chapter 2 in *Overcoming Endometriosis*, edited by M. L. Ballweg and the Endometriosis Association (New York: Congdon & Weed, 1987), pp. 20–29.

21. K. Hurlbutt "Report on Pain Management in Women with Endometriosis," Chapter 20 in *Overcoming Endometriosis*, edited by M. L. Ballweg and the Endometriosis Association (New York: Congdon & Weed, 1987), pp. 268–271.

Chapter 2

1. D. L. Olive, E. A. Pritts, and A. J. Morales, "Evidence Based Medicine: Study Design for Evaluation and Treatment," *Journal of the American Association of Gynecologic Laparoscopy* 5 (1998): pp. 75–82.

2. E. G. Hughes, "Systematic Literature Review and Meta-Analysis," *Seminars in Reproductive Endocrinology* 14 (1996): pp. 161–169.

3. I. D. Cooke and E. J. Thomas, "The Medical Treatment of Mild Endometriosis," *Acta Obstetricia et Gynecologica Scandinavica* 150 Suppl. (1989): p. 27.

4. T. M. D'Hooghe, C. S. Bambra, M. Isahakia, et al., "Evolution of Spontaneous Endometriosis in the Baboon (*Papio anubis, Papio cynocephalus*) over a 12- Month Period," *Fertility and Sterility* 58 (1992): p. 409.

5. G. Jones, S. Kennedy, A. Barnard, et al., "Development of an Endometriosis Quality of Life Instrument: The Endometriosis Health Profile 30," *Obstetrics and Gynecology* 98 (2001): pp. 258–264.

6. A. Kauppila, J. Puolakka, and O. Ylikorkala, "Prostaglandin Biosynthesis Inhibitors and Endometriosis," *Prostaglandins* 18 (1979): p. 655.

7. D. L. Olive and A. F. Haney, "Endometriosis Associated Infertility: A Critical Review of Therapeutic Approaches," *Obstetrics and Gynecology Survey* 41 (1986): p. 538.

8. R. Goebel and H. K. Rjosk, "Laboratory and Clinical Studies with the New Antigonadotropin, Danazol," *Acta Endocrinology* 85 Suppl. 212 (1977): p. 134.

9. W. S. Floyd, "Danazol: Endocrine and Endometrial Effects," *International Journal of Fertility* 25 (1980): pp. 75–80.

10. R. L. Barbieri, J. A. Canick, A. Makris, et al., "Danazol Inhibits Steroidogenesis," *Fertility and Sterility* 28 (1977): pp. 809–813.

11. R. McGinley and J. H. Casey, "Analysis of Progesterone in Unextracted Serum: A Method Using Danazol [17 α-pregn-4-en 20 yno (2,3-

d) osoxazol-17-ol], a Blocker of Steroid Binding to Proteins," *Steroids* 33 (1979): pp. 127–138.

12. V. C. Buttram Jr., J. B. Belue, and R. Reiter, "Interim Report of a Study of Danazol for the Treatment of Endometriosis," *Fertility and Sterility* 37 (1982): pp. 478–483.

13. R. G. Alvarado, J. Y. Liu, and R. M. Zwolak, "Danazol and Limb Threatening Arterial Thrombosis: Two Case Reports," *Journal of Vascular Surgery* 34 (2001): pp. 1,123–1,126.

14. P. Vercellini, L. Tresid, S. Panazza, et al., "Very Low Dose Danazol for Relief of Endometriosis Associated Pelvic Pain: A Pilot Study," *Fertility and Sterility* 62 (1994): pp. 1,136–1,142.

15. T. I. Janicki, "Treatment of the Pelvic Pain Associated with Endometriosis Using Danazol Vaginal Suppositories. Two Year Follow-Up," *Fertility and Sterility* 77 (2002): p. S52.

16. M. Igarashi, M. Iizuka, Y. Abe, et al., "Novel Vaginal Danazol Ring Therapy for Pelvic Endometriosis, in Particular Deeply Infiltrating Endometriosis," *Human Reproduction* 13 (1998): pp. 1,952–1,956.

17. W. P. Dmowski and M. R. Cohen, "Treatment of Endometriosis with an Antigonadotropin, Danazol: A Laparoscopic and Histologic Evaluation," *Obstetrics and Gynecology* 46 (1975): p. 147.

18. R. L. Barbieri, S. Evans, and R. W. Kistner, "Danazol in the Treatment of Endometriosis: Analysis of 100 Cases with a 4-Year Follow-Up," *Fertility and Sterility* 37 (1982): p. 737.

19. A. Doberl, S. Jeppsson, and G. Rannevik, "Effect of Danazol on Serum Concentrations of Pituitary Gonadotropins in Postmenopausal Women," *Acta Obstetricia et Gynecologica Scandinavica* 123 Suppl. (1984): p. 95.

20. V. C. Buttram Jr., R. C. Reiter, and S. Ward, "Treatment of Endometriosis with Danazol: Report of a Six-Year Prospective Study," *Fertility and Sterility* 318 (1985): p. 485.

21. M. R. Henzl, S. L. Corson, K. Moghissi, et al., "Administration of Nasal Nafarelin as Compared with Oral Danazol for Endometriosis," *New England Journal of Medicine* 318 (1988): p. 485.

22. S. Telimaa, J. Puolakka, and L. Ronnberg, et al., "Placebo Controlled Comparison of Danazol and High Dose Medroxyprogesterone Acetate in the Treatment of Endometriosis," *Gynecological Endocrinology* 1 (1987): p. 13.

23. S. R. Bayer and M. M. Seibel, "Medical Treatment: Danazol," in *Endometriosis: Contemporary Concepts in Clinical Management*, edited by R. S. Schenken (Philadelphia, PA: J. B. Lippincott, 1989), pp. 169–187.

24. J. D. Miller, R. W. Shaw, R. F. Casper, et al., "Historical Prospective Cohort Study of the Recurrence of Pain After Discontinuation of Treatment with Danazol or a Gonadotropin Releasing Hormone Agonist," *Fertility and Sterility* 70 (1998): pp. 293–296.

25. S. R. Bayer, M. M. Seibel, D. S. Saffan, et al., "Efficacy of Danazol Treatment for Minimal Endometriosis in Infertile Women: A Prospective, Randomized Study," *Journal of Reproductive Medicine* 33 (1988): pp. 179–183.

26. S. Telimaa, "Danazol and Medroxyprogesterone Acetate Inefficacious in the Treatment of Infertility in Endometriosis," *Fertility and Sterility* 50 (1988): pp. 872–875.

27. K. L. Bruner, E. Eisenberg, F. Gorstein, et al., "Progesterone and Transforming Growth Factor Beta Coordinately Regulate Suppression of Endometrial Matrix Metalloproteinases in a Model of Experimental Endometriosis," *Steroids* 64 (1999): pp. 648–653.

28. D. L. Olive, "Medical Treatment: Alternatives to Danazol," in *Endometriosis: Contemporary Concepts in Clinical Management*, edited by R. S. Schenken (Philadelphia, PA: J. B. Lippincott, 1989), pp. 189–211.

29. O. Muneyyirci Delale and M. Karacan, "Effect of Norethindrone Acetate in the Treatment of Symptomatic Endometriosis," *International Journal of Fertility and Women's Medicine* 43 (1999): p. 24.

30. L. Fedele, S. Bianchi, G. Zanconato, et al., "Use of a Levonorgestrel Releasing Intrauterine Device in the Treatment of Rectovaginal Endometriosis," *Fertility and Sterility* 75 (2001): pp. 485–488.

31. T. M. Lau, B. Affandi, and P. A. W. Rogers, "The Effects of Levonorgestrel Implants on Vascular Endothelial Growth Factor Expression in the Endometrium," *Molecular Human Reproduction* 5 (1998): pp. 57–63.

32. E. C. Hamblen, "Androgen Treatment of Women," *Southern Medical Journal* 50 (1957): p. 743.

33. E. Hirvonen, M. Malkonen, and V. Manninen, "Effects of Different Progestogens on Lipoproteins During Postmenopausal Replacement Therapy," *New England Journal of Medicine* 304 (1981): p. 560.

34. L. Fahraeus, A. Sydsjo, and L. Wallentin, "Lipoprotein Changes During Treatment of Pelvic Endometriosis with Medroxyprogesterone Acetate," *Fertility and Sterility* 45 (1986): p. 503.

35. S. Telimaa, J. Puolakka, L. Ronnberg, et al., "Placebo Controlled Comparison of Danazol and High Dose Medroxyprogesterone Acetate in the Treatment of Endometriosis," *Gynecological Endocrinology* 1 (1987): p. 13.

36. P. A. Regidor, M. Regidor, M. Schmidt, et al., "Prospective Randomized Study Comparing the GnRH Agonist Leuprorelin Acetate and the Gestagen Lynestrenol in the Treatment of Severe Endometriosis," *Gynecological Endocrinology* 15 (2001): pp. 202–209.

37. R. F. Harrison and C. Barry-Kinsella, "Efficacy of Medroxyprogesterone Treatment in Infertile Women with Endometriosis: A Prospective, Randomized, Placebo Controlled Study," *Fertility and Sterility* 74 (2000): pp. 24–30.

38. M. E. Hull, K. S. Moghissi, D. F. Magyar, et al., "Comparison of Different Treatment Modalities of Endometriosis in Infertile Women," *Fertility and Sterility* 47 (1987): p. 40.

39. M. C. Andrews, W. C. Andrews, and A. F. Strauss, "Effects of Progestin Induced Pseudopregnancy on Endometriosis; Clinical and Microscopic Studies," *American Journal of Obstetrics and Gynecology* 78 (1959): p. 776.

40. R. B. Scott and L. R. Wharton Jr., "The Effect of Estrone and Progesterone on the Growth of Experimental Endometriosis in Rhesus Monkeys," *American Journal of Obstetrics and Gynecology* 74 (1957): p. 852.

41. A. D. Noble and A. T. Letchworth, "Medical Treatment of Endometriosis: A Comparative Trial," *Postgraduate Medical Journal* 55 Suppl. 5 (1979): p. 37.

42. G. F. Meresman, L. Auge, R. I. Baranom, et al., "Oral Contraceptive Treatment Suppresses Proliferation and Enhances Apoptosis of Eutopic Endometrial Tissue from Patients with Endometriosis," *Fertility and Sterility* 76 (2001): pp. S47–S48.

43. P. Vercellini, L. Trespidi, A. Colombo, et al., "A Gonadotropin Releasing Hormone Agonist Versus a Low Dose Oral Contraceptive for Pelvic Pain Associated with Endometriosis," *Fertility and Sterility* 60 (1993): p. 75.

44. G. Frontino, P. Vercellini, O. De Giorgi, et al., "Continuous Use of Oral Contraceptives (OC) for Endometriosis Associated Recurrent Dysmenorrhea Not Responding to Cyclic Pill

Regimen," *Fertility and Sterility* 77 (2002): pp. S23–S24.

45. K. L. Sharpe-Timms, R. L. Zimmer, W. J. Jolliff, et al., "Gonadotropin Releasing Hormone Agonist (GnRH-a) Therapy Alters Activity of Plasminogen Activators, Matrix Metalloproteinases and Their Inhibitors in Rat Models for Adhesion Formation and Endometriosis: Potential GnRH-a Regulated Mechanisms Reducing Adhesion Formation," *Fertility and Sterility* 69 (1998): pp. 916–923.

46. W. P. Dmowski, "The Role of Medical Management in the Treatment of Endometriosis," in *Endometriosis: Advanced Management and Surgical Techniques*, edited by C. R. Nezhat, G. S. Berger, F. R. Nezhat, et al. (New York: Springer-Verlag, 1995), pp. 229–240.

47. R. L. Barbieri, "Endometriosis and the Estrogen Threshold Theory: Relation to Surgical and Medical Treatment," *Journal of Reproductive Medicine* 43 (1998): pp. 287–292.

48. B. S. Hurst, S. C. Gardner, K. E. Tucker, et al., "Delayed Oral Estradiol Combined with Leuprolide Increases Endometriosis Related Pain," *Journal of the Society of Laparoendoscopic Surgeons* 4 (2000): pp. 97–101.

49. A. M. Dlugi, J. D. Miller, and J. Knittle, "Lupron Depot (Leuprolide Acetate for Depot Suspension) in the Treatment of Endometriosis: A Randomized, Placebo Controlled, Double Blind Study," *Fertility and Sterility* (1990): pp. 419–427.

50. "Goserelin Depot Versus Danazol in the Treatment of Endometriosis: The Australian/New Zealand Experience," *Australian and New Zealand Journal of Obstetrics and Gynecology* 31 (1996): pp. 55–60.

51. S. P. Chang, H. T. Ng, "A Randomized Comparative Study of the Effect of Leuprorelin Acetate Depot and Danazol in the Treatment of Endometriosis," *Chinese Medical Journal (Taipei)* 57 (1996): pp. 431–437.

52. U. Cirkel, H. Ochs, and H. P. G. Schneider, "A Randomized, Comparative Trial of Triptorelin Depot (D-Trp6-LHRH) and Danazol in the Treatment of Endometriosis," *European Journal of Obstetrics and Gynecology Reproductive Biology* 59 (1995): pp. 61–69.

53. P. G. Crosignani, A. Gastaldi, P. L. Lombardi , et al., "Leuprorelin Acetate Depot Versus Danazol in the Treatment of Endometriosis: Results of an Open Multicentre Trial," *Clinical Therapeutics* 1(4) Suppl. A (1992): pp. 29–36.

54. W. P. Dmowski, E. Radwanska, Z. Binor, et al., "Ovarian Suppression Induced with Buserelin or Danazol in the Management of Endometriosis: A Randomized, Comparative Study," *Fertility and Sterility* 51 (1989): pp. 395–400.

55. I. S. Fraser, R. P. Shearman, R. P. Jansen, et al., "A Comparative Treatment Trial of Endometriosis Using the Gonadotropin Releasing Hormone Agonist, Nafarelin, and the Synthetic Steroid, Danazol," *Australian and New Zealand Journal of Obstetrics and Gynecology* (1991): pp. 158–163.

56. G. D. Adamson, L. Kwei, and R. A. Edgren, "Pain of Endometriosis: Effects of Nafarelin and Danazol Therapy," *International Journal of Fertility and Medical Studies* 39 (1994): pp. 215–217.

57. J. M. Wheeler, J. D. Knittle, and J. D. Miller, "Depot Leuprolide Versus Danazol in Treatment of Women with Symptomatic Endometriosis: Efficacy Results," *American Journal of Obstetrics and Gynecology* 167 (1992): pp. 1,367–1,371.

58. M. Y. Dawood, J. Ramos, and F. S. Khan-Dawood, "Depot Luprolide Acetate Versus Danazol for Treatment of Pelvic Endometriosis: Changes in Vertebral Bone Mass and Serum Estradiol and Calcitonin," *Fertility and Sterility* 63 (1995): pp. 1,177–1,183.

59. Nafarelin European Endometriosis Trial Group (NEET), "Nafarelin for Endometriosis: A Large Scale, Danazol Controlled Trial of Efficacy and Safety, with One Year Follow-Up," *Fertility and Sterility* 57 (1992): pp. 514–522.

60. R. Rolland and P. F. van der Heijden, "Nafarelin Versus Danazol in the Treatment of Endometriosis," *American Journal of Obstetrics and Gynecology* 162 (1990): pp. 586–588.

61. S. H. Kennedy, I. A. Williams, J. Brodribb, et al., "A Comparison of Nafarelin Acetate and Danazol in the Treatment of Endometriosis," *Fertility and Sterility* 53 (1990): pp. 998–1,003.

62. J. A. Rock, "A Multicenter Comparison of GnRH Agonist (Zoladex) and Danazol in the Treatment of Endometriosis," *Fertility and Sterility* 56 (1991): p. S49.

63. R. W. Shaw, "An Open Randomized Comparative Study of the Effect of Goserelin Depot and Danazol in the Treatment of Endometriosis. Zoladex Endometriosis Study Team," *Fertility and Sterility* 58 (1992): pp. 265–272.

64. A. Prentice, A. Deery, S. Goldbeck-Wood, et al., "Gonadotropin Releasing Hormone Analogues for Pain Associated with Endometriosis (Cochrane Review)," in *The Cochrane Library*, Issue 3 (Oxford: Update Software, 1999).

65. F. W. Ling "Randomized Controlled Trial of Depot Leuprolide in Patients with Chronic Pelvic Pain and Clinically Suspected Endometriosis," *Obstetrics and Gynecology* 93 (1999): pp. 51–58.

66. E. Surrey and H. Judd, "Reduction of Vasomotor Symptoms and Bone Mineral Density Loss with Combined Norethindrone and Long Acting Gonadotropin Releasing Hormone Agonist Therapy of Symptomatic Endometriosis: A Prospective Randomized Trial," *Journal of Clinical Endocrinology and Metabolism* 75 (1992): pp. 558–563.

67. L. Makarainen, L. Ronneberg, and A. Kauppila, "Medroxyprogesterone Acetate Supplementation Diminishes the Hypo Estrogenic Side Effects of Gonadotropin Releasing Hormone Agonists Without Changing Its Efficacy in Endometriosis," *Fertility and Sterility* 65 (1996): pp. 29–34.

68. O. Tabkin, A. H. Yakinoghe, S. Kucuk, et al., "Effectiveness of Tibolone on Hypoestrogenic Symptoms Induced by Goserelin Treatment in Patients with Endometriosis," *Fertility and Sterility* 67 (1997): pp. 40–45.

69. D. Edmonds and R. Howell, "Can Hormone Replacement Therapy Be Used During Medical Therapy of Endometriosis?" *British Journal of Obstetrics and Gynaecology* 101 (1994): pp. 24–26.

70. P. Kiiholma, M. Korhonen, R. Tuimala, et al., "Comparison of the Gonadotropin Releasing Hormone Agonist Goserelin Acetate Alone Versus Goserelin Combined with Estrogen Progestogen Addback Therapy in the Treatment of Endometriosis," *Fertility and Sterility* 64 (1995): pp. 903–908.

71. K. S. Moghissi, W. D. Schlaff, D. L. Olive, et al., "Goserelin Acetate (Zoladex) with or Without Hormone Replacement Therapy for the Treatment of Endometriosis," *Fertility and Sterility* 69 (1998): pp. 1,056–1,062.

72. E. S. Surrey, B. Voigt, N. Fournet, et al., "Prolonged Gonadotropin Releasing Hormone Agonist Treatment of Symptomatic Endometriosis: The Role of Cyclic Sodium

Etidronate and Low Dose Norethindrone 'Addback' Therapy," *Fertility and Sterility* 63 (1995): pp. 747–755.

73. M. D. Hornstein, E. S. Surrey, G. W. Weisberg, et al. (Lupron Add Back Study Group), "Leuprolide Acetate Depot and Hormonal Addback in Endometriosis: A 12 Month Study," *Obstetrics and Gynecology* 91 (1998): pp. 16–24.

74. P. I. Lee, J. B. Yoon, K. Y. Joo, et al., "Gonadotropin Releasing Hormone Agonist (GnRH-a) Zoladex (Goserelin) and Hormonal Addback Therapy in Endometriosis: A 12 Month Study," *Fertility and Sterility* 77 (2002): p. S23.

75. L. Fedele, F. Parazzini, E. Radici, et al., "Buserelin Acetate Versus Expectant Management in the Treatment of Infertility Associated with Minimal or Mild Endometriosis: A Randomized Clinical Trial," *American Journal of Obstetrics and Gynecology* 166 (1992): pp. 1,345–1,350.

76. F. J. Cornillie, I. A. Brosens, G. Vasquez, et al., "Histologic and Ultrastructural Changes in Human Endometriotic Implants Treated with the Antiprogesterone Steroid Ethylnorgestrinone (Gestrinone) During Two Months," *International Journal of Gynecologic Pathology* 5 (1986): p. 95.

77. C. Robyn, J. Delogne-Desnoeck, P. Bourdoux, et al., "Endocrine Effects of Gestrinone," In *Medical Management of Endometriosis,* edited by J.-P. Raynaud and M. L. Ojasoot (New York: Raven Press, 1984), p. 207.

78. L. Fedele, S. Bianchi , T. Viezzoli, et al., "Gestrinone Versus Danazol in the Treatment of Endometriosis," *Fertility and Sterility* 51 (1989): p. 781.

79. M. Worthington, L. M. Irvine, D. Crook, et al., "A Randomized Comparative Study of the Metabolic Effects of Two Regimens of Gestrinone in the Treatment of Endometriosis," *Fertility and Sterility* 59 (1993): p. 522.

80. M. D. Hornstein, R. E. Gleason, and R. L. Barbieri, "A Randomized Double Blind Prospective Trial of Two Doses of Gestrinone in the Treatment of Endometriosis," *Fertility and Sterility* 53 (1990): p. 237.

81. Gestrinone Italian Study Group, "Gestrinone Versus a Gonadotropin Releasing Hormone Agonist for the Treatment of Pelvic Pain Associated with Endometriosis: A Multicenter Randomized, Double Blind Study," *Fertility and Sterility* 66 (1996): pp. 911–919.

82. E. Thomas and I. Cooke, "Successful Treatment of Asymptomatic Endometriosis: Does It Benefit Infertile Women?" *British Medical Journal* 294 (1987): pp. 1,117–1,119.

83. J. Jiang, R. Wu, Z. Wang, et al., "Effect of Mifepristone on Estrogen and Progesterone Receptors in Human Endometrial and Endometriotic Cells in Vitro," *Fertility and Sterility* 77 (2002): p. 995.

84. B. Tjaden, D. Galetto, J. D. Woodruff, et al., "Time Related Effects of RU486 Treatment in Experimentally Induced Endometriosis in the Rat," *Fertility and Sterility* 59 (1993): p. 437.

85. L. M. Kettel, A. A. Murphy, J. F. Mortola, "Endocrine Responses to Long Term Administration of the Antiprogesterone RU486 in Patients with Pelvic Endometriosis," *Fertility and Sterility* 56 (1991): p. 402.

86. R. C. Jones, "The Effect of a Luteinizing Hormone Releasing Hormone Antagonist on Experimental Endometriosis in the Rat," *Acta Endocrinology* 114 (1987): pp. 379–382.

87. J. M. Woolley, A. M. De Paoli, M. E. Gray, et al., "Reductions in Health Related Quality of Life in Women with Endometriosis (Abstract)" (presentation at the Seventh Biennial World

Congress on Endometriosis, London, May 14–17, 2000).

88. S. E. Bulun, K. M. Zeitoun, K. Takayama, et al., "Molecular Basis for Treating Endometriosis with Aromatase Inhibitors," *Human Reproduction Update* 6 (2000): pp. 413–418.

89. S. Yano, Y. Ikegami, and K. Nakao, "Studies on the Effect of the New Non Steroidal Aromatase Inhibitor Fadrozole Hydrochloride in an Endometriosis Model in Rats," *Arzneimittelforschung* 46 (1996): pp. 192–195.

90. T. M. D'Hooghe, S. Cuneo, N. Nugent, et al., "Recombinant Human TNF Binding Protein-1 (r-hTBP-1) Inhibits the Development of Endometriosis in Baboons: A Prospective, Randomized, Placebo and Drug Controlled Study," *Fertility and Sterility* 76 (2001): p. S1.

91. J. Donnez, P. Smoes, S. Gillerot, et al., "Vascular Endothelial Growth Factor (VEGF) in Endometriosis," *Human Reproduction* 13 (1998): pp. 1,686–1,690.

92. A. Fasciani, G. D'Ambrogio, G. Bocci, et al., "High Concentrations of the Vascular Endothelial Growth Factor and Interleukin-8 in Ovarian Endometriomata," *Molecular Human Reproduction* 6 (2000): pp. 50–54.

93. J. L. Mahnke, M. Y. Dawood, J. C. Huang, "Vascular Endothelial Growth Factor and Interleukin-6 in Peritoneal Fluid of Women with Endometriosis," *Fertility and Sterility* 73 (2000): pp. 166–170.

94. E. Barcz, P. Kaminski, and L. Marianowski, "VEGF Concentration in Peritoneal Fluid in Patients with Endometriosis," *Ginekologia Polska* 72 (2001): pp. 442–448.

95. Z. Levine, J. A. Efstathiou, D. A. Sampson, et al., "Angiogenesis Inhibitors Suppress Endometriosis in a Murine Model," *Journal of the Society of Gynecologic Investigation* 9 (2002): p. 264.

96. T. Mori, S. Yamasaki, F. Masui, et al., "Suppression of the Development of Experimentally Induced Uterine Adenomyosis by a Novel Matrix Metalloproteinase Inhibitor, ONO-4817, in Mice," *Experimental Biological Medicine* 226 (2001): pp. 429–433.

97. A. Audebert, P. Descampes, and H. Marret, "Pre or Postoperative Medical Treatment with Nafarelin in Stage III–IV Endometriosis: A French Multicentered Study," *European Journal of Obstetrics, Gynecology and Reproductive Biology* 79 (1998): pp. 145–148.

98. S. Bianchi, M. Busacca, and B. Agnoli, "Effects of Three Month Therapy with Danazol After Laparoscopic Surgery for Stage III–IV Endometriosis: A Randomized Study," *Human Reproduction* 14 (1999): pp. 1,335–1,337.

99. S. Telimaa, L. Ronnberg, and A. Kauppila, "Placebo Controlled Comparison of Danazol and High Dose Medroxyprogesterone Acetate in the Treatment of Endometriosis After Conservative Surgery," *Gynecological Endocrinology* 1 (1987): pp. 363–371.

100. F. Parazzini, L. Fedele, M. Busacca, et al., "Postsurgical Medical Treatment of Advanced Endometriosis: Results of a Randomized Clinical Trial," *American Journal of Obstetrics and Gynecology* 171 (1994): pp. 1,205–1,207.

101. M. D. Hornstein, R. Hemmings, A. A. Yuzpe, et al., "Use of Nafarelin Versus Placebo After Reductive Laparoscopic Surgery for Endometriosis," *Fertility and Sterility* 68 (1997): pp. 860–864.

102. P. Vercellini, P. G. Crosignani, R. Fedini, "A Gonadotropin Releasing Hormone Agonist Compared with Expectant Management After Conservative Surgery for Symptomatic Endometriosis," *British Journal of Obstetrics and Gynaecology* 106 (1999): pp. 672–677.

103. L. Muzii, R. Marana, P. Caruana, et al., "Postoperative Administration of Monophasic Combined Oral Contraceptives After Laparoscopic Treatment of Ovarian Endometriomas: A Prospective, Randomized Trial," *American Journal of Obstetrics and Gynecology* 183 (2000): pp. 588–592.

104. G. Frontino, P. Vercellini, O. DeGiorgi, et al., "Levonorgesterel Releasing Intrauterine Device (Lng-IUD) Versus Expectant Management After Conservative Surgery for Symptomatic Endometriosis. A Pilot Study," *Fertility and Sterility* 77 (2002): pp. S25–S26.

105. G. Morgante, A. Ditto, A. LaMarca, et al., "Low Dose Danazol After Combined Surgical and Medical Therapy Reduces the Incidence of Pelvic Pain in Women with Moderate and Severe Endometriosis," *Human Reproduction* 14 (1999): pp. 2,371–2,374.

106. L. Alvarez-Gil and V. Fuentes, "Raloxifene and Endometriosis," *Fertility and Sterility* 77 (2002): p. S37.

Chapter 3

1. P. Crosignani and P. Vercellini, "Conservative Surgery for Severe Endometriosis: Should Laparotomy Be Abandoned Definitively?" *Human Reproduction*, 10(9) (1995): pp. 2,412–2,418.

2. J. Blythe, "Back to the Future: Values and Consequences in Gynecologic Surgery Training," *American Journal of Obstetrics and Gynecology*, 177(6) (1997): pp. 1,293–1,297.

3. J. Rosser Jr., L. Rosser, et al., "Objective Evaluation of a Laparoscopic Surgical Skill Program for Residents and Senior Surgeons," *Archives of Surgery* 133 (1998): pp. 657–661.

4. J. Hulka and H. Reich, *Textbook of Laparoscopy*, 3rd ed. (Philadelphia, PA: W. B. Saunders Co., 1998), pp. 121–125.

5. R. Azziz, "Operative Endoscopy: The Pressing Need for a Structured Training and Credentialing Process," *Fertility and Sterility* 58(6) (1992): pp. 1,100–1,102.

6. AAGL Board of Trustees, "Credentialing Guidelines for Operative Endoscopy," American Association of Gynecologic Laparoscopists, formally adopted at meeting of September 23–27, 1992.

7. Joint Commission on Accreditation of Healthcare Organizations, *CAMH Refreshed Core, January 2001, MS-7–MS-12.*

8. C. J. Levinson, "Credentialing in the United States." *Journal of the American Association of Gynecologic Laparoscopists* 2(4) Suppl. (August 1995): p. S26.

9. A. Luciano, "A System of Credentialing Physicians in Advanced Gynecologic Endoscopy," *Journal of the American Association of Gynecologic Laparoscopists* 8(2) (May 2001): pp. 176–178.

10. H. Nieburh et al., "Laparoscopic Surgery: Mistakes and Risks When the Method Is Introduced," *Surgical Endoscopy* 7 (1993): pp. 412–415.

11. T. Russell, "Statement of the American College of Surgeons to the Quality Interagency Coordination Task Force for the National Summit on Medical Errors and Patient Safety Research," September 11, 2000.

Chapter 4

1. K. Lamb and T. R. Nichols, "Endometriosis: A Comparison of Associated Disease Histories," *American Journal of Preventative Medicine* 2(6) (1986): pp. 324–329.

2. T. R. Nichols, K. Lamb, and J. A. Arkins, "The Association of Atopic Diseases with Endometriosis," *Annals of Allergy* 59(11) (1987): pp. 360–363.

3. C. R. Mabray, "Obstetrics and Gynecology and Clinical Ecology (Part I)," *Clinical Ecology* 1(2) (1982–83): pp. 103–113.

4. M. Han, L. Pan, B. Wu, et al., "A Case-Control Epidemiologic Study of Endometriosis," *Chinese Medical Science Journal* 9(2) (June 1994): pp. 114–118.

5. V. P. Baskokov and V. N. Latysh, "Increased Sensitivity to Drugs and Endometriosis," *Akusherstvo; Ginekologia* 2 (1989): pp. 55–58.

6. R. Desowitz, *The Thorn in the Starfish: The Immune System and How It Works* (New York: W. W. Norton, 1988), pp. 14–15.

7. J. Joneja and L. Bielory, *Understanding Allergy, Sensitivity & Immunity* (New Brunswick and London: Rutgers University Press, 1990).

8. L. Schindler, "Understanding the Immune System" (Washington, DC: National Institutes of Health, 1993).

9. F. S. Goulart, "Allergies," *Milwaukee Journal,* October 6, 1986, pp. D1–D2.

10. Joneja and Bielory, *Understanding Allergy, Sensitivity & Immunity,* pp. 121, 135.

11. Joneja and Bielory, *Understanding Allergy, Sensitivity & Immunity,* pp. 124–125.

12. Joneja and Bielory, *Understanding Allergy, Sensitivity & Immunity,* p. 121.

13. *Newsletter of The Environmental Medicine Foundation,* Spring 1992.

14. *Human Ecologist* (Winter 1993), p. 21.

15. *Family Practice News* (March 1–14, 1987).

16. Health Studies Collegium, *Information Handbook for Use with Your Immune Enhancements Program* (Sterling, VA: Serammune Physicians Lab, 1993).

17. "Indoor Allergens Endanger Health," *Environmental Health Perspectives* 101(4) (September 1993): p. 286 (reporting a National Academy of Sciences, Institutes of Medicine Report).

18. Z. Blumenfeld, "Menstrual Asthma: Use of Gonadotropin-Releasing Hormone Analogue for the Treatment of Cyclic Aggravation of Bronchial Asthma," *Fertility and Sterility* 62(1) (1994): pp. 197–200.

19. J. Salvaggio, "Allergists, Immunologists Urged to Unite Societies," *Skin & Allergy News* 17(6) (June 1986): p. 3.

20. T. Morris, "Family Ordeal: Boy's Stubborn Allergies Affected an Entire Household," *Milwaukee Journal* (January 5, 1987): pp. D1–D2.

21. W. G. Crook, *The Yeast Connection and the Woman* (Jackson, TN: Professional Books, 1995), p. 498 (citing J. Brostoff and S. J. Challacombe).

22. Crook, *The Yeast Connection and the Woman,* p. 491.

23. M. L. Ballweg, "It's All in Your Head," *The Endometriosis Sourcebook* (Chicago: Contemporary Books, 1995), pp. 295–314.

24. T. Guilford, "The Yeast-Human Interaction" (presentation at the Yeast-Human Interaction 1985 Conference, San Francisco, CA, 1985).

25. M. Crandall, "Allergic Predisposition in Recurrent Vulvovaginal Candidiasis," *Journal of Advancement in Medicine* 4(1) (1991): p. 28.

26. D. J. Beer and R. E. Rocklin, "Histamine-Induced Suppressor-Cell Activity," *Journal of Clinical Immunology* 73 (1984): pp. 439–451.

27. T. Ruzick and J. Ring, "Enhanced Releasability of Prostaglandin E2 and Leukotrienes B4 and C4 from Leukocytes of Patients with Atopic Eczema," *Acta Dermato-Venereologica* 67 (1987): pp. 469–475.

28. C. Jessop, "Clinical Features and Possible Etiology of CFIDS, Chronic Fatigue, and Immune Dysfunction Syndrome: Unravelling the Mystery" (presentation at the CFIDS Association of America Conference, Charlotte, NC, November 18, 1990). *Summary: The CFIDS Chronicle* (Spring 1991): pp. 70–73.

29. M. L. Ballweg, "Fibromyalgia/Endo Link?" *Endometriosis Association Newsletter* 12(3) (1991): pp. 6–8.

30. S. Mathur, M. R. Peress, H. O. Williamson, et al., "Autoimmunity to Endometrium and Ovary in Endometriosis," *Clinical and Experimental Immunology* 50 (1982): pp. 259–266.

31. N. Gleicher, A. El-Roeiy, E. Confino, et al., "Is Endometriosis an Autoimmune Disease?" *Obstetrics and Gynecology* 70 (1987): p. 115.

32. N. Gleicher, "Endometriosis: A New Approach Is Needed" *Human Reproduction* 7 (6) (1992): pp. 821–824.

33. A. El-Roeiy, W. P. Dmowski, N. Gleicher, et al., "Danazol but Not Gonadotropin-Releasing Hormone Agonist Suppresses Autoantibodies in Endometriosis," *Fertility and Sterility* 50 (1988): pp. 864–871.

34. S. Z. A. Badaway, V. Cuenca, A. Stitzel, et al., "Immune Rosettes of T and B Lymphocytes in Infertile Women with Endometriosis," *Journal of Reproductive Medicine* 32 (1987): p. 194.

35. J. A. Hill, H. M. P. Faris, L. Schiff, et al., "Characterization of Leukocyte Subpopulations in the Peritoneal Fluid of Women with Endometriosis," *Fertility and Sterility* 50 (1988): p. 216.

36. D. S. Cunninghan, K. A. Hansen, and C. C. Coddington, "Changes in T-cell Regulation of Responses to Self Antigens in Women with Pelvic Endometriosis," *Fertility and Sterility* 58(1) (1992): pp. 114–119.

37. E. Winger, "Anti-Endocrine Antibodies in Patients with Candidiasis" (presentation at the Conference on the Yeast-Human Interaction, San Francisco, CA, 1985).

38. C. O. Truss, "Metabolic Abnormalities in Patients with Chronic Candidiasis: The Acetaldehyde Hypothesis," *Journal of Orthmolecular Psychiatry* 13(2) (1983): pp. 66–92.

39. G. F. Kroker, "Chronic Candidiasis and Allergy," in *Food Allergy and Intolerance*, edited by J. Brostoff and S. J. Challacombe (London: Bailliere Tindall, 1987), pp. 850–872.

40. A. V. Jones, M. Shorthouse, P. McLaughlin, et al., "Food Intolerance: A Major Factor in the Pathogenesis of Irritable Bowel Syndrome," *Lancet* 2 (1980): pp. 959–964.

41. C. E. Bayliss, H. K. Bardley, A. V. Jones, et al., "Some Aspects of Colonic Microbial Activity in Irritable Bowel Syndrome," *Lancet* 2 (1980): pp. 1,115–1,117.

42. J. O. Hunter and A. V. Jones, "Studies on the Pathogenesis of Irritable Bowel Syndrome Produced by Food Intolerance," in *The Irritable Bowel Syndrome*, edited by N. W. Read (New York: Grune and Stratton, 1985), pp. 185–190.

43. A. V. Jones, A. J. Wilson, J. O. Hunter, et al., "The Aetiological Role of Antibiotic Prophylaxis with Hysterectomy in Irritable Bowel Syndrome," *Journal of Obstetrics and Gynecology* 5 Supp. 1 (1984): pp. S22–S23.

44. K. Akiyama, Y. Yui, T. Shida, et al., "Relationship Between the Results of Skin, Conjunctiva and Bronchial Provocation Tests and RAST with *Candida Albicans* in Patients with Asthma," *Clinical Allergy II* (1981): pp. 345–351.

45. S. Lanson, "Immune Complexes to Candida Mannan: An Objective Marker of Candida Overgrowth," *Journal of Advancement in Medicine* 10(3) (Fall 1997): pp. 179–186.

46. N. H. Axelson, "Analysis of Human Candida Precipitins by Quantitative Immunoelectro-phoresis: A Model for Analysis of Complex Microbial Antigen-Antibody Systems," *Scandinavica Journal of Immunology* 5 (1976): pp. 177–190.

47. R. D. Nelson, N. Shibata, R. P. Podzorski, et al., "Candida Mannan: Chemistry, Suppression of Cell-Mediated Immunity, and Possible Mechanisms of Action," *Clinical Microbiology* (Rev. 1991): pp. 1–19.

48. W. G. Crook, *Chronic Fatigue Syndrome and the Yeast Connection* (Jackson, TN: Professional Books, 1992), p. 94.

49. J. Goodwin and J. Ceuppen, "Regulation of the Immune Response by Prostaglandin," *Journal of Clinical Immunology* 3 (1983): pp. 295–309.

50. J. E. Domer, "Candida Cell Wall Mannan: A Polysaccharide with Diverse Immunologic Properties," *Critical Reviews in Immunology* 17 (1989): pp. 33–51.

51. A. Kalo-Klein and S. S. Witkin, "Prostaglandin E2 Enhances and Gamma Interferon Inhibits Germ Tube Formation in *Candida Albicans*," *Infection and Immunity* 58 (1990): pp. 260–262.

52. S. Mathur, J. M. Goust, E. O. Harger III, et al., "Immunoglobulin E Anti-Candida Antibodies and Candidiasis," *Infection and Immunity* 18(1) (1997): pp. 257–259.

53. D. J. Beer and R. E. Rocklin, "Histamine-Induced Suppressor-Cell Activity," *Journal of Allergy Clinical and Immunology* 73 (1984): pp. 439–452.

54. S. S. Witkin, A. Kalo-Klein, L. Galland, et al., "Effect of *Candida Albicans* Plus Histamine on Prostaglandin E2 Production by Peripheral Blood Mononuclear Cells from Healthy Women and Women with Recurrent Candidal Vaginitis," *Journal of Infectious Diseases* 164 (1991): pp. 396–399.

55. N. M. Kudelko, "Allergy in Chronic Monilial Vaginitis," *Annals of Allergy* 22 (1971): pp. 594–597.

56. H. J. Palacios, "Hypersensitivity as a Cause of Dermatologic and Vaginal Moniliasis Resistant to Topical Therapy," *Annals of Allergy* 37 (1976): p. 110–13.

57. N. Rosedale and K. Browne, "Hyposensitisation in the Management of Recurring Vaginal Candidiasis," *Annals of Allergy* 43 (1979): pp. 250–252.

58. J. Sclafer, "L'Allergi à *Candida Albicans* (Clinique, Diagnostique et Traitment)," *Semain Hopitale Paris* 33 (1957): pp. 1,330–1,340.

59. P. N. Kasckin, N. A. Krassilnikov, and V. Y. Nikachalov, "Candida Complications After Antibiotic Therapy," *Mycopathologia et Mycologia Applicata* 14 (1961): pp. 173–188.

60. A. Liebeskind, "*Candida Albicans* as an Allergenic Factor," *Annals of Allergy* 20 (1962): pp. 394–396.

61. G. Holti, "Some Skin Hazards and Allergy Problems in Dentistry," *Newcastle Medical Journal* 30 (1969): pp. 245–254.

62. M. Planes, D. Brunet, H. Dalayeun, et al., "Allergi à *Candida Albicans* Chez l'Enfant," *Rev. Franc. Allerg.*

63. W. G. Crook, *Chronic Fatigue Syndrome and the Yeast Connection* (Jackson, TN: Professional Books, 1992), p. 94 (citing S. S. Witkin).

64. M. Das and A. Datta, "Steroid Binding Protein(s) in Yeast," *Biochemistry International* 11 (1985): pp. 171–176.

65. D. S. Loose, D. J. Schurman, and D. Feldman, "A Corticosteroid Binding Protein and

Endogenous Ligand in *Candida Albicans* Indicating a Possible Steroid Receptor System," *Nature* 293: pp. 477–479.

66. D. S. Loose and D. Feldman, "Characterization of a Unique Corticosteroid Binding Protein in *Candida Albicans*," *Journal of Biological Chemistry* 257 (1982): pp. 4,925–4,930.

67. D. S. Loose, D. A. Stevens, D. J. Schurman, et al., "Distribution of a Corticosteroid Binding Protein in *Candida* and Other Fungal Genera," *Journal of General Microbiology* 129: pp. 2,379–2,385.

68. B. L. Powell and D. J. Drutz, "Confirmation of Corticosterone and Progesterone Binding Activity in *Candida Albicans*," *Journal of Infectious Diseases* 147 (1983): p. 359.

69. R. Skowronski and D. Feldman, "Characterization of an Estrogen Binding Protein in the Yeast *Candida Albicans*," *Endocrinology* 214(4) (1989): pp. 1,965–1,972.

70. O. S. Kinsman and A. E. Collard, "Hormonal Factors in Vaginal Candidiasis in Rats," *Infection and Immunity* (1986): pp. 498–504.

71. O. S. Kinsman, K. Pitblado, and C. J. Coulson, "Effect of Mammalian Steroid Hormones and Luteinizing Hormone on the Germination of *Candida Albicans* and Implications for Vaginal Candidosis, *Mycoses* 31 (1988): pp. 617–626.

72. D. Metzger, J. H. White, and P. Chambon, "The Human Oestrogen Receptor Functions in Yeast," *Nature* 334(7) (1988): pp. 31–36.

73. K. Wright, "Yeast Meets Est(rogen): A Microorganism Responds to a Vertebrate Hormone," *Scientific American* (1988): pp. 28–32.

74. S. Buratowski, S. Hahn, P. A. Sharp, et al., "Function of a Yeast TATA Element-Binding Protein in a Mammalian Transcription System," *Nature* 334(7) (1988): p. 37.

75. C. O. Truss, "Metabolic Abnormalities in Patients with Chronic Candidiasis: The Acetaldehyde Hypothesis," *Journal of Ortho-molecular Psychiatry* 13(2) (1983): pp. 66–92.

76. M. Fiore et al., "Chronic Exposure to Aldicarb-Contaminated Groundwater and Human Immune Function," *Environmental Research* 41(2) (1986): pp. 633–645.

77. D. Feldman and A. Krishan, "Estrogens in Unexpected Places: Possible Implications for Researchers and Consumers," *Environmental Health Perspectives* 103(57) (October 1995): pp. 129–133.

78. B. Zondek and Y. M. Bromberg, "Clinical Reactions of Allergy to Endogenous Hormones and Their Treatment," *Journal of Obstetrics and Gynaecology British Empire* 54 (1947): p. 1.

79. G. P. Heckel, "Endocrine Allergy and the Therapeutic Use of Pregnanedial," *American Journal of Obstetrics and Gynecology* 66 (1953): p. 1,297.

80. E. W. Phillips, "Clinical Evidence of Sensitivity to Gonadotropins in Allergic Women," *Annals of Internal Medicine* 30 (1949): p. 364.

81. C. R. Mabray, "Obstetrics and Gynecology and Clinical Ecology (Part I)," *Clinical Ecology* 1(2) (1982–83): pp. 103–113.

82. C. R. Mabray, M. L. Burditt, T. L. Martin, et al., "Treatment of Common Gynecologic-Endocrinologic Symptoms by Allergy Management Procedures," *Obstetrics & Gynecology* 59(5) (1980): pp. 560–564.

83. W. Konetzki, "Immune Therapy for Endometriosis: The Newest Treatment Frontier," Tape #103, Endometriosis 15th Anniversary Conference audiotapes. (Milwaukee, WI: Endometriosis Association, 1995.)

84. S. Mathur, J. T. Melchers III, E. W. Ades, et al., "Anti-Ovarian and Anti-Lymphocyte Antibodies in Patients with Chronic Vaginal Candidiasis," *Journal of Reproductive Immunology* 2 (1980): pp. 247–262.

85. A. Vojdani, P. Rahimian, H. Kalhor, et al., "Immunological Cross Reactivity Between *Candida Albicans* and Human Tissue," *Journal of Clinical and Laboratory Immunology* (1996): pp. 1–15.

86. M. Vasquez and F. M. Kenny, "Ovarian Failure and Antiovarian Antibodies in Association with Hypoparathyroidism, Moniliasis, Addison's and Hashimoto's Diseases," *Obstetrics and Gynecology* 41 (1973): pp. 414–418.

87. A. S. Kunin, B. R. MacKay, S. L. Burns, et al., "The Syndrome of Hypoparathyroidism and Adrenocortical Insufficiency, a Possible Sequel of Hepatitis: Case Report and Review of the Literature," *American Journal of Medicine* 34 (1963).

88. F. M. Kenny and M. A. Holliday, "Hypoparathyroidism, Moniliasis, Addison's, and Hashimoto's Disease: Hypercalcemia Treated with Intravenously Administered Sodium Sulfate," *New England Journal of Medicine* 271 (1964): p. 708.

89. K. D. Wuepper and H. H. Fudenberg, "Moniliasis, 'Autoimmune' Polyendocrinopathy, and Immunologic Family Study," *Clinical Experiments in Immunology* 2 (1967): pp. 71–82.

90. R. M. Blizzard and J. H. Gibbs, "Candidiasis: Studies Pertaining to Its Association with Endocrinopathies and Pernicious Anemia," *Pedia* 42 (1968): p. 231.

91. M. B. Block, L. M. Pachman, D. Windhorst, et al., "Immunological Findings in Familial Juvenile Endocrine Deficiency Syndrome Associated with Chronic Mucocutaneous Candidiasis," *American Journal of Medical Science* 261 (1977): p. 216.

92. S. M. Baker, M. McDonnell, and C. Truss, "Double-Blind Placebo-Diet Controlled Crossover Study of IgG Food ELISA" (presentation at the American Academy of Environmental Medicine Advanced Seminar, Virginia Beach, VA, October 1994).

93. S. L. Vargas, C. C. Patrick, G. D. Ayers, et al., "Modulating Effect of Dietary Carbohydrate Supplementation on *Candida Albicans* Colonization and Invasion in a Neutropenic Mouse Model," *Infection and Immunity* 61(2) (1993): pp. 619–626.

94. K. A. Gazella, "Controlling Candida Naturally," *Health Counselor* 7(3) (June/July 1995): pp. 27–31.

95. E. White, "Candidiasis," Lamberts Bulletin, Lamberts Health Care Ltd.

96. L. Seachrist, "Food for Healing: Oral Tolerance Therapy Aims to Neutralize Autoimmune Disease," *Science News* 148 (1995): pp. 158–159.

97. W. H. Konetzki, "The Immunologic Aspects of Endometriosis," in *Endometriosis and Endometrium*, edited by Diamond and Osteen (Malden, MA: Blackwell Science Inc., 1997), pp. 347–352.

98. J. Wright, "The Unappreciated Role of Adrenal Cortical Hormone Dysfunction in Difficult Patients," Audiotape #2 (presentation at the 29th Annual Meeting of the American Academy of Environmental Medicine, Virginia Beach, VA, October 1994).

99. H. Santelmann, E. Laerum, J. Roennevig, et al., "Effectiveness of Nystatin in Polysymptomatic Patients: A Randomized, Double-Blind Trial with Nystatin Versus Placebo in General Practice," *Family Practice* 18(3) (2001): pp. 258–265.

100. M. T. Bailey and C. L. Coe, "Endometriosis Is Associated with an Altered Profile of Intestinal Microflora in Female Rhesus Monkeys," *Human Reproduction* 17(7) (2002): pp. 1,704–1,708.

101. S. S. Witkin, A. Kalo-Klein, L. Galland, et al., "Effect of *Candida Albicans* Plus Histamine on Prostaglandin E$_2$ Production by Peripheral Blood Mononuclear Cells from Healthy Women and Women with Recurrent Candidal Vaginitis," *Journal of Infectious Diseases* 164 (1991): pp. 396–399.

102. P. N. Kasckin, N. A. Krassilnikov, V. Y. Nikachalov, "Candida Complications After Antibiotic Therapy," *Mycopathologia et Mycologia Applicata* 14 (1961): pp. 173–188.

103. S. S. Witkin, "Defective Immune Responses in Patients with Recurrent Candidiasis Infections," *In Medicine* (May/June 1985): pp. 129–132.

104. *Candida Dysbiosis Information Foundation Newsletter* 2(2) (January 1996): p. 7.

105. L. Galland, "Leaky Gut Syndrome: Breaking the Vicious Cycle," *Townsend Letter for Doctors* (August/September 1995): pp. 62–68.

106. M. Burnhill, "Taking a Serious Approach to Vulvovaginitis," *Contemporary Ob/Gyn* (September 1986): pp. 69–79.

Chapter 5

1. L. L. Gabel, P. J. Fahey, C. R. Gallagher-Allred, et al., "Dietary Prevention and Treatment of Disease," *Supplement to the American Family Physician* 46(5) (November 1992): p. 41s.

2. U. Erasmus, *Fats and Oils* (Vancouver, BC: Alive Books, 1986), pp. 256–259.

3. D. Horrobin, "Nutritional and Medical Importance of Gamma-Linolenic Acid," *Progress in Lipid Research* 31(2) (1992): pp. 163–194.

4. W. N. Burns and R. S. Schenken, "Pathophysiology," in *Endometriosis: Contemporary Concepts in Clinical Management,* edited by R. S. Schenken (Philadelphia, PA: J. B. Lippincott, 1989), pp. 113–15.

5. H. Koike, T. Egawa, M. Ohtsuka, et al., "Correlation Between Dysmenorrheic Severity and Prostaglandin Production in Women with Endometriosis," *Prostaglandins, Leukotrienes, Essential Fatty Acids* 46 (1992): pp. 133–137.

6. M. Morita, Y. Yano, K. Otaka, et al., "Minimal and Mild Endometriosis: Nd:Yag Laser Treatment and Changes in Prostaglandin Concentrations in Peritoneal Fluid," *Journal of Reproductive Medicine* 35(6) (1990): pp. 621–624.

7. H. P. Bartram, A. Gostner, W. Scheppach, et al., "Effects of Fish Oil on Rectal Cell Proliferation, Mucosal Fatty Acids, and Prostaglandin E$_2$ Release in Healthy Subjects," *Gastroenterology* 105(5) (1993): pp. 1,317–1,322.

8. "Fish Oil Component Improves Clinical Status in Active Arthritis," *Family Practice News* 116(17): p. 23.

9. "Fish Oil Supplements: Efficacy in Active Rheumatoid Arthritis," *Modern Medicine* 55 (1987): p. 169.

10. A. Covens, P. Christopher, and R. F. Casper, "The Effect of Dietary Supplementation with Fish Oil Fatty Acids on Surgically-Induced Endometriosis in the Rabbit," *Fertility and Sterility* 49 (1988): pp. 698–703.

11. Z. Harel, F. M. Biro, R. K. Kottenhahn, et al., "Supplementation with Omega-3 Poly-unsaturated Fatty Acids in the Management of Dysmenorrhea in Adolescents," *American Journal of Obstetrics and Gynecology* 174(4) (1996): pp. 1,335–1,337.

12. N. D. Barnard, A. R. Scialli, D. Hurlock, et al., "Diet and Sex-Hormone Binding Globulin, Dysmenorrhea, and Premenstrual Symptoms," *Obstetrics and Gynecology* 95(2) (February 2000): pp. 245–250.

13. B. Deutch, "Menstrual Pain in Danish Women Correlated with Low n-3 Polyunsaturated Fatty Acid Intake," *European Journal of Clinical Nutrition* 49 (1995): pp. 508–516.

14. R. E. Frisch, "Fatness and Fertility," *Scientific American* (March 1988): pp. 88–95.

15. D. W. Cramer, E. Wilson, R. Stillman, et al., "The Relation of Endometriosis to Menstrual Characteristics, Smoking, and Exercise," *Journal of the American Medical Association* 255 (1986): pp. 1,904–1,908.

16. J. J. Challem and R. Lewin, "Managing Endometriosis Through Improved Nutrition," *Let's Live* 57(4) (1989): pp. 34–38.

17. M. S. Biskind, "Nutritional Deficiency in the Etiology of Menorrhagia, Cystic Mastitis, and Premenstrual Tension, Treatment with Vitamin B Complex," *Journal of Clinical Endocrinology and Metabolism* 3 (1943): pp. 277–334.

18. "Can B_6 Add to Asthma Therapy?" *Medical World News* 11 (August 1986): p. 63.

19. W. Phipps, "Diet and the Menstrual Cycle," (American Society for Reproductive Medicine) San Francisco, 1994.

20. B. R. Goldin et al., "Estrogen Excretion Patterns and Plasma Levels in Vegetarian and Omnivorous Women," *New England Journal of Medicine* 307 (1982): pp. 1,542–1,547.

21. B. R. Goldin et al., "Effect of Diet on Excretion of Estrogens in Pre- and Post-Menopausal Women," *Cancer Research* 41 (1981): pp. 3,771–3,773.

22. Spallholtz et al., "Immunological Responses of Mice Fed Diets Supplemented with Sclenite Selenium," *Proceedings of the Society of Experimental Biology Medicine* 143: pp. 685–689.

23. S. E. Rier, D. C. Martin, R. E. Bowman, et al., "Endometriosis in Rhesus Monkeys (*Macaca mulatta*) following Chronic Exposure to 2, 3, 7, 8-tetrachlorodibenzo-p-dioxin," *Fundamental & Applied Toxicology* 21(4) (1993): pp. 433–441.

24. S. E. Rier, D. W. Martin, R. E. Bowman, et al., "Immunoresponsiveness in Endometriosis: Implications of Estrogenic Toxicants," *Environmental Health Perspectives* (1995): p. 103.

25. M. L. Ballweg, "Avoiding Toxins and PCBs: What You Can Do," *The Endometriosis Sourcebook* (Chicago: Contemporary Books, 1995), p. 393.

26. T. Colborn, D. Dumanoski, and J. P. Myers, *Our Stolen Future* (New York: Penguin Books, 1995), p. 214.

27. T. B. Clarkson, M. A. Anthony, C. L. Hughes Jr., "Estrogenic Soybean Isoflavones and Chronic Disease," *Trends in Endocrinology and Metabolism* 6(1) (1995): pp. 11–16.

28. D. C. Knight and J. A. Eden, "A Review of the Clinical Effects of Phytoestrogens," *Obstetrics and Gynecology* 87(5) (1996): pp. 897–904.

29. S. Leaner Barr, "Don't Overdo the Tofu," *Longevity* (March 1995): p. 12.

30. J. P. Ehrlich, "Captive Cheetahs' Reproductive Ills Linked to Soy Feed," *Medical Tribune* (December 17, 1986).

31. E. J. Thomas, "Preventive, Symptomatic and Expectant Management of Endometriosis," *Current Concepts of Endometriosis* (1990): p. 323.

32. D. Mills, "Nutritional Aid to Pain Relief," Lamberts Bulletin, LambertsHealth Care Ltd.

33. P. Muller, "First International Symposium on Magnesium Deficit in Human Pathology" (1971).

34. R. Sherwood, B. Rocks, A. Stewart, et al., "Magnesium and the Premenstrual Syndrome," *Annals of Clinical Biology* 23 (1986): pp. 667–670.

35. N. Fletcher, "Mitral Valve Prolapse," *Endometriosis Association Newsletter* 13(2) (1992): pp. 1–2.

36. L. Galland, "Nutrition and Candidiasis," *Journal of Orthomolecular Psychiatry* 14(1) (1984): pp. 50–60.

37. "Magnesium Deficiency and Asthma," *Human Ecologist* 59 (1993): p. 21.

38. S. Davies, "Magnesium, Candida and Food Allergies," Tapes #8 and #26, Physicians Candida Update Program (Memphis TN: International Health Foundation, 1988), audiotapes.

39. L. Galland, "Metabolic Basis of Clinical Syndromes," Tape #3 (presentation at the Yeast-Human Interaction Conference, San Francisco CA, March 29–31, 1985), audiotape.

40. M. S. Seelig, "The Requirement of Magnesium by the Normal Adult," *American Journal of Clinical Nutrition* 14 (1964).

41. L. Galland, "The Chemistry of Healing II: Magnesium and the Battle for Light," *Gesell Institute of Human Development Update* 4(2) (Spring 1985): pp. 3–5.

42. M. L. Ballweg, "Alternative Treatments for Endometriosis," *Overcoming Endometriosis* (Chicago; Contemporary Books, 1987), p. 85.

43. *Understanding Vitamins and Minerals* (Emmaus PA: Rodale Press, 1984), pp. 28–29, 56–59.

44. B. Woller, "The Immune Boost of Vitamin E Experimentally Buoys Hope," *Medical Tribune* 28(36) (September 23, 1987): pp. 1, 8.

45. R. S. London et al., "The Effect of Alpha-Tocopherol on Pre-Menstrual Symptomatology: A Double Blind Trial," *Journal of the American College of Nutrition* 2 (1983): pp. 115–122.

46. J. Joseph, "An Interview with Dr. Evan Shute," *Bestways Magazine* (1975): pp. 1–7.

47. "Beta-Carotene in Vitamins," *Medical Advertising News* (April 15, 1990).

48. R. Londer, "Anti-Aging Eating," *Health* (July 1986): pp. 41–44.

49. C. Bateson-Koch, *Allergies: Disease in Disguise* (Burnaby, BC: Alive Books, 1996), p. 182.

50. W. P. Leary and C. J. Lockett, "Newer Understanding of Zinc Metabolism," *Internal Medicine* 6(12) (1985): pp. 90–97.

51. "Nutrition and Aging," *Whole Life Times* (November/December 1984).

52. *For Tomorrow's Children: A Manual for Future Parents* (Blooming Glen, PA: Preconception Care, Inc., 1990), p. 71.

53. K. H. Sullivan, "The Iron File," *Vegetarian Times* (July 1996): pp. 58–65.

54. B. D. Reed, M. L. Slattery, and T. K. French, "The Association Between Dietary Intake and Reported History of Candida Vulvovaginitis," *Journal of Family Practice* 29(5) (1989): pp. 509–515.

55. W. G. Crook, *The Yeast Connection and the Woman* (Jackson TN: Professional Books, Inc., 1995), pp. 669–670.

56. E. Cranton quoted in *Healthline*, W. G. Crook, ed., Vol. 4, No. 2, October 1992: p. 7.

57. D. Mills, "The Nutritional Status of the Endometriosis Patient," Institute for Optimum Nutrition Project (September 1991).

58. J. R. Mathias, R. Franklin, D. C. Quast, et al., "Relation of Endometriosis and Neuromuscular Disease of the Gastrointestinal Tract: New Insights," *Fertility and Sterility* 70(1) (1998): pp. 81–88.

59. B. Sears and B. Lawren, *The Zone* (New York: HarperCollins, 1995), p. 15.

Chapter 6

1. A. Murphy, "Clinical Aspects of Endometriosis," *Annals of the New York Academy of Sciences* 955 (2002): pp.1–10.

2. R. Barbieri and S. Missmer, "Endometriosis and Infertility: A Cause-Effect Relationship?" *Annals of the New York Academy of Sciences* 955 (2002): pp. 23–33.

3. B. Lessey, "Implantation Defects in Infertile Women with Endometriosis," *Annals of the New York Academy of Sciences* 955 (2002): pp. 265–280.

4. D. Lebovic, M. Mueller, and R. Taylor, "Immunobiology of Endometriosis," *Fertility and Sterility* 75(1) (2001): pp. 1–10.

5. "Environmental Panel [Eighth World Congress on Endometriosis]," *Endometriosis Association Newsletter* 34(2) (2002): p. 5.

6. R. Blackwell, B. Carr, R. Chang, et al., "Are We Exploiting the Infertile Couple?" *Fertility and Sterility* 48(5) (1987): pp. 735–739.

7. For a good overview, read T. Weschler, *Taking Charge of Your Fertility* (Quill, 2001).

8. S. Marcoux, R. Maheux, and S. Bérubé for The Canadian Collaborative Group on Endometriosis, "Laparoscopic Surgery in Infertile Women with Minimal or Mild Endometriosis," *New England Journal of Medicine* 337(4) (1997): pp. 217–222.

9. F. Parazzini, "Ablation of Lesions or No Treatment in Minimal–Mild Endometriosis in Infertile Women: A Randomized Trial," *Human Reproduction* 14(5) (1999): pp. 1,332–1,334.

10. D. Olive and E. Pritts, "The Treatment of Endometriosis: A Review of the Evidence," *Annals of the New York Academy of Sciences* 955 (2002): pp. 360–372.

11. R. Schenken, "Endometriosis and Infertility," *Practice Committee of the American Society for Reproductive Medicine Report* (2001): pp. 1–9.

12. J. Deaton, M. Gibson, K. Blackmer, et al., "A Randomized, Controlled Trial of Clomiphene Citrate and Intrauterine Insemination in Couples with Unexplained Infertility or Surgically Corrected Endometriosis," *Fertility and Sterility* 54 (1990): pp. 1,083–1,088.

13. I. Tummon, L. Asher, J. Martin, et al., "Randomized Controlled Trial of Superovulaton and Insemination for Infertility Associated with Minimal or Mild Endometriosis," *Fertility and Sterility* 68 (1997): pp. 8–12.

14. D. Adamson, "Endometriosis: Traditional Perspective, Current Evidence, and Future Possibilities," *International Journal of Fertility* 46(3) (2001): pp. 151–168.

15. A. Whittmore, R. Harris, and J. Intyre, "Characteristics Relating to Ovarian Cancer Risk: Collaborative Analysis of 12 U.S. Case-Control Studies—II. Invasive Epithelial Ovarian Cancers in White Women," *American Journal of Epidemiology* 136 (1992): pp. 1,184–1,203.

16. B. Mosgaard, O. Lidegaard, S. K. Kjaer, et al., "Infertility, Fertility Drugs, and Invasive Ovarian Cancer: A Case-Control Study," *Fertility and Sterility* 67 (1997): pp. 1,005–1,012.

17. S. Soliman, S. Daya, J. Collins, et al., "A Randomized Trial of In Vitro Fertilization Versus Conventional Treatment for Infertility," *Fertility and Sterility* 59 (1993): pp. 1,239–1,244.

18. K. Barnhart, R. Dunsmoor-Su, and C. Coutifaris, "Effect of Endometriosis on In Vitro Fertilization," *Fertility and Sterility* 77(6) (2002): pp. 1,148–1,155.

19. S. Spandorfer and Z. Rosenwaks, "Endometriosis: Is IVF the Answer for Infertility? Stage-Related Success Rates in 1,417 Consecutive IVF-ET Cycles" (Controversies in

Obstetrics, Gynecology, and Infertility World Congress, Paris, 2002).

20. D. Dicker, J. Goldman, T. Levy, et al., "The Impact of Long-term Gonadotropin-Releasing Hormone Analogue Treatment on Preclinical Abortions in Patients with Severe Endometriosis Undergoing In Vitro Fertilization-Embryo Transfer," *Fertility and Sterility* 57 (1992): pp. 597–600.

Chapter 7

1. Private correspondence with the FDA, 1989–1990.

2. *Ann. Dermatol. Venereol.* (French toxicology journal) 113(13) (1986), pp. 31–41.

3. *Ugeskr Laeger* (Danish toxicology journal) 153(13) (1991), pp. 939–40.

4. Candida Research and Information Foundation survey, *CRIF Newsletter* (1990).

5. J. Jones et al., "Evaluation of Workers with Multiple Chemical Sensitivities."

6. C. Shim and M. H. William, "Affects of Odors in Asthma," *American Journal of Medicine* 80 (1986).

7. N. Ashford and C. Miller, *Chemical Exposures: Low Levels, High Stakes.* New York: Van Nostrand Reinhold, 1991), p. 61.

8. U.S. House Committee on Science and Technology, *Neurotoxins: At Home and the Workplace*, Report 99-827 (September 16, 1986).

9. P. S. Spencer et al., "Neurotoxic Properties of Musk Ambrette," *Toxicology and Applied Pharmacology* 75 (1984).

10. P. S. Spencer et al., "Skin as a Route of Entry for Neurotoxic Substances," in *Dermatoxicology*, edited by F. N. Marzulii and H. I. Mailback (1984), pp. 629–630.

11. D. L. Opdyke, *Monographs on Fragrance Raw Materials*, published on behalf of the Research Institute for Fragrance Raw Materials (Oxford: Pergamon Press, 1979), pp. 37, 87, 279–280, 498.

12. U.S. House Subcommittee on Business Opportunities, Chaired by R. Wyden and the National Institute of Occupational Safety and Health (1988).

13. J. Kendall, "Making Sense of Scents," *Citizens for a Toxic-Free Marin*.

14. Private correspondence with the FDA (1989, 1990).

15. A. S. Adamson, "Consumer Products Perfumery in the '80s and '90s," *Perfumer & Flavorist* (July/August 1989), pp. 8, 10.

16. University of Minnesota School of Social Work, Notice of Environmental Issues, 1993.

17. "No Scents," *Montreal Gazette*, May 29, 1995.

18. W. Lambert, "More Claim Chemicals Made Them Ill," *The Wall Street Journal*, January 17, 1996.

19. Allen and Handsbury's Respiratory Institute, *Air Currents* (London: Glaxo, Inc.).

20. J. E. Lessenger, "Occupational Acute Anaphylactic Reaction to Assault by Perfume Spray in the Face," *Journal of the American Board of Family Practice* 14(2) (2001): pp. 137–140.

21. "Samantha Turner," *Washington Post* (March 16, 2002), obituaries, p. B07.

22. S. Eisenhardt, B. Runnebaum, K. Bauer, et al., "Nitromusk Compounds in Women with Gynecological and Endocrine Dysfunction," *Environmental Research* 87(3) (2001): pp. 123–130.

Chapter 8

1. S. McDonough, "Cancer and Endometriosis," *Overcoming Endometriosis* (New York: Congdon & Weed, Inc., 1987), pp. 236–240.

2. E. Cameron and L. Pauling, *Cancer and Vitamin C* (Philadelphia: Camino Books, 1979), pp. 6–9; 18–19.

3. S. Steingraber, *Living Downstream: An Ecologist Looks at Cancer and the Environment* (Reading, MA: Addison-Wesley Publishing Co., 1997), p. 240.

4. P. Hersey, A. Edwards, M. Honeyman, et al., "Low Natural-Killer-Cell Activity in Familial Melanoma Patients and Their Relatives," *British Journal of Cancer* 40(1) (1979): pp. 113–122.

5. G. Garzetti, A. Ciavattini, M. Provinciali, et al., "Natural Killer Activity in Stage III and IV Endometriosis: Impaired Cytotoxicity and Retained Lymphokine Responsiveness of Natural Killer Cells," *Gynecologic Endocrinology* 9 (1995): pp. 125–130.

6. Y. Kikuchi, N. Ishikawa, J. Hirata, et al., "Changes of Peripheral Blood Lymphocyte Subsets Before and After Operation of Patients with Endometriosis," *Acta Obstetricia Gynecologica Scandinavica* 72 (1993): pp. 157–161.

7. H. Kanzaki, H. S. Wang, M. Kariya, et al., "Suppression of Natural Killer Cell Activity by Sera from Patients with Endometriosis," *American Journal of Obstetrics and Gynecology* 167 (1992): pp. 257–261.

8. G. Grunert and R. Franklin, "Pathogenesis of Infertility in Endometriosis," in *Endometriosis: Advanced Management and Surgical Techniques* (New York: Springer-Verlag, 1995).

9. J. Kupryjanczyk, D. Bell, D. Yandell, et al., "p53 Expression in Ovarian Borderline Tumors and Stage I Carcinomas," *American Journal of Cancer Prevention* 102(5) (1994): pp. 671–676.

10. P. Vercellini, D. Trecca, S. Oldani, et al., "Analysis of p53 and *ras* Gene Mutations in Endometriosis," *Gynecology & Obstetrics Investigation* 38 (1994): pp. 70–71.

11. O. Abulafia and D. M. Sherer, "Angiogenesis of the Endometrium," *Obstetrics and Gynecology* 94(1) (1999): pp. 148–153.

12. R. N. Taylor, I. Ryan, E. S. Moore, et al., "Angiogenesis and Macrophage Activation in Endometriosis," *Annals of New York Academy of Science* 828 (1997): pp. 194–207.

13. S. K. Smith, "Angiogenesis," *Seminars in Reproductive Endocrinology* 15(3) (1997): pp. 221–227.

14. X. Jiang, S. Morland, A. Hitchcock, et al., "Allelotyping of Endometriosis with Adjacent Ovarian Carcinoma Reveals Evidence of a Common Lineage," *Cancer Research* 58 (1998): pp. 1,707–1,712.

15. R. C. Kline, J. T. Wharton, E. N. Atkinson, et al., "Endometrioid Carcinoma of the Ovary: Retrospective Review of 145 Cases," *Gynecologic Oncology* 39 (1990): pp. 337–346.

16. M. Mostoufizadeh and R. Scully, "Malignant Tumors Arising in Endometriosis," *Clinical Obstetrics and Gynecology* 23(3) (1980): pp. 951–963.

17. J. Heaps, R. Nieberg, and J. Berek, "Malignant Neoplasms Arising in Endometriosis," *Obstetrics and Gynecology* 75(6) (1990): pp. 1,023–1,028.

18. K. L. Bruner-Tran, S. E. Rier, E. Eisenberg, et al., "The Potential Role of Environmental Toxins in the Pathophysiology of Endometriosis," *Gynecologic Obstetric Investigation* 48 (1999): pp. 45–56.

19. H. Gebel, D. Braun, A. Tambur, et al., "Spontaneous Apoptosis of Endometrial Tissue

Is Impaired in Women with Endometriosis," *Fertility and Sterility* 69(6) (1998): pp. 1,042–1,047.

20. L. Brinton, G. Gridley, I. Persson, et al., "Cancer Risk After a Hospital Discharge Diagnosis of Endometriosis," *American Journal of Obstetrics and Gynecology* 176(3) (1997): pp. 572–579.

21. P. Vercellini, F. Parazzini, G. Bolis, et al., "Endometriosis and Ovarian Cancer," *American Journal of Obstetrics and Gynecology* 169(1) (1993): pp. 181–182.

22. M. Hornstein, P. Thomas, A. Sober, et al., "Association Between Endometriosis, Dysplastic Naevi and History of Melanoma in Women of Reproductive Age," *Human Reproduction* 12(1) (1997): pp. 143–145.

23. F. Nezhat and M. L. Ballweg, "Risk of Gynecologic and Breast Cancer in Women with Endometriosis and Their Families," *Journal of the American Association of Gynecologic Laparoscopists* 6(3), Suppl. (August 1999).

24. R. Doll and R. Peto, "The Causes of Cancer: Quantitative Estimates of Avoidable Risks of Cancer in the United States Today," *Journal of the National Cancer Institute* 66(6) (1981): pp. 1,191-1,308.

25. K. Obata, S. Morland, R. Watson, et al., "Frequent PTEN/MMAC Mutations in Endometrioid but Not Serous or Mucinous Epithelial Ovarian Tumors," *Cancer Research* 58 (1998): pp. 2,095–2,097.

26. Z. Shoham, "Epidemiology, Etiology, and Fertility Drugs in Ovarian Epithelial Carcinoma: Where Are We Today?" *Fertility and Sterility* 62(3) (1994): pp. 433–448.

27. B. Rosen, J. Irvine, P. Ritvo, et al., "The Feasibility of Assessing Women's Perceptions of the Risks and Benefits of Fertility Drug Therapy in Relation to Ovarian Cancer Risk," *Fertility and Sterility* 68(1) (1997): pp. 90–94.

28. B. Zakarian, *The Activist Cancer Patient: How to Take Charge of Your Treatment* (New York: John Wiley & Sons, Inc., 1996), p. 21.

29. S. Epstein, *The Politics Of Cancer* (San Francisco: Sierra Club Books, 1978.

30. D. Davis and C. Muir, "Estimating Avoidable Causes of Cancer," *Environmental Health Perspectives* Nov: 103, Suppl. 8 (1995): pp. 301–306.

31. J. Brotons, M. Olea-Serrano, M. Villalobos, et al., "Xenoestrogens Released from Lacquer Coatings in Food Cans," *Environmental Health Perspectives*, 103(6) (1995): pp. 608–612.

32. "Conference on Breast Cancer and the Environment," *Health Facts* 22(8) (1997): pp. 1, 4–5.

33. M. Wolff, P. Toniolo, E. Lee, et al., "Blood Levels of Organochlorine Residues and Risk of Breast Cancer," *Journal of the National Cancer Institute* 85(8) (1993): pp. 648–652.

34. K. J. Aronson, A. B. Miller, C. G. Woolcott, et al., "Breast Adipose Tissue Concentrations of Polychlorinated Biphenyls and Other Organochlorines and Breast Cancer Risk," *Cancer Epidemiology, Biomarkers and Prevention* 8 (2000).

35. E. Dewailly, A. Demers, P. Ayotte, et al., "Plasma Organochlorine Concentrations and Breast Cancer Aggressiveness," *Epidemiology* 10(4) (1999): p. S100.

36. T. Zheng, T. Holford, S. Mayne, et al., "Environmental Exposure to Hexachlorobenzene (HCB) and Risk of Female Breast Cancer in Connecticut," *Cancer Epidemiology, Biomarkers & Prevention* 8 (1999): pp. 407–411.

37. D. Schottenfeld and J. Froumeni, eds., *Cancer Epidemiology and Prevention* (New York: Oxford University Press, 1996).

38. "Mammography Controversy," *Network News* (National Women's Health Network) 6 (March/April 1997).

39. National Institutes of Health, National Cancer Institute, "Understanding Breast Changes: A Health Guide for All Women," NIH Publication No. 97-3536 (1997), p. 5.

40. R. G. Steen, *A Conspiracy of Cells: The Basic Science of Cancer* (New York: Plenum Press, 1993), p. 48.

41. S. Epstein, *The Breast Cancer Prevention Program* (New York: Macmillan, 1997), pp. 38–40.

42. S. Love and K. Lindsey, *Dr. Susan Love's Breast Book* (Reading, MA: Addison-Wesley, 1995), pp. 176–194.

43. R. D. Gambrell, "Role of Progestins in the Prevention of Breast Cancer," *Mauritas* 8 (1986): p. 169.

44. L. Bergkvist, H. Adami, I. Persson, et al., "The Risk of Breast Cancer After Estrogen and Estrogen-Progestin Replacement," *New England Journal of Medicine* 321(5) (1989): pp. 293–297.

45. E. Barrett-Connor, "Postmenopausal Estrogen Replacement and Breast Cancer," *New England Journal of Medicine* 321(5) (1989): pp. 319–320.

46. D. C. Martin, "Cancer and Endometriosis: Do We Need to Be Concerned?" *Seminars in Reproductive Endocrinology* 15(3) (1997): pp. 319–324.

47. R. Lobo, "Benefits and Risks of Estrogen Relacement Therapy," *American Journal of Obstetrics and Gynecology* 173 (1995): pp. 982–990.

48. National Black Women's Health Project, "Breast Cancer and African American Women," (statistics from the National Cancer Institute, Washington, DC).

49. E. Keough, ed., *The Complete Book of Cancer Prevention: Foods, Lifestyles & Medical Care to Keep You Healthy* (Emmaus, PA: Rodale Press, 1988), pp. 40–41.

50. G. M. Cooper, *The Cancer Book* (Boston: Jones & Bartlett, 1993), p. 46.

51. C. Fuchs, M. J. Stampfer, G. A. Colditz, et al., "Alcohol Consumption and Mortality Among Women," *New England Journal of Medicine* 332(19) (1995): 1,45–1,250.

52. P. Wingo, "Cancer Incidence and Mortality, 1973–1995: A Report Card for the U.S.," *Cancer* 82(6) (1998): pp. 1,197–1,207.

53. M. Ciotti, "Screening for Gynecologic and Colorectal Cancer: Is It Adequate?" *Women's Health Issues* (Jacobs Institute of Women's Health) 2(2) (1992): pp. 83–93.

54. American Cancer Society, "Facts & Figures," American Cancer Society website (1999) cancer.org/statistics/cff99/selectedcancers.html.

55. M. S. Piver and G. Wilder, *Gilda's Disease: Sharing Personal Experiences and a Medical Perspective on Ovarian Cancer* (Amherst, MA: Prometheus Books, 1996), pp. 35–46.

56. P. D. DePriest, E. R. Banks, E. D. Powell, et al., "Endometrioid Carcinoma of the Ovary and Endometriosis: The Association in Postmenopausal Women," *Gynecologic Oncology* 47 (1992): pp. 71–75.

57. M. Fukanaga, K. Nomura, E. Ishikawa, et al., "Ovarian Atypical Endometriosis: Its Close Association with Malignant Epithelial Tumours," *Histopathology* 30 (1997): pp. 249–255.

58. Gilda Radner Familial Ovarian Cancer Registry website (1999) rpci.med.buffalo.edu/departments/gynonc/grwp.html.

59. A. Whittemore, "Characteristics Relating to Ovarian Cancer Risk: Collaborative Analysis of 12 U.S. Case-Control Studies," *American*

Journal of Epidemiology 136 (1992): pp. 1,175–1,203.

60. American Society for Reproductive Medicine, "Risks of In Vitro Fertilization (IVF)," Fact Sheet (American Society for Reproductive Medicine website, December 1997).

61. B. J. Mosgaard, O. Lidegaard, S. K. Kjaer, et al., "Infertility, Fertility Drugs, and Invasive Ovarian Cancer: A Case-Control Study," *Fertility and Sterility* 67(6) (1997): pp. 1,005–1,011.

62. D. Cramer, W. Welch, R. Scully, et al., "Ovarian Cancer and Talc," *Cancer* 50(2) (1982): pp. 372–376.

63. A. Whittemore, M. Wu, R. Paffenbarger Jr., et al., "Personal and Environmental Characteristics Related to Epithelial Ovarian Cancer," *American Journal of Epidemiology* 128(6) (1988): pp. 1,228-1,240.

64. K. Costigan, "Fertility Shots: Linked to Cancer?" *Health* (September, 1993).

65. American Society for Reproductive Medicine, "Ovulation Drugs: A Guide for Patients" (1995).

66. Leukemia Society of America, "Hodgkin's Disease and the Non-Hodgkin's Lymphomas," Publication P-38 40M 8/94, p. 8.

67. S. Watstein and K. Chandler, *The AIDS Dictionary* (New York: Facts on File, 1998), pp. 192–193.

68. L. Hardell and M. Eriksson, "A Case-Control Study of Non-Hodgkin's Lymphoma and Exposure to Pesticides," *Cancer* 85(6) (1999): pp. 1353–1359.

69. C. Poole, *Melanoma Prevention, Detection & Treatment*, (New Haven, CT: Yale University Press, 1998).

70. National Cancer Institute, "Moles and Dysplastic Nevi," Publication #93-3133 (March 1993).

71. R. Arnot, *The Breast Cancer Prevention Diet: The Powerful Foods, Supplements, and Drugs That Can Save Your Life* (Boston, MA: Little Brown, 1998), pp. 105–107.

72. D. Haney, "'Breast Cancer Prevention Diet' Protested," *Milwaukee Journal Sentinel*, November 23, 1998, sec. G, p. 2.

73. L. Kohlmeimer et al., "Lifestyles and Trends in Worldwide Breast Cancer Rates," *Annals of the New York Academy of Science* 609 (1990): pp. 259–268.

74. U. Erasmus, *Fats and Oils* (Vancouver, BC: Alive Books, 1986), pp. 256–259.

75. A. Weil, "Pollutants Linked to Breast Cancer," *Natural Health* (November/December 1993), pp. 10–11.

76. N. Barnard, "Women and Cancer: Opportunities for Prevention," (Physician's Committee for Responsible Medicine) *Update* (September/October 1991).

77. B. C. Chiu, J. R. Cerhan, A. R. Folsom, et al., "Diet and Risk of Non-Hodgkin's Lymphoma in Older Women," *Journal of the American Medical Association* 275(17) (1996): pp. 1,315–1,321.

78. P. Schedin and T. Byers, "Adolescent Diet and the Risk of Breast Cancer in Adulthood: A Role for Vitamin A?" *Nutrition* 13(10) (1997): pp. 924–925.

79. R. R. Watson, R. H. Prabhala, P. M. Plezia, et al., "Effect of Beta-Carotene on Lymphocyte Subpopulations in Elderly Humans: Evidence for a Dose-Response Relationship," *American Journal of Clinical Nutrition* 316 (1991): pp. 22–28.

80. J. Welsh, "Vitamin D Compounds as Potential Therapeutics for Estrogen-Independent Breast Cancer," *Nutrition* 13(10) (1997): p. 915.

81. G. Studzinski and D. Moore, "Sunlight: Can It Prevent as Well as Cause Cancer?" *Cancer Research* 55 (1995): pp. 4,014–4,022.

82. K. Colston, U. Berger, and R. Coombes, "Possible Role for Vitamin D in Controlling

Breast Cancer Cell Proliferation," *The Lancet* (January 28, 1989)1: pp. 188–191.

83. E. John, G. Schwartz, D. Dreon, et al., "Vitamin D and Breast Cancer Risk: The NHANES I Epidemiologic Follow-up Study, 1971–1975 to 1992. National Health and Nutrition Examination Survey," *Cancer Epidemiology, Biomarkers & Prevention* 8(5) (May 1999): pp. 399–406.

84. D. Hunter, S. Hankinson, F. Laden, et al., "Plasma Organochlorine Levels and the Risk of Breast Cancer," *New England Journal of Medicine* 337(18) (1997): pp. 1,253–1,258.

85. T. Beardsley, "Trends in Cancer Epidemiology: A War Not Won," *Scientific American* 270 (1994): pp. 130–138.

86. Citizens for a Better Environment, "Defending Your Right to Know Before the U.S. Supreme Court," Fact Sheet (1997).

87. S. Epstein, "Environmental and Occupational Pollutants Are Avoidable Causes of Breast Cancer," *International Journal of Health Services* 24(1) (1993): pp. 45–50.

88. D. Adalberto, P. Crosignani, F. Robutti, et al., "Triazine Herbicides and Ovarian Epithelial Neoplasms," *Scandanavian Journal of Work, Environment, and Health* 15 (1989): pp. 47–53.

89. F. Perera, "Environment and Cancer: Who Are Susceptible?" *Science* 278 (1997): pp. 1,068–1,073.

90. L. M. Gibbs and the Citizens Clearinghouse for Hazardous Waste, *Dying from Dioxin* (Boston, MA: South End Press, 1995), p. 1.

91. Selected Cancers Cooperative Study (SCS) Group, "The Association of Selected Cancers with Service in the U.S. Military in Vietnam," *Archives of Internal Medicine* 150 (1990): pp. 2,473–2,481.

92. N. Dalager, H. Kang, V. Burt, et al., "Non-Hodgkin's Lymphoma Among Vietnam Veterans," *Journal of Occupational Medicine* 33(7) (1991): pp. 774–779.

93. S. Hoar, A. Blair, F. Holmes, et al., "Agricultural Herbicide Use and Risk of Lymphoma and Soft-Tissue Sarcoma," *Journal of the American Medical Association* 256(9) (1986): pp. 1,141–1,147.

94. M. Fingerhut, W. Halperin, D. Marlow, et al., "Cancer Mortality in Workers Exposed to 2,3,7,8-Tetrachlorodibenzo-*p*-dioxin," *New England Journal of Medicine* 324(4) (1991): pp. 212–218.

95. L. Roberts, "Dioxin Risks Revisited," *Science* 251: 624–626.

96. N. M. Brown et al., "Prenatal TCDD and Predisposition to Mammary Cancer in Rats," *Carcinogenesis* 19(9) (1998): pp. 1623–29.

97. H. Becher, K. Steindorf, and D. Flesch-Janys, "Quantitative Cancer Risk Assessment for Dioxins Using an Occupational Cohort," *Environmental Health Perspectives* 106, Suppl. 2 (1998): pp. 663–670.

98. *Rachel's Environmental and Health Weekly News*, no. 636 (February 4, 1998).

99. M. Kogevinas, H. Becher, T. Benn, et al., "Cancer Mortality in Workers Exposed to Phenoxy Herbicides, Chlorophenols, and Dioxins," *American Journal of Epidemiology* 145(12) (1997): pp. 1,061–1,075.

100. T. Schreiber, "Misleading and Irresponsible, Cancer Activists Decry Harvard Report," *Resist* newsletter 6(3) (1996).

101. Telephone interview with Randy Billings, Director of Development, Harvard School of Public Health, June 29, 1999.

102. J. R. Harris, S. Hellman, et al., *Breast Diseases* (Philadelphia: J. B. Lippencott Co., 1987), pp. 98–100.

103. "Physical Exercise and Reduced Risk of Breast Cancer in Young Women," *Journal of the*

National Cancer Institute 86 (1994): pp. 1,403–1,408.

104. G. Logsdon, *The Contrary Farmer's Invitation to Gardening* (White River Junction, VT: Chelsea Green Publishing, 1997), p. 84.

105. R. Abrams, *Will It Hurt the Baby? The Safe Use of Medications During Pregnancy and Breastfeeding* (Reading, MA: Addison-Wesley Publishing Co., 1990), p. 9.

106. Institute of Medicine, National Academy of Sciences "Nutrition During Lactation: A Report from the Subcommittee on Nutrition During Lactation" (1991): 178–179.

107. M. Maiman, V. Seltzer, and J. Boyce, "Laparoscopic Excision of Ovarian Neoplasms Subsequently Found to be Malignant," *Obstetrics and Gynecology* 77 (1991): pp. 563–565.

108. J. Hsiu, F. Given, and G. Kemp, "Tumor Implantation After Diagnostic Laparoscopy: Biopsy of Serous Ovarian Tumors of Low Malignant Potential," *Obstetrics and Gynecology* 68 (1986): pp. 905–935.

109. G. Kindermann, V. Maassen, and W. Kuhn, "Laparoscopic Management of Ovarian Tumors Subsequently Diagnosed as Malignant," *Journal of Pelvic Surgery* 2 (1996): pp. 245–251.

110. D. A. Tsin and K. Haghighi, "Endometriosis and Cancer," (presentation at the World Congress of Gynecologic Endoscopy, September 23–28, 1997).

111. M. Piver, ed., "The Gilda Radner Familial Ovarian Cancer Registry Newsletter," (1998) 3.

112. "Odds in Your Hand," *Prevention* (June 1996): p. 30.

113. S. Piver, "Routine Ovarian Cancer Screening for a Subset of At-Risk Women," *The Female Patient—Ob/Gyn* (February 1997): pp. 71–87.

114. D. W. Cramer, R. F. Liberman, M. D. Hornstein, et al., "Basal Hormone Levels in Women Who Use Acetaminophen for Menstrual Pain," *Fertility and Sterility* 70(2) (1998): pp. 371–373.

115. "Breast Cancer, rBGH and Milk," *Rachel's Environment & Health Weekly* no. 598 (May 14, 1998): pp. 8–10.

116. S. E. Hankinson, W. C. Willett, G. A. Colditz, et al., "Circulating Concentrations of Insulin-Like Growth Factor-1 and Risk of Breast Cancer," *The Lancet* 351 (1998): pp. 1,393–1,396.

117. J. Holly, "Insulin-Like Growth Factor-1 and New Opportunities for Cancer Prevention," *The Lancet* 351 (1998): pp. 1,373–1,374.

118. M. Estok, "How Concerned Should You Be About Ovarian Cancer (Part II)," *A Friend Indeed: For Women in the Prime of Life* 13(6) (1996): p. 1.

119. M. S. Piver and R. E. Hempling, "Screening for Gynecologic Malignancies in Primary Care, Ovarian Cancer," *Emergency Medicine* (March 1993): pp. 141–148.

120. "Bright Lights and Breast Cancer," *Country Journal* (November–December 1993): p. 36.

121. R. C. Kline, J. T. Wharton, E. N. Atkinson, et al., "Endometrioid Carcinoma of the Ovary: Retrospective Review of 145 Cases," *Gynecologic Oncology* 39 (1990): pp. 337–346.

122. G. Wyshak, R. E. Frisch, N. L. Albright, et al., "Lower Prevalence of Benign Diseases of the Breast and Benign Tumours of the Reproductive System Among Former College Athletes Compared to Non-Athletes," *British Journal of Cancer* 54 (1986): pp. 841–845.

123. J. Gofman, *Preventing Breast Cancer: The Story of a Major, Proven, Preventable Cause of this Disease* (San Francisco: Committee for Nuclear Responsibility, Book Division, 1996.

124. J. Elmore, M. Barton, V. Moceri, et al., "Ten-Year Risk of False Positive Screening Mammograms and Clincial Breast Examinations," *New England Journal of Medicine* 338(16) (1998): pp. 1,089–1,096.

125. C. Reznick, "Chemical Carcinogenesis and Chemoprevention: The Role of Nutrition in Cancer," (presentation at the 33rd Annual Meeting of the American Academy of Environmental Medicine, Baltimore, MD, November 6–8, 1998, syllabus), pp. 417–437.

126. S. Austin, *Breast Cancer: What You Should Know (but May Not Be Told) About Prevention, Diagnosis, and Treatment* (Roseville, CA: Prima Publications, 1994), p. 288.

127. L. C. Clark, G. F. Combs Jr., B. W. Turnbull, et al., "Effects of Selenium Supplementation for Cancer Prevention in Patients with Carcinoma of the Skin," *Journal of the American Medical Association* 276(24) (1996): pp. 1957–63.

128. P. Quillin, *Beating Cancer with Nutrition* (Tulsa, OK: Nutrition Times Press, Inc., 1998), pp. 187–189.

Chapter 9

1. J. Fallon, "Endometriosis in Youth," *Journal of the American Medical Association* 131 (1946): p. 1,405.

2. D. L. Chatman, "Endometriosis and the Black Woman," *Journal of Reproductive Medicine* 16 (1976): p. 303.

3. D. L. Chatman and A. B. Ward, "Endometriosis in Adolescents," *Journal of Reproductive Medicine* 27 (1982): pp. 156–160.

4. D. P. Goldstein, C. D. Cholnoky and S. J. Emans, "Adolescent Endometriosis," *Journal of Adolescent Health Care I* 37 (1980): p. 41.

5. S. J. Emans and D. P. Goldstein, "Pelvic Pain, Dysmenorrhea, and the Premenstrual Syndrome," in *Pediatrics and Adolescent Gynecology*, 3rd ed. (Boston: Little, Brown & Co., 1990), pp. 273–300.

Chapter 11

1. "Best Clinical Practices Chapter 13 from the International Position Paper on Women's Health and Menopause: A Comprehensive Approach," National Heart, Lung, and Blood Institute, NIH Office of Research on Women's Health, Giovanni Lorenzini Medical Science Foundation (March 2002): pp. 5–26.

2. A. Weber, "Effects of Estrogens and Androgens on the Libido of Women Following Surgical and Natural Menopause," *Menopausal Medicine* 7(1) (Spring 1999): pp. 5–7.

3. L. Mayo, "A Natural Approach to Menopause," *Clinical Nutrition Insights* (July 1997): pp. 1–8.

4. R. L. Barbieri, "Endometriosis and the Estrogen Threshold Theory: Relation to Surgical and Medical Treatment," *Journal of Reproductive Medicine* 43 Suppl. 3 (March 1998): pp. 287–292.

5. E. Gold, J. Bromberger, S. Crawford, et al., "Factors Associated with Age at Natural Menopause in a Multiethnic Sample of Midlife Women," *American Journal of Epidemiology* 153(9): pp. 865–874.

6. "Postmenopausal Hormone Replacement Therapy," Harvard Medical School Health Publications Group, 1993.

7. J. Sach, *What Women Should Know about Menopause* (New York: Dell, 1991).

8. R. Punnonen, P. J. Klemi, and V. Nikkane, "Postmenopausal Endometriosis," *European Journal of Obstetrics, Gynecology, and Reproductive Biology* 11 (1980): p. 195.

9. S. Boschert, "New Onset Endometriosis Seen in Many Postmenopausal Women," *Ob. Gyn. News* (May 1, 2002), http://www2.eobgynnews.com.

10. C. H. Nezhat, W. A. Saleh, and F. Nezhat, "Endometriosis in Women with Surgically Removed Ovaries Presenting Chronic Pelvic Pain," *Abstracts of the Scientific Oral and Poster Sessions, 50th Annual Meeting, The American Fertility Society, Program Supplement* (1994): p. S209.

11. B. Namnoum, N. Hickman, and B. Goodman, "Incidence of Symptom Recurrence After Hysterectomy for Endometriosis," *Fertility and Sterility* 64(5) (November 1995): pp. 898–902.

12. A. Prentice, "Clinical Review, Regular Review: Endometriosis," *British Medical Journal* 323 (July 14, 2001): pp. 93–95.

13. Society of Obstetricians and Gynaecologists of Canada, *Hysterectomy*, "Clinical Practice Guidelines," no. 109 (January 2002): pp. 1–12.

14. R. Witt and H. Barad, "Management of Endometriosis in Women Older than 40 Years of Age," *Obstetrics and Gynecology Clinics of North America* 20(2) (June 1993): pp. 349–363.

15. D. B. Redwine, "Endometriosis Persisting After Castration: Clinical Characteristics and Results of Surgical Management," *Obstetrics and Gynecology* 83(3) (March 1994): pp. 405–413.

16. K. L. Molpus, "Pathophysiology and Management of Endometriosis in Menopause," *Infertility and Reproductive Medicine Clinics of North America* 6(4) (1995): pp. 805–828.

17. R. D. Kempers, M. B. Dockerty, A. B. Hunt, et al., "Significant Postmenopausal Endometriosis," *Surgical Gynecology and Obstetrics* 111 (1960): p. 348.

18. A. Babaknia, *Endometriosis: The '90s Outlook (Endometriosis FAQ)*, Frontiers in Bioscience USA (June 30, 2002) http://www.bioscience.org/books/endomet/end01-33.htm.

19. L. Speroff, R. H. Glass, and N. G. Kase, "Endometriosis and Infertility," in *Clinical Gynecologic Endocrinology and Infertility*, 4th ed., edited by L. Speroff, R. H. Glass, and N. G. Kase (Baltimore, MD: Williams and Wilkins, 1989), p. 547.

20. S. E. Bulun, K. Zeitoun, K. Takayama, et al., "Estrogen Production in Endometriosis and Use of Aromatase Inhibitors to Treat Endometriosis," *Endocrine-Related Cancer* 6 (1999): pp. 293–301.

21. S. Hulley, D. Grady, T. Bush, et al., "Randomized Trial of Estrogen Plus Progestin for Secondary Prevention of Coronary Heart Disease in Postmenopausal Women" *Journal of the American Medical Association* 280 (1998): pp. 605–613 (reporting on the Heart and Estrogen/Progestin Replacement Study Research Group).

22. Writing Group for the Women's Health Initiative Investigators, "Risks and Benefits of Estrogen Plus Progestin in Healthy Postmenopausal Women: Principal Results from the Women's Health Initiative Randomized Controlled Trial," *Journal of the American Medical Association* 288(3) (July 17, 2002): pp. 321–333.

23. "HRT: Four Experts Chart a New Course," *OBG Management* 14(9) (September 2002): pp. 72–88.

24. W. H. Utian, "New HRT Dosing Options for Menopausal Symptom Relief," *Medscape for WebMD* (retrieved July 26, 2002) http://www.medscape.com/viewprogram/293.

25. M. Notelovitz "Tailoring Hormone Therapy to Patients' Needs," *Menopausal Medicine* 8(3) (Fall 2000): pp. 1–5.

26. M. Ahlgrimm and J. M. Kells, *The HRT Solution* (New York: Avery, 1999).

27. J. T. Hargrove and K. G. Osteen, "An Alternative Method of Hormone Replacement Therapy Using the Natural Sex Steroids," *Infertility and Reproductive Medicine Clinics of North America* 6(4) (October 1995): pp. 653–674.

28. "The Real News About the Women's Health Initiative," *Women's Health Access* Issue 106 (September/October 2002): p. 2.

29. M. Ahlgrimm, *Natural Hormone Replacement: What You Need to Know* (Madison, WI: Women's Health America, Inc., 2002).

30. G. Bachmann, J. Bancroft, G. Braunstein, et al., "Female Androgen Insufficiency: The Princeton Consensus Statement on Definition, Classification, and Assessment," *Fertility and Sterility* 77(4) (April 2002): pp. 660–668.

31. M. Ahlgrimm, "DHEA: Is It a Fountain of Youth?" *Natural Hormone Replacement Therapy* (Madison, WI: Women's Health America, Inc., 2002).

32. A. D. Genazzani, M. Stomati, C. Strucchi, et al., "Oral Dehydroepiandrosterone Supplementation Modulates Spontaneous and Growth Hormone–Releasing Hormone-Induced Growth Hormone and Insulin-Like Growth Factor-I Secretion in Early and Late Postmenopausal Women," *Fertility and Sterility* 76(2) (August 2001): pp. 241–248.

33. R. Matorras, M. A. Elorriaga, J. I. Pijoan, et al., "Recurrence of Endometriosis in Women with Bilateral Adnexectomy (with or Without Total Hysterectomy) Who Received Hormone Replacement Therapy," *Fertility and Sterility* 77(2) (February 2002): pp. 303–308.

34. M. M. Gelfand, "Role of Androgens in Surgical Menopause," *American Journal of Obstetrics and Gynecology* 180 (March 1999): pp. S235–S237.

35. M. M. Seidl and D. E. Stewart, "Alternative Treatments for Menopausal Symptoms: Systematic Review of Scientific and Lay Literature," *Canadian Family Physician* 44 (June 1998): pp. 1,299–1,308.

36. F. Chandler, ed., *Herbs: Everyday Reference for Health Professionals* (Ottawa, ON: Canadian Pharmacists Association, Canadian Medical Association, 2000).

37. L. Barclay, "Black Cohosh Controls Menopausal Symptoms," *Medscape from WebMD* (retrieved July 25, 2002) http://www.medscape.com/viewarticle/437037.

38. "Menopause, Estrogen Loss, and Their Treatments," *Reuters Health* (retrieved May 10, 2002) http://www.reutershealth.com/wellconnected/doc40.html.

39. D. Schardt, "Got Soy? A Good Food . . . but No Miracle Worker," *Nutrition Action Healthletter* 29(9) (November 2002): pp. 8–11.

40. M. L. Finkel, M. Cohen, and H. Mahoney, "Treatment Options for Menopausal Women," *The Nurse Practitioner: The American Journal of Primary Health Care* 26(2) (February 2001): pp. 5–7.

41. S. S. Weed, *New Menopausal Years: The Wise Woman Way, Alternative Approaches for Women 30–90* (New York: Ash Tree Publishing, 2002).

42. Osteoporosis Society of Canada, *Osteoporosis Online* (retrieved May 30, 2002) http://www.osteoporosis.ca.

43. N. Sinaii, S. D. Cleary, M. L. Ballweg, et al., "High Rates of Autoimmune and Endocrine Disorders, Fibromyalgia, Chronic Fatigue

Syndrome and Atopic Diseases Among Women with Endometriosis: A Survey Analysis," *Human Reproduction* 10(10) (2002): pp. 2,715–2,724.

44. D. L. Schneider, E. L. Barrett-Connor, and D. J. Morton, "Timing of Postmenopausal Estrogen for Optimal Bone Mineral Density: The Rancho Bernardo Study," *Journal of the American Medical Association* 277 (1997): pp. 543–547.

45. C. E. Cann, "Bone Densitometry as an Adjunct to GnRH Agonist Therapy," *Journal of Reproductive Medicine* 43 (1998): pp. 321–330.

46. R. F. Spark, "Dehydroepiandrosterone: A Springboard Hormone for Female Sexuality," *Fertility and Sterility* 77(4) Suppl. 4 (April 2002): pp. S19–S25.

47. P. P. Zandi, M. C. Carlson, B. L. Plassman, et al. for the Cache County Memory Study Investigators, "Hormone Replacement Therapy and Incidence of Alzheimer's Disease in Older Women," *Journal of the American Medical Association* 288 (2002): pp. 2,123–2,129.

Chapter 12

1. A. Audebert, "How to Prevent Endometriosis?" in *The Second World Congress on Controversies in Obstetrics, Gynecology & Infertility, Proceedings* (N.p.: Monduzzi Editore, 2001), pp. 375–384.

2. N. Sinaii, S. D. Cleary, M. L. Ballweg, et al., "High Rates of Autoimmune and Endocrine Disorders, Fibromyalgia, Chronic Fatigue Syndrome and Atopic Diseases Among Women with Endometriosis: A Survey Analysis," *Human Reproduction* 17(10) (2002): pp. 2,715–2,724.

3. R. G. Lahita, "Systemic Lupus Erythematosus: Learning Disability in the Male Offspring of Female Patients and Relationship to Laterality," *Psychoneuro-Endocrinology* 13(5) (1988): pp. 385–396.

4. H. L. Ross, F. Z. Bischoff, and S. Elias, "Genetics of Endometriosis," in *Endometrium & Endometriosis*, edited by M. P. Diamond and K. G. Osteen (Malden, MA: Blackwell Science, 1997), pp. 70–74.

5. S. Kennedy, H. Mardon, and D. Barlow, "Familial Endometriosis," *Journal of Assisted Reproductive Genetics* 12(1) (1995): pp. 32–34.

6. J. W. Fanton and J. G. Golden, "Radiation-Induced Endometriosis in *Macaca Mulatta*," *Radiation Research* 126 (1991): pp. 141–146.

7. A. Van Langendonckt, F. Casanas-Roux, and J. Donnez, "Oxidative Stress and Peritoneal Endometriosis," *Fertility and Sterility* 77(5) (2002): pp. 861–868.

8. K. Lamb and T. R. Nichols, "Endometriosis: A Comparison of Associated Disease Histories," *American Journal of Preventive Medicine* 2(6) (1986): pp. 324–329.

9. T. R. Nichols, K. Lamb, and J. A. Arkins, "The Association of Atopic Diseases with Endometriosis," *Annals of Allergy* 59(11) (1987): pp. 360–363.

10. "Characteristics of Women with Endometriosis," *Endometriosis Association Newsletter* 10(2) (1989) (partial publication of data from Endometriosis Association Research Registry).

11. M. L. Ballweg, "Fibromyalgia/Endometriosis Link? . . ." *Endometriosis Association Newsletter* 12(3) (1991).

12. D. A. Grimes, S. A. LeBolt, K. R. T. Grimes, et al., "Two-Fold Risk of Endometriosis in Hospitalized Patients with Lupus," *American*

Journal of Obstetrics and Gynecology 153(179) (1985).

13. M. G. Brush, "Increased Incidence of Thyroid Autoimmune Problems in Women with Endometriosis," in *Endometriosis: A Collection of Papers Written by GPs, Researchers, Specialists and Sufferers About Endometriosis,* compiled by the Coventry Branch of the Endometriosis Society (March 1987).

14. M. L. Ballweg, "The Puzzle of Endometriosis," *Endometriosis: Advanced Management and Surgical Techniques* (New York: Springer-Verlag, 1994), pp. 275–285.

15. M. L. Ballweg, "The Puzzle of Endometriosis," *The Endometriosis Sourcebook* (Chicago: Contemporary Books, 1995), pp. 409–430.

16. C. R. Mabray, "Obstetrics and Gynecology and Clinical Ecology," *Clinical Ecology* (Part 1) 1(2) (1982–83): pp. 103–113.

17. D. W. Cramer, E. Wilson, R. J. Stillman, et al., "The Relation of Endometriosis to Menstrual Characteristics, Smoking, and Exercise," *Journal of the American Medical Association* 255(14) (1986): pp. 1,904–1,908.

18. M. Han, L. Pan, B. Wu, et al., "A Case-Control Epidemiologic Study of Endometriosis," *Chinese Medical Sciences Journal* 9(2) (1994): pp. 114–118.

19. K. Arumugam and J. M. H. Lim, "Menstrual Characteristics Associated with Endometriosis," *British Journal of Obstetrics & Gynaecology* 104 (1997): pp. 948–950.

20. R. Matorras, F. Rodiquez, J. I. Pijoan, et al., ""Epidemiology of Endometriosis in Infertile Women," *Fertility and Sterility* 63 (1995): pp. 34–38.

21. S. Berube, S. Marcoux, and R. Maheux, "Characteristics Related to the Prevalence of Minimal or Mild Endometriosis in Infertile Women. Canadian Collaborative Group on Endometriosis," *Epidemiology* 9 (1998): pp. 504–510.

22. S. L. Darrow, J. E. Vena, R. E. Batt, et al., "Menstrual Cycle Characteristics and the Risk of Endometriosis," *Epidemiology* 4(2) (1993): pp. 135–142.

23. P. Vercellini, O. DeGiorgi, G. Aimi, et al., "Menstrual Characteristics in Women with and Without Endometriosis," *Obstetrics and Gynecology* 90(2) (1997): pp. 264–268.

24. G. B. Candiani, V. Danesino, A. Gastaldi, et al., "Reproductive and Menstrual Factors and Risk of Peritoneal and Ovarian Endometriosis," *Fertility and Sterility* 56(2) (1991): pp. 230–234.

25. S. H. Woodworth, J. S. Sanfilippo, M. Singh, et al., "A Prospective Study on the Association Between Red Hair Color and Endometriosis in Infertile Patients," *Fertility and Sterility* 64 (1995): pp. 651–652.

26. R. E. Frisch, G. Wyshak, L. S. Albert, et al., "Dysplastic Nevi, Cutaneous Melanoma, and Gynecologic Disorders," *International Journal of Dermatology* 31 (1992): pp. 331–335.

27. J. W. Huffman, "Endometriosis in Young Teen-Age Girls," *Pediatric Annals* 10(12) (December 1981): pp 44–49.

28. D. L. Olive and D. Y. Henderson, "Endometriosis and Müllerian Anomalies," *Obstetrics and Gynecology* 69 (1987): p. 412.

29. B. Kirshon and A. N. Poindexter, "Contraception: A Risk Factor for Endometriosis," *Obstetrics and Gynecology* 71(6) Part 1 (June 1988): pp. 829–831.

30. H. Sangi-Haghpeykar and A. N. Poindexter, "Epidemiology of Endometriosis Among Parous Women," *Obstetrics and Gynecology* 85(6) (1995): pp. 983–992.

31. T. Paull and L. G. Tedeschi, "Perineal Endometriosis at the Site of Episiotomy Scar," *Obstetrics and Gynecology* 40 (1972): p. 28.

32. P. Rovito and M. Gittleman, "Two Cases of Endometrioma in Cesarean Scars," *Surgery* 100 (1986): p. 118.

33. P. E. Stroup, "Endometriosis in Laparotomy Scars," *Journal of Reproductive Medicine* 16 (1976): p. 85.

34. H. Fakih, R. Tamura, A. Kesselman, et al., "Endometriosis After Tubal Ligation," *Journal of Reproductive Medicine* No. 30 (12), (December 1985): pp. 939–941.

35. S. M. Ismail, "Cone Biopsy Causes Cervical Endometriosis and Tuboendometrioid Metaplasia," *Histopathology* 18 (1991): pp. 107–114.

36. J. Benifla, E. Darai, F. Filippini, et al., "Operative Hysteroscopy May Transport Endometrial Cells into the Peritoneal Cavity: Report of a Prospective Longitudinal Study," *Gynaecological Endoscopy* 6 (1997): pp. 151–153.

37. H. Depypere, M. Coppens, H. van Kets, et al., "Pelvic Spreading of Endometrial Tissue During Endometrial Ablation," *Gynaecological Endoscopy* 6 (1997): pp. 155–156.

38. K. W. Schweppe and D. Ring, "Peritoneal Defects and the Development of Endometriosis in Relation to the Timing of Endoscopic Surgery During the Menstrual Cycle," *Fertility and Sterility* 78(4) (2002): pp. 763–766.

39. M. L. Ballweg and the Endometriosis Association, *The Endometriosis Sourcebook* (Chicago: Contemporary Books, 1995), p. 411.

40. Ballweg and the Endometriosis Association, *The Endometriosis Sourcebook*, pp. 197–210.

41. A. H. A. Wynn and M. Wynn, *The Case for Preconceptual Care in Men and Women* (Bicester, England: AB Academic Publishers, 1991), pp. 32–33.

42. T. Colborn, F. S. vom Saal, and A. M. Soto, "Developmental Effects of Endocrine-Disrupting Chemicals in Wildlife and Humans," *Environmental Health Perspectives* 102(3) (1994): pp. 256–257.

43. J. D. Buckley, L. L. Robison, and R. Swotinsky, "Occupational Exposures of Parents of Children with Acute Nonlymphocytic Leukemia: A Report from the Children's Cancer Study Group," *Cancer Research* 49 (1989): pp. 4,030–4,037.

44. F. Sharara, D. Seifer, and J. Flaws, "Environmental Toxicants and Female Reproduction," *Fertility and Sterility* 70(4) (1998): pp. 613–622.

45. J. W. Fanton and J. G. Golden, "Radiation-Induced Endometriosis in *Macaca Mulatta*," *Radiation Research* 126 (1991): pp. 141–146.

46. J. E. Haddow, G. E. Palomaki, W. C. Allan, et al., "Maternal Thyroid Deficiency During Pregnancy and Subsequent Neuropsychological Development of the Child," *New England Journal of Medicine* 341(8) (1999): pp. 549–555.

47. A. J. Wolfberg and D. A. Nagey, "Thyroid Disease During Pregnancy and Subsequent Congenital Anomalies," Abstract (January 17, 2002).

48. A. M. Mandl, "Factors Influencing Ovarian Sensitivity to Gonadotropins," *Journal of Endocrinology* 15 (1957): p. 448.

49. N. D. Barnes, A. B. Hayles, and R. J. Ryan, "Sexual Maturation in Juvenile Hypothyroidism," *Mayo Clinical Procedures* 48 (1973): p. 849.

50. D. C. Morse, E. K. Wehler, W. Wesseling, et al., "Alterations in Rat Brain Thyroid Hormone Status Following Pre- and Postnatal Exposure

to Polychlorinated Biphenyls (Aroclor 1254)," *Toxicology and Applied Pharmacology* 136 (1996): pp. 269–279.

51. J. L. Jacobson and S. W. Jacobson, "Intellectual Impairment in Children Exposed to Polychlorinated Biphenyls in Utero," *New England Journal of Medicine* 335(11) (1996): pp. 783–789.

52. B. Burrows, F. D. Martinez, M. Halonen, et al., "Association of Asthma with Serum IgE Levels and Skin-Test Reactivity to Allergens," *New England Journal of Medicine* 320(5) (February 1989): pp. 271–277.

53. Preconception Care, Inc., *For Tomorrow's Children: A Manual for Future Parents* (Blooming Glen, PA: Preconception Care, Inc., 1990), pp. 104, 109.

54. C. R. Mabray, M. L. Burditt, T. L. Martin, et al., "Treatment of Common Gynecologic-Endocrinologic Symptoms by Allergy Management Procedures," *Obstetrics and Gynecology* 59(5) (1980): pp. 560–564.

55. C. J. Ansell and C. C. Gorchoff, "A Descriptive Investigation of the Perinatal Clinical Courses of Women with Endometriosis," Yale University School of Nursing (1987).

56. A. Carosso, C. Ruffino, N. Bugiani, et al., "The Effect of Birth Season on Pollenosis," *Annals of Allergy* 56 (April 1986): pp.300–303.

57. D. E. Johnstone, "Born Under the Sign of the Sneeze," *Journal of Respiratory Diseases* (April 1987): p. 8.

58. "Curtailing Allergies in Child with Atopic Family History," *Family Practice News* 16(22) (November 15–30, 1986).

59. *Medical Tribune*, June 10, 1993.

60. J. Vickerstaff Joneja, L. Bielory, *Understanding Allergy, Sensitivity, & Immunity: A Comprehensive Guide* (New Brunswick, NJ: Rutgers University Press, 1990), p. 241.

61. K. Mortimer et al., *American Journal of Respiratory and Critical Care Medicine* (October 2000).

62. B. Xu, J. Pekkanen, A. L. Hartikainen, et al., "Caesarean Section and Risk of Asthma and Allergy in Childhood," *Journal of Allergy and Clinical Immunology* 107(4) (2001): pp. 732–733.

63. M. Kalliomäki, S. Salminen, H. Arvilommi, et al., "Probiotics in Primary Prevention of Atopic Disease: A Randomised Placebo-Controlled Trial," *The Lancet* 357 (2001): pp. 1,076–1,079.

64. *The Lancet* 346 (1995): pp. 1,065–1,069.

65. B. Baker, "Breast-Feeding's Role in Pediatric Asthma Debated," *Family Practice News* (June 1, 1999): p. 49.

66. Reuters Medical News, "Breast-Feeding Cuts Risk of Respiratory Disease" (October 23, 2001).

67. P. S. Clyne and A. Kulczycki Jr., "Human Breast Milk Contains Bovine IgG: Relationship to Infant Colic?" *Pediatrics* 87(4) (April 1991): pp. 439–444.

68. P. Vadas, Y. Wai, W. Burks, et al., "Detection of Peanut Allergens in Breast Milk of Lactating Women," *Journal of the American Medical Association* 285(13) (April 4, 2001): pp. 1,746–1,748.

69. N. Sigurs, G. Hattevig, and B. Kjellman, "Maternal Avoidance of Eggs, Cow's Milk, and Fish During Lactation: Effect on Allergic Manifestations, Skin-Prick Tests, and Specific IgE Antibodies in Children at Age 4 Years," *Pediatrics* 89(4 pt. 2) (1992): pp. 735–739.

70. C. Bateson-Koch, *Allergies: Disease in Disguise* (Burnaby, BC: Alive Books, 1994), p. 129.

71. L. S. Birnbaum, "Developmental Effects of Dioxin," *Environmental Health Perspectives* 103 Supp. 7 (1995): pp. 89–94.

72. U.S. Environmental Protection Agency, "Health Assessment Document for 2,3,7,8-tetrachlorodibenzo-p-dioxin (TCDD) and Related Compounds," External Review Draft EPA/600/BP-92/001c (August 1994).

73. K. Patel, "Is Breast Milk Safe from a Chemically Sensitive Mother?" (presentation at the American Academy of Environmental Medicine annual meeting, Baltimore, Maryland, November 8, 1998).

74. O. Tsutsumi, M. Momoeda, Y. Takai, et al., "Breast-Fed Infants, Possibly Exposed to Dioxins in Milk, Have Unexpectedly Lower Incidence of Endometriosis in Adult Life," *International Journal of Gynecology & Obstetrics* 68(2) (2002): pp. 151–153.

75. Leo Galland, M.D., *The Four Pillars of Healing* (New York: Random House, 1997), p. 139.

76. J. Raloff, "What's Coming out of Baby's Bottle?" *ScienceNewsOnline* 156(6) (August 7, 1999).

77. A. Ivarsson, O. Hernell, H. Stenlund, et al., "Breast-Feeding Protects Against Celiac Disease," *American Journal of Clinical Nutrition* 75(5) (2002): pp. 914–921.

78. M. Kelly and E. Parsons, *Mother's Almanac* (New York: Doubleday and Company, 1975), p. 42.

79. *Pediatrics* 86 (1990): p. 541.

80. A. Munir et al., "Exposure to Indoor Allergens in Early Infancy and Sensitization," *Journal of Allergy and Clinical Immunology* 100 (1997): pp. 177–181.

81. L. Lawson, *Staying Well in a Toxic World* (Evanston, IL: Lynnword Press, 1993), p. 305.

82. M. Kelly, *The Mother's Almanac II: Your Child From Six to Twelve* (New York: Doubleday, 1989), p. 171.

83. Jacobsen, "Allergy Treatment Can Prevent Development of Asthma in Children," *Clinical Immunology* (February 2002).

84. S. H. Arshad, S. Matthews, C. Gant, et al., "Effect of Allergen Avoidance on Development of Allergic Disorders in Infancy," *The Lancet* 339(8808) (1992): pp. 1493–1497.

85. L. J. Stevens, *The Complete Book of Allergy Control* (New York: Macmillan Publishing Company, 1983), p. 115.

86. *Journal of Allergy and Clinical Immunology* 85 (1990): pp. 65–74.

87. Centers for Disease Control, "Asthma: United States, 1980–1990," *Journal of the American Medical Association* 268(15) (1992): pp. 1,995, 1,999.

88. R. McConnell, K. Berhane, F. Gilliland, et al., "Asthma in Exercising Children Exposed to Ozone: A Cohort Study," *The Lancet* 359 (February 2002): pp. 386–391.

89. B. Lanphear, *Pediatrics* (March 2001).

90. J. J. K. Jaakkola, L. Oie, P. Naftad, et al., "Interior Surface Materials in the Home and the Development of Bronchial Obstruction in Young Children in Oslo, Norway," *American Journal of Public Health* 89(2) (January 1999): pp. 188–192.

91. K. Wickens, N. Pearce, J. Crane, et al., "Antibiotic Use in Early Childhood and the Development of Asthma," *Clinical and Experimental Allergy* 29 (1999): pp. 766–771.

92. M. R. Laufer, "Premenarcheal Endometriosis Without an Associated Obstructive Anomaly: Presentation, Diagnosis, and Treatment" (abstract presented at the Annual Meeting of the American Society for Reproductive Health, 2000), p. S15.

93. Letter from William G. Crook, M.D., to the Endometriosis Association (May 17, 1988).

94. C. O. Truss, *The Missing Diagnosis* (Birmingham, AL: 1983 [self-published]), p. 108.

95. B. Björksten, P. Naaber, E. Sepp, et al., "The Intestinal Microflora in Allergic Estonian and Swedish Two-Year-Old Children," *Clinical and Experimental Allergy* 29 (1999): pp. 342–346.

96. H. Koike, T. Egawa, M. Ohtsuka, et al., "Correlation Between Dysmenorrheic Severity and Prostaglandin Production in Women with Endometriosis," *Prostaglandins, Leukotrienes, Essential Fatty Acids* 46 (1992): pp. 133–137.

97. B. Deutch, "Menstrual Pain in Danish Women Correlated with Low n-3 Polyunsaturated Fatty Acid Intake," *European Journal of Clinical Nutrition* 49 (1995): pp. 508–516.

98. A. Covens, P. Christopher, and R. F. Casper, "The Effect of Dietary Supplementation with Fish Oils Fatty Acids on Surgically Induced Endometriosis in the Rabbit," *Fertility and Sterility* 49 (1988): pp. 698–703.

99. Z. Harel, F. Biro, R. K. Kottenhahn, et al., "Supplementation with Omega-3 Polyunsaturated Fatty Acids in the Management of Dysmenorrhea in Adolescents," *American Journal of Obstetrics and Gynecology* (1996): pp. 1,335–1,338.

100. S. K. Weiland, E. von Mutius, A. Hüsing, et al., "Intake of Trans Fatty Acids and Prevalence of Childhood Asthma and Allergies in Europe," *The Lancet* 353(9,169) (June 12, 1999): pp. 2,040–2,041.

101. L. Kohlmeimer et al., "Lifestyles and Trends in Worldwide Breast Cancer Rates," *Annals of the New York Academy of Science* 609 (1990): pp. 259–268.

102. D. Gislason et al., "Sensitization to airbourne and food allergens in Reykajavik and Uppsala," *European Respiratory Journal* 10 (1997): pp. 6–12.

103. D. Gislason et al., "Sensitization to airbourne and food allergens in Reykajavik and Uppsala," *Allergy* 54 (November 1999): pp. 1160–1167.

104. M. R. Gazvani, L. Smith, P. Haggarty, et al., "High Omega-3: Omega-6 Fatty Acid Ratios in Culture Medium Reduce Endometrial-Cell Survival in Combined Endometrial Gland and Stromal Cell Cultures from Women with and Without Endometriosis," *Fertility and Sterility* 76(4) (2001): pp. 717–722.

105. L. Pauling, "On Vitamin C and Infectious Diseases," *Executive Health* 19(4) (1983).

106. C. Anah, L. Jarike, and H. Baig, "High Dose Ascorbic Acid in Nigerian Asthmatics," *Journal of Allergy & Clinical Immunology* 62(5) (1981).

107. R. Matthew and B. Altura, *Magnesium and Trace Elements* (Basel, Switzerland: 1993).

108. M. A. Zeligs, "Diet and Estrogen Status: The Cruciferous Connection," *Journal of Medicinal Food* 1(2) (1998): pp. 67–82.

109. S. L. Rosenthal and F. M. Biro, "Communication with Adolescents and Their Families," *Adolescent & Pediatric Gynecology* 4 (1991): pp. 57–61.

110. A. Kimbrell, *Fatal Harvest: The Tragedy of Industrial Agriculture* (Washington: Foundation for Deep Ecology and Island Press, 2002), p. 211.

111. R. J. Barnard and G. Heuser, "The Estrogen-Like Effect of Herbicides: A Patient Report," *Clinical Pediatrics* 37 (1998): pp. 633–634.

112. *Canary News* "Children and Non-Hodgkin's Lymphoma," January/February 2001, p. 14.

113. "Pesticide Exposure and Childhood Immunological Abnormalities," *Human Ecology* (Fall 2001): p. 6 (report on "Assessing Environmental Exposure in Children: Immunotoxicology Screening," *Journal of Exposure Analysis and Environmental Epidemiology* 10 (2000): pp. 769–775).

114. "Estrogenic Agents Leach from Dental Sealant," *Science News* 49 (April 11, 1996): p. 214.

115. N. Olea et al., *Environmental Health Perspectives* (March 1996).

116. F. Clavel-Chapelon and the E3N-EPIC Group, "Evolution of Age at Menarche and at Onset of Regular Cycling in a Large Cohort of French Women," *Human Reproduction* 17(1) (2002): pp. 228–232.

117. M. E. Herman-Giddens, "Secondary Sexual Characteristics and Menses in Young Girls Seen in Office Practice: A Study from the Pediatric Research in Office Settings Network," *Pediatrics* 99(4) (April 1997), pp. 505–512.

118. M. E. Herman-Giddens, "Prevalence of Secondary Sexual Characteristics in a Population of North Carolina Girls Ages 3 to 10," *Adolescent & Pediatric Gynecology* 4 (1991): pp. 21–26.

119. BBC News, "Girls Reach Puberty at Eight," June 19, 2000, BBC News website (www.bbc.co.uk).

120. *Pediatrics* 2000 CDC report.

121. A. P. Burgess and J. L. Burgess, "The Growth Pattern of East African Schoolgirls," *Human Biology* 36 (1964): pp. 177–193.

122. L. Zacharias and R. J. Wurtman, "Age at Menarche," *New England Journal of Medicine* 280(16) (April 17, 1969): pp. 868–875 (describing results reported in N. Michaelson, "Studies in Physical Development of Negroes: IV. Onset of Puberty," *American Journal of Physical Anthropology* 2 (1944): pp. 151–166.

123. C. M. Tiwary, "Premature Sexual Development in Children Following the Use of Placenta and/or Estrogen Containing Hair Product(s)," *Pediatric Research* 135 (1994), p. 108A.

124. T. A. Foster, A. W. Voors, L. S. Webber, et al., "Anthropometric and Maturation Measurements of Children, Ages 5 to 14 Years, in a Biracial Community: The Bogalusa Heart Study," *American Journal of Clinical Nutrition* 30 (1977): pp. 582–591.

125. C. A. Kozinetz, "Sexual Maturation and Blood Pressure Levels of a Biracial Sample of Girls," *American Journal of Diseases of Children* 145 (1991): pp. 142–147.

126. D. S. Freedman, S. R. Srinivasan, L. S. Webber, et al., "African-American–White Differences in Serum Lipoproteins During Sexual Maturation: The Heart Study," *Journal of Chronic Disease* 40, (1987): pp. 309–318.

127. National Heart, Lung, and Blood Institute Growth and Health Study Research Group, "Obesity and Cardiovascular Disease Risk Factors in Black and White Girls: The NHLBI Growth and Health Study," *American Journal of Public Health* 82 (1992): pp. 1,613–1,620.

128. G. S. Lemaire, "The Relationship of Illness, Psychosocial, and Cognitive Factors to Perceived Uncertainty Among Women with Endometriosis," dissertation submitted to the Faculty of the Graduate School of the University of Maryland (1996).

129. F. Parazzini, C. LaVecchia, E. Negri, et al., "Menstrual Factors and the Risk of Epithelial Ovarian Cancer," *Journal of Clinical Epidemiology* 42 (1989): pp. 443–448.

130. F. Parazzini, S. LaVecchia, and S. Franeschi, "Risk Factors for Endometrioid, Mucinous, and Serous Benign Ovarian Cysts," *International Journal of Epidemiology* 18 (1989): pp. 108–112.

131. H. A. Risch, N. S. Weiss, J. L. Lyon, et al., "Events of Reproductive Life and the Incidence of Epithelial Ovarian Cancer," *American Journal of Epidemiology* 117 (1983): pp. 128–139.

132. A. S. Whittemore, R. Harris, J. Itnyre, and Collaborative Ovarian Cancer Group,

"Characteristics Relating to Ovarian Cancer Risk: Collaborative Analysis of 12 U.S. Case-Control Studies," *American Journal of Epidemiology* 136 (1992): pp. 1,212–1,220.

133. B. A. Stoll et al., "Does Early Physical Maturity Influence Breast Cancer Risk?" *Acta Oncologica* 33(2) (1994): pp. 171–176.

134. D. Apter, "Hormonal Events During Female Puberty in Relation to Breast Cancer Risk," *European Journal of Cancer Prevention* 5(6) (1996): pp. 476–482.

135. J. L. Kelsey, M. D. Gammon, and E. M. John, "Reproductive Factors and Breast Cancer," *Epidemiological Reviews* 15 (1993): pp. 36–47.

136. L. M. Butler, N. A. Potischman, B. Newman, et al., "Menstrual Risk Factors and Early-Onset Breast Cancer," *Cancer Causes and Control* 11 (2000): pp. 451–458.

137. C. J. Grossman and G. A. Roselle, "Estrogen, a Strong Suppressor of Cell-Mediated Immunity," *Journal Steroid Biochemistry* 19 (1983): p. 461.

138. S. M. Garn, M. LaVelle, K. R. Rosenberg, et al., "Maturational Timing as a Factor in Female Fatness and Obesity," *American Journal of Clinical Nutrition* 43 (1986): pp. 879–883.

139. Francesca Lyman, "Coming of Age Too Soon?" MSNBC (March 1, 2001).

140. M. E. Herman-Giddens, A. D. Sandler, and N. E. Friedman, "Sexual Precocity in Girls: An Association with Sexual Abuse?" *American Journal of Diseases of Children* 142 (1988): pp. 431–433.

141. K. Vigilante and M. Flynn, *Low Fat Lies: High Fat Frauds and the Healthiest Diet in the World* (Washington, DC: Regnery Publishing, 1999).

142. D. Shepperson Mills and M. Vernon, *Endometriosis: A Key to Healing Through Nutrition*, 1st ed. (Boston, MA: Element Books, Inc., 1999), pp. 189–190.

143. R. E. Frisch, "Fatness and Fertility," *Scientific American* (March 1988): pp. 88–95.

144. O. Stark, C. S. Peckham, and C. Moynihan, "Weight and Age at Menarche," *Archives of Diseases in Childhood* 64 (1989): pp. 383–387.

145. J. E. Brody, "Risk for Cancer Can Start in Womb," *New York Times*, December 21, 1999.

146. H. Aldercreutz and F. Martin, "Biliary Excretion and Intestinal Metabolism of Progesterone and Estrogens in Man," *Journal of Steroid Biochemistry* 13 (1980): pp. 231–244.

147. H. Aldercreutz, K. Höckerstedt, C. Bannwart, et al., "Effect of Dietary Components, Including Lignans and Phytoestrogens, on Enterohepatic Circulation and Liver Metabolism of Estrogens and on Sex Hormone Binding Globulin (SHBG)," *Journal of Steroid Biochemistry* 27 (1987): pp. 1,135–1,144.

148. D. P. Rose, "Dietary Fiber and Breast Cancer," *Nutrition Cancer* 13 (1990): pp. 1–8.

149. B. R. Goldin, H. Adlercreutz, S. L. Gorbach, et al., "Estrogen Excretion Patterns and Plasma Levels in Vegetarian and Omnivorous Women," *New England Journal of Medicine* 307(25) (1982): pp. 1,542–1,574.

150. C. G. Whitten and T. D. Schultz, "Binding of Steroid Hormones *in Vitro* by Water-Insoluble Dietary Fiber," *Nutrition Research* 8 (1988): pp. 1,223–1,235.

151. T. D. Shultz and J. E. Leklem, "Nutrient Intake and Hormonal Status of Premenopausal Vegetarian Seventh-Day Adventists and Premenopausal Nonvegetarians," *Nutrition Cancer* 4 (1983): pp. 247–259.

152. B. R. Golden, H. Adlercreutz, S. L. Gorbach, et al., "The Relationship Between Estrogen Levels and Diets of Caucasian American and Oriental

Immigrant Women," *American Journal of Clinical Nutrition* 44 (1986): pp. 945–953.

153. B. K. Armstrong, J. B. Brown, H. T. Clarke, et al., "Diet and Reproductive Hormones: A Study of Vegetarian and Nonvegetarian Postmenopausal Women," *Journal of the National Cancer Institute* 67 (1981): pp. 761–767.

154. V. W. Persky, R. T. Chatterton, L. Van Horn, et al., "Hormone Levels in Vegetarian and Nonvegetarian Teenage Girls: Potential Implications for Breast Cancer Risk," *Cancer Research* 52 (1992): pp. 578–583.

155. F. Diamond, "The Function of Adipose Tissue," *Growth, Genetics, and Hormones* 18(2) (2002): pp. 17–22.

156. M. Duenwald, "Body's Defender Goes on the Attack," Vaccinationnews.com (January 2002).

157. M. E. Herman-Giddens, L. Wang, and G. Koch, "Secondary Sexual Characteristics in Boys: Estimates from the National Health and Nutrition Examination Survey III, 1988–1994," *Archives of Pediatrics & Adolescent Medicine* 155(9) (September 2001): pp. 1,022–1,028.

158. Feminist Majority Foundation, "Empowering Women in Sports," no. 4 (1995).

159. W. Rogan, *Journal of Pediatrics* (Spring 2000).

160. *Epidemiology* 11(6) (November 2000).

161. E. Marshall, "Search for a Killer: Focus Shifts from Fat to Hormones," *Science* 259 (1993): pp. 618–621.

162. I. Colon, C. J. Bourdony, and O. Rosario, "Identification of Phthalate Esters in the Serum of Young Puerto Rican Girls with Premature Breast Development," *Environmental Health Perspectives* 108(9) (September 9, 2000): p. 895.

163. J. H. Petersen and T. Breindahl, "Plasticizers in Total Diet Samples, Baby Food and Infant Formulae," *Food Additives and Contaminants* 17(2) (2000): pp. 133–141.

164. B. C. Blount, M. J. Silva, S. P. Caudill, et al., "Levels of Seven Urinary Phthalate Metabolites in a Human Reference Population," *Environmental Health Perspectives* 108(10) (2000): pp. 979–982.

Chapter 14

1. J. P. Myers, "Environmental Threats to Women's Health: Protecting a Human Right" (speech to United Nations Commission on the Status of Women, 1998).

2. B. Moyers, "Trade Secrets: A Moyers Report," PBS March 2001.

3. Agency for Toxic Substances and Disease Registry, "Children's Exposures," *Public Health and the Environment* 1(1/2) (2002): p. 1.

4. U.S. Environmental Protection Agency, Office of Children's Health Protection, "Our History: Office of Children's Health Protection," (retrieved December 4, 2002), EPA website www.yosemite.epa.gov/ochp.

5. N. Sinaii, S. D. Cleary, M. L. Ballweg et al., "High Rates of Autoimmune and Endocrine Disorders, Fibromyalgia, Chronic Fatigue Syndrome and Atopic Diseases Among Women with Endometriosis: A Survey Analysis," *Human Reproduction* 17(10) (2002): p. 2,715.

6. S. E. Rier et al., "Endometriosis in Rhesus Monkeys (*Macaca Mulatta*) Following Chronic Exposure to 2,3,7,8,-tetrachlorodibenzo-*p*-dioxin," *Fundamental and Applied Toxicology* 21 (1993): pp. 433–441.

7. John Quaid, "Mystery in the Blood," *Amicus Journal* 23(1) (Spring 2001): p. 34.

8. U.S. Environmental Protection Agency, National Center for Environmental Assessment, "Database of Sources of Environmental

Releases of Dioxin-Like Compounds in the United States," March 2001.

9. U.S. Environmental Protection Agency, Endocrine Disruptor Screening Program, Report to Congress, August 2000.

10. F. I. Sharara, D. B. Seifer, and J. A. Flaws, "Environmental Toxicants and Female Reproduction," *Fertility and Sterility* 70(4) (1998): p. 615.

11. J. P. Myers, "Environmental Threats to Women's Health: Protecting a Human Right" (speech to United Nations Commission on the Status of Women, 1998).

12. J. Houlihan, C. Brody, and B. Schwan, "Not Too Pretty: Phthalates, Beauty Products & the FDA" (2002): nottoopretty.org.

13. Environmental Research Foundation, "The Environmental Movement: Part 6, Changing the Climate of Opinion," *Rachel's Environmental and Health Weekly News* no. 746 (2002): p. 3.

14. L. M. Gibbs, *Dying from Dioxin* (Boston: South End Press, 1995), pp. 30–31.

15. Gibbs, *Dying from Dioxin*, p. 33.

16. National Toxicology Program, Center for the Evaluation of Risks to Human Reproduction "NTP-CERHR Expert Panel Report on Di(2-Ethylhexyl)Phthalate" (October 2000).

17. J. Kielhorn, C. Melber, U. Wahnschaffe, et al., "Vinyl Chloride: Still a Cause for Concern," *Environmental Health Perspectives* 108(7) (2000): p. 1.

18. B. Moyers, "Trade Secrets: A Moyers Report," PBS March 2001.

19. Plaintiffs' First Supplemental Disclosure, *McKinley v. Gencorp*, Ohio, 2002.

20. Environmental Research Foundation, "The Environmental Movement: Part 6, Changing the Climate of Opinion," *Rachel's Environment & Health Biweekly* no. 746 (2002): pp. 3–4.

21. Wingspread Statement on the Precautionary Principle, January 1998.

22. Environmental Research Foundation, "The Environmental Movement: Part 4, Rebuilding the Movement to Win," *Rachel's Environmental and Health Weekly News* no. 744 (2002): p. 4.

23. Environmental Research Foundation, "The Environmental Movement: Part 6, Changing the Climate of Opinion," *Rachel's Environmental and Health Weekly News* no. 746 (2002): pp. 3–4.

Contributors

Ellen Agger, Mahone Bay, Nova Scotia, is a freelance health writer and Web content manager who specializes in plain language. She has been an Endometriosis Association member for years and has a keen interest in and extensive experience using alternative therapies for her health needs.

Ann Beckmann is a website developer for Antioch University, Seattle, Washington, and a writing coach who works one-on-one with writers at all skill levels. She previously worked at metro daily newspapers in Edmonton, Alberta; Madison and Milwaukee, Wisconsin; and Seattle and Everett, Washington.

P. Fay Campbell, Milwaukee, Wisconsin, has a B.A. in communications and an M.S.Ed. in counseling from Western Illinois University. Her background is in mental health counseling, specializing in women's issues.

Lynn Castrodale, the Association's former Environmental Coordinator, has conducted seminars for Association support groups on dioxin, PVC, and endo. She has a degree in marketing and international business from Drake University.

Gary O. Caviness, B.S., M.S., Connecticut, is a researcher for Boehringer Ingelheim Pharmaceuticals, Inc. and is also the owner and CEO of BioGrafix, a biological sciences graphic arts company.

Kim Collier is a middle-school language arts teacher from Connecticut and a long-time Association member and environmental justice advocate. She is also a cofounder of the Endometriosis Walk for Awareness, and was the Association's first Environmental Coordinator. Collier raises awareness about the harms of PVC, dioxins, and phthalates (as well as other toxins such as pesticides and diesel exhaust) through her work with the Connecticut Coalition for Environmental Justice.

The late **Eleanor DiBiasi, Ph.D.**, wrote her doctoral dissertation, "The Meaning of Endometriosis to Females Experiencing the Disease," in 1996. She included poems and stories by women with endo about their disease. She wanted to share these descriptions in the hope of enlightening others about how it feels to live with endometriosis.

Kelly Dobert, Queensbury, New York, is a wife, mother of two, Association Lifetime Member, lifetime endo activist, a cofounder of the Endometriosis Walk for Awareness, and a twenty-three-year endo survivor who's pain free at last!

Elizabeth Dougherty, an Association member, is a freelance writer and editor based in Palo Alto, California.

Linda Duczman earned her B.A. in journalism from Marquette University. She has authored a children's book and was associate creative director for a communications company in Milwaukee before becoming a freelance writer. She has written articles for trade magazines and newsletters and has scripted award-winning video productions for business, industry, education, the arts, and nonprofit organizations.

Marge Fundarek, now forty-six, feels she may finally be free of endo after having a radical hysterectomy for cervical cancer. She lives happily with her husband and their pets in Pickering, Ontario.

Lauren Gottschalk, Milwaukee, Wisconsin, is a student at Brandeis University.

Crystal Grotberg is a graduate student. She was Education/Publications Associate for the Endometriosis Association at the time she wrote her article in this book.

Since beginning alternative therapies, **Jennifer Hochgesang** has been almost consistently symptom free from endo for almost five years. She lives in Oak Park, Illinois, with her two dogs, two cats, and one fiancé.

Russell Jaffe, M.D., Ph.D., C.C.N., Sterling, Virginia, is a physician, biochemist, and molecular biologist. He has developed a number of laboratory procedures that measure the function of cells and cell systems including the ELISA/ACT LRA tests. He has published over fifty peer-reviewed articles and contributed to a variety of texts. He also teaches physicians how to practice integrative and comprehensive medicine.

Clara Klein, Nevada, writes, "I was told after my first operation that I had to have a child right away or never. What I didn't have was someone I wanted to have a child with—not until years later. By then (early thirties), it was too late. I was raw with emotion when I wrote my poem. Since then, I have come to peace with my destiny. I am now a successful career woman and have a successful marriage. But I will always feel like I missed something."

Meri Lau, Madison, Wisconsin, is an art teacher for the Madison, Wisconsin, Metropolitan School District at the elementary level, taught art in the Milwaukee Public Schools for seven years, earned a master's of science in art education at the University of Wisconsin–Milwaukee, and continues to advocate for the inclusion of children with severe disabilities in art.

Nancy Merrill, Milwaukee, Wisconsin, was education and development assistant/associate editor for the Association at the time she wrote her article in this book. She was a nurse in gynecology and obstetrics before earning her B.A. and M.A. in English and working in editing and writing positions.

Deborah Metzger, M.D., Ph.D., is renowned for her integrative approach to the management of endometriosis. She has a Ph.D. in molecular endocrinology from Baylor College of Medicine, an M.D. from the University of Texas Medical School at Houston, and a fellowship in reproductive endocrinology from Duke University. She has served on the faculties of the University of Connecticut, Yale University, and Stanford University. She has lectured worldwide, has written extensively about endometriosis and chronic pelvic pain, and has a private practice in San Jose, California, specializing in endometriosis, chronic pelvic pain, and other complex gynecologic problems.

Before beginning her current work on an M.D./Ph.D. at Dartmouth Medical School, **Grace Migaki**, New Hampshire, spent five years as a scientist in the department of immunology at Boehringer Ingelheim Pharmaceuticals, Inc.

David L. Olive, M.D., is professor of obstetrics and gynecology and director of the Division of Reproductive Endocrinology and Infertility at the Unversity of Wisconsin Hospital in Madison. He earned his medical degree at Baylor College of Medicine, performed a residency in Ob/Gyn at Northwestern University and a fellowship in Reproductive Endocriology and Infertility at Duke University. Dr. Olive is Board Certified in both Ob/Gyn and Reproductive Endocriology and Infertility and is accredited in advanced laproscopy and hysteroscopy. He has been a faculty member at the University of Arkansas, the University of Texas, and Yale University. Dr. Olive is an internationally recognized expert in infertility, endoscopic surgery, Asherman syndrome, endometriosis, and uterine fibroids. He has written more than 250 scientific publications and several books and is on the editorial board for numerous journals.

Lori Price is the former president of the Kitchener-Waterloo Association Support Group. After the birth of her twin boys—miracle IVF babies—she is a busy stay-at-home mom who savors her miracles daily.

Brenda W. Quinn's history of Wisconsin's oldest private hospital won the Council for Wisconsin Writers (CWW) Non-Fiction Book Award in 1999. She was Education and Outreach Coordinator at the Association from 2000 through 2002. Quinn holds an M.A. from the University of Wisconsin–Milwaukee.

Corey Resnick, N.D., is president of Integrative Health and Nutrition, Inc., consultants in Lake Oswego, Oregon. He received his doctor of naturopathic medicine degree from the National College of Naturopathic Medicine in Portland, Oregon. He currently serves on the board of directors of the American Association of Naturopathic Physicians and is cofounder of Tyler Encapsulations.

Cindy Rice, Milwaukee, Wisconsin, wrote her article in this book as part of her high school independent study program. She is now a college student.

Suzanne Rohrer founded the Houston Chapter of the Endometriosis Association and served as its first president. She is a semiretired science teacher, having taught physics, chemistry, and biology at both the primary and secondary levels.

Canadian **Marielle Saint-Louis** (a pseudonym) wrote her article in this book to celebrate the one-year anniversary of her hysterectomy.

Lori Schott, a leader of the Akron, Ohio, Endometriosis Association Support Group, and **Steve Schott** are the parents of a young woman who has been struggling with severe endo for many years.

Maria H. Schulz, B.A.S., B.S.N., R.N., was diagnosed at twenty-three with endo, though she first had symptoms at fourteen. After ten surgeries, she is finally pain free, thanks to surgery with an endo specialist. Maria is a registered nurse for an acute rehabilitation facility. She and her husband live in Indiana with their miracle son through adoption.

Lyse Tremblay, Montreal, is also the author of "Is Your Home a Health Hazard?" which appears in *The Endometriosis Sourcebook*.

Christel Wendelberger, Milwaukee, Wisconsin, is a freelance writer and founder of Forward Communications, a strategic communications consulting firm.

Jean Wiswesser, Northampton, Pennsylvania, has suffered with endo symptoms since age fourteen, has had nine endo-related surgeries, graduated from college, and "found a wonderful, compassionate employer and loving, gentle fiancé." Of her poem in this book, Jean writes, "This poem is dedicated to my mother and best friend, Kathy Wiswesser."

Wanna Wright, J.D., is a women's health advocate, performance poet, and playwright residing in Emeryville, California. She has survived cervical cancer for twenty-six years and breast cancer for twenty-three years.

Index

Vanderbilt Medical Center

Cultivate a Cure

The Cultivating a Cure Garden, blooms outside the
Endometriosis Association Research Program at
Vanderbilt University School of Medicine,
the Association's flagship research program,
in Nashville, Tennessee. The Association's Memorial Garden at
International Headquarters in Milwaukee, gives people another
opportunity to plant seeds of hope for a cure with their generous gifts to the
Association's endowment or Open Research Fund.
These places of beauty remind us all that as long as there is hope,
together we will make a difference!
To plant seeds of hope with your donation, contact:

Endometriosis Association
International Headquarters
8585 N. 76th Place
Milwaukee, WI 53223, U.S.A.
online at www.EndometriosisAssn.org
or call (414) 355-2200

Karen Bain, an Endometriosis Association member and artist from Astoria, Oregon,
produced this original art to signify that when we all work together, we will reach a
cure. Add a person to the line with your gift for research!

More than "Cramps," Ongoing Pelvic Pain is the Leading Sign of Endometriosis, a Common, Serious, Disease.
Are You at Risk?

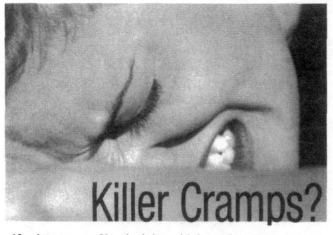

For at least six months have you had. . . .

	Yes	No
1. Pelvic pain? The pain may have a monthly pattern, for example being worst during your period and/or mid-cycle. Some have constant pain.	☐	☐
2. Fatigue, exhaustion, low energy?	☐	☐
3. Diarrhea, painful bowel movements, or other stomach upset at the time of your period?	☐	☐
4. Stomach bloating and swelling?	☐	☐
5. Heavy or irregular menstrual bleeding?	☐	☐

10 points or more: You clearly have risk factors for endometriosis. If you said yes to any question, regardless of your score, you should tell your doctor about your symptoms. You are not alone. Contact us today!

10 points if you said yes to question #1.
5 points for each yes to questions #2—5. ☐ ☐

Endometriosis Association Membership/Donation Form

_____
(last)   name   (first)

_____
street   apt.#

_____
city   state/province

_____
zip/postal code   country

_____
phone   email

Charge to   VISA   MASTERCARD
              ☐   ☐

_____
card number   exp. date

Make checks payable to:
ENDOMETRIOSIS ASSOCIATION
International Headquarters
8585 N. 76th Place
Milwaukee, WI 53223 U.S.A.

Join online www.EndometriosisAssn.org
Call or fax your membership:
(414) 355-2200 phone   (414) 355-6065 fax

☐ I am interested in helping start a chapter or group in my area if one does not exist. (local support group information will be sent with your membership package) Please send guidelines.

☐ am willing to serve as a Contact Person—women with endo y call me to share information and support.

Please check one: ☐ I have/had endometriosis
                     ☐ I have not had endometriosis

MEMBER (for those who have/had endometriosis)
   1 year dues. $35 U.S./52 Canadian
   2 year dues $60 U.S./89 Canadian
   3 year dues $105 U.S./156 Canadian
   (free book with 3 year membership, circle one:
   Our Stolen Future or _Overcoming Endometriosis_)
   5 year dues $140 U.S./208 Canadian
   (one year free with 5 year membership) $_____

FAMILY MEMBERSHIP (includes _TeenSource_ newsletter, teen support program with all other benefits of membership. Not available separately.)
1 year add $15 U.S./22 Canadian per year $_____

ASSOCIATE (for those who have not had endo)
   1 year dues. $40 U.S./59 Canadian
   2 year dues. $70 U.S./104 Canadian
   3 year dues. $120 U.S./ 178 Canadian
   (free book with 3 year membership, circle one:
   Our Stolen Future or _Overcoming Endometriosis_)
   5 year dues $160 U.S./238 Canadian
   (one year free with 5 year membership) $_____

DONATION (optional) $_____

ADDITIONAL POSTAGE for international shipping
Canadian members add: $5.00
Countries other than U.S. or Canada add $15.00 $_____

TOTAL $_____

Welcome and thank you!